Mountford John Byrde Baddeley, Charles Slegg Ward

North Wales

Part 1, Third Edition

Mountford John Byrde Baddeley, Charles Slegg Ward

North Wales
Part 1, Third Edition

ISBN/EAN: 9783337325459

Printed in Europe, USA, Canada, Australia, Japan

Cover: Foto ©Andreas Hilbeck / pixelio.de

More available books at **www.hansebooks.com**

Thorough Guide Series.

NORTH WALES

(PART I.)

CHESTER, RHYL, LLANDUDNO, BANGOR, LLANRWST
BETTWS-Y-COED, CARNARVON, LLANBERIS, BEDDGELERT, AND
FFESTINIOG SECTIONS.

M. J. B. BADDELEY, B.A..

AUTHOR OF "THE ENGLISH LAKES," &C.

AND

C. S. WARD, M.A..

AUTHOR OF "NORTH DEVON AND NORTH CORNWALL," &C.

14 MAPS AND PLANS

By BARTHOLOMEW.

THIRD EDITION—REVISED.

" From Tudno's cell to Mynach's deep-toned glen."

LONDON :
DULAU & CO., 37, SOHO SQUARE, W.
1889.

MAP INDEX.

To face Page

Index Map (inside cover)

Plan of Chester - - - - - - - - 3

Chester, Rhyl, Llandudno (¼ inch) . - - - - 11

Llandudno, Bettws-y-Coed, Holyhead (¼ inch) - - - 21

Plan of Rhyl - - - - - - - - - 23

    ,, Llandudno - - - - - - - - 44

Llandudno, Bangor, and Eastern Part of the Snowdon
Group (½ inch) - - - - - - - - 47

Plan of Conway - - - - - - - - 55

Bangor and neighbourhood - - - - - - 79

Snowdon and district (½ inch) - - - - - - 105

Carnarvon Castle - - - - - - - - 134

Criccieth, Pwllheli and the Lleyn Promontory (¼ inch) - 156

Ffestiniog, Beddgelert, Harlech, Portmadoc (½ inch) - 165

Sketch of Blaenau Ffestiniog - - - - - - 167

CONTENTS.

———o———

		Page
Map Index		viii
Introduction		ix
The Scenery		ix
Geology		xi
Accommodation		xii
Fishing		xii
Pronunciation		xv
Glossary		xvii
Heights of Mountains		xxi
Skeleton Tours		xxii
Approaches		1
CHESTER SECTION: **Chester**		3
Hawarden		11
Chester to Mold and Ruthin (over Moel Fammau)		12
Chester to Carnarvon (rail)		16
RHYL SECTION: **Rhyl**		23
Rhuddlan and Dyserth		25
Bodelwyddan		27
St. Asaph		29
Cefn Rocks		31
Denbigh, &c.		33
Ruthin		36
Moel Fammau		37
Abergele and Pensarn		40
LLANDUDNO SECTION: **Colwyn Bay**		42
Llandudno		44
Great Orme's Head		46
Little Orme's Head and Creuddyn		48
Conway		55
,, to Penmaenmawr (over Sychnant Pass)		57
,, to Llanfairfechan or Aber (over Bwlch-y-ddeufaen)		58
Penmaenmawr		61
,, Excursions		62
,, to Conway by Sychnant Pass		65
Llanfairfechan		69
,, Excursions		70
,, to Conway Valley (by Bwlch-y-ddeufaen)		72
,, to Trefriw (by Pen y-gaer)		73
Aber		74
,, to Bethesda (over Moel Wnion)		76

CONTENTS.

	Page
Bangor Section : **Bangor**	79
Penrhyn Castle	81
Menai Straits and Anglesey	83
Beaumaris	90
Penmon Priory (p. 92) Puffin Island, Red Wharf Bay	93
Bangor to Holyhead	94
Holyhead	96
,, Mountain and the Stacks	97
Bangor to Bettws-y-Coed (rail and road)	99
Bethesda to Aber (Mountain walk)	100
,, to Llanberis	101
Llanrwst and Bettws-y-Coed Section :	
Llandudno to Bettws-y-Coed (rail)	105
Tal-y-Cafn to Llanrwst (walk)	106
Deganwy or Conway to Trefriw (steamer)	108
Llanrwst	109
Trefriw	110
Llanrwst to Trefriw (by Llanrhwchwyn)	111
Trefriw to Llanrwst (,, ,,)	113
Llanrwst to Capel Curig (direct)	113
,, ,, by Llyn Crafnant	114
,, ,, by Llyn Cwlyd	115
,, Bettws-y-Coed by Llyn-y-parc	116
Bettws-y-Coed	118
,, Short Excursions	119
,, to Llanrwst by Llyn-y-parc	124
,, ,, and Conway (rail)	125
,, Corwen (road)	126
,, Blaenau Ffestiniog (rail)	127
,, Bangor, Llanberis and Beddgeler	129
Carnarvon and Llanberis Section :	
Bangor to Carnarvon (road)	133
Carnarvon	133
,, to Llanberis, Bettws-y-Coed, &c.	135
Llanberis	137
,, to Bethesda	138
,, to Snowdon Ranger	138
,, to Capel Curig and Beddgelert	139
Pen-y-gwryd to Dolwyddelen	140
Carnarvon to Beddgelert (rail and road)	140
Snowdon Ranger to Llanberis	141
Rhyd-ddu to Criccieth (walk)	142
,, to Nantlle	142
Carnarvon to Nevin or Pwllheli	142
Pen-y-groes to Clynnog	143
Ascent of Rivals	144
Carnarvon to Pwllheli or Criccieth (rail)	145
Pen-y-groes to Nantlle or Rhyd-ddu (rail)	146
Criccieth	147

CONTENTS.

	Page
Pwllheli - - - - - - - -	149
The Lleyn - - - - - - - -	150
Pwllheli to Aberdaron and back - - -	151
Aberdaron to Nevin - - - - -	154
Nevin - - - - - - - -	155
,, to Pwllheli - - - - - -	156
.. to the Rivals - - - - - -	156
BEDDGELERT SECTION :	
Carnarvon to Beddgelert (road) - - - - -	157
Snowdon Ranger or Rhyd-ddu to Nantlle (walk) -	158
,, to Criccieth - - - -	158
Beddgelert - - - - - - -	158
,, to Carnarvon - - - - -	159
,, to Llanberis or Bettws-y-Coed - - -	160
,, to Ffestiniog - - - - - -	161
.. to Portmadoc - - - - - -	163
Portmadoc to Beddgelert - - - - - -	164
FFESTINIOG SECTION :	
Portmadoc to Ffestiniog (Toy railway) - - -	165
Blaenau Ffestiniog (Duffws) - - - -	167
.. to Bettws-y-Coed - - - - -	168
,, to Portmadoc - - - - - -	168
Mynffordd Junction to Barmouth - - - -	169
Ffestiniog Village and neighbourhood - - -	169
,, ,, to Beddgelert - - -	174
.. .. to Barmouth (road) - -	176
.. .. to Bala or Bettws y-Coed (road)	176
,, ,, to Bala (rail) - - - -	177
Trawsfynydd to Dolgelley - - - - -	177
Palmerston Slate Quarry (Blaenau Ffestiniog) - -	178
MOUNTAIN SECTION : Heights and Introductory - - -	180
Carnedd Dafydd and Carnedd Llewelyn, &c. - -	181
Elidyr-fawr and Elidyr-fach - - - -	189
Glyder-fawr and Glyder-fach - - - -	191
Moel Hebog - - - - - - -	195
,, Siabod - - - - - - -	197
Moelwyn and Cynicht - - - - - -	200
Snowdon - - - - - - - -	203
Y Tryfan - - - - - - -	210
APPENDIX : Snowdon by Cwm-glas, &c. - - - -	211A

Introduction.

The district described in this guide to North Wales includes the pleasure resorts of the six northern counties and part of Cardiganshire, as far south as Aberystwith and the Devil's Bridge. To secure portability we issue it in two parts, corresponding to the two divisions into which both physically and in a railway point of view it naturally falls. In *Part I.* (this volume) is comprised the area bounded on the south by the water-sheds of the Clwyd, the Conway and the Dwyryd (the Ffestiniog river); in other words the northern seaboard of the principality and Snowdonia. This is the district served almost entirely by the London and North Western Company, though it is also tapped by the Great Western at Chester and Ffestiniog, and by the Cambrian at Portmadoc. *Part II.* deals with the districts of the Great Western, and the main line of the Cambrian Railways, and has for its distinctive natural features the lovely valleys of the Dee, the Dyfi and the upper Severn and the noble cliffs of Cader Idris. In each Part the connecting routes between the two districts are described, *e.g.* in this part we conduct the traveller from Rhyl to Corwen, and from Bettws-y-Coed and Ffestiniog to Dolgelley and Barmouth, where Part II. is referred to for further explorations.

The Scenery. The natural features which have long made North Wales one of the chief tourist districts of these islands are mountains and the streams to which they give birth, and the genuine admiration that these objects call forth is thoroughly deserved. Of course, if mere size and volume are to be the basis of our estimate of scenery, then Snowdon, with its trifling elevation of 3,500 feet and the cataracts of the Mynach (Devil's Bridge) 300 feet in all, are insignificant. It is, however, on composition and proportion that the impressiveness or beauty of a scene really depends, and so it results that Snowdon is as grand an example of a mountain as are heights of four times its altitude amid larger surroundings, and the Devil's Bridge scenery well holds its own among ravines and glens of a similar character, but on a far larger scale.

North Wales has also the advantage of being compassed on two sides by the sea, and its shore-line, though nowhere assuming the grandest forms of cliff-scenery, is almost everywhere interesting. The distinctly bold parts of the actual seaboard are Penmaenmawr, Holyhead Island, the extremity of the Lleyn promontory and, in a lesser degree, the Little and Great Orme's Head, but from nearly every point in its circuit the mountain girdle inland lends great attractiveness. That the coast-line is an important element in the views from the mountains need scarcely be mentioned.

In the rugged and shapely character of its mountains North Wales may challenge comparison with any of its competitors. Cader Idris is a worthy second to Snowdon; the Tryfan is one of the boldest masses of rock in the kingdom; Cynicht seen from the west and Elidyr-fawr from the east are perfect pyramids; and Glyder-fach is almost as chaotic a wilderness of crag and boulder as are the adamantine ranges of Skye and Arran. Still, perhaps, the valleys are the most distinctive features of Welsh scenery. Except under peculiar atmospheric conditions the wilder valleys of Great Britain are apt to disappoint expectations based on the too glowing descriptions that have so often been given of them. Size has a much greater effect on the eye in this class of scenery than in others. A rocky pass which creates a feeling of awe when looked down upon from the rocks that overhang it often fails to sustain that emotion when the stand-point is the valley itself and the crags are viewed from below. Admitting this, we know no valley in Great Britain that is more wildly beautiful than the Pass of Llanberis, while that of Nant Ffrancon, when entered at its lower end, almost vies with Glencoe in the uncompromising sternness of its features. It is, however, in those valleys of softer character, where stream and woodland and rich pasture display their ever-varying combinations, that Wales is pre-eminent. None of its valleys present, indeed, in one scene such a perfect blending of the varied elements of natural beauty as is afforded by Borrowdale in Cumberland, but we may travel far and wide before finding so long a continuance of luxuriant valley scenery, with so little admixture of tameness, as that on which we feast our eyes between Llangollen and Barmouth — the Dee, the Wnion, and the Mawddach. Dolgelley is at the focus of some of the sweetest glens in the kingdom; Ffestiniog, too, with all its slate quarries has hardly lost that charm which more than a hundred years ago drew from Lord Lyttleton his oft-quoted eulogium. Of the others the Vale of Llanrwst has been, perhaps a little, and the Vale of Clwyd, without doubt a great deal, over-praised.

Speaking generally, Welsh scenery has, to some extent, the straggling character but not the full grandeur of that of the Highlands of Scotland; and while, with one important exception, its elements are equal to those which compose the scenery of the English Lake District, it very seldom presents them in that compact and concentrated form which distinguishes Cumberland and Westmorland from all other tourists districts. The exception alluded to is of course the lakes, or rather the lack of them. To enumerate all the llyns of Wales would take pages, but except Bala, there is scarcely one freshwater lake which is a main factor in any landscape of which it forms part. Llyn Gwynant and Llyn-y-Ddinas are lovely lakelets, but the mass of Snowdon sinks them into insignificance.

Of the mountain tarns, Llyn Idwal, Llyn-y-Cau (under Cader Idris), and Llyn Llydaw (under Snowdon) may vie with the finest in the kingdom, but by far the most beautiful sheet of water in Wales is the estuary of the Mawddach. Of this famed prospect we need hardly speak here, but those who have seen it under favourable conditions, when the tide is up, from Barmouth Bridge or the "Panorama Walk," will agree with us that it is of ideal loveliness, unmarred by a single ingredient of even commonplace quality.

Geology. The rocks of North Wales, from the vale of Clwyd westward are entirely Palæozoic, and the amateur, provided he has already mastered the rudiments of the science, will find *Records of the Rocks* (Palæozoic) by Rev. W. S. Symonds, published by Murray, price 12s., at once succinct and sufficient. Here it is enough to say that the bold headlands, Great and Little Orme's Head are limestone, a formation that is finely developed both at Cefn Rocks on the Elwy, near St. Asaph and in Eglwyseg Rocks above Llangollen; Penmaenmawr (mountain) is a huge mass of igneous rock that has been forced up through the black slates of the Cambrian formation. It marks the north-east limit of the eruptive rocks, which mainly form the bolder features of Carnarvon and Merioneth. Snowdon consists of a base of slates and grits, above which we get porphyry containing felspar (the flesh coloured crystals seen in granite), succeeded by beds of volcanic ashes. The summit of the mountain is of felspathic lava, which once covered the whole surrounding group, but this is now

represented only by isolated masses that have escaped
denudation. Between Bangor and Carnarvon, between
Nevin and Bardsey, and on the west of Holyhead Island,
are found pre-Cambrian beds, the oldest formation in these
islands and possibly contemporary with the Laurentian of
Canada, the most ancient rocks known to Geology.

Accommodation. In the body of the book will be
found particulars as to hotel and inn accommodation, and
here it need only be mentioned that the economically
minded tourist can almost everywhere get good treatment
for 10s. to 12s. per diem, and in the less frequented
localities for a smaller sum. At the best hotels in the
most fashionable places 15s. per diem is about the average.
From several tariffs before us, the following may be taken
as a sample bill, exclusive of liquors.

					s.	d.	s.	d.
Breakfast	...	...	...	...	1	6 to	2	6
Luncheon	...	...	...	...	1	6 „	2	6
Dinner	...	...	...	...	3	0 „	5	0
Bed ...	...	...	...	...	2	6 „	3	6
Attendance	...	..	...	...	1	6 „	1	6
					10	0 „	14	6

Lodgings are good and abundant in all the regular tourist
resorts, and during August range from 15s. to 40s. a room
per week. The latter price is demanded and very easily
obtained in the best situations at Llandudno. Of course
in unfashionable districts, such as the Lleyn promontory,
primitive quarters can be obtained for a nominal sum, but
the tourist must be prepared to find them more or less
humble in their appointments. It is no libel on the Welsh
housewife of the humbler sort to say that she appears to
be more fond of finery than orderliness.

While speaking of accommodation, we may opportunely
suggest to a by no means small number of wayside inn-
keepers that charging two different prices for the same
article served under the same conditions is not a happy
method of redeeming Taffy's character from the reproach
which is proverbially and, as a rule, very unfairly attached
to it. For a fair glass of beer no thirsty tourist can
object to pay twopence, but for a mysterious compound
which it need scarcely shame a " blue ribboner " to drink, it
is objectionable to be charged that sum, when—say—half-
a-dozen natives are paying at least 25 per cent. less in the
same apartment. Ask for *cwrw da !*

Fishing. Trout-fishing in minor streams and in
numerous small lakes can be had either gratis or for

a nominal sum, particulars of which can be obtained on the spot. The following details have been supplied by hotel keepers and others interested.

River **Conway** (Gwydir Estate) for *Salmon*:

			£	s.	d.
For the whole season	... ...	... ...	10	10	0
From 1st May to 31st August, inclusive	... ...		4	0	0
For one month }			1	0	0
For one week } May 1 to June 30	... ...		0	10	0
For one day }			0	2	6
For one month }			2	0	0
For one week } July 1 to August 31...	... ...		0	15	0
For one day }			0	4	0
For the whole period }			3	0	0
For a fortnight } September	... ...		2	0	0
For a week }			1	0	0
For the whole period }			7	0	0
For a fortnight } Oct. 1 to Nov. 15	... ...		3	0	0
For a week }			2	0	0

Tickets can be obtained at the Eagles Hotel, Llanrwst; the Royal Oak, Waterloo, Gwydir and Glanaber Hotels, Bettws-y-Coed; and Penisa'r Pentre Shop, and Belle Vue Hotel, Trefriw.

Rivers **Lledr & Llugwy** for *Salmon:*

On the Baroness Willoughby de Eresby's Fishery above Pont Lledr, and from the south bank of the river Llugwy from Pont-y-pair, to the confluence of that river with the Conway.

			£	s.	d.
From 1st May to 15th Nov.	... ...		3	0	0
For one month }			0	15	0
For one week } May 1 to Oct. 31	... .		0	5	0
For one day }			0	2	0
For one week } Nov. 1 to 15	... ...		0	10	0
For one day }			0	3	0

Tickets can be obtained at the Eagles Hotel, Llanrwst; the Royal Oak, Waterloo, and Gwydir Hotels, Bettws-y-Coed; Pont-y-pant and Benar View Hotels, Dolwyddelen; also from Mr. Ellis Pierce, Bookseller, Dolwyddelen.

For 3s. 6d. per annum trout fishing on Conway, Llugwy, Lledr, Cwlyd, Eigiau, Crafnant, Alwyn, Elwy, Voelas, &c. rivers and most of the lakes connected therewith. There are boats on the principal lakes for which there is no fixed charge, and fishermen can generally be obtained for a moderate fee.

The **Seiont, Gwyrfai, and Llyfni** fishery district, for which Carnarvon and Llanberis are the principal head quarters, embraces all the lakes and tarns (with 2 or 3 exceptions) in the neighbourhood in addition to the above rivers, and also the Cefni in Anglesey. Salmon and sewin in the Seiont for which a licence 20s. is required, in addition to following tickets:—5s. *for season* ; 2s. 6d. *a week* ; 1s. *a day. Boats* 1s. *an hour on* Llyn Padarn—*no boats on* Llyn Peris. *For tickets apply at the principal Hotels.*

River Dwyryd, Llyn Tecwyn and Llyn Garnedd. In the river are trout and salmon, and in the lakes (no boats) small trout. *Season,* 20s. ; *month,* 10s. ; *week,* 5s. ; *day,* 2s. 6d. These are all within easy reach of Maentwrog, Tan-y-Bwlch and Ffestiniog.

From Nevin within 2 miles by road, are the streams Edeyrn, Abergeirch, and Penpryd, where plenty of trout and possibly salmon may be had. *Season,* 18s. 6d. ; *month.* 5s.. *week.* 2s. 6d. *Tickets at Ty-Cerrig Hotel, Nevin.*

Welsh Place-Names. At the risk of abridging the amusement which visitors may derive from their phonetic perplexities, it must be said that, with the exception of the sounds of *ch* and *ll*, the difficulties of Welsh pronunciation are apt to be greatly exaggerated.

The Welsh *ch* may be described as an English *k* stopt in the middle of pronunciation, like the *k* in *sunken*, if you attempt to pronounce that word without sounding the *e*. It may therefore be approximately represented by the symbol *k'*, as :—*bach, bychan*, pronounced *bak', buk'an*.

The *ll* has the sound of the English *hl* (nearly), as :—*llan*, pronounced *hlan*; but at the end of a syllable it is rather like *lh* than *hl*, as :—*pwll*, pronounced *pōolh*.

According to these rules, the apparently unpronounceable name Llanuwchllwyn may be fairly represented in pronunciation as Hlan-e ōok'-lin. It is quite a mistake to try (as many Englishmen do) to pronounce *ll* as if it were *thl*, for instance *Dolgelley* as Dolgethly : there is no *t* sound in the word. It is really pronounced more like *Dol-gĕh-hly*.

Another difficulty, that of the vowels, is comparatively imaginary. At first sight, a word bristling with *w*'s and *y*'s appears to be all consonants, but these letters are vowels or semi-vowels, and, indeed, among those commonly used, *w* is always *ōo*, and *y* has two sounds (see *p.* xvi), both of which are illustrated in the name Dyffryn, pronounced *Duffrin*.

One great help towards attaining a passable pronunciation arises from the fact, that, as in German, the sounds are constant, and present no such bewildering varieties as, for instance, the English *ou* in 'bough,' 'tough,' 'though,' 'thought,' 'through.' Of the sounds given in the following list two are specially noteworthy : *dd = th*, as in 'then,' and *ff* = English *f* (but a single *f* in Welsh = *v* in English). As samples of the comparative ease of pronouncing words which look almost hopeless, we may instance Dwygyfylchi (*Doo-c-guv-ul-k'y*) and Llanfairpwllgwyngyll (*Hlan-va-pōolh-gwin-gilh*).

Consonants.

C, always hard like K.
Ch, strong guttural, like a stopt k (see *p.* xv).
Dd = soft *th*, as in *then*, whi*th*er (never as in *th*in).
F = V.
Ff = F.
G, always hard; *ng* as in le*ng*th.
H, as in English.
Ll, as nearly as possible like *hl*, or at the end of a syllable *lh* (see p. xv).
R, as in English, but always **distinctly** pronounced before a consonant, as well as before a vowel.
S, always hard as in *s*ay; never soft as in chee*s*e.
Th, hard as in *th*in (not like *dd*, see above).

Vowels.

A, long, as in f*a*ther; or short, as in m*a*t (never as in m*a*te).
E, long, like *a* in m*a*te; or short as in m*e*t.
I, long *e*, as in m*e*; or short *i*, as in f*i*t.°
O, long, as in n*o*te; or short as in n*o*t.
U, long, as *e* in m*e*; or short, as *i* in th*i*n.
W, short, as *oo* in g*oo*d; rarely long, as *oo* in b*oo*t.
Y, short, as *u* in f*u*n; but in monosyllables or final syllables like *i* in th*i*n: e.g. *hyny* is pronounced exactly like 'honey.' There are, however, a few monosyllables ending in *y*, including the article y (=the), which have the short *u* sound, as *Pen-y-Gwryd*, in which the single *y* is sounded just like the *a* in 'two-a-penny.'

Diphthongs.

The exact sounds of those of the Welsh diphthongs which **differ** but slightly from one another, can only be learnt by careful observation and practice. They may, however, be roughly grouped as follows :—

ae, ai, au, like English *ay* in 'aye,' or German *ai* in 'Kaiser.'
ei, eu, ey, like *i* in 'hide,' but the *ey* in Lleyn like *ee* in 'seen.'
aw, ow, like *ou* in 'out.'
oe, oi, like *oy* in 'boy.'
ew, iw, yw, like *u* in 'duty.'

The **combination** *wy* is not strictly a diphthong, both vowels being distinctly sounded, **and the** y (even in the middle of a word) has the sound of the English short *i*, for **instance**, *dwy* corresponds almost exactly in sound with the English word 'dewy.'

Mutations.

All *initial* consonants (excepting *ff*, *h*, *r*, and *s*) admit of change in certain positions, being influenced by the word immediately preceding. The general object of these "mutations" is to afford an easy transition from one word or syllable to another, and in place-names they are in most cases influenced by the *gender* of the following noun or adjective, the tendency of the feminine gender being to produce an initial change from a "hard" to

---

° An initial *i* before a vowel has the sound of the English consonant *y*, thus *ie* = yea, in sound and meaning.

its corresponding "soft" consonant. Take the following examples :—

C changes to G, as Pen-y-Gader (from Cader).
P changes to B, as Pen-y-Bont (from Pont).
T changes to D, as Glan-y-Don (from Ton).
B changes to F, as Glyder-Fach (from Bach).
D changes to Dd, as Moel-Ddu (from Du).
G is lost altogether, as Maen-or (from Gor).
M changes to F, as Careg-Fawr (from Mawr).

In certain cases, the rules for which we omit, Ll and Gl change to L, as Rhudd-lan (from Glan), Rh changes to R, as Tref-riw (from Rhiw). Many more examples will be found in the accompanying list of place-names with their derivations.

Observe also that the preposition *yn*, "in," produces what is called the "nasal" mutation in the succeeding word; for example, *c* changes to *ngh* in the name Llanfair-yn-*ngh*ornwy (a village in Anglesey), the last word being in its original state Cornwy.

Accent. The rule, in words of more than one syllable, is to lay the stress on the last syllable but one, and this will hold good in all place names, so that exceptions need not be noted; thus: "Dolwyddélen," not "Dolwýddelen;" "Maentwrog," not "Máentwrog;" "Arénig," not "A'renig."

Real compounds, however, (as place names often are) have their accent upon the last element only, as: "Llan-rẃst," "Pen-y-bónt," "Twll-dú," "Llan-fáir," &c., each part being treated as a separate word, and this tends to throw the chief accent on what seems to be the last syllable. The fact also that the first element is usually the generic, and the last the distinctive part of the word, endorses the propriety of this accentuation. *Crib* signifies "crest," or "top." "What crest?" is the natural question, and the natural reply Crib-góch—"Red crest." The order of the two elements is reversed in English, but the Cumberland folks are quite correct when they say Whitehaven, and not Whitehá ven.

Glossary.

Aber, a confluence, river-mouth.
Afon, a river.
Allt (from *Gallt*), a cliff.
Aran (or *Arran*), a high place, an alp.
Bach } masc. *Fach* } fem.
Bychan } masc. *Fechan* } fem.
little.

Bala, an outlet.
Bedd, a grave.
Ber, a hill-top.
Bettws, a corruption of English "bede-house," *i.e.* house of prayer, chapel.
Blaen, pl. *Blaenau*, a summit.
Bod, a dwelling, abode.
Borth, see *Porth*.

Braich, an arm.
Bron (fron), pap or breast.
Bryn (fryn), a hill.
Bwlch, a mountain pass.
Bwrdd, a table.
Cader (gader), a seat, a chair.
Cae, a meadow.
Caer (Gaer), a fort.
Cain, fair.
Careg, a rock or stone.
Carn, Carnedd, a cairn, heap of stones.
Cau, a hollow.
Cefn, a ridge.
Celli (Gelli), a bower, grove.
Cil, a recess.
Clogwyn, a precipice.
Clunllom, a haunch.
Clynog, bosky, bushy.
Coch, fem. Goch, red.
Coed, a wood.
Cor (gor), a choir, church.
Cors, a bog.
Craig, pl. Creigiau, a craig.
Crib, pl. Cribiau, a crest.
Croes (Groes), a cross.
Cwm, a valley.
Cymmer, a confluence.
Dau, (fem. Dwy), two.
Din, Dinas, a hill-fort.
Dôl, a dale.
Drosgl, a hump (lit. awkward).
Drws, a door.
Du (ddu), black.
Dwfr (dwr), water.
Dyffryn, a valley.
Eglwys (Lat. Ecclesia), a church.
Esgair, a shank, a leg.
Fach, fechan, see Bach.
Fawr, see Mawr.
Ffordd, a (high) way.
Foryd (from Moryd) an estuary.
Ffridd, a forest.
Ffynnon, a well, a spring.
Gelli, see Celli.
Glan, a bank, a shore.
Glas (las), blue or green.
Glyn, a glen.

Gogof (Ogof), a cavern.
Gwalch, a hawk, or heron.
Gwern, a swamp, an alder-grove.
Gwy (wy,) water.
Gwyn (wyn), fem. gwen (wen), white.
Hafod, a summer dwelling.
Hên, old.
Hir, long.
Isel, low; is, lower; isaf, lowest.
Llam, a stride, step.
Llan, a churchyard, church.
Llech, a rock, a flag-stone.
Lleyn, a peninsula.
Llwyd, brown.
Llyn, pl. Llyniau, a lake.
Llwyn, a grove.
Llys, a court, a hall.
Maen (Faen), pl. Meini, a stone.
Maes (Faes), a field.
Mawr (Fawr), great.
Melin (Felin), a mill.
Moel (Foel), a bare hill.
Morfa, a marsh, lit. a place by the sea.
Mynach, a monk.
Mynydd (Fynydd), a mountain, a moorland.
Nant, a brook, hence a vale.
Neuadd, a hall.
Newydd, new.
Pant, a hollow.
Pen, a headland.
Pentref (Pentre), a village.
Perfedd, a centre.
Pistyll, a spout.
Plâs, a palace.
Pont (Bont), a bridge.
Porth (Borth), a port, a harbour.
Prysor, brushwood.
Pwll, a pool.
Rhaiadr, a waterfall.
Rhiw, a slope, a brow.
Rhos, moorland.
Rhudd, red.
Rhyd, a ford.
Sarn, a causeway.
Sych, dry.

Tal, a headland, a point.
Talar, a headland in a field.
Tan, under.
Tomen, a mound.
Towyn (Tywyn), a strand.
Traeth, a beach.
Traws, cross (adj. and noun).
Tref (Tre), a house.
Tri, three.
Trwyn, a point.
Twll, a pit.

Ty, a house.
Tyddyn, a farm.
Uchel, high ; *uch (uwch)*, higher, *uchaf*, highest.
Wen (see Gwyn).
Y (Yr before a vowel), the ; *Yn*, in, at, into.
Ychain, (pl. of *Ych*), oxen.
Ynys, an island.
Yspytty, an hospital, an inn.
Ystrad, a vale.

Meaning and Pronunciation of the more important places.

(Pronounce *th* hard, as in *thin*, *dd* soft, as in *then*.)

Abergele [Aber-gelly].
Aberglaslyn, outlet of the blue lake.
Bangor, high choir (one having the full number of monks, &c.).
Beaumaris, the (town on) beautiful marsh. French.
Beddgelert, [Beth-gelert], Gelert's grave.
Bettws-y-Coed [Bettoos-i-coyd]. Chapel in the wood.
Bod-ysgallen, abode of the thistle.
Bwlch-y-ddeufaen [Boolk'-i-thi-ven], pass of the two stones.
   ,, *y-maen*, pass of the stones.
Capel Curig [Cappel-kerrig], S. Curig's chapel.
Carnarvon, the fort opposite Mona.
Cerrig-y-Druidion, stones of the Druids.
Clwyd [Cloo-id].
Colwyn, white summit.
Conway (river). Clear water.
Criccieth [Cricketh].
Denbigh, hill fort.
Duffws [Diffoos].
Dolbadarn, St. Padarn's dale.
Dwygyfylchi [Doo-e-guv-ul-k'y], the joint passes.
Dolwyddelan [Dol-wythélan], Gwyddelan's dale.
Ffestiniog, the place of hastening (Lat. *festinare*).
Harlech, on the rock (or the fine rock).
Llanbedr, church of St. Pe er.
   ,, *beris*,   ,,   ,, Peris.
   ,, *ddulas*, perhaps black or dark church.
   ,, *dudno*, church of St. Tudno.
   ,, *fair*,   ,,   ,, Mary.
   ,, *gollen*,   ,,   ,, Collen.
   ,, *rwst*,   ,,   ,, Grwst.
   ,, *saintffraid*, ,,   ,, Bride or Bridget.
Maentwrog [Män-toorog], the stone of Twrog.
Nantlle [Nant-hly].

Penmaenmawr, the big stony headland.
Penrhyn, the promontory.
Pensarn, head of the causeway.
Pen-y-gwryd [Pen-a-gŏōrid], head of the ridge (lit., " chain ").
Portmadoc, see *Tremadoc*.
Pwllheli [Poolh-elly], the salt pool.
Rhyl, a rift or cleft.
Ruthin, red castle (= rhudd-din).
Tal-y-Bont, front of the bridge.
Tal-y-llyn [properly **Tal-a-hlyn** but in practice Tath-lyn], front
   of the lake.
Tan-y-Bwlch [Tan-i-bŏŏlk'], under the pass.
Trawsfynydd [Trowsvunith], cross moor.
Trefriw [Trev-roo], house on the slope.
Tremadoc, House of Madoc.

HEIGHT, &c., OF CHIEF MOUNTAINS.

Name.	County.	Feet.	Meaning.
Snowdon	Carnarvon	3571	Hill of Snow.
Carnedd Llewelyn	,,	3482	Llewelyn's Cairn.
,, Dafydd	,,	3430	David's Cairn.
Y Glyder-fawr	,,	3275	————
,, fach	,,	3262	————
Y Garn	,,	3107	Heap of Stones.
Y Foel-fras	,,	3091	Humpy Mount.
Elidyr-fawr	,,	3033	
Y Tryfan	,,	3009	Three-headed (hill)
Aran Mawddwy	Merioneth	2970	High place.
Yr Arryg	Carnarvon	2874	
Cader Idris	Merioneth	2929	Chair of Idris.
Aran Benllyn	,,	2902	High place at head of
Moel Siabod	Carnarvon	2865	———— [lake
Pen Helig	,,	2850	
Arenig-fawr	Merioneth	2800	Great Arenig.
Y Foel-goch	Carnarvon	2726	Red Mount.
Moel Perfydd	,,	2750*	Central Mount.
Carnedd-y-Filiast	,,	2694	Greyhound Cairn.
Moel-sych	Merion.& Montg.	2718	Dry Mount (sych).
Pen Llithrig-y-Wrach	Carnarvon	2623	Slippery Hag's Head.
Llwyd-mawr	,,	2600*	Big brown (hill).
Drum	,,	2579	Ridge.
Moel Hebog	,,	2578	Falcon Mount.
Cader Fronwen	Merion.& Montg.	2573	White-breasted Seat.
Moelwyn	Carnarvon	2529	White Mount.
Y Drosgl	,,	2478	Hump.
Diphwys	Merioneth	2467	
Plynlimon	Cardigan	2469	Five Beacons.
Rhobell-fawr	Merioneth	2409	————
Llethr	,,	2475	Smooth.
Rhinog-fawr	,,	2362	————
Cynicht	Carnarvon	2362	————
Y Garnedd-goch	,,	2315	Red Cairn.
Moel Eilio	,,	2382	
Mynydd-mawr	,,	2293	Great Mount.
Manod-mawr	Merioneth	2171	Great Mass.
Moel Wnion	Carnarvon	1905	
,, -y-gamelin	Denbigh	1897	Mount of the winding stream.
Yr-Eifl (Rivals)	Carnarvon	1887	The Forks.
Moel Fammau	Denbigh, Flint	1823	————
Penmaenmawr	Carnarvon	1553	Big stone headland.
Moel Offrwm	Merioneth	1328	Mount of Sacrifice.
Breidden Hills	Montgomery	1250*	————
Carn Madryn	Carnarvon	900*	Fox Cairn.
Conway Mountain	,,	800*	————
Great Orme's Head	,,	750*	————
Holyhead Mount.	Anglesey	719	————

* Approximate

SUGGESTIONS FOR TOURS.

*₊*North Wales affords scope for the gratification of so many different tastes in touring that a list of tours adapted to each taste would occupy many pages. Lovers of sea and land in combination will include Llandudno, Penmaenmawr, Llanfairfechan, Beaumaris, Barmouth and Aberystwith in their tour; mountaineers will be at pains not to omit Snowdon or Cader Idris, and will appreciate the other ascents described in our "Mountain Section"; archæologists will lay stress on the castles, Rhuddlan, Conway, Beaumaris, Carnarvon, and Harlech, not forgetting Valle Crucis Abbey. The ancient town on the Rivals, and a number of cromlechs, will also attract them; while everybody will wish to see as mnch of the districts of Snowdonia, Ffestiniog, Barmouth and Dolgelley as time permits. The following outline tours only profess to secure the tourist who wishes to make the most of his time against going wrong. He might go right in a hundred different ways. We must also draw attention to the circular tours of the railway companies, the routes of which are noted in our yellow sheet.

A FORTNIGHT FOR NON-PEDESTRIANS.

DAY.
1. Chester.
2 and 3.—Llandudno.
4 and 5.—Bettws-y-Coed.
6 and 7.—Menai Bridge.
8.—Llanberis.
9.—Beddgelert.
10.—Ffestiniog.
11 and 12.—Barmouth.
13 and 14.—Dolgelley.
15 and 16.—Llangollen.
or,
13 — 16.—Aberystwith and Machynlleth.

A WEEK'S TOUR IN SNOWDONIA. (For fair walkers).

Sleeping Quarters in Italics.

Day.
1. Rail to Llandudno, walk or drive round Great Orme, *Llandudno Junction.* or *Conway.*
2. Conway Castle; rail to Llanfair (Anglesey); walk back to Bangor by Anglesey Column and Menai Bridge; train to *Bethesda.*
3. Walk up Nant Ffrancon, visiting Llyn Idwal (whence the route may be continued by the Devil's Kitchen over Glyder-fawr to Pen-y-gwryd and Capel Curig) to Capel Curig and *Bettws-y-Coed* (17 *m.* direct, including Llyn Idwal; 18 *m.* over Glyder-fawr).
4. Fairy Glen and Conway Falls (5 *m.* there and back); rail to Blaenau Ffestiniog and Portmadoc; walk to *Beddgelert* (7—8 *m*).
5. Ascend Snowdon, descending to Pen-y-gwryd or *Llanberis.*
6. Carnarvon (by rail from Llanberis); home.

A PEDESTRIAN FORTNIGHT.

Sleeping Quarters in Italics.

Day.
1. Chester to Mold by train; walk over Moel Fammau to *Ruthin,* 12 *m.*
2. Denbigh by train; walk to Cefn Caves, &c., and St. Asaph; train to *Llandudno Junction* or *Conway.*
3. Llandudno by train; walk round Great Orme; rail to Llanfair (Anglesey): walk to Bangor; train to *Bethesda.*
4. Walk up Nant Ffrancon to Llyn Idwal and by the Devil's Kitchen over Glyder-fawr to Capel Curig and *Bettws-y-Coed.*
5. Walk by Fairy Glen, Conway Falls, the Cromlech and Capel Garmon back to Bettws-y-Coed; train to *Dolwyddelen.*
6. Over Moel Siabod to Pen-y-gwryd and *Llanberis.*
7. Over Snowdon to *Beddgelert.*
8. Walk to Portmadoc or Tan-y-Bwlch; rail to Duffws; walk to *Ffestiniog Village.* Or walk all the way by Tan-y-Bwlch, or over Moelwyn.
9. Walk by Cynfael Falls, Rhaiadr and Raven Fall to Talsarnau Station; rail to *Harlech,* or by old road from Maentwrog to *Harlech.*
10. Walk by Cwm Bychan, Roman Steps, Bwlch Drws-Ardudwy to Dyffryn Station; train to *Barmouth.*
11. Over Cader Idris to *Dolgelley.*
12. Walk to Tal-y-llyn and Corris, train to *Machynlleth.* Or train to *Berwyn;* walk to *Llangollen.*

NOTE TO THE THIRD EDITION.—Some additional excursions in the Snowdon range, including the ascent of the mountain from Cwmglas, will be found on *p.* 211A, &c.

These are from the pen of an experienced climber, one of many travellers from whom we have received valuable suggestions for the improvement of the volume. We beg to invite further communications from any who may detect errors or omissions. The pages of the introduction which deal with Welsh pronunciation have had the advantage of revision by a scholar of distinction.

In this edition the hotels on the list of the *Cyclists' Touring Club* (Aug. 1889) are distinguished by H.Q. (head-quarters), and Q. (quarters), and the Temperance Houses with sleeping accommodation have been added. Many of the latter are of a humble character.

Approaches.

The tourist district of North Wales borders so closely on the region of the well known and characteristic scenery of the Midland counties of England, and the transition from the one to the other is so devoid of special feature that a detailed description of the routes by which it is approached would be quite superfluous. Taking Chester, Llangollen and, say, Welshpool as places at which the tourist may be fairly advised to commence his explorations, we need only say that the London and North Western and the Great Western Railway companies convey passengers with comfort, speed, and reasonable fares to them from all parts of the kingdom. Approaching from the South by the former line, the only object likely to arrest the attention is **Beeston Castle**, perched on a lofty sandstone rock on the left of the line, 9 miles short of Chester. The picturesque ruins of the Castle, and the wide-spread view from it, extending over the estuaries of the Dee and the Mersey in the north, and to the Clwydian range in the west, may tempt the leisurely tourist to break his journey for an hour or two, especially as the attraction is enhanced by a "good hotel"—the *Beeston Castle*—"in the foreground." The hotel is close to the Station, the Castle is about ¾ m. from it, and the latter is open to visitors on every weekday except Tuesday and Thursday. A mile beyond it the mansion of *Peckforton* is seen.

On the *Great Western route*, between Wellington and Shrewsbury, the Wrekin rises bold and isolated on the left of the line. (This is also part of the L. and N.W. route from London to Aberystwith, &c.) There is also a very pretty view from the viaduct between Gobowen and Chirk, and a still finer one—of which every traveller has heard—from that over the Dee between Chirk and Ruabon. The latter prospect extends up the valley to Llangollen and the hills beyond it. The Gresford valley, between Ruabon and Wrexham, also presents a richly diversified landscape, but this will be spoken of in our description of the Great Western route from Chester to Barmouth.

Of the Welshpool approach we shall speak more fully in our description of the beautiful route from Shrewsbury or Whitchurch to Aberystwith and Barmouth by the Cambrian line.

The following table gives an approximate idea of the time

occupied on the journey from London, Birmingham, and Manchester to the favourite tourist resorts in the Principality.

	From London	From Birmingham	From Manchester.		From London.	From Birmingham	From Manchester.
	Hrs.	Hrs.	Hrs.		Hrs.	Hrs.	Hrs.
Aberdovey ...	8	4¼	5¾	Ffestiniog ...	8½	5¼	4¼
Abergele ...	6	3¾	2¼	Harlech ...	8¼	6½	7
Aberystwith ...	7½	4¾	6	Llanberis ...	8½	6½	5
Bala ...	7½	4	4¼	Llandudno ...	6¼	4¼	2¾
Bangor ...	7	4½	3¼	Llanfairfechan...	6¾	4½	3¼
Barmouth ...	9	5¼	5½	Llangollen ...	6¼	2¾	3
Beaumaris ...	8	5½	4¼	Llanrwst ...	7¼	5¼	3½
Bettws-y-coed ...	7½	5½	3¾	Machynlleth ...	6¾	4	5¼
Borth ...	7¼	4½	5¼	Menai Bridge ...	7¼	5½	3½
Carnarvon ...	7¾	5¼	4	Penmaenmawr...	6¾	4½	3¼
Chester ...	4½	2½	1¼	Portmadoc ...	9½	7	5½
Conway ...	6½	4½	3	Pwllheli ...	9¼	6¾	5¼
Colwyn Bay ...	6¼	4	2¾	Rhyl ...	5¼	3½	2¼
Dolgelley ...	8	4¾	4¾	Welshpool ...	5¼	2½	3¼

Liverpool to Llandudno, Bangor, &c., by Sea.—During the season there is a regular service of passenger-steamers between Liverpool and North Wales once or twice daily. The calling places are Llandudno, Beaumaris, and Bangor (Menai Bridge); the time occupied,—about 3 hours to Llandudno, 4½ hours to Bangor; and the fares,—*first class*, about 4s. 6d. to Llandudno, 5s. to Beaumaris or Bangor; *second class*, 2s. 6d. and 3s.; *return*, about two-thirds as much again. Excellent views of the coast and mountains are obtained during the voyage, the Clwydian range, Penmaenmawr, and the heights of Eastern Snowdonia, dominated by Carnedd Llewelyn, and then Snowdon itself appearing in turn.

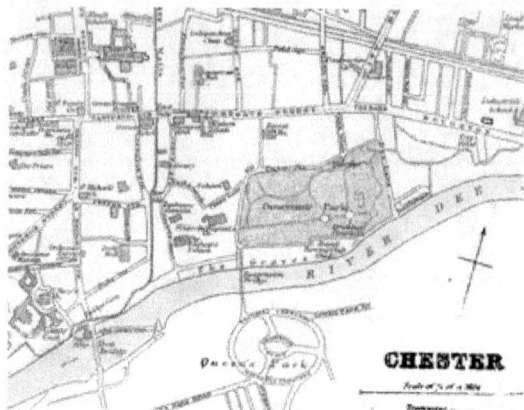

CHESTER

Chester.

—◆—

Hotels : *Queen's,* close to General Station; *Grosvenor,* near the city cross; *Blossoms* (H.Q.), *Golden Lion* (Q.), both in Foregate St. ; *Westminster* (temperance), City Road.

Post Office in St. John's Street. *Principal mails arr. abt.* 7 *a.m. and* 3 *p.m.* ; *dep. abt.* 11 *a.m.* and 10 *p.m.*

Population, 36,788.

Railway Stations: *General Station* for G.W.R. and L. & N.W.R. *Northgate Station* for "Cheshire Lines" The latter station is in Victoria Road, and from it the shortest route to the General Station is by St. Anne Street, Black Diamond Street, and Brook Street. The distance is a trifle over half-a-mile.

Tramways : From the Station, by Foregate, Eastgate, and Bridge Streets, Grosvenor Road and Bridge, to within a few yards of the Grosvenor Lodge entrance to Eaton Park.

Chester, if we regard the general style of its domestic architecture, is not only the most picturesque, but the most antique town in Britain. Elsewhere there are buildings of equal or greater age, but here relics of the Roman, Norman and Plantagenet periods occur in a setting that has altered little since the days of the Stuarts. The old-world appearance of the place is dear to the citizens, and most of the modern work rendered necessary by lapse of time has been executed in the happiest manner, so as to preserve or reproduce the ancient aspect. The history of the city carries us back to the Roman occupation of Britain. From about A.D. 60, down to the time of the withdrawal of the imperial forces early in the 5th century, the famous xxth Legion, surnamed *valens victrix,* had its headquarters on the banks of the Dee. By the Romans the spot was called *Deva,* after the river, and the name Chester, the Saxon form of the Latin *Castra,* commemorates the camp whose main outlines are still shown by the rectangular arrangement of the walls and principal streets. Many memorials of this period - altars, statues, coins, tiles, &c., as well as a hypocaust, or heating-apparatus—have from time to time been brought to light, and may be seen in and about the Museum (*see page* 5). The earliest inscription that has been discovered bears the name "Commodus," and is referred to Ceionius Commodus (d. A.D. 138), who was adopted by Hadrian, and was the first to be styled Cæsar as a mark of heirship of the imperial throne. He does not appear to have had any direct connection with Britain. After the departure of the Romans, Chester was twice reduced to ruin—first in 607, by Æthelfrith, King of Northumbria, who at the same time destroyed the monastery at Bangor-Iscoed, and slew 1200 monks; and secondly by the Danes, in 894. It was rebuilt by Æthelred I.

nearly on the old lines, the only important alteration being its extension southward as far as the river-bank, and the inclusion thereby of the site of the Castle. At the time of the Norman Conquest, Chester was the last place of importance to yield to William, which it did not do till 1069, when it was conferred, with the county of Cheshire, on Hugh Lupus, the Conqueror's nephew and chief huntsman (*grosveneur*), who was created Earl of Chester and Count Palatine, and given *carte-blanche* to enlarge his borders at the expense of the Welsh. The last earl of this line died in 1237; in 1246 the title was annexed to the Crown, and in 1301 was bestowed on Edward, Prince of Wales, afterwards Edward II. From that date downwards the eldest son of the Sovereign has been Earl of Chester. The palatinate jurisdiction was only abolished by Parliament in 1830. In 1471 a large part of the city was burnt, and in 1645 it yielded, after three months' siege, to the forces of the Parliament. Since then, with the exception of the Fenian scare, in February, 1867, its history has been uneventful.

Walk through the city. The principal objects of interest are the *Walls*, *St. John's Church*, the *Rows*, and the *Cathedral*, and these we propose to examine in the order just given, though, owing to the compactness of the city, it matters little with which we begin. The services at the Cathedral on weekdays are at 10.15 a.m., and 4.15 p.m.,* and whilst they are going on, the interior of the building cannot be examined. Leaving the General Station by City Road, which passes the Queen's Hotel and crosses the Shropshire Union Canal, we enter Foregate Street, and, turning to the right, at once make acquaintance with Old Chester. Rather more than half-a-mile from the Station, the line of the Walls is reached at *East Gate*, and we are then almost equally near the Rows (straight on through the Gate); the Cathedral (through the Gate, and then to the right by St. Werburg Street), and St. John's Church (to the left, from the outside of the Gate by John Street, and left again by Little John Street).

The Walls. These mark the outline of the Roman *Castra*, except on the south side, where they follow the river-bank and enclose a somewhat larger space. Their foundations are usually said to be Roman, but it is more probable that they are Norman, and date from the days of Hugh Lupus, who first built the Castle. The walls themselves, except a small portion, possibly Norman, on the north side overlooking the canal, are not older than the 14th century. A paved footway runs along the top of them, and their circuit is nearly two miles. We ascend by some steps on the right hand, just outside East Gate, and turn to the right, commanding in a few yards the best attainable view of the exterior of the Cathedral—the south transept, the choir, lady chapel, central tower, and presently of the chapter-house and

* Mondays not choral.

refectory. We next arrive at the **Phœnix Tower**, so called from the crest of one of the city guilds which it bears, whence, as an inscription tells us, Charles I. witnessed the defeat of his troops on Rowton Moor, " September 24, 1645." The date is wrong and should be September 27. The wall now turns westward, and has the Shropshire Union Canal as a deep moat along its north side. *Northgate* is crossed, and then a raised platform of masonry, called *Morgan's Mount*, and beyond it a half-moon tower, known as *Pemberton's Parlour*, are passed on the way to the N.W. angle of the walls, which is marked by *Bonwaldesthorne's Tower*. This tower is connected by a bridge (now dry), with the **Water Tower**, and here, until the embankment altered the course of the river, vessels used to be moored. Bonwaldesthorne's Tower is now used as a **Museum**, where a good many local antiquities may be seen, and on the small green plot immediately below are a hypocaust, or warming apparatus, and sundry altars, &c., of Roman date. Altogether, the red and crumbling towers, the bright patch of verdure and the trees make a pleasant little group. The railway line, which here is close to the walls, is used by the G.W.R. from London, and the L. & N.W.R. to Holyhead, and travellers over it may get a hasty glance at the Water Tower, and at the antiquities on the plat. We now turn southward, past the Infirmary, the Queen's School, and the Linen Hall (at the end of Stanley Place), to the *Water Gate*. Then on the outside of the wall, enclosed between it, the railway and the Dee, is the famous but dangerously curved race-course, the **Roodee**. Just short of the river, Grosvenor Road leads to **Grosvenor Bridge**, a single arch of 200 feet span over the Dee, across which are seen the wooded suburb of Curzon Park and the city cemetery. We are now close to the so-called **Castle**, which might more properly be denominated the County Buildings, since it consists of the Shire Hall and Assize Courts, the Gaol, and the Barracks, the last-named having an enclosed parade-ground in front of it. At the back of these buildings, which are of classical design, and nearer the river, is an old square block known as **Julius Cæsar's Tower**. This is now a magazine, but a small vaulted chapel is still preserved in the upper part. The church of *St. Mary-in-the-Castle*, or *on-the-Hill*, is close by, but need not detain the tourist. Nearly opposite the entrance to the Castle are the **Militia Barracks**, and a short distance citywards the Franciscan Monastery and church of St. Bridget. Opposite the Monastery is the **Grosvenor Museum**, opened in 1886.

Resuming our walk along the walls, we pass below the old castletower above mentioned, and have in front the *Dee Mills*, and the picturesque **Old Bridge**. The road over the latter enters the city through *Bridge Gate*, which we next cross. A causeway, or weir, at this point interrupts the tranquil flow of the Dee, which a little further up is spanned by the Suspension Bridge. It is advisable to quit the wall-top after reaching Bridge Gate, as the rest of the circuit to the East Gate is devoid of interest. Keeping

alongside the river, here known as the *Groves*, a good choice of
boats offers itself to those disposed for a water excursion to Eaton
Hall, 5 *m.* up-stream. When the *Suspension Bridge* is reached
we turn to the left, and in a few yards arrive at *St. John's Church*,
to the east of which is Grosvenor Park, presented to the city in
1872 by the then Marquis of Westminster.

St. John's Church, in spite of its being but a fragment
of a Norman church, is of great interest. Begun about 1075, it
was originally meant to be the cathedral of the vast diocese that
included both Lichfield and Chester, but did not attain to that
dignity, as Coventry was eventually preferred. When entire its plan
was cruciform, with a central tower, and it appears to have been
finished not later than 1225. The central tower fell in 1574, and
crushed the east end of the church, which was never rebuilt, and
is now a picturesque ruin, showing beautiful Transitional Norman
work. [*The ruins can be fairly seen without entering the enclosure,
which is kept locked. For the key apply to the sexton, who is generally to be found in the church.*] During the 15th century, a lofty
detached belfry-tower was built at the west end, but this, too, fell
April 14th, 1881, and only the shell of its lower part remains.
The existing church consists of the nave, with its aisles, and the
base of the tower of the original fabric. The arches of the nave
date from about 1095, and the graceful double triforium, with four
pointed arches in each tier, answering to each bay of the nave, is
about a century later. The north porch, rebuilt in 1883, is excellent. The N.E. clock-tower and belfry were added in 1887.

We now proceed by Little John Street, which begins opposite
the porch of the church, to John Street, and turn to the
right along it to Foregate Street and the East Gate, passing
through which we find ourselves in front of the handsome timber-
built *Grosvenor Hotel*. Just beyond this, on the same side of the
street, the **Rows** begin. These consist of covered ways, or porticos, formed by the setting back of the front of the first-floor of
the houses, while the higher stories, supported by pillars, align in
elevation with the ground floor. These porticos are found in
each of the four streets that meet at right angles at High Cross,
but those in East Gate Street and Bridge Street are the principal
ones. The first floor thus set back is utilised for a second row of
shops, which is made accessible from the street by flights of steps
at frequent intervals. Many of the best shops are to be found in
Eastgate Row, and in the Row on the east side of Bridge Street.
Perhaps the best plan, in order fully to see these peculiar features
of the city, is to ascend to *Eastgate Row*, and follow it round into
Bridge Street Row and as far as St. Michael's Church. Then
cross to the opposite side of the street, and thread the low-
pitched and much more old-fashioned *Scotch Row*, back to High
Cross. In this way a good view of the delightfully irregular and
quaint street-fronts will be obtained. *Watergate Row* is rather
uninviting, and many will prefer to go and return by the street of
that name, which should by no means be left unexplored, as it

contains two houses, on the south side, that are fine specimens
of unrestored 17th century work. The first of these is *God's
Providence House*, so named from the inscription that it bears—
" God's Providence is mine inheritance, 1652."—which is supposed to allude to the preservation of the family then occupying
it from the plague. It is now used as a shop. Further down the
street is the richly-carved front of *Bishop Lloyd's House*. Lloyd
was translated from the Manx See to that of Chester in 1605. A
panel, dated 1615, bears his arms. A little beyond this house, on
the opposite side, is Trinity Church, where the poet Parnell (*d.*
1717), and Matthew Henry (*d.* 1714), the commentator, were buried,
the latter "beneath the commandments." *Derby House*, once
a palace of the Stanleys but now divided among several humble
tenants, is another relic of old times. To reach it go through
a small passage on the left, after passing the end of Nicholas
Street. Returning to High Cross and St. Peter's Church, we next
turn up Northgate Street, and can if we choose make our way
along the left-hand side by *Shoemaker's Row* to the market, and
so to St. Werburg Street and the South-porch of

The Cathedral.

Weekday Services: 10.15 a.m., 4.15 p.m.

The **Cathedral** stands on ground that is considered, and not
improbably, to have been the site of a Christian church from the
middle of the 2nd century. The existing fabric is of various dates
from the 12th to the 16th century, and was the church of the
Benedictine Abbey founded by Hugh Lupus, who brought over
monks from Bec, in Normandy. Of these Anselm, who shortly
afterwards was made Archbishop of Canterbury, was the leader.
The church was dedicated to St. Werburg, or Withburga, fourth
Abbess of Ely, early in the 8th century, whose remains had been
brought to Chester and enshrined in a Saxon church on or near
this spot by Elfreda, daughter of King Alfred. When Henry VIII.
dissolved the Abbey, Chester was made the seat of a bishopric,
and the Abbey church became the Cathedral, for although the
title Bishop of Chester occurs long before that time, it appears to
have been used to designate the prelate whose see was at Lichfield.

As we approach from Northgate Street, the new block of buildings connected with the north-west angle is the *King's School*,
founded by Henry VIII. in the Abbot's Lodgings. The **West
Front** of the cathedral has a fine Perpendicular window, but
is lacking in dignity, and, speaking generally, it must be added
that the re-facing of the outside, necessitated by the wasting of
the new red sandstone of which it is built, has imparted an air of
newness to the whole building that, combined with its comparatively small size, detracts much from its impressiveness as a
whole. Two noticeable features of the building are the floor
level, which, owing to the fall of the ground eastward, is highest

at the west end, and the very large south transept, which **from**
the end of the 15th century has been the parish church of St.
Oswald, and until recent years was the only place of worship **for**
the parishioners. Entering by the south porch and standing on
the raised part of the floor under the west window, the first thing
that strikes us is the warm tone of the interior, due to the colour
of the stone, and in no other cathedral, except perhaps Hereford,
so noticeable. In the course of the thorough restoration, which
is approaching completion, the cumbrous organ screen that
formerly cut the church in half has been removed, and now the
full length is seen at once. The westernmost part of the **Nave**,
with which we begin our survey, is Late Perpendicular, and except
for the elaborate west window, very plain. On the south wall
hangs a tapestry of Raphael's "Elymas the **Sorcerer**." In the
south-west angle, in the base of an unfinished tower, is the
Consistory Court with Jacobean fittings, while at the north-west
angle is a fine fragment of the Norman Church. Here is the new
Baptistery, with an old Italian font. Along the N. aisle wall
(Norman), between the Baptistery and the (Norman) N.E. doorway
leading to the cloisters, are some magnificent **mosaics**. They were
given (1886) by Mrs. Platt, of Durham, in memory of her husband
who was a great benefactor of the King's School. The Nave, its S.
aisle, and the S. Transept (restoration incomplete, 1887), are Late
Decorated. From the space below the central tower, whence there is
a good general view of the Choir, we pass through the elegant
Screen, whereon is the handsome **Organ**, into the small **North
Transept**, which is Norman below and Perpendicular above. In
the Norman work two periods are easily detected—the earlier of
small stones widely jointed, the later of large well fitted stones. Of
the Perpendicular windows the north one is a happy restoration by
the late Sir G. Scott, who also designed the roof, in which observe
the arms of Wolsey, who is supposed to have been a benefactor to
the abbey, and is similarly commemorated by a boss in the north
cloister. The large canopied **tomb** on the floor of this transept
marks the present resting place of the learned Bishop Pearson
(d. 1686). Around the recumbent effigy are heads of the Apostles
with sentences from the creed. He was buried at the east end of
the choir, where his coffin was discovered in 1844. Strange to say,
until the present monument was erected, a few years ago, from the
designs of Mr. A. W. Blomfield, **nothing** indicated the grave of
Chester's best known bishop.

The **Choir**, which is in the Early Decorated style, has been
completely restored, and is a rich and beautiful work. The exquisite *canopies* of the *Stalls*, 48 in number, are the finest in
England, and some of the so-called *Misereres** are very quaint and
include one (sixth on the north side) of St. Werburg and the Stolen
Goose. The *Bishop's Throne*, with stalls for his Chancellor and

---

* For complete description of all the Misereres see Dean Howson's Handbook, 1s.

Chaplain, is modern, and the gift of the clergy of the diocese. The *Pulpit*, with representations of the building of Solomon's Temple, St. John the Baptist in the Wilderness, and the Revelation to St. John the Apostle of the Heavenly Jerusalem, is the gift of the Freemasons of the shire. To the Freemasons of that part of Lancashire formerly included in the diocese is due the restoration of the *Sedilia*. The *Altar*, constructed of |materials brought from the Holy Land, is decorated with carvings representing the plants connected with our Saviour's Passion. A noteworthy architectural feature of the choir is the *Triforium*, with four arches answering to each bay below.

The **Choir Aisles**, like the choir itself, belong to the Decorated period. That on the south side ends in an apse, and so reproduces the features of the original work, which was thus restored as a memorial of Mr. Thomas Brassey, the railway contractor, by his sons. The south door of this aisle was discovered during the restoration, and near it was found a grave, believed to be that of Ralph Higden, author of the "Polychronicon," who died about 1367. The so-called *Emperor's Tomb*, traditionally assigned to Henry IV. of Germany (d. 1106), belongs to some person unknown. Note on the floor of the aisle, near its west end, the course of the Norman apse. The north aisle is terminated eastward by a Late Perpendicular addition, and shows what the corresponding aisle was like before it reverted to its early 14th century form; and on its floor westward the line of the original Norman apse is preserved. The *Canon's Vestry*, already mentioned as pertaining to the North Transept, should be seen. It is Early English, except the west side, which is Norman. The easternmost extension of the Cathedral is the **Lady Chapel**, which is entered from the north aisle of the Choir. Originally Early English, and standing out clear from the rest of the church, it was in the 15th century hemmed in for two bays of its length by the eastward additions to the choir aisles. At the same time the Perpendicular windows were inserted in the eastern bays and at the east end. Now, with the exception of the two western bays on the north side, it has been restored to its former condition, and the lofty high-pitched roof opened out, after having long been hidden by a mean ceiling. Note a boss portraying the murder of Thomas à Becket. All the windows have been filled with stained glass. The subjects of the three southern ones, and of the single northern one, are almost wholly taken from the Acts of the Apostles.

The **Cloisters.**—We enter these through the Norman doorway at the east end of the north aisle of the nave. The east, west, and north sides of the square, though dilapidated, are picturesque; the south side, which had perished, has been rebuilt. The style throughout is Perpendicular, and the arcade, on the south and partly on the west side, is double. Near the spot where we enter, the early abbots were buried, and the inscribed slabs relating to the third and fourth should be noticed. Proceeding westward we have visible proof of the Norman character of the wall of the adjoining aisle of the cathedral. At the south-west corner a passage, also Norman, leads to the West Front. Along the west side of the cloister is a long vaulted chamber of Early Norman work, the purpose of which is doubtful. The north side was bounded by what was the old Refectory. [A fine Early English reader's pulpit, with staircase in the wall, is still preserved, but the noble chamber has had its western portion severed from it by a passage.] The lavatory of the monks is indicated by the Early English arches, spoilt by the passage just mentioned.

The East cloister is bounded by the *Fratry* (restored) and the vestibule of the *Chapter* House. Between the two is a passage called the *Maiden's Aisle*.

The Chapter House and its *Vestibule*, which may be entered either from the north transept or the east cloister, should be seen even by the most hurried visitor. Both date from the last half of the 13th century, and are, therefore, Early English at its best. A singularly graceful feature of the vestibule is the way the mouldings of the pillars run up unbroken into the vaulting. In the Chapter House, which is also the *Cathedral Library*, the beautiful five-light east window is filled with excellent modern glass, by Heaton & Butler, pourtraying the story of the foundation from St. Werburg downwards. Notice the bust of Charles Kingsley by *Belt !*

Those who have time should complete their survey of the outside of the cathedral. Amongst other details of the restored South Transept will be observed, near the south-west angle, memorials of Lord Beaconsfield, Dr. Kenealy, and Mr. Gladstone, with his Vatican pamphlets.

We have but indicated some of the chief objects of interest in this most interesting of English cities, such as all visitors would desire to see. Those who are antiquarians should also inspect the vaulted crypts or cellars, respectively under Crypt Chambers, in East Gate Street, and Messrs. Newman & Crittall's premises in Bridge Street.

For Eaton Hall, the splendid seat of the Duke of Westminster, the route lies over Grosvenor Bridge, a short distance beyond which is the *Grosvenor Lodge*, a costly structure, imitated from St. Augustine's Gateway, at Canterbury. Thence it is three miles to the Hall. The distance by river from the Groves, above the Old Bridge to Eccleston, is 3 miles, and to the iron bridge beyond the Hall, 5½ miles. In summer a steamer plies between Chester and Farndon, calling at these points.

The Park is at all times open to the public, but inquiry as to the Hall should be made at the Hotels or principal booksellers.

Hawarden (pron. "Harden").

Route 1. *Broughton Station* (*Mold Branch*) 5 m; *Hawarden* 7½ m.

   ,,   **2.** *Queen's Ferry* (*main Holyhead line*) 7 m; *Hawarden* 8¾ m.

   ,,   **3.** *Hope Station* (*Mold Branch*) 9 m; *Hawarden* 12 m.

Hawarden Castle is reached by a short foot-path from the junction of the three drives—from Hawarden, Broughton and Hope respectively, but visitors are accompanied by the lodge-keeper from the *Village Gate* opposite the inn, to which all our distances are calculated.

Regulations as to the Park and Castle. Visitors are allowed upon the gravel drives between noon and sunset. The old castle is open, without charge, rom 1 to 6 p.m. from May to October inclusive. At other times there is a charge of one shilling for each party of six or less. Dogs not admitted.

There is a more satisfactory motive than that idle curiosity which befits the tripper rather than the tourist for visiting Hawarden, and few travellers who are not going at Yankee speed will grudge the few hours which are required for this excursion. Hawarden Park is pleasant rambling ground; what little remains of the Castle is picturesque; the church, though simple, has a kind of miniature cathedral look about it, and the views from the castle and churchyard are good and extensive.

All things considered, perhaps the best plan is to start from *Broughton Station* and, after proceeding about a mile, during which we take the right-hand branch beyond Broughton Church and cross Broughton Brook, to enter the Park by the *East Lodge*. If we start from Queen's Ferry we shall enter the Park from the village, by the *Wynt Gate*, opposite the *Glynne Arms* (n.q.), and, if from Hope, by the *South* or "*Top*" *Lodge*, which is 1½ miles from the station, and reached by turning to the right at the second crossroads. In this case we approach by a fine gravel drive through the *Bilberry Woods*.

The Broughton and Hope routes meet after a long mile's walk through the Park, just south of the Castle, the first view of which, crowning the thickly wooded eminence in front, is striking. From Broughton you bend to the left as you approach the modern residence of Mr. Gladstone (Hawarden Park). From Hope the ravine of the Broughton Brook is crossed.

Little remains of the **Old Castle** except the huge circular keep, and that gives an impression of great strength. It is 20 yards across, and its walls are nearly 5 yards thick. A modern wall has been substituted for the battlements, and from the summit there is a wide view extending in one direction to the Clwydian Hills, in the others across the Dee estuary, and over Chester to Beeston Hill.

Hard by are the scanty remains of the *Chapel.*

The ruin dates from an indefinite period—perhaps a little earlier than that of the first Edward. Simon de Monfort and Llewelyn held colloquy within the space occupied by its present walls, and the upshot was its surrender to the latter. Then it reverted to the Crown, but was again taken, this time by Dafydd, brother of Llewelyn, about which time the present keep was probably built. To describe its subsequent fortunes in detail would be tedious, but the last important scene in its eventful history was its surrender to General Mytton in the Parliamentarian war, after which it was dismantled and fell by purchase into the hands of Sergeant Glynne in whose family, represented by Mr. W. H. Gladstone, it still remains.

Hawarden Church stands north of the village street, on an eminence overlooking the Dee Estuary. It has a central tower surmounted by a short spire, a nave and two aisles, and a chancel which does not geometrically fit in with the nave. The roof and fittings suffered from a fire in 1857, after which a restoration was effected by Sir Gilbert Scott. The *Reredos,* a representation in alabaster of the Last Supper, is in memory of the Rev. Henry Glynne, Rector for 38 years, and in the side chancel is a fine figure, by Noble, of his brother, Sir Stephen Glynne, who died in 1874. The communion plate was stolen in 1821, and again in 1835.

The **Modern Mansion** is north-east of the Castle, between it and the high-road. It was originally a square brick building, but besides being encased in stone and turreted, it has received so many additions as to retain no resemblance to its original self.

For a full description of all that is interesting about Hawarden, the tourist should refer to the " Hawarden Visitors' Handbook," published at Chester.

Chester to Mold and Ruthin (over the Clwydian range).

Chester to Mold (rail), 13 *m.   Mold to Ruthin (by old road),* 9 *m ; (over Moel Fammau),* 11 *m.*

There is only one reason—but that a very good one—for including this route in a Tourist hand-book. The pedestrian by adopting it, has a very easy walk to begin with and, if favoured by weather, will gain during his few hours' experience a general view of the country he is about to explore as pleasing as it is comprehensive. From the ridge of the Clwydian range, he will have a great part of it modelled out before him. As we shall describe the Vale of Clwyd in our Rhyl section, we content ourselves with saying here that though it has been greatly overpraised, it affords when seen from this walk as rich a prospect of characteristic English rather than Welsh scenery,—green meadows, yellow corn-fields and waving woods—as the eye can wish to rest upon. The chief Welsh mountains are a considerable distance away, but their respective summits are easily distinguished.

Mold may also be reached from Wrexham by a line which joins our present route at *Hope Junction,* 2½ m. short of which and close to *Bridge End Station* it passes close to the fragmentary ruin of *Caergwrle Castle,* on the left, and the British Post of *Caer Estyn* on the right. The alleged discovery of a hypocaust or warm air bath at the former place gives it a claim to Roman origin, but all we are told about its later existence is that it served as a resting place for Queen Eleanor on her way from Carnarvon, and was presented to her by her husband, Edward I. The fragments are those of a round tower and walls.

Hope Mountain, 1½ miles from Bridge End Station, is 1,080 feet high, and commands a wide prospect.

There are half-a-dozen or more trains from Chester to Mold running the distance in from half-an-hour to 40 minutes. The line passes through an ordinary country, with here and there indications of mining industry. For 3½ miles it is identical with the main line to Holyhead; then it branches inland to the left and passes within sight of the low range of hills on which Hawarden (*p.* 11) stands. At the next station, *Hope,* the mineral line from Wrexham to Connah's Quay is crossed. The only view of any note on the way is that of the Clwydian Hills which extend north and south for about 20 miles—a long waving outline in which the highest summit Moel Fammau is rendered doubly conspicuous by its huge monument.

Mold.

Hotels. *Black Lion* (H.Q.), in the main street, between the station road and the Church; *Temperance,* Chester Street.

Mining and agriculture divide the attention of the people of Mold. The tourist should take a peep at the church, view the surrounding country from Bailey Hill (both places are within a few minutes' walk of the inn and station), and then proceed on his way to Ruthin.

The **Church,** in the higher part of the town, between the hotel and Bailey's Hill, is a fine one. It was built in the reign of Henry VII., and has been restored by Scott. The principal features of the interior are the richly-panelled roof and the broad band of quatrefoils and stone panels above the nave arcades. Many of the windows are filled with good glass by Wailes. In the church-yard rows of tombstones serve as a border to the main walk.

The **Bailey Hill** at the north end of the main street, rises just high enough above the town to admit of a panoramic display of the surrounding country, in which the most noteworthy object is Moel Fammau heading the Clwydian range in the west,—" with awful pre-eminence," says an old guide-book writer. On the top of the mound are a clump of trees and a bowling green. The public notice in regard to the use of the latter suggests an almost puritanical austerity on the part of the local authorities. There are no traces of the fortifications which are said to have originated the name, " ballium " signifying a portion of a fortified castle.

The *Ruthin Road* is a continuation of the one which comes up from the station at right angles to the main street. The one used for carriages diverges from the old one 3½ miles on the way and, crossing the range further south at a lower elevation, adds nearly two miles to the distance. Pedestrians should follow the old one. The first two miles are on the flat or up-hill, and as we rise there is a pleasant retrospect of the town. A little to the left of the road is a Jesuit College (formerly Mold Gaol), and, if our walk be taken in the afternoon, the number of clerically dressed trios taking their daily constitutional, and speaking any language but English, will suggest to us that it is in a flourishing condition.

From the top of the hill, 250 feet above sea-level and somewhat disfigured by one or two mines and quarries, a descent is made through a nicely wooded country past the entrance to Co-omendy Hall, to the **Loggerhead's Inn** in the **Alyn** valley. This favourite house-of-call has a signboard painted by Richard Wilson more than a century ago, and now quite undecipherable. It represents, we are told, **two** heads back to back, and the inscription is " we three loggerheads be." The third head you evolve from your inner consciousness.

There is a very pretty walk from here along the east side of the Alyn river —flanked by trees and limestone rocks —to *Rhydymwyn Station* on the Mold and Denbigh line. to which we have described the descent of Moel Fammau, when the ascent has been made from the Vale of Clwyd.

Beyond the "Loggerheads," our road crosses the Alyn, **and in** ¾ mile reaches a smithy, whence the new road curves away to **the** left, and the old one, continuing almost straight on. soon gets **between** the hills. In less than another mile, when the last farm on the left across the streamlet has been passed, it is best to diverge to the right (there is a gate a little further on) and enter a cart-track which leads up a marshy hollow and after a toilsome ten minutes brings us in sight of Moel Fammau. Keeping well to the left we cross some rough heathy ground sprinkled with trees of so moribund a character that the most genial spring sunshine can hardly quicken them into foliage, whilst their twisted branches might even have furnished Gustave Doré with a subject. Then, gaining the ridge. we join the track from Ruthin, and in a few moments are clambering up the ' disjecta membra ' of the monument.

For the view from Moel Fammau see p. 37. **The way** from the summit to Ruthin is **by a track which** goes a little west of **the ridge** to the top of Bwlch-pen-barras.

To reach Ruthin without climbing **Moel Fammau** you keep straight on along the old road, which affords capital walking up its grass-grown slope, to the pass of *Bwlch-pen-barras*, 1150 feet above sea-level. The contrast between the dark heather on one side and the (in winter) russet bracken on the other is striking. Hence a delightful view across the rich vale of Clwyd—none the worse for its being narrowed by the frame of the flanking hillsides, opens out in front. Close at hand is a grassy glade, falling to a plantation, and beyond it the vale of Clwyd backed in the distance by Snowdonia. Ruthin with its castle and modern spire is just in front, and lower down the valley, the castle of Denbigh rises from the plain on a low mound. St. Asaph Cathedral is seen, and the coast west of Rhyl.

Three tracks strike northwards from here along the ridge in the direction of Moel Fammau. The middle one is the shortest for pedestrians.

In descending you proceed down the easy slope of the road till you come to a plantation on the left, a little short of the farm of *Rhiwlas*. Here it is best to leave the road and descend the hill on the left. Other paths are soon reached, which leave the open ground through a gate leading into a lane. This lane rejoins the new road in less than half-a-mile. The pretty little new church and inn (the " Griffin ") of *Llanbedr* are only a few minutes' walk further, and from them you may either pursue the road, or make straight for the station by a foot-path which commences at once and goes almost in a direct line to it, the landmark being the spire of Ruthin church. A road is entered only a few yards short of the wooden bridge at the south end of the station.

Chester and Holyhead Railway.

Chester to Rhyl, Llandudno, Bangor, and Carnarvon.

Chester to Rhyl, **30** *m*; *Abergele,* **34** *m*; *Colwyn Bay,* **40½** *m*; *Llandudno Junction,* **44½** *m*; (*Llandudno,* **47½** *m.*) *Conway,* **45** *m*; *Penmaenmawr,* **49½** *m*; *Llanfairfechan,* **52** *m*; *Aber,* **54** *m*; *Bangor,* **59½** *m*; *Menai Bridge,* **61** *m*; (*Holyhead,* **84** *m.*) *Carnarvon,* **68** *m.*

This line affords one of the pleasantest railway journeys in the country. For nearly the whole distance between Chester and Carnarvon it has the sea close at hand on one side, and on the other a series of landscapes which, though they seldom attain to the highest rank in respect of foreground, include more or less distant views of some of the finest Welsh scenery. Among the most striking prospects on the route we may mention that across the Conway estuary during the descent to Llandudno Junction, the more circumscribed one while rounding the abrupt bluffs of Penmaenbach and Penmaenmawr, the charming peeps across the Menai Straits between Bangor and Carnarvon, and, on the Holyhead route, the retrospect of Snowdonia after passing through the Tubular bridge. The Vale of Clwyd, the limestone cliffs about Colwyn, and the town of Conway are also noteworthy features during the journey. The first part of the route as far as Mostyn, we must fairly own, is greatly marred by the chimneys of chemical works and other branches of local industry.

The Route. Issuing from the joint station of the L. & N. W. and G. W. Companies the line passes through a short tunnel, a sandstone cutting, and the city wall. A hasty glimpse is caught on the right of the Water Tower, a picturesque Edwardian structure, and close by at its foot is a collection of Roman antiquities prominent among which is a hypocaust or warming apparatus. Then follows an embankment which commands a full view of the *Roodee.* Over this famous race-course the town-hall, the tower of the cathedral, and the castle, or rather gaol, are seen—the last named a little left of the Grosvenor Bridge. whose single arch is more remarkable for width and height than picturesqueness. Crossing the Dee ourselves, we soon enter Wales. On the left a wide alluvial valley extends to the foot of the hills which culminate in the Clwydian range. Along this valley goes the main line of the Great Western to Shrewsbury, which we shall describe further on. In another mile or so the Mold branch strikes off on the same side. Away to the west we gain our first introduction to the hills of Wales in the Clwydian range, running due north and south.   A little further and a flagstaff rising from a wooded ridge on the left marks the position of Hawarden Castle (p. 11), beyond which the fine church of Hawarden also comes into view with the tower-crowned summit of Moel Fammau beyond.   A straight road leads up to Hawarden from Queen's Ferry station, 7 m. from Chester.

For the next fifteen miles the line skirts the Dee estuary, a dreary enough waste of sand with a line of low hills on its further shore, a little way up which the sand-side resort of Parkgate may be seen.   Opposite to it, and the first station of any note upon our route, is Flint (Royal Oak, H.Q.).   The only object of interest to the tourist—and that a scant one—in this town is the Castle.   We can see it from the railway and read its history as we go along.   The neighbourhood is utterly spoilt by chemical and other works, which have, however, given a considerable fillip to the town from a commercial point of view.   In former days, we read, "the haut ton came here to bathe"!   This suggests that mud-baths were even then appreciated.

Flint Castle stands on a slightly elevated rock between the railway and the sea.   It is a bare and square ruin consisting of four towers, of which one, called the *Double Tower*, is considerably larger than the others, and the fragments of walls connecting them.   Originally, it appears to have been a Plantagenet stronghold.   Two unfortunate kings of that line are associated with its history—Edward II. and Richard II.   The former, we are told, met his favourite, Piers Gaveston, within its walls, and outside them Bolingbroke, if we may believe Shakespeare, offered his mock homage to the latter.   Previous to these events the castle was taken by Llewelyn, and in the interval it was presented by Edward III. to the Black Prince.   In due course it fell into the hands of the Percies, of Northumberland; Sir Roger Mostyn garrisoned it for Charles I. and Sir William Brereton took it for Cromwell, but it only survived its capture a few years.

The next object of any note is **Basingwerke Abbey**, which stands in a belt of trees on the left of the line, 4 miles beyond Flint, and a few yards short of **Holywell Station**.

Basingwerke Abbey and Holywell.   Both of these may be visited in a walk of 2⅓ miles there and back from Holywell Station, which is distant 17 miles from Chester and 13 from Rhyl.   Take the road which runs inland from the down-side of the station, and, where it divides at an *inn*, bear to the left for the Abbey, which is on the right and above the road some 250 yards from the turn.

Basingwerke Abbey, now a neglected ruin, situated amid surroundings of the ugliest, is itself interesting and picturesque, and the remains, though very fragmentary, are considerable, and date from about 1170—1200.   The House was Cistercian, and was founded by Ranulph, 2nd Earl of Chester, in 1131, at which time a community of monks was already settled here, probably attracted to the spot by the neighbouring holy well of St. Winifred, which is

described below. It is difficult to allot the remains to their original position in
the structure. The chief parts belong to the south transept of the Church and
the adjoining refectory. Most of the arches and windows are pointed, but there
are two small round-headed doorways, and two well-preserved round arches
with a shaft between them. These arches led from the refectory into a small
chamber. Some of the buildings have been used for farm purposes, and one
chamber, now a roofless shell of three walls, but whose purpose is doubtful,
should be examined. To enter it, pass round to the right of the farm-yard and
go through a gate beyond. One wall still has 4 lancet lights, and along the
inside is a well-preserved arcade, rounded above. The abbey was dissolved in
1535, but one small square-headed Perpendicular window is the only remnant
of its later architectural history. It is much to be desired that some care were
taken to preserve the ruins from further decay. At a trifling outlay the immediate precincts, which are still graced by some good sycamores, might be made
quite an oasis in this manufacturing desert.

For **Holywell** we return as far as the Inn and take the other road,
which ascends the valley past a succession of works of various kinds in whose
b half the copious brook that issues from St. Winifred's well is dammed back
into a series of anything but crystal pools. There is no mistaking the way, for
the road is straight and the **well** is on the left-hand side, a few hundred yards
beyond a ramshackle bridge that crosses the road. The church and the vaulted
canopy beneath it, under which is the sacred spring, form a charming whole of
Late Perpendicular work, and were built by Margaret, mother of Henry VII. The
spring itself—so the legend runs—burst from the spot where for a while rested
the head of Winifred, a virgin who lived in the 7th century, and whom a too
ardent lover—Caradoc, Prince of Wales—enraged at the rejection of his suit,
had decapitated. Of the virtues of the spring none can doubt who view the
many mouldering crutches and other votive offerings that still hang about its
arches, like the drenched garments which the shipwrecked mariners of old hung
up in the temple of the sea-god. Just below the spring a bath has been made,
and its zinc-covered roof is in keeping with the spirit of the age, which informs
us that the sweet moss on the stones is *Jungermannia asplenioides* and the blood
stains *Byssus iolithus*. A fee of 2d. is charged for admission to the well. To
inspect the *old church* the care-taker, who lives across the road, must be found.
The building contains nothing of any particular interest. It is now used for
Welsh service and as a Sunday-school. Close by is a singularly ugly church
built in the last century, and in charge of the same custodian, who will point
out a Pennant monument, dated 1623, and show the mutilated effigy of a priest
holding a chalice, which used to be exhibited as the statue of St. Winifred, but
is now treated with small respect. The town of *Holywell* (*King's Head*, H.Q.)
is of less importance as a trading centre than formerly, and now only numbers
about 3,000 inhabitants. The *Church* has been restored.

About Holywell the sea-shore is a bare, shadeless waste—a
salt-marsh—but at **Mostyn** (*Mostyn Arms*, H.Q.) the scenery
improves, pleasant-looking woods shelving down a steep bank to
the side of the line. The entrance to *Mostyn Hall* is opposite
the station, but the Hall itself, though less than half-a-mile
away, is not seen. It is the seat of Lord Mostyn, and is
interesting from the fact, that had not Henry of Richmond been
apprised of the arrival of a contingent of Richard the Third's

army in time to escape through the " King's Window "—as it has since been called—the course of English history might have been very different from what it has been. The house dates from the reign of Henry VI., but has been much altered. It contains a great variety of Welsh antiquities.

A little beyond Mostyn the end of the estuary of the Dee is reached by a wilderness of sand-hills stretching to *Aire Point*, on which is a light-house. The low-lying cluster of houses at its opposite termination is Hoylake. On the left the hills grow higher. One of them is crowned by a white building, which was one of the stations of the semaphore system for announcing the arrival of ships before the telegraph came into use. Another building for the same purpose is seen a little further on. Then we pass *Prestatyn* Station (*Railway*, Q.), beyond which the Vale of Clwyd opens on the left, and the old cliff-line retires. The west side of the long and straight Clwydian range is now in sight, and Moel Fammau once more lords it over the rounded summits on either hand. From about here, too, the Great Orme's Head comes into view—the furthest point seawards—and to the left of it we may detect Penmaenmawr, the north-east limb of Snowdonia.

The next Station is **Rhyl**—the centre-point of the wide seaboard of the Vale of Clwyd, here a dead level. *For a full description of the town, &c., see page* 23. The hotels close to the Station, which is on the south side of the town, and about ¼ *m.* from the sea, are the *Alexandra*, the *Dudley Arms*, and the *Bee*.

A mile beyond Rhyl the line crosses the estuary of the Clwyd, and the scenery becomes more interesting. Looking up the river we may see Rhuddlan Castle and, on a slight eminence to the right, the bulky tower of St. Asaph Cathedral. More to the right is the white steeple of Bodelwyddan Church, the richest example of modern ecclesiastical architecture in Wales. The scene on the right, while crossing the estuary, is rather picturesque, and a little beyond *Foryd Station* we reach the real sea and look across it to the Little and Great Orme's Head. On the left richly wooded hills advance towards the line. Then come Abergele and the modern suburb which entitles it to be called a wateringplace, **Pensarn**. The latter is a row of lodging-houses, with a little iron church and two hotels. (*For particulars, see Rhyl Section.*)

The modern, and seemingly vast baronial mansion of *Gwrych* (R. B. Hesketh, Esq.) rising from a hill-side which is wooded from head to foot, monopolises the attention of the traveller as he leaves Abergele. It shows a frontage of a quarter of a mile, and its chief tower is nearly 100 feet high. Numerous other towers and turrets, square or round, and some of them ivy-clad, lend an imposing air to the building, which is, however, in great part only a shell built for effect. The hills that border the west side of the Vale of Clwyd and abut on the sea from about here to the two

Orme's Heads are of mountain limestone, and a little beyond Gwrych they are characteristically pierced by a large cave conspicuous from the line, and called *Yr Ogof*. It lends its name to the hill above—Cefn-yr-Ogof.

Hereabouts the beach is of white limestone pebbles, and the line is carried some way above it. About *Llandulas* Station the scenery is much disfigured by chimneys connected with lime-works. Then we pass through a short tunnel that pierces the headland called *Penmaen Rhos*, and on issuing from it overlook the fine sweep of Colwyn Bay, which bids fair in the course of time to form a continuous watering-place. The original village, **Old Colwyn (Station)** looking very like "New" Colwyn, is only a little beyond the tunnel, and from it the line skirts the shore, high up, to **Colwyn Bay Station**, 1½ miles beyond Old Colwyn. Large Hotels, a Hydro', and an ever increasing number of lodging houses and shops testify to the popularity of this bright-featured watering-place. A short distance further along the shore its little rival, *Llandrillo-yn-Rhos*, is seen.

Picturesque limestone cliffs now appear; the Little Orme's Head becomes a prominent object on the right front, and the line goes inland across the broad neck of the promontory of which, together with its "big brother," the Great Orme, it forms the chief natural feature. From the summit of a short ascent, the eye strikes for the first time into the heart of "Wild Wales." Looking out on the left we have the Conway estuary in the foreground, and behind it a broken outline of mountains. Forming the centre piece is the green gently rounded summit of Y Foel Fras; to the left of it and further away, the ridge of Carnedd Llewelyn, the peak of Penllithrig, with a steep southern slope, and the more rounded height of Moel Eilio; to the right of Y Foel Fras is Tal-y-fan. As we proceed the castle and bridges of Conway come into view, and over them the summit of Penmaenmawr may be discerned. *Mochdre and Pabo Sta. is 2 m. W. of Colwyn Bay Sta.*

A few minutes more and we are at **Llandudno Junction** (*Refreshment rooms*, and *hotel* close by), which is separated from Conway by the width of the estuary only. Northwards, the Llandudno branch strikes away. Southwards up the charming Conway valley, winds that to Llanrwst, Bettws-y-Coed, and Ffestiniog. "Old Conway's foaming flood" is the poetical description of the river we are crossing, and when the tide is rushing in under the "twa brigs," the epithet is something more than alliterative, but we have scarcely time to notice it before we are whisked along an embankment, through the "tubular," under the walls and the castle into **Conway** Station. Up the valley on the left are seen Tal-y-fan and Penllithrig. *For the town and its surroundings, see Llandudno Section.*

Beyond Conway we look across a flat sea-board of grass and gorse to the western side of Llandudno and the Great Orme. On the left the hill called Conway Mountain rises abruptly from the line, and we may notice that the limestone has given place to

the slate of which Snowdonia almost entirely consists. One of
the Rocks on the Conway Mountains shows a clear-cut human
profile. A tunnel under *Penmaenbach* (the "little" head of the
rock, as opposed to *Penmaenmawr*, the "great" ditto) succeeds, on
issuing from which we are in sight of Puffin Island and Anglesey,
Beaumaris being distinctly visible. In a wooded hollow on the
left is the terribly named village of Dwygyfylchi (Doo-e-guv-
ul-k'y), beyond which, after passing under the bluff of Foel Llys,
intermediate between Penmaenbach and Penmaenmawr, we
come upon the green crater-like recess, which is occupied by
the pleasant watering-place of **Penmaenmawr**. Huge stone
and slate quarries disfigure the bold headland which gives its
name to the village and drops almost sheer to the sea a little
beyond it. The high-road skirts the side of this headland, and
the rail goes through its base, emerging from the tunnel upon
the less confined but still more silvan belt of park and meadow
land that contains the old inland village, but quite modern
sea-side resort of **Llanfairfechan**. Behind this the mountains
are loftier than any of those whose feet we have yet skirted,
Tal-y-fan and Llwydmor being the chief heights.

The village of **Aber**, 2 miles beyond Llanfairfechan, has
altered but little except as regards its hotel, which is now a very
fair and convenient one, since the time—many years ago—when
a voluminous guide-book compiler wrote in the " English as she
is spoke " of the period : " At the inn here, tho' respectable,
there is no post-horses. It is a convenient place whence he
ascend the summit of Penmaenmawr." Here we are almost
opposite Beaumaris, behind which rises the Bulkeley Monument.
Nearly all the intervening space of 4 miles is occupied by the
Lavan Sands. Southwards the beautiful Aber glen opens, and on
the left of its entrance is a pointed wooded hill called *Maes-y-gaer*,
the " field of the fortress."

The next object of interest beyond Aber is the square tower of
Penrhyn Castle, rising above the woods on the right of the line.
On the left, the Nant Ffrancon mountains are seen at the head of
the Ogwen Valley, the nearest, on the right of the valley, being
Moel-perfydd; behind it, Y Garn and the Glyders, and on the left,
Carnedd Dafydd. The pretty Ogwen glen is crossed, and then,
through two short tunnels, between which the new line to Bethesda
strikes off on the left, we enter the **Bangor Station**. (*Refreshment Rooms.*)

For Bangor and the route hence to Holyhead, see Bangor Section.

For Carnarvon the main line is followed through a tunnel to
Menai Bridge Station, which is close to the Suspension Bridge
over the Straits, and just beyond the favourite *George Hotel*.
Between the tunnel and the station there is a good view of the
bridge and straits. The Tubular Bridge is some way further west,
and a little way short of it the Carnarvon branch ascends south-

wards, affording fine glimpses of the straits, the bridges, and the Anglesey Monument.   Then the straits disappear for a time behind the oak groves of *Vaenol Park*, to reappear at the busy-looking little *Port Dinorwic*.   After passing this station, there is a delightful view up the straits, including, on the Anglesey side, the silvan grounds of *Plas-Newydd* (Marquis of Anglesey).

Hence to **Carnarvon** the line is carried above the straits, of which pleasing views are here and there obtained.

For Carnarvon, see Carnarvon Section.

RHYL

RHYL SECTION.

𝕽𝖍𝖞𝖑.

———◆———

Hotels: *Westminster, Belvoir, Queen's,* opposite the pier, ½ *m.* from station; *Royal* (H.Q.), *Mostyn Arms, George, Albion,* between station and sea; *Alexandra, Dudley Arms, Bee,* close to station; *Vaughan's Temperance,* Queen's Street. **Hydro'**, ½ *m.* E. of station.

Post: Chief deliveries, 7 *a.m.,* 1.30, 4.30 *p.m.*; despatches, *abt.* 10 *a.m.,* 12.10, 9.0 *p.m.*

Population: About 6000.

Distances from the Parade (pier): *Walks*: Rhuddlan, 3 *m*; Dyserth (new road), 3½ *m*; Prestatyn (by the sands), 4 *m*; Pensarn, 4 *m*.

By rail (Eastward): Prestatyn, 3½ *m*: Mostyn, 10 *m*; Holywell, 14 *m*; Chester, 30 *m.* (*Southward*): Rhuddlan, 3½ *m*; St. Asaph, 6 *m*; Denbigh, 11 *m*; Ruthin, 18 *m*; Corwen, 30 *m.* (*Westward*): Abergele. 4 *m*; Colwyn Bay, 10½ *m*; Llandudno, 18 *m*; Conway, 15 *m*; Bettws-y-Coed, 30 *m*; Bangor, 30 *m*.

To the unencumbered tourist this large and still expanding watering-place can only be recommended as a convenient station at which to leave the main line and visit the two or three objects of real interest in the Vale of Clwyd. It occupies a central position on the perfectly level seaboard which extends across the mouth of that valley from the Clwydian range on the east to the limestone cliffs behind Abergele on the west, a breadth of about 8 miles. It is true that some of the highest Carnarvonshire mountains, including Carnedd Llewelyn, and possibly Snowdon itself, may be seen either from the esplanade or its immediate neighbourhood, but they are too far off to be taken into serious account in connection with the natural attractions of the locality. Except for the long waving line of the Clwydian hills, the limestone eminences behind Abergele and the towers of Rhuddlan Castle, there is nothing in the way of scenery to raise this dull end of the Vale of Clwyd above the standard of Southport or Blackpool.

But there is another and a large class of holiday-makers for whom Rhyl possesses sterling merits as a set-off to its natural unpicturesqueness. It is the *beau ideal* of a bathing-place—perfectly safe, and when the tide is out you have a good ride thrown in for your money. Paterfamilias, with an eye for the beautiful, and, may be, a rising family of disproportionate length to his purse, will find here a healthy, lively, and not unattractive town,

where he may locate himself and family at a cheaper rate than
that which prevails in the picturesque resorts further west, with
the comfortable assurance that the bairns will thoroughly enjoy
themselves on mile upon mile of good, firm sand, on which there
is not the slightest fear of their being surrounded by the tide or
tumbling off anywhere—because there is nowhere to tumble off—
while he himself may take train, and within the space of a day's
travel explore some of the finest scenes of Snowdonia. If disposed
to energy he may even make a push for Snowdon itself, while the
less ambitious visitor may spend several pleasant days in forming
acquaintance with the lesser beauties of the Vale of Clwyd, with
the agreeable variation of a sea-trip to Llandudno. Rhyl is
15 miles short of Llandudno Junction, which may be regarded as
the threshold of "Wild Wales."

The **Esplanade** at Rhyl is nearly a mile long, and ½ mile from
the station, whence it is reached by a street running at right
angles to it. The general plan of the town is rectangular, and the
principal shops are in High Street. The houses are for the most
part plain, well-to-do dwellings, without any pretence to the architectural dignity of Llandudno, and equally devoid of the detached-
villa style of Penmaenmawr and Llanfairfechan. At the west end
of the esplanade an extensive area has been walled in and laid out
with gardens, lawns, &c., so as to furnish the recognised requirements of modern seaside existence. It is needless to add that
what some people regard as the nuisances of that existence
correspondingly present themselves.

The **Pier** (*single admission*, 2*d*.) is 700 yards long, and affords
a comprehensive, though distant, view of the mountain-land
which occupies almost the entire area between Conway, Bettws-y-
Coed, Capel Curig and Bangor. Take the many-towered Gwrych
Castle on the wooded hill behind Abergele as your centre-point.
Above it you have Carnedd Llewelyn—a good second to Snowdon
in the skyward competition of Welsh mountains; then, more to
the right and rather nearer, Y Foel Fras, succeeded by Tal-y-fan,
1,000 feet lower. But the boldest slope of this range is that of
Penmaenmawr, which rises to the right of the chimneys of the
limeworks at Llandulas. The Great Orme brings to an end the
coast in this direction, and nearer at hand the Little Orme hides
Llandudno. South of Carnedd Llewelyn, Penllithrig is the chief
height. Turning eastwards you see the Clwydian range sinking
to the sea.

The shore between the Parade and **Foryd Bridge**, 1 mile
west of the pier, is rather rough. From the bridge (*toll*, 1*d*.), you
may proceed to Pensarn, either by road or by the sands, or by
ferry across the river-mouth, from opposite the little inn, some
way short of the bridge. Foryd is the port of Rhyl. The
slight elevation of this bridge makes it command a view up the
Vale of Clwyd. The massive ivy-clad towers of Rhuddlan Castle
are the most conspicuous object. Right of them are the tower of

St. Asaph Cathedral and the slim white spire of Bodelwyddan
Church. The full extent of the Clwydian range is seen from its
commencement near Dyserth, above which Newmarket Cop crops
up, to the monument-crowned Moel Fammau, and the round top
of Moel-y-Gamelin, only half-a-dozen miles beyond which, but of
course unseen, lie the town and sweet vale of Llangollen.

Excursions from Rhyl.

Under this head we include visits to Holywell (St. Winifred's
well), and Basingwerke Abbey; Rhuddlan Castle; Dyserth Castle
and waterfall; Bodelwyddan Church; St. Asaph Cathedral; Cefn
Caves and Ffynnon Fair (St. Mary's well); Denbigh Castle, &c.;
Ruthin Castle, &c.; Abergele and Gwrych Castle; the ascent of
Moel Fammau.

All of these, except the last, may be reached in an hour or less
by making use of the railway, and those who wish to make the
most of a day may without difficulty include Ruthin, Denbigh,
Cefn caves, St. Asaph, and Bodelwyddan Church in one excursion;
thus: first train to Rhuddlan; walk 2 *m.* to Bodelwyddan Church,
thence 2½ *m.* to St. Asaph Cathedral, and another 2½ *m.* to Ffynnon
Fair (St. Mary's well). Then to Cefn Caves ¾ *m.*, and thence by
Henllan to Denbigh Castle and Station, 4¾ *m.* further. Leave
Denbigh about 4 p.m. by rail to Ruthin, whence return by last
train about 8.45 p.m. to Rhyl. The total walk, including the
necessary détours to visit points of interest, is 13 miles, and
8 hours or thereabouts between Rhuddlan and Denbigh will afford
plenty of time both for sightseeing and rest. The railway journeys
amount to 30 *m.*

Rhuddlan Castle and Dyserth.

Rhuddlan is 3 *m.* from Rhyl by road, and 3¼ *m.* by rail; Dyserth 3¼ *m.* by new
road over Gladstone Bridge. Breaks run frequently to both places; pedestrians
should eschew the direct walk from Rhyl—it is as dull a one as could be taken.
Their best plan is to drive or take train to Rhuddlan, and then to walk by
the Castle, Bodrhyddan and Dyserth to Prestatyn Station, the distance a-foot
being about 6 miles.

Those who walk from Rhyl must leave the town by the bridge
which crosses the railway at the east end of the station, and
keep as straight on as may be over *Morfa Rhuddlan* ("the Marsh
of Rhuddlan") till they turn sharp to the right about half-a-mile
short of Rhuddlan.

The *Railway Route* from Rhyl keeps on the main line to the
far side of the Clwyd estuary, which it crosses south of Foryd
Bridge, and then follows the west bank of the stream. From
Rhuddlan Station cross the river and proceed up the village till
you come to a turn on the right, just beyond a house, in the walls
of which is inserted a stone, inscribed "This fragment is the re-

mains of the building where King Edward I. held his Parliament A.D. 1283 ; in which was passed the Statute of Rhuddlan, securing to the Principality of Wales its judicial rights and independence." Passing round this house you will soon come in sight of the castle.

Rhuddlan Castle (*Amission, 2d ; key kept at cottage opposite entrance*) is a rectangular building, with a massive tower at each corner, and double ones at the entrance gates. One of them may be ascended. They are connected by walls of great thickness, but within the area nothing whatever remains. The castle was founded by Robert of Rhuddlan, a nephew of Hugh Lupus, but was rebuilt about 1160. Edward I. used it as a store-house, if not as a residence, and Queen Eleanor is said to have given birth to a princess in it. Richard II. had a meal in it on his way to Flint. Dafydd, brother of Llewelyn, tried to take it, but was imprisoned in it instead, and finally, after being taken by General Mytton, it was dismantled by order of the Parliament.

Dyserth is nearly 3 miles from Rhuddlan and Prestatyn Stations, and 3½ by the new road which crosses the railway by Gladstone Bridge—the second from the station.

We shall here take it on the way from Rhuddlan to Prestatyn, because the country lying between it and Rhyl is unutterably dull.

From Rhuddlan the road is for nearly half-a-mile the same as that to Rhyl.* Then just where the latter strikes away to the left a drive commences on the other (right) side to *Bodrhyddan House*, and this is by far the most interesting route to take. **Bodrhyddan** is a red-brick mansion, Elizabethan in style, and surrounded by fine timber. It has for several centuries belonged to the Conwy family, and contains a fine collection of ancient armour. There is no recognised admission to the house, but strangers are allowed to walk through the grounds, re-entering the main road about 1½ miles from the point at which they left it, and ¾ mile beyond the house. A few yards further we come to cross-roads, the left hand turn leading to Rhyl, and the right-hand one to Dyserth village. For the *Castle* we keep straight on for a short distance, and then enter a path on the right, which leads through a field and a scrubby plantation and across a mineral railway. The *Castle* is simply a few fragments of stonework, roughly indicating the walls, on the crest of a steep limestone hill, 300 feet high, grass-grown but showing a bold rocky face on two sides. It commands a view west and north across Rhuddlan Marsh, including Rhuddlan itself, St. Asaph Cathedral, Bodelwyddan Church, the two Ormes, and the range of the Carnarvon mountains extending from Penmaenmawr over Carnedd Llewelyn to Moel Siabod. The building is supposed to be of Norman origin, but its actual history

---

* Nothing shows the modern character of Rhyl more plainly than the fact that it is neither traversed nor approached by any real high road. The nearest is that which passes more than 2 miles south of it through Abergele, Rhuddlan, and Dyserth.

is probably shorter than that of any castle in the kingdom. Henry III. strengthened it in 1211, and Llewelyn pulled it down 20 years afterwards. A little south of it are the ivied ruins of a building called *Siamber-wen* (the " White Chamber ? "), variously stated to have been the residence of the Constable of the Castle, a chapel, and a sacred well.

From the castle a path will be seen leading through a field, past the church to **Dyserth** village. (*Red Lion*, Q.)   *The Church*, re-built about 1872, is a neat structure, with a belfry, and an old wooden porch. It contains a Jesse window (so-called from the pictorial genealogical tree springing from the patriarch), the stained glass of which is said to have come from Basingwerke Abbey. In the yew-shaded churchyard is an old cross, *said* to be —Dyserth is the most unauthentic place we ever visited—in honour of a native warrior.

Opposite to the *inn* (a good one) is the *Waterfall*, greatly spoilt in appearance by the proximity of a large wheel.

The conspicuous, tree-crested height, called **Newmarket Cop**, is 2½ miles east of Dyserth. On its summit, which com-mands a wide view, is a large mound said—yet another fable!— to mark the burial place of Boadicea. The *churchyard* of Newmarket contains a 14th century cross. It is nearly 3 miles thence to Prestatyn Station, by the Dyserth Road for half-a-mile, and then by a by-road to the right. A little to the right of the latter, between it and the Cop, are the ruins of *Ffynnon-wen* (the "white well "), and a little further the village of *Gwaenysgor*.

Another ascent worth making from Dyserth is that of *Moel Hiraddug*, ¾ m. S.E. of the village, on the far side of the New-market road. The view will be understood from foregoing de-scriptions.

Between Dyserth and Prestatyn we pass the *Talargoch Lead Mine* and the village of *Meliden*. There is an inn at Prestatyn Station.

Bodelwyddan Church.

From Rhyl, by road through Rhuddlan, 5½ m.; from Rhuddlan Station, 2¼ m.; from St. Asaph Station, 3 m.

Excursion breaks from Rhyl several times a day during the season at nominal fares.

Those who prefer to walk may in a pleasant round of about 6 miles include Rhuddlan Castle, Bodelwyddan Church, and St. Asaph Cathedral. Take the train to *Rhuddlan Station*, 3½ m. visit the Castle (n. 26), and then returning by the Station cross the line, take the left-hand road, and in about a quarter-of-a-mile turn to the right. The spire of the church is seen ahead. *Pengwern* was formerly a seat of the Mostyn family.

[From *St. Asaph Station* proceed through the city past the Cathedral (*p.* 29) and down to the bridge over the Elwy. Turn to the right and then in ⅛ m. to the left and keep straight on for 1½ m. to a lodge of Bodelwyddan Park (Sir W. Williams, Bart.). During the walk from St. Asaph the many-towered mansion is seen amongst the trees on the left front, and the spire of the church comes into sight more to the right. From the lodge bear round by the park wall to the right.]

Bodelwyddan Church (*Key at Schoolhouse, near west end of the Church*) was built, 1856—1860, by the late Lady Margaret Willoughby de Broke in memory of her husband. The architect was Mr. John Gibson, of Westminster, and the cost, exclusive of gifts, *e.g.* pulpit, font, lectern. &c., is said to have been £60,000. The style is pure Decorated, and the building consists of chancel, nave, with north and south aisles, and western tower and spire. The material of the outside is the local limestone, which has almost the whiteness of unpolished marble, and is still apparently as unsullied as ever. The sense of newness detracts somewhat from the interest of the exterior, but the lofty tower and spire, 202 feet, is extremely graceful, and the whole church, especially as seen from the south-east, is of great beauty. Entering at the west-end by a singularly cramped doorway under the tower, we pass beneath the organ loft and choir gallery, which occupy the stage above. The general effect of the interior is rich almost to excess, and much of the cost is at once accounted for by the clustered shafts of the *Nave Arcade*, which are monoliths of polished Belgian red marble. The carving of the limestone capitals should be noticed as well as that of the corbels supporting the shafts that carry the roof.

The *Font*, in the north aisle, is a shell held by two children (portraits of daughters of Sir H. Williams), and over it is a good window to their mother's memory.

The *Pulpit* is an exquisite specimen of oak carving by Earp. A *Lectern* of unusual design was presented in 1883. It is of oak, and represents a huge pinnacle of rock, surmounted by an eagle. Of the quality of the carving there is no question, but it was bold of the artist thus to represent a crag by wood, and in introducing such soft details as ferns and flowers into the haunt of the king of birds he must be held to have sacrificed consistence to his desire to render his work elaborate. The *Chancel* is even richer than the nave. On both sides are canopies of Caen stone, and at the east end similar ones, of richer design, in alabaster. Note, too, the clustered shafts of red Griotte marble, set off by narrow lines of black Irish marble in the hollows. Throughout the church the pavement is in keeping with all the rest, and an abundance of stained glass, of unequal merit, completes the feast of colour. A good window, in memory of the foundress of the church, has been placed in the south side of the chancel. The visitor should ascend to the organ loft, in order to obtain the best view of the whole building. It is strange that, in so modern a building, the organ was not placed in or near the chancel, and made a decorative feature.

From Bodelwyddan the road past the south side of the church leads direct to St. Asaph, which is entered in about 2 miles.

St. Asaph.

----◆----

Hotels: *Plough* (H.Q.), half-a-mile from the Station and near the Bridge, over the Elwy River, by which the main road from Rhyl enters the city; *Kimmel Arms* (Q.), near the Cathedral.

Post: *Arr. about* 7 *a.m.,* 2 *p.m.; dep.* 9 *a.m.,* 11 *a.m.,* 8.30 *p.m.*

Population: *About* 2,000.

This smallest of cities is 5½ miles by road and 6 miles by rail from Rhyl. It is a large, well to do village, on the right bank of the River Elwy, and though a pleasant-enough resting-place for the traveller exploring the Vale of Clwyd, will not on its own account long detain him. The only object of interest is the **Cathedral.** (*Services on Sundays:* 11, 3¼, 6¼; *week days:* 8¼, (11½ *Thursdays*), 3¼ (5 *in winter*). *Choral on Sundays, Thursday Mg., and Saturday Evg., and on Saints' Days at* 11½. *At other times the Cathedral is closed. The key is kept by Mr. W. H. Robinson, a few yards below, on the same side of the street. A small fee is charged for ascending the tower.*)

History makes Kentingern, an exiled bishop of the British church in Strathclyde, its founder. He established a monastery here about 560, and built the church from which the place got its old name of Llanelwy, *i.e.,* the church on the Elwy. His successor was Asa, or Asaph (*d.* 596), under whom the monastic church became the cathedral of the diocese, which, from about the middle of the 12th century, has been known by his name. For many centuries the church was a wooden one, and in 1245 and 1278 it is known to have been destroyed by fire. Bishop Anian II., who died before 1293, rebuilt it, and from his time parts of the nave and aisles of the present structure date. In 1402, however, it was again nearly destroyed by Owen Glyndwyr, and was not restored till 1482, under Bishop Redman. Thenceforward its history down to the commencement of its restoration, by the late Sir Gilbert Scott, is little more than a record of successive disfigurements at the hands of repairers. The restoration has still to be carried out in regard to the transepts, and the chapter-house, removed in 1780, has not yet been rebuilt, but with these exceptions the Cathedral is now probably a finer church than at any previous period of its history. The principal dimensions are : extreme length, 182 feet; breadth of the nave, with its aisles, 68 feet; length of transepts from N. to S., 108 feet; height of central tower, 100 feet. The exterior of the church is extremely plain, its principal feature being the bulky tower, but the interior, open from west to east, while generally plain, is that of a spacious and dignified parish church, chiefly of Decorated style, but with Early English windows in the chancel. The arches are all without capitals to their pillars, and the clerestory of the nave is lighted by small squares, with foliated tracery. The *Choir-stalls*, as far as they are old, are Perpendicular and Bishop Redman's work. The new work, including the *Bishop's Throne*, is a happy reproduction in the same style. The form of the side windows of the chancel is due to the traces of Early English work, discovered during the process of restoration, but the *East Window* is Decorated and filled with excellent glass depicting scenes from the life of our Lord. Beneath this is a handsome *Reredos*, designed by Scott. Most of the glass in the Cathedral is satisfactory, except the west window, which is painfully coarse in colouring. The window next the choir on the north side of the chancel, with subjects from the songs of Miriam and Deborah, is to the memory of Mrs. Hemans, the poetess, to whom there is also a plain tablet in the south aisle of the nave. She is not buried in the Cathedral, but in Dublin, where she died in 1835.

The *north transept* is occupied by the organ (excellent by Hill and Son), and behind this is the *Luxmoore Monument*, which commemorates the Bishop who died in 1830, and his two sons, the Dean and the Canon.

The *south transept*, which has been fitted as the *Consistory Court* of the diocese, and is used as the Chapter Room, contains the library and two monuments worth notice: one to a bishop, possibly Bishop Leoline (*d.* 1375), and certainly not older than the middle of the 14th century; the other to Dean Shipley (*d.* 1825) by Ternouth.

Outside the west door is the restored *altar-tomb* of Bishop Isaac Barrow (*d.* 1680), and that of Bishop Vowler Short (*d.* 1872).

N.B.—The unseemly conduct of excursionists from Rhyl and elsewhere is answerable for the Cathedral being kept under lock and key. The fee charged for ascending the tower (wide view of the Vale of Clwyd) has been imposed in order to protect it against a repetition of the wilful damage from which it suffered in the days of free access.

The **Parish Church**, Perpendicular, restored in 1872, is at the foot of the hill, near the Elwy. Like most of the churches in the Vale of Clwyd it consists of two aisles of equal length. The south aisle has a fine roof. In the churchyard is buried R. R. Jones, *alias* " Dic Aberdaron " the self-taught linguist, who died in 1843.

ffynnon ffair (St. Mary's Well) and Cefn Rocks and Caves.

Distance from Rhyl to the Caves, 9 m.; *from St. Asaph Station,* 3½ m.; *from Trefnant Station,* 2½ m. *The well is ¾ m. short of the Caves from either station.*

Excursion Breaks from Rhyl during the season.

The Elwy glen about **Cefn Rocks** is the most picturesque spot within an hour's inland excursion from Rhyl. The pleasantest and easiest approach for pedestrians is from Trefnant Station, and the return thither by a different route can be included in a round of 5½ m. This round we shall first describe, and then give the direct routes from Trefnant and St. Asaph.

(1) *From Trefnant Station to Cefn Caves and back.* Leave the Station by the road between the two inns hard by. *Trefnant Church,* erected in 1855 from designs by the late Sir G. G. Scott, is passed, and we keep straight on past the entrance (left) to *Plas Heaton.* The road is pleasantly timbered and next passes the drive (right) leading to Galltfaenan. When it bends sharply round to the left take a narrow road on the right. This at first is up and down, but soon drops rapidly into the silvan glen of the *Afon-y-Merchion,* with the bold cliff, Cefn Rocks, at its lower end. Just before reaching a bridge—*Pont Trap*—go through a wicket-gate on the right, whence a foot-path by the side of the stream leads through the wood to the bank of the Elwy river, which is crossed a short distance down by a foot-bridge, *Pont-yr-Onen.* Beyond this bridge turn up stream past some cottages, and then, almost immediately, the track leads through a rugged limestone archway. The **Caves** are in the face of the cliff above, and are reached by striking up one of the paths that hereabouts ascend more or less steeply. When to bend back again cannot be described in writing, but will be obvious to anyone who has noted the entrance to the caves whilst descending the glen we have come down. The entrance is closed by a door, the key of which is kept at a cottage below, but the attendant is always on the look out for visitors. One perforation of a limestone cliff is apt to be very like another, and as far as anything to be seen is concerned, these Cefn Caves have little to boast of. Their chief interest arises from the remains that have been found in them of the Old-World life of man and of animals long extinct in these islands. To the lover of natural beauty the charm of the spot will be the glen of the Elwy, which is gracefully wooded, and here narrow and abrupt, with just enough of meadow to add richness. Plenty of rustic seats allow of the scene being enjoyed restfully. On the opposite bank is *Dolben,* a small country-house, delightfully placed in full view of the cliff on which we stand.

To reach **Ffynnon Fair** follow the path down-stream by the
Elwy. When a considerable breadth of meadow is reached, the
ruins of the Chapel are seen on the left in a clump of trees surrounded by a railing and the well itself is on its west side. The
Chapel is partially buttressed in its decay by trees. It appears to
be in no part earlier than the 14th century, and is mainly late
Perpendicular. The *Well* is open to the sky. It once had a
canopy, but now only the curbstones remain. Returning to the
river-bank we follow the path to a mill, where a road begins
which leads into the main road from Denbigh to St. Asaph, close
to *Pont-yr-allt-goch*, a single-arch bridge over the Elwy. For *St.
Asaph* we should turn to the left, but for *Trefnant* cross the bridge
and ascend the hill. When the road forks take the left-hand
branch; this leads direct to Trefnant station.

(2) *From Trefnant Station to Cefn Caves, direct,* 2½ *m.*

When facing the Inns, take the road to the right, and where
this forks keep straight on by the left-hand branch, and so down
to Pont-yr-allt-goch, from which a pretty view up and down the
Elwy is obtained. At the fork beyond the bridge take the left-
hand road, and then. avoiding a couple of farm-tracks that go off
left to Glanllyn Farm, at the next fork take the left branch, and
descend to a mill. Here the route becomes a foot-path by the
bank of the Elwy. The mill-leat keeps us company on the right,
and towards the end of the meadows we cross it by a little bridge,
and so reach the *Chapel* and *Well* of *St. Mary* (*Ffynnon Fair*, see
above). Returning to the river-bank, the path presently passes
in front of a couple of cottages, and so by an archway through
the rock to the foot of *Cefn Cliff.*

For the Caves, see p. 31.

(3) *From St. Asaph to Cefn Caves either by Cefn or the Denbigh
Road.*

The route by Cefn. From the bridge turn to the left, and in a
few hundred yards to the right, along the Abergele Road, and
then in a quarter of a mile to the left. Thence the road is fairly
straight, and passes *Cefn* (Mrs. Wynne), and so to the top of the
bluff overlooking the Elwy glen, to which a cart track descends
in zig-zag fashion.

The *Denbigh-road* route joins that described under (2), close
to Pont-yr-allt-goch.

At **Tremeirchion** (abt. 2 *m.* from Bodfari; 3 *m.* from Trefnant; 5 *m.*
from St. Asaph) are some recently explored **Caves** that have proved richer in
old-world remains than those at Cefn. *Key at Ffynnon Beuno Inn, close by.*
There is also a fine Jesuit College at Tremeirchion.

Denbigh.

Hotels: *Crown, Bull* (H.Q.) : both in High Street, and about ½ m. from the Station ; *Clwyd* (Temperance), Vale Street.

Post: *Arr. abt.* 7 *a.m. and* 3 *p.m.* ; *dep.* 8.30 *a.m. and* 7 *p.m.*

Population: 6,491.

Distances : St. Asaph, 5 *m.* : Rhyl, 11 *m.* : Ruthin, 8 *m.* ; Corwen, 19 *m.*

This well-to-do and pleasant country town occupies the top of a considerable hill on the west side of the Vale of Clwyd, and with its castle is a conspicuous object as we approach by rail in either direction, but especially from the southward. It is an important market town (Wednesdays), and in its butter and poultry trade vies with Newtown in Montgomeryshire.

A broad street runs up hill from the station to the picturesque *High Street*, which from its width has the character of a market-place. Here are the hotels, the post-office, and many good shops. The principal object of interest to visitors is the Castle, and this may be reached by any of the narrow streets running up on the south side from the west end of High Street. One of these side streets leads to *Burgesses' Tower*, part of the original defences of the town. The old gateway through which we here enter the castle precincts still shows the portcullis grooves. On our way to the Castle two objects call for mention. **St. Hilary's Church**, now dilapidated and closed, was for many years the only church within easy reach of the townsmen, whose parish church is at Whitchurch (*see* p. 34). The *Chancel*, supposed to have been the garrison chapel, is still cared for, but the rest of the building is of various dates, and plain almost to ugliness. Hard by are the *ruins of a large church*, begun by Dudley, Earl of Leicester, in 1579, but never finished, owing, it is said, to the funds for its completion having been borrowed by Essex on his way to Ireland, and never repaid. It is generally stated to have been intended by Leicester as a new cathedral, but this idea is probably due to its size.

The **Castle** (*admission*, 2d.) occupies the site of a British hill-fort. It was built about 1300 by Henry Lacy, Earl of Lincoln, whose mutilated statue is in a niche over the main entrance. This entrance, which is flanked by one octagonal tower and part of another, is the only portion sufficiently intact to give any idea of the original building, and it too would have soon disappeared but for the timely arrest of decay by the Crown, to whom the Castle belongs. A good deal of plain substantial masonry has been built up, which, though somewhat unsightly from within, does not mar

Guide VIII.   D the appearance of the outside. Within the area is a greensward partly fitted up as a gymnasium. The ruins are difficult to make out, and are lacking in architectural details of any interest, but one of the stairs should be ascended for the sake of the wide and, under favourable weather, beautiful view of the Vale of Clwyd. The man-in-charge has, in the "refreshment room," a small collection of curiosities that have been dug up from time to time.

The *History* of the Castle may be briefly told. As already stated, it was built about 1300 by the Earl of Lincoln, from whom it passed to the Earl of Lancaster, and on his attainder was bestowed on Hugh Despenser, but again reverted to the Crown on the execution of this favourite and his son in 1326. Thereupon it was given to Roger Mortimer, 1st Earl of March, Isabella's favourite, but on his attainder and execution in 1330, Edward III. bestowed it on Montacute. It appears to have been again possessed by the Earls of March in Richard II.'s reign, and from Roger, the fourth Earl, who was Lieutenant of Ireland, it at length descended by marriage to the Crown. Elizabeth granted it to Dudley, Earl of Leicester, and was once sumptuously entertained here by him. During the Civil War it was visited by Charles I. in 1645, but was taken by the Parliamentary forces under Mytton late in the following year. After the Restoration it was reduced to utter ruin by order of Charles II., in which state, except for the repairs already mentioned, it has remained.

The handsome modern **Church of St. Mary**, consecrated in 1874, has now worthily supplied the requirements of the town, so long obliged to be content with St. Hilary's. It is Decorated, and was erected from the designs of Williams and Underwood, at a cost of nearly £10,000. The principal material used is the local limestone. The *reredos*, by Earp, a beautiful work, was the subject of litigation on account of its design, which includes in its central compartment a representation of the Crucifixion in bold relief. It was the gift of the late Miss Mesham (*d.* 1873), of Pont Ruffydd, whose munificent contributions, amounting in all to £4,000, also supplied funds for the organ and the lofty tower, with its clock and fine peal of bells.

Of the *Whitefriars' Priory*, known as the Abbey, little more than the site remains, E. of the railway and close to the station. Howell's School and the Lunatic Asylum are fine buildings.

The Parish Church of Denbigh, long disused, except for funerals, is **Whitchurch**, about a mile east from the Station, and reached by turning to the left ¼ m. along the Ruthin road. It is a large Perpendicular building of two equal aisles, and a western tower. Parts of the old rood-screen have been converted into a reredos and a screen at the west-end of the north aisle. Two of the roof corbels in this aisle are conjectured by Mr. Thomas to represent Archbishop Chicheley, the founder of All Soul's, Oxford, and Margaret, Countess of Derby— "a noble church builder in the 15th century, the period of this work." There are several *monuments* of interest. A portrait.

brass in the porch commemorates Richard Myddleton (d. 1575). He was Governor of Denbigh Castle, and is represented with his wife, 9 sons, and 7 daughters. " Several of these sons became very distinguished men. William, the 3rd son, a sea captain, was the first to translate the Psalms into Welsh metre. Sir Thomas, the fourth, became Lord Mayor of London, and with Heylin shared the expense of the first portable edition of the Bible and Prayer book in Welsh, 1630 ; and Sir Hugh, the sixth, brought the New River to London."—*Thomas*. Of other memorials should be noticed : Humphrey Llwyd, the Antiquary, d. 1563 ; the altar tomb with effigies of Sir John Salisbury, d. 1578, and his wife ; Thomas Edwards, d. 1810, (Twm o'r Nant) the Cambrian " Hudibras."

Those who make Denbigh their temporary head-quarters and are interested in churches, should visit **Llanrhaiadr** (2½ *m.* *towards Ruthin and close to the junction of the two roads from Denbigh. That leaving the town by the Castle should be taken by pedestrians*) a mile distant from the Station of that name. The " Jesse " east window and the chancel roof are especially noteworthy. The window, *not* brought from Basingwerke, though generally so accounted for, is fine 15th century glass, and may be compared with that at Dyserth (*page* 27). Tradition says that it was purchased with offerings made by pilgrims to the Holy Well, *Ffynnon Ddyfnog*, the copious spring hard by, which gives its name to the church.

Denbigh to Ruthin, (*by rail*), 8 *m.* The line continues up the Vale of Clwyd, passing in less than 3 miles *Llanrhaiadr Church*, and *Hall* on the right, and nearly a mile further *Llanrhaiadr Station*. In another 1½ miles, the diminutive church of *Llanychan* appears nearly a mile away on the left of the line. From this part of the journey the highest summits of the Clwydian range are well seen across the valley, the huge ruin on Moel Fammau being specially prominent ; in fact the nearest station to it is *Rhewl*, 5 miles from Denbigh and 3 short of Ruthin. We have preferred to describe in detail the ascent from Ruthin and other places (*pp.* 37, 14), and those who start from Rhewl, a study of the map and a word of enquiry at the station will enable to find their way. The distance is about 4 miles, and there is a road most of the way.

Ruthin.

Hotels : *Castle* (H.Q.) in St. Peter's Square; *Wynnstay Arms*, old fashioned : *Cross Foxes* ; *Williams' Temperance*, Well Street.

Post : *Arr. about* 7 *a.m. and* 4.45. *p.m.* ; *dep.* 8.15 *a.m. and* 7.30 *p.m.*

Population : 3034.

Distances : Corwen, 12 *m.* ; Denbigh, 8 *m.* ; St. Asaph, 13 *m.* ; Rhyl, 23 *m.*

This quaint little borough, now widely known for its mineral waters, stands on a small knoll above the east bank of the river Clwyd, which is here an insignificant stream. *St. Peter's Square*, the centre of the town and its principal business part, is a short quarter of a mile from the Station. At the north end of the Square some good iron gates lead to **St. Peter's Church**, a foundation partly collegiate and partly parochial dating from about 1300. Of the exterior of the original building only the lower part of the tower remains, and the surmounting spire that rises to a height of 180 feet is modern. The churchyard is pleasantly secluded and in front of the Porch are two fine beech trees. Within, the tower-arches and the fine Perpendicular oak roof of the north aisle are the principal items of archæological interest. The old chancel was pulled down in the 17th century, and the rest of the church until the restoration of 1856–59 was in an unworthy condition. Now, in spite of its general newness, it is an ornament to the town. The contiguity of the cloisters, which once connected it with the canons' houses, prevents their being any windows on the north side. After the Dissolution the collegiate property passed into lay hands, but enough of it was redeemed by Gabriel Goodman, a native of the town, Dean of Westminster, to found and endow *Christ's Hospital Ruthin*, whose warden was appointed to serve the church. Goodman also founded the *Grammar School*, which still flourishes close by. Of many *monuments* that of Goodman, a bust, and the brasses to his parents and their children on the north wall, should be noticed.

The **Castle** (*admission at the Lodge at the top of Castle Street, which leaves the Square at the south end*) is the residence of Major W. Cornwallis West, Lord-Lieutenant of Denbighshire. The inhabited portion, which is Elizabethan in style, was built early in the present century within the circuit of the old Edwardian stronghold. Its most noticeable feature is a lofty and severe looking clock-tower. To view the old part of the castle turn down to the right after entering by the lodge. Here the deep-red towers and walls, mantled with greenery and looking down on a richly wooded glade, are delightful. The circuit of the castle can thus be made, and in the course of it will be passed some exceedingly fine evergreen oaks. The Eagle tower commands a fine view of the vale.

The *History* of the castle has been comparatively uneventful. It was built about 1280 and conferred on Reginald de Grey, son of the founder of the College of Priests, and remained in his family till the end of the 15th century. In 1400 it successfully baffled Owen Glyndwr, and during the Civil War it was held for Charles I., but succumbed like its neighbours, Denbigh and Rhuddlan, to Mytton, after a 3 months' siege in the spring of 1646. Since then it has been a ruin. From the time of the de Greys it was for nearly 200 years the property of the Crown. Then it was sold to Sir Thomas Myddleton of Chirk, from whom the present owner inherited it through the female line.

Moel Fammau, 1823 feet.

From Ruthin, 5 m., from Mold, 6½ m., from Rhydymwyn, 5 m.

(As this mountain is to many tourists their first experience of Wales, it may not be superfluous to remark that Fammau is pronounced " Vamma", Ruthin " Rithin ", and Rhydymwyn " Rhidymooin ").

Moel Fammau (the bare high-places) is the highest point of the Clwydian range, which extends from almost due north to south in a billowy line of green summits from Prestatyn, on the Chester and Holyhead railway 4 miles east of Rhyl, to the high ground between the vales of Clwyd and Llangollen,—a distance of nearly 20 miles. This range is far more conspicuous than its average height would suggest for two reasons—its continuity and isolation. There are very few gaps of any great depth in it, and it is the most elevated ground between the Peak of Derbyshire and Snowdonia. It was this conspicuousness that caused Moel Fammau to be chosen as the site of the Jubilee Column erected in 1810 to celebrate the fiftieth year of the reign of George III. This column was an enormous structure raising the height of the hill to nearly 2000 feet, but it was blown over in 1862, and now lies a shapeless mass of ruin about which, as there can hardly be any original subscribers left to feel aggrieved at our remarks, we may once for all observe that nothing can well be imagined more ugly except its original self.

The **view** from Moel Fammau is remarkable for its extent, and comprises a bird's eye prospect of the Vale of Clwyd which excuses if it does not justify the extravagant praise bestowed by many writers on that fair and fertile but not pointedly picturesque region. North and south you look along the line of the Clwydian summits, underneath which, to the west, lies the whole length of the valley. Rhyl, the quadrangle of Rhuddlan Castle, the white spire of Bodelwyddan, the tower of St. Asaph, Denbigh with its castle, and the tall spire of Ruthin Church, are the chief artificial adornments of the luxuriant strath, which is brought to an end southward by the round summits of the Gamelin hills, separating it from the vale of Llangollen and the dark level line of the Berwyns. Then, in the south-west, the peaks of Arran and Cader Idris are distinct and much nearer at hand to the right of the latter, the Arenigs. Of Snowdonia, the most clearly-marked summits are Moel Siabod, Snowdon itself, the Tryfan, Penllithrig, Carnedd Llewelyn, and Penmaenmawr. Then comes the sea and the Great Orme, while from the north-east to the south-east the view extends over the " Sands o'Dee " and Chester to the Peak hills near Buxton. Beeston Castle is due east. Cumberland and the Isle of Man may possibly be included in the prospect.

The most effective walk over the mountain is undoubtedly from east to west, as by far the finest scenery is on the latter side. Taking it in that direction the easiest way to follow is that from Mold, already described in the walk thence to Ruthin (*p.* 13). Starting from Rhyl we may still climb from the east, but a more convenient place for beginning the walk will be Rhydymwyn, the next station to Mold on the line between that town and Denbigh. We will, therefore, describe the ascent from Rhydymwyn as well as from Ruthin.

(1) *Denbigh to Rhydymwyn (rail),* **13** *m.   Rhydymwyn to Moel Fammau, 5 m; Ruthin,* 10 *m.*

Starting from Denbigh we retrace the route by which we have come from Rhyl for 1¼ miles. Then turning eastwards and crossing the River Wheeler the line enters a narrow gap in the Clwydian range at **Bodfari** (*Inn*). On *Moel-y-Gaer,* ¾ *m* north of the station, the remains of an ancient camp may be traced, and a mile or two farther we have another Clwydian summit, *Moel-y-parc,* about the same distance on the right. Hereabouts the line ascends a long and steep gradient, passing **Caerwys** (*Buck* (Q.) ; supposed to be of Roman origin, and once noted for its Eisteddfods, is a mile north of the station), and reaching a height of over 400 feet at *Nannerch.* Beyond this we get good views of the Clwydian range. A picturesque park is passed on the right, the quarries of *Hendre* on the left and winding down the valley of the Alyn, we arrive at *Rhydymwyn Station* (inn).

From *Rhydymwyn* the first part of the walk as far as Cilcain village is intricate. It is best to ask for particulars at the *Antelope Inn,* close to the station. From it you cross the line, and taking the first turn to the left, keep alongside the *Alyn* stream for half-a-mile. Then when the road forks both ways, enter a footpath which crosses a park, and, after passing through a plantation, re-enters a lane which goes—directly, for a lane—to the little village of **Cilcain** (*two small inns*). The church here has a brick band round the tower and a remarkable oak-roof, said, of course, to have been brought hither from Basingwerke Abbey near Holywell (p. 17). The rest of the way is simple enough. Turn to the left round the church and, after crossing the little Cain stream, take a field-path and proceed up a grassy hollow, from the end of which you struggle up a narrow path to the column.

(2) *From Ruthin, 5 m.* Follow the Mold road, which crosses the railway ¼ m. south of the station to **Llanbedr** (Inn: the *Griffin*).* Here is an ornate little modern church, and in the churchyard a monument to David Lloyd (d. 1620), 16th in descent from Tudor Trevor, Lord of the Marches, buried in the old church, which is about 100 yards from the Hall.

From the *Griffin* continue along the Ruthin road to the right of the church till it bends sharply to the right. Here go straight on up a narrow lane. This is the old road, and in ¼ mile, where it turns abruptly to the left and crosses a stream, keep straight on till you come out on to the hill-side at a gate. Here turning up to the left you will rejoin the old road and continue up it to **Bwlch-pen-Barras**, the *col* of the Clwydian range between Ruthin and Mold. Care must be taken at the gate to avoid a path which ascends the most likely-looking valley with a little stream on the right. The walk up the pass is a pleasant grassy one and commands a charming retrospect. From the *col* there are three tracks going left towards the summit. The middle one is the best for pedestrians. Half-way, on a shoulder stretching westward, is a circular British camp, called *Moel-y-guer.*

For the View see p. 37.

Descents. (1) *To Mold.* Go south-eastwards, leaving the ridge, but not dropping into the valley on the left. Soon you will enter a cart-track which descends a marshy hollow to the old Ruthin and Denbigh road, which it enters half-a-mile east of the *col* of *Bwlch-pen-Barras.* In 2 miles this enters the new road, and in less than 3 reaches the *Loggerheads Inn* (p. 14). Hence it is 8 miles to Mold.

(2) *To Rhydymwyn.* The village of Cilcain is seen rather north of north-east. To reach it you cross a stile and descend a steep spur of the hill into a green hollow which is skirted on the left by a grass-lane. Cross the road at the end of this and enter a field-path. For *Cilcain, see p.* 38. The rest of the way is rather intricate. Take a lane to the right a few yards beyond the second inn. Cross a brook and a lane beyond, and when the road goes right and left take a field-path opposite and enter a wood at once. The path continues through it and a park beyond, coming from the latter into a road which skirts the Alyn stream on the right and, turning across it to the right in half-a-mile, reaches ¼ m. further *Rhydymwyn station.* Close to this is the *Antelope Inn.*

(3) *To Ruthin, see p.* 15.

---

* There is a direct foot-path from the station to this point (*see p.* 15).

Abergele and Pensarn.

————◆————

Hotels: (Pensarn) *Cambrian* (Q.) ; *Railway.*
　　(Abergele) *Hesketh Arms* (Q.) ; *Bee.*
Post: (Pensarn) *Arr. abt.* 6.20 *a.m.* and 3.20 *p.m.; dep.,* 7.30 *p.m.*
　　(Abergele) *Arr. abt.* 7 *a.m.* and 1.20 *p.m.* ; *dep.* 11.30 *a.m.* and 8.30 *p.m.*
Distances: Rhyl, 4 *m.* ; Bodelwyddan Church, 5 *m.* ; St. Asaph, 8 *m.* ; **Cefn**
Caves, 10 *m.* ; Colwyn Bay, 8 *m.* ; Conway, 13 *m.* ; Llandudno, 16 *m.*

Pensarn, a small watering-place consisting of a street and a
terrace, is close to the station on the inland side of the railway,
which here skirts the shore.

Abergele is a village about a mile inland and with the exception of the Hotels makes less provision for visitors.　There is nothing about either place that calls for description, and both
are chiefly frequented by quiet folk who like to enjoy their
whiff of the sea in peace and to avoid the fancy prices of fashionable resorts.　*Abergele Church* (restored) is associated with two
tragical occurences.　In the graveyard are interred the bodies of
seven persons out of 178 who perished by the burning of the Ocean
Monarch in the bay, Aug. 24th, 1848, and close by a granite
monument commemorates the 33 persons who lost their lives
by the burning of the Irish mail train, Aug. 20th, 1868.

The coast hereabout is quite uninteresting, but the hills south
and west are near at hand for pleasant rambling and at all times
are a pretty feature in the view from the terrace at Pensarn.
The conspicuous tower on the hill-top southward is an object of
frequent and generally futile enquiry.　It is or rather was, we
are told, a windmill.

Half a mile along the Bangor road is the east Lodge of **Gwrych
Castle** (R. B. Hesketh Esq.), at which privileged carriages and
pedestrians by special permission are admitted to explore the
delightful grounds.　A striking feature of them is the abundant
growth of cypress.　The castle is a modern antique of many
towers, square and round, and is in great part a shell built only for
effect.　Behind it rises a fine escarpment of limestone, and nature
and art combine to make up a charming whole.　Those who are
journeying westward by road should by all means endeavour to
go through the Park, as its beauties as well as the castle are hidden from the high road by a huge wall.　The *West Lodge* is 2
miles along this road from Abergele and outside it sundry tablets
record the associations, historical and otherwise, of the " pass "

at the foot of the cliff, by which in early days, as now, lay the route
from east to west. Of these associations the most recent is that
of the betrayal of Richard II. to Bolingbroke by Earl Percy, when
the wretched king was carried off to Flint Castle. From just
within this western Lodge a path goes up through plantations to
the *Yr Ogof Cave*, a huge orifice in the limestone cliff immediately
westward. The cave is, however, in spite of its great mouth only
a shallow affair and in itself of no interest, but a good view seaward and eastward is obtained from it. There are two or three
smaller caves.

Several walks of more or less interest may be taken, but none is
better than the one to the top of **Cefn yr Ogof**, the hill in whose
seaward face these caves are. Proceed either through the Park or
by the Bangor road a short distance beyond the west Lodge.
Then turn to the left, and ascend the valley which opens to the
sea at Llandulas.

[**Llandulas Village**, with its new Decorated *Church*, by Street, and an
inn, the *Valentine Hotel*, is half-a-mile onward along the main road, which then
ascends past a large quarry. A long mile from the church a road on the right
goes down a quarter of a mile further to *Llandulas Station*, the neighbourhood
of which is disfigured by tall chimneys and lime works.]

When clear of the Gwrych grounds the ascent is best made by
a path that, ¾ *m.* from the main road, bends back up the hill, the
top of which is some 700 feet above sea-level. The view from the
summit is well worth the climb. Near at hand southward across
an intervening dip are the earth-works of *Gorddyn-mawr*, and of
mountains we note in succession from west to south-west Penmaenmawr, Carnedd Llewelyn, Penllithrig, the Tryfan, and Moel
Siabod. How far in other directions must depend on the atmo-
spere, but the Isle of Man and Liverpool are among possibilities,
and Anglesey and Puffin Island are visible in ordinary weather.

Another and longer excursion for which rail may be used to
Llandulas station, is to the summit of **Llysfaen Hill**, an old
semaphore station commanding a superb view of the mountains
behind Conway. The distance from Llandulas is a little over
a mile.

Llysfaen Church, restored by Street, is a good example of
the two-aisled churches of this district.

LLANDUDNO SECTION.

Colwyn Bay and Old Colwyn.

---◆---

Hotels : (Colwyn Bay) *Pwllycrochan*, ¾ *m.* from the station and sea ; *Colwyn Bay*, on the sea, 3 min. from station ; *Imperial*, *Coed Pella*, *Railway*.

Hydropathic Establishment, close to the sea, ½ *m.* from station.

(Old Colwyn) *Marine*, ½ *m.* from the station; *Ship* (Q.).

(Llandrillo-yn-Rhos), *Rhos Abbey*, *Blue Bell*.

Post : *Arr. abt. 7 a.m. and 2.45 p.m.; dep. 12.15 and 8.45 p.m.*

Distances (from Colwyn Bay): Rhyl, 10½ *m.*; Abergele 6½ *m.*; Conway, 5 *m* ; Llandudno, 7 *m.* (*rail*), 6 *m.* (*road*).

Colwyn Bay and Old Colwyn are distinct stations. **Old Colwyn** (*Marine Hotel* and a fair number of *lodgings*) is a village about a mile east of Colwyn Bay and a trifle back from the shore, to which hereabout, pretty little glens run down. **Colwyn Bay** is a large and much frequented watering-place that, thanks to its pleasant situation and, possibly too, to its much-advertised claims on visitors, has rapidly sprung up since 1866, when Lady Erskine's mansion Pwllycrochan was opened as an hotel. The advantages and disadvantages of Colwyn Bay as a seaside resort are alike obvious. To dismiss the latter at once we may say that it has only a short promenade on its sea-front unless we reckon the station platforms and the limited strip of shore at the foot of the railway embankment. A further drawback is the huge ballast pit that in addition to the railway intervenes between the main body of the place and the sea. This pit is said to be nearly exhausted, and for the well-being of the town the sooner it is quite so the better, though what can be done with it is by no means clear. A winter garden—that last resource of summer watering-places that long for a season all the year round—would here be buried rather than sheltered.

The advantages of the place are happily, however, far in excess of these drawbacks. The sweep of the bay, enclosed between Penmaen Rhos, on the east, and Little Orme's Head on the west, is delightful. The accommodation for visitors in regard to hotels and lodgings is abundant and excellent, and there is about the town, and especially on the slopes and hillsides behind it, that great desideratum in a summer retreat, abundance of wood. The bathing too, to the west of the town, where the bend of the railway inland leaves a larger margin of shore, is both safe and good. Endless pretty walks and drives are within easy reach at the back of the town, and not the least pleasing features of the neighbour-

hood are the valleys, each with its brook and greenery, that
descend to the shore towards and about Colwyn village. The exploration of the upper part of these little glens affords short and
delightful strolls.

About a mile west of Colwyn Bay, but rapidly becoming almost
a part of it is the seaside village of **Llandrillo yn Rhos** (Hotels:
Rhos Abbey, *Blue Bell*), where a parade has been made and a good
many lodgings are springing up. Unfortunately here the shore is
somewhat rough, but a constant source of amusement is the *fish
weir*, at which large catches are frequently made. For *Llandrillo
church* and *Llys Euryn*, &c., *see p. 52.* About a quarter of a mile
along the cliff beyond the Rhos Abbey Hotel is the ancient **Capel
Trillo**, a small barrel-vaulted building over a spring. It measures
inside about 11 feet by 8 feet, the walls are 2 feet thick and are
pierced by widely splayed lancets. It is sadly neglected, and now
that it is between two fires as it were, Llandudno and Colwyn
Bay, will, it may be feared, suffer positive injury. In January,
1884, we found the little spring choked with rubbish, and the
inside of this primitive oratory blackened with the remnants of
a fire.

The walk or drive from Colwyn Bay to Llandudno is described
the reverse way page 52.

Llandudno.

◆

Hotels (see plan): *St. George's*; *Imperial*; *Adelphi*; *Queen's*; on or close to the **Parade**; *Royal*; *Prince of Wales*; *Tudno Castle*; *Baths*; *Alexandra*; *Washington* (½ m. toward Little Orme); *Stanley* (Q.).

"**Hydros.**": in Nevil Crescent, **and** a large one, *Craigside*, **on S. side** of Little Orme's Head.

Principal Boarding Houses : *Moon's Private Hotel*; *Lockyer's*; *Heath House*; *Wheeldon's*; *Rugby House*.

Hotels in the Neighbourhood: *Deganwy Castle*, on Conway Bay, 2¼ m. adjoining Deganwy Station, and (smaller **but** comfortable), *The Junction*, at Llandudno Junction ; *Ferry Farm*, 100 yards from it.

Post : chief deliveries, *abt. 7 a.m. and 3.30 p.m.* ; despatches, 9 a.m., 8.15 p.m.

Population : 4,838.

Distances : (*by rail*) Llandudno Junction, 3 m. ; Conway, 4 m. ; Penmaenmawr, 8 m.: Llanfairfechan, 10¾ m ; Aber, 12½ m. ; Bangor, 17¼ m. ; **Menai** Bridge, 19 m.; Carnarvon, 26¾ m.

Colwyn Bay, 7 m.; Rhyl, 17½ m. ; St. Asaph, 23¼ m. ; Chester, 48 m.

Llanrwst, 14 m.; Bettws-y-Coed, 18 m.; Dolwyddelan, 23½ m.; Blaenau Ffestiniog, 30¼ m.

Steamers: The Liverpool, Llandudno, and Welsh Coast Steamboat Company's vessels, on week-days, ply twice each way between Liverpool and Menai Bridge, calling at Llandudno, Beaumaris, and Bangor.

Llandudno is in size and importance at the head of the pleasure resorts of North Wales, and the number of its inhabitants, given above from the census of March. 1881, requires to be multiplied at least by three if it is to represent the condition of things at the height of the season, in August and September. The popularity of the place is easily accounted for, and is the product of three main factors—the situation of the town, its first-class provision for the health and comfort of visitors, and its convenience as a base for excursions.

Its *situation*, on the level neck of a promontory, under a mile in width. at once between two bold headlands, Great and Little Orme's Head, and between two seas, Orme's Bay and Conway Bay, is unique amongst English or Welsh watering-places. In the matter of sea breezes, it enjoys the advantages of an island position without the drawback of isolation from the mainland. The Great Orme, which rises abruptly to a height of over 700 feet, shelters it from the dry but chilly north-west winds, but to all

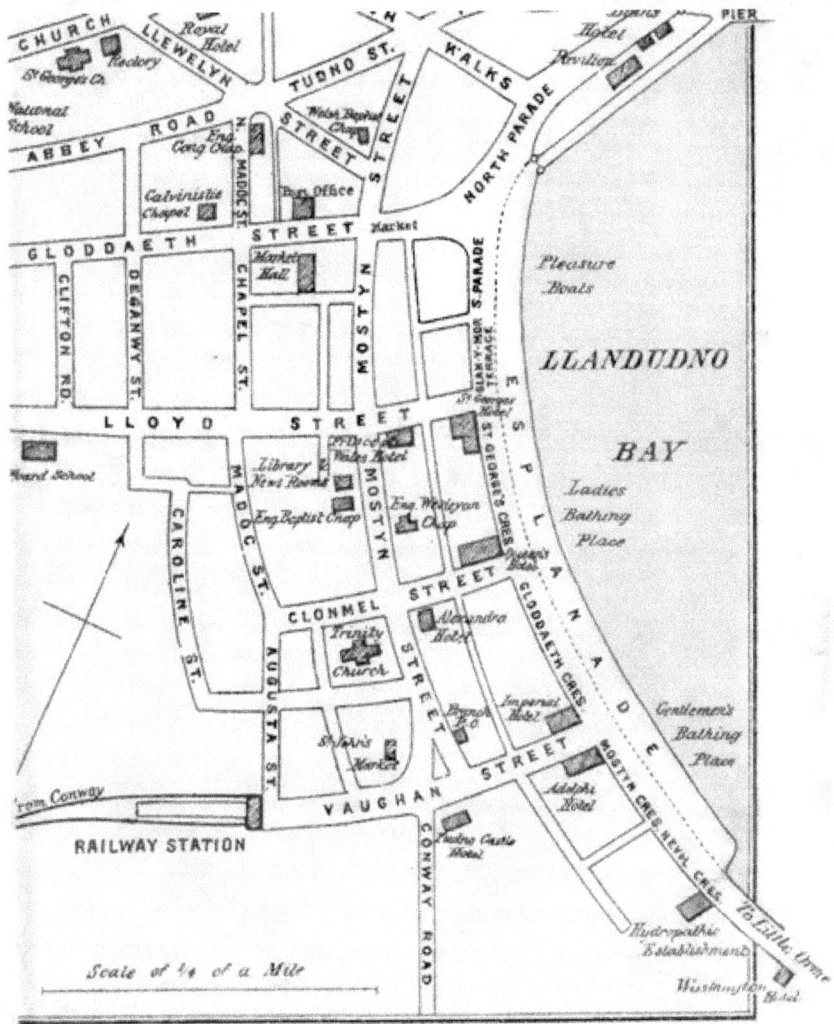

other points it lies open. The whole town, which has come into being since 1850, is laid out regardless of the cost of space, and is on handsome lines. The principal sea-front, the **Parade**, overlooks Orme's Bay, and contains the chief hotels. Its aspect is north-east and north, and consequently in summer has the merit of coolness. If visitors, when they come to explore the site of the town, wonder why a place so obviously built on a settled plan, seems to face the wrong way, and has been made to turn its back on the fine scenery of Conway Bay and the mountains of Snowdonia, they will soon find a partial reason. North-eastwards, between the two Ormes, which form the horns of the bay, the shore slopes with fair rapidity, and even at the lowest ebb the water retires to no excessive distance, whereas westwards, when the tide is out, the Conway sands form a patchwork of sand and mud, interspersed with stagnant pools, neither sightly to the eye nor pleasant to the feet.

The drawback to Llandudno is its shadelessness. Neither on the Great Orme nor on the flat between it and the Little Orme is there anything worthy to be called a tree. The nearest ones are those of Gloddaeth, on the line of heights which extend westwards from the Little Orme.

As to the second factor mentioned above, the provision for the health and comfort of visitors, Llandudno need not fear comparison with any competitor for public patronage. The drainage is perfect, and the water supply, brought from Llyn Dulyn, a precipice-girt lake near Carnedd Llewelyn, abundant and pure. The hotel and lodging accommodation is excellent, and the former, considering its quality, is not, perhaps, unduly expensive, but the charge for apartments, not only in the best situations but throughout, is during the August rush of visitors very high, the excuses pleaded being the shortness of the season and the high rating of the town.

Mostyn Street, the principal business thoroughfare, a fine street of first-rate shops, is at the back of the Parade, and contains a Public Reading Room.

The *Sea Bathing* in Orme's Bay is both good and safe, and the Conway shore is available when the sea on the other side is too rough, while for those who prefer a swimming bath (*admission, including Pier, 6d.*), there is the largest in the kingdom in the basement of the **Pavilion**, a spacious public room recently erected. From the west end of the sea-front, under shelter of Gt. Orme's Head, runs out an elegant **Promenade Pier** (*toll 2d.*), 1,200 feet long, and with its head so shaped as to afford a leeside landing-place in all weathers. Here, as well as on the Parade, an excellent band plays during the season. The view, without being remarkable, is pleasant, and includes the ridge of Tal-y-fan behind the Conway mountain, Y Foel Fras at the head of the Aber glen on its right and Pen-llithrig, some three miles short of Capel Curig, on its left.

Boating is of course one of the staple amusements of Llandudno, but all that we need say about it is that there are two caves on the more easterly side of the Little Orme, called respectively *Eglwys Wen* ("White Church"), and the "Demon's Cave," which can only be visited by water, and that a fine view is obtained by sailing round the Great Orme.

Great Orme's Head.

Round this interesting headland a good carriage-road of easy gradients, known as the **Marine Drive** (*tolls : foot passengers,* 1*d.*; *saddle horses,* 3*d.*; *carriages,* 6*d. per horse*), winds along the face of the cliffs, and between the toll-houses measures 4¾ m. The complete circuit of the Head, 6 miles, is made several times a day by public conveyances that carry passengers at 1s. each. The round may of course be made in either direction, but all who are free to choose should start from the end near the pier, in order to have the view of the Conway estuary and the mountains in front of them during the latter half of the journey. We accordingly so describe it.

After passing the *Pavilion* and the entrance to the *Pier*, just short of the *Toll House*, at the beginning of the drive, we see on the left what, for reasons best known apparently to nursemaids and their charges, is called the *Happy Valley*, and then, soon after passing the Toll House, have above us great beetling masses of carboniferous limestone, the rock of which the Great Orme wholly consists. When *Pen-trwyn*, the north-east corner of the promontory, is reached, we get a view eastward of the Clwydian range and of the coast-line about and beyond Rhyl. Rounding the point, the rocks on our left soon present a good example of erosion, due to springs, and then for a little distance cliff gives place to a steep green slope, up which a foot-track leads to "Old Farm Refreshments," but not to **St. Tudno's Church**, the path to which is about a quarter-of-a-mile further on, near a flagstaff. This little church, which is only a trifling distance from the drive, is a favourite resort on Sunday evenings, when service is often held in the churchyard. It is the parish church of Llandudno, and is said to stand on the site of the cell of St. Tudno, a hermit of the 7th century, about whom little is certainly known. During the Early English period a church was built, and the west end of the north wall is possibly a part of it, but the rest of the building as far as it is old belongs to the 15th century. From 1839 to 1855 the church was in ruins, but in the latter year it was restored, and in part rebuilt by Mr. W. H. Reece, of Birmingham. On either side of the east end is a 13th century coffin-slab, and the old circular font rescued from base uses has been reinstated. The *grave yard* is the parish cemetery, and its marble monuments are in striking contrast to the humble little edifice. The key of the church is kept at the

" Old Rectory Refreshments " close by. For the road over the hill from Llandudno to St. Tudno's, *see below.*

Returning to the Drive, a steady ascent of about ¾ mile brings us to the *Lighthouse*, which exhibits a fixed light visible 24 miles. In the cliff below is *Hornby Cave*, so named from the brig *Hornby*, which was wrecked at this point on New Year's Day, 1824, all the crew perishing except one man who managed to scramble up the cliff. Leaving the lighthouse and passing a steep green terraced hollow on the right, we in a few yards reach a point in the road commanding a magnificent view of the Conway estuary, the coast westward to Anglesey and Puffin Island and of the mountains of East Carnarvon. The peaked summit of Snowdon is among the possibilities of a clear day, and the direction to look for it S.W. by S. over the right shoulder of Carnedd Llewelyn which itself appears a trifle to the right of the green rounded outline of Y Foel Fras. It is a steady decline from the point we have now reached, and the details of the opposite shore including the beautiful ruin, Conway Castle, come out distinctly as we descend. Below us on the right a level strip intervenes between the steep hill-side and the sea, and on it we see the scanty remains of *Gogarth Abbey.* Passing through the Toll Bar we reach the low ground and turn to the left along Abbey Road to Church Walks, by which Llandudno is re-entered.

Great Orme direct.—A road, fitter for walking or riding than driving, leads from Church Walks, a little west of the end of Mostyn Street, up to the top of the Great Orme ; and the same point may be reached by proceeding up the so-called Happy Valley from the Marine Drive. By keeping straight on, *i.e.*, in a direction north-west, the Old Semaphore Telegraph Station (750 feet) may be reached, whence the view is both wide and beautiful. The road to St. Tudno's Church (*see above*) branches to the right a few hundred yards short of the *Telegraph Station* (now licensed as an inn), whence, crossing a stiff wall by a step-stile, the walk can be continued right over the Head to the *Lighthouse* at its north-west extremity. Those who wish to spend a day rambling over this bare but breezy headland will find light refreshments at " Old Farm " and " Old Rectory " (the former somewhat to the east of the church, and the latter close to it), as well as at the Telegraph Inn. It is usual to enumerate certain British antiquities as to be found on the headland ; but in truth there is nothing of any importance or real interest, unless the *Copper Mining Works*, at the back of Pen-y-Dinas, above Happy Valley, be so reckoned. The rocking-stone, *Cryd Tudno*—" Tudno's Cradle " —does not rock, and quarrying has destroyed much of the Dinas.

Little Orme's Head and walks south of Llandudno.

General Remarks.—That part of the Llandudno promontory which lies south of the town, between it and the Chester and Holyhead main line, and called *Creuddyn*, is a tract of country of no special beauty in itself, but rendered interesting by the several limestone knolls which diversify the surface, and one or two mansions rising from their wooded slopes. These knolls attain a height of from 350 to 500 feet, and are all reached in a few miles with very little exertion. A line of them, comprising the Little Orme's Head, Mynydd Pentre (the "mountain headland"), the Gloddaeth Hill, and Brynmaelgwyn stretches from N.E. to S.W. about 1½ miles from the town. These hills are wooded on their southern slopes, and Brynmaelgwyn, has a complete girdle of trees and brushwood. The pleasantest short stroll—easily accomplished between breakfast and luncheon—is to take the shore road until you are between the Little Orme and Mynydd Pentre, and then, after making the *détour* to the top of the Little Orme or not—to climb the ridge in the other direction, south westwards, and follow it until you drop on to the Conway-road, under Brynmaelgwyn, about 1½ miles from Llandudno.

Beyond this first ridge, and separated from it by a green valley, is a second one, following the same points of the compass, and consisting of Bryn Euryn, Penrhynmawr, and Pabo. From the latter height you may reach Llandudno Junction in 1½ miles, and return to Llandudno by train; there is also a station near Mochdre.

Both these walks should be taken from east to west. As we have said elsewhere, there is no really first-class scenery in this part of North Wales east of the Conway river; so that, if you walk from west to east, you have your back to the view all the way. To describe this view in detail from each height would be tedious repetition—" Anglesey, Puffin Island, Carnedd Llewelyn" *ad nauseam.* We will therefore, once for all, give some account of it from **Pabo Hill**, which, though in itself a mere green hump with a semicircular limestone quarry on one side, is the best view-point of all, because it has the fine lower reach of the Conway in the immediate foreground, and the mountain group (of which Carnedd Llewelyn is the crowning height) fully displayed in the background. From the other heights the mountain view is pretty much the same, but the foreground is tamer. From one and all there is a more or less wide expanse of sea, the mouths of the Dee and Mersey being the limits in one direction, and Puffin Island and Anglesey in the other. The mountains visible constitute that part of Snowdonia which lies between the vales of the Conway (or Llanrwst), Llugwy, and Nant Ffrancon. Highest and most central of these are the almost level summits of Y Foel Fras (the "big bare hill"—an expressive title—) and Carnedd Llewelyn. Of the latter only a strip is visible. It lies to the left of Y Foel Fras, and farther away. Still more to the left, Pen-

llithrig may be recognised by its **more pronounced** outline, pointed
to the south and sloping **gradually to the north**. Then, separated
from the last named by a couple of smaller, tapering peaks, we
have the **eastern** shoulder of Moel Siabod, which rises on **the far
side of the Llugwy valley**. From several of the heights, Arenig-
fawr and Arenig-fach, near Bala, are seen far away to **the south**.
To the right of Y Foel Fras the range drops seawards to Penmaenmawr, the **Conway Mountain** and Penmaenbach, the chief intervening height being Tal-y-fan. The **town** and castle of Conway
give a picturesqueness and animation to the foreground, which
would be still further enhanced by the Suspension Bridge, if its
light elegance were not counteracted by the heavy bulk of the
"tubular" beside it. From Pabo **you have only** one peep of the
Clwydian range, over a dip **in the nearer hills, through** which the
railway goes; but from the more **eastern heights a much more**
extensive view of them is obtained. Another feature **of the Pabo**
view is the appearance **of** Llandudno itself, framed, **as it were**, by
the woods of Brynmaelgwyn and Gloddaeth, **to the exclusion of**
the dreary stretch of marsh which **so** greatly **detracts from its**
picturesqueness from most points of view.

We will now give such general directions for these walks as
will, we hope, enable the pedestrian **to** reach the particular point
he is making for, without binding him to any precise way of getting there. In a country so scored with lanes and paths, **it is**
easier and pleasanter to lose one's self for a few minutes, **now**
and again, **than to** follow **minute** directions. A variety **of**
pleasant walks may be planned to one or more of these knolls ;
or, if something **more than a** *dilettante* stroll be desired, the whole
of **them**, including the grounds of the Gloddaeth mansion, may
be tramped over within the space of a few hours.

(1) **The Little Orme.**—Though about 300 feet lower than
its neighbour, the Great Orme, this headland presents decidedly
finer and sheerer cliffs, while the walk round it is as easy and
pleasant a one as can be wished for. On trip days, when the
Happy Valley and the Telegraph Station are in the full swing of
their popularity, a stroll over this comparatively neglected height
will specially commend itself to the less exuberant class of visitors.
The whole round may be accomplished in from $1\frac{1}{2}$ to 2 hours, and
very little direction is needed.

Keep along the shore-road till it ascends between the Little
Orme and Mynydd Pentre. Here there is a break for some
distance in the wall on the left hand, and a path, passing through
a wicket-gate, a little way up the hill, leads on to the headland.
Beyond this gate you may reach the cairn at the top in a few
minutes, by bending to the left, but it is much better to keep on
by an obvious route, so as to make the entire circuit. The views
all the way are delightful, and by taking the walk in this direction,
you have the softer aspects of nature in front to begin with, and
the grander ones as a climax. Amongst the former, the grace-

fully graduated outline of the Clwydian range, culminating in the monument-crowned Moel Fammau (*p.* 37), is a noteworthy feature. In front of it are the tower of St. Asaph Cathedral and the white spire of Bodelwyddan Church and the coast round Colwyn Bay to Abergele, still nearer at-hand being the plain church-tower of Llandrillo-yn-Rhos. Then, as you approach the cliff, you look down upon a little opening, called *Trwyn-y-fuwch* (the "Cow's Ness"), in which are huge blocks of limestone, evidently torn away from the softer earth above them. Continuing northwards, the cliffs become higher and more imposing, in places rising almost sheer for upwards of 300 feet, broken here and there by recesses whose shelving sides are overgrown with grass. There is no sharp rim of actual precipice, but the views down to the wave-worn base of the rocky wall do not lack impressiveness. Presently, as we proceed over the short dry grass, which, broken in places by masses of rock, forms the upper surface of the headland, Llandudno comes into view, and then Penmaenmawr, with Anglesey to the right of it. A short ascent then takes us to the cairn, and the full panorama is disclosed. The mountain features will be understood from the previous description (*p.* 48). The depression of the Conway valley is traceable, but not the river itself. Conway Castle peers over the Gloddaeth woods, and in the background Penllithrig is to the left, and Y Foel Fras and Carnedd Llewelyn to the right of it. Far away in the south, the square outline of Arenig-fach is overtopped by the peak of Arenig-fawr, near Bala.

In descending, make southwards for the wicket-gate again, which is, in reality, the only portal of the headland. Then, after descending to the main road, either return by it to Llandudno, or, if bound for Gloddaeth, proceed along it, for a few hundred yards, to a point at which four roads meet. The one down-hill to the left is the comparatively modern road to Llandrillo-yn-Rhos and Colwyn Bay. Either of the two others may be followed. If (1) you continue along the broader main road, you will in about a mile, at the second turn to the left, hit the direct route to Gloddaeth, described below. (2) By climbing the narrower middle road, only fenced on one side, you will pass a small inn, the *Penrhyn Arms*, whence you may ascend, almost at once, to the common-land, or you may continue along the lane—avoiding a turn downhill to the left—and enter, close to a cottage which at first sight forms a *cul-de-sac*, a path traversing the upper part of a wood. This path crosses a lane, and then continues through a couple of fields to the rear of *Gloddaeth House*.

(2) **Direct route to Gloddaeth**, *abt.* **2** *m.* Follow the shore-road past Craig-y-don Parade, and then turn to the right and proceed across another road ($\frac{1}{4}$ *m.* distant) up a steep lane which winds upwards past some quarries and resolves itself into indefinite tracts near an old *windmill* (without sails) on the high com-

mon-land at the edge of the Gloddaeth woods. The all-round view from hereabouts is very good.

It is a pleasant walk from this point along the ridge to the right, keeping the woods on the left and descending a steep pitch to the hollow between the hill you are on and Brynmaelgwyn, where the direct path from Gloddaeth to Llandudno by the Conway road is entered. The map is the best guide.

A little beyond and below the old windmill the Gloddaeth woods are entered by a gate opening on to a cart-track that descends to the back of Gloddaeth House.

Gloddaeth House dates from the days of Elizabeth, but has been greatly altered of late years. It is an old seat of the Mostyn family. The public path passes behind it, and being skirted by an intervening wall affords no view of it. The grounds in front can only be visited by privilege, and perhaps the chief attraction of the place to the sojourner in shadeless Llandudno is its umbrageous surroundings.

In returning you may take the direct path between the Gloddaeth hill and Brynmaelgwyn, or—much better—the one which crosses a meadow and the south side of the latter woody height to Eglwys Rhos church, half a-mile distant. These routes diverge close to the gate through which the main drive passes, a little west of the house. *For Eglwys Rhos, see p.* 54.

(3) **To Pabo Hill** (5 m.) and **Llandudno Junction**, abt. 6½ m. Pabo Hill is the chief object of this walk, which may be taken and enjoyed, by the laziest visitors, between breakfast and a 5 o'clock dinner. To reach it you have to cross the green valley which we have already described as lying between the Pabo range and the nearer Gloddaeth one. Starting along the shore-road towards the Little Orme, you may either go between that promontory and Mynydd Pentre, or you may cross the ridge of the latter by Castell Bodafon. In the former case you leave the Colwyn road (p. 52) at cross-roads just beyond the Little Orme, bending to the right up a narrow but very fair road—fenced on one side—which soon passes a little inn. Thence the road, or rather lane, drops at the first turn to the valley and joins the Llandrillo and Eglwys Rhos road. This it leaves again by turning to the right just beyond an old windmill with two sails. Going left again, in a third of a mile it climbs by a steep zig-zag to a ragged-looking group of houses on the brow of the next range. If you cross the hills by Castell Bodafon, leave the shore-road beyond Craig-y-don Parade, turn left in ¼ mile and right again by a path a little further, and then go as straight as you can over the hill till you pass through a gate on to the Llandrillo and Eglwys Rhos road, a few yards west of the point at which the previously described route joins it. Then, right for a ¼ mile towards Eglwys Rhos; left, past a smithy till you actually join Route 1, at the foot of a zig-zag close to a pond. At the top of this zig-zag, a little past a school-house, turn to the right to the

group of cottages before-mentioned. Here turn left again, and
after bending round to the right you will reach the top of Pabo by
taking a cart-track, also to the right, where the road begins to
descend. **Pabo Hill** is easily recognised by the fact that its
south side has been hollowed out into a semi-circular quarry.
The view from the top—a pleasant greensward—has been already
described (*p.* 48.) *Bod-yscallen* House is close at hand.

From Pabo go a little north-westwards and you will enter by a
gate the *Bod-yscallen woods*—noticeable for their parasitic growth
of ivy, which conduces to picturesqueness rather than vitality.

In a few hundred yards, where the main track bends to the
right to Bod-yscallen House, keep straight on by a foot-path
which leads over an immense stile and then drops to *Marl House*
(half ruin). Hence a footpath, at first a cart-track, leads almost
directly to Llandudno Junction.

Bod-yscallen, itself a large foreign-looking mansion, owned
by the Mostyn family, is very pleasantly situated on the slope of
the hill.

The nearest way to it from Llandudno is by the Conway road
as far as the second turn to the left beyond Eglwys Rhos Church
(*see map*). By this route the distance is about 2½ miles.

(4) To **Llandrillo-yn-Rhos** and **Colwyn Bay**, 6 *m*. Proceed along the shore as if bound for the Little Orme's Head,
and ascend the main road that winds round between it and
Mynydd Pentre. When a junction of four roads is reached, take
that on the left, which leads down by *Penrhyn Farm*. The tower
of a large, broken-down windmill is then seen away on the right
front, and, avoiding a cart-road which goes off at the bottom of
the hill directly towards it, we take the next road on the right
hand. This, beyond a toll-bar, crosses the main streamlet of the
valley, and then ascends to Llandrillo-yn-Rhos Church, affording
on the way a pleasant peep of the hills on the far side of the
Conway estuary, and, looking back, of the Gloddaeth Woods.
Two short towers that break the sky-line in this latter direction
are the remains of wind-wrecked mills.

Llandrillo Church, chiefly Perpendicular and externally
plain, has Irish-like stepped battlements. There are traces of
E.E. and Dec. work in the tower and northern half of the building. The churchyard, in spite of its exposed situation, as
evidenced by the wind-blasted yews, is well cared for. *The Lich-
gate*, very plain, is dated 1677.

Just beyond the church is a good roadside house, the *Ship Inn*,
where, turning to the right, we have, in a hundred yards or so,
the ruins of *Llys Euryn* in a field on the right. What these ruins
are is doubtful, but they probably represent a late 15th cent.
manor-house, partially fortified. (The fireplace arch, obviously
modern, was rebuilt about 1854.) On the spot, however, it is kind
not to question the curious jumble of facts and fiction, that they are
the remnant of a palace of Maelgwyn Gwynedd, whose later resi-

dence was Deganwy Castle, itself pulled down to provide material for Conway Castle ! On the top of *Bryn Euryn*, the grassy hill south of the ruins, is the trace of an encampment, possibly a stronghold of the above named prince, whence there is a wide but not particularly beautiful view. Returning to the road, we next pass a National School, and, turning left, arrive at Colwyn Bay.

Llandrillo Church by Capel Trillo and Llandrillo to Colwyn Bay (*Pedestrian only*). Just short of the Ship Inn turn down a cart track on the left, and at the end of it sharply to the right, and again along a hedgerow to the left. This brings us to the cliff close to *Capel Trillo* (*p* 43), whence by a footpath and the shore the way is unmistakeable to *Colwyn Bay* (*p.* 42).

(5) **Llandudno to Conway.** This short excursion of 2 to 4 miles can be made with equal convenience by rail, water, or road, and it is one that no visitor, for however brief a sojourn, should omit to make. The routes by rail and water are, as regards scenery, practically the same. On the left hand, just at the actual mouth of the Conway river, we reach **Deganwy** *Station* with the *Deganwy Castle Hotel* close by, and behind it a small hill (*abt.* 250 *ft. high*) on which are the very scanty remains of *Deganwy Castle*. This rude castle was built by Hugh Lupus, soon after the Conquest, and was at one time held by Henry III., who was besieged in it by the Welsh. In 1262 Llewelyn dismantled it, and much of its material was, we are told, afterwards used in the construction of Conway Castle. An old tower about ½ *m.* north of it was an outpost.

The ascent of *Deganwy Hill* is best made by footpath either from the hotel or from the new chapel a little further on, and beyond the station. The view from the top is extensive, and includes the lowest reach of the Conway river and the mountains as far south as Arenig-fawr near Bala.

There is quite a hamlet of little lodging houses close to Deganwy Station, and then, as we near Llandudno Junction, the fir-clad knoll of *Bodlondeb* on the western side of the river is a charming foreground to the bracken-covered Conway mountain behind it. Conway Town and Castle are now in full view as well as the Suspension and Tubular Bridges, which we must honestly confess, when looked at in connection with the long embankment connecting them with the " Junction," are the reverse of an improvement to the scenery. In the old " ferry " days the prospect about here must have been charming, but it was a clear case for the submission of the picturesque to the convenient, and the only actual eyesore is the " Tubular " itself, which quite spoils the light and graceful lines of the Suspension Bridge. Arriving by boat we can disembark, if we will, close to the Castle. If by rail it will be well to alight at *Llandudno Junction*, to which point the road-route from the south end of Mostyn Street, and *viâ* Eglwys Rhos, converges. Close to Llandudno Junction Station is the *Junction Hotel*, a small but well-managed house affording good quarters at reasonable charges. **A hundred** yards or so towards Llandudno is another inn, the *Ferry* **Farm,** whose name recalls the former, not **seldom** perilous, passage of **the Conway river.** At one or other of these houses the tourist who does not care for the **joys and sorrows of a** popular watering-place could **do worse than locate himself, as** the railway gives rapid and **inexpensive access to all the chief** points of North Wales. **From no direction does Conway Castle appear to** greater advantage than as **we approach it from the eastward by** the main, Chester and **Holyhead, road, which is carried across the** Conway first by an **embankment 670 yards long, and then by a** graceful **Suspension Bridge** (*toll*, 1*d*.). This bridge was erected by Telford, 1824-6, and is **377 feet in** extreme length and **32 feet** wide. Its chains are on the east side fixed to what was once **an** islet, and on the west are carried **many** feet into the rock beneath the castle. Only too **close to it,** from a picturesque point of view, is the **Tubular Bridge** that carries the railway. This is one of George **Stephenson's works, "the** firstborn **of a** giant race," and consists of two parallel rectangular tubes, each 412 ft. long, 25½ ft. high in the middle, and 22½ ft. at either **end.** The clear span of the bridge is just **400 ft., and** therefore only 60 ft. less than that of the two main spans of **the Menai** Tubular Bridge. Of the **towers** that stand at **each** end of the tubes, built, it is alleged, to **harmonise** with those of the adjoining Castle, the less said the better.

By road, 4 *m.* The first part of this, a straight stretch of a mile across *Morfa Rhianedd,* is monotonous. Then, at *Eglwys Rhos,* we have **a** pretty church (containing memorials of the Mostyn family) and a small inn, the *Mostyn Arms,* on the left. On the right is a new and very tastefully-built school-house. A yew tree in the churchyard shows, better than any words could do, which way the wind blows hereabouts. Just beyond the church the footpath to Gloddaeth (*p.* 51) commences. Then the road breasts a slight rise between Deganwy Hill on the right and Body-scallen on the left. A very slight ascent about here is sufficient to open out the country to the eye, and there is a very pleasing view from the top of this one. *Bod-yscallen* (*p.* 52) is reached by the second turn to the left beyond Eglwys Rhos.

The descent to Llandudno Junction passes at its foot a small hamlet, beyond which the road goes alongside the railway to the station.

CONWAY.

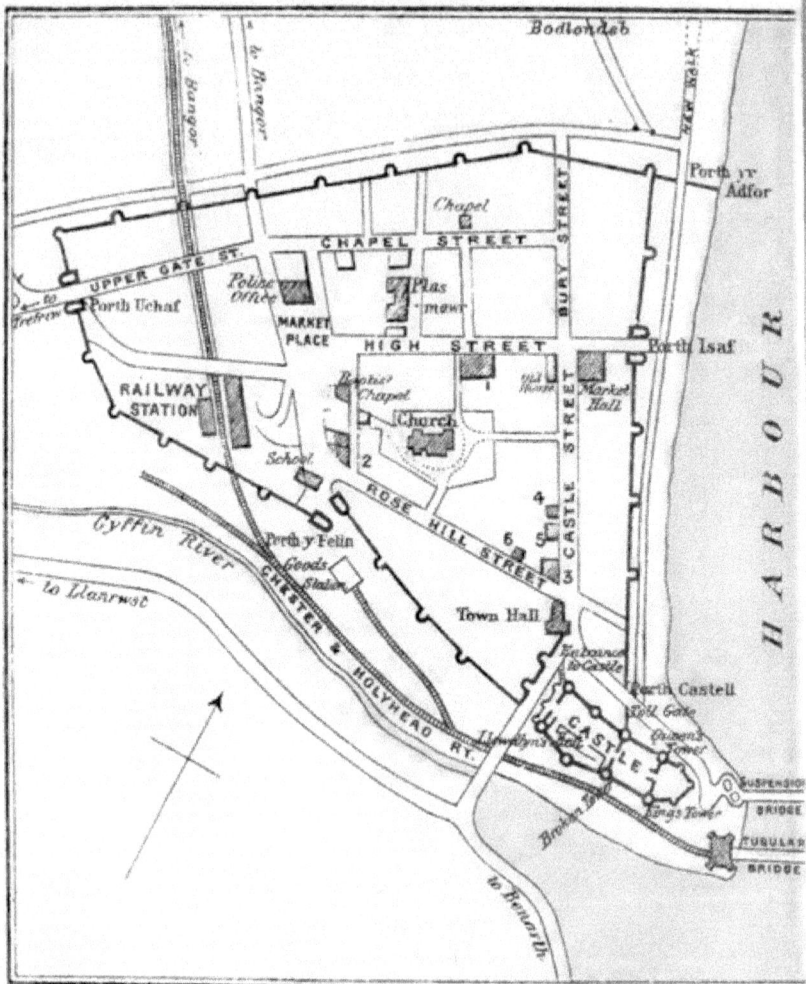

Scale of Quarter of a Mile.

REFERENCE.

1. Castle Hotel
2. Erskine Arms Hotel.
3. Castle View Hotel
4. House with Stanley Arms
5. Post Office
6. English Wesleyan Chapel

Conway.

———◆———

Hotels: *Castle*; *Erskine Arms*, Q. (both near to **station**); *Castle View*.
Post: *Arr. abt. 7 a.m. and* 2.30 ; *dep.*, 9.20 *a.m. and* 8.45 *p.m.*
Population: 3,179.

This ancient town is still almost entirely intramural, and its walls, though no longer in a defensive condition, are nearly perfect. Their circuit has been, not inaptly, compared to the shape of a Welsh harp. There is no walk along the top, and no particular architectural details about them call for notice, but their broken outline against the sky, caused by the slope of the ground on which they are built, and the number of round towers that rise at very short intervals, is very striking—especially at their western angle, which attains a considerable elevation.

The Castle (*admission 3d. Entrance close to the toll-house of Suspension Bridge*) is at the eastern angle of the walls. Those who enter the town by the Suspension Bridge pass under the shadow of the four large northern towers, and so to the entrance-gate. The same point is reached from the Railway Station by turning to the right along Rose Hill Street. From the flight of steps at the entrance the four northern towers, answering to four similar towers on the south, present a bold and impressive front. Then, crossing a drawbridge, we pass three small towers, from the walls between which the town-walls may be traced to their highest point. Turning to the left we enter the *Great Court* at its western end, and in doing so note the great thickness of its walls, 15 feet at least. On the right-hand (south) side of this court is the *Great* or *Llewelyn's Hall*, 130 feet long by 32 feet wide. Its roof has perished, and is now represented by one old and one restored arch. The floor too has perished, but its level is indicated by the fireplaces and a walk on the north side. Beneath the floor were formerly cellars, and these, being now thrown into the hall, injure its proportions, but any beauty thus lost is more than compensated for by the festoons of ivy which drape the arches and walls. The *Chapel* was at the east end of the hall, and a round window still remains. From the Great Court we pass into a smaller one having four drum-towers, each with a turret, at its angles.

The *north-east tower*, called the *Queen's*, contains an interesting little oratory, with small chambers for the priest on either side, similar to those at Beaumaris. The *south-east*, or *King's Tower*, has a dungeon in its basement, and the tower next to it on the south side, long known as the *Broken Tower*, is the one that used to be so conspicuous a shell from the railway. Only recently it has been repaired, and in very uncouth fashion, quite regardless of appearances. Beyond the eastern tower is a small embattled platform, whence a good view is obtained of the two bridges and down the Conway as far as Glan Conway, and from the Deganwy hills to the Great Orme, while the wooded knoll of Bodlondeb, on the left bank of the estuary, is a pretty feature. The ascent to the top of the walls should not be omitted, as a good and wide view is thence obtainable, and Conway itself is completely commanded.

A few words must suffice for the *History* of the Castle. It was built about 1284 by Henry de Elreton (the architect of Carnarvon Castle) for Edward I., who more than once visited it, and on one occasion at some risk. With only a few of his men he had preceded the body of his army and crossed the river, soon after which the tide flowed in and prevented his men from following. The Welsh in the mountains learning this fact made a descent on the Castle, which they furiously attacked. The handful of defenders, who, we are told, had no other provisions than a little bread and honey, held out with difficulty, though with success, until relieved by their comrades. It was from Conway that Richard II. started to meet Bolingbroke, to whom he was betrayed by Northumberland, and carried off to Flint. In the Civil War Archbishop Williams of York held it for a while for the King, and was succeeded by Rupert, who was obliged to surrender it in Nov., 1646, to the Parliamentary forces, and in 1665 it was dismantled by the Earl of Conway, who carried off such materials as were of value, but lost them at sea.

Those with time at command should visit the **church** (restored). It is mainly of the Decorated period and contains a good roodloft, screen and stalls, and there is a beautiful niche on the south side of the nave. Malthusian philosophers will not fail to enquire for the tomb of Nicholas Hooke, a 17th century worthy who was the 41st child of his father, and himself father of 27.

Plas Mawr (just off High-st.), sometimes called *Queen Elizabeth's Palace*, is a fine specimen of an Elizabethan house, with stepped gables and an octagonal tower. It has been saved from destruction by th Royal Cambrian Academy of Art, which holds its exhibition in it annually, from about Whitsuntide to the end of October. (*Adm. 6d.*) It contains 52 doors and 365 windows. Inside the ceilings and walls are richly and quaintly decorated. The **College**, in Castle Street, near the Post Office, is another remnant of old Conway, but has now only a coat-of-arms of the Stanleys to show the visitor.

The **New Walk**, as it is called, round the fir-clad knoll and mansion of Bodlondeb affords a delightful half-hour's shady stroll, especially when the tide is up. You enter it by the water-side at the north end of the main street, and, passing between low rocks on the left and the sea-shore on the right, come out near some new villas on Conway Marsh. Thence a road goes left and joins the main Bangor road just opposite the raised foot-bridge over the railway, by which the ascent of Conway Mountain (*p. 57*) is commenced.

At Conway the curfew-bell is still rung.

Conway to Penmaenmawr by Sychnant Pass (or Conway Mountain, 800 *ft.*), **Dwygyfylchi**, and **Foel Llys**, 1,200 *ft.*

For a miniature mountain **excursion**, within the powers of every-one who can walk at all, nothing can well be imagined **easier and more enjoyable than this**. There is a good road, 4½ miles in length and reaching its summit in the Sychnant Pass (550 *ft.*), all the way from Conway to Penmaenmawr, but to make the most of the day the route should be over the Conway mountain and Allt-wen, down to the Dwygyfylchi inn, up again to Foel Llys (by the Fairy Glen, or direct), and down to Penmaenmawr. This means a good half-day's outing. Pedestrians who like a full day's excursion should continue from Foel Llys, round the basin in which Penmaenmawr village lies, passing the Druid Stones (*or* Meini Heirion), over Penmaenmawr Mountain (1,553 *ft.*), and down to Penmaenmawr village or Llanfairfechan. The direct Sychnant Pass route loses nine-tenths of the views, and in its highest part the proprietor of a new house has erected a wall with the result, if not the aim, of entirely excluding what view there is. A description of the far more interesting hill-route will cover every object included in the road-route.

The Route. Quitting Conway by the Bangor road, which goes side by side with the railway from the station, we go through the Walls, past a new stone bridge, which crosses the line on the left, and over a raised iron foot-bridge a few hun-dred yards further. This joins an adjacent cart-road, from which, in a few hundred yards, a green track starts up the south side of the **Conway Mountain** (or *Town Hill*) and reaches its summit, a little right of the track, about 2¼ miles from the town. During the ascent the road over the Sychnant Pass may be seen in the valley about half-a-mile to the left. As we approach the top there is a charming view down the vale of Llanrwst, to the right of which Tal-y-fan and the lofty green upland of Y Foel Fras form the culminating heights, and we can see back along the coast to Colwyn and the Clwydian range. From the top, Llan-dudno and the two Ormes come into the view, as well as Puffin Island and the north-east part of Anglesey. Penmaenmawr, with its three cairns, rises in front over Allt-wen, to the right of which Penmaenbach drops steeply to the sea. Here, too, on the summit, are traces of a fortified camp, called *Castell-caer-seion*, and of stone circles which, to the eyes of the antiquarian, suggest an old British town, but about which the unlearned tourist may be pardoned for being sceptical.

Pursuing our journey along the ridge, we pass a depression leading down to the sea on the right, and containing a small re-servoir. By diverging seaward beyond this the top of *Penmaen-bach*, a few feet lower than the Conway Mountain, may be reached, but there is nothing particular to be gained by making the détour. It is better to continue to the left of a few green enclosures and a

farm to the summit of **Allt-wen**, which is a little higher than
either of its companion **heights**, and introduces us to **a new and
most attractive** view into the fertile hollow of *Dwygyfylchi*
(pronounced Doo-e-guv-ul-k'y. The little village is seen **in the
centre of the hollow, and** Foel Llys rises beyond it. Southwards
we see the road descending from the Sychnant Pass, and where
it reaches the level of the valley, a narrow opening in **a hill,
prettily wooded and headed by a** little waterfall, indicates **the**
position of the Fairy Glen.

In descending it is best to strike southwards, almost retracing
our steps till we enter a farm-track, which drops sharply round **a**
face of rock and enters the Sychnant road a little west **of the top
of the pass.** Then, descending to the valley, we **reach the comfortable little** *Dwygyfylchi Inn*, whence, if we wish **to include the**
Fairy Glen (*admission 4d.*, p. 66.) we must turn **up a by-lane
and.** after our visit, proceed by the old Llanfairfechan **track,**
which commences with a steep zig-zag between the **inn and the**
entrance to the glen; or we may begin the ascent from the **main**
road by a path which starts almost opposite a school-house. **In**
either case special direction is needless. A little hole **in the**
steep side of Allt-wen on the opposite side of the valley **is an**
old copper mine.

Foel Llys is about 1,200 feet above the sea, and from it **we**
have a bird's-eye view of the village of Penmaenmawr, fronting
the sea at the mouth of a green semi-circular recess, which **may**
be described as a somewhat larger edition of the one in which
Dwygyfylchi stands. The side of Penmaenmawr mountain which
forms the western flank of this recess is sadly **marred by huge**
quarries, but the general view is most charming. *

From Foel Llys it is best to bend left again till we reach the
crest of a green glade, up which comes a road direct from Penmaenmawr village. Descending this glade we pass through a gate,
and the road becomes enclosed. Continuing as straight **as may**
be, we enter the village close to the *Mountain View Hotel.*

The continuation of the route from the crest of **the green** glade
(*see above*) to the stones of *Meini-hirion*, and over the Penmaenmawr mountain to the village, or to Llanfairfechan, is
described in the Penmaenmawr excursions (*p.* 67).

Conway to Aber (or **Llanfairfechan**, 11 *m.*) over **Bwlch-
y-ddeufaen**, alt. 15 *m.* *Inn at Roe-wen*, 5 *m.*

Three miles of walking may be saved by taking train to *Tal-y-cafn Station*, on
the Ffestiniog line, and there crossing the ferry and proceeding by a direct
road over a slight eminence to *Roe-wen*.

As a mountain pass, Bwlch-y-ddeufaen—said to be part of **a**
Roman road from Conovium (Caerhun) to Aber—has no special
features, but the walk over it is an easy and bracing one, **and**
affords extensive and pleasing views of land and sea from the

---

* A good path has lately been made all round Foel Llys, near the top.

long level which constitutes its highest part, as well as an interesting descent to Aber. It also gives pedestrians who make an early start the fine alternative of breasting the main ridge of Eastern Snowdonia from the top of the pass (1,400 *ft.*), and making the tour of Carnedd Llewelyn and Carnedd Dafydd to Bethesda or Capel Curig. We shall describe this variation in our " Mountain Section." Those who wish to make it should take the early train from Llandudno or Conway to Tal-y-cafn.

The Route. There is a good carriage-road from Conway to Roe-wen, 5 miles on the way. It commences either by the old lower road which goes under the railway from the entrance to the Castle, or by a turn to the left on the Bangor side of the railway station. The two routes unite at *Gyffin*, a little village half-a-mile from Conway, and thence the Llanrwst road is followed for 2 miles, the first half of which is up-hill. In front are the green broken slopes of Tal-y-fan, and in the distance the peak of Penllithrig. At first the Conway river is hidden by the hill of *Benarth*, but in about 2 miles from Conway, its winding course comes into full view. The valley below on the right is well cultivated and sprinkled with farmsteads and cottages, with here and there a more imposing villa residence, showing that its quiet beauty is not unappreciated.

A long 2½ miles from Conway we turn to the right out of the Llanrwst road at the *Commercial Inn*, and descend gradually to the *Afon Roe* valley, passing on the right the unprepossessing modern church of *Llangelynin*. The old church—probably the highest ecclesiastical building in Great Britain—is on the eastern shoulder of Tal-y-fan, and reached by turning to the right nearly half-a-mile beyond the modern one. It is disused except for a 6 p.m. service on the last Sunday in the summer months.

Roe-wen, a few yards short of which we turn sharp to the right, at the point where the road from Tal-y-cafn converges, is the chief part of the parish of *Llangelynin*. It is styled on the Ordnance Map " Y Ro," and contains a small inn. The brook, babbling over stones and rocks along the south side of it, enhances the picturesqueness of the scene. Here begins the rough part of the route. Taking the right-hand turn, at the west end of the village, we climb a very steep hill, by a narrow lane metalled in places with nothing but bare rocks of slate. On reaching the high ground, pretty views of the Conway valley open up behind and southward, the hills of Pen-y-Gaer and Pen-y-Gader being prominent in the latter direction, and the green slopes of Drum and Y Foel Fras in front. The road about here is very sloppy, and continues so until we reach the lane coming up on the left from Llanbedr, half-a-mile short of which point there is a small *cromlech* a few yards to the right. Beyond the Llanbedr lane the " going" improves, and presently we come out on to open ground. The top of the bwlch (*abt.* 1,400 *ft.*) is more than half-a-mile further. It is marked by an iron gate and a cross-wall, and a little short of it is an upright stone about 8 feet high. The companion stone, said to be prostrate, we have failed to discover.

Passing through the gate we look over a bare plateau, from which Penmaenmawr rises steeply on the right, and over a high depression in Y Drosgl on the left the slopes of Llwyd-mor are seen. The sea, Anglesey, Beaumaris and Penrhyn Castle come into view. Llanfairfechan is hidden by Carreg-fawr, but about 1¼ miles beyond the gate at the summit a track leads down to it by the side of a wall. A little further a cross-track, also leading to Llanfairfechan, comes down Yr Orsedd on the left, and a mile further our own route, hereabouts but faintly marked, is joined by one from Llyn-yr-afon, and commences a sharp descent into the Aber glen.* An enclosed road is entered through an iron gate, beyond which the descent is continued steeply. During it there is a view up the glen to the waterfalls. The round hill in front is Moel Wnion. Passing through Aber village we enter the Conway and Bangor road, and turning to the right in a few yards opposite the church reach the *Bulkeley Arms Hotel* and the *Railway Station.*

---

* There is a lovely view into the glen, with a peep across the Menai Straits beyond it. Hereabouts, too, a stone step-stile leads on to the winding drive by the side of Maes-y-Gaer, and down to Llanfairfechan.

Penmaenmawr.

Hotels : *The Penmaenmawr*, close to the Station, overlooking the sea :
Mountain View, in the village.

Post : *Chief del. abt. 7 a.m.* ; *desp. abt. 8.30 p.m.*

Both in itself and its surroundings **Penmaenmawr** is one of the
most enjoyable of the many marine resorts which have sprung up
during the last half century along the coast of North Wales. A
sensational account of the mountain Penmaenmawr, written early
in the century, and attaining its climax in the expression " superabundantly horrid," does not so much as hint at the existence of
a village of the same name further than remarking that " on its
western side there is a public-house, once a place of much
resort." The terrors of the pass over the side of the mountain
have served a large number of writers with an excuse for much
" high-falutin " description ; when, however, they exhaust their
eloquence upon the risks which the wayfarer formerly encountered from falling rocks and the *débris* of the precipice, these
writers forget that travellers now-a-days are subject to exactly the
same danger, whatever it may be, except that those by rail have
the protection of a short tunnel while passing under the extreme
shoulder. The only thing " superabundantly horrid " about Penmaenmawr at the present time is the quarries which disfigure the
side of the headland with vast heaps of rubbish, and threaten in
the more or less distant future to destroy the beauty of the valley
below altogether. In a century or two, if the work of destruction
goes on at its present pace, the stoutest pedestrian will be able to
walk in a bee-line from Penmaenmawr to Llanfairfechan without
turning a hair.

The most modern part of Penmaenmawr occupies the centre of
the deep green hollow which, though the work of the road and
rail-maker have rendered it as accessible as any place in the kingdom, is by nature almost excluded from the outer world by Penmaenmawr Mountain (1,553 *ft.*) on the west side, and Foel Llys
(1,181 *ft.*) on the east. On the west side of the hollow, and close
under the former mountain, is the comparatively old part, *Penmaenan*, as it is called, a regular street of insignificant looking
houses (inn, *Black Lion*). The railway, following the coast-line at
only a little distance from it, separates the inhabited part from
the sea, but the slope of the hill prevents its obstructing the sea
view, and besides prospective improvements there is a good
promenade along the shore between the line and the sea. On a

tablet at the entrance to the new roads a quotation from a letter of Mr. Gladstone bears witness to the salubrity of the place.

The architecture of Penmaenmawr proper is to a great extent of the villa type, the only continuous line of houses being along the main road, and this consists principally of shops. From the Station the main road is reached in a few hundred yards in both directions by carriage-roads, and by a foot-road between.

The sands below the pebbles are good and firm and there is excellent bathing at nearly all states of the tide, the distance between high and low-water mark being comparatively little, and the exception being, oddly enough, for a short time, about high-water.

Excursions from Penmaenmawr.

Beauty, rather than variety, is the feature of the walks in the immediate neighbourhood of Penmaenmawr, and those who do not take kindly to hill-climbing will find their walking area rather limited. Fair climbers, however, may reach with moderate effort several of the most interesting spots in north-east Snowdonia, and if the rail be made use of, a great part of the scenery of North Wales may be visited between breakfast and sundown. These mixed rail-and-coach excursions will be found described under the heads of Bettws-y-coed, Bangor, Carnarvon, &c., and the ascents of Y Foel Fras and Carnedd Llewelyn—the two most accessible of the higher mountains—in the "Mountain Section." The specialities of the place are comprised in the following delightful rambles:—

(1) **Ffrith Demonddydd** (abt. 650 ft.) It is a very pleasant stroll of an hour or more there and back to the top of this green little knoll, which lies like a footstool under Foel Llys. To reach it, leave the main road at the *Mountain View Hotel*, and in a few yards turn up to the right. In less than half-a-mile, after passing two cross-roads, you bear to the left, and passing a little farm get on to the hill-side. From the greensward on the top there is a charming view of Penmaenmawr and its surroundings, and across the sea to Puffin Island and Anglesey. *Permission should be asked at a farm close to the foot of the hill.*

(2) **Penmaenmawr Mountain, 1** hr.; (**Llanfairfechan Station, 2** hrs.) **Meini Hirion, 2** hrs.; **Penmaenmawr Village, 3** hrs.

This walk may be called the tour of Penmaenmawr. You climb, as it were, to the brim of the broken bowl in which the village lies, and walk round it, having no occasion to descend again till you have completed the semi-circle, and reached the summit of Foel Llys. The walk may be extended at the cost of another hour or so, down into the almost similar little hollow between Foel Llys and Allt-wen, wherein lie Dwygyfylchi and the Fairy Glen, but we shall here content ourselves with the former circuit.

From the station or village go about half-a-mile along the main road towards Bangor. Then, a few yards beyond the *Black Lion Inn*, at Penmaenan, turn up to the left. A new Wesleyan Chapel confronts you. From it turn again to the right, up a narrow lane, which bends again to the left at a conspicuous gate, and right again a little higher up. A few yards further you enter a foot-path on the left, just short of a cottage, and continue upwards through a wood with the *débris* of a huge quarry on the right. Passing a path that leads into the quarry you go through a wall by a wicket-gate. Beyond this the path, after approaching a little hollow, bends back towards the quarry and reaches a wall, by the side of which it zigzags up till it passes through it by an opening just when a cross-wall bars further direct progress. Beyond this point there can be little mistake. The cross-wall turns up the hill in a few yards, and continues pretty much in the direction of the one you have already skirted, and the top of the mountain lies some way to the right of it, marked by three cairns. Upon it are the ruined walls of the ancient fort of *Dinas Penmaen*, or *Braich-y-Dinas*, wherein, says an old authority, there were once a hundred towers and space for 20,000 soldiers!

Penmaenmawr (Mountain) is, thanks to its bold and comparatively isolated position, seen from more points than any other mountain near the coast of North Wales, and for the same reason the view from it is very extensive. Over the sea it commands the lowland plain—as it seems from high ground--of Anglesey, the Menai Bridges, the Anglesey and Bulkeley columns and the white sea-frontage of Beaumaris being conspicuous. The Isle of Man and Black Combe, in Cumberland, are questions of atmosphere. Of Llandudno and its twin Ormes you might almost draw a ground-plan. Southwards all is mountain and moorland, the central position, due south, being occupied by Y Foel Fras, which hides the loftier heights of Carnedds Llewelyn and Dafydd. A little to the right of Y Foel Fras, and forming a lower part of the same ridge, is Y Drosgl, and beyond it in clear weather the sharp-cut peak of Snowdon. Then, as the Foel Fras range sinks seawards, we may note in the hollow between it and Moel Wnion, a silvery or rather, perhaps, milky streak. This is the less interesting of the two Aber waterfalls, and far away beyond it the Rivals are as distinct as outline and isolation can make them. Between them and Snowdon the horizon is cut by the nearer heights on the far side of Nant Ffrancon.

Penmaenmawr appears to have been identified by some with the

> "rock whose haughty brow
> Frowns o'er old Conway's foaming flood."

whence Gray's " bard " denounced the " ruthless Edward." As a fact, however, neither Conway nor its " foaming flood " are to be seen from any point on the mountain.

Three cairns mark the summit of Penmaenmawr, and if we
go down a little east of them, we shall soon find a track which
roughly descends to the wall of which we saw so much during
our ascent. Surmounting it by the tallest step-stile in Wales, we
wind through a network of walls behind a cottage, and then traversing a field cross another wall, just where a rough cart-track
comes up from Llanfairfechan. The descent to Llanfairfechan
from this point is obvious, but in making our tour of Penmaenmawr we must continue south-eastward, alongside of another
wall, and by a track which only exists in the Ordnance survey, till
we reach the old track from Llanfairfechan to Conway, a little
east of the point at which this too emerges through a gate on to
the open, and close to a farm-building called *Pen-y-cafn*.   All
this is quite plain sailing in fair weather, but in foggy you must
be careful after entering this track not to follow any of the diver-
gencies to the right, which lead over boggy ground to the lonely
region of Bwlch-y-ddeufaen, between Tal-y-fan and the Foel
Fras ridge. The hill on which the Meini Hirion stand is due east,
beyond the round top of *Moelfre**, and our course to it soon comes
to a wall on the left hand which turns down towards Penmaenmawr village almost opposite the circles. On the far side of this
wall are a mound and a little stone circle, called *Carneddau*
("heaps of stones") on the Ordnance Map.

For Meini-Hirion see next excursion, p. 65, where also attention is drawn to the lovely bird's-eye view of the Penmaenmawr
combe from the green spur in front of the stones.

The nearest way down from here to the village is by a path
which crosses the last-named wall by a ladder-stile a few yards
below its turn. Thence the route, crossing some step-stones,
turns out of the main track by a path to the right, at first very
faint but soon more distinct, and keeping a little above the stream
enters a road at *Craig Llwyd Farm*. Turn along this road to the
right, and in about ¼ mile you will come to a footpath on the left
which crosses a new road, and passing the English Presbyterian
Chapel enters the main road close to the *Mountain View Hotel*.

To continue the circuit of the hills from Meini-Hirion you must
go on first on one and then on the other side of a wall, bending
to the right a little in one place, till you pass through a gate a
little short of Tyn-y-ffrith Farm.   Then bending to the left, you
enter the Green Gorge, and by a lane descend straight to the
village.

If you wish to include **Foel Llys** in the excursion, you must
diverge to the right at the top of the Green Gorge, or you may continue along the old Conway track, past *Tyn-y-ffrith*, and descend
to the *Dwygyfylchi Inn*, near the entrance to the Fairy Glen, the

---

* This hill was, we are told, once crowned by three stones of different colours
—three women who, like the "Merry Maidens" between Penzance and the
Land's End, were petrified for Sabbath breaking.

upper part of which is a very little **distance to** the right of the
track, and a **little** beyond Tyn-y-ffrith.

Foel Llys, Dwygyfylchi (pron. Doo-e-guv-ul-k'y), **Fairy
Glen (Nant Daear Llwynog), Sychnant Pass**, Conway, &c.

To the Fairy Glen and back, *direct*, 4 m. *Ditto, over Foel Llys,
and back by road*, **5 m.** *Top of Sychnant Pass, direct*, 2 m.
Conway, 4½ m.

We have grouped all these places together because they lie in
the same direction, and the pedestrian may advantageously combine them in one walk of half a day's duration. The most
popular excursion included in the list is that to the Fairy Glen
and back by road (public conveyances run frequently).

This is the old road to Conway. The new one goes side by side
with the railway and the sea round the foot of Penmaenbach and
the Conway mountain, leaving the hollow in which Dwygyfylchi
lies on the right hand.

(1) *To the Fairy Glen direct.* The road passes to the right of the
Mountain View Hotel, and in half a mile goes under the rocky
shoulder of Foel Llys, called *Trwyn-y-wylfa* ("the headland of
watching"), sometimes the "Weeping Rocks," from a legend
in respect of a causeway made from Puffin Island to this point
by a philanthropic hermit, St. Seiriol. The floods, however,
came and, as they swept away for ever this great engineering
work, here stood the people bewailing its destruction. A little
beyond this and opposite a by-road to Dwygyfylchi church, a
wide track turns to the right up the eastern side of Foel Llys (an
easy route to the summit) but our route goes straight on to the
Dwygyfylchi Inn, a comfortable little house, close to which a
by-lane leads up to the Fairy Glen (*see page 66*).

(2) *Over Foel Llys to the Fairy Glen.* The road passes to the
right of the Mountain View Hotel, and a few yards further we
take the by-road on the right which leads up the hill past several
villas, and leaves the green mound of Ffrith Denomddydd on the
left. In less than a mile this road, after bending to the right
opposite this mound, passes through a gate into a deep green
hollow, sometimes called the *Green Gorge*. Here the road bends
back to the left, so as to break the steepness, but you may take
a path straight up the gorge and leave it for Foel Llys as soon
as you see your way comfortably to the top. Once there, you are
nearly 1,200 feet above the sea, and in the enjoyment of a delightful prospect. The twin hollows, if we may so call them, of Penmaenmawr and Dwygyfylchi lie far down on either side. The sea-
view is similar to that from Penmaenmawr mountain (*p.* 63),
except that the greater elevation of that height intercepts a portion of the Menai Straits, while eastwards you have, by way of
compensation, a glimpse of Conway Castle and the estuary of the
Conway river to the right of Allt-wen—the hill which rises so
abruptly from the far side of the Dwygyfylchi basin. Southwards

Guide VIII.   F

Tal-y-fan and its loftier continuation towards Y Foel Fras bar further prospect.

In *descending* we strike eastwards, and soon gain a path which brings us down into the road a minute or two's walk short of the Dwygyfylchi Inn.

The **Fairy Glen** has been fenced in, and made a highly remunerative possession to the proprietor, 4*d.* a head being charged for admission. This circumstance is not calculated to **increase one's** appreciation of its charms, but perhaps the worst **we can say of** it is that the composer of the placard describing **it as** " the loveliest piece, in miniature, of silvan rock and river scenery in Wales " would have done well to put " in miniature " in italics. It is a succession of little cascades, of which the two **chief** ones are near the top, and as we thread our way upwards, **crossing** and recrossing the **stream,** we gain delightful peeps **through** the abundant foliage which overhangs it—none the less **pleasing from their intermittent character.** The glen is only too **trimly kept.** The old Conway and Llanfairfechan track zigzags up from a point between the entrance to it and the inn.

From Dwygyfylchi the ascent of the *Sychnant Pass* (the " **dry** valley," *abt.* 575 *ft.*) begins at once. On the left is the steep **scree** of *Allt-wen* (the " white cliff " though " red " would be more **appropriate.)** Everything here, mountain and pass, as well as **glen, is** miniature, **and** allowing this, we cannot **help drawing attention to** the striking similarity in shape of Allt-wen, as **seen** from the bottom **of the pass,** to Great Gable as it appears from Wasdale Head.

We have already, on page 57, commented on **the great pains which have** been taken to wall **off** the view from the top **of the** Sychnant Pass, and for this reason, if for no other, we strongly **advise the pedestrian** to strike off to the left before reaching the **highest point by a** cart-track, which **crosses the top of the** gully **under a face of rock,** and make for Conway **Mountain.** The dis- **tance is only** slightly longer, and a pleasant détour may be made **to the top** of Allt-wen (or **of** Penmaenbach) on the way. A description of these hills is given in the reverse route (*p.* 57).

3. By the " Green Gorge" **to Meini Hirion,** 2½ *m* ; **Penmaenmawr Mountain,** 4½ *m* ; **and back to the village,** 6 *m.*

We have already described this **delightful** ramble the reverse way on page 63, to which we **must refer the** visitor for details of the latter half of it, commencing **from Meini** Hirion.

The shortest way to Meini Hirion is by the Craig Llwyd Farm, which is reached by turning out of the main road by a footpath leading up past the Presbyterian Church, a little west of the Mountain View Hotel. Above the church go about 15 yards to the left along a new road and then continue the ascent to a second parallel road. The Farm is some distance to the right along this road, and is reached by passing through a gate where another bit of road goes off to the left. Then, leaving the farm on the right, we pass through the right-hand one of two gates and make a direct ascent by a pleasant footpath about half-way between the quarries above and the streamlet below. This path, after becoming very faint, enters a good one from the quarries close to some stepping stones which cross the streamlet at its head. Beyond them is a stepstile; go over this and continue up along the side of the wall, till it turns sharp to the right, and you cross the old Conway and Llanfairfechan track. The Meini Hirion are straight ahead just over the brow of the hill.

From the village take the right-hand (upper) fork of the road at the Mountain View Hotel, as in the route to Foel Llys, and in a few yards turn up the by-road which strikes up the hill—also to the right. This road, after passing two cross-roads and bending sharp to the right under Ffrith Denomddydd (p. 62), enters the so-called "Green Gorge" by a gate, beyond which you ascend between heathery slopes, with Foel Llys on the left and Craig-y-fodwch on the right, to the old Conway and Llanfairfechan track. If you break the ascent by bending abruptly to the left at the gate, you will see the "Stones" standing out against the sky-line; or from the gate you may take a steep path to the right and go over the heathery Craig-y-fodwch—a delightful stroll.

Towards the top of the *Green Gorge* you bend to the right round Craig-y-fodwch, and leaving the little farm of Tyn-y-ffrith a little on the left, enter the old Llanfairfechan track, which passes through a gate and then continues by the side of a wall till, after passing through another gate, it bends to the right out of the straight course, which is continued by a newer track. Then it rejoins the wall, and, going through or over it by gate or step-stile, continues along it till in about ¼-mile a pathway leads up to the "Stones" which are on the brow of the hill a little to the left.

Meini Hirion means simply "long stones," *meini* being the plural of *maen*, a "stone." Whether these particular ones are Druidical or merely sepulchral monuments, we must leave the learned to decide, but anyhow the situation greatly resembles in its wild and bleak character those of Stonehenge, Callernish in the Lews, the Circle near Keswick and other Druidical remains. There are a score or so of stones forming a rough circle, nearly 30 yards in diameter. Four of them are about 5 feet high, the others insignificant. A short distance to the west of them is another collection, covering a smaller area, and lying confusedly about without any appearance of regular order.

There is a wide view from the larger circle, but à more beautiful one from the grassy knoll which overlooks Penmaenmawr from the north side of the road by which we have approached.

The direct way down again commences with a step-stile in the wall just after it has turned seawards a little west of the circles. It is fully described on page 64.

For *Penmaenmawr Mountain* we continue, with a wall on our right, along the old Llanfairfechan track, not over clear in places, almost as far as a gate through which it passes out of the unenclosed ground. Then bending to the right we skirt the wall that goes from the gate in the direction of the top of the mountain till we come to a track leading down towards Llanfairfechan through another gate. Over another wall and across a field from this point we reach a cottage behind which a huge step-stile lands us at the foot of the rough stony cone of the mountain.

For the View &c, see page 63.

The way down is back to the last wall which we crossed and alongside of it, first on the left hand and then on the right, till the path bends to the right above the stone quarries, and approaches a shallow cwm. Here it goes left again, and, passing through a wicket-gate, descends through some trees at the foot of the aforesaid quarry. A lane is soon entered whicn comes out into the main road in the hamlet of Penmaenan, a good half-mile west of the fashionable part of the village.

Ascent of Carnedd Llewelyn, Y Foel Fras, &c. from Penmaenmawr. These longer excursions will be found described in our " Mountain Section." *For the railway journey to Bangor, Carnarvon, &c., see p.21.*

Llanfairfechan.

Hotels: *Queen's* (H.Q.); *Castle*; *Llanfairfechan (small)*, ½ to ¼ m. from Station.

Post: *Arr. abt.* 7.15 a.m., 1.30 p.m.; *dep.* 8.30 p.m.

Population: about 2,200.

Distances: *Eastward*: Penmaenmawr, 3 m; Conway, 7½ m; (Llandudno, 11½ m; Llanrwst and Trefriw, 19 m; Bettws-y-Coed, 22½ m.); Rhyl, 22½ m; Chester, 52½ m. *Westward*: Aber, 2 m; Bangor, 7½ m; Menai Bridge, 9 m; (Carnarvon, 16 m; Beaumaris, 14 m.) Holyhead, 32 m.

Of the minor watering-places along this north coast, none is more favoured in beauty or in convenience of access to the most attractive scenes of North Wales than **Llanfairfechan**. In a situation at once open, yet sheltered and well wooded, at the foot of Penmaenmawr Mountain, which rises immediately to the east, it commands a charming seaward view across the entrance of the Menai Straits to Anglesey and Puffin Island. Behind it rises the picturesque mountain outline of Carreg-fawr, Yr Orsedd, and the hills south of Aber, while westward, immediately adjoining the village, are the flourishing plantations and park of *Bryn-y-Neuadd* (S. Platt, Esq.). The place is still only a large village, but there are plenty of good lodgings, devoid of pretentiousness, and well placed. Bright little gardens are a pleasant feature, and but for its turbulent character after rain, which makes protecting walls necessary, the little Llanfair stream which here enters the sea, would be another. That *sine qua non* of a prosperous holiday resort, a good water-supply, has been assured by the construction of a reservoir on Glan Sais, 1000 feet above the sea. There are two *churches*: *Christchurch*, modern and good, adjoining the lower part of the village, and the *Parish Church* higher up the valley. The former is used for English, the latter for Welsh services. Along the shore is a *parade*, or rather, level track of humble character, and thereabouts provision is duly made for boating and bathing when the tide is in. At low tide there is a large stretch of sand, which, at any rate, is a safe playground for the little ones. The bathing is second rate.

Of *Walks* close at hand, those to Penmaenmawr village and Aber, respectively three and two miles by high road, call for no description, and the railway is available if preferred. Of other walks, one of the first that should be taken in clear weather is the easy climb to the top of *Carreg-fawr (Llanfairfechan Hill)*

This little height (about 1,150 feet) not only affords a picturesque view, but will at once enable the visitor to grasp the general lie of the land in the neighbourhood. Accordingly we describe the prospect from it in some detail with a view to making clear the routes for other and more ambitious excursions.

(1) **Ascent** of **Carreg-fawr.** (¾ hr.) From the station follow the road up to the village, crossing the main (Bangor and Conway) road in ⅓ mile and at the fork, 100 yards further, taking the right-hand branch. There either cross the foot-bridge between the two churches and follow the path that goes round the higher one (with the bell-turret), or cross the carriage-bridge 100 yards further up-stream. Path and road re-unite just beyond the church.

Then (a) ten yards further take a lane on the left, which soon becomes a path winding along the edge of a cliff that hangs over the Llanfair stream. Stick to this path for nearly ½ mile; then, a little after it has become a lane, turn abruptly to the right, and, almost at once, left again over a wooden step-stile. Hence the path, after passing a ruinous and an inhabited cottage, winds up the steep hill and passes through a gate on to the open moorland ¼-mile short of the top, which is unmistakable.

(b) Continue along the road for ½ mile past the church; then, at a double white-washed cottage, turn up the hill to *Bryngoleu Farm*, whence the road ascends steeply to the right and passes through an iron gate on to the open fell with a walled-in preserve on the right.

The *view* westward embraces nearly the whole of the Anglesey. Beaumaris is plainly seen at the mouth of the straits, and over it Baron Hill (Sir R. Bulkeley), and the Bulkeley monument. To the right of this is Llanfaes church, Castell Lleiniog, the Light-house at the extremity of the island, and then Puffin island with its ancient tower. On this side of the straits Bangor is out of sight, but Penrhyn Castle is conspicuous. Now turning to the coast-line, near at hand we observe Aber station, 2 miles west of Llanfair-fechan, while close below us is the park and castellated mansion of Bryn-y-neuadd. Looking north-east, the view is limited by the bold cairn-crowned summit of Penmaenmawr, while nearly due east, just across the Llanfair glen, is the abrupt scarp of the little hill marked Dinas in the map. Inland, to the right of Dinas and so round to south, the prospect extends over a somewhat dreary upland, but it will be useful to note some of its details. The broken ridge that bounds the view to the right of Dinas is Tal-y-fan (2,000 feet) with Foel-lwyd at its near end, just over a bit of road seen crossing the ridge. This road marks Bwlch-y-ddeufaen, the pass by which the Roman* road led from Aber to Conovium (Caerhun), in the Conway valley. The track on the south side of Carreg-fawr joins this road about 1¼ m. short of the bwlch, and by it it is almost a straight route of 8 miles from Llanfairfechan to Tal-y-cafn Ferry across the Conway. Now observe another cart-track running across the low ground south-eastwards and gradually ascending by the east flank of Yr Orsedd to the tame ridge of

---

* On *Rhiwiau Uchaf Farm*, about a mile south of Carreg-fawr, a *Roman milestone* (now in British Museum) was found in January, 1883. The inscription showed that it was erected in A.D. 119. It marked the 8th Roman mile from Conovium.

Y Drosgl in that direction. This track marks the easiest route from Llanfairfechan to Llyn-yr-Afon (Aber Lake—fair trout-fishing), which lies in the curve beyond and south of Y Drosgl, at the foot of the steep northern face of Y Foel Fras. A glance at the map will show that this same track puts us well on our way towards the summits of Drum (2,527 ft.), Y Foel Fras (3,091 ft.), and Carnedd Llewelyn (3,482 ft.). The distances and times of these three summits from Llanfairfechan are, roughly speaking, 4¼ m. (2 hrs.), 5½ m. (2½ hrs.) and 8½ m. (4½ hrs.), and the route to the most distant of them lies past, though not necessarily over, the actual summit of the other two. Directions as to the route, &c., will be found under Carnedd Llewelyn in the "Mountain Section" at the end of the volume. More to the right of the track, which has thus caused us to write at such length, is the round top of Moel Wnion, and descending from it is seen a little burn that, after rain, has the appearance of a long white thread. It is the Afon-y-garn, and joins the main Aber stream some half-mile below the cascade.

(2) **Ascent of Dinas** (abt. 1,050 ft.). This is a little hill crowned by the remains of an earthwork. It rises almost precipitously on the right bank of the Llanfair stream, about two miles up the valley from the sea. The point to make for is *Tyn-y-llwyfan Farm*. Take the road through the village (straight across the main road, and the right fork beyond), and keep the stream on the right-hand side till you come within 100 yards of the third bridge (wood with iron rails) ¾ m. beyond the churches. Here turn up to the left by the new road that in ¼ mile reaches *Tyn-y-llwyfan Farm*. Go through the gate and turn left by the barn with a zinc waggon-roof. The stony side of Dinas is now straight ahead but keep to the lane as far, or nearly as far, as the second gate (½ m.), almost to the ridge, and then turn up to the right, doubling round still further so as to avoid an awkward wall.

The Farm may also be reached by the road along the west bank of the Llanfair stream, which is also the way up to the *reservoir*.
The **view** from the top is similar to that from Carreg-fawr except so far as it is obstructed by that slightly superior height.

(3) **Ascent of Penmaenmawr** (1,553 ft.). Take the road that leads up to the village from the east side of the bridge by which the Chester and Holyhead road crosses the Llanfair stream. Where this forks, follow the left-hand branch, which in half-a-mile reaches the small farm called *Henar*. Hence you may (*a*) pursue the zigzags of the track, and, after passing through three gates or gateways, turn sharp to the left and gain the first top of the mountain, or (*b*) you may save the zigzags and make the ascent a more impressive one by striking up the slope, and using the quarrymen's path and ladders, which lead also to the first top. Hence you may go right or left to the actual summit. The last part of the way is in any case very stony. *For a description of the summit, the view from it, and the descent to Penmaenmawr village direct or by Meini Hirion circles, see pp. 63 and 64.*

Llanfairfechan (or Aber) over Bwlch-y-ddeufaen to the Vale of Conway.

Distances from Llanfairfechan (from Aber add 1 mile) : to the Bwlch, 3¼ *m; Roe-wen (small inn),* 6½ *m; (Conway,* 11½ *m. Trefriw,* 13 *m; Llanrwst,* 14½*m; Bettws-y-coed,* 18 *m.) Tal-y-cafn ferry and station (Inn),* 8½ *m.*

Route fully described the reverse way on p. 58.

The walk from either Llanfairfechan or Aber over the Bwlch to Tal-y-cafn station, and the return thence by rail is an easy half-day's excursion. On either side of the Bwlch the country traversed is bleak and somewhat dreary, but the views obtained, though not of the highest order, are sufficiently varied to render the route a pleasant one to those who like for a while to get out of the stream of tourist traffic. The archæologist will find some traces of the Britons, and for the greater part of the way will be following the Roman mountain-road from Aber to Conovium (Caerhun). For the 8th milestone, recently discovered, see p. 70. The ascent to Pen-caer-helen (or Pen-y-gaer), one of the best preserved of British strongholds, will involve an addition of about 2½ miles to the round *viâ* Tal-y-cafn, but only about a mile extra on the way to Trefriw.

Route from Llanfairfechan. Proceed as for the ascent of Carreg-fawr (*p.* 70), as far as the gate above Bryngoleu Farm. Thence the road, which soon becomes only a well-defined bridle-track, crosses the southern ridge of Carreg-fawr. When it runs into a similar track turn to the left, and then in a few hundred yards the track from Aber is joined, just where the latter reaches the wall.

Route from Aber. Proceed up the glen as for the water-falls (*p.* 75), but at Pont Newydd cross the stream, and continue along the road, which ascends with the stream below on the right for a mile and then passes through a gate on to open ground. Hence by a sharp bend right and left in turn you breast the hill, being careful to avoid the green and more distinct path which goes up the valley on the right, high on the hill-side, to Llyn-yr-Afon. Ascending more gradually, you recognise the already familiar top of Penmaenmawr on the left front, and soon join the Llanfairfechan track.

From the meeting of the tracks it is a rather drear and viewless mile and a half to the top of **Bwlch-y-ddeufaen** (about 1,400 feet), so called from the two stones, of which one only, standing to the right of the track some distance beyond the gate in the cross-wall at its highest point, is now erect. The Pass has the rocky steep of *Foel-lwyd* on the left, and Y *Drosgl*, a featureless ridge, on the right. It must formerly, from the nature of the surrounding country, have afforded the only practicable route for direct traffic between the lower part of the Conway valley and the coast opposite Anglesey. Now it is only fit for pedestrians and

horsemen. Eastward of its highest point the track continues
some way above and to the left of the cwm which commences
here, and in about ¾ mile it becomes enclosed again. As we
proceed along the southern slope of Tal-y-fan, which is the
broken range extending eastward from the pass, the prospect is
still a lonesome one, and is now bounded on the right by the
ridge that runs down from Y Foel Fras towards the Conway. The
archæologist will note sundry longstones, and a heap or two supposed to mark the remains of huts. A mile from the bwlch the
route—a rough, but enclosed one—for Llanbedr and Trefriw goes
off on the right, and those who desire to visit Pen-y-Gaer must
here turn off (see below). The way to Tal-y-Cafn is straight on,
and soon a good cromlech is conspicuous on the left of the road.
It is three-legged, and with a top-stone about 8 feet by 7 feet.
Beyond the Llanbedr turn the road has become sloppy, and the
descent to Roe-wen is very rough and steep. Fine views of the
Conway valley are obtained in front and southwards. In the
village of *Roe-wen* is a roadside public-house. Hence the direct
road to **Tal-y-Cafn station** is 2 m., but a prettier walk, that
only involves an additional mile, is to take the road on the right.
This descends the valley of the little Afon Roe for about a mile,
and then soon runs into the main road from Conway to Trefriw,
almost opposite Caerhun church. **Caerhun** is the Roman station
Conovium, and a good many "finds" have there been made, but
the most attractive things now to be seen are the fine yews in the
churchyard. From the road just north of, and a little beyond the
church, a foot-path runs near the river direct to *Tal-y-cafn* Ferry,
where there is a small public-house kept by the ferryman. The
charge is 1d. per head for transfer across the river to the station,
which is close to the water.

Bwlch-y-ddeufaen to Trefriw by Pen-caer-Helen (Pen-y-gaer).

A mile west of the pass, take the road on the right that at once descends
to the Afon Roe and then ascends the opposite side of the valley. The
round summit of Pen-caer Helen is conspicuous ahead with Pen-y-gader on its
right. The road takes us direct to its foot. To ascend it turn to the right at a
sharp angle in the road and follow the cart-track that makes for the top of the
ridge a little west of the summit. The stronghold, "one of the most perfect
British forts in Wales, is defended on the only approachable side (the west) in an
unusual manner, the ground being thickly planted with upright stones projecting from 1 to 3 feet from the ground." Apart from the interest of the fort as
a relic of the past, the non-professional visitor will find ample reward for the
small fatigue of the ascent to it in the charming view over the vale to the
Denbighshire hills. Returning to the road it is an easy mile and-a-half past
Llanbedr Church to the main road at Tal-y-Bont, where is a fair roadside inn.

For the route to Trefriw, &c., see page 106.

Aber.

Hotel : *Bulkeley Arms* (H.Q.), close to the station. **Post Town**, Bangor. Box closes about 5 p.m.

To write of Aber as a seaside resort would be trifling with our
readers. It is nearly four miles from the village, as the crow,
or rather the gull, flies, across the mouth of the Menai Straits to
Beaumaris; and, in former days, people used to walk nearly the
whole distance when the tide was out. The immediate shore,
too, is not adapted for bathing or walking. Consequently, Aber
has been left behind in the race for popularity by all its modern
competitors along the coast, and its appearance may be described
as even primitive, the only positively new looking things about it
being the church and the hotel, both of which have been rebuilt.
For the tourist, however, bent on land excursions by rail or on
foot, there cannot well be a more convenient starting point than
the comfortable little hotel close to the station. The village is
nearly half-a-mile inland, and in the jaws of one of the most
delightful little glens in the Principality. Down it babbles the
Aber river, after a course over fall and rapid—one branch from
the remote lake of Llyn-yr-Afon, under Y Foel Fras, the other
from a wild upland valley on another side of the same mountain. Rising from the village itself, the wooded height of
Maes-y-gaer on the left, and the loftier but barer slope of Moel
Wnion on the right, leave only just enough space for road and
river to escape from the glen. A long trough by which water is
conveyed from the glen to turn a mill-wheel close to the station is
among the *notabilia* of the place.

The full name of the village is, we are told, *Aber-gwyn-gregin*,
Whether this be derived from *gwyn*, meaning " white," and *cregyn*,
" shells," or from a secondary meaning of *gwyn*, " blessed," and
greg a " cackling," we leave the philologist to decide. The readi-
ness with which the double suffix has been allowed to drop may,
perhaps, favour the latter theory, but our business is with scenery,
not derivations.

The *Excursions by Rail* from Aber need no special remark.
The opportunities are the same as those from Penmaenmawr and
Llanfairfechan, except as far as arises from the fact that several
of the trains which stop at the latter two places do not stop at
Aber. On foot, the specialities are Maes-y-gaer, the Aber Falls,
the mountain road into the Conway valley, over Bwlch-y-ddeufaen,
the delightful walk over Moel Wnion to Bethesda, and the more

ambitious ascent of Y Foel Fras, Carnedd Llewelyn and Carnedd Dafydd.

In the village, between the road and the stream, is a woody little mound, flattened at the top, and called Y *Mwd*. This is said to have been the site of a castle in which Llewelyn received the summons of Edward I. to surrender Wales. Here, too, the Welsh Prince is said to have put to death in a very atrocious fashion a Norman knight, William de Breos by name, who had first won his friendship as his captive, and afterwards lost it through certain clandestine love passages with his wife, Joan Plantagenet, daughter of King John. Of the spot called *Cae gwilym Ddu* ("Black William's field), on a mountain 4 miles south of Aber," where the Norman knight was buried, we wot not, nor yet of the tree, hard by the hamlet, on which he was hung.

Maes-y-gaer ("Field-of-the-fort," 753 *ft.*) the steep wood-covered hill which hems in the glen on the left, and is perhaps its most beautiful feature, is now surrounded by a slate fence, and closed to the public. The way up is from Pont Newydd on the way to the falls (ask at the cottage), and we believe no objection is offered to quietly-disposed visitors making the ascent. The coast-view is very good; southward the waterfalls are seen, but the extent of prospect is curtailed by loftier heights close at hand.

The Aber Falls are nearly 3 miles from the station and hotel, and at the end of the glen, which comes to an abrupt end close to them in a manner that is more characteristic of limestone than other mountain districts. The walk is a very attractive one throughout, and, at the cost of an hour's exertion, the interest may be doubled by returning over the smooth dry ridge of Moel Wnion.

Starting from the station or hotel we reach the main road opposite the church, and after following this for a few yards to the left, we leave it by the by-road which passes through the village at the entrance to the glen—a narrow opening with the wooded slopes of Maes-y-Gaer on the left and Fridd Ddu on the right. The latter is the northern shoulder of Moel Wnion, which flanks the glen throughout. This part of the walk may remind tourists of the East Lyn in Devonshire, but while the mountain screen is on a larger and bolder scale, the stream bears no comparison in beauty.

At the first bend in the road the larger fall comes into view at the head of the valley, and a little further on the *road* crosses the stream by *Pont Newydd*, noticeable for its graceful arch and light parapet, whence it strikes up a lateral valley for Bwlch-y-Ddeufaen. Instead of crossing the bridge, we continue along a path on the right of the stream for a few yards and then, just beyond the waters-meet, cross the western branch of it by a wooden foot-bridge, beyond which the path keeps the water on the right hand all the way to the fall, separated from it at first by a margin of trees, and then traversing at a greater distance from it a grassy tract, sprinkled with alder, thorn, and other bushes. As we pass to the left of a little cottage, called *Nant*, the valley opens into a bowl-shaped cul-de-sac—its sides green or russet, according to the time of year, with bracken, and its head formed of almost sheer masses of rocks, down which the larger fall makes a succession of leaps; the lowest cannot be much less than 120 feet in perpendicular height, and the basin at its foot is 600 feet above the sea-level. The smaller fall is nearly $\frac{1}{2}$ a mile to the right, and is rather a broken slide than a continuous fall. After heavy rain there is, perhaps, no more decided fall in Wales than the larger one, but as a fall it owes its impressiveness entirely to height and volume, and lacks that varied and intricate beauty of surroundings which is the chief contributor to the beauty of most British scenes of this kind. Walls of rock, from whose narrow ledges spring a few trees, flank it on both sides. The path extends to the bottom of the fall and, given a fair force of wind and water, you may enjoy an impromptu shower-bath at some distance from the basin into which the water leaps.

The *smaller cascade* is on the way to Moel Wnion—otherwise there is nothing to be gained by diverging to it. Beyond it you may climb to the ridge of Moel Wnion almost any where—the easiest route is to keep rather to the left till you get on to the *col* (*about* 1,500 *feet*), which separates the Aber glen from the one leading down to Bethesda on the other side. Thence for the route on to Bethesda (3 *m.*) see page 77 ; for the return to Aber, p. 101.

As you are approaching the larger fall, you may have noticed the line of a track crossing the scree on the left-hand well up the hill-side. This track, which may be easily reached by doubling back some way from the fall, leads into the wild upland hollow of *Cwm-yr-Afon-goch* (the "valley of the red river"), and thence the route may easily be continued to the summit of Y Foel Fras, and along the ridge to Carnedd Llewelyn. The first part of it, however, just over the Aber Falls, is very narrow, and at the risk of being laughed at by "experienced climbers" we say that it is not a route which a guide-book writer is justified in recommending. In slippery weather the awkwardest part of it is a few yards of rock just over the falls. More than one fatal accident has occurred here or hereabouts.

Aber to the Conway Valley by the Bwlch-y-ddeufaen Pass. *See* n. 71.

Aber to Bethesda over Moel Wnion, 6 *m.* 2-3 *hours.*

Moel Wnion (pron. "Oonion ") is 1,905 feet above sea-level, and our reason for introducing it here instead of in our " Mountain Section " is that it affords the easiest and driest walk over so great an elevation that we have ever discovered in Great Britain. By following its ridge throughout, instead of skirting its side by paths, you will obtain the maximum of enjoyment in combination with the minimum of superfluous exertion.

The Route. There are two ways of starting from Aber. (*a.*) By

the lane on the west side of the church, which ascends to a group
of cottages, and, continuing up to the right of them, enters the
open ground through a gate, beyond which a green path turns
sharply up the hill to the left. (*b.*) Through the village as far as
a stile on the right, just opposite the spot at which the mill-leet
reaches the road-side. By this route you must avoid a green track
to the left, just above the stile, and in a few hundred yards you
will enter, at right angles, the track (*a.*) coming up from the
church.

From the junction of the two paths you continue along the one
from the church, and at a fork a little short of the first wall follow
the greener and apparently less used right-hand branch, crossing
almost at once a wide green drive, beyond which you keep the
wall on the left. Then, crossing an iron fence, the track makes
for a gate in a wall some way to the right of the first cairn. From
all this part of the walk there is a lovely view across the Menai
Straits to Beaumaris, than which no watering-place in the kingdom wears a more inviting aspect at a distance. Behind it, are
the Bulkeley monument, the tarn and Redwharf Bay, beyond
which is the so-called Parys Mountain, and to the left of it in the
far distance that of Holyhead. The square towers and the woods
of Penrhyn Castle are effective objects in the foreground.

A second cairn now appears higher up the mountain, and our
track, after passing a little to the left of it, disappears altogether
for a short distance. The chief Aber waterfall, with the hills
culminating in Y Foel Fras, now comes into view on the left, and
in a few minutes we reach a cross-track, which comes up from the
west and is continued round the head of the Aber glen into the
remote upland valleys beyond. Cross this track, and make right
ahead for the top of Moel Wnion, a wide almost level area with
nothing attractive about it except the fine all-round view. This
includes the charming prospect across the Menai Straits already
commented on, and a long array of mountain summits in the
south. The valley between Bangor and Nant Ffrancon is seen
west and south west, and beyond it, some way to the right, rise the
hills on the other side of Nant Ffrancon itself and the peak of
Snowdon. The furthest height visible in Nant Ffrancon is the
Glyder-fawr, to the left of which, nearer at hand, are Carnedds
Dafydd and Llewelyn.

In descending to Bethesda we may go as we please in a south-
westerly-direction. First we cross a cart track in a hollow; to
the left is the *col* between Aber and Bethesda (1,520 *ft.*) ; then we
go over the top, or to the right or left of a stony height, called
Gyrn (1,777 *ft.*). The best route is over the top of it, the next
best to the left of it. Other tops on a descending scale follow. If
we are in a hurry, it is best to keep to the left of them. A long half-
mile beyond Gyrn we pass a narrow green gap on the right, through
which the vista of Penrhyn Park and castle, backed by Anglesey,
is only spoilt by the Llanllechid slate-quarry in the foreground.
Then, passing to the left of *Moel Faban* (1,300 *ft.*) we enter a path

by the side of the leet which conveys the water round the hill-side
from Afon Caseg, underneath Carnedd Llewelyn. Follow this
path till you come to a gate opening on to a lane on the left.
This lane leads with more or less directness down to Bethesda.
After passing through another gate it enters a cross-road close to
the Welsh Calvinistic chapel on the right. Opposite the chapel,
continue the descent till you come to a complicated meeting of
roads. These, too, must be crossed, and then you come again to
cross-roads, at which you must go a few yards to the right.
Immediately below is the new church. The track goes to the
right of this, and just below it enters the Bangor and Capel
Curig road in the main street of Bethesda, a little north of the
" Douglas Arms." All the ways into Bethesda, except the main
one, are very puzzling.

Aber to Llyn-yr-afon, Carnedd Llewelyn, &c. *See
Mountain Section.*

Aber to Bangor, *see p.* **21,**

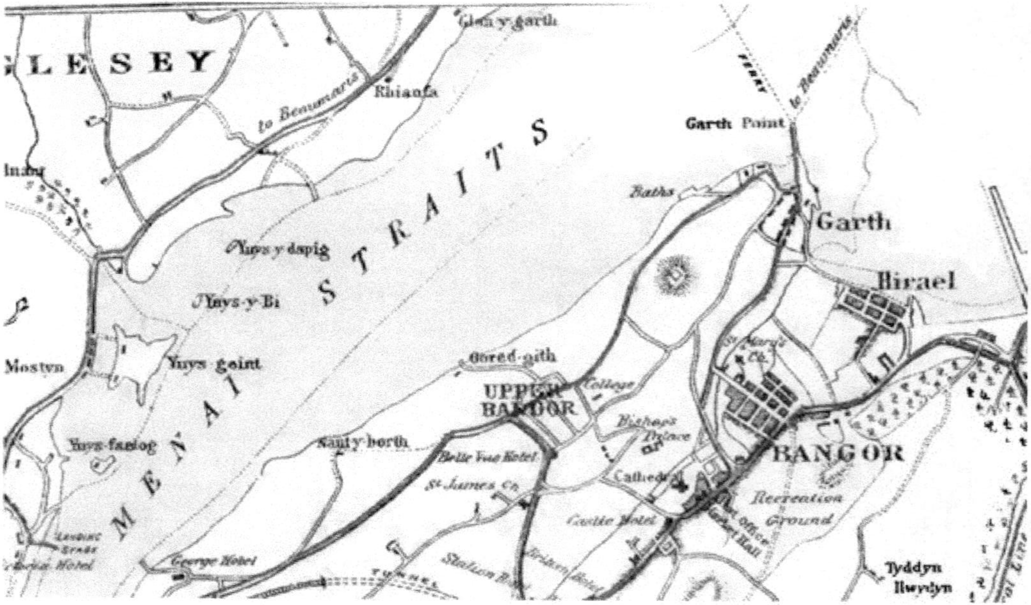
LESEY
to Beaumaris
Rhianfa
Glan-y-garth
MENAI STRAITS
Ynys-y-dapig
Ynys-y-Bi
Mostyn
Ynys-gaint
Ynys-faelog
George Hotel
Garth Point
FERRY
to Beaumaris
Baths
Garth
Hirael
Gored-gith
UPPER BANGOR
College
Bishops Palace
Nanty-borth
Belle Vue Hotel
St James Ch.
Cathedral
Castle Hotel
BANGOR
Recreation Ground
Station Road
TUNNEL
Tyddyn Llwydyn

BANGOR SECTION.

Bangor.

---◆---

Hotels : in Lower Bangor : *British*, near the station ; *Castle* (B.Q.), near the Cathedral, ½ m. from station ; in Upper Bangor : *George*, 1¼ m. from the station, overlooking the Straits and near the Suspension Bridge ; *Belle Vue*, ½ m. from the station on the way to Menai Bridge ; *Railway, Station, William's Temperance*, close to the station ; *Albion* (Q.), High-street.

Post Office : High-street. *Chief deliveries abt. 7 a.m.,* 4.30 p.m. ; *despatch·s,* 8.30, 10.20 a.m. 8.15 p.m. *Open on Sundays, 7—10 a.m.*

Population : abt. 8,000.

Distances : (*By rail*). Aber, 5½ m ; Llanfairfechan, 7¼ m ; Penmaenmawr 10 m ; Conway, 14¼ m ; (Llandudno, 18 m ; Llanrwst, 26½ m ;) Rhyl, 30 m ; Chester, 60 m. Bethesda 5½ m. Menai Bridge, 1½ m ; (Carnarvon, 8¼ m ; Llanberis, 17¼ m.) ; Holyhead, 24¼ m. (*By road*), Beaumaris, 6¼ m. Bethesda, 5½ m ; Capel Curig, 15 m ; Bettws-y-Coed, 20¼ m. (*By water*), Beaumaris, 4 m.

Steamers : During the summer season there is double service each way of boats each weekday between Menai Bridge, Bangor, and Beaumaris, and Llandudno and Liverpool. A small steamer plies at frequent intervals between Bangor (Garth) and Beaumaris.

Omnibuses, &c., meet the principal trains.

Bangor, one of the **chief pleasure-centres of North Wales is,** on first acquaintance, a little perplexing to the stranger who, on arriving by rail, finds himself almost out of sight of the city, halfway between it and its modern and favourite tourist suburb, the " Upper Town." If, instead of patronising one of the several omnibuses or vehicles that compete for his custom at the station, he determines to explore a bit before deciding on his inn, or other resting-place, he may find the accompanying sketch-plan (enlarged from the 1-inch ordnance map in the absence of any more recent survey) and a few words of comment upon it useful. The station, it will be noted, is at the south end of a devious street that wriggles in a north-east direction, past the Cathedral, down a somewhat cramped valley to the Harbour—*Port Penrhyn.* This street constitutes the main part of **Lower Bangor,** and leads past the once favourite Penrhyn Arms Hotel (now closed) to the entrance to Penrhyn Park. The *George Hotel,** an excellent

---

*Sometimes called the Bangor Ferry Hotel, **from the old ferry, now** superseded by the Suspension Bridge.

house with a well-earned reputation, is in the opposite direction from the Station, nearly due west from it, over the ridge, and distant 1¼ m. by the winding road shown in the plan. The grounds command a delightful view of the Straits, the Menai Bridge, and the well-wooded opposite shore of Anglesey. The situation of other hotels will be sufficiently indicated by the plan. Chief of them are the British and the Castle.

Along the ridge, from the George Hotel towards Garth Point, is the modern suburb of **Upper Bangor**, and here is a plentiful supply of lodgings that, for situation and outlook, leave nothing to be desired, and at *Garth*, whence the ferry (*fare 2d., return free*), plies across the Straits, there is also a considerable choice of lodgings of various qualities and prices.

As a seaside resort, the weak point about Bangor is the bathing, which, at high water, is not much to boast of, and at other states of the tide, is, from the shore, impossible. Its strong points are the delightful marine and mountain views and the easy access it affords to the very heart of the Snowdon range.

The **Cathedral** (*Services: Sundays*, 8 *and* 11.30 *a.m.*, 4 *p.m.*; *week-days* 8 *a.m.*, 3 *p.m.*, *except June-Sept.* (*choral*) 5 *p.m.* *Open daily from* 9 *a.m. to* 4 *p.m.*) was originally founded by Deiniol Wyn, son of Dinothus, the reputed founder of the great monastery at Bangor Iscoed,* in Flintshire. This Daniel, who was its first bishop, died in 584, and was buried at Bardsey Isle. Of his church, it need hardly be said, not a trace remains and, not to mention minor disasters, two succeeding cathedrals were destroyed—one by the English in 1071, and another by Owen Glyndwr in 1402. In 1496 the choir was rebuilt, and in 1532 the nave and western tower was completed. From that date down to 1869 no material alteration was made, though at the hands of repairers a good deal of disfigurement took place. At the last named date Sir Gilbert Scott's restoration began and the building, like that of St. Asaph, is now probably a handsomer church than at any former period. In the process of removing unsound portions of the Perpendicular structure, abundant remains of the one wrecked by Glyndwr were discovered built up in the walls. Guided by these fragments and incorporating them with new work, the architect has bequeathed to us a church of much beauty which only needs tone to be interesting. The nave-arcades of six bays, the clerestory and N. aisle windows are Perpendicular; the windows of the South aisle are Decorated. The north and south transepts and choir have Early Decorated windows, except the east window, which is Perpendicular. Not the least pleasing feature of the exterior is the north transept. The central tower which, so far, has only been carried just above the roof is alone wanting to

---

* *Bangor-ys-ycoed*, i.e. Bangor-under-the-wood. The name *Bangor*=High Choir, and the epithet in both cases denotes dignity rather than elevation or conspicuousness, *cf.* High Mass.

complete the restoration. Unfortunately the low site òn which
the church is built must always detract from its effectiveness.
Close by is the unpretending Palace of the bishop.

Between the Cathedral and the station is the Free **Museum** and
News Room. In the former is a collection of curiosities from
China and the Eastern Seas, and also several relics of the French
Revolution and Reign of Terror.

The Recreation Grounds. These occupy the steep side of
the hill south of the main street. The principal entrance is at the
top of Dean Street, on the left, nearly half-a-mile from the
Cathedral towards the Harbour, but a pleasant stroll of an hour or
so may be enjoyed by taking a foot-path which turns up the hill
sharp to the right on the road from the station to the Cathedral.
This crosses the station end of the tunnel, and $\frac{1}{4}$ mile further joins
the Pentir road. Take the first turn to the left out of this, and
turn left again in the direction of the town $\frac{1}{3}$ mile further. Where
the road thus entered bends sharply down to the town, a turn to the
right will take you to the highest part of *the Recreation Grounds.*
The mountain prospect eastward is, according to the local custom,
shut out by a high and foolish wall, and we have to be content
with a bird's eye view of Bangor, a mass of slate. The ramble
we have described is a very pleasant one, and affords a view of
the mountains about Llanberis and Nant Ffrancon.

From the Recreation Ground stile it is also a pleasant half-mile
ramble southwards as directly as you can go to *Felin Esgob,* "the
Bishop's Mill," on the Cegid stream, and thence either up again
to the first turn to the right, and so into a by-road which leads
direct to the old Penrhyn Arms, or eastwards by an obvious path
across the stream and two mineral lines to the model village of
Llandegai (p. 82).

Penrhyn Park and Castle, the seat of Lord Penrhyn, is to
the east of the city, and on the east of the main road to Bethesda.
(*Admission to the castle on Tuesdays and Thursdays by tickets obtainable at the Hotels, and at Bethesda. 2s. for one person, and 1s. extra
for each additional member of the party. Half the proceeds goes to the
Carnarvon and Anglesey Infirmary.*) There are three entrances to
the Park, viz., at *Port Penrhyn, Llandegai,* and *Tal-y-Bont,* and its
circuit, which is guarded by a huge wall that effectually hinders
all view of it from the road, is about 7 miles in length. It occupies the sea-ward end of the ridge that divides the valley of the
Cegid stream from that of the Ogwen, and extends eastward across
the latter. The views obtainable from the hill on which the Castle
stands are charming, and include the entrance of the Straits, the
mountains, and the coast as far as the Great Orme. The Castle
is a modern erection of severe Norman style, and as a whole is
heavy, but impressive from its size. At the north end is the keep
of 5 stories, which is really fine and after the pattern of Rochester,
but even this, with its plate-glass windows and roller blinds, is a

rather incongruous combination of the antique and **the modern.**
Within the castle the demerits of Norman architecture when
adopted for a 19th century mansion are everywhere obvious, but
there is a rich abundance of costly workmanship in the fittings
and furniture.   In the hall the stained glass by Willement is
excellent.   Among other curiosities to be noticed are a bedstead
wrought in slate, and the *Hirlas Horn*, an Elizabethan relic, well
known from the martial song, " Fill high the blue hirlas that shines
like the wave," by Mrs. Hemans.   A visit will of course be paid
to the *stables*, where the fittings are also of slate, the omnipresent
material of these parts.

Close to the principal entrance to the park is the model village
of **Llandegai** where the *Church* (restored) in its pretty surroundings should be visited.   It contains, besides a monument to
Abp. Williams, a handsome alabaster tomb of uncertain date
brought from Llanfaes Priory (*p.* 92), and a Penrhyn monument
by Westmacott.   From Llandegai it is about a mile and a
half (somewhat less by the field-walk and *Felin Esgob*),
to the heart of the city.   From Llandegai the walk may
also be pleasantly extended to *Llanllechid* (2 *m.* away) on the
slope of Moel Wnion, and commanding a fine view of the Nant
Ffrancon mountains.   Hence it is a charming stroll, chiefly by
the little Afon-y-Llan streamlet, into the main road, which is
entered just where it crosses the Ogwen, 3 *m.* from Bangor.

The Menai Straits and Anglesey.

The first part of the following descriptions treats of the charming scenery on both sides of the Menai Straits. The north side of this beautiful water-way, Redwharf Bay and Holyhead Island, are the only parts of Anglesey attractive to the general tourist. Its inland scenery is monotonous to a degree, the long undulations of its hills—if hills they may be called—being equally undistinguished by grace of outline or richness of vegetation. Lovers of coast scenery may find their account in trudging from Amlwch to Holyhead, a distance of about 30 miles, but we confess that we have not been tempted to make the excursion ourselves.

The island has, indeed, one recommendation that to the archæologist atones for its general dulness—the abundance of its antiquities; but these hardly fall within the lines of a guide-book intended for general use, and we have, therefore, only mentioned the few that come in the way of the routes which seem to us to call for description.

Menai Bridges, Anglesey Column, &c. *Bangor to Llanfair (rail)*, 4 m; *Llanfair to Bangor by Menai Bridge and Garth (road)* 6-7 m.

These lions of Wales are all within an easy stroll of the hotels at Bangor and Menai Bridge. The difficulty in describing such a stroll is to decide where to begin and where to end it. Nothing can well be more picturesque than the scenery on both sides of the Menai Straits, but we can only pretend to give such a general description of it as will prevent visitors from missing any of its salient points. These are the Straits, the Bridges, and the panoramic views of Snowdonia from the higher ground on the Anglesey side of them. These views may, of course, be obtained from the Carnarvonshire side, but in that case we miss the exquisite foreground afforded by the long-drawn wood-fringed windings of the Straits themselves. All the vantage ground is within a narrow area, but inside that area we may wander as we will.

For the information of those who wish simply to inspect the bridges we may state that the Menai Bridge Station is within 300 yards of the Suspension Bridge; Treborth Station, on the Carnarvon branch, is about the same distance from the "Tubular." A man is stationed at each end of the latter, but visitors are not admitted without a pass, which may be obtained from the

engineer of the line at Bangor Station. The shortest route, from bridge to
bridge, is along the drive through the grounds of Treborth, but these are now
closed to the public, and the only way is to cross the line by the Carnarvon
road a few yards on the Bangor side of Menai Bridge Station, and to take the
by-road to Treborth a mile further, making the entire distance about 2 miles.
To ordinary tourists, however, we recommend the following route.

From *Bangor* take train to Llanfair, 4 miles distant and the
first station in Anglesey, and thence walk, ascending the Column,
visiting Llanfair and Llandisilio churches, crossing the Suspension
Bridge and returning by the road above the Straits from Upper Bangor
to Garth. From the *George Hotel*, on the Carnarvonshire side of the
Straits, the train may be taken at Menai Bridge Station, half-a-
mile distant; while from *Menai Bridge Village* on the Anglesey
side, the Column is reached in a walk or drive of nearly two miles.
Beyond the Column there is no scenery whatever, and the views
of Snowdonia become less interesting as you recede from it.

The route from Bangor by rail to Llanfair is described on page
94. From Llanfair (*two inns*), retracing our course by the
Holyhead road, which runs side by side with the railway, for half-
a-mile, we are at the foot of the **Anglesey Column.** It stands
on a rocky knoll, 250ft. above the sea, a little to the left of the
road, and is approached by a short gravel-walk through a shrub-
bery. Threepence is charged for admission. There is an unob-
structed view from the base, but from the top, 90ft. higher, and
reached by 115 steps, the panorama is considerably extended.
Immediately below, the southern part of Anglesey is spread out,
with the Holyhead Mountain just peering over a low intervening
ridge, in the north-west. Beaumaris is hidden by somewhat
higher ground, but the two "Ormes" with Llandudno between
them are well seen. Then to the right the great Carnarvonshire range commences with Penmaenbach and Penmaenmawr,
continued by the higher ridge of Tal-y-fan. In the foreground in
this direction the port and shipping of Bangor give animation to
the scene, and farther away, to the right of Tal-y-fan, the round-
backed Moel Wnion, between Aber and Bethesda, brings the
mountain range much nearer. Still more to the right Carnedds
Llewelyn and Dafydd make apparently a dead-heat of it for
supremacy in this direction. Then comes the entrance of
Nant Ffrancon with Bronllwyd (over the Penrhyn slate quarries),
and the mass of Elidyr-fawr between it and the Pass of Llanberis.
West of this the Crib-goch spur of Snowdon protrudes, and then
comes the topmost peak itself, succeeded by a long and less interesting succession of heights till the three peaks of the Rivals (the
Skiddaw of Wales) drop steeply to Carnarvon Bay, and dwindle
away westward into the lesser hills of the Lleyn promontory.
The foreground in this direction is, perhaps, the gem of the scene,
the serpentine course of the Straits, between the wooded demesnes
of Plas-Newydd on the right and Vaenol Park on the left, being
of ideal beauty. The whole of the "Tubular," and the greater
part of the Suspension Bridge are included in the prospect.

The Column is a memorial of the Marquis of Anglesey who was distinguished in the Peninsula War, and second in command at Waterloo. It was erected in 1816. On the top is a bronze statue of the Marquis by Noble. This was added in 1860.

Returning to the road we may turn down to the right in a few minutes and, passing under the line, reach *Llanfair Church* (modern), occupying a secluded position, a field's space away from the Straits, on the banks of which, hard by, is the *Nelson statue* on a low pedestal. There is no way beyond the church, but returning under the railway we may take a foot-path to the right, and descend to the shore under the north end of the " Tubular." This path leads only to the Tubular Bridge and the shore below it. As before mentioned a man is stationed at the bridge, and with a pass we may inspect it.

The **Britannia Tubular Bridge** was commenced in 1846, and completed in 1850. It is a third-of-a-mile long, and its roadway is 100 ft. above high-water mark. The central support is the Britannia Tower, 230 ft. high, said to be so named from the fact that its foundation is a rock on which a ship called the Britannia was wrecked. There are two other towers. The depth of the tubes is from 30 feet at the centre to 23 feet at the abutments, and the towers rise to a considerable height above the tubes. It is needless to say that strength and stability were the two things aimed at in designing the bridge ; at the same time, we must, in fairness add that, owing to the great extent of open space, due to the vast spans and the great headway, the impression of heaviness which bulk and rectangular outline might otherwise create, is very much mitigated, while as a monument of engineering resource and skill the structure will always command admiration. The great strength of the bridge arises from the rectangular form of the tubes, which are built up of wrought iron plates, and have the top and bottom composed of rectangular cells so arranged as to meet the strain caused by changes of temperature. Stephenson originally designed a two-arch iron bridge, but this was found incompatible with the free navigation of the straits.

Returning to the high-road we have a very pleasant walk along it to Menai Bridge, 1½ miles distant. Immediately below, on the right, are the Straits with the island of *Gored-goch*, the house on which looks at spring-tides as if it were flooded, and nearer the Suspension Bridge, the old church of Llandisilio, connected with the main part of the island by a causeway. Behind the latter the tower of the new church rises above a fir-covered promontory and, if we watch the mountain outline as we proceed, we shall see the two little humps of the Tryfan at the far end of Nant Ffrancon, to the right of Carnedd Dafydd. The mansion on the opposite side of the water is Treborth, and during our walk we shall see Plas-newydd set between the piers of the Tubular Bridge.

Half-a-mile short of the Suspension Bridge the road turns sharp to the right, two other roads joining it. That on the left is from Llangefni (*Bull's Head*, H.Q.), a place of importance, in consequence of its fairs. The one straight on drops to the Beaumaris road. Our course, however, is along the main road for 200 yards further till we pass through a gate on the right into a lane which leads through the fir-plantation, and across the causeway to Llandisilio Church. This is, perhaps, the most suggestive memorial in the neighbourhood of its condition when railways. colossal bridges, and tourist hotels were undreamt of. About fifteen yards long, and half as many wide, utterly destitute of architectural ornamentation, with three windows and a tottering bell-turret, this little place of worship is by no means the weakest contribution to a scene of remarkable picturesqueness, and the many families who from sentiment or other cause have selected the surrounding graveyard for their last resting-place, would, we think, have been more true to the *genius loci* if they had adopted a simpler and less ostentatious design in their monuments. Morning and evening services are held in the church.

You may return to the high-road or work your way round the promontory into a lane, one branch of which goes under the Suspension Bridge and past the pier of the Liverpool steamers, the other into the high-road again (*see map*). The **Village** of **Menai Bridge** is on the Anglesey side of the Straits, and contains several hotels and inns, the chief of which are the *Victoria* (H.Q.) and the *Bulkeley Arms*, both on the Beaumaris-road. In itself, however, it has little to attract. Speaking of hotels, we may observe that additions, regardless of the cardinal laws of proportion, have greatly spoilt the attractive appearance which that excellent one, the *George*, on the Bangor side of the Straits, once presented. Many charming bits of British landscape—the Menai Straits amongst them—are on too small a scale to be unscathed by the architectural incongruities which, on the pretext of keeping abreast of modern requirements, are perpetrated in their midst.

For the route from Menai Bridge to Beaumaris see p. 89.

The **Menai Suspension Bridge** (*toll* 1*d.*), was part of Telford's work in constructing his Chester and Holyhead Road. Its graceful lines and extreme lightness make it a pleasant feature in all views that include it. The suspended part is 580 feet long, and the headway for ships below is 100 ft. The piers from which the chains, 16 in number, are hung, are each of them 53ft. in height above the roadway. A guide may be had from the cottage, at the Anglesey end, to the place where the chains are fastened in the solid rock.

Looking westward from the bridge, we see a little short of the "Tubular," on the Anglesey side, the mansion of Pant Rhydderch. In this direction the view does not extend beyond the "Tubular," but eastward it reaches the Great Orme.

On reaching the Lodge at the other side of the bridge, the right-hand road is the nearest way to *Menai Bridge Station*, a little beyond which it becomes private at the entrance to *Treborth*

(R. Davies, Esq., M.P., Lord Lieutenant for Anglesey). For Bangor we turn left, and pass another approach to the station close to the *Antelope Inn*. Our road then continues on high ground between the railway and the Straits, affording across the latter an excellent view of the sloping wooded shore all the way to Beaumaris. The modern mansions of *Rhianfa* and *Glyn-y-garth* are conspicuous a little above the water's edge, and almost close to one another. Behind them, on the hill-top, the stump of an old windmill suggests a most tempting view-point.

When the main road bends to the right for Bangor station and city, it is best to keep on along the equally good road which gradually winds down to Garth. *Upper Bangor*, as the high ground between this road and the city is called, is a delightful suburb, rapidly growing as a residential locality. Here and there seats are placed by the road-side, and from one of these you can see Llandudno and Beaumaris at the same time, with the great Orme filling up the space between them. At *Garth* (inn) you pass the *Anglesey Ferry*, whence, bending sharp to the right along a level road, you reach the Cathedral in rather less than a mile, and the station in 1½ miles.

Plas-Newydd. This mansion, which occupies so fine and conspicuous a position on the north side of the Menai Straits, is the seat of the Marquis of Anglesey. Visitors are allowed to walk through the grounds (tickets of Mr. Jones, the agent, Anglesey Estate Offices, Graig, LlanfairP.G.) when the family is from home. They may be reached by boat from Bangor, or by taking the first turn to the left out of the Holyhead road, after passing the Anglesey column, 4 miles from Bangor. From Llanfair this by-road is joined in a few hundred yards by crossing the line a little on the Bangor side of the station. From the junction of these two roads the entrance to the park is reached in 300 yards, just where the wood begins. Hence to the mansion the distance is a mile; first through wood and then across an open greensward—a charming walk. The house is surrounded by woods on every side except towards the Straits. George IV. halted here on his way to Ireland. The Queen, then Princess Victoria, was a visitor during the summer of 1832. Behind the house are two *Cromlechs*, one of which has an enormous cap-stone 10 to 12 feet square and more than 3 feet thick. The second and smaller one is hard by, "eleven inches" distant, to quote the precise language of an old writer.

From the Cromlechs we may continue southwards, and in a long ½ mile pass to the right of a *tumulus*, behind which is *Kistvaen*, or stone-lined grave. It is in the shape of a quadrant, and the cap-stone is 7 ft. square. Thence entering the public road in half-a-mile we may turn to the left, and, passing Llanedwen Church, reach in another mile, **Moel Don Ferry**, opposite *Port Dinorwic (p. 22)*.

Bangor to Carnarvon by boat, *about* 10 *n. man and boat*, **12s. 6d.** This pleasant excursion can only be undertaken when the tide serves, the currents being very strong. There is not much to describe upon it, as we have already drawn attention to the chief places visible on the route. As we quit the landing-place at **Garth Ferry** (1 *m. from centre of town*) we look back

upon Beaumaris, the two Ormes, and Penmaenmawr. Directly
opposite are the mansions of *Glyn-y-garth* and *Rhianfa*. Then
come the *George Hotel* on the left and the *Village* of *Menai
Bridge* on the right. Passing under the Suspension Bridge we
have the grounds of *Treborth* on the left, *Llandisilio Church* (p.
86) on the right, and in front, just short of the "Tubular," *Pant
Rhydderch*. Then comes the big bridge itself, and beyond it, on
the right, *Llanfair Church*, *Plas Llanfair* and the *Nelson statue*;
on the left *Vaenol Park*, opposite to which is *Plas Newydd* (*p.* 87).
Port Dinorwic, to which the slates come from Llanberis, succeeds
on the left; then the shores grow tamer and less wooded, the 3
peaked Rivals are seen far ahead, a peep of Snowdonia reveals
itself, and we reach Carnarvon.

Bangor to Menai Bridge, 2 *m*; *and Beaumaris,* 6½ *m. (by
road). Distances reckoned from the station; from the centre of the
town add ½ m.*

Omnibuses in connection with most trains. Fare 1s. 6d.

** The shortest way to Beaumaris is by **Garth** Ferry, which, on the
Bangor side is nearly 1½ miles from the Station (1 *m. from centre of town*). On
the Anglesey side the landing-place is about 2 miles short of Beaumaris, the
distance across being ¾ mile (*fare 2d., return free*). *Total distance,* 4 *m.* There
is also a small steamer from Garth to Beaumaris direct several times a day.
Fare, 6d.

This route, as far as Menai Bridge village, is over the same
ground as the one described the reverse way on page 87 in the
return from the Anglesey Column, except that we do not make the
détour by Garth.

Ascending from the town by the Holyhead-road, past the station,
we soon gain the high ground of **Upper Bangor,** a rapidly
growing suburb with villas, lodging-houses, and shops. The view
begins at once. Looking to the right the mountains are seen from
Penmaenmawr to Carnedd Dafydd, and then, as we breast the
ridge, the Straits appear in front with the Suspension Bridge in
one direction and Llandudno and the Great Orme in the other.
The Anglesey coast is seen from the Bridge to Beaumaris, charmingly wooded throughout and rising to an almost uniform height of
from 200 to 300 feet. An old windmill is a conspicuous object
about the centre of this ridge and, beneath it, close to the water's
edge, are the modern mansions of *Rhianfa* and *Glyn-y-garth.*
Beyond the latter is the Anglesey end of the Garth ferry. A
little further on our way we may note the railway emerging from
a tunnel on the left, and a few yards further a road goes off on the
right to the beautifully situated *George Hotel*. Just short of the
Suspension Bridge one of the Carnarvon roads diverges on the
left, passing close to the Menai Bridge station. We turn sharp to
the right on to the Bridge (*toll* 1d.), which is crossed by two
carriage-ways and a foot-path. *For a description of it, see p.* 86.

The view in crossing is very pleasing in both directions, though it cannot be said that the village of Menai Bridge enhances its charm. Westward we look over the islet of *Gored-goch*, with a cottage upon it that, at flood-tide, might be mistaken for an ark floating on the water, to the north-end of the "Britannia Tubular," a little short of which, on the north side of the water, is the mansion of *Pant Rhydderch*. The Anglesey column is also conspicuous. Eastward are several islets and the pier at which the Liverpool steamers land their passengers.

On the Anglesey side of the bridge you may, if so disposed, be conducted to the spot at which the chains are imbedded in the solid rock.

A few yards past the bridge the Beaumaris road diverges to the right, and descends through *Menai Bridge Village* (hotels, *Victoria, Bulkeley Arms*) to the level of the water, by or near the side of which it continues all the way to Beaumaris. For the most part it is well shaded, and on the way it passes close to the mansions we have already drawn attention to as seen from Upper Bangor. Beyond them the Ferry route strikes in (there is a small inn by the water-side), and a little further are the handsome gates of a new drive to *Baron Hill* (Sir Richard W. Bulkeley, Bart.) A short two miles more, and we are at *Beaumaris*.

A variation on this walk may be obtained at the cost of half-an-hour's extra walking, with fine views of Snowdonia as compensation, by turning up the hill to the left just after crossing a cwm about a mile beyond Menai Bridge Village. This route goes through the village of *Llandegfan*, and rejoins the main road a few yards short of Beaumaris. Beyond Llandegfan, however, it offers no special attraction.

Beaumaris.

Hotels: *Bulkeley Arms, Liverpool Arms,* Q., both in the main street.

Post : *Chief arr. abt. 7.0 a.m., 5.30 p.m.; dep. 7.50 a.m., 7.20 p.m.*

Population : 2,241.

Distances: Bangor (*road*), 6½ *m.*; (*water*), 4 *m.*; (*ferry*), 4 *m.*

Modes of access: '*Buses* in connection with principal trains at Bangor Station, *via* Menai Bridge. *Steamer* from Garth Point, fare 6d. *Ferry* from Garth Point, whence road 2 *m.*

The Liverpool and Llandudno steamers call once or twice a day each way during the season.

Beaumaris, though yearly increasing in favour as a summer resort, is, in itself, only a quiet little town of three streets with a regularly built and somewhat ambitious row of white lodging-houses, &c., overlooking the green, and facing the sea. Its advantages are its south-east aspect, the charming view up the coast and across the bay to the mountain girdle from Penmaenmawr to Snowdon, the pretty strolls to objects of interest near at hand, and not least its comparative freedom from the hurry-scurry of the full tide of tourist traffic. The bathing is fair, and for boating it is better off than Bangor, because the deep water channel here hugs the Anglesey shore. For those who only pay it a flying visit there are two objects calling for description,—the *castle* and the *church*.

Beaumaris Castle (*admission 2d.*), like the town, was the creation of Edward I. Its position on low marshy land, but with a lovely prospect all around, accounts for its name. The architect was Henry de Elreton, the same who built Conway and Carnarvon, but those graceful many-turreted exteriors, set off by all the advantages of situation, here find no counterpart. And yet, as a ruin to be explored, Beaumaris will, by many, be deemed of greater interest even than Conway, and far more so than the comparatively empty shell of Carnarvon.

At the end of *Castle Street* we enter between two low towers, and are at once on the site of the filled-up moat that is now girdled with trees. Before proceeding to examine the inside of the castle we should first get a glimpse of its exterior defences, and so taking the walk on the right we pass through an archway* in the *Gunner's wall* a supplementary defence of the main approach;

---

* This is now reported to be closed.

We then get a view of the east side of the structure, which is square and has large drum towers at each angle with three smaller ones intervening. Here, too, the mound on the off-side indicates the limits of the moat, and one of the springs that supplied it with water still runs and makes the ground boggy so as to prevent our walking round in this direction.

Returning through the archway, we enter the works by the gate on the south side close by, and at once have an impressive view of the massive towers and curtain-wall, now richly ivied. Before penetrating to the central quadrangle the visitor should walk round between the two lines of defence. Here the turf is kept short by a numerous colony of grey rabbits, pets of Lady Bulkeley, that are on no account to be molested. On the north-side we pass the *main entrance* (now closed) to the inner quadrangle flanked by two towers, which even among the many massive ones all around are conspicuous by their huge bulk. In the course of this peregrination we may, if so minded, ascend to the top of the outer wall at various points. On completing the circuit, we pass beneath a pointed arch into a vaulted passage, now crossed by 5 arches and showing the grooves of two portcullises, into the *central court*, which, as an ideal interior, quite compensates for the lack of outside attractiveness. In front of us are the five large windows that lighted the **Great Hall**, perfectly framed in the glorious ivy that almost completely drapes the whole of the court. The domestic and other buildings are in excellent preservation for a ruin, and endless passages and small chambers will interest the curious in such matters. Thanks to the rabbits, the whole area is a well kept lawn. One item on the east side of the quadrangle every visitor should inspect, viz., the **Chapel**. To reach it, turn up to the left of the now dilapidated racquet-court, and when on the first-floor level turn along to the left. It is Early English in style, and measures about 27 feet by 22, with an apsidal termination eastward. The roof is groined, and round the walls is an Early Decorated arcade. The chapel is lit by five lancets, and at the west end are 4 squints presumably to afford a view of the altar to the retainers, who, from its small size, could not have found room in the chapel itself. On either side of the west end is a small chamber, each with a stone seat, and similar to those adjoining the oratory in Conway Castle.

The *history* of the castle, excluding the "massacre of the bards" by Edward I., which is not history, is marked by no event of importance except that it was held by the Bulkeley of that day for Charles I., and had to yield to General Mytton.

The **Church**, which is a trifle north of the main street, is late thirteenth century, with a sixteenth century chancel. It is sadly in need of judicious restoration, and except to the professed archæologist not particularly interesting. In the middle of the chancel, facing the altar, is a memorial by Ternouth to Charlotte Mary Lady Bulkeley (*d.* 1829), which good in itself is painfully prominent. Another monument worth notice is that to the last

Lord Bulkeley (d. 1822), by Westmacott, "Hope encouraging the widow." It stands to the left of the altar, on the S. side of which a stone commemorates the father of Sir Philip Sidney (d. 1363). Note also the old chancel stalls and two recumbent marble figures in the vestry. The churchyard contains a good many old grave slabs and a forest of nettles. To the south of the chancel is a curious arched tomb.

Baron Hill, the seat of the Bulkeleys, is close by, on the hillside above the castle. Till 1881 visitors were allowed to visit the grounds, but this privilege, which was much esteemed, was then withdrawn owing to the repeated vandalism and rudeness of excursionists. It is now restored, on Th. and Sun. 1—dusk.

Penmon Priory.

This is a favourite drive or walk from Beaumaris. The distance by road is about 4½ miles, but nearly a mile may be saved by keeping to the coast when the road makes an angle inland. By water this excursion may include a visit to Puffin Island, which is about five miles from Beaumaris.

We leave the town by the road past the castle, and where this, a good half-mile onwards, forks close to Friars, a modern house that takes its name from the destroyed Llanfaes Priory*, we take the right-hand branch, which, in a few hundred yards, turns inland. Pedestrians can, however, follow the coast, and rejoin the road in a trifle over a mile, and those who so do will pass close to Tre'r-castell, a farmhouse on the site of an old fourteenth century mansion of the Tudors, whose cellars supplied Queen Elizabeth with her favourite mead. If the road be kept, then at cross-roads, ¾ m. from the turn inland, we bear to the right and soon pass a little to the right of Castell Lleiniog, a square shell on a thickly wooded mound, which is attributed to Hugh Lupus. It is hardly of sufficient interest to tempt the tourist to delay his journey by turning aside to it. The shore is now quickly regained, and the road, after passing the famous Penmon quarries, turns a trifle inland to the Priory. This was founded in the sixth century (i.e., supposing it, and not the one on Puffin Island, to have been the parent house), and Seiriol, who gave his name to Ynys Seiriol (now known as Friestholm or Puffin Island), was its first ruler. The Church (key at the Clerk's, near the Lighthouse) is cruciform and chiefly Norman, except the chancel which is not older than 1400. To about this period must also be attributed the doorway on the south side of the nave, which has a quaint animal in a chain-stitch pattern enclosure above. As is common in monastic churches, the chancel is larger than the nave, but the comparatively small size of the whole building, total length 87 ft., points to the fact that the house never rose to any great importance. To the south of the church, and once con-

---

* Joan, wife of Llewelyn, and daughter of King John of England, was buried here.

nected with it by the prior's lodgings, which occupied the site of the present seventeenth century building, is the thirteenth century *Refectory*, under which was the hall, whose south doorway has for its lintel an old gravestone. The Refectory S.E. window lintel is still older, and is formed of an ancient British cross, whose base now forms the Font. Above the refectory is a large dormitory.

East of the refectory is a large *dovecote-tower*, with a curious stone roof, and in the deer-park on the hill above is an interesting *cross*, about 6½ feet high, on the east face of which formerly decipherable, but now quite weathered away, was the " mocking of our Lord."

About half-a-mile north of the Priory over the hill is the **Lighthouse**, connected with the shore by an iron bridge.

Puffin Island (*Priestholm* or *Ynys Seiriol*) so conspicuous an object in almost all Snowdonian coast-views, is separated from the east point of Anglesey by a channel about half-a-mile wide. There is not much to see except the ruins of the *church-tower*, which is by some antiquaries held to be of the seventh century. The island is still frequented by puffins in considerable numbers during the breeding season, and rabbits abound.

Red Wharf Bay. *By carriage-route through Pentraeth*, 8 m. *Direct pedestrian route*, 7 m.

The excursion to *Red Wharf Bay*, a wide and picturesque inlet, is a favourite one from Beaumaris, though the routes to it above indicated are thoroughly commonplace—fair samples of inland Anglesey scenery. The pedestrian should take the direct route, which turns to the right beyond Baron Hill, 1 mile out of Beaumaris, and, passing the *Bulkeley Monument* on *Tower Hill*, continues almost straight for another 1½ miles. Then, after crossing a streamlet the road forks, and those who wish simply to see Red Wharf Bay may, with advantage, take the right-hand branch, which in 1½ miles reaches the little village of *Llanddona*, overlooking the Bay from its eastern extremity. At low tide the whole inlet is a waste of sand and little pools. Northwards, beyond it, the coast is seen to the north-east extremity of the island. The tiny islet of *Moelfre*, where the "Royal Charter" was wrecked in Oct., 1859, with the loss of nearly 450 lives, appears about half way.

In returning from Llanddona the route may be varied in several ways, best suggested by the map. The best is by Llanfihangel, and *Bwrdd Arthur* (" Arthur's Table ")—the latter an old fortification, commanding a view which, if not, as Pennant described it, " savagely great," is at all events comprehensive and delightful, and goes far towards atoning for the dullness of the country you have to traverse in order to obtain it.

If, on the outward journey, instead of taking the turn to Llanddona at the fork of the road, you take the left branch, you will descend to the shore of the bay in 1½ miles, and proceeding round it for about 3 miles, almost to its western extremity will reach *Min-y-Don Hotel*, a comfortable but unpretentious hostelry, with accommodation for a considerable number of visitors. *Red Wharf Bay* calls for no special description of its scenery. Its girdle of low hills, its pleasant sands, its clear water, and its quietude, combine to give it an attractiveness which would be lost if it became a popular resort. Those, and those only, who like to enjoy themselves quietly will appreciate it. Besides the hotel on the bay, there are one or two small inns at Pentraeth, a good mile inland. (2 *m. walk from Min-y-don.*)

Bangor to Holyhead, 24 *m. by rail or road.*

Except for the views of which the Menai Straits are the chief feature, and the retrospect of Snowdonia after crossing them, there is little calling for description in a tourist's guide-book between Bangor and Holyhead. The railway is the more interesting route of the two, as it affords the occasional variety of a sea-view. Of the **Road Route** our personal experience suggests the opinion that no one who has tried it once will wish to repeat the experiment. Mile after mile of hard high-road with a stone wall of uniform height on each side, and never a square foot of grass to relieve the feet or to shake off the dust upon for more than half the distance—such are its peculiarities. The milestones cheer the wayfarer with the expectation of a Half-way House—Mona Inn —but the roofless shell is all that remains of this once important stage-house, and there is now no hostelry between the Holland Arms, 8 miles from Bangor, and the Valley Hotel, 4 miles short of Holyhead. The country consists of a succession of flats and slight undulations from the crests of which the Carnarvonshire heights, from the Rivals in the west to Penmaenmawr in the east, are well seen.

Railway Route.—Issuing from the tunnel at the west end of Bangor station, we get pretty peeps of the Straits and Suspension Bridge through the trees as we approach the *Menai Bridge Station* (1½ *m.*). Here the Carnarvon branch continues the upward gradient on the left, while the Holyhead line slightly falls again for the Tubular Bridge, on issuing from which, by looking in quick succession, first to the right and then to the left, you will obtain two very charming views of the Menai Straits. The Suspension Bridge, with Penmaenmawr to the left of it, is very effective in the former direction, and in the latter Llanfair Church, a statue of Nelson looking as if he were taking a " header " into the straits, and further away the demesne of Plas Newydd (the Marquis of Anglesey) are the chief features. Then comes the Anglesey Column, high up on the right and the station of **Llanfair** (*inns*). The full name of this parish is *Llanfairpwllgwyngyll* (" pooth gwingeeth ") or, more briefly, Llanfair P. G. The addition " trisiliologogoch " has no more foundation in fact than has the bill for the proposed railway to commence here and end at Pontrhydfendigaedmynachlogfawr.

The back view over the straits from about here is very fine, the whole range of the Carnarvonshire mountains being visible from Penmaenmawr in the east to the triple-peaked Rivals (Yr Eifl) in the west. The top of Snowdon comes out as a sharp peak just rising over the huge round shoulder of Crib-y-ddysgyl. The first dip to the left of it is the Pass of Llanberis, the second Nant Ffrancon, between which and Penmaenmawr Carnedds Dafydd and Llewelyn raise their slightly tapering and very similar peaks a little above the rest of the range, the next highest point being Y Foel Fras.

At the next station, *Gaerwen*, the Amlwch branch diverges on the right.

The distance from *Gaerwen* to **Amlwch** (Hotel, *Dinorben Arms*, H.Q.) is 18 m., but the chief resort of visitors is the *Bull Bay Hotel*, on the shore, 1¾ m. north-west of the town.*

The line now descends to and crosses *Malldraeth Marsh*, a wide and perfectly flat expanse of reedy pasture, on the far side of which we cross an embanked tidal river that opens on to *Malldraeth Sands*, half-a-mile to the south. The Mansion and grounds of *Bodorgan* (Sir George Meyrick) are on the west side of the Bay, about halfway between the railway and the open sea.

A short tunnel—the only one in Anglesey—pierces the low range of hills which extends all along the west side of Malldraeth Marsh, and then we reach **Bodorgan Station**. Here is a good inn (*Meyrick Arms*, H.Q.) frequented by anglers who come to fish *Llyn Coron*, a featureless sheet of water close at hand. Four miles from here on the other side of the Marsh is the Village of *Newborough*, which owes its name to the fact that it was once formed "into a corporate body, and had annexed to it the royalties of the Prince of Wales by Edward I." At *Aberffraw*, nearly 3 miles S.W. of Bodorgan, there was once a Palace of the Prince of Wales.

The next Station is *Ty-Croes* ("house of the cross"), and a little beyond it *Llyn Faelog*, somewhat similar to Llyn Coron, is passed on the left. Then we cross another waste of sand-hills and grass and reach *Valley Station (Inn)*, whence to Holyhead, it is 4 miles, road and rail going side by side, and crossing by an embankment on to Holyhead Island.

* Amlwch is a poor town with a long straggling and very untidy suburb extending to the high ground round its harbour. From its centre a tortuous road leads to the **Bull Bay Hotel** (1¾ m.), where visitors may enjoy quiet and healthy surroundings at 2 guineas a week. The coast is rocky, but there is a little bathing basin filled at high tide. West of the hotel the coast becomes bolder, and from a cairn a good mile in this direction there is a wide view including the sea, the Carnarvonshire mountains, and the Holyhead Mountain.

Holyhead.

———◆———

Hotels: *North Western*, at the station; *Marine* (H.Q.), on the road from the railway to the town pier.

Post Office (*centre of town*): *Del.*, abt. 7 a.m. and 1.45 p.m.; despatches, abt. 7.30 and 11.10 a.m., 7.30 and 10 p.m.

Holyhead is in itself the dullest and least interesting of towns. It has a most commodious station, with a first-class hotel attached to it for the accommodation of the Irish traffic, but the small account in which the town itself is held may be judged from the fact that, though the station is close to it, there is no communication between the two without going at least a quarter of a mile round by the bridge over the line a little way south of both.

The *Clock Tower* in front of the hotel, between the arrival and departure platforms, commemorates the completion of the new Harbour Works, and their opening by the Prince of Wales in 1873. A conspicuous *Obelisk* on an eminence east of the town is in memory of Captain Skinner, who was washed overboard off one of the Irish mail packets which he commanded in 1833.

Another memorial is an *arch* on the pier at the north end of the town in honour of a visit from George IV. in 1821.

The Welsh name of Holyhead is *Gaer Gybi*, and the church is dedicated to Saint Cybi, whose statue is under a canopy on the south porch. It is an old embattled building with incongruous additions, and chiefly remarkable for the curious scrolls and carving under the battlements. The churchyard is surrounded by a thick wall, which is said to be Roman, and gives it a very gloomy appearance.

As a tourist resort Holyhead's sole attraction is its " Mountain," and the coast scenery beyond, its special "lion " being, of course, the South Stack Lighthouse.

The distance to this lighthouse is a short four miles, and carriage-folk have no choice but to drive directly to it round the south side of the Mountain,—a route of no special interest till the lighthouse is reached. Pedestrians may vary their route in many ways, the Mountain itself being scored by tracks innumerable.

The particular spots to be visited are the South and North Stacks, the top of the Mountain, and the old Telegraph station between the last-named and the North Stack. There are no inns on any of the routes.

(1) The *shortest way* for the Mountain and South Stack is by the street which turns slightly left up the hill beyond the Royal Hotel, opposite to, but ¼-m. from the station. This ends at the British Schools close to a new church with a spire. Here turn to the left by the road that goes straight for the Mountain. As you go along this road you will see, besides the cairn on the top of the hill, a second one on a lower shoulder to the south of it. The best route to follow is about half-way between these cairns.

In less than a mile from the town you come to a shabby hamlet. Pass to the left through this; out of it to the right, and, where in a few yards the road goes left* again, leave it, and ascend through another shabby collection of houses, in which, as is not unusual in these parts, the pig seems to be the chief proprietor. Thence you may either take an obvious path to the top of the Mountain or, as above stated, follow the one half-way between the two cairns, and so on to the lighthouse, on the way to which a rough carriage-track is crossed two or three times. The lighthouse is not seen till you are close upon it.

(2) *A more interesting route, including all worth seeing.* Four hours is enough for this, but a day may well be devoted to it.

Continue along the level road leading by the side of the railway wall till you come to *Cross-street*, a little short of the Marine Hotel and the entrance to the pier. This street takes you on to the brink of the harbour, along which a good road goes to the breakwater. When the road forks, about half-a-mile from the town, keep to the right, winding past a large villa and another building which, with its grounds, forms a mimicry of a mediæval castle. Immediately beyond the latter is the **Break-water**, a most substantial monument of engineering skill. It is nearly 1½ miles long, and occupied 30 years in construction. From it a wide tramway leads to the quarries that supplied the material of which it is built.

Walk along the tramway to the quarries and then, ascending from the lowest working to a higher one, enter a track which rises to the rough ground strewn with heather, gorse and stones. Luckily there are numerous tracks, for without them the going would be as bad as possible. Keep the one nearest the cliff. This will bring you, in ten minutes or so, to the point opposite the **North Stack**, which is reached by passing a shed. Immediately above are the old **Telegraph Buildings** and enclosures (*about* 560 *ft. above the sea*), pleasant green patches in the surrounding sterility. These buildings fell into disuse when the electric telegraph was extended to the South Stack.

From hereabouts we get a good idea of the general character of the scenery. The cliffs, with the steep gorse-clad slopes rising from them and the sea dashing against their feet, are impressive, though they are only intermittently sheer and lack that boldness

---

* A good many hut-circles, &c., occur on this road, a short distance from this turn.

and variety of rock-form which marks the **granite buttresses of** the Land's End district. They are more like their opposite neighbours **at the end of** the Lleyn promontory. The South Stack **is** just **visible from the** Telegraph ruins, but, instead of making direct **for it, you may** reach the top of the mountain by obvious **tracks.** There is no direct route between the North and South Stacks, **as the highest part of** the cliff, **about 300 feet sheer, intervenes.**

The view from **Holyhead "Mountain"** (719 *ft.*) is, of course, **entirely dependent for** extent upon atmospheric conditions. **There is sea in almost every** direction and Anglesey, **more extensive than beautiful, is** mapped out below. Off its north-western extremity the *Skerries Lighthouse*, more than 100 feet high, appears. **The whole** Carnarvonshire range, from Penmaenmawr **to the** Rivals, Carn Madryn and the Lleyn promontory, is visible, the **peak of** Snowdon forming **its** centre-piece, and to the left of **Penmaenmawr are the** Great and Little Ormes Head on either side of Llandudno. The possibilities include the Wicklow mountains in Ireland, the Isle of Man, and **Black** Combe on the far side of Morecambe Bay.

The South Stack is not seen from the top of the mountain, but its **direction is shown by a couple of** reservoirs. Descend to the road **on the left hand of these, and a** few minutes' walking beyond them will bring you **to** the **top of** the 398 steps leading down to the little suspension bridge by which the abyss between the **mainland and** the **Stack is** spanned at a height **of about** 60 **feet.** **The descent** is tiring but simple, and **during it you may note the** extraordinary crumpled character **of the cliff behind.** White seams of quartz give it a rough resemblance to the dog-tooth ornamentation of Norman architecture.

The **South Stack** is occupied **by** the *Lighthouse*, **and the** white-washed buildings appertaining **thereto, the** whole suggesting **anything but** discomfort **or** danger, notwithstanding the exposed situation. The **Lighthouse** was erected in 1809 and is 212 feet above high-water. Visitors are shown **over it, and,** if the weather be clear, they **can see** across the **sea to Ireland and the Isle of** Man. The chain suspension bridge has taken **the place of** a rope-bridge, which was itself preceded **by** a mere **basket, like the one** which formerly existed at Noss, in Shetland. **From** February to August the rock is the resort of countless sea-**birds.**

In *returning to Holyhead* the best route is the one we have de-**scribed** as the shortest in coming. After ascending **the** steps—a **more fatiguing climb we** never experienced unless it **was** that of **the iron spire of Rouen** Cathedral—you **will see** in a few yards a foot-track striking across the moor up a slight hollow. This takes **you** a little to the right **of** the reservoirs, and then the two cairns— one on the top of the mountain and **the** other on a shoulder south **of** it come into view. **The** path, or rather paths—for they are legion,—cross several times a carriage-track, and then leave it **to** ascend between the **cairns.** Beyond **them** you pass the two **shabby groups of houses** already described, and at the latter join the main road, which enters Holyhead close to a new church with a spire.

Bangor to Bethesda, 5½ m (5 *by rail*); Capel Curig, 15 m; and Bettws-y-Coed, 20½ m.

The milestones reckon from a point nearly a mile east of Bangor Station and half-a-mile from the centre of the town.

Train or **coach** to **Bethesda**, thence **coach.**

(1) **By road to Bethesda.**—This is a section of the Great Holyhead road. Starting from the station, it goes the whole length of the town, past the British and Castle Hotels and the Cathedral, and then turns southwards at a sharp angle near the north-west entrance to Penrhyn Park. For the next mile we have on the left a characteristically high wall that affords through the only gap in it a fine setting of Penrhyn Castle, with Penmaen-mawr in the background. Except a pretty retrospect across the Straits, there is nothing else noteworthy until the wall ends at the massive gateway which forms the main entrance to the Park. Here, too, the Conway road strikes off on the left, and the railway to the same place emerges from a tunnel. Hard by is the model village of **Llandegai** (*p.* 82). Then, as we proceed, a fine view opens up to the left and in the rear, including the sea, Anglesey, Puffin Island, the Great Orme, and Penmaenmawr. Penrhyn Castle rises very finely from the luxuriant woodland around it. In front the mountains present a formidable barrier on both sides of Nant Ffrancon. Carnedd Llewelyn and Carnedd Dafydd on the left are pre-eminent, the former rising behind its bold out-post, Yr-Elen. At the head of the valley are the Glyders, and on the right of it the peaks of Y Garn and Foel-goch, and the round back of Elidyr-fawr.

Soon after this the road, crossing the Ogwen, which hereabouts comes briskly down a very pretty glen, continues somewhat more steeply than before along and above its east side to Bethesda.

Pedestrians may with advantage follow up the course of the stream on its west side by entering a cart-track on the Bangor side of the bridge. The walk for some distance is a very charming one, and, on a hot day especially much pleasanter than the high-road route, which, however, may be re-entered by crossing *Pont-y-coetmor* in about a mile. The next bridge is the one under the slate quarries, and the road over it enters the main road half-a-mile beyond Bethesda town.

(2) By rail. The Bethesda branch quits the main line a few
yards beyond the far end of the tunnel which commences at the
east (Chester) end of Bangor Station. Thence turning south it
follows for two miles the picturesque valley of the Cegid. The
tramway from the Penrhyn quarries also threads this valley. A
fine view of the mountains clustering round Nant Ffrancon presents itself at once, the most prominent heights being Carnedd
Llewelyn and Carnedd Dafydd on the left of the pass, and Elidyr-
fawr on the right. Where the main valley bends to the right,
towards Pentir, the railway turns to the left, and reaches the stations of *Felin-hen*, and *Tregarth*. Then, passing through a tunnel
300 yards long, it enters the Ogwen valley a short distance from
Pont-y-coetmor and a mile short of its terminus at **Bethesda**.
The station is at the north end of the town, $\frac{1}{4}$ mile from the
Douglas Arms Hotel, and a mile from the slate quarries.   .

Bethesda [Hotels: (all on main road) *Douglas Arms* (**H.Q.**),
$\frac{1}{4}$ *m.* from station; *Victoria* and *Waterloo* (both smaller), *Elias'
Temperance. Post arr. 7 a.m., 6 p.m.; dep. 6.50 p.m.*] is a large
village devoted almost entirely to slate-quarrying, and, in itself,
possessed of no attraction for the tourist. It is, however, a good
starting point for several mountain ascents—notably those of
Carnedds Dafydd and Llewelyn, and the range along the west
side of Nant Ffrancon, which culminates in the Glyders.
   The **Penrhyn Slate-quarries** are reached by crossing the
bridge about half-a-mile south of the centre of the village. Visitors
are allowed to inspect them. They are the largest in Wales, and
the men employed at them are numbered by thousands. To the
eye they present the appearance of a succession of terraces rising
one above another on the mountain-side, the natural features of
which, it is needless to say, have been destroyed by them. The
process of working the slate is simple. First. the hill-side is
cracked by blasting; huge blocks are detached by crow-bars, and
conveyed on trollies to the sheds, where they are split and dressed;
lastly they are piled up edgewise in wagons, and conveyed down
the little narrow-gauge line to Port Penrhyn at Bangor.

Bethesda to Aber over Moel Wnion.   (1905 *ft.*)   *abt.* 6 m.
Route described the reverse way on page 76.

   In clear weather this is a delightful walk, and for reasons given in the reverse
description, it is far better to follow the ridge of Moel Wnion (pron. "Oonion")
from end to end than to effect the small saving of exertion afforded by following the track along the side of the same mountain from Llanllechid (*see
map*). In bad weather there is nothing got by going from Bethesda to Aber
at all.

   The only real difficulty in the route is to extricate oneself from Bethesda,
and to do this successfully explicit directions are needed.

   Standing in the main road a few yards north of the "Douglas Arms," and
looking up between the new church and the schools you will see high up on the
hill-side a chapel—as ugly a building as the church is the reverse. To reach it

take the first turn to the right, nearly 100 yards north of the hotel. Passing round the church you ascend by intermittent steps to a cross-lane. Turn right for a few feet, and then continue the ascent by a path which brings you out at a complicated meeting of roads. Cross these and go on ascending by a path with a wall on one side and a fence of slate slabs on the other till you reach the chapel ("Welsh Calvinistic"). The route is continued upwards by a road on the right of this, which after becoming a mere cart-track passes through two gates on to the open fell. You have now the green height of **Moel Faban** (1,300 *ft.*) directly in front. The track goes to the right of this and presently ceases. Between Faban and the next height (*Llefn*) there is a narrow green gap, *Ffos Rhufeiniaid*, through which the vista of Penrhyn Castle, the wooded coast of Anglesey, and Red Wharf Bay beyond is only marred by the Llanllechid slate-quarry in the foreground. Hence you may steeply climb to the top of **Llefn** (1,450 *ft.*), or keep to the right of it and take the next height **Gyrn** (1,777 *ft.*), or (a third course) leave that, too, on the left, and not make for the ridge until you are on the *col* (1,520 *ft.*) between Bethesda and Aber and at the foot of the round summit of Moel Wnion.

The Aber glen is now before you and if the weather is unfavourable you may descend at once into it and reach the Aber Hotel in 3 miles.

A cart-track crosses the dip between Gyrn and Moel Wnion, and a little further on another doubles round the head of the Aber Glen and traverses the eastern slope of Moel Wnion only a few hundred feet below its summit. Our course, however, is straight up and along the ridge. The top of **Moel Wnion** is a wide plateau with a cairn upon it. The view from this part of the walk is very beautiful. Westwards we have the Menai Straits with its bridges, Beaumaris, looking like a gem of the sea, the Anglesey monuments and the whole breadth of the island to the far-off Holyhead mountain There is nothing but atmosphere to prevent our seeing the Isle of Man, and even Ireland. Eastwards a forcible contrast is presented by the deep and lonesome hollows which pierce the flanks of Y Foel Fras and its lower dependencies. The Carnedds rise to the right of these due south, and the peak of Snowdon may be seen over the heights on the far side of Nant Ffrancon.

Continuing along the ridge you soon see two more cairns in front. The track recommences a few yards to the right of the first—our route having in the interval crossed the cart-track already spoken of as traversing the east side of the mountain. A good view of the chief Aber waterfall is now obtained. The second cairn is left some way on the right, and the track, passing through a gate about opposite to it, continues to the left of another wall, and presently crosses an iron fence, whence, looking to the right, you see Maes-y-gaer and Penmaenmawr in a line. Then, crossing a broad green drive, you bend to the left and see Aber below you. You may either turn to the right out of the main track by a narrower one and enter the village at its south end, or you may continue to the left and enter a lane which, passing in a few yards a group of cottages, enters the high-road on the left side of the church and a few yards west of the by-road to the hotel and station. The latter is the shorter route.

Bethesda to Llanberis, 8 m. No particular object is to be gained by taking this ramifying route except that of getting by the shortest way from one place of interest to another. The road begins and ends with slate quarries. In starting you cross the Ogwen by the bridge which leads to the slate quarries half-a-mile south of the Douglas Arms Hotel ; then ascend by *St. Ann's Church*, the conspicuous one with a spire, whence, passing south of *Moel-y-ci* and

Drysgol-faur you again reach slate-quarries, and crossing the main road that leads to the upper Dinorwic quarry, descend first over the flat *débris* of a quarry, and then by a path, to the road which crosses the isthmus between the two Llanberis lakes, and enters Llanberis itself between the Station and the **Victoria Hotel.**

During the first part of the walk there is a good retrospect of the Carnedd Llewelyn range, then Anglesey and Carnarvon are seen to the right, and Elidyrfawr and fach to the left, and lastly Snowdon comes into view in front over the Llanberis valley.

From the busy town and unkempt surroundings of Bethesda, first to the pleasant woods of *Ogwen Bank*, and from them to the sterile grandeur of Nant Ffrancon, we have two of the most abrupt transitions to be met with in the kingdom. There is no finer scene of its kind in Wales than **Nant Ffrancon** (the "Vale of the Beavers"), and none whose effectiveness depends so much on the conditions under which it is seen. When first entered from its upper end by Llyn Ogwen, its limited length, together with the proximity of the Penhryn slate-quarries, and the cultivated lower country between them and Bangor, almost entirely counteract the sensations which its immediate surroundings are fitted to inspire, but as we enter it at its lower end, passing in an instant from woodland luxuriance and all that savours of every-day life, into an amphitheatre of steep and rugged mountains, scarred by torrents and broken by jagged splintered rocks, with a feebly cultivated strath at our feet, a feeling akin to awe comes over us. Thus entered, Nant Ffrancon is the Glencoe of Wales, and its impressiveness, like that of Glencoe, is only fully felt when its summits are made indistinct by mist, or scudding clouds are running riot amid the fantastic rock-outlines which they both veil and magnify. As a rule Nant Ffrancon appears to much greater advantage in winter than in summer.

The road rises gradually along the eastern side of the valley, forming a terrace whence the wide level strath—probably the bed of an old lake—comes out in bold contrast with the broken slopes on either side. This strath is half cultivation and half marsh; a number of small farmsteads besprinkle it, giving a human association to the scene without robbing it of its wildness.

At the foot of the pass, 1½ miles beyond Bethesda, a new bridge has been thrown across the stream. This leads to the farm-road under the mountains that form the west flank of the valley. This route, being lower down, is not such an effective one as the main road, but it brings before the eye a view of the **Falls of Ogwen**, a broken series of fully exposed cataracts at the head of the glen, which the main road does not admit of. Those who are returning to Bangor or Bethesda should ascend by the main road and return by this one.

The mountains on each side of the valley, as we ascend it from Bethesda are: on the west, Bronllwyd—the spur that ascends from the upper part of the slate quarries,—Carnedd-y-Filiast, Moel Perfedd, Foel-goch and Y Garn; then encircling its head are **Glyder-fawr**, Glyder-fach—the centre-piece—and, coming into view as we near the top, Y Tryfan, marked by two rocky peaks. The east side is monopolised by the long sloping shoulder of Braich-du—an abutment of Carnedd Dafydd, very rough and steep in its descent to the pass. The front presented by the Glyders and the Tryfan is particularly bold and rugged.

At the top of the pass, 4½ miles from Bethesda, and just above the Ogwen Falls, which you may see by a little clambering, there is the solitary cottage of *Benglog*, recently enlarged, and often occupied by artists or fishermen. This is the point at which to turn off for Llyn Idwal, to start across the Glyders to Pen-y-Gwryd, or to begin the ascent of Y Tryfan. The last two excursions are described in our "Mountain Section."

Llyn Idwal and **Twll-du** (the "**Devil's Kitchen**"). The scenery connected with these two much visited spots is amongst the severest in North Wales, equalled only, perhaps, by the Llyn-y-Cau recess of Cader Idris, and one or two of the cwms of Snowdon. It is half-a-mile to the outlet of Llyn Idwal, and 2 miles to the foot of Twll-du, but a couple of hours is not too much to devote to the excursion.

A rough path ascends from the west side of the cottage and, bearing to the right over boggy ground in a few hundred yards, continues to ascend till it reaches the lake close to its outlet. **Llyn Idwal** is deep-set between the rocky heights of Y Garn on the right and Glyder-fawr on the left, both of which descend to it so steeply as to apparently bar further progress. Looking across it we may note, high up above and a little to the right of its far end, a narrow rift in the rocky wall. This is **Twll-du** (literally the "black hole"), and to reach it either side of the lake may be taken ; the left-hand route is rather the shorter of the two, but the right-hand the drier, if the tops of the moraine heaps, which appear in every direction about here, be followed. From the end of the lake to the "Kitchen" (Twll-du) the climb is a very steep and rough one, first up the ridge of a moraine, and then over rough stones. The height of Llyn Idwal above sea-level is about 1,200 feet, of the kitchen (the bottom of the chasm), 1,700 feet, and the top of the chasm 2,000 feet. Idwal, so runs the legend, was son of Owen Gwynedd, prince of North Wales. He was thrown into the lake by his foster-father. No bird, it was long believed, would fly over the waters of the lake.

Twll-du (the **Devil's Kitchen**) is only a few yards wide, and the perpendicular rocks which form its walls are from 200 to 300 feet high. It is quite impassable, the small stream which threads it leaping from rock to rock in the wildest fashion. It is to Wales what Pier's Gill, under Scafell, is to the Lake District.

To reach the top of the chasm you must bend to the left from its foot, and climb a steep ledge of rock, down which trickles a streamlet. With care the ascent is quite safe, but it is not one to be recklessly made. In its lower part the streamlet tumbles over a precipice, to reach the top of which you must work a little way round to the right. Then its course is followed till you reach the ridge some way to the left of the top of the fissure, a little beyond which is the small lake, *Llyn-y-cwm.*

For the routes thence up Glyder-fawr to the left, Y Garn to the right, or to Llanberis over the spur of Y Garn, see "Mountain Section."

The routes from Benglog to Pen-y-gwryd over the Glyders, and the ascent of Y Tryfan are described in the " Mountain Section."

From Benglog the road turns eastward and skirts the southern shores of **Llyn Ogwen**, a wild but featureless sheet of water, a mile long, and in its broadest part ¼ mile wide. There is fair fishing in it. From its further end Y *Tryfan* rises precipitously on the right, and down gentler slopes on the left comes the stream that feeds Llyn Ogwen from the lakelet of *Ffynnon-y-lloer*. The highest point on the road (900 ft.) is gained a little further on, just beyond the hollow of *Cwm Tryfan*. Then we cross the *Llugwy*, which descends from Ffynnon Llugwy on the left. The road onward to Capel Curig is bare and desolate. *Capel Curig* and the rest of the way to Bettws-y-Coed are more fully described in the Bettws Section (p. 129). There is a grand view of Snowdon as we pass the village, and Moel Siabod monopolises the front view. Then come several small hotels, the bridge and romantic falls of *Pont-gyfyng*, *Ty-Hyll*, where the river is crossed and a hill-road strikes off for Llanrwst; the *Swallow Falls* and, nearly 2 miles further, **Bettws-y-Coed** (*p.* 118).

Llanrwst and Bettws-y-Coed Section.

Llandudno to Llanrwst and Bettws-y-Coed, by rail.
*Llandudno to Llandudno Junction, 3 m; Glan Conway, 4 m;
Tal-y-cafn, 8½ m; Llanrwst 14 m; Bettws-y-Coed, 18 m. From
Conway the distances are 2 miles less.*

This railway threads the Vale of Conway, or Llanwrst, as it is
indifferently called, and besides presenting a series of very charming landscapes from its own course, affords to sojourners at Llandudno and other watering-places along the coast the opportunity
of making a day's excursion into the deepest recesses of eastern
Snowdonia. The longest round—except for those who like to
spend the greater part of the day on the rail in accomplishing the
circuit of Ffestiniog, Portmadoc and Carnarvon—is that by rail to
Bettws-y-Coed, thence by coach to Bangor (through Nant Ffrancon),
or to Llanberis (through the Pass of Llanberis), and back by an
evening train to the starting-place. Very interesting excursions,
involving less rail and more walking made be made from the
smaller stations on the route as follows :—

From Tal-y-cafn : (1) Over Bwlch-y-ddeufaen to Penmaenmawr, Llanfairfechan or Aber (*p.* 59). (2) To Llanbedr and Pen-y-gaer (*p.* 73). (3) To
Llyn Eigiau, Carnedd Llewelyn and Bethesda (*see* "Mountain Section").
(4) By the high-road past Porth-lwyd and Dolgarrog falls to Trefriw and
Llanrwst (*p.* 106).

From Llanrwst : (1) To Trefriw, Llyn Cwlyd and Capel Curig. (2) To
Trefriw, Llyn Crafnant and Capel Curig. (3) To Llanrhwchwyn. (4) To Llyn-
y-parc and Bettws-y-Coed.

The Route. From Llandudno Station the line crosses the
flat isthmus cn which Llandudno stands, and reaches the sea-
shore at *Deganwy*—close to the mouth of the Conway estuary.
The view westwards over the sea includes the town, castle, woods
and bridges of Conway, the Conway Mountain, Penmaenbach and
Penmaenmawr, Puffin Island, and Anglesey ; while eastwards
Deganwy Hill is succeeded by a small limestone-ridge, extending
from Gloddaeth to the Little Ormes Head.

At *Llandudno Junction*, we probably change trains, and then the
line follows for several miles the windings of the Conway estuary.
The low wooded knoll of *Benarth*, on the opposite (western side), is
succeeded by a green cultivated slope that rises to the mountains,
amongst which Y Foel Fras, with a flat top but a scarped eastern

front, is the most conspicuous.   Farther away are Penllithrig, sloping abruptly to the left and gently to the right, and, in its right rear, Carnedd Llewelyn, the crowning height of Eastern Snowdonia.

Tal-y-cafn (*inn.* behind station) to **Pen-y-gaer, Porth-lwyd** and **Dolgarrog Waterfalls, Trefriw** and **Llanrwst.** 3–4 *hrs.* **walk.**

Cross the ferry (1*d.*) to the little inn on the opposite side, and continue along the road till in ¾ mile you come to a group of houses at the crossing of the Conway and Llanrwst road.   Turn to the left down this, and if you are bound for Pen-y-gaer, take a lane to the right in a little over a mile.   (The little church of Caerhun, mentioned below in the main route, is very prettily situated ¼ mile left of the road a short distance before the turn.   There is a path to it from near the little inn opposite Tal-y-cafn).   This lane leads to *Llanbedr Village,* whence a road reaches in 2½ miles the Bwlch-y-ddeufaen road, a mile short of the top of the pass.   Pen-y-gaer is easily reached by taking a by-road to the left about ¾ mile along this road.   The earthworks round this British post are still well defined, and there is a fine view from it across the Conway vale in one direction, and in the other up the bare hollow that is brought to an abrupt termination by Llyn Dulyn and Melynllyn under the slopes of Carnedd Llewelyn and Y Foel Fras.   *Llyn Dulyn* supplies Llandudno with water.   It is a wild out-of-the-way lake with precipitous sides, but the way to it is dreary and monotonous.   Half-a-mile south of it is the smaller lake *Melynllyn.*

Continuing along the main road from the turn for Llanbedr, we reach in a long half-mile the hamlet of *Tal-y-bont* (*inn*), and ¾ m. further cross the **Porth-lwyd** stream just where it recovers its composure after its wild rush down the cliffs from Cwm Eigiau.   Both this fall and the next one, Dolgarrog, are a succession of cataracts eminently picturesque, and, to the Cumbrian tourist, somewhat suggestive of Lodore.   The *Porth-lwyd* is reached by a track which starts from the north side of the bridge, and, after passing some cottages, goes through a gate on the left.   From it you may proceed along the upland valley to Llyn Eigiau and Carnedd Llewelyn, but we have preferred to reach these remote spots by the clearly defined road from Tal-y-bont.   (*See* " *Mountain Section.*")

The **Dolgarrog Falls** are a mile south of Porth-lwyd, and are reached in the same way, by a track north of the bridge over the *Afon-ddu* ("Black stream "), but they are not so easy to get at, the way and the view being a great deal obstructed by trees.   The stream which contributes them comes down from Llyn Cwlyd, to which we shall describe the route from Trefriw (*p.* 115).

The objects of interest on the route to Llanrwst are described in connection with that town and Trefriw (*p.* 110).   The Trefriw " Spa " is ¾ mile south of Dolgarrog, the village 1½ mile further, Llanrwst station another mile, and Llanrwst town just beyond it.

A mile beyond Tal-y-cafn, the little church of *Caerhun,* with its bell-turret, its grassy grave-yard and belt of yew-trees, is a very pretty object on the far side of the river.   It occupies the site of the Roman *Conovium.*   Beyond it a little further south, is the hill of *Pen-y-gaer* (the " hill of the fort,") so-called from an old camp, whose entrenchment may still be traced on the summit.   The hills on the right now **draw nearer,** and become very steep and

richly wooded. Descending them from the upland valleys beyond
are two picturesque waterfalls,—*Porth-lwyd*, or *Rhaiadr-mawr*,
nearly 2 miles past Caerhun, and *Dolgarrog*, ½ mile further. In
both, the water falls from ledge to ledge in a succession of graceful cascades, partly hidden by the abundant foliage which decks
the cliffs on either side.

In less than a mile beyond Dolgarrog a mine may be noticed
on the hill-side and another small stream coming down from
it to a small building at the edge of the strath. These are
the waters and Spa of Trefriw (*p.* 110). Then comes the hotel
(*Belle-vue*), and pier of the same village, and ¼ mile further on,
the village itself, which is seen to greater advantage from this
(the east) side of the valley, than from closer quarters, a circumstance due chiefly to the graceful curve of the Crafnant valley,
which forms a charming background to the picture. (*For Trefriw*,
see p. 110.)

Llanrwst Station is now close at hand, but the town is half-
a-mile further, and almost hidden by the side of a cutting through
which the line passes. Coming out on to the open, however, we
look back on to the bridge and church, and directly opposite we
have the grounds and woods of Gwydir, amongst which rises the
Falcon Rock. Then, crossing the Conway, the line enters Carnarvonshire, and, approaching Bettws-y-Coed, affords a brief
glimpse of Moel Siabod up the Llugwy valley.

The scenery all along this part of the Conway valley is very
charming, though it has perhaps been somewhat over-praised,
both by those who think that by foolishly comparing it with the
Rhine they flatter Wales, and by others who have written of it as
the finest valley in Wales. It has little of that winding character,
which, aided by the nearness and abruptness of the flanking hills,
causes such a constant change of picturesque settings in the valley
of the Wye, and it is in every respect surpassed by the Mawddach
river and estuary.

Other routes from Llandudno to Bettws-y-Coed. *Scenery
and objects of interest described in the route by rail* (*p.* 105).

There is a road on each side of the Conway Valley all the way.
That on the *east side* passes through Llanrwst, and is 17 miles in
length, nearly a mile of which may be cut off by crossing the river
at Llanrwst, and finishing the journey by the road on the west
side. This road, lying a little further back from the mountains
than the railway, the river and the other road, affords somewhat
fuller views than are obtained from any of those three routes.
The extra length of the east-side road between Llanrwst and
Bettws-y-Coed arises from there being no way across the river
until the Waterloo Bridge, half-a-mile beyond Bettws, is reached.

The *West Road* goes round the wooded hill that rises immediately south of Conway, and does not fairly enter the valley for
about 5 miles. We have described the part of it between the

cross-roads, ⅔ mile from Tal-y-cafn station, and Llanrwst on page 106.

Deganwy or Conway to Trefriw by steamer. *Once or twice during the day according to tide. Fares : Single,* 1s. 6*d.*, *and* 1s. ; *Return,* 2s. 6*d.*, 1s. 6*d.* This is a very pleasant sail, but as the railway runs side by side with the river almost the whole distance, and is never more than ¼ mile from it, a separate description is quite unnecessary (*see p.* 105). The landing-place at Trefriw is opposite the Bellevue Hotel, ¼ *m.* north of the village, 1½ *m.* of Llanrwst station, and a mile south of the Spa. *For Trefriw see p.* 110.

Llanwrst.

Hotels: *Victoria* (H.Q.), by the river-side, opposite the bridge; *Eagles &
Gwydir Arms*, in the Square; *Queen's*, a small house near the station.

Post: *Arr. abt.* 7 a.m., 4.30 p.m.; *d.p.* 6.30 p.m. (7.45 *in summer*)

Population: Abt. 2,500.

The station is fully half-a-mile from the centre of the town, and so placed as
to accommodate Trefriw also, which village is reached in 1 mile by a new road,
not yet put on the Ordnance Survey.

The natural situation of Llanrwst on the level strath of the
Conway valley, on the banks of its river, and in one of the richest
parts, with a cliff-like line of hill wooded from head to foot
on the west side, and gentler slopes of alternate mead and woodland on the east, is delightful in the extreme, and the town,
when seen from the neighbouring heights, has a most inviting
appearance.

Art, however, has hardly seconded Nature. The streets, narrow
and confined to begin with, have been rendered more oppressively
so by modern improvements, the chief object of the builders
having apparently been to prevent the visitor, while passing
through the town, seeing any indication whatever of the character
of its surroundings. Old houses, over which it may have been
possible to catch a glimpse of the hills and woods, have given place
to new ones several stories high, and chapels of ostentatious
ugliness almost abut upon the roadway. An exception must
be made in favour of St. James' English Wesleyan Chapel on the
left hand of the road from the station, and built partly in the
domestic Queen Anne style. The only open space in the town is
the Square, and that is partly occupied by an old building.

The hotel accommodation is good. The *Victoria* is just far
enough out of the town to command a view of the valley, and
the *Eagles and Gwydir* is also near the bridge and the bank of
the river.

The only objects of interest connected with the town itself are
the church and the bridge. The **Bridge** bears date 1636, and it is
said that Inigo Jones had a hand in designing it. It is curious
rather than graceful, and rises to a sharp point in the centre. If
it ever did shake, it has been shaken till it will shake no more.

The **Church** (*key at a house close to gateway*), is reached from
the corner of the Square, close to the Eagles Hotel. Yew trees
and the river flowing close by give it a pleasing appearance, but

the main body of the building, which has a short tower, is in no
way remarkable, except for a large and finely-carved oak screen,
which graces the interior and is said to have been brought from
Maenan Abbey.

The **Gwydir Chapel**, however, assigned to Inigo Jones in 1634,
and projecting at the S.E. corner of the building, contains much
that is of enduring interest.   On entering, the visitor may read a
full description of the different **memorials** on the walls and
floor of the apartment.   The **chief curiosity** is the suggestively
capacious stone coffin of Llewelyn, which is said to have been
brought to Maenan Abbey, and thence, at the dissolution of
that monastery, to Llanrwst.   A pedigree, extending over 500
years, from Owen Gwynedd, **Prince** of Wales, to Sir Richard
Wynne, of Gwydir, 1633, is inscribed in white marble in the N.E.
corner; but the most admirable piece of work in the chapel is,
perhaps, a portrait-brass of Dame Sarah Wynne, daughter of the
old chevalier, Sir Thomas Middleton, by one Wm. Vaughan.   Two
pyramidal columns of variegated marble decorated with martial
insignia, and a stone effigy of a natural son of David, Prince of
of Wales, bearing the terrible name of Howel Coytmor-ap-Gruff-
Vychan-ap-Gruff-Gam (or *breviter* "Goch,") should also be
mentioned.   From the descendants of "Goch," Gwydir was
bought by the Wynnes.

Gwydir Castle (*open weekdays; up the straight road*, ⅓ m.
across the bridge) has little noteworthy in its exterior, having been
to a great extent rebuilt, though parts date back to the 16th cent.
The interior, however, is most interesting.   It abounds in
carved oak and designs in Spanish leather.   A chair, made by a
native artist, is as elaborate as it is uncomfortable.   There is the
coronation chair of George II. and a stool of Queen Caroline, the
cradle of Richard Wynne (1634), and a wonderful carving in high
relief of uncertain date brought from Belgium ; also, among the
tapestry, a screen accredited to Mary Queen of Scots ; and we must
not omit a door with which, we are told, a lady spiritualist held
converse for an hour and a-half, with results known only to her-
self.   The housekeeper shows the rooms, which include the dining
and drawing rooms, the study, and a number of bedrooms.

From the Castle we may proceed to the **Chapel** which peers out from the
richly wooded hill-side above the junction of the Llanrwst road with that from
Trefriw to Bettws-y-Coed.   A flight of steps leads up to it.   It was built in
1673, is of plain exterior, and has been lately in the repairer's (restorer's) hands.
Service is held in it during the summer months.

From the west end of the chapel proceed a short distance by the farm-road
which leads into a broad wood-track.   Turning to the right along this, you
will enjoy a lovely view of the Vale of Llanrwst, and in ¼ m. join the Llyn-y-
parc route (*p*. 116), opposite the *Forester's Cottage*.

* **Trefriw** (*pron*. **Trev-ru**) Hotel, *Bellevue*, is a charmingly
situated village, 1 *m*. from Llanrwst Station, 1½ *m*. from the town
by the new road commencing at the station.   The hotel, how-

---

* *There is a path beginning with a lane from the far side of Llanrwst Bridge.*

ever, is a quarter of a mile further north, opposite the little dock to which the steamer from Deganwy and Conway comes during the tourist season, the river being tidal up to this point.

Like Llanrwst, Trefriw looks best from a little way off, and from nowhere better than from the railway, the beautiful bend of the valley which winds upwards from it to Llyn Crafnant being a special feature from this view-point. There are one or two public-houses in the village itself.

The **Chalybeate Wells** are 1½ miles from Trefriw village, and 1 mile from the hotel, on the Conway road. You may have your pennyworth either in the building by the road-side, or mount to the old mine above, where the waters issue from the ground. They are said to be inconceivably nasty and correspondingly efficacious.

Llanrwst to Trefriw by Llanrhwchwyn, *about* 5 m. This is the most interesting short excursion from Llanrwst, except, perhaps, that to Bettws-y-Coed by Llyn-y-Parc. Llanrhwchwyn is one of the most remarkable parishes in the kingdom. Possibly there is not one so near to, and yet so far from, the " madding crowd." You can hear the railway whistle, and yet be lost to the world altogether. The church is a curiosity, and the two or three ramshackle uninviting farmsteads, which presumably form the parish, look as if they had dropped into their positions by mistake, and nobody had ever taken the trouble to remove them.

The Route. Cross the bridge, and, when you have passed Gwydir Castle on the left, turn to the right for a few yards along the Trefriw road ; then to the left up the hill-road to Capel Curig— a milestone at the corner says " Capel Curig, 6½ m." After ascending this road for a few hundred yards you come to the *Forester's Cottage* on the right.* Here take the lane striking off to the right. A stream is at once crossed, which a few yards below makes a tiny but picturesque fall, fancifully styled the " Grey Mare's Tail." After rain the name is appropriate. Keep along this road for ¼ mile, and then, close to a cottage, turn left again through a wood. This brings you to the side of a silvan dingle, down which a streamlet hurries to the Llanrwst vale. After a short ascent, instead of following the lane across this streamlet, enter a footpath by a step-stile on the left. A few yards up this path you will discover the position of **Llanrhwchwyn** Church by the yew trees which surround it. The path leads almost straight up to it, and past the cottage at which the key is kept.

Entering by the lich-gate, which bears the enigmatical inscription " IT. ID. OT. 1462. WO," we find ourselves in a small graveyard, overshadowed by seven venerable yew trees. In the midst is the church, as rude a specimen of ecclesiastical architecture as

---

* You may reach this spot from Gwydir Chapel (*p.* 110) by turning to the right beyond it, along a wood-track, which comes out at a gate opposite the Forester's Cottage.

your eye has probably ever rested on. It is called " Llewelyn's Old Church," the Welsh patriot having, during his residence at Trefriw, attended service at it until his wife " objected to the hill," and induced him to build another church on a more come-at-able spot. We know very few ladies of the present day who would not sympathise with the princess in the matter. The church is over 500 feet above the Llanrwst Valley.

St. Rhychwyn lived in the 7th century, and was a son of Helig Foel, the Carnarvonshire chieftain, whose submerged lands are now represented by the Lavan Sands, between Llanfairfechan and Beaumaris.

The **Church** consists of two aisles of equal length and a bell-turret. Its antiquity is specially evidenced in the primitive arrangement of its roof-timbers, the thickness of its walls, and its massive doors. The window at the east end of the north aisle contains some stained glass representing the Crucifixion. The Font is also very old.

Bedd Taliesin. Crossing a step-stile outside the N.W. corner of the churchyard, and going to the right along the lane for 100 yards or so, we may turn to the left along an unfenced road that passes a farm and works round in about a mile to Llyn Geirionydd, at the foot of which, reached by a footpath, is an upright slate slab, surmounted by a cross and supported by steps—the whole about 25 feet high. This marks the supposed grave of the Welsh bard. Taliesin, who flourished in the sixth century. The monument was erected by Lord Willoughby D'Eresby. The earliest record of Taliesin is like that of Moses, if we substitute the mud of the Dyfi estuary for the bulrushes of the Nile, a coracle for a cradle, and Elphin, son of Gwyddno for Pharaoh's daughter; the latest reminds us of Macbeth, for like that monarch he seems to have been buried in two different places, 40 miles apart—by the shores of Llyn Geirionydd, and among the hills between Aberystwith and Machynlleth—so at least says the Ordnance Survey, which marks " Bedd Taliesin " in both spots.

Llyn Geirionydd is bordered on the west by a steep craggy mountain, and on others by grass slopes. From the monument you may take a path that drops to the Crafnant valley, at the risk of wetting your feet in crossing the stream where the two waters meet, or you may take the cart-track along the east side of the lake to Talyllyn—a small farm—and thence cross the hill by a quarry, beyond which there is no particular path until you drop by a farm to the Capel Curig road, ½ m. beyond Ty-Hill Bridge.

Continuation to Trefriw. Passing from Llanrhwchwyn church into the lane at its west end, you keep to the right for about a quarter of a mile, and then turn left by a sloppy track, which goes to the left of a hill called *Clunllom.* The top-level of this hill is very little above the track, and it should be made for as soon as you get on to open ground. It lies immediately above the wooded steep that flanks the Llanrwst valley on the west. From its southern end the town of Llanrwst and the adjacent part of the vale are immediately below us. Far away in the south is a mountain pointed on the right and sloping to the left. This is Arenig-fawr between Bala and Ffestiniog, and just in front of it is the square-topped Arenig-fach, but the finest mountain outline in sight is that of Moel Siabod, which rises alone above the lower level of the nearer range. To the right of it is Snowdon. The long, even ridge of Cefn Careadwydd hides the loftier summits in the north-west, except Penllithrig, which shows a round outline to the left of it. Trefriw is hidden by the dense fir-wood which clothes the whole side of the hill, but the valley ascending from it to Llyn Crafnant is fully seen, and the Conway valley looks very charming as it extends northwards towards its outlet. Eastwards the long line of high ground which separates the Conway from the Clwyd basin bars further prospect.

From this spot there are two ways to Trefriw. (a) By path round the south end of the wood, and then through it into the direct road from Llanrhwchwyn; (b) By the hollow glade on the west, between us and the Crafnant valley. A path leads down this to the Methodist Chapel above the village.

Trefriw to Clunllom, Llanrhwchwyn and Llanwrst, abt. 5 m.

This route will be understood from the foregoing description of it taken the reverse way. You may either start by the Methodist Chapel and go up the hollow glade, bending to the left for the top of Clunllom as soon as you get to open and almost level ground, or you may reach the same spot by following the Llanrhwchwyn road from the upper part of the village, and, continuing along a path through the wood till you get into an open field, above which, on the right hand, is the top of the hill (*Clunllom*).

Hence the position of Llanrhwchwyn Church is indicated by the yew trees which surround it, and from the church the pathway leading down the hill, past a small reservoir, and into a woody lane, cannot well be missed. You follow the lane till, in about ¾ mile, you reach the *Forester's Cottage*, just after crossing a stream which forms a waterfall on the left, and thence you may either go straight down to *Llanrwst*, or pass through a gate into a wood opposite the cottage and make a little détour by *Gwydir Chapel* (p. 110).

Llanrwst to Capel Curig direct, by Ty-Hyll, 7 m.

This route cuts off the corner made by the rail and high-road route through Bettws-y-Coed, and presents during the descent of the hill between Llanrwst and Ty Hyll some fine views.

The road crosses Llanrwst Bridge and, continuing through an avenue for nearly half-a-mile, joins the road that skirts the west-side of the valley from Trefriw to Bettws-y-Coed. In the left hand angle of the two roads is Gwydir Castle (*p*. 110) with its formally trimmed yew-trees.

Follow the Trefriw road for a few yards, and then turn up the by-road which at once begins to climb the hill. In a few

hundred yards you pass a cottage on the right. A little beyond
this, avoid the track which goes alongside of the wall on the left,
and follow that which crosses a small stream a little further on,
and then ascends through the wood again. Shortly a lead-mine
with two wheels is passed on the right, and another on the left.
On the right is a new chapel.

The highest point of the road is reached nearly 3 miles
from Llanrwst. From it there is a fine mountain outline in
front. Moel Siabod is the nearest and most prominent height.
To the right of it the peak of Snowdon may be detected, and
then, nearer at hand the Glyder-fach, with the three points of
Y Tryfan still more to the right.

A little further on the road another lead-mine is passed. Avoid
the road which descends through a gate on the left. The rest of
the way cannot well be mistaken. The road drops rapidly to the
Bettws and Capel Curig high-way, which it joins a few yards
beyond *Ty-Hyll Bridge*, and ¾ m. west of the Swallow Falls. During the descent there is a good view down into the glen which
contains the latter. This is not a carriage-route.

Llanrwst or Trefriw to Capel Curig by Llyn Crafnant.
(*Pedestrian route.*) *Llanrwst to Trefriw*, 1½ *m.* ; *Llyn Crafnant*,
4 *m* ; *top of Pass (about 1,250 feet)*, 6 *m* ; *Capel Curig*, 7½ *m.*

This is the finest of the comparatively easy routes between the
Conway valley and Capel Curig. It has two special excellences,—
the first view of Llyn Crafnant, and the prospect from the top of
the pass beyond that lake.

Leave Llanrwst by the new road which passes close to the railway station, and crosses the river (*toll* 1*d.*) and the level strath
to Trefriw. At Trefriw, cross the Crafnant stream, and turn up
the steep road to the left at once. After crossing one or two roads
you come to a fork, where you must take the left branch, so as to
keep up the valley along the north side of the stream. On the
left, across the water, is the steep, fir-clad height of *Clunllom*; on
the right the long ridge of *Cefn Careadwydd* rises, and in front
is the rocky *Mynydd Daulyn*—its summit disfigured by a slate-
quarry. To the left of the last-named mountain is Llyn
Geirionydd (p. 112), by the side of which an alternative, but
less interesting route leads to Capel Curig. From the lake a
tributary stream comes tumbling down its valley.

Two miles from Trefriw our road crosses the stream and enters
a narrow opening immediately under Mynydd Daulyn, which has
been absurdly likened to the Gap of Dunloe, near Killarney.
From the top of it **Llyn Crafnant**, its level artificially raised a
few feet, comes suddenly into view. It is about a mile long, and
nearly half-a-mile wide. On either side the hills slope to the water
steeply, but without much variety of outline or colouring, the left
hand ones being heathery, those on the right fairly sprinkled with
wood and carpeted with bracken. In front, however, at the far

end of the glen, is a sharp outline of rock and greenery, which goes far to make amends for the shortcomings of the flanking hills, and is more suggestive of Westmorland than Wales.

The road traces the southern shore of the lake, and comes to an end about half-a-mile beyond its head, at a re-built farmhouse. Hereabouts the bottom of the valley is occupied by meadows, but beyond the farm a steep green barrier, dotted with thorn and other bushes, faces us. The route may be continued to the left or right of this obstacle. The right is decidedly to be preferred, and in this direction a faint path winds steeply up the corrie, under the finely cut rocks of *Craig-wen*. At the top it traverses a narrow green hollow, and then passes through a gap in a wall, beyond which is, apparently, the bed of an old lake, carpeted with heath and moss and long grass, that shows a rich brown tint in the flowerless season. Moel Siabod now comes into view in front.

It is best to keep to the left of this lake-bed, and to quit it through a small opening on the same side. The rest of the way is over broken and, in places, boggy ground, well up above and to the left of the valley. Snowdon and the Capel Curig lakes come into view in front, and on the right, separated from them by the triple-peaked Tryfan and the Glyder range, the bare valley up which the road goes to Nant Ffrancon may be traced, with Carnedds Dafydd and Llewelyn flanking it on the right.

There is no track in this part of the route, but as you descend to Capel Curig you will, after crossing a wire fence, come to a wall. Keep this on the right till you escape through a gate, whence the evident route to the village is by a cart-track, which enters the road close to the new church, and just at the junction of the Bangor, Llanberis, and Bettws-y-Coed roads.

Llanrwst or Trefriw to Capel Curig by Llyn Cwlyd, (*abt.* 10 *m.,* 3½–4½ *hrs.*).

This is a longer and wilder route across Eastern Snowdonia than the one previously described by Llyn Crafnant. At the cost of an hour's extra travel the ascent of Penllithrig (2,623 *ft.*) may be included in the excursion.

From Llanrwst the route is by the new road, which diverges close to the station, and crossing the Conway (*toll,* 1*d.*) reaches Trefriw in 1½ miles. Here cross the bridge over the Crafnant stream, and turn up at once to the left, keeping straight on till the road forks. Take the right-hand branch, skirting a wood on the right, and a cemetery on the left. When you have passed through a gate, and the road sweeps round to the right by the side of the wood, go through another gate on the left and pass a farmhouse, beyond which the track leads on to and over the hill, affording a peep of Llyn Crafnant and Llyn Geirionydd on the left hand during the ascent. After passing the long and almost level ridge of Careadwydd, a tiresomely boggy one, you see two farms,

Bryniog-isaf and *Bryniog-uchaf*, "Lower and Upper Bryniog," by which the path goes, crossing the stream by a bridge at the bottom of the valley. During the descent a corner of Llyn Cwlyd comes into view, with Penllithrig towering beyond it. From the stream the path leads past two shepherd's cottages, *Craig-wen* and *Cwm Cwlyd*, about ¾ mile apart, and then bears down to the lake, with which it runs parallel, about 100 feet above the water.

Llyn Cwlyd is over 1½ miles long by ¼ mile wide, and about 1,100 feet above the sea. Its south side is a steep green slope, with a crest of dark rock, *Creigiau Gleision*. The north side is not so steep, and the path is distinct throughout. The *col* beyond it is about 200 feet higher than the lake, and is marked by a cairn, whence by turning sharp to the right you may easily ascend Penllithrig. The Tryfan, with its three humpy peaks, and the Glyders here come into view.

Beyond the *col* the path is at first indistinct, but the direction to be taken is shown by two or three cairns, and is at first southwards to the right of the rocky ridge of *Craig-wen*. Then the track becomes plainer, but a considerable part of it is over very boggy ground. It passes to the left of a prominent piece of broken wall to a gate. Then it keeps to the right of a stream which is crossed at another gate. Beyond this it passes a farm-steading and, crossing another stream at a gate, drops to the high-road, which has been seen for some time, a long half-mile on the Bangor side of Capel Curig.

Llanrwst to Bettws-y-Coed by Llyn-y-parc, *abt.* 6 *m.*

This is another delightful walk. The first part is through shady woods, and the last over open ground from which there is a very fine view of Snowdonia.

Pursue the Llanrhwchwyn route (*p.* 111) as far as the *Forester's Cottage*, making the détour described in that route to Gwydir Chapel or not, as you please. From the cottage, leaving first the Llanrhwchwyn and then the Capel Curig route on the right, you follow the lane southwards, by the side of a wall. Presently a track strikes off to the right to some lead-mines but, continuing straight a-head, you pass over a stile and proceed alongside of **Llyn-y-parc** at a considerable height above it. The lake itself is almost, if not quite, hidden by the trees (fir and oak) which clothe its banks on this side throughout, except where the ground may have been lately cleared. It is nearly ¾-mile long, and very narrow; on the other side it is flanked by low but steep hills, only sprinkled by wood, chiefly birch. Pretty and secluded are the most appropriate epithets to apply to it.

From nearly opposite the south end of the lake several wood-tracks fork. By following that which keeps nearest the streamlet issuing from it you will make a steep descent, partly by a tramway, to the Llanrwst and Bettws-y-Coed road, reaching it a mile short of Bettws; but by far the best plan is to take the right-hand branch,

which will bring you to two ladder-stiles at the foot of the lake.
Cross the right-hand one and beyond the next wall you will find a
carriage-way which comes to an abrupt end at the wall itself. It
was made, we are told, in connection with some mining enterprise,
which happily came to nothing.

Keeping to the left of this road, and a little above it, you will
have a splendid mountain view westwards, Moel Siabod and the
Tryfan, with its three humps, being specially prominent. Between them are the Glyders and Snowdon, while southwards over
the lower hill-country beyond Bettws the peak of Arenig is conspicuous. To the left of Siabod the Moelwyn group appears.

Dropping again to the new road, we pass through the farm called
Pen-'r-allt, and here again, instead of turning to the right at once
down the road, it is well worth while to make for the little hump
in front with the cairn upon it.* From this point there is a
charming peep down into Bettws-y-Coed and the valley beyond.

Thence bend back again to the road, and descending through a
hollow not far from a streamlet, you will come into the track
along the north side of the Llugwy, close to the old vicarage and
the commencement of a foot-path which leads down to the *Miners'
Bridge* (p. 121). You may either take this path and join the
main (Bangor) road a mile west of the village or, turning at once
to the left, enter the village by the bridge called *Pont-y-Pair*.
The latter is considerably the shorter route.

---

* The cairn has disappeared (1887).

118

Bettws-y-Coed.

---

**Hotels**: *Royal Oak, Gwydir Arms, Glan Aber* (H.Q.), in the village near the station ; *Waterloo,* ½ *m.* on the way to Waterloo Bridge.

₊ The hotel accommodation of Bettws-y-Coed is good without being unduly pretentious. The **Royal Oak** and **Waterloo** are the largest houses, and the **Gwydir** and others are thoroughly comfortable.

Post : *Del.*: **7** *a.m.* ; **3.40** *p.m.* (July-Sept.) ; **5.15** *p.m.*; Sunday (to callers) **7-10** *a.m. Desp.* : **10.10** *a.m.* ; **6.15** *p.m.* ; **7.35** *p.m.* (July-Sept.) ; Sundays 6.15 *p.m.*

Distances : (*By rail*) Llanrwst, 4 *m* ; Conway, 16 *m* ; Llandudno, 18 *m*. Dolwyddelen, 5½ *m* ; **Blaenau Ffestiniog**, 12½ *m* ; (Ffestiniog Village, 16 *m.*) ; Portmadoc, 25½ *m* ; Barmouth, 42½ *m*. (*By road*), Corwen, 22 *m*. Capel Curig, 5½ *m* ; (Pen-y-gwryd, 9½ *m* ; Beddgelert, 17½ *m* ; Llanberis, 16 *m.*) Bethesda, 15 *m* ; Bangor 20½ *m*. *Short Walks*: Miner's Bridge, 1 *m* ; Swallow Falls, 2¼ *m*. Fairy Glen, 1¼ *m*. Capel Garmon, 2 *m*. Llyn Elsi, 2 *m*. Llyn-y-Parc, 2¼ *m*.

From an artist's point of view Bettws-y-Coed and its surroundings form, perhaps, the most beautiful region in the British Isles. David Cox visited the village periodically for forty years, and painted the sign-board of the Royal Oak Inn, still to be seen in the entrance-hall of the enlarged hotel. If you visit the Royal Academy and refer to your catalogue to identify a lovely river-bit, the chances are about even that it is on the Llugwy or the Lledr, while Moel Siabod with, may be, the warm tint of sunset on its graceful peak—the Schiehallion of Wales—is equally distinguished among mountains. The Llugwy and the Lledr contribute their waters to those of the Conway, the one in the village itself, the other 1½ miles away, and Moel Siabod (pronounced "Shab'-od") is almost but not quite visible from it. Speaking generally, though we may wonder a little that such neighbourhoods as those of Dolgelley, Borrowdale, Patterdale, and the Brathay have not had their charms equally recognised by the brethren of the brush, we must all admit that the title Paradise of Wales may fairly be given to Bettws-y-Coed. It is a lovely spot, and the scenery by which it is surrounded is, of its kind, the best, though, strange to say, from the village itself there is not a single mountain visible. Bettws-y-Coed occupies the same position in Wales as Dunkeld does in Scotland, and Matlock in the Peak District. All around is richness to profusion, waving wood and beetling precipice, but of the wild or grand there is absolutely nothing.

At the same time, though it cannot be described as a centre, Bettws-y-Coed is an excellent head-quarters from which to visit a great deal of the finest scenery of North Wales. There is a considerable variety of delightful short walks, and you may avail yourself of rail or coach to visit the inmost recesses of Snowdonia between breakfast and sunset.

The village itself lies in a green and luxuriant recess on the south bank of the Llugwy, a little above and to the south-west of the junction of that stream with the Conway. Between the valleys thus formed rise precipitous hills, wooded from head to foot, except where sheer faces of rock overhang the scene. The great Holyhead road runs through the village, entering it from the Conway valley on the south and leaving it by the Llugwy valley to the west. A long half-mile in the former direction it crosses the Conway river by the **Waterloo Bridge,** so named from its having been built in the year of that battle. It is a latticed iron structure with a single arch. Much more ancient and picturesque is the bridge over the Llugwy in the village itself. It is called **Pont-y-Pair,** and over it goes the nearest way to Llanrwst. The broken course of the stream below adds much to the effect of the scene. Another old bridge—in reality a ladder by which the rock on the far side of the stream is reached—is called the **Miner's Bridge,** and is situated nearly a mile up the Llugwy, in a part where the stream pursues a romantic course over a rough bed of rock and boulder.

The *Old Church* of Bettws-y-Coed is in a yew-shaded enclosure near the station, but it is now only used as a cemetery. Its successor, built on somewhat heavy Norman lines, is on the south of the road in the village. The old building contains the recumbent effigy of Gruffydd, nephew of the great Llewelyn.

Short Excursions from Bettws-y-Coed.

The lovers of silvan river-scenery—on a small scale, but thoroughly beautiful—will find much to delight them on both the Conway and the Llugwy, while the natural craving to find out what is to be seen from a place as well as at it, will be satisfied by a visit to the hill above Capel Garmon, a little village on the hills, 1½ miles south-west of Bettws-y-Coed.

(1) **Fairy Glen, Conway Falls, &c.**--The favourite stroll from Bettws-y-Coed is to the Fairy Glen, 1½ miles distant, but the walk may with great advantage be extended so as to cover 7 or 8 miles out and in, and thus be made to include the best parts of the Conway and Machno streams. Regarded simply as falls, none of those seen on this route are in any way extraordinary, but the ravine in which they occur is very beautiful.

The Route. Cross the Waterloo Bridge, half-a-mile south of the village, and a few yards further take the right hand, or Lledr Valley road, keeping along it. with the river and railway on the right, till you come to a bridge over the former. Do not cross, but take a rough lane on the left, entered by a wooden step-stile. You travel along this lane for a few hundred yards. A notice-board, opposite a cottage on the left, states that the key to *Ffos Noddyn*—better known as the **Fairy Glen**—is kept there, and the attendant is usually on the look-out. A little further, a wicket-gate on the right admits to a path which descends through a second gate, followed by some rude steps, to the north end of the glen—the only point from which a satisfactory view up it can be obtained. On the scale which its name suggests—for all fairies seem to have been sma' folk,—the scene is an exceedingly pretty one. The stream forms a succession of cascades and pools, overhung by sheer rocks of no great height, but pleasantly shaded by dwarf-oak, ash, and other trees. There is no path alongside the water.

Re-entering the road through the gate by which you left it, you turn to the right and proceed upwards to a cottage, beyond which the road becomes a green cart-track. Above, on the left, is the main Corwen road, and looking back. a splendid view of Moel Siabod is obtained, with the two Lliwedd peaks of Snowdon on its left and Glyder-fach and the triple-crested Tryfan on the right. A little short of the point at which the main road is entered a path descends to the river-side on the right, and in a few yards reaches the **Conway Falls**. The cliffs hereabouts are higher, and the scene is altogether more imposing than at the Fairy Glen. The falls are not more than 50 feet in height and do not make a sheer leap. Between them is a salmon ladder which, to speak impartially, would be accounted a great dis-figurement if its object were commerce and not sport. A little higher up, the Conway and **Machno** unite their waters in a bold and abrupt gorge.

It it necessary to return to the main path, progress alongside of the stream being effectually stopped by the deep chasm of the Conway. Then, entering the main road, you turn down the Penmachno road in about 175 yards, and, crossing the bridge over the Conway gorge, reach, in half-a-mile, the old toll-gate of *Pant Bridge*. The gate is abolished, but the enterprising *janitor* announces himself as guide to the "grandest waterfall, the most surprising ruins and sceneries in Wales." He also affords "accommodation to drink" a variety of non-intoxicants. The "sceneries" lie on your return route, which is commenced by crossing the bridge.

To Penmachno and Ffestiniog, 13—14 m.

The **Village of Penmachno** (*country inns*) is nearly 2 miles higher up the valley (4½ m. from Bettws). It is a quiet little place amid scenery of no great account. Beyond it the road continues alongside the Machno stream for 2 miles, after which it follows the course of a tributary, and passes about a mile to the right of *Llyn Conway*, the source of the Conway river. Then it joins a road from Pentrevoelas, and a little further strikes into the Bala and Ffestiniog road, 3½ miles short of the latter village and just above the deep

defile called *Rhaiadr-cwm*. Near the junction there is, or was, a small roadside
inn. The full distance from Bettws-y-Coed to Ffestiniog is from 13 to 14 miles.
The road is one of the many which have been left desolate since railways were
brought into the neighbourhood, and, except to those who like desolation for its
own sake, offers little attraction. The front view, however, during the descent
to Ffestiniog is fine, the Moelwyn group appearing to great advantage.

From the bridge there is a view up the troubled boulder-strewn
course of the stream to *Moel Pen-y-bryn*, a bulky height overlooking
Penmachno. The arch of an older bridge is seen below. Then,
turning down the left bank of the stream, we proceed by a
delightful cart-track, which passes, in a few hundred yards,
Pandy Mill, much patronised by the artistic fraternity.
Immediately below it are the picturesque Machno Falls, higher
than those of the Conway, and more confined. Beyond this,
we proceed through a wood only separated by a strip of verdure
from the deep chasm of the stream and, reaching a fork of the
road just beyond a row of cottages, descend by the right-hand
branch to the Lledr stream, which is crossed by a bridge leading
to the Bettws and Dolwyddelen road. From the junction, a high
rock, high up on the left, presents a striking human profile.
You may liken it to William the Third, or the Duke of Wellington, or any other man whose nose has been an index to his
character. Your grandchildren will probably call it, in no uncom-
plimentary spirit, William Gladstone—that is, if it has not been
smoothed down into a slate-quarry by their time—and no part of
North Wales is making more rapid advances in that direction
than the fairy-haunted Lledr valley.

In returning to Bettws you need not cross the bridge which
you passed on your way out a little short of the Fairy Glen, but
you may continue along the left side of the river, going underneath the railway, and entering the main road ¾ *m.* short of the
station.

(2) **The Miner's Bridge**, 1 *m*; and **Swallow Falls**, 2½ *m*.

Both these charming scenes lie a few yards to the right of the
main (Holyhead) road. The former is reached by a foot-path
which leaves the road just opposite to it, but you may pass
through the wall some way short of it and follow a path through
the trees and above the water. **The Miner's Bridge** is a step-
ladder which leads down from the top of a rock on one side of the
stream to one only just above the surface of the water on the
other side. The scene owes its natural picturesqueness to the
river itself, which all the way from the Swallow Falls has its bed
strewn with rocks and boulders, and its steep banks beautifully
fringed with trees.

Return to Bettws. Crossing the bridge you may ascend by a foot-path,
through the wood and enter the narrow road which reaches the village again
at *Pont-y-Pair* in less than a mile.

Rejoining the road, which hereabouts is well shaded, we reach in 1¼ miles the **Swallow Falls** ("Rhaiadr-y-Wennol") opposite to which is a good inn, the *Swallow Falls Hotel*.

These celebrated falls are, partly owing to their accessibility, more visited than any in Wales, and perhaps the Devil's Bridge and the remote Pistyll Rhaiadr afford the only superior scenes of the kind. There is a good rush of water, forming several cataracts, of which the middle one makes the cleanest leap. The one above it is rather a row of silver streaks hurrying down a steep slope of broken and splintered rock, and of the lowest one it is difficult to get a good view. Walks lead to the top of the highest and to the foot of the middle fall. The dell below is finely wooded and the stream flows between sheer cliffs. High up on the opposite side is an old summer-house now falling into decay.

(3) **Capel Garmon**, 2 *m*; the **Cromlech**, 3 *m*; **Bettws-y-Coed**, 6½ *m*. This is a grand walk in respect of the views which it commands, apart from the interest attached to the Cromlech. Most of the view may be obtained by merely ascending Gallt-y-foel (1 *to* 1½ *hrs. up and down*), but the entire round is to be strongly recommended.

The road to Capel Garmon crosses the Waterloo Bridge and then makes a very sharp angle to the left to break the steepness of the hill. Pedestrians, however, may ascend the hill direct by a foot-path commencing with some steps a few yards to the right after crossing the bridge. This path joins the road at the bend above, and from about here the top of **Gallt-y-Foel** (800 *ft.*) may be reached in about 20 minutes. The view comprises the valley of the Conway downwards as far as Llanrwst, and by going west as far as a wall above a wood, you will add Bettws itself and the rich valley of the Llugwy above it. Otherwise, the prospect is mainly the same as that described a little further on.

From the junction of the foot-path with the road the latter goes straight on for nearly ¾ mile and then turns up to the right to the village of **Capel Garmon** (*country inn*). There is nothing to be noted here, but in the next half-mile along the same road we have as fine a panoramic view of the Carnarvonshire range as can be imagined. The only point missed is Snowdon itself, which is hidden by Siabod—the mountain *par excellence* of this neighbourhood. To the right of Siabod are Glyder-fach, the triple-peaked Tryfan, Carnedd Dafydd and Carnedd Llewelyn—the last named the highest summit of a long waving line which stretches northwards almost to Conway Bay. East of Siabod the conical peak of Yr Aran—part of Snowdon—is seen, and as we proceed, the double crest of Lliwedd—another part of Snowdon—comes into view. The richly-wooded Llugwy valley, above Bettws, forms a striking contrast to the wildness beyond.

The point at which to turn off for the Cromlech is two-thirds of a mile beyond Capel Garmon, just after losing sight of the village for the second time. Passing through a gate on the right we

enter a cart-track, which leads past *Tyn-y-Coed* farm to the
Cromlech, which is in a square-walled enclosure, containing dwarf
oak, in a stony field beyond. It lies in a trench and is scarcely
visible till you are close upon it. A flat stone, four or five yards
square, rests on about half-a-dozen supporting stones, and there
is an open chamber, 7 yards long, on the north side.

From the cromlech cross a stone stile just south of the enclosure.
Proceed along the footpath to a second stone stile. Do not cross
this but follow the wall a few yards to the right and cross another
low stone stile. Then go down hill bearing to the right. In
50 yards, at a gateway on the right, a defined path descends
through the scanty woodland to another stile, whence turn left
(*i.e.*, south) and go through a gateway as though aiming for Penmachno, clearly seen at the foot of the grassy Pen-y-bryn. In a
few minutes you will cross a stile and enter a cart-road a little to
the right of a farm. This track enters the main (Corwen) road
close to a milestone, 2¼ miles from Bettws, and opposite the divergence of the Penmachno road. From it the peak of Snowdon is just
visible over the western slope of Moel Siabod. The return hence
to Bettws along the high-road commands a fine view up the Lledr
valley; or, by taking a path on the left in about 175 yards, you
may include the Conway Falls and the Fairy Glen in the excursion.

(4) **Llyn Elsi** (2 *m.*) occupies a slight hollow on a broken
heathery plateau south-west of the village. The lake itself has
no special attraction, but the bluff overlooking it (where the track
ends) is a pleasant breezy spot for a pic-nic. The mountain view
is extensive, and, of its kind, remarkably good.

Starting * by either of the two lanes which meet behind the
new church, you ascend steeply, with fine, wooded cliffs towering
above on the right, and the Llanrwst valley below. The track is
rough, but there are plenty of seats whence to enjoy the view. At a
direction stone, "to Elsie Lake," we turn to the right, and then have
only to keep to the track thus entered on. When it reaches the
open ground, beyond a deserted farmstead, it is defined by a ditch
on either side. The lake, nearly half-a-mile long, is of irregular
outline, and its surface is broken by an islet or two.

Moel Siabod, rising due west, stands out almost without a rival,
as seen from about here. Snowdon lies exactly behind it. To the
right are the Glyders, Tryfan and the Carnedds, and to the left
the Moelwyn group beyond Ffestiniog. Due south Arenig-fawr
rises above everything around it.

The return may be varied by skirting the lake to its north end
and thence descending by the side of the stream which issues from
it, passing a slate-quarry and thence following a track down to the
main (Bangor) road, which is entered half-a-mile west of Bettws.

---

* A footpath from the other end of the village, a little short of the Waterloo
Hotel, joins the above route.

(5) **To Llanrwst by Llyn-y-parc,** *abt. 6 m. Described the reverse way,* p. 116.

Every sojourner at Bettws-y-Coed, whether he goes the whole of this route or not, should wander up on to the hills over which the first portion of it lies, the moorland, to wit, extending behind the wooded cliffs that beetle over the village on the north.

Cross the river by *Pont-y-Pair,* and turn up the lane to the left. In half-a-mile this lane passes the old vicarage on the left, and a few yards further a very fair but little-used road strikes up the hollow on the right, through a plantation. Following this road upwards and bending with it to the right, you will soon come to the farm called *Pen 'r Allt.* The view from all the eminences of the high ground about here is very fine. Westward, Moel Siabod and the Tryfan, with its three little humps, present very bold outlines, and between them are the Glyders and Snowdon. To the left of Moel Siabod the Moelwyn group is seen, and due south Arenig.

About a mile to the north-west of this point a flagstaff is conspicuous on the top of a somewhat higher hill. By strolling to it you will get a nearer and still finer view of the mountains.

At Pen-'r-Allt turn sharp to the left, and then keep along the new road (or a little above it on the right) till it comes to an unexpected end at a wall, the reason being, we are told, that the mining speculation, for the purposes of which it was constructed, met with a similar fate. There is, however, a stile a little way to the right, and from it the path continues over another stile to the foot of **Llyn-y-parc** (*p.* 116), whence the route, passing to the right of the lake and gradually climbing to a considerable height above it, cannot well be missed, though it may be varied by taking one which goes to the very top of the hill. The direct route passes through a gate beyond the end of the lake, and then descends a woody and narrow hollow, called *Nant Gwydir,* at the foot of which it joins the hill-road from Capel Curig, a few yards short of the *Forester's Cottage.* From this point you drop directly to *Llanrwst,* or enter the wood by a gate on the right opposite the cottage and reach your destination by *Gwydir Chapel* (p. 110).

(6) **To the old Summer-house** (over the Swallow Falls), **3 m; Ty-Hill Bridge, 4** *m;* **Bettws-y-Coed, 7** *m.* This round is hardly so interesting a one as those we have already described, but in fairly dry weather it is very enjoyable.

Cross Pont-y-Pair and proceed as in the Llyn-y-parc route, last described, but instead of turning to the right near the old vicarage (here a path drops through the wood to the Miner's Bridge) keep straight on. Larch plantations succeed, and a view of a very pretty reach of the Llugwy, above the Miner's Bridge, is obtained.

Presently the lane zigzags up to the right away from the river. The summer-house is seen straight ahead, but to get there it is best to continue up the lane past the farm of *Pen-craig*, and then to turn to the left near a shed, and cross a field by a path which leads into the wood through a gate at the corner of a wall. Hence there is a wood-path to the *Summer-house*. The view is very attractive, but the trees below only allow one side, if that, of the Swallow Falls to be seen.

The only orthodox route back is the one you came by, as far as the shed, near which, turning to the left, you enter at once the hill-road from Llanrwst to Capel Curig by Ty-Hill Bridge (*p.* 114). A short cut may be made into this road from the summer-house at your discretion. The road drops through a pleasant wood to the bridge, whence the return is by the main road past the Swallow Falls to *Bettws-y-Coed*.

Bettws-y-Coed to Llanrwst and Conway by rail.

Llanrwst, 4 *m*; *Tal-y-cafn,* 9½ *m*; *Glan Conway,* 14 *m*; *Llandudno Junction,* 15 *m*; *Conway,* 16 *m.*

We have described this route in detail the reverse way on page 105, and shall, therefore, be very brief here. Besides the rail there are two roads from Bettws-y-Coed to Conway: one along the east side of the valley, passing over the Waterloo Bridge and through Llanrwst, 17 miles in length; the other, along the west side, leaving Llanrwst a short half-mile on the right and passing Trefriw. The length of this route is 15 miles. From Trefriw a steamer goes once or twice a day to Conway and Deganwy, according to tide. The western road passes through the best scenery, but the eastern one commands the best views. The description of the railway route, which passes between them, will suffice for both.

The Route. Quitting Bettws-y-Coed, the line affords a view up a tract of the Llugwy valley, and of Moel Siabod beyond it. Then it passes close under the richly-wooded cliffs of *Carreg-y-gwalch* on the left, and, after crossing the river, allows a prospect of the grounds of Gwydir Castle, and a peep at Llanrwst Bridge and Church before entering a tunnel and cutting, which cause the town to be passed unseen. (*For Llanrwst, see p.* 109). The station is half-a-mile beyond it.

We have now reached the east side of the valley and, looking out on the left, we get a charming view of *Trefriw* standing at the entrance to the graceful curve of the Crafnant valley. A mile or so further, we may note a mine just above the place at which the Trefriw waters are drunk. Trickling down the hill-side, and further north, in quick succession, the beautiful falls of *Dolgarrog* and *Porthlwyd* descend in broken cascades from the upland vales above. Then, as the hills retire and become less wooded, the mountains come into view behind them. The green round height, not more than two miles away, is Pen-y-gaer, and further away are seen Tal-y-fan, Y Foel Fras, a strip of Carnedd Llewelyn, and Penllithrig, the last-named marked by a steep southward and gradual northward slope.

The *Church of Caerhun*, standing in a verdant little enclosure on the far side of the stream, on the site of the Roman *Conovium*, is a very attractive object as we approach *Tal-y-Cafn Station* and *Ferry*. Beyond these the river widens out into an estuary and the line follows its windings, very soon affording a view of the Castle and Bridges of Conway at the north end of the woody knoll of Benarth. *Glan Conway* is passed, and in another mile we join the main Chester and Holyhead line at *Llandudno Junction*. Thence, passing through the " Tubular " and under the walls of the Castle, we enter Conway Station.

For Conway Town, see p. 55.

Bettws-y-Coed to Pentre Voelas, 6½ *m*; **Cerrig-y-Druidion,** 12 *m*; **and Corwen,** 22 *m*.

Route more fully described the reverse way in " Part II."

This road, part of the great Holyhead one, is of great interest till the summit-level is reached a little short of Pentre Voelas. After that, except to cyclists, for whom the whole distance from Pentre Voelas to Corwen is as good going as could be wished for, there is nothing above the standard of ordinary scenery—and a good deal below it—except a charming river-bit at *Pont-y-Glyn*, all the way.

The Route. After crossing Waterloo Bridge (½ *m*.) the road commences a long ascent, and affords a lovely view up the *Lledr Valley*, the graceful peak of Moel Siabod occupying the place of honour in the middle distance. Immediately below, a mile beyond the bridge, is the *Fairy Glen*, and a mile further the *Conway Falls*. To the right of Siabod appear the Glyders, and over its left slope two peaks represent Snowdon. A little further, and the sharp point of the Tryfan is seen to the right of the Glyders, and as we rise still higher, the smoother outlines of Carnedd Dafydd and Carnedd Llewelyn appear still more to the right. All this time our road is above the Conway stream, falling into which a very pretty tributary may be noticed a little more than 4 miles on our way. From the brow a little short of *Pentre Voelas*, Snowdon again displays two peaks to the left of Siabod.

Beyond remarking that there are good inns at *Pentre Voelas* (Voelas Arms, H.Q.) and *Cerrig-y-Druidion* (White Lion, H.Q.), and that *Pont-y-Glyn* is 6 miles short of Corwen, we shall not repeat our description of this route given in our " Second Part." The central point is *Cernioge*, a farm-house which the milestones show to have once been more important. The inn, however, has ceased to exist for many a long year, except on the maps, where, by the way, no mention is made of those at Pentre Voelas and Cerrig-y-Druidion.

Bettws-y-Coed to Blaenau Ffestiniog.

Pont-y-pant, 4 m; Dolwyddelen, 5½ m; Roman Bridge, 7½ m; Blaenau Ffestiniog, 12½ m.

The first part of this route is the finest. Slate-quarries are being developed in the upper region of the Lledr valley to an extent which threatens to entirely destroy its picturesqueness. The railway route follows so nearly the road one that a separate description of the latter is superfluous. The only material difference is that where the railway goes through a tunnel more than 2 miles long, between Roman Bridge and Ffestiniog, the road passes over the hill. There is nothing, however, calling for special comment during this part of the journey. We advise tourists who have already visited the **Fairy Glen** scenery, to go by rail to Pont-y-pant, and walk thence to Dolwyddelen rather than foot it all the way.

The Route.—Quitting Bettws-y-Coed, the line goes due south for 1½ miles under steep wooded slopes on the right and with the river and road on the left. Then, opposite the confluence of the Lledr with the Conway, and within a very short distance of the Fairy Glen, the depths of which, however, are hidden by trees, it turns sharply to the right up the valley of the former stream. The **Lledr Valley**, though, with the exception of Moel Siabod, the height of its flanking hills seldom attains four figures, is eminently picturesque. The rocky character of its surface, the eccentricities of its stream, and the rich colouring which it shows have made it the delight of the artist, but it has, of late years, been sadly cut up by quarries, and the position of the viaduct by which the railway crosses the road and the stream about a mile up it, is unfortunate, the valley being thoroughly blocked, as it were, for scenery. It is, however, the traveller by road and not by rail that suffers. For the latter, as soon as the screen is crossed, there is a glorious view of the finest side of Moel Siabod on the right, and in about 2 miles we reach *Pont-y-pant*, where is a conveniently-placed tourist inn in the midst of very characteristic scenery. Then, after passing through a short tunnel, the peak of Snowdon comes into view, and, a little further, we reach **Dolwyddelen**, whence is the best ascent of Moel Siabod.

Dolwyddelen (*Post arr. abt. 7 a.m.; dep., 7.30 p.m.*) is a half tourists', half quarryman's village, with three fair-sized inns (*Bexar View Hotel, Elen's Castle Hotel,* and the *Gwydir Arms*), which cater for the tourist, and are ¼ to ½ mile from the station. The only artificial object of any interest is the *Castle,* a mile up the valley on a knoll close to the road. It now consists of but a single square tower, quite devoid of architectural beauty, but the spot commands a good view down the valley.

Dolwyddelen to Pen-y-gwryd. *Pedestrian route.* 7½ *m.*

The most remunerative route between these points is over Moel Siabod, and is described in our "Mountain Section." For those who prefer an easier route, or who are hampered by fog on the higher summits, there is an easily found way across the lower spurs of that mountain and over Bwlch-chediad to the Gwynant valley. The views on the way, under such conditions, are not of the highest order, but there is always the chance of the weather clearing after a start has been made, and in that case, without serious increase of distance or fatigue, Siabod can be made for. The alternative route by Llyniau-duwaunedd (twin lakelets of no particular merit), and over Bwlch Rhiw-r-ychain is shorter, but more fatiguing. We describe both.

Route. Half-a-mile west of Dolwyddelen turn to the right by the road that leads up to the Castle and passes it on the left. A mile further a farm called *Ffridd* is reached. Here take a rough cart-track to the right. This crosses the stream in half-a-mile. From the crossing (*a*) the *Bwlch-chediad* route ascends by an intermittent path almost due west, with the steep ridge of *Cribiau* on the right-hand and a boggy valley on the left. The *Bwlch* is reached in 1¼ miles. From it and during the descent on the other side there is a grand view of Snowdon with Yr Aran and Moel Hebog on the left and the Glyders on the right of it. A sharp descent of half-a-mile brings us into the main road a little above Llyn Gwynant. *Pen-y-gwryd* is a good two miles to the right, and *Beddgelert* six miles to the left. (*b*) For *Bwlch Rhiw-r-ychain* continue up the valley and skirt the north side of the two lakes above mentioned. Beyond them there is a sharp ascent by the stream-side to the Bwlch (1,800 ft.) ; when this is gained Snowdon rises proudly in front and the pass of Llanberis is seen to the right of it. Descend in the direction of the latter. The Capel Curig lakes appear on the right, and a lovely peep of Llyn-y-Ddinas with Moel Hebog behind it on the left. Keeping over the higher ground you will strike the Beddgelert road about 150 yards west of the Pen-y-gwryd Hotel.

Southward from Dolwyddelen Station runs a narrow trough-shaped cwm and up it the old Roman road, *Sarn Helen,* upon which we shall light more than once in our travels. Then, as we proceed Ffestiniog way, *Dolwyddelen Castle,* a simple square tower, is conspicuous half-a-mile to the right, and a fine view of the peaks of Snowdon is obtained across a neck of low and barren ground. All this time Siabod is in full view on the right. At the next station, **Roman Bridge** *—so called, presumably, from a vague idea that the Romans, having left a road behind them in the neighbourhood, might also fairly be credited with a bridge—the rail and road part company. The road makes directly over the hill for Ffestiniog, and the railway, after following up the valley for another 1½ miles, turns sharp to the left and plunges into the bowels of the earth, from which it only emerges at the far end of the colossal slate-heaps of Blaenau Ffestiniog. The *London and North Western Hotel* is close to the station. The narrow-gauge station for Portmadoc is side by side with the L. and N. W. station, and that for Ffestiniog village and Bala nearly half-a-mile distant, close to the *Victoria Hotel.*

---

* The bridge (called Pont-y-saruddi in Ordnance) is wholly modern and was nearly rebuilt in 1883.

Bettws-y-Coed to Bangor, Llanberis and Beddgelert.

Bettws-y-Coed to Capel Curig, 5½ m; Nant Ffrancon (Benglog), 11 m; Bethesda, 15 m; Bangor (by rail), 20 m; (by road), 20½ m.

Capel Curig to Pen-y-gwryd, 4 m; (Beddgelert 12 m.); Llanberis Station, 10½ m.

Routes described the reverse way, pp. 99, 139.

These are the chief coach-routes through the highlands of Wales. During the season, coaches run from Bettws-y-Coed daily to Bangor, to Llanberis, and through Beddgelert to Portmadoc. Additional ones to Capel Curig only. **Average** Fares: Capel Curig, 2s.; Pen-y-gwryd, 3s.; Llanberis, 4s.; Beddgelert, 5s.; Portmadoc, 7s. 6d.; Bangor, 6s. *Return, about half as much again.* **Time**: *to Llanberis, abt.* 3½ *hrs.; Beddgelert,* 3½ *hrs.; Portmadoc,* 5 *hrs.; Bangor,* 3½ *hrs.*

Circular tickets are also issued by all these routes from the principal stations on the Chester and Holyhead line and its branches. Particulars will be found in the *North Wales Tourist Guide* issued annually by the L. & N. W. Company.

The scenery during the greater part of these three routes is of a very high order, and it is difficult to assign to any one of the three the pre-eminence. We may say, however, that the Bangor one is better taken the reverse way, inasmuch as Nant Ffrancon appears to much greater advantage when entered from its lower than from its upper end, whereas the descent of the Pass of Llanberis is as fine as the ascent, if not finer. The roads are good—that to Bangor too good for pedestrians, who, in hot or dry weather especially, may be excused a feeling of irritation at the scrupulous care with which, except on the wildest part between Capel Curig and Nant Ffrancon, the entire width of it is kept clear of the slightest border of grass, and the enclosing walls maintained in repair as perfect as it is unpicturesque.

The Route. Quitting Bettws we at once begin to ascend the sweetly wooded Llugwy glen the river chafing and fretting down its rocky channel on the right hand. *The Miner's Bridge* (p. 121) passed, we reach, in 2¼ miles, the **Swallow Falls** ("Rhaiadr-y-Wennol"), opposite to which is the *Swallow Falls Hotel. (For a description of the Falls see p.* 122). Hereabouts, the road bends somewhat to the left and brings us in view of the finely-pointed *Moel Siabod* (pronounced "Shab'-od"), with the peaks of Snowdon peering over its long northern shoulder— the left-hand one is the summit. A strip of the Glyders is seen more to the right. A little further, we cross the stream by *Ty-Hyll Bridge*, on the far side of which a hill-road from Llanrwst converges. For the next mile or more the river flows through flat meadows; then, as its course turns abruptly to the right, the valley again narrows, the eastern spur of Moel Siabod assumes

Guide VIII.   K

a conical shape, and we pass on the left the rebuilt single-arched
Pont-gyfyng, under which the stream forms a succession of fine
falls, best seen from a recess in the wall below the bridge. Hereabouts, too, Carnedd Dafydd and Carnedd Llewelyn come into
view on the right front. Beyond this is the small *Tyn-y-Coed
Hotel*, and a little further the larger *Tan-y-bwlch Hotel*, not to be
confounded with the one of the same name in the Ffestiniog
valley. The river-bit, opposite the last-named inn, is very charming.

*For the ascent of Moel Siabod from Tan-y-bwlch, see "Mountain
Section."*

And now, as the road bends round again for **Capel Curig**, Snowdon appears before us in its finest aspect—a line of bold yet gracefully tapering peaks, which is certainly unrivalled in Wales, and
with which no view of the monarch of English mountains, still less
of the Scottish one, can compete. Taken from left to right, the
points are *Lliwedd* (triple-crested) *Y Wyddfa* (the summit), *Crib
goch* (in front of the rest), and *Crib-y-ddysgyl*. The intervening
space, occupied by the two tarns of Capel Curig and the valley
leading up to Pen-y-gwryd, is, it must be confessed, bare and uninteresting. (In respect of foreground, Cader Idris is far finer
than Snowdon, and the chief mountains of Scotland and the
English Lake District derive a similar advantage from the lakes
which occupy that position in regard to them). To the right of
this valley rises the range which culminates in the stony wilderness of the Glyder-fach.
   The large and old-established *Royal Hotel*, Capel Curig, is $\frac{1}{4}$ m.
away from our present route on the road to Llanberis. There is a
small house—the *Bryntyrch*—a little short of the turn for it.

For route to **Trefriw** and **Llanrwst**, by **Llyn Crafnant**, *see p.* 114.

For continuation to Llanberis and Beddgelert see p. 131.

The Bangor road now goes northwards for a little way round
the extremity of the Glyder range, and then rises to the west
through a desolate boulder-strewn valley, with the Llugwy still
on the left hand. On the right the valley is hemmed in by the
heights of Penllithrig, Carnedd Llewelyn and Carnedd Daffydd.
All of these present their most gradual slopes in this direction,
and for that reason the sudden appearance—to the south of the
valley—of one of the most remarkable mountains in Wales is all
the more impressive. This is *Y Tryfan*—the "three-peaked" hill.
It rises abrupt and isolated from a scene of great desolation to a
triple-forked summit (though from some points it shows only
double, or even single), and the hollow to the left of it is filled by
the Glyder-fach.
   The highest point on the Holyhead road is reached $3\frac{1}{2}$ miles
beyond Capel Curig, and a few yards beyond the 36th milestone
from Holyhead. The mountain mass which appears to block the
road in front consists of Y Garn and Foel-goch. On the left are

the Tryfan and the steep side of Glyder-fach; on the right Braich-du—the southern spur of Carnedd Dafydd—sends down a wild rocky slope into **Llyn Ogwen**. This desolate lake—or rather tarn—is a mile long, and beyond its environment of mountains shows nothing to attract the eye. It is very shallow. At its far end, close to a recently enlarged cottage, called *Pen-y-Benglog*—whereat artists often find a bed—the road turns abruptly to the right and enters **Nant Ffrancon**.

The rest of the route to Bangor we have preferred to describe in detail the reverse way, chiefly because it is only by being ascended from Bangor that the features of Nant Ffrancon can be at all appreciated. Taken in the direction we are now following, the rich cultivated lowland which commences at the foot of the glen presents itself as soon as ever the glen is entered, and quite counteracts the impression of solemnity created by the uncompromising sternness of the immediate surroundings. As we descend, the transition from utter wildness to rich cultivation is remarkably sudden, and before we have realised the change we are in the busy street of a quarrying village—the most important in North Wales, for on the left hand, half-a-mile short of it, are the mammoth *Penrhyn slate quarries*. The village is **Bethesda** (*p.* 100).

From Bethesda the *road* follows in turn the right and left bank of the Ogwen as far as the colossal portals of *Penrhyn Castle*, 2 miles short of Bangor. The stream threads a beautiful glen all the way.

There is a fine retrospect of mountains, including Carnedds Llewelyn and Dafydd, Glyder-fawr, Moel-perfydd, and Elidyr-fawr. On the right is the whale-back of Moel Wnion, and afterwards Penmaenmawr. Then, 1¼ miles short of Bangor Station, the road, after skirting the wall of Penrhyn Park, turns sharply to the left.

The *railway* begins on the north side of Bethesda, and runs parallel with the road for a little distance. Then it enters a tunnel, and coming out into a tributary valley, joins the main line a few yards short of the tunnel that ends at Bangor Station.

Capel Curig to Pen-y-gwryd, 4 *m*; (**Beddgelert**, 12 *m*.) **Llanberis**, 10½ *m*.

There is nothing to relieve the bare monotony of the four-mile ascent from Capel Curig to Pen-y-gwryd except the shapely outline of Snowdon in front. Siabod shows its stupid side on the left, and the Glyder range, whose green southern slope the road skirts all the way to Pen-y-gwryd, has no beauty of outline to attract the eye.

The mountain inn of **Pen-y-gwryd** (950 *ft.* above the sea) needs no praise from us. There is another inn which lays itself out for tourists a mile further on the Llanberis road, the

Corphwysfa (or "resting-place"), which some barbarian has hybridized into Pen-y-Pass.'

For Pen-y-gwryd to Dolwyddelen, see p. 140, and for the ascents of Snowdon, Moel Siabod, and the Glyders, see "Mountain Section." For Pen-y-gwryd to Llyn Ogwen, see p. 211.

From the front of the inn, just where the roads to Beddgelert and Llanberis diverge, there is a lovely view down Nant Gwynant, —one of the sweetest valley prospects in Wales. A wide strip of Llyn Gwynant washing the base of Gallt-y-Wenallt, a rocky shoulder of Snowdon, is an effective feature of it. To the left of it, beyond a lower ridge, the shoulder of Cynicht appears.

To Beddgelert. A sharp descent, during which the old road is seen below on the right, is made between Pen-y-gwryd and Llyn Gwynant. On the way the Glyders are in view behind, and the Dyli stream falling from Glaslyn and Llyn Llydaw in a deep recess of Snowdon is seen joining the Gwynant. This side of Snowdon is a grand example of rugged mountain scenery, and the green slopes beyond Llyn Gwynant. with their little plots of fir-trees, make a telling contrast.

Llyn Gwynant is a mile long and about 500 yards wide. Beyond it we look up a hollow between the razor-like Lliwedd ridge on the right and Yr Aran on the left till the towering peak of Y Wyddfa reappears. Moel Hebog, rising beyond Beddgelert, is seen in front. A mile beyond Llyn Gwynant our road crosses the Glaslyn, and less than a mile further skirts *Llyn-y-Ddinas*, smaller than Llyn Gwynant, but scarcely, if at all, inferior in beauty. Beddgelert is reached in another 2¼ miles.

From Pen-y-gwryd the Llanberis road continues upwards round *Y Foel-perfedd*, a "cub" of Glyder-fawr (and a remunerative hour's stroll up and down from the inn). Snowdon itself is seen no more all the way; but as we turn sharp to the right, *Crib-goch*, its almost inaccessible eastern spur (2,900 *feet high*), is a fine substitute, and just before we reach the top of the pass a strip of Moelwyn appears to the left of Cynicht. At the top of the **Llanberis Pass** (*abt.* 1,200 *feet*), the *Corphwysfa Hotel* is on the right, and the commencement of the track to Snowdon on the left. The pass at once assumes almost its finest aspect, but we have described it more in detail the reverse way (*p.* 139). As we descend, we have the crags of *Esgair-felyn*, an arm of Glyder-fawr, on the right and, after descending a little way, the grand rock-amphitheatre of *Cwm-glas* on the left. The stream is then crossed at *Pont-y-Gromlech*, and a few yards further the huge boulders, fancifully named the "*Cromlech*," abut on the road. Cottages and cultivation commence, and soon the broken glen widens into the strath that contains *Old Llanberis* (*roadside inn*). Then come *Llyn Peris*, with the terraces of the *Dinorwic quarries* disfiguring the green slope of Elidyr-fawr, the *Victoria Hotel*, *Dolbadarn Tower*, and **Llanberis Station**, (*For Llanberis, see* **p. 137**).

Carnarvon and Llanberis Section.

◆

Bangor to Carnarvon, *by road,* 9 *m.*

There are two roads from Bangor to Carnarvon, one by Menai Bridge Station (already described as far as that point, *p.* 88), the other passing under the railway at the Bangor Station and ascending the valley. The two meet a little short of Port Dinorwic. The former is far the more interesting, though, after leaving Menai Bridge, it passes on the wrong side of *Treborth* and *Vaenol Park,* both of which are protected from the *profanum vulgus* by the high walls which hereabouts constitute so large a part of the scenery. Good views of Snowdonia are, however, obtained in the opposite direction.

Port Dinorwic (chief inn, the " Half-way House "), is the shipping-port of the Llanberis slate-quarries, with which it is connected by a mineral line. For the rest of the way the road continues side by side with the railway, and commands a view of the less interesting end of the Menai Straits. *Carnarvon* is entered by the railway station and the Royal Hotel.

Carnarvon.

◆

Hotels: *Royal* (late *Uxbridge Arms*), in North Road, near the station; *Royal Sportsman* (H.Q.), close to the Castle, in Castle Street, both old-established first-class houses; *Castle,* in Castle Square; *Queen's* and *Prince of Wales* in Bangor Street; *Arvonia* (Temp.) Bangor Street.

Post Office : (Post-office in Castle Square). *Arr. abt.* 7 *a.m.,* 4.45 *p.m.* ; *dep.* 7.50 *a.m.,* 7.40 *p.m.*

Population : 10,237.

Distances : Llanberis, 9 *m.* Snowdon Ranger, 10½ *m* ; Rhyd-ddu, 12½ *m* ; Beddgelert, 16½ *m.* Nantlle, 8½ *m.* Treborth, (for Tubular Bridge), 6¼ *m* ; Menai (Suspension) Bridge, 7¼ *m* ; Bangor, 8¼ *m.*

Carnarvon [i.e., *Caer-yn-ar-Fon* (*Mon*), the "Fort opposite Mona" (Anglesey)], the capital of the shire, is just within the western entrance of the Menai Straits, and at the mouth of the river Seiont. It is the modern representative, but not quite on the site, of the Roman *Segontium*, and for many centuries was a post of great military and considerable mercantile importance. The scenery in its immediate neighbourhood hardly merits a stronger epithet than pretty, as the shores of the straits are here comparatively tame, the Anglesey bank being low and deficient in wood. Much of the present prosperity of the town is due to the thousands of visitors whom the summer brings to see its celebrated castle, and though the railway facilities carry many of them farther afield into the heart of the mountains at Llanberis and Beddgelert, it has a large supply of good lodgings that are eagerly sought after. The tourist who arrives by rail and wishes at once to get a general idea of the neighbourhood, will do best to make for **Twt Hill**, a rocky knob reached by a lane a few yards on the town side of the Royal Hotel, at the back of which it stands. Its height is insignificant, only 192 feet, but the panorama is complete, and includes not only the Straits up and down and a considerable part of Anglesey, but also the fine amphitheatre of mountains from Penmaenmawr, in the N.E., to the Rivals in the S.W. The town lies fully revealed below, and on its far side the many-turreted castle is well seen.

The **Castle** (*admission 4d.*) was begun in 1283 by Edward I., but owing to interruptions in the work was not finished, or rather it was left unfinished, till 1322. Architecturally it belongs to the middle period of Edward II. It was twice besieged by Owen Glyndwr without success. In the time of Henry VIII. it had become much dilapidated, and in 1540 and following years was restored. During the civil war it more than once changed hands, but was finally taken by the Parliamentary forces in 1646. The warrant for its demolition in 1660 was happily allowed to become a dead letter, and it is now well cared for by the Crown, to whom it belongs. The ground-plan is an irregular oval, and consisted of two courts now thrown into one. The main entrance is a few steps to the right from the end of Castle Street. Over the *Gateway*, between the flanking towers and under an elaborate canopy, is a statue of Edward I. (face obliterated). Notice the massive doors and the grooves for the four portcullises. Within the gates we find ourselves in what was the *Upper Quadrangle*, at the far end of which, *i.e.*, on our left, was the Queen's Entrance, now closed, as is a smaller one—a postern in the lower part of the Eagle Tower, which is at the opposite end of the castle. A reference to the plan will sufficiently explain the principal details of both courts. In justice to our readers it is only fair to say that, if they are already familiar with the best exterior views of the Castle, they will find its interior disappointing, and from the entire absence of ivy, devoid of picturesqueness. As seen from the water, or from the railway south of the town, it is exceedingly beautiful, but the inside is only a bare shell kept in excellent repair. Those who care so to do can explore the galleries that are carried along inside the walls. The *Eagle Tower*, with its graceful turrets, will, of course, be ascended, and the mean little passage-chamber, about

CARNARVON CASTLE.

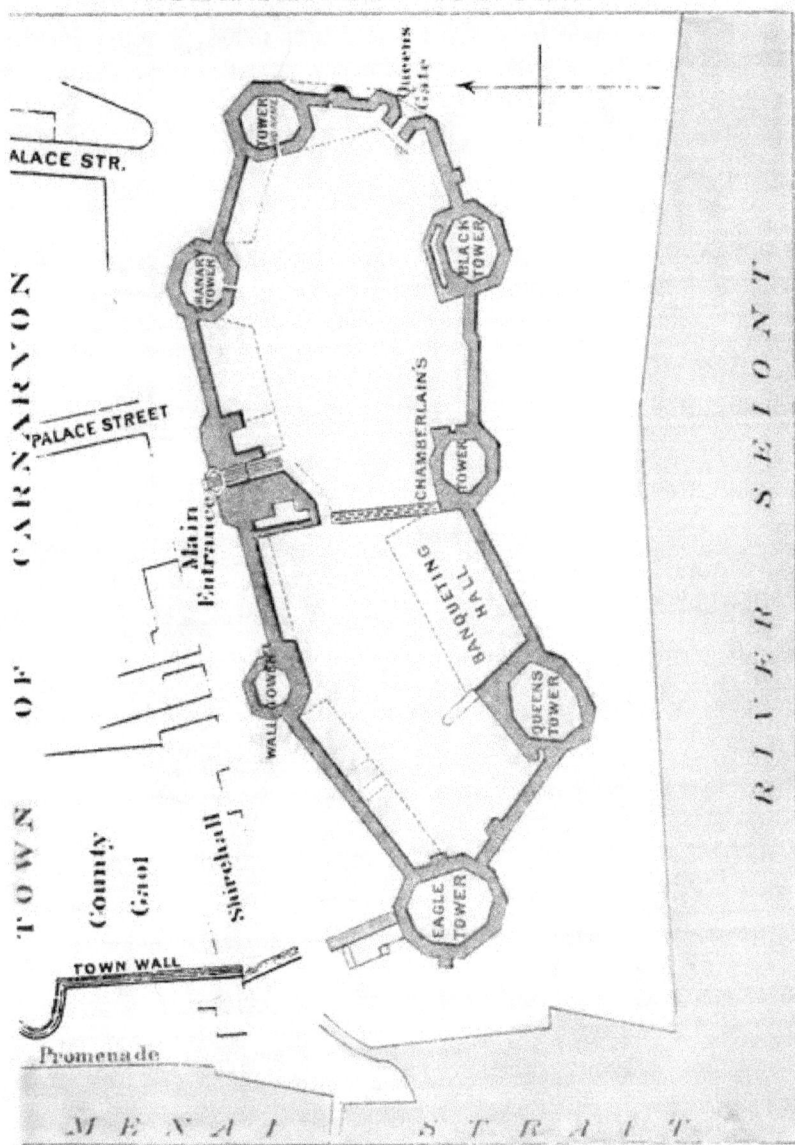

PALACE STR.

TOWN OF CARNARVON

PALACE STREET

Main Entrance

WALL TOWER

County Gaol

Shirehall

TOWN WALL

Promenade

Queens Gate

BLACK TOWER

GRANARY TOWER

CHAMBERLAIN'S TOWER

BANQUETING HALL

QUEENS TOWER

EAGLE TOWER

RIVER SEIONT

MENAI STRAIT.

John Bartholomew & Co. Edin.

12 ft. by 8 ft. that it contains, will be examined on account of its traditional connection with the birth of the first Prince of Wales of English blood, who, however, had already been king for 9 years before the tower was roofed in! There is a fine view of Snowdonia.

On leaving the Castle the circuit of the **Town Walls**, which also date from Edward I., is worth making, and this may best be done by turning to the right so as to pass round the Castle along its river-front. On the Quay are endless rows of slates from the Llanberis quarries, and then, after passing the Eagle Tower, we reach a *Promenade* running below the western wall of the town, the towers and top of which have been variously appropriated by the townsfolk. Close to the north-west angle notice the *Town Church*, or *St. Mary's*, built partly through the wall. Continuing still outside the walls, which now turn eastward, many towers are passed, and, if so disposed, we can make our way round to the point whence we started.

Castle Square has a picturesque appearance, and on the occasion of the cattle-fairs is a busy scene.

Carnarvon is not itself a parish, but belongs to *Llanbeblig*, whose church is half a mile south-east along the road to Beddgelert, on the site of *Segontium*, of which but slight fragments remain above ground.

There is a modern church (English) near Carnarvon Station.

Carnarvon to Llanberis, Bettws-y-Coed, &c.

Carnarvon to Llanberis (rail), 9 m ; *Pen-y-gwryd (road)* 15½ m ; (*Beddgelert,* 23½ m.) *Capel Curig,* 19½ m ; *Bettws-y-Coed,* 25 m.

Route described the reverse way, p. 129.

This route, whether it be followed direct to Bettws-y-Coed, or the branch taken from Pen-y-gwryd to Beddgelert, introduces the tourist to the heart of Snowdonia. The interesting part commences at Llanberis, and scarcely flags all the rest of the way. Coaches in connection with morning trains run daily from Llanberis both to Bettws-y-Coed and to Beddgelert. *Time:—Llanberis to Bettws-y-Coed, about* 3¼ *hrs.; to Beddgelert, about* 2¼ *hrs. Fares : Llanberis to Bettws-y-Coed, abt.* 4s. ; *to Beddgelert, abt.* 4s. Holders of circular tickets proceed from Bettws-y-Coed by train. Passengers to Beddgelert may proceed almost at once to Portmadoc, or they may return to Carnarvon either by the way they came, or by taking 'bus to Rhyd-ddu Station (4 m.), and there joining the North Wales narrow-gauge line to Dinas and Carnarvon.

The Route.—Quitting the town we look back on the right hand over the masts on the Seiont river to the castle, which from this point displays its many turrets to great advantage. The Seiont comes down from Llanberis, and is accompanied at a greater or

less distance by the railway during the whole of its course. Its
lower part—the first mile or two of our journey—forms a pretty
glen crossed by the line seven times. and not unlike the glen of
Southey's Greta, just above Keswick. Then, after passing *Pont Rug
Station* (3½ *m.*), we come on to a ragged-looking, poorly cultivated
country. with little to arrest the eye until the foot of the Lower
Llanberis lake—*Llyn Padarn*—is reached, a little beyond *Cwm-y-
glo* Station.   The peak of Snowdon. never very striking from this
side, is intermittently visible on the right hand, but Carnedd
Dafydd and the broken ridge of Elidyr-fawr are more prominent.

Llyn Padarn never ranked high among lakes, even in Wales.
for scenery, and it is now utterly ruined by quarries.   It is 2 miles
long, and the railway skirts or makes short cuts over the whole
length of its south-west side, affording a view of the high and
humpy Elidyr-fach on its far side, and of Dolbadarn Castle and
the entrance to the Pass of Llanberis some distance beyond its far
end, close to which is **Llanberis station**, the terminus of the
railway.

For continuation of main route, see page 139.

Llanberis.

Hotels: *Victoria*, 300 yards south of the Station; *Padarn Villa, Dolbadarn* (H.Q.), close to the Station; *Castle, Snowdon Valley*, in the village a little further away.

Post: *Arr. abt.* 8 *a.m.; dep.* 5.40 *p.m.*

As the starting-point for the easiest ascent of Snowdon and many other excursions *modern Llanberis* enjoys a reputation exceeding its intrinsic merits. *Old Llanberis* is much more picturesque, but it is 2 miles away, on the level strath at the foot of the pass. The new village extends for about half-a-mile north of the station, in a line with the margin of Llyn Padarn. The *Victoria* is considerably the most important hotel, and is well placed on rough and rising ground at the foot of the smaller lake, Llyn Peris, and close to Dolbadarn Castle. The others, though smaller, will commend themselves to tourists both in charges and accommodation. The staple industry of the place is slate-quarrying, on a scale second only to that of Bethesda. The two objects to be visited close at hand are Dolbadarn Castle and the Waterfall. The rest is coaching or mountaineering.

Dolbadarn Castle.—This solitary tower is just above the Victoria Hotel, and may be reached from the grounds of that house, or by a bridge from the road which crosses the stream that connects the two lakes or, again, from the main road to the pass a few hundred yards beyond the hotel. The present building is probably not many centuries old, but the site is historic, for it was held, we are told, in the sixth century by Maelgwyn Gwynedd, Prince of North Wales. In the castle of that date Llewelyn-ap-Iorwerth kept his rebellious brother, Owen Goch, a prisoner for twenty years or more, and in the time of Edward I. it was defended by Dafydd, brother of the great Llewelyn, against the attack of the Earl of Pembroke. A flight of stone steps leads some way up on to a platform that goes round it. The view from it up the Pass of Llanberis is complete and compact, and but for the huge Dinorwic quarries, whose *débris* threatens in time to choke up the lake altogether, Llyn Peris would be a very charming foreground.

If bound for the Pass you can make a short cut into the road without returning either to the village or the " Victoria."

The **Waterfall** (*Ceunant-mawr*, the " big ravine ") is reached by taking the lane to the right after crossing the stream south of the station, a little short of the Victoria Hotel (or by passing the church from the Dolbadarn). In 300 yards re-cross the stream by a bridge, and a little way further turn to the left round a pair of new cottages up a path which leads to the foot of the fall. The water makes a twist as it comes down the slanting face of a rock, and is only effective after heavy rain, and even then it is too exposed to rank high among scenes of the kind. From the foot you may reach the top by a steep pitch on the right of the stream.

A handsome church has recently been erected at Llanberis.

Llanberis to Bethesda, 8 m.   *Route described the reverse way, p.* 101. There are extensive views from the high ground between Llanberis and Bethesda, but few tourists will take a walk so beset with quarries at both ends for its own sake. The way is over the bridge between the two lakes, and then to the left, commencing the ascent almost at once, and passing through a wood. During the first 8 minutes of every hour blasting goes on at the quarries, and during that time the road is kept clear. The first and most intricate part of the route is described in the ascent of Elidyr-fawr (*see* " *Mountain Section* "), but instead of turning to the right up Elidyr-fach, after entering the main road you keep pretty straight on over a dreary moor with a cheerless reservoir in the middle, and the low heights of *Drysgol-fawr* and *Moel-y-ci* on the left, and the Carnedds Dafydd and Llewelyn rising finely in front. Afterwards the prospect northwards includes Beaumaris and the Straits. Then you go by *St. Ann's Chapel* (new with a steeple), and down to the *Ogwen* river, which is crossed by the bridge that connects the quarries with the main Holyhead road and Bethesda. *For Bethesda, see* p. 100.

Llanberis to Snowdon Ranger, 4 m. 1½ hrs. This is an easy and fairly interesting walk. The summit of the route is at Bwlch-y-maes-cwm, some 1,100 feet above sea-level, and there is a well-defined bridle-track all the way. The start may be made either by proceeding to Llanberis Waterfall (*see above*), or by the lane leaving the village nearly opposite the *Padarn Villa Hotel*. From the Waterfall the latter route is quickly reached across two or three fields. For some distance the route is parallel with that from Llanberis to the top of Snowdon, but along the west instead of the east side of the valley. When the valley divides, it climbs gently up the west side of *Maes Cwm*, which is flanked on either hand by green slopes now and again broken by a bit of crag and scree. As soon as a gate at the top of the Bwlch is reached a good view of Snowdon is obtained. The path for a couple of hundred yards or so is now ill-defined ; but passing through a second gate on the brow it soon becomes good again. Then, as it bears round to the right and soon commences a steady descent, Llyn Cwellyn comes into full view, with Y Garn rising by a narrow ridge from Llyn-y-dywarchen, and to the right of it, near the foot of Cwellyn, Mynydd Mawr (2,295 feet), and the fine Craig Cwm-bychan. The path passes by a small farm-house, and the station and inn are immediately below.

For the ascents of Snowdon, the Glyders, &c., from Llanberis, see " *Mountain Section.* "

Llanberis to Capel Curig or Beddgelert (*continuation of main route.   Distances, &c, p.* 129).

From the station the road crosses the stream coming down from the Waterfall, of which we catch a glimpse on the right, and, passing the *Victoria Hotel* and *Dolbadarn Tower* above it, reaches the side of the upper lake—*Llyn Peris.* On the opposite side the huge *Dinorwic slate quarries*, rising tier above tier, spoil what must once have been a very pleasing scene. Above them rises the smooth slope of Elidyr-fawr with a deep hollow between it and Foel-goch. On the right the long northern shoulder of Snowdon, which rises like a rampart over the Pass of Llanberis, commences at once. We pass an octagonal castellated building, about which curiosity is not easily satisfied, on the left, and make a slight descent to the green strath in which lies the picturesque village of **Old Llanberis** (roadside inn, the *Vaenol Arms*). Nearly a century ago, when New Llanberis was not in existence, this now pleasant resort was described as "a small and rude village, surrounded by vast rocks, the cloud-capped summits of which are seldom visible to the inhabitants below." The church was a "miserable-looking place resembling an ancient cottage more than a house." Matters are very different now. The village is picturesque, with little or no sign of squalor, and the church has by restoration been made an harmonious contributor to the characteristic beauty of the scene. It contains a 15th century timber roof, "likened," says Murray, "to a ship with the keel uppermost." Even the natural features around seem to have cheered up to some extent, for the "cloud-capped summits" often doff their vapour covering and display their full height to the passing tourist. This is the best point at which to quit the road for a ramble over the many-peaked range of mountains which separates the Pass of Llanberis from Nant Ffrancon (*see* "*Mountain Section*").

Soon after quitting the village we begin to ascend, and the valley grows narrower. Two deep hollows on the right—*Cwm-glas-bach* and *Cwm-glas*, the latter deep-set beneath the towering crags of Crib-goch and Crib-y-ddysgyl—break the cliff-line on that side, and on the other side of the road close to it are some huge boulders, one of which is improperly called the *Cromlech.* They are even larger than the famous Bowder-stone in Borrowdale, but not so nicely poised. In the one first passed a resemblance to the prow of a ship may be noticed.

The **Pass of Llanberis** is unquestionably the finest mountain defile traversed by a carriage-road in Wales, and many will think it not surpassed in the whole kingdom. It is longer and much narrower than Nant Ffrancon, which by reason of the breadth of its strath is more of the Glencoe order of grandeur, while the chief features of Llanberis are the proximity of the mountains on each side to one another, and the steep rocky character of their slopes. The valley itself is almost choked with

the *débris* of the impending crags, and great effect is added by
the wild hollow called Cwm-glas, which forms, as it were, a bowl
high up between Crib-goch and Crib-y-ddysgyl. The rude rampart of rock on the left is Esgair-felen, an arm of Glyder-fawr,
whose summit comes into view before the top of the Pass is
reached. The peak of Snowdon itself is visible from no point in
it, being hidden first by Crib-y-ddysgyl and then by Crib-goch.
The top of the Pass (about 1,200 ft.) is reached at *Corphwsyfa*
(the "Resting-place," barbarised into *Pen-y-pass*), where is a
fair-sized inn and a ragged group of houses. Here the Capel
Curig ascent of Snowdon quits the road, and, as soon as we have
passed the point of divergence, the Lliwedd shoulder of Snowdon
appears on the right, and the Crib-goch one behind us; but the
summit Y Wyddfa is still hidden. As we commence the descent,
a strip of Moelwyn appears on the right front. Then, at a sharp
bend in the road, a lovely view down Nant Gwynant, with a part
of Llyn Gwynant backed by Cynicht, breaks upon us on the right
hand, a most refreshing sight after so long a stretch of unrelieved
wildness. Moel Siabod, from this side a featureless ridge, also
becomes conspicuous in front, and at the fork of the road we come
to the well-known **Pen-y-gwryd Inn..**

For the route from Pen-y-gwryd to Beddgelert, see p. 132.

Pen-y-gwryd to Dolwyddelen, 8 *m.*, 2¼ *hrs.*—This is described in
some detail the reverse way, page 132. The easiest route is to leave the road
at the end of the wall, 150 yards towards Beddgelert, and to proceed southwards over the broken ground, with the Pass of Llanberis and Snowdon behind,
till you come to the lowest part of the green shoulder descending from Moel
Siabod, called *Bwlch Rhiw-r-ychain.* From this point a sharp descent of a few
hundred feet brings us to the two lakes called *Llyniau Duwaunedd,* passing to
the north of which we cross the stream issuing from them and enter a cart-
track that, after crossing a spur of Moel Siabod, runs into the road to Dolwyddelen at the hamlet of *Ffridd,* a mile short of *Dolwyddelen Castle,* which
is itself another long mile from the village (*p.* 127) and station.

The four miles of descent from Pen-y-gwryd to Capel Curig call
for little description. Moel Siabod is on the right, and the dull
side of the Glyder range on the left. The valley itself, *Nant-y-
gwryd*, is dreary and featureless, and only partly relieved by the
two Capel Curig Lakes at its far end.

For Capel Curig, see p. 130, *and for the road thence to Bettws-
y-Coed, p.* 104.

Carnarvon to Snowdon Ranger, 10¼ *m.*; **Rhyd-ddu,**
12½ *m.* (rail); **Beddgelert,** 16½ *m.* ('bus).

This route lies along the Afonwen branch of the North-Western
for 3¼ miles as far as *Dinas Station.* Thence it is continued by
the North Wales Narrow Gauge Railway to Rhyd-ddu (*pron.* Rhid-
the), and is completed by a 'bus journey of 4 miles to Beddgelert.
Both Snowdon Ranger and Rhyd-ddu are recognised starting-

points for the ascent of Snowdon, the latter place, or Pitt's Head, three-quarters of a mile nearer Beddgelert, being equally convenient for those who start from that place. (*For all these ascents see " Mountain Section.*")

The Route.—From Dinas the line, as it rises rapidly, affords a fine view of the triple-peaked Rivals and glimpses of the peak of Snowdon. There is also a wide prospect of the Menai Straits and Anglesey, but the panoramic display is still finer from Bryngwyn, to which a branch goes from the first station, *Tryfan Junction.* From Tryfan the line goes above the pretty little glen of the *Gwrfai stream* to *Waenfawr* and *Bettws Garmon*, the nearest station for the much-sketched **Nant Mill**, of which we get a good general view on the left hand from the rail. That the grouping of rock, pine-woods, winding stream and falls, offers delightful studies for the artist is undeniable, but the scene as a whole is likely to disappoint those who have formed their expectations from pictures. On the opposite side of the valley the abrupt *Craig Cwm-bychan* is a fine feature, especially when **Llyn Cwellyn** is reached. This lake, which is about a mile long and contains trout and char, has no noteworthy surroundings except this crag, but ahead we get a good view of Snowdon with the minor peak of Aran on the right of it. *Snowdon Ranger Station* and *Inn* (H.Q.), rather more than half-way along the lake, are both primitive and, after leaving them behind, the line crosses a romantic little glen with a waterfall on the left, and affords an effective view of Llyn Cwellyn. Then, pursuing a snake-like course, it reaches **Rhyd-ddu** (*Roadside Inn*), where Snowdon is the dominant feature.

Snowdon Ranger to Llanberis, 4 m; 1¼ hrs.

This route for the best part of a mile is identical with that of the Snowdon Ranger ascent of Snowdon. It follows a well-defined bridle-track past a little farm just above the station and inn, and then bears to the right round the hill. Soon, looking back, we obtain a good full-length view of Llyn Cwellyn with the fine Craig Cwm-bychan rising abruptly from the water's edge at its foot, and behind this Mynydd Mawr (2,293 *ft.*). Across the head of this lake appears the tarn Llyn-y-Dywarchen, from which a steep and narrow ridge runs up to the north flank of Y Garn. In front, Snowdon rises—a finely scarped peak at the head of Cwm Clogwyn.

When the bridle-track reaches a bit of wet ground on the near side of a gate we turn up-hill with a wall on our right hand. In a hundred yards and through two gates we then gain the top of the pass, and henceforward have but to follow a broad path down *Maes Cwm*. This *cwm*, green for the most part but broken here and there by crag and scree, is in no wise remarkable, and the view over Llanberis and Llyn Padarn which is obtained as we descend it is likewise devoid of striking features. When the main valley is reached the Llanberis route up Snowdon is traceable on the hill-side on the right. Just short of Llanberis we can by crossing a couple of fields reach the *waterfall* and thence enter the village near the *Victoria Hotel*. If, however, we prefer to follow the path which has now become a road it will bring us into the village close to the *Padarn Villa Hotel*, and only a trifling distance from the station, for which we must turn to the right.

Rhyd-ddu to Llanfihangel-y-Pennant, 8 *m*; **Dolbenmaen,** 12 *m*; **Criccieth,** 16 *m*.   This is a foot-track but little traversed.   It goes between Moel Hebog on the left and Mynydd-mawr on the right, attaining a height of about 1,200 feet.   There is an inn at Dolbenmaen, whence the nearest road to Criccieth (*see p.* 145) should be specially ascertained.

Rhyd-ddu or Snowdon Ranger to Nantlle, 6 *m*.   From the Cwellyn Arms Inn at Rhyd-ddu a winding road ascends past *Llyn-y-Dywarchen*, which has been enlarged by its waters being dammed up, to *Bwlch-gyfelin*, abt. 750 feet.   Thence a steep descent leads to a copper mine and some cottages, near which the track from Snowdon Ranger, which leaves the road near the south end of Llyn Cwellyn, converges.   Half-a-mile onward the road crosses the stream.   On the left is the stony face of *Y Garn*, and looking back we get a fine view of Snowdon above the *col*.   The *Upper Nantlle Lake* is featureless, and the lower one is quite lost in the slate-quarries.   At **Nantlle** is a small hotel about ¼ *m.* short of the station.

From Rhyd-ddu, where we exchange rail for road, the first mile past the bog-surrounded *Llyn-y-Gader*—a square featureless lake on the right—is comparatively poor.   When the summit of the route is gained, Pitt's Head is the name given to the rock profile on the right, and just beyond it the Beddgelert route up Snowdon strikes off on the left.   Then we begin the descent of the *Colwyn glen*, which gradually increases in beauty, getting more and more wooded, and having the fine mountain Moel Hebog (2,578 feet) on the right hand.   For **Beddgelert**, in a lovely situation at the junction of the Colwyn and Gwynant valleys, *see page* 157.

Carnarvon by yr Eifl (= the Rivals) to Nevin or Pwllheli.

Road all the way : *Nevin,* 20 *m.*, or *Pwllheli,* 20 *m.*

Pedestrian route: rail to Pen-y-groes, 6¾ *m.*, *thence walk to Clynnog fawr,* 4½ *m.*, *whence Nevin* (*by Bwlch-yr-Eifl*), 8 *m.*, or (*by Llanaelhaiarn*), 10 *m* ; *Llanaelhaiarn to Pwllheli,* 6 *m.* (*Station,* 6½ *m.*)   *Llanaelhaiarn to Llangybi Station,* 6 *m.*

The above distances are exclusive of the ascent to Tre'r Ceiri, the fortified British town on the easternmost peak of the Rivals. Llanaelhairn is the starting-point for this climb, and allowing say ¼-hour on the summit, the détour will increase the time to Nevin by about 2 hrs., and to Pwllheli or Llangybi by about 2½ hrs. The pedestrian route indicated above has the recommendations of affording a glance up Cwm Nantlle from Pen-y-groes (*Victoria,* Q.), and of reducing the walking distance to Clynnog from 9½ m., to 4½ m.   Nothing, moreover, is lost in the way of scenery, as rail and road are nearly coincident as far as Groeslon Station,

5 miles from Carnarvon. For those who make the Rivals the
object of a day's excursion from Carnarvon, Llangybi is the
nearest railway station at which to take the train for the return
journey, and supposing the tourist to reach Pen-y-groes about
10 a.m., he will have 9 hours for his walk. At Llanaelhaiarn
there is a good roadside house, "The Rival Inn," and another
at Four Crosses, 2½ miles short of Pwllheli ; but the Newborough
Arms, at Clynnog, has been closed for years, and that village
now has only the humblest of beershops. In Llangybi village
there is a small roadside inn, but none at the Station.

The road from **Carnarvon to Clynnog**, 9½ m., calls for
little description. In ¾-m. it crosses the river *Seiont*, and at *Pont
Newydd*, 2 m., the *Gwrfai* stream, which drains Llyn Cwellyn on
the road to Snowdon Ranger and Beddgelert. Then, passing to
the left of *Llanwnda Church* and *Dinas Station*, the narrow gauge
railway to Rhyd-ddu is crossed, and the main line itself, close to
Groeslon Station, 3½ m. by road. Thence to Clynnog there is
nothing to note except the church of *Llandwrog*, a short distance
on the right, and 5 miles from Carnarvon, and on the left the
great wall that bounds and hides *Glynllifon Park* (Lord Newborough). *For Clynnog, see below.*

Pen-y-groes Station to Clynnog, 4½ m. On leaving the *up*-side of
the station the road that crosses the line from Nantlle is at once entered on,
and turning to the left along it we very shortly take another road on the
right. In about half-a-mile from the turn and near the top of the hill a foot-
path over the left-hand wall is to be followed, and as we turn out of the road
we leave behind us a good view of the Nantlle *cwm*, and have on our right the
ample woods of *Glynllyfon* (Lord Newborough), above which rise an antique
castle-like lodge and the towers of the mansion more to the left. Ahead, the
Rivals and an intervening range present a fine mountain profile, while across
Carnarvon Bay is seen the long low line of Anglesey. The path passes to the
right of a farmstead and presently develops into a cart-track, which soon joins
a farm-road at right angles. Here we turn to the left through a meadow and at
the next junction of roads to the left again. [A little to the left of our route is
the hill-fort *Craig-y-dinas* on the near side of the Afon Llyfni (the stream from
the Nantlle lakes) whose steep banks guard it on three sides. A bit of wall and
ditches indicate the north-west defences.] After crossing the Llyfni at *Pont-y-
Cim* (pronounced Kim) we soon bear to the right past a cottage or two and join
the main road from Carnarvon about 1½ m. short of Clynnog-fawr.

Clynnog (*a small beer-shop only*) is a considerable village, with
a fine Perpendicular **Church**, dating from the reign of Henry
VII. Here, in 616, St. Beuno founded a monastery, which, after
lasting some 600 years, was suppressed, and the church made
collegiate. A solid oak chest, with three locks, is still preserved.
In it were deposited the proceeds of the sale of such calves and
lambs as were born with the Nôd Beuno. This mode of providing
alms for the poor, and money for the repairs of the church is said
to have continued down to the end of the 18th century. The
rood-screen (good) is still in position, but no part of the present

church or its furniture is earlier than the end of the 15th century.
Connected with the church, but distinct from it on the south side,
is the *Eglwys Beuno*, once famous for the cures wrought by
the tomb of the saint, but for many years used as a school. **St.
Beuno's Well**, still a principal source of the village water-supply,
is on the left of the road, about ¼ *m.* from the church. It is
square and surrounded by steps or seats, and traces of two niches
remain. Out of sight from the road, but between it and the sea,
and about ½ *m.* from the church, is a fine three-legged **Cromlech**:
to reach it we turn down a lane close to the church and then left
through the fields.

The scenery improves as we leave Clynnog, and the steep green
slopes and screes of the conical *Gyrn* mountains overhang the
road. As we bend round the foot of *Moel Penllechog*, the three
Rivals rise boldly in front, and at the foot of the seaward peak is
a small pier and harbour, whence the products of stone quarries
are shipped.

Our road now crosses a brook, and passes a small roadside
house, the *Waterloo Tavern*, and then after half a mile of collar-
work we reach *Llanaelhaiarn* (*Inn*: Rival), situated at the top of
the pass.

Ascent of the Rivals. The easiest route is to follow the
Nevin road for rather more than a mile from Llanaelhaiarn
Church, and then to strike obliquely up the hill to a green track,
and ascend by it to the fortified British town **Tre'r Ceiri** (= the
town of fortresses), which crowns the easternmost of the three
peaks. The builders of this stronghold, whether Gaels or Kymry,
are unknown, and no thorough investigation has as yet been
made of its site. In spite, however, of the long ages that have
elapsed since it was deserted the main outlines are unmistakable.
A single, almost coffin-shaped, enclosure, with parts of two other
walls on its western side, where only it was seriously open to
attack, constitute the existing defences. At the northern end a
cairn marks the look-out, and just west of this the remains of a
sally-port may be noticed. The main entrance is at the south
end, where the converging western walls were also strengthened
by outer works, and another and smaller entrance on the west side
is still in fair preservation. The inside of the town is occupied
by several groups of buildings of various shapes and sizes, all reduced now to more or less ruined enclosures, one of which, a
square not far from the cairn, Pennant dignified with the name of
the Prætorium. The view from the hill on a clear day is striking,
and embraces an amphitheatre of mountains from Cader Idris
round to the Snowdon group. The coast of Wales from Anglesey
northward to St. David's Head, in the south, is in full view, and
near at hand the shore line of the Lleyn peninsula can be almost
completely traced. To enumerate the mountains and places
within sight would be useless, as the map is a far better guide.
Suffice it to say, that, as the finely-shaped outline of the Rivals

is in view from most of the chief summits of Carnarvon and Merioneth, so *they* are to be made out from our present stand-point. The peak immediately west of Tre'r Ceiri is the highest of the three (1887 *feet*), and the ascent of it can easily be made by rounding the head of the intervening cwm. The view from it is, we think, on the whole hardly so pleasing as that from the lower height, but it has the advantage of looking right down into Nant Gwrtheyrn. Those who make the ascent and are bound for Nevin are recommended to descend to the cliff-route mentioned on page 156.

From **Llanaelhaiarn** to **Pwllheli** is an almost straight road of 6½ miles, and devoid of special features. At 2 miles from the former place the road to *Llangybi village*, 2¾ *m*, goes off on the left, and on the right is the entrance lodge of the well-wooded grounds of *Trallwyn*. Another short mile brings us to *Pont-y-rhyd-goch*, where the grouping of stream and bridge and cottages is picturesque. **Four crosses** (*Inns*) is, as its name implies, a hamlet at cross-roads, and here, by turning to the left, *Chwilog Station* can be reached in 2½ *m*. From this point the road for a couple of miles follows the ridge, west of the Erch valley, and then drops quickly to Pwllheli.

Llanaelhaiarn to Nevin, 6 *m*. The road crosses a rather desolate heath at the southern foot of the Rivals to the hamlet of *Llithfaen*, 2 *m.*, where there is a small public-house. (The name *Llithfaen* means "loadstone," and preserves the tradition that the neighbouring heights possessed the fatal power of drawing vessels from their course.) Thence it is 2 *m.* to Pistyll, whose little church is seen on the right of the road, and Nevin 2 *m.* further. For **Nevin** see p. 155

Llanaelhaiarn to Llangybi Station, abt. 6 *m*. Turn to the left at Trallwyn lodge, 2 *m.*, and avoid all branch roads till 1½ *m.* further cross-roads are reached a quarter of a mile after crossing a small stream. Then turn to the left to Llangybi, 1 *m.* Here there is a roadside inn. For the station we turn to the right at the entrance of the village. The road winds, but is unmistakable.

Carnarvon to Afonwen, 18 *m*; Pwllheli, 22 *m*; (or Criccieth, 22 m.)

As soon as the town is left behind look out on the right in a backward direction for a fine view of Carnarvon Castle. Then the *River Seiont*, flowing beneath a steep and wooded bank is crossed, and in about a mile onward the *Forydd* stream. At *Dinas Station* (3¼ *m*.) the North Wales narrow-gauge railway goes off on the left for Snowdon Ranger, &c. (*see p.* 140), and *Llanwnda Church* is close by on the right. Then nothing calls for notice till we reach *Pen-y-groes Station*, 7 *m.*, the junction for Nantlle (pronounced "Nant-thly").

Looking up the valley on **the left** Snowdon is the peaked summit that completely blocks it, while **much nearer** and **to the** right of it is a rocky knoll shewing **the** upturned face, chiefly nose, of *Old Meredith*.

Pen-y-groes to Nantlle (*rail*), 1¼ *m* ; **Rhyd-ddu or Snowdon Ranger** (*road*), 7½ *m*.

Nantlle (*small hotel*, ¼ *m. from station*), is a jumble of slate quarries, and the only justification for including this route in a tourist's guide book springs from the splendid view of Snowdon which it presents through the pass by which the road enters the Carnarvon and Beddgelert valley. As we wind along from the station and hotel between the yawning gulfs which form the quarries and the towering heaps of slate débris above them, we presently come into full view of the *Upper Nantlle Lake* (the lower one is quite lost in the quarries). This is surrounded by a belt of meadow and pasture land, and has no special feature. The road forms a kind of terrace, and looking straight ahead we see the peak of Snowdon rising above the hollow between the bold scarp of *Y Garn*, which forms a wall of rock and assumes grotesque outlines, on the right, and a projection of Mynydd-mawr on the left. Gradually ascending we presently cross the stream and come to a *copper-mine* and some cottages under Y Garn. Hence the main road ascends steeply to a height of about 750 feet and then winds down to the road from Carnarvon to Beddgelert, passing on the way *Llyn-y-Dywarchen*, which has been artificially enlarged by the erection of an embankment and wall close to the road-side. The main road is entered at the *Cwellyn Arms Inn*, ¼ *m*. from Rhyd-ddu Station.

The shortest way to *Snowdon Ranger* is by a track to the left near the copper mines. This takes us over the depression which has the rocky knob of *Clogwn-y-gureg* on the right, and a steep green slope of Mynydd-mawr on the left. Then it descends into the main Beddgelert and Carnarvon road, which it enters close to the bridge a little south of *Llyn Cwellyn*, whence it is a short mile to the Snowdon Ranger. By taking this path you save about 1½ miles, and reach the Ranger almost as soon as you would reach Rhyd-ddu, the distance from Nantlle being in both cases about 6 miles.

Onward to Afonwen **the scenery is** of little interest, and less **beauty.** Moel Hebog **comes into view,** with Snowdon over it to **the left** after passing *Brynkir Station*, and on the other side rise, **ever** gracefully, **the Rivals. At** *Chwilog Station* tickets are called **for, and then** in a minute **or** two we reach **Afonwen** the junction of the North-Western and Cambrian railways. Here there is a small refreshment-house **close** to the station, but no village. The mountain view is very beautiful. North-east Snowdon is the right hand of two peaks close together. To the right of this is the bulky Moel Hebog. Following the sky-line southward we have the sharp peak of Cynicht peering over an intervening ridge. Criccieth Castle is due east in the mid-distance, and across the bay is the twin fortress of Harlech. Above the latter are the Rhinogs, while more to the right is a well-defined strip of the scarped northern face of Cader Idris.

From Afonwen **Pwllheli** is 4 miles west, and **Criccieth** 4 miles **east.** *For Pwllheli see p.* 149.

Criccieth.

Hotels: *George IV.* (H.Q.), *White Lion*, both near the station.
Post: *Arr. abt. 7 a.m.; dep.*, 6.15 p.m.
Population: *abt.* 1,400.
Distances: Beddgelert (*rail to Portmadoc*, 5 m; *coach*, 8 m.), 13 m. (*Walk over Moel Hebog*), 4½—5½ hrs. Carnarvon (*rail*), 22½ m. Ffestiniog (*rail to Blaenau*, 18 m; *to Ffestiniog village*, 22 m.) Harlech (*rail*), 13½ m. (*by sea*), 7 m. Nantlle (*rail*), 17 m. Nevin (*rail to Pwllheli*, 7½ m; *road*, 7 m.), 14½ m. Rhyd-ddu Station (*footpath most of the way*), *abt.* 14 m. Tan-y-Bwlch (*rail*), 11 m.

From the sightseer's point of view, Criccieth has little to boast of beyond the shell of its old castle, but as the nearest (open) sea-side resort to the finest part of Snowdonia, it is growing in favour with those who like to combine sea and mountain air. Moreover, it is in itself a pleasant little spot, half watering-place and half village (it has even a village green), with a fair beach, a clear sea and a charming view across the water. For bathing there is a small supply of tents and a patch of sand, but on the whole the margin of the sea hereabouts is too largely composed of weedy boulders to be thoroughly enjoyable. Exception must be made in favour of a delightful little sweep of shore east of the town, and consisting of a rim of pebbles bordering a good expanse of sand. This is close to the railway and main road, and bathers require to pitch their tents.

Of *Old Criccieth* a few poor cottages remain, just below the landward side of the Castle rock. The *modern town* has a row of about thirty lodging houses west of the Castle, parallel to the sea, and on a low cliff above it, while about ¼ mile from the sea there is a yearly increasing collection of villas on pleasantly rising ground. Here, too, are the two small hotels. There is a fair sprinkling of wood in the neighbourhood. Close to the Castle is a smaller green boss, surmounted by a flagstaff.

For the pleasures of the water there are a few boats and an abundant supply of canoes, which in calm weather are a pleasing feature as they sail and paddle in the neighbourhood of the shore. Withal the place is very healthy.

Criccieth Castle (*toll* 1d.) is within 300 yards of the station, and is reached therefrom by a foot-path starting from the down platform. It consists of a tower-guarded gateway, a small irregular shaped court, and a few fragments. The towers are round, and of rough, unhewn stone, and little or no wrought stone now appears anywhere. It is quite uncertain when the castle was built, but it is generally said to have been either erected or largely restored by Edward I. in 1286. It is in every way far less interesting than its larger neighbour at Harlech, which is seen across the bay some 7 miles distant.

A new church (Early Dec.), built of the local grey stone, has recently been opened.

The view from the Castle extends westwards down the Carnarvonshire coast, along which are seen the Gimlet Rock at Pwllheli and the St. Tudwal Isles.   More to the right are the sharply peaked Rivals; then comes the long, regular range of Llwyd-mawr, and in the north-west, close at hand, Moel Hebog, over whose left shoulder the peak of Snowdon appears.   Rather north of east Moelwyn and Moelwyn-bach contribute a bold outline, while south eastwards is the equally broken range consisting of Rhinog-fawr, Rhinog-fach, and Llethr, the two latter separated by a deep hollow, with Harlech Castle in front of them.   These are continued by the Llawllech range, which drops to the sea at Barmouth, and over which the peak of Cader Idris may be seen.   A long line of coast beyond Aberystwith completes the panorama.

The **walks in the neighbourhood** of Criccieth are tame, but the archæologist will find two **Cromlechs**, each some 2½ miles distant, and a good mile apart.   To visit these, take the road running north from the town across the green.   There is a wide view from the higher part of this road, extending to Bardsey and the other points mentioned in the view from the Castle. (A low hill, half-a-mile to the right of this road and marked by a flagstaff, commands a still finer panorama.)   In a long mile the road forks, and we turn to the right, and in 200 yards or so enter a private road on the left, through an iron gate.   Half-a-mile onward another turn to the left takes us by Ynys-ddu farm, about 3 furlongs beyond which are some outbuildings.   Hence we see our first *Cromlech* in and over a wall a furlong ahead.   It is seven feet high, has four legs—the space between them filled up with stones—and an almost triangular top-stone, 14 feet from apex to base.   Hence, crossing the brow of the hill—a ladder-stile shows the way—we cross the Dwyfawr stream by a high plank-bridge close to a cottage, and bear to the left up to the brow of the next hill, beyond which is a low cottage close to two or three firs.   The second *Cromlech* is just beyond this cottage, a little left of a fence.   It is smaller than the other and consists of one round-backed stone with four supporters, one of them much bigger than the rest and standing on its side so as to form a wall.   Hence, going south, you will enter a path that comes out into the main road a little west of a bridge over the Dwyfawr, 2 miles from Criccieth (*see map*).

Criccieth to **Dolbenmaen**, 4 m; **Llanfihangel-y-pennant,** **6 m; and Rhyd-ddu**, 14 m.   This is a little frequented route, and most tourists will prefer crossing Moel Hebog to Beddgelert and there taking the conveyance which runs in connection with the trains at Rhyd-ddu.   The latter route is described in the "Mountain Section," and the direct route to Rhyd-ddu is identical with it till we pass through a gate and enter at right angles the road leading to Dolbenmaen (¾ m. to the left, small inn). From this point a shorter route than that through Dolbenmaen is to continue the Hebog route as far as the little inn, and then to turn sharp to the left for a bridge visible for some time previously. (This sharp angle may be cut off by taking a foot-path leading down to the bridge, by a white cottage, from a point a little short of the inn.)   A quarter-of-a-mile after crossing the bridge you turn left and cross the main *Dwyfawr* stream by another bridge, turning to the right at once from the other side. *Llanfihangel* is reached in a mile, and from it the track continues up the narrowing valley, over the dip between Moel Hebog and Y Garnedd-goch, till it joins the Nantlle and Rhyd-ddu road (*p.* 146), ¼ *m.* short of the inn and ½ *m.* from the station at Rhyd-ddu. The writer has not travelled the portion between Llanfihangel and the junction with the Nantlle road.

Afonwen to Pwllheli, 4 *m.* The line runs near the sea and passes the well-wooded grounds of Broomhall, beyond which is the village of Abererch.

Pwllheli.

Hotels: *Crown, Tower* (H.Q.), *Madryn Arms*, abt. ½ *m.* from the station.
Post: *Arr. abt.* 8 *a.m.,* 7 *p.m.; dep.* 5.45 *p.m.* **Pop.** *abt.* 3,500.

A sandy beach, good bathing, easy access to fine scenery, and a very moderate bill, are the attractions which Pwllheli offers to the holiday-maker, and possibly, if it troubled itself a little more to turn these attractions to account, it might take a more prominent position among Welsh watering-places. At present there are few houses on the beach, and the town, though a fair representative of Welsh towns generally, is not an inviting one to strangers. As we enter it from the station a fishy odour suggests one of its staple commodities—*crustacea.* The anticipation of perpetual feastings on crabs and lobsters easily reconciles us to this peculiarity, but the next one has no such set-off to redeem it. The streets—roadway and footway—are paved with "kidneys." The reason assigned by the natives for this—that there is a local prejudice against being able to distinguish the degree of a man's sobriety by his gait—we only repeat because we had it from one of them. The most abstemious tourist, if he happen to have nails in his boots, will certainly feel qualms about his condition before he has got fairly through the town.

There are two view-points within the limits of a short stroll from Pwllheli—one, just out of it and a little to the right of the Nevin Road, the other an isolated rock standing out to sea at the mouth of the harbour and called *Careg-y-rimbill* or the *Gimlet Rock.* From the latter in particular there is a fine prospect extending along the coast both ways and across the sea to the mountains about Barmouth, including Cader Idris, Diphwys, and the range which extends northwards from the latter, consisting of Llethr, Rhinog-fach and Rhinog-fawr. Looking along the coast we see Cynicht and Moelwyn, with Moel Hebog and the peak of Snowdon to the left of them, and the Rivals due north.

The Lleyn Promontory.

To ensure the tourist against disappointment, let us **at once** confess that the Lleyn promontory, as this far stretching **tract of** Carnarvonshire is called, **looks** its best from a distance. The long hill-outline commencing at its extreme point, and continuing with little break to the **western** skirts of Snowdon, is, perhaps, as **graceful as anything of the kind in the country,** unless it be the **Malvern range in Worcestershire, and plays an** important **part in the views from the mountains that** overlook the watering-**places along the eastern** sweep of Cardigan Bay. Speaking **generally, these hills are on a** declining **scale** of altitude **from east to west.** Each **single** height, **or group, rises** from its **own base, apart from the others,** at a **slope** which, **though nowhere abrupt, is sufficiently steep to** make **the** particular **hill to which it belongs a distinctive part of one** harmonious whole. **Standing in their midst, however, we lose the** combined effect, and from **the Rivals, westwards, the separate** heights degenerate into grassy "tumps," **more remarkable for** the extensive views of sea and mountain, **which they** one and all command, than for **any** special beauty or interest of their own. The valleys **stretching between them from sea to** sea **are** wide, almost **level, and** cultivated throughout, while **the** countless enclosures and small detached **farmsteads—white** and fairly prosperous-looking—that strike **the eye** from any eminence, tell of the multitude of small holdings into which the land is divided. Cattle-rearing is carried on extensively, and as we shall see in the **course of** our wanderings, **the** pig is **treated with** an almost Hibernian degree of consideration, while **geese** form one of the most flourishing branches of the community.

Of all this extensive **district Pwllheli is the one market and** business centre, and the visitor who quits that town by any of the **roads** leading westwards from it **on** the morning of a fair-day **will very** quickly be disabused of any previously-formed notion, **that he is** entering a wild and sparsely populated region. A **strange one** it may seem to the "Seisoneg," for so far the **tourist-tide has not set** towards it with sufficient strength to induce **the inhabitants to** grapple with the English language, and in many places—Aberdaron, to **wit—there** is scarcely a word of English spoken.

From a picturesque point of view the most interesting parts of the **Lleyn** promontory **are** the tract extending north-eastward from Nevin to the Rivals **and** the few square miles of hilly country lying between Aberdaron and Braich-y-pwll, the "Land's End" of Wales, as the extreme point of the country is not inaptly called. The road from Pwllheli to Nevin **is** exceptionally rich in timber **of forest growth, and presents scenery** more resembling **that of** some favoured English shire than such as is characteristic of the rest of the promontory or of Wales generally. We shall suppose the tourist to make Pwllheli his starting-point, and to return either to the same place or to Nevin. Allowing one day for the journey to Aberdaron and Braich-y-pwll, another for Bardsey, and a third for the return, he will, if favoured by weather, see all that is noteworthy in the district.

Pwllheli to Aberdaron, abt. 14 m.

Mail-cart by Llanbedrog, 4 m. and Sarn, 11 m.; abt. 8 a.m. 'Bus by Sarn to Tocia Farm, 3½ m. short of Aberdaron, abt. 4 p.m. Fare by either route, 2s.

The travelling in either of the above conveyances is of the rough-and-ready order, intended mainly to satisfy local requirements. The mail route turns inland at Llanbedrog, and the 'bus route follows the Nevin road as far as the *Farmer's Arms*, 2 miles from Pwllheli, beyond which it proceeds inland, as shown on the map, to *Nanhoron*, prettily placed at the entrance of Nant Bodlas, where it joins the mail route. At **Sarn**, 3½ miles beyond Nanhoron, there are two or three very fair inns—the Penrhyn Arms being the chief, and of better class than any others west of Pwllheli and Nevin. The full name is *Sarn Meyllteyrn*, but it is locally known as Sarn. It is prettily placed in a narrow dell, watered by a streamlet, and, in comparison with the surrounding country, well wooded. The road onward to *Tocia* (pron. "Tockya") *Farm*, where the 'bus stops unless there is a sufficient number of passengers to warrant its proceeding to Aberdaron, is over a dull upland. The mail-cart goes through to Aberdaron, to which village the road, after continuing on high ground for a couple of miles, gradually descends.

Pedestrian Route, abt. 14 m. The scenery along this route, or rather the views from it, give it a decided advantage over the two carriage ones. There is a road all the way, to be followed or not, as the tourist pleases. A pleasant détour adding a few miles to the route, may be made from Llanbedrog to the fishing village of Abersoch, 7 miles from Pwllheli, but for general views the direct route cannot be well improved upon.

Quitting Pwllheli we may either follow the Llanbedrog road, which runs parallel to the shore nearly half-a-mile inland, or taking the left branch where the main street forks, reach the sands by a straight road half-a-mile long. The latter route is the pleasanter of the two, and by adopting it we may, before starting westward, visit the **Gimlet Rock**, a long half-mile in the opposite direction. The view from it across Cardigan Bay extends from Aberystwith to the estuary of the Ffestiniog river, and includes the heights of Cader Idris, Diphwys and the Rhinogs, seen across the water, as well as Moelwyn, Cynicht, and Snowdon over the land. Nearer at hand, between Snowdon and Cynicht, the round top of Moel Hebog appears.

Turning westward from the Gimlet Rock, if we have visited it, or from the end of the road by which we reached the shore, we have 3 miles of tolerably firm sand, backed by a low sand-bank, before us. An impromptu bathe may generally be indulged in. Then, where the shore bends south to the little height of *Careg-y-defaid*, a short lane takes us from the sands into the Llanbedrog road. The village of **Llanbedrog** is a mile further on. At its entrance, where we turn up the hill to the right, is the church, prettily placed in a park which contains some fine trees. Half-way up the hill the Abersoch road turns off at the *Glyn Weddw Arms*.

[**Abersoch** (*Inns*) is a small fishing village, 3 miles beyond Llanbedrog. Tourists who like to follow the coast should proceed through it to *Porth-ceiriad* a square-shaped bay guarded by steep rocks, at the foot of which is a belt of sand. Thence they may strike across the promontory, and follow the coast-line of *Porth Nigel* (" Hell's Mouth", as it is most inaptly called) till they reach the main route again at the foot of Rhiw hill. The map is by far the best guide to this détour.]

Continuing up the hill from the *Glyn Weddw Arms*, we turn sharp to the left opposite a smithy, and pass through a part of the village, characteristically called *Pig Street*. Here is another small inn. Then ascending to a considerable height we obtain a glorious retrospect of sea and mountain, easily improved by climbing the second of two eminences on the right hand (the first is crowned by a round tower). A new school-house marks the point from which to climb. The prospect includes, in addition to the objects to which we have drawn attention in our description of the Gimlet Rock, a bird's-eye view of Abersoch and the two isles of St. Tudwal. Westwards it extends to the Rhiw heights, which lie between us and Aberdaron.

Descending again, we hit the main road some distance beyond the point at which we left it, and a third of a mile further take the left hand branch (the right hand one is the main route by Nanhoron and Sarn, described above). Our route continuing along a lower level, crosses in 1½ miles the *Nant Bodlas* brook, a little beyond which it turns sharp to the left, and then again to the right, reaching, a couple of miles further, the shore of **Porth Nigel**, or " Hell's Mouth." There is nothing in the appearance of the long sandy crescent of this bay to account for the latter name. Such names, however, oftener have regard to the hidden dangers of the sea than to the physical characteristics of the land, and not unfrequently a bit of a spar standing out of the water suggests their origin. There is another Hell's Mouth on the coast of Anglesey, near Amlwch.

Our road, after skirting for a short distance the edge of the low cliffs, commences the ascent of the **Rhiw Hill**, half-a-mile long, and steep. This little ridge is the obstacle which makes it easier for carriages to adopt the longer route through Sarn to Aberdaron. To pedestrians, however, it furnishes the salt of the journey. The **rearward** views during the ascent are increasingly fine. The various peaks **visible across** Cardigan Bay will have been identified from the descriptions already given of the prospect in this direction.

On the top of the pass (**Bwlch-y-Rhiw**, the " pass of the steep slope "), is the *Penponcyn Inn*, a welcome little roadside house. Looking north from it we have the Sugarloaf, as the little hump which crowns the Rhiw ridge is called, and southwards across a field a remarkable line of broken crags. It is quite worth while to turn aside and scale the latter—the way is obvious, and the détour only occupies a few minutes. From the top you see Bardsey Island, and, in the far west, a long line of Wicklow summits. Holyhead is due north, Snowdon almost over Pwllheli, and the Rivals are the most striking of the nearer hills.

Reaching the road again, we keep an almost straight course for about 3½ miles, mostly on the descent to

Aberdaron (Principal inn *the Ship*, very small. *Post arr. about* 11 *a.m.*, *d.p. about* 2 *p.m.*) This is only a small and not very comely village. There is little English spoken even at the inns, but if the two or three bedrooms at the shop between the two little bridges are not already engaged, visitors will find there very fair accommodation at extremely moderate charges. A milestone, also between the bridges, gives the road-distances as 16 m. to Pwllheli, 13 m. to Nevin, 33½ m. to Carnarvon, and 5½ m. to Sarn. The old *church* of Aberdaron is a heavy, melancholy looking building by the side of the bay. As a place of worship it has been superseded by perhaps a still uglier erection with two towers on the higher ground a little inland. The historical interest of the village is centred in "Dick of Aberdaron," who was born at the end of the last century, and is accounted to have had a baker's dozen of languages at his tongue's end. Notwithstanding this, and the fact that he found a patron in Mr. Roscoe, of Liverpool, he never appears to have been many stages above beggary. He died in 1843, and was buried at St. Asaph.

A curious example of Aberdaron arrangements is afforded by the pigsties, which occupy the most eligible building sites at the street corners.

The bay of Aberdaron has a beach of sand besprinkled with pebbles, and boulders. and is backed by cliffs of loose earth. At its horns the beach disappears, and the cliffs are of hard slaty rock. Two islets, *Ynys-gwylan fawr* and *fach* ("big and little"), lie opposite the village.

Aberdaron to Braich-y-pwll (the "Land's End" of North Wales), 3 m.; and **back by Mynydd Anelwog** (635 *ft.*), 8 m.

Whether the tourist make the Bardsey expedition, which is the subject of our next description, or not, he will find this a very pleasant and remunerative little walk. With the exception of the Rhiw Hills, already described, it includes all that is of real interest near Aberdaron.

Ascend the hill by the road which goes westward from the north side of the shop between the two bridges, and take the left turn in about half-a-mile opposite a new house (the road straight on goes to the skirts of Mynydd Anelwog, by which we shall return). The rest of the way is as direct as may be. The top of Bardsey soon comes into view a little to the left of our course. In 2 miles we reach the second and last milestone and the last cottage. Hence a green path leads down to the promontory, reaching it by a rough staircase of rock a little south of its most westerley point. **Braich-y-pwll.** On the closely cropped greensward, a little above and to the right of the path is an enclosure overgrown with bracken and circumscribed by a square grass walk, marking the site of **Eglwys Fair**, the "chapel of Our Lady," as to the history of which we have been unable to gain any particulars. The other supposed object of special interest is **Ffynnon Fair**, "Our Lady's Well," which occupies a hollow in the cliff a little to the right of the bottom of the rock-staircase we have spoken of above, and is only accessible at low tide. It is a little basin of salt water, and the pilgrim who was skilful enough to convey a palmful to the top of the cliff without spilling any had his fondest wishes gratified. On the rock beside the well is the impression of "Our Lady's" hand, also of the shoe of her horse. The basin is filled every tide.

The coast scenery about here, though the cliffs are much broken by steep grass slopes and nowhere rise to any great perpendicular height, lacks neither boldness nor beauty. Bardsey Island, rising several hundred feet above the sea is a strong feature in the foreground, and all around it is a vast expanse of sea beyond which, in clear weather, the Irish hills may be discerned. Northwards, when we have risen to the higher ground, Holyhead Island contrasts with the almost dead level of the rest of Anglesey. The best route to take is well up above the northern side of the promontory till a descent is perforce made into the hollow separating us from **Mynydd Anelwog.** A turf fence or two has to be crossed and then we hit a path leading round the north side of this hill, the top of which, marked by a small cairn, is easily gained. The view is a repetition of the one we have already described in our walk to Aberdaron. Eastward, at our feet, stretches a wide belt of cultivation—turf-fenced fields and white cottages innumerable ; little woodland—and that of stunted growth ; no sign of great prosperity and none of slovenly poverty. Farther away the Rhiw Hills, Carn Fadryn, and Carn Boduan rise from the plain, and beyond them the three peaks of the Rivals give character to the sky-line. Snowdonia itself is too far off to assert individuality.

In descending we have only to make for the road which is seen below going directly to Aberdaron, and which may be entered pretty much where we please. It joins our outward route half-a-mile short of the village.

Bardsey Island. *5-6 m. from Aberdaron. Charge for a boat, about £1.* The time occupied on the sail, in fact, the possibility of making it at all, depends on the state of the sea. Under any but favourable conditions few tourists will care to venture forth. With them the island may be reached in a little over an hour. The tide race between the mainland and the island is very swift. Hence its Welsh name, *Ynys Enlli*, the "island of the current."

Sailing out of Aberdaron Bay we pass beneath the cliffs of *Parwyd*, the loftiest in the neighbourhood, and, crossing the Sound, are landed in a little bay at the south end of the broad part of the island. Hence a road leads northwards up the centre, passing to the left of the lofty hill which occupies the north-west corner. Alongside this lane are the half-dozen or so farmsteads which shelter the inhabitants of the island, and at its northern end, nearly a mile from the landing-place, the scanty remains of **the Abbey**, founded in the sixth century. They consist of the *Abbot's House*, still used as a dwelling-place, and a fragment of a tower. A number of graves lined with stone may or may not be accepted as evidence that 20,000 saints lie buried in Bardsey. At any rate, Lord Newborough, the owner of the island, has erected a monument, 9 feet high, to their memory.

Near the south end of the island, on its narrow part, is the *Lighthouse*, from which the coast of Cardigan Bay, as far, it is stated, as St David's Head, may be seen in clear weather, but the best view is to be had from the top of the hill which occupies nearly the whole of the north-east side of the island.

The inhabitants of Bardsey occupy themselves with farming and fishing. Tuesday is their day for visiting the mainland.

Aberdaron to Tocia, 3½ *m* ; **Sarn,** 6 *m* ; *and* **Pwllheli,** 16 *m* ; *or* **Nevin,** 15 *m.*

Tourists who have reached Aberdaron by the pedestrian route we have described from Pwllheli, may vary their return route whether they are making for Pwllheli or Nevin. If they have come from Nevin, or by conveyance from Pwllheli, we advise them to adopt the pedestrian route in returning. The detailed description given the reverse way on page 151 will suffice for guidance. We need only remind them here that there are way-side inns at Bwlch-y-Rhiw, 8½ *m.*, and Llanbedrog, 9½ *m.*; also that the charm of the walk lies in the views from Bwlch-y-Rhiw and the high ground a little short of Llanbedrog. From the latter place they may reach the sands in a little over a mile, and follow them all the way to Pwllheli.

By Sarn (*Meyllteyrn*). An omnibus leaves Tocia for Pwllheli early in the morning, and the mail-cart goes through from Aberdaron to the same place about 2 in the afternoon.

From Aberdaron the road rises at once and, leaving the modern church on the left hand, proceeds along a monotonous upland called *Rhos Hirwaen.* A little to the left of it, 1¼ miles on the way, is a large circular camp called *Castell Odo. Tocia,* whence the 'bus starts, is only a farm-house. Half-a-mile further one road to Nevin, passing through Llangwnadl, strikes away at right angles to the left, but another, the one we are describing and which is to be preferred, goes on direct to **Sarn.** Inns: the *Penrhyn Arms, Pen-y-bont,* &c. *Post arr. about* 10 *dep. about* 3·30 *p.m.* This hamlet, the chief part of the village of Meyllteyrn, lies in the prettily wooded little hollow watered by Afon Soch. It contains the best, almost the only inn accommodation west of Pwllheli, to which town there are two routes from it. One of them is followed by the 'bus, and joins the Nevin and Pwllheli high-road at the *Farmer's Arms,* 2 miles short of the latter town; the other, travelled over by the mail-cart, joins the pedestrian route from Aberdaron to Pwllheli about 2 miles short of *Llanbedrog.* Both pass through a pretty bit of scenery at *Nanhoron,* to which point they are identical (*see p.* 151).

For *Nevin* there are also two routes from Sarn —one retracing the Aberdaron road for a few yards and then going north to **Tudweiliog** (3 *m., small inns mail-cart to Nevin and Pwllheli, about* 3 *p.m.,* and thence through *Edeyrn* (6¼ *m. small inn*), and past *Porth-dinlleyn* (*p.* 156) unmistakeable all the way; the other climbing steeply for a few hundred yards, and then turning sharp to the left. The latter, which passes close to the northern slope of Carn Fadryn, is, perhaps, to be preferred, but neither presents anything more than ordinary scenery.

Nevin.

Inn: *Nanhoron Arms* (Q.). *Post arr.* 9.45 *a.m., dep.* 4.25 *p.m. Pop.* 2,000.

Nevin is a small town consisting of one longish street, leading towards, but not to the sea, and two or three short ones branching from it. It has considerable natural attractions, but to the casual visitor it seems to have been even less mindful of them than Pwllheli, and yet we read that Edward I. after celebrating "his seizin of Wales upon the summit of Snowdon, adjourned to "conclude the ebullitions of joy for victory by solemn rites upon "the plains of Nefyn .... the concourse on this occasion was pro-"digious; the chief nobility of England, and many foreigners of "distinction were present at this proud but disgraceful festival." Whether it be that the town has never fairly recovered from this disgrace, or for some other reason, we know not, but so far it appears not to have discovered that it is on the sea. Your first impulse on entering it, is to walk down the street to some vantage point, from which looking down upon the water, you may admire the fine and abrupt coast-scenery in the direction of the Rivals. Such a point, however, is not attainable. From the bottom of the street the road turns to the right and never reaches the cliff at all.

Retracing your steps, you find that you must go a few hundred
westwards on the Porth-dinlleyn road, and then turn down a lane
leading to Port-Nevin to get the view you want, which even then
is only to be obtained by scrambling up and walking along the top
of a turf-fence.   Thence its features are the cliff of *Careg-y-llam*
dropping sheer from a height of several hundred feet into the sea,
and the bold outline of *Yr Eifl* (The Rivals) beyond.   Northwards
is Anglesey emphasized by Holyhead Island.

A mile or more west of Nevin is **Morfa Nevin** (the " Marsh
of Nevin," a name which need not make the visitor apprehensive),
a collection of detached houses, at some of which lodgings may be
had.   In fact, in this direction there are houses at short intervals
all the way to *Porth-dinlleyn*, 1½ miles from Nevin, and the terminus of the main road from Pwllheli.   **Porth-dinlleyn** (the
" haven of the low-lying fortress ") has threatened Holyhead with
competition as a packet-station for Ireland in the days both of
road and of rail, and its natural advantages for such a purpose are
undoubted.   On one occasion the casting-vote of the Speaker
sealed its fate.   It is protected from the west by a long spit on
which is the site of an ancient fortress that presumably originated the name.   As we look back over Nevin, from the road hereabouts, the hills present a fine and rocky outline.   One of them,
Careg-lefain, would be called in a more enterprising neighbourhood the Lion Rock.   Carn Boduan to the right of it is steep and
abundantly wooded.

Nevin to Pwllheli (*town, 7 m; station 7½ m.*)   '*Bus daily at*
9 a.m. ; *mail-cart, 4.30 p.m.   Returning at 8 a.m., 5 p.m.   Fare*, 1s.

The road starts in a south-westerly direction so as to get round
the obstacle interposed by *Carn Boduan*, and joins, one mile from
Nevin, the high-road which starts from Porth-dinlleyn.   Thence
it is continued by a succession of straight reaches all the way to
Nevin.   The scenery is rather that of a finely-wooded English
road—such as that from Coventry to Leamington—than what one
expects in Wales.   This is especially noticeable in the neighbourhood of *Boduan Hall*, a seat of Lord Newborough, which stands
a little way to the left, 3 miles from Nevin.   Hereabouts, the road
goes through a long avenue, and 2 miles further it passes the
Farmer's Arms Inn, opposite to which the omnibus route from
Aberdaron strikes in.   Between this and Pwllheli, a height on the
left commands a fine view across the bay to the coast of Merioneth
and Cardigan.   *Pwllheli Station* (*p.* 149) is half-a-mile beyond
the town.

The Rivals (Yr Eifl), 5½ *m.* (*see p.* 144).   Carriages from
Nevin can go to *Llithfaen* (4 *m.*), where is a small public-house :
pedestrians should quit the road at *Pistyl* (2 *m.*), and take the
cliff-route by *Careg-y-llam* (" rock of the leap ") and *Nant
Gwrtheyrn* (" Vortigern's Valley"), a deep hollow between Yr Eifl
and the sea.   The names are connected with a story about
Vortigern having fled hither for refuge, and, on being discovered
by his subjects, having leapt into the sea !

English Miles

0 1 2 3 4 5 6 7 8

Trwy.
For
Carvg y

Porth Dinllen B.
Porth Nevin

Porth Dinllen Pt
Porthwen
NE.
Aber geirch
Mynt
Nevin
Bo
Edern
Ceidio
Bodvea
Porth Sgadan
Plas y Ran
Llandudwen
Porthygwaylau
Tudweiliog
Madryn
Rhyd yea
park Fadryn
Penllech B.
1224
Llanf
Bâch
Pt Coalman
Penllech
Cefn
amwlch
Porth Llefenig
Porth Whiling
Llangwnnal
Llaniestyn
Gween fau
Porth Ferin
Sarn
Meilteyn
Saethon Llanbedr
Pt Glas
Botlwan
Rhos
Pig Sty
Maen Mellt
Botwnog
Porth oer
Rhiw Hirwaun
Bryncroes
Tudta
Gelliwig
Llandegwning
Castell mardd
Mynydd y
Rhiw
Rhiw
Llangian
Tripod
Bank
Mynydd Anelwg
835 ft
Mynydd y graig
Llanenge
Porth Uan Hawen
Md Mawr
Plas
Pe
Braich y pwll
Mynydd
Llanundrhys
Talavarch P.
D
St Mary's Well
Aberdaron
Castell
PORTH NIGEL
OR
HELLS MOUTH
Porth Cadlan
Maen gwenonwy
BARDSEY SOUND
Aberdaron B.
The Trwyn
Ynis Gwylan
Md
Cilan
Peny kil
Penllan Hd
BARDSEY
IS?
St Mary's Abbey
Light
Landing Place

Beddgelert Section.

Carnarvon to Beddgelert by road.

*Carnarvon to Snowdon Ranger, 7½ m ; Rhyd-ddu Station, 9 m ; Beddgelert,
12½ m. Add half-a-mile to Carnarvon Station. For route by rail from Carnarvon
to Rhyd-ddu, see p. 140.*

The tour of Snowdon by Beddgelert, Pen-y-gwryd and Llanberis is daily
made during the season by coach leaving Carnarvon about 11.30 a.m. and reaching it again about 6 p.m. *Fare for the round, abt. 8s.*

The Beddgelert road goes south by the Market Place and, after
ascending a hill, passes on the left *Llanbeblig Church*, the mother
church of Carnarvon. Then, after a slight descent, it crosses the
river Seiont, which comes down from Llanberis, and the Llanberis
railway. A steady and almost straight ascent, with one break,
follows to the long hamlet of *Waen-fawr*. The country traversed
during this part of the journey is of no interest, but there is a
fine retrospect over Anglesey and on the right the Rivals appear
to advantage.

The road now gradually drops to the *Gwrfai* valley, down which
comes the little railway already described (p.141). *Waen-fawr station*
is at the meeting point of the road and rail, and a mile further we
pass *Capel Garmon station*, a little beyond which is a very fair inn.
The scenery now improves. Moel Eilio, green and round, is on
the left and *Mynydd-mawr*, sending down an abrupt shoulder—
Craig Cwm-bychan—into Llyn Cwellyn, is in front. Rail, road
and river go side by side, and in another mile the river is crossed
by a by-road at **Nant Mill** (*Nant Melin*). This scene is in high
favour with artists, which, perhaps, accounts for the somewhat
extravagant praise lavished upon it. The Mill itself is nothing
but four bare walls. The stream forms some pretty cascades
under the bridge, and Craig Cwm-bychan is a fine background, as
is also a fir-clad recess in Moel Eilio on the left, above which are
some good crags.

Llyn Cwellyn, whose eastern side we now skirt is 1¼ miles
long and nearly half-a-mile wide. It affords fair trout-fishing
which may be enjoyed *ad lib.* by sojourners at the *Snowdon
Ranger Hotel*, a comfortable tourist inn half-way up it. The only
striking natural feature upon it is the crag of Mynydd-mawr—
Craig Cwm-bychan—which falls almost sheer into its northern
end. As we proceed along it the peak of Snowdon comes into

view.   *For the ascent from Snowdon Ranger* or *Rhyd-ddu see* " *Mountain Section.*"   **Rhyd-ddu** (*small inn*), is 1½ miles beyond the "Ranger."

Snowdon Ranger or Rhyd-ddu to Nantlle, *abt.* 6 m.   The road-route, unmistakable, branches off at Rhyd-ddu, and, after ascending to a height of about 700 feet, drops at first steeply and then gently between Mynydd-mawr and Y Garn to Nantlle (pron. "Nant-thly"). From Snowdon Ranger the shortest way is by a path which begins after crossing the bridge a little south of Llyn Cwellyn.   This path goes to the north of the rocky little knob called *Clogwen-y-Gureg*, and joins the road near a copper-mine a mile further.

The only strong recommendation for this walk is the grand view of Snowdon obtained near Nantlle, but as this is always at one's back it is much better to take the route in the opposite direction (*see p.* 146).

There is a track from Rhyd-ddu to **Llanfihangel**, 8 m. ; **Dolbenmaen**, 9 m. ; and **Criccieth** (*road*), 14 m.   It is entered from the Nantlle road, just where the latter turns to the right ¼ m. from Rhyd-ddu.   There is a direction-post at the fork.   Thence the route is between Moel Hebog on the left and Carnedd-goch on the right.   We have not travelled the whole route.   *For a description of it beyond Llanfihangel the reverse way see p.* 148.

Half-a-mile beyond Rhyd-ddu we pass to the left of the square-shaped uninteresting expanse of *Llyn-y-Gader*, and a little further attain the highest point on our route, about 600 ft. above sea-level.   The detached rock called **Pitt's Head** is close to the road on the right hand, and as we approach it from this side not only the profile but the shape of the rock altogether is very striking.   There is nothing else noteworthy, except the general improvement of the scenery, till we reach Beddgelert.   Moel Hebog rises finely on the right but the **lower slope of** Snowdon on the left is monotonous.   A rock in the way is **inscribed** *Llam Trwsgyll*.   Llam means "step," and Trwsgyll was a **giant** who made a prodigious one to the other side of the stream, where for nearly a mile the old road runs.

Beddgelert.

Hotels : *Royal Goat* (H.Q.), a furlong out of the village on the Portmadoc road; *Prince Llewelyn* and *Saracen's Head* (Q.), in the village.

Post : *Arr. abt.* 8.40 *a.m.; dep., abt.* 4.50 *p.m.*

Distances : Carnarvon, 13 m.   Pen-y-gwryd, 8 m ; (Llanberis, 14½ m.) Capel Curig, 12 m ; Bettws-y-Coed, 17½ m.   Ffestiniog (*carriage road through Penrhyn*), 16 m. (*old road*, 13 m.).   Portmadoc, 8 m.

No village in North Wales is more romantically placed than Beddgelert.   The difference between it and Bettws-y-Coed is that which may be expected to exist between a mountain and a hill district. Beddgelert is as pre-eminent in the mountainous as Bettws-y-Coed is in the hilly characteristics of its surroundings. Of towns Dolgelley is, perhaps, even more romantic, though less wild in its environs, and Llangollen has equally beautiful ones of a softer type. We can think of no other rivals.

The village, though somewhat mean in its general appearance, affords very satisfactory tourist accommodation. The Royal Goat is considerably the largest and most fashionable hotel, and a good one, but the other two we have mentioned leave little to be desired by the tourist who prefers more homely quarters.

The village is placed on the north side of a triangular green-sward, from which the slopes of Snowdon rise on the north, of Moel Hebog on the west, and the abrupt cliff of Craig-y-Llan on the east. Close to it the Glaslyn stream, coming down from the cwms of Snowdon, is joined by the Colwyn stream, which commences a few miles northward in the Carnarvon direction.

The name *Beddgelert* (the " grave of Gelert ") has its origin in the legend—as well known as its kindred one of Helvellyn—of the faithful hound of the great Llewelyn, which was killed by its master under the impression that it had worried his infant son, when in reality it had rescued him from the jaws of a ravenous wolf. The lasting voucher for the truth of the legend is the grave itself, —a group of rude stones in a shaded enclosure in the second meadow south of the village, and reached by the foot-path which commences close to the wooden bridge at the junction of the streams, or by a direct path from the Goat Hotel.

The mountainous character of the neighbourhood of Beddgelert will suggest that it is a spot rather for definite walks than for casual strolls, and this is the case, though the ramble to Pont Aberglasglyn (*p.* 161) by footpath and road on the west side of the stream, returning by foot-path on the east side is a favourite one, and the Pen-y-gwryd road will repay the rambler for every step he may choose to take along it. If he proceed about half-a-mile beyond Llyn-y-Dinas (3 *m. from Beddgelert*), and then turn to the right over a bridge across the Glaslyn, he will in less than 2 miles further enter *Nant-y-mor*, down which a track leads into the Ffestiniog road about 1½ *m.* south of Pont Aberglaslyn. Cynicht is the prominent mountain to the south of this route, which is about 12 miles in length out and in.

For the ascents of Snowdon, Moel Hebog, and Cynicht from Bedd-gelert, see " Mountain Section."

Beddgelert to Carnarvon. *By road to Rhyd-ddu,* 3¾ *m* ; *and thence by train,* 12¾ *m.* *Total,* 16½ *m.* *Through communication 4 or 5 times a day.* *By road throughout,* 13 *m.*

Route described more fully the reverse way, p. 140.

From Beddgelert the road ascends for nearly 3 miles to a height of nearly 600 ft. Moel Hebog rises steeply out of the valley on the west, and on the east the slopes of Snowdon commence at once. The summit comes into view some distance before reaching the isolated boulder on the left called *Pitt's Head*, which is said to be a wonderfully good likeness, and is most striking when looked back upon after passing it. Then, after passing the featureless *Llyn-y-Gader*, we soon reach **Rhyd-ddu** station, ¼ *m.* beyond which is a small inn, the *Cwellyn Arms*.

Hence the **railway** passes considerably east of the road. and from its more elevated position affords better views. The routes come close together again about half-way down *Llyn Cweilyn* (*p.* 157). Beyond this the end of the lake is soon reached, *Craig Cwm-bychan* descending boldly into its waters on the opposite side. *Nant Mill* (*p.* 157), between the railway and road, is soon passed and we reach *Bettws Garmon* (*inn*). In another mile, at *Waen-fawr station*, the railway turns away to the east up the pretty *Gwrfai glen* and joins the Afonwen branch of the London and North-Western at *Dinas* (*change carriages*) 3 *m.* short of Carnarvon.

The **Road** ascends gradually through the long hamlet of Waen-fawr. From the top of the hill there is a fine view in front over Carnarvon and Anglesey to the Holyhead mountain, and as we descend, the three peaks of the Rivals are conspicuous on the left. We have quitted the mountains, and there is nothing more of special interest till we enter *Carnarvon* (*p.* 133).

Beddgelert to Pen-y-gwryd, 8 *m*; (Llanberis, 14½ *m.*) Capel Curig 12 *m*; Bettws-y-Coed, 17½ *m.*

Coaches daily, early in the afternoon.   **Fares**: *Llanberis*, 4s.; *Capel Curig*, 3s. 6d.; *Bettws-y-Coed*, 6s.

The route to Pen-y-gwryd is described the reverse way, p. 132.

There is no finer valley in Wales, except the wider one of the Mawddach, than the one through which this route passes. The verdure of its strath and the rich, glossy character of the mountain slopes that sink into it, can hardly fail to remind the Cumbrian tourist of Borrowdale. At first the Yr Aran arm of Snowdon descends abruptly into it, on the left, and lower heights on the right. The fine peak of Moel Siabod is seen filling up the gap in front as soon as we leave the village. In 2 miles we reach the charming little *Llyn-y-Ddinas*, beyond which an opening on the left reveals the top of Snowdon itself at the head of *Cwm-y-Llan*. The flanking heights of this cwm are Yr Aran and Lliwedd. Then we pass on the left *Llyn Gwynant* and a long ascent, during which the rocky Glyders bar the prospect in front, takes us to the Pen-y-gwryd Inn, 950 feet above sea-level.

For Pen-y-gwryd to Llanberis, see p. 132; *to Capel Curig and Bettws-y-Coed, p.* 140.

Beddgelert to Ffestiniog.

(1) *Carriage-route by Penrhyn,* 9 m; *Tan-y-Bwlch (Hotel),* 13 m; *Ffestiniog,* 16 m.

(2) *By old-road to Tan-y-Bwlch,* 10 m; *Ffestiniog,* 13 m.

(3) *By mountain-road to Tan-y-Bwlch, about* 8 m; *Ffestiniog,* 11 miles.

(4) *Over or between Cynicht and Moelwyn, see "Mountain Section."*

The interest of these routes varies in proportion to their roughness, the least attractive being the carriage one, and the most attractive that over the mountains. To the pedestrian who wishes to reach Ffestiniog in a few hours without undue exertion, we recommend No. 3, but in any case he will prefer No. 2 to No. 1. All are identical to the far side of Pont Aberglaslyn. No. 3 rejoins No. 2 close to Tan-y-Bwlch station, and No. 2 rejoins No. 1 at Tan-y-Bwlch Hotel. Travellers by No. 2 or 3 may join the train at Tan-y-Bwlch station, 7 or 9 miles on the way, but by No. 1 little is gained by so doing, inasmuch as it is a mile's steep ascent from the hotel to the station in a retrograde direction. The narrow-gauge line from Tan-y-Bwlch has its terminus at Duffws (Blaenau Ffestiniog), whence it is 4 miles by ordinary gauge (G. W. R.) to Ffestiniog Village. The trains do not run in connection, and the stations are about 150 yards apart.

Going by route 4, over Cynicht and Moelwyn, or between them by Cwm Croesor and Cwm Orthin, you descend to Tan-y-grisiau Station, on the narrow-gauge line, 1½ m. short of Blaenau Ffestiniog, or 3 miles by road across the valley from Ffestiniog village.

The Route. From the village of Beddgelert the pedestrian may save the angle formed by the road past the Goat Hotel, by taking a field-path which starts on the right of the wooden bridge at the junction of the streams and, passing near the Church and Gelert's Grave, re-enters the road in a short half-mile. From this point the valley contracts, and road and stream wind side by side through the defile which terminates at *Pont Aberglaslyn.*

Pont Aberglaslyn. The scenery which centres in this famous bridge may without affectation be described as sub-alpine in character; that is, it might be mistaken for several scenes in the Alps—and those, amongst the most beautiful—in miniature, notably points on the roads which lead from the end of the Swiss lakes to the great passes into Italy. Judged from this standard, it may also be fairly urged that what the Welsh scene loses in size and grandeur it very nearly recovers in the beauty and purity of its stream and the rich colouring of its rocks.

The *Bridge* itself is a single-arched, ivy-clad structure, thrown from rock to rock just before the stream ceases to be a mountain

torrent and enters upon the last stage of its brief career in the
quiet waters of Traeth-mawr. The water below, clear as crystal,
and green-tinted, flows through a deep rocky channel, and the
cliffs, abundantly sprinkled with fir, rise steeply to a height of
several hundred feet on either side. For the best view of the
scene, walk a little way along the Portmadoc road, and then return leisurely. Thus seen, the rock, on the east of the bridge, has
a conical outline, and the whole picture is more compact and
complete than from other points of view.

From the Bridge you may return to Beddgelert by a path along the east side
of the stream, or you may climb the rock on the same side and make your way
back along the ridge of Craig-y-Llan. You will re-enter Beddgelert by the
wooden bridge before mentioned, or by one a little higher up the stream.

The **old bridle-route** to Tan-y-Bwlch, in parts not much more than a
track, turns to the left (or, rather, the carriage-road turns to the right out of
it) after crossing a streamlet ½ m. beyond Pont Aberglaslyn. The way is described in the ascent of Moelwyn (*Mountain Section*), the first-half of it from
Beddgelert, the last from Tan-y-Bwlch.

We have fully described the rest of both the new and the old
carriage-road to Tan-y-Bwlch and Ffestiniog in the Ffestiniog
Section (*p.* 174). They are identical for about 4 miles, winding
round the base of the hills that rise from the east side of Traeth-
mawr. There are two fair inns—the *Alfred* (3 *m.*), close to the
crossing of the Cwm Croesor stream and tramway, and the *Brondanw Arms*, ⅔ *m.* further. A capital view of Cynicht is obtained
on the way. Then at the old *Pen-y-gyffiniau toll-house* the old
road strikes up the hill to the left and, after affording fine views
of Cynicht and Moelwyn on the left and across Traeth-mawr to
Portmadoc and Harlech on the right, drops steeply from the
station to the hotel of Tan-y-Bwlch.

The new road (omitted on the Ordnance map between Pen-y-
gyffiniau and Penrhyn) continues south along the level of Traeth-
mawr to the little rocky ridge, near the top of which are the *village*
and *station* of **Penrhyn**, straggling and unkempt. From the station
it drops sharply into a minor valley, through which the road passes
from Portmadoc to Ffestiniog. Turning back up this at an acute
angle, there is nothing of interest till you descend through a
wooded part into the Ffestiniog valley, on entering which you see
the church of Ffestiniog, and the mountain Manod-mawr right
ahead. Then, passing the beautiful grounds of *Plas* on the left,
you rejoin the old road at *Tan-y-Bwlch Hotel* (*p.* 174). Maentwrog (*p.* 176), is half-a-mile further, on the other side of the river,
but the road to Ffestiniog turns to the left beyond the bridge,
without entering it. *For Ffestiniog, see p.* 167.

Beddgelert to **Glaslyn Inn**, 4½ *m*; **Tremadoc**, 7 *m*; **Portmadoc**, 8 *m*. (*or by short cut from Glaslyn Inn, 7 m.*).

Several coaches during the day. Fare, 2s. 6d.

This road is the same as the one to Ffestiniog as far as Pont Aberglaslyn, instead of crossing which it continues along the west side of the widening valley at the foot of the pleasant slope of *Moel-ddu* (pron. "Moel thee"). As the valley grows in breadth the river becomes a sluggish stream, and the level strath across it is only interesting as forming—by contrast—a most effective foreground to the rugged heights of Moelwyn, Cynicht, and Snowdon. As we advance, Cynicht assumes the appearance of a pyramid, and from nowhere does the peak of Snowdon show to greater advantage than from the neighbourhood of Portmadoc and Tremadoc. The *Glaslyn Inn* is a comfortable little house, and the shortest way from it to Portmadoc is along a straight foot-path which leads to the Cwm Croesor tramway; proceeding along this you reach the Cambrian railway a little east of the station. The road makes an acute angle through *Tremadoc* (*p.* 164), before reaching which town it passes under a fine range of cliff—more like limestone than slate in its appearance—overgrown with ivy and with a wood-covered scree at its foot. The hill in front is Moel-y-Gest.

Portmadoc [Hotels: *Sportsman* (H.Q.), near Cambrian Sta., *Royal Commercial*, in town; *Queen's* (Q.), opp. station; *Hughes' Temp.*, High St. *Post arr. abt.* 8.15 *a.m.*; *dep.* 5.45 *p.m. Pop.* 2,000], between the stations of the Cambrian and Ffestiniog railways, owes its importance to its position as shipping-port for the Ffestiniog slates. Though not in itself a tourist resort, the meeting of the railways and the commencement of the road-route to Beddgelert and Snowdon combine to cause a constant flow of tourists through it, and a few hours may be very agreeably spent in walking by the *Terrace Road*, which turns to the right at the Market Hall, to the little bay called *Borth*, and in ascending the adjacent height of Moel-y-Gest. The distance between the two stations is about half-a-mile.

Moel-y-Gest (*abt.* 750 *ft.*, 2 *hrs. up and down*) is the rough little hill rising immediately west of Portmadoc between the Cambrian railway and the sea. The sharpness of the climb up it is fully atoned for by the view, which derives its excellence from the isolated position of the hill itself, though it must be admitted that Traeth-mawr, when seen *in extenso*, as it is from the heights surrounding it, is a poor foreground.

The way up from the Cambrian Station is by the right-hand turn beyond the Sportsman Hotel (from the Ffestiniog Station by the left-hand turn, a little short of the same house). Then left, past the elegant new *Church of St. John*. A few yards further you pass behind a large house and enter a lane which tra-

verses a wood. It is best to keep to this lane, avoiding paths upward to the left, until you come out of the wood and see the
highest part of the hill before you. A steep scramble up the
rocky slope places you on the first top, which overlooks Portmadoc.
There is a higher one reached by crossing a small gulley and a
wall, some way to the west and looking towards Pwllheli.

The *View* extends southwards past Harlech Castle along the coast
and inland to the Rhinog range; **eastward up** the vale of Ffestiniog; then, more **to the left,** across Traeth-mawr to Moelwyn,
Cynicht, and Snowdon. To the north, Moel-ddu and Moel Hebog
are close at hand over Tremadoc; and westward there is a wide
prospect, including the Rivals and the coast of the Lleyn promontory over Criccieth and Pwllheli to St. Tudwal's Isles.

The return route may be made through *Tremadoc*, and in
that case a little care is required to avoid the quarries which lie
on the north slope of the hill a little below the summit. You may
go to the right or the left of them (in the latter case you skirt a
wood), and the rest of the way, as well as that back from Tremadoc to Portmadoc, cannot be mistaken. The whole round is
from 4 to 5 miles.

Portmadoc to Tremadoc, 1¼ *m*; *and* Beddgelert, 8 *m*.

Coaches several times a day.   Fare, 2s. 6d.

*Route described the reverse way, p. 163. Pedestrians may save
a mile by following the Cwm Croesor tramway and a foot-path as far
as the Glaslyn Inn.*

The road goes past the Cambrian Station (the tramway some
distance east of it), and crosses the strath to **Tremadoc** (*small
pub. houses*). This village, built by Mr. Madocks,[*] M.P., early
in the century, has been commercially superseded by Portmadoc.
It lies under the abrupt and picturesque cliff of *Yr-allt-wen* (the
"white cliff"), the foot of which is skirted by the road on to
Beddgelert for a considerable distance. On the other (right-hand)
side the dead-level of Traeth-mawr offers a strong contrast. A
long 2 miles from Tremadoc, we pass the pleasant little *Glaslyn
Inn*, at which the foot-route from Portmadoc converges. Thence
the river is close at hand on the right all the way to Pont Aberglaslyn. Over the strath there is a fine view, heightened in effect
by the contrast between the level valley and the rugged peaks
of Moelwyn, Cynicht and Snowdon. Approaching from this
side, too, we obtain the most compact and admirable view of
Pont Aberglaslyn. (*For full description see p.* 161). *Beddgelert* is 1½ miles further, but those bound for the village may save a
little by taking a foot-path where the road turns away from the
stream. *Gelert's Grave* is in a small shaded enclosure in the last
field but one before entering the village. For the "*Goat*" stick
to the road. *For Beddgelert, see p.* 158.

---

[*] This gentleman also reclaimed Traeth-mawr by building the "cob" or
embankment across its mouth.

ffestiniog Section.

Portmadoc to Ffestiniog* by the "Toy" Railway.

Portmadoc to Mynffordd Junction, 2¼ m; Penrhyn, 3¼ m; Tan-y-Bwlch, 7¾ m; Tan-y-grisiau, 11¾ m; Blaenau Ffestiniog, 13 m; Duffws, 13¼ m.

‚ Passengers proceeding Bettws-y-Coed way by the L. & N.W. railway should book to Blaenau Ffestiniog ; those for the Great Western, or to Ffestiniog Village, to Duffws, 2 minutes' walk from the Great Western terminus.

The Ffestiniog railway came into existence as a tram-line along which slate-laden wagons descended by their own gravitation from Ffestiniog to Portmadoc, and were dragged up again, empty, by horse-power. At first the abruptness of the curves forbade all idea of working it by locomotives, but the application of the "bogie" principle—by which each set of wheels, working on a central pivot underneath a vehicle, can follow the curvature of the line without being affected by the rigidity of the vehicle itself—overcame this difficulty, and the Fairlie double bogie-engines not only promoted the tramway to the rank of a steam railway, but enabled it very shortly to come out as a full-blown passenger line. Its first appearance in that character produced a sensation which put all the other " Wonders of Wales " as deeply into the shade as an electric light puts an ordinary street lamp, and though the wonder has somewhat worn off, still no orthodox tourist visits Wales without taking a turn, one way or the other, on the "Toy" railway; and indeed, apart from its sensational character, the journey is a most interesting one.†

As lately as 1876, Mr. Spooner, to whom as engineer and manager the prosperity of the line is mainly due, had the honour of conducting over it a Royal Commission, headed by the Duke of Sutherland and containing distinguished representatives from all parts of Europe. The gradients of the line are only remarkable for the skill with which severe ones have been avoided. The rise from Portmadoc to Ffestiniog is about 700 feet. The average gradient is thus less than 1 in 100, and the greatest is 1 in 68.

* We retain the double F in the spelling of Ffestiniog for consistency's sake (*see Introductory Remarks*). In Welsh the English sound of F is represented by double F, the single F being pronounced like the English V, as Moel Fammau (pron. "Moel Vamma "). There is no more real excuse for spelling Ffestiniog with a single F than there would be for writing Llandidno instead of Llandudno. The inconsistency is, perhaps, best shown by the fact that in the case of Mynffordd, on this very line of railway, the double F is retained.
† The lines from Dinas to Rhyd-ddu, from Machynlleth to Abercorris, and from Towyn to Abergynolwyn are equally "Toy" in regard to gauge.

This comparative evenness has been attained by accommodating
the course of the line as far as possible to the slope of the
mountains, and by an unstinted use of blasting powder where
necessary. The original cost, we are told, was about £6,000 a
mile.

Commercially, the line has been a great success, and though,
of course, the slate-quarries have irretrievably ruined the natural
attractions of the immediate locality in which they are hewn, it
cannot be fairly asserted that the railway has seriously affected
the physical character of the country through which it passes.
From the valley below its presence can hardly be detected except
by the passing of a train, and in itself it forms a terrace-route
from which the beauties of the Ffestiniog valley are seen to great
advantage. The coaches and trucks, again, are small and unob-
trusive, and the most sensitive tourist need have no fear of
sustaining such a shock as that which is inflicted on his better
nature by—say—the first sight of the shrieking iron monstrosity
which takes lovers of the beautiful—save the mark!—up the
Rigi.

The Route. Quitting Portmadoc, the line at once crosses the
long embankment by which the extensive flat of Traeth-mawr is
protected from the sea (*p.* 164). Side by side with it runs the
road, and while crossing, we have a grand head-to-foot view of
Moel Hebog, Snowdon, Cynicht and Moelwyn. The tapering peak
of Snowdon itself shows to great advantage over its outlier **Yr
Aran.** On the other side, Harlech Castle is seen across the water.

At **Mynffordd Junction** we cross the Cambrian line, and pick
up passengers from Barmouth and other places along the coast.
Beyond it Cynicht and Moelwyn are again prominent. Then
comes *Penrhyn* (called *Penrhyn Deudraeth* on the Cambrian line).
It lies below us on the right, and is the abode of quarrymen.
A stretch of dullish moorland succeeds. Then, as we ascend,
lovely peeps are obtained through the intervals in the oak-copse,
which skirts the line for a long distance, into the lower part, or
strath of the Ffestiniog valley, watered by the winding stream of
the Dwyryd, which is seen flowing through a low rocky defile into
the sea. We pass immediately above and behind the finely
placed mansion of *Plas*; Maentwrog appears at the foot of a
rocky knoll far below, and the steeple of Ffestiniog church
crowning a green hill at the far end of the valley. Another
minute, and we are going almost back again—right away from
the depths into which the line seemed about to plunge. This,
the sharpest curve upon it, works round the Tan-y-Bwlch glen,
on the far side of which is **Tan-y-Bwlch** station. If our train
happens to be crossing another there, the latter will very likely
be seen running in the same direction, and parallel with us. Tan-
y-Bwlch station is 400 feet above the sea, a long mile above
Tan-y-Bwlch Hotel, and 1½ miles from Maentwrog. Just beyond it
a little fall is noticeable on the left, and a lake on the right. Then

we pass through a short tunnel and, on emerging from it, get a
pretty view of Ffestiniog village. The next bend affords a more
extensive one down the green strath seawards, and then comes
a tunnel ¾ m. long. Issuing from it, the valley has vanished, and
we are traversing barren hollows at the foot of Moelwyn. On the
left, the mountain-side is strewn with rocky debris. **Tan-y-
gristau** station, 630 feet above the sea and the best starting
point for the summit of Moelwyn, is soon reached, and beyond it
comes a green upland over which Ffestiniog Church re-appears,
but our journey is almost over. Cyclopean walls of slate pierced
by black caves, break-neck inclines, and tramways that look as if
they were off in search of the moon, indicate our arrival at the
new Ffestiniog:—The old one is 4 miles further, on the Great
Western line to Bala. If bound thither, we must go on to the
"Toy" terminus, Duffws. The platform at Blaenau Ffestiniog is
adjacent to the L. and N. W. station.

Blaenau Ffestiniog (Duffws).

Hotels: *North Western*, close to the L. and N.W. station ; *Queens*. close to
Duffws and Great Western stations.

Post: *Arr. abt.* 7 *a.m.* ; 4.15 *p.m. (callers only)* ; *dep.* 5.30 *p.m.* (*abt.* 7 *p.m* in
summer).

Distances (*by rail*) : Dolwyddelen, 6¾ *m* ; Bettws-y-Coed, 12¼ *m*. Ffestiniog
Village, 3¼ *m* ; Bala, 25 *m*. Portmadoc, 13¼ *m* ; Barmouth. 28 *m*.

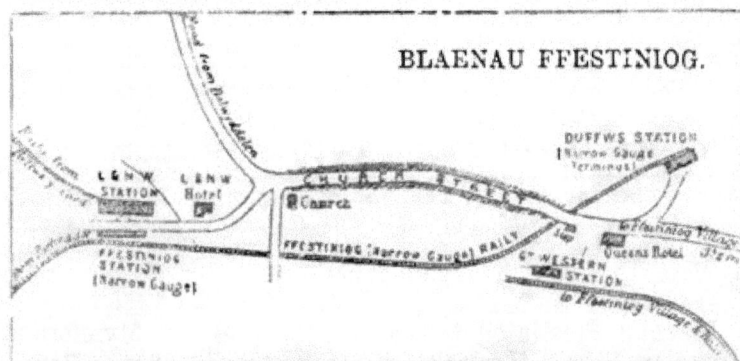

BLAENAU FFESTINIOG.

Ffestiniog and **Blaenau Ffestiniog** are 4 miles apart. The
former is the original village ; the latter the modern town, the centre
of the slate-quarries and the nucleus of the three railways—

L. & N. W., **G. W. and Ffestiniog. We follow** the authority of the Post **Office, which has been accepted by the** L. & N. W. and G. W. Railways. **The Ffestiniog Company, however,** call their terminus, which is within a stone's **throw of the** G. W. Blaenau Ffestiniog, *Duffws* (pronounced " Diffoos "). As a town, Blaenau is the creation of a few years. Its situation at the head of one of the branches of the Ffestiniog valley is naturally a fine one, but the mountains which rise immediately behind and beside it **have** been mutilated in such wholesale fashion by slate-quarries, large and small, that it is impossible even to guess what its present natural features **are—it has none.** The town possesses no attractions for tourists, **except** such as wish to explore quarries. The hotel accommodation, however, is good, the North-Western being in the hands of the L. & N. W. Company, and the " Queen's " maintaining a well-earned reputation, so no tourist need be afraid of having to stay **a night or more** here.

Blaenau is the **nearest resting-place** from which to ascend Moelwyn. *For the ascent see* " *Mountain Section.*" The mountains east of the town are bulky, and of no interest. The principal ones are *Manod-mawr* and *Manod-bach*, between which lies *Llyn-y-Manod*, a considerable **sheet of** water. From Manod-mawr there is, however, a fine full-length view of the Ffestiniog valley. *For description of a quarry see p.* 178.

Blaenau Ffestiniog **to** Dolwyddelen, 6¾ m; *and* **Bettws-y-Coed**, 12½ m. (*by rail*).

Route fully described the reverse way, p. 127.

A tunnel two **miles long passes** from the slate-quarries of Ffestiniog to the Lledr **valley, in** its higher part bleak and ragged. (The road goes over the hill.) Issuing from the tunnel, we have Moel Siabod in its most impressive aspect on the left front, and a strip of the Glyders over its western **slope;** then, between Roman Bridge and Dolwyddelen stations, the peaks of Snowdon come into view over a depression, still **more to the left.** The shell of *Dolwyddelen Castle* **is passed,** also on **the left, a** mile short of *Dolwyddelen* (p. 127) Station. The rest of the way is through the best part of the Lledr valley, specially beautiful at *Pont-y-pant*. Then, as we approach the meeting of the Lledr and the Conway, the retrospect of Siabod **is** perfect. Hereabouts the line turns sharp to the left for *Bettws-y-Coed*. The Fairy Glen is close at hand on the right, but **not seen.**

Blaenau Ffestiniog to Tan-y-Bwlch, 5½ m; **Mynffordd Junction, 11** m; **(Harlech,** 18 m; Barmouth, 28 *m.*); **Portmadoc,** 13½ m.

Route to Portmadoc fully described the reverse way p. 166.

Starting from *Duffws* (pron. " Diffoos "),—the Ffestiniog terminus, **close to** that of the Great Western,—or from *Blaenau* itself, the change-point with the **London and** North-Western, **the line** bends round **the quarry-seamed side of** Moelwyn and, beyond *Tan-y-grisiau*, **enters a tunnel from which** it emerges high **up** above the main Ffestiniog valley. **Then comes its most beautiful part.** Winding like a serpent along the slopes of Moelwyn-bach it affords delightful **glimpses of Ffestiniog village,** Maentwrog, and Tan-y-Bwlch. **The** *Tan-y-Bwlch hotel* **is a mile below** the *station* of **the same name.** About here the line is so tortuous as almost to render **excusable the hyperbole that** the engine-driver **of** a long **train can shake hands with the guard** (at least the **train** need **only be a mile and a half and the** driver's and guard's arms **an eighth of a mile long).** Beyond **this** loop we pass just over the **mansion and** grounds of *Plas*, and get **a** good view down the Ffestiniog river to its estuary. The rest of the way is featureless, until beyond *Mynffordd Junction* we cross the long embankment by which Traeth-mawr is saved from the encroachments **of the sea.** Looking to **the right up this** there is a splendid view **of Moel** Hebog, Snowdon, **Cynicht, and Moelwyn.** Then we enter *Portmadoc* station (*for the town, &c., see p.* 163).

Mynffordd Junction to Harlech, 7 m; Barmouth, 28 m.

The two stations ("Ffestiniog" and "**Cambrian**") adjoin one another.

From Mynffordd the line descends to the **sea-level**, which it reaches at *Penrhyn-Deudraeth*. Thence it bends sharp to the right, crossing the mouth of the Ffestiniog valley and revealing, before the bend, a view of Harlech Castle and, after it, of Snowdon and its satellites, all on the right hand. The run on to *Harlech* is across a level marsh. The Castle is just above the station, on the left-hand. Then, after passing *Penarn* there is a very pretty view, on the left, up the Artro glen. Rhinog-fawr, Rhinog-fach and Llethr are seen beyond it, and the green round hill nearer at hand is Moelfre. Dull slopes intersected by stone walls succeed on the left, and across the sea on the right the Rivals and the lessening range which extends to Bardsey island at the far end of Carnarvonshire, come into view. Entered from this side Barmouth displays none of the characteristic beauty of its neighbourhood. *For the town, see Part* II.

Blaenau Ffestiniog (G.W.R.) to Ffestiniog Village, 3¾ m.

This little **line was formerly of the** same **gauge as** the Ffestiniog railway, but having been bought by the Great Western Company, and made part **of their Bala and** Ffestiniog branch, it has been widened into the ordinary gauge. It is carried high up above the end of the Vale of Ffestiniog and affords a fine view seawards along the length of that charming valley. Moelwyn limits the view to the north-west, the humpy Manods appear to the east, and southwards is the high ground which separates the valley from the barren moor of Trawsfynydd and the rocky Rhinog hills.

Ffestiniog Village (Hotels: *Pengwern Arms, Abbey* (H.Q.). Inn: *Newborough Arms*. *Post, arr.* 8 *a.m.; dep.* 4.50 *p.m.*) owes its attractiveness to the commanding position which it occupies at the head of the Ffestiniog valley. The *Church* crowns a green knoll

that drops at once almost to sea-level. For the view go through
a gate on the south side of the churchyard and pass along the
side of the wall to the west end. There are no special features in
the prospect beyond the valley itself and Moelwyn, but it is certainly one of the best set views in Wales, and will charm every
beholder. With a few mundane attractions thrown in, "a loving
wife, a bosom friend, and a good set of books," a former Lord
Lyttleton once wrote that he could "pass an age here and think
it a day," and Ffestiniog has reason to be grateful for the
words.

The **Cynfael Falls, Rhaiadr-cwm, &c.** No one stays
many hours at Ffestiniog without strolling across the fields to the
"Falls," and they are well worth visiting, not so much for themselves as for the charming little dell in which they occur. The
stroll may be turned into a walk of 7 or 8 miles, by continuing
across the railway to Rhaiadr-cwm and returning by the deserted
Bala road.

Go down-hill for a few yards past the church towards Maentwrog,
and pass through a gate on the left opposite the Newborough
Arms—the one that leads into a farm-yard. Pass through the
yard and, being careful not to descend at once to the valley, follow
an obvious path which soon crosses a little hollow. In about $\frac{3}{4}$ m.
the way down to the lower fall, passing some farm-sheds, is
equally obvious. A rude flight of steps leads down to a little
bridge which spans the stream, and is put there to afford a view of
the *Lower Fall*. There is nothing remarkable either in height or
volume, but the ravine through which the stream forces its way
between walls of rock, broken by green shady slopes and festooned
with ferns and mosses, is delightful.

The bridge is a *cul-de-sac*, but a path continues along the north
side of the stream for about $\frac{1}{4}$ mile, during which we pass an
isolated rock, rising about 15 feet above the water. This is called
Hugh Lloyd's Pulpit from the story that a Welsh enthusiast of that
name used to preach from the platform which forms its summit.

A little beyond this the path crosses the stream by a wooden
bridge, and continues along its southern side. On the side we
have just left the rocks hang perpendicular, and in a few hundred
yards we may descend to a good view-point called the *Goat's
Bridge*. A large flat-topped boulder apparently blocks the stream-
bed, and it is only when we reach the little slab that forms an
arch connecting this boulder with the bank that we discover what
has become of the water.

A little further on we come to the *Higher Fall*, which consists
of two—the one shelving, the other sheer, dropping from 30 to
40 feet in all. Above these the gorge ceases, the path emerging
from the wood and continuing under the railway-bridge. By
following the stream for a few hundred yards further we reach
the Ffestiniog and Trawsfynydd road at *Pont Newydd*, $1\frac{1}{4}$ miles
from Ffestiniog.

For **Rhaiadr-cwm** cross Pont Newydd and take the lane to the right on the other side. In ¼ m. turn right again by a road which descends to the stream and continues along its northern side. Follow this, avoiding the ford and the stepping-stones where the stream is first reached. In about a mile you will reach *Cwm Cynfael*, the highest house in the valley.

A field or so beyond this the road, which has become a mere cart-track, winds abruptly up to the left, leaving a rocky knoll between itself and the stream.

The *cataracts* of *Rhaiadr-cwm*, by which the waters descend from the upland wastes, now appear in front. At the severe Easter-tide of 1883, when the writer visited this spot, they were a group of icicles.

Above Rhaiadr-cwm our track joins the high-road—high indeed as any in Wales. About half-a-mile further, and just where the Penmachno road strikes off to the left, is, or was, a little way-side house called *Aber-mignant* (6 days license). Hence it is 3½ miles back to Ffestiniog by the main road. About half-a-mile on the way we pass ¼ m. south of **Llyn-y-Morwynion** (the "lake of the maidens"), so called from a tradition so like that of the Sabine Women, that in its appropriation we can hardly acquit "Taffy" of that thievish propensity which has been, generally speaking, so libellously attributed to him. The men of Ardudwy, says the story, made a successful foray into the Vale of Clwyd after wives. Returning with their booty they were hotly pursued by the men of Clwyd, and overtaken at this spot ; a bloody battle ensued ; the Clwydians triumphed and the men of Ardudwy were slain to a man. The wives, however, had become such willing prisoners that rather than return to their native homes they rushed down the steep hill-sides and were drowned in the lake.

About a mile down the stream issuing from the lake and on the right bank is a place called **Beddau-gwyr-Ardudwy** (the "graves of the men of Ardudwy"). All trace of these graves has disappeared. In Pennant's time only a few upright stones remained. The site is half-a-mile north of the main road and on the old Roman way, *Sarn Helen*, 2 miles from Ffestiniog village.

During the descent to Ffestiniog a fine view of the Moelwyn range presents itself and, as we approach the village, the Vale of Ffestiniog appears in front in all its characteristic beauty.

Tomen-y-mur, Rhaiadr Du, the Raven Fall, &c.

A very pleasant walk from Ffestiniog village may be made to include all these more or less attractive spots, which may with equal ease be visited from Maentwrog (pronounced "Mentoorog"), or Tan-y-Bwlch ; except that from Ffestiniog about 2 miles of walking may be saved by taking train to Maentwrog Road Station. *Approx. Dist.* :—Ffestiniog to Tomen-y-mur, 3¼ *m* ; Rhaiadr-Du, 6¼ *m* ; Raven Fall, 6½ *m* ; Maentwrog, 8½ *m* ; Tan-y-Bwlch, 9 *m*.

Tomen-y-mur is simply a Roman or British mound crowning an eminence amongst desolate but not uncultivated scenery, and commanding a wide panoramic view ; while the Falls are, not only in themselves but also in respect of the glen in which they are placed, amongst the most picturesque objects of their kind in Wales.

Pedestrians may include in the walk the Ffestiniog (Cynfael) Falls by following the route described on page 170, and continuing from the foot-bridge above Hugh Lloyd's Pulpit, by path

up the hill, under the line and out into the road, a long half-mile
short of Maentwrog Road Station. Otherwise, if the train-time
fits, the journey so far is best made by rail, as the road goes a
long way round and affords no compensating interest.

From Maentwrog Road Station follow the road for a few hundred yards till it joins that coming up from Maentwrog, opposite a
school-house. Here turn to the left, and in 350 yards leave the
high-road by the second cart-road on the left (the first passes
through a gate and has a building between it and the railway).
This road goes under the line at once and is very rough to begin
with. Then it improves, and after a few minutes' walking you see
Tomen-y-mur crowning a grassy knoll behind a farm-stead. It
is a double-topped mound, about 25 feet high—Roman, British, or
what else we must leave to individual judgment. The view
from this commanding site is extensive, and northwards,
over the vale of Ffestiniog, remarkably fine. Moel Hebog
rises to the left, and Moel Siabod to the right of Moelwyn—the latter in the gap between it and the lumpy Manods.
Southward, over the dreary upland in which Trawsfynydd appears amid its firs, like an oasis, we see Cader Idris; to the left
of it and nearer at hand, Rhobell-fawr, and farther away again
the Arans. The dark, rocky Rhinog range commences in the
south-east with Diphwys, and extends due south. Between
Rhinog-fawr and Rhinog-fach is the dip called Bwlch-drws-Ardudwy.

A few yards south-west of Tomen-y-mur was, according to
Ordnance Survey, *Heriri Mons*, a crossing-place of two Roman
roads, the chief one being Sarn Helen, running from South to
North Wales.

Returning to the road and the school-house we may either
descend direct to Maentwrog (*p.* 176) or, after proceeding ¼ mile
down the road in that direction, take a lane on the left just opposite the divergence of the private road to that village. This lane
turns to the right in half-a-mile opposite a gateway leading to a
farm, and ¼ mile further forks, the right-hand branch descending
to the Maentwrog road again, and the left-hand continuing
slightly up on to open ground. Take the latter. From it there is
a beautiful view across and up the Ffestiniog valley, and in
another short half-mile you will pass a cottage on the right, from
which the road commences a steep descent into the lovely glen
that contains Rhaiadr-du and the Raven Falls. After a short
descent you will see a wall with a door in it some way below on
the left. Passing through this door and dropping steeply for a
few yards through the wood, you enter the track that leads up the
valley to the higher Fall (*Rhaiadr-du*). Turn up this to the
left, and a few minutes' walking places you opposite one of the
most charming scenes of its kind in the country. **Rhaiadr-du**
(the "Black Fall") occurs at the bend of the stream, and has the
peculiarity of a vertical twist during its descent. On both sides
are sombre rocks crowned with oak-trees, and at its foot is a deep

:auldron-like hollow, in which the water lies still and dark for a
ew yards before resuming its torrent-rush down the glen.

The Raven Fall (*see below*) is a little lower down the glen.
To reach it return by the path, but instead of ascending to the
loorway, keep straight on till you pass through a wicket, and con-
inue along the path until you come to an old lime-kiln close to
he crossing of a streamlet. Here a path strikes sharply back to
he left (you may cut off this corner by scrambling down at once
after passing through the wicket). Follow this for 300 yards, and
hen, diverging a little to the right, you will get a fair view of the
'all, but hereabouts it is rather the general beauty of the stream
han any one particular fall that forms the enchantment.

Hence returning to the main track, you re-enter the road you
eft when descending to the doorway, just short of a gate, and after
a sharp descent of half-a-mile, enter the high-road a mile S.W. of
Maentwrog, and 1½ miles of *Tan-y-Bwlch*.

Raven Fall, 2 m; and Rhaiadr-du, 2¼ m; from Maentwrog (½ m. more from Tan-y-Bwlch). *Guide at the Ivy Bridge
Cottage,* 1 m. on way. A lovely walk.

The way is rather intricate, and those who do not take the guide
hould particularly note the following directions :—

Take the Harlech road for ¾ mile, and then turn up the lane on
he left, which for a short distance runs a little above the high
oad, and then turns sharply up the glen opposite the guide's
ottage. A little way up you pass a farm called *Y-Felin-Rhyd-
ach,* and hereabouts the glen is cultivated. Then you come to a
rate, beyond which take the grassy cart-track which diverges to
he right and soon comes to an old lime-kiln. A few yards short
of this there is another fork, whence the right hand branch takes
ou to the *Raven Fall,* the left hand to *Rhaiadr-du.* The view-
oint for the former is a little off the track, 300 yards beyond the
iln. A cross-path marks the exact spot, and the fall is seen from
n overhanging bit of cliff under some birch trees—a place to be
n no account visited in anything but broad daylight. Far down
elow, the water tumbles about 30 feet almost sheer into a cavern-
us hollow, and then, after forming a dark pool, slides over one or
wo shelves of rock.

Thence for Rhaiadr-du the simplest plan is to return to the
iln and take the other path, but a corner may be cut off by
crambling up the cross-path before mentioned. The path from
he kiln comes to a wall in which, a little to the right, is a wicket
eading into a wood. Thence it continues direct to Rhaiadr-du.
For description see p. 172.)

You may vary the return by going only half-way back to the
vicket, and then turning up by a rough path that goes through a
oor in the boundary-wall of the wood. A little higher up you
nter the cart-track which you left when you first diverged to the
iln. Go right up this road, passing a cottage on the left, and in

another half-mile, when you rejoin a fenced road after enjoying
a fine view of the Ffestiniog valley, turn to the left. The lane
thus entered leads into the Maentwrog and Trawsfynydd road, a
mile above Maentwrog.

Ffestiniog Village to Tan-y-Bwlch (3 m.), and Beddgelert, 16 m.

Pedestrians may save 3 miles by following the old road (very
rough for carriages) from Tan-y-Bwlch Hotel to the old toll-gate
at Pen-y-gyffiniau.   This is still the only one marked on the
Ordnance Survey ; or they may cut the distance still shorter and
make the route more interesting by taking a still older track that
quits the old road close to Tan-y-Bwlch station and rejoins it a
few hundreds yards short of Pont Aberglaslyn.   *For this route see
ascents of Moelwyn and Cynicht in "Mountain Section."*
From Ffestiniog the road descends rapidly round the south side
of the church and reaches the strath of the valley at Tal-y-bont,
underneath which flows the Cynfael stream from the picturesque
glen containing the waterfalls. Moelwyn monopolises the north
side of the valley for several miles.   Maentwrog bridge is 1½ miles
further.   The village of Maentwrog (*p.* 176) rests under a steep
rock a few yards to the left, but, instead of entering it, our road
crosses the bridge, and a third of a mile beyond it reaches the
Tan-y-Bwlch Hotel, as pleasant a place to sojourn at as any
in the neighbourhood.   The situation of the hotel is delightful,
and, happily, no misguided proprietor has ever attempted to
cockneyfy it.   In front of it the house and beautifully-timbered
grounds of *Plas* (visitors are admitted to the grounds by order)
occupy the valley and adjoining slopes, and there is a good view
over the green strath of the Dwyryd beyond.

Old road (*very rough for carriages*).   This ascends through the
woods from the hotel and in a mile passes underneath the
Ffestiniog railway a little to the left of *Tan-y-Bwlch station.*
Thence it passes over a rough moorland to its highest point at
Bwlch-y-maen, where the descent commences to Traeth-mawr.
So far we have had the slopes of Moelwyn on the right-hand all
the way.   Now the sharp clear-cut Cynicht appears on the same
side and Moel Hebog in front.   Then, as we descend with the
deep dell of the Gyffiniau stream on the right-hand, we look
seaward over the wide area of Traeth-mawr to Portmadoc and
Cardigan Bay.   The new road is rejoined a little beyond the foot
of the hill and close to a new church.

The **main road** continues along the valley from Tan-y-Bwlch,
passing the park, woods, and house of *Plas* on the right, and soon
reaching the side of the river, which hereabouts becomes tidal, only
to leave it again in half-a-mile, the last part of the way to
Penrhyn Deudraeth being between gentle and uninteresting hills.

Penrhyn Deudraeth (Inns *Griffin, Osmond*), consists mainly of quarrymen's houses, and is of no interest to the tourist. From it the direct road proceeds to Portmadoc, passing over the Cambrian line at Mynffordd Junction, and crossing the Portmadoc embankment side by side with the Ffestiniog railway.

From the embankment there is a splendid view up the strath, the perfect level of which serves to emphasize, by the force of contrast, the ruggedness of the surrounding peaks of Moel Hebog, Snowdon, Cynicht and Moelwyn.

For **Beddgelert** the new road turns very sharp to the right and ascends to the *station* at Penrhyn, whence, after rising for a short distance, it drops again to the flat area of Traeth-mawr. During the ascent Harlech Castle is a prominent object in the rear, and on gaining the summit there is a grand amphitheatre of mountains in front—Moel Hebog, Snowdon, Cynicht and Moelwyn displaying their most striking outlines. The view is improved by climbing one of the rocky hillocks on the right of the road.

Proceeding due northwards along Traeth-mawr we rejoin the old road 1½ miles beyond Penrhyn, and half-a-mile further pass the *Brondanw Arms Inn*, and about the same distance further, the *Alfred Inn*, opposite to which our road turns sharp to the left. We are now at the opening of Cwm Croesor, and, looking up it, we have a very fine view of the pyramid-like peak of Cynicht, one of the most striking in Wales. (*See* "*Mountain Section.*") A little further on our road doubles round a woody knoll which is the commencement of the rise from the strath to the mountains. A little distance, but no time, may be saved by taking a path across it. The views up the woody glens on the right during this part of the journey are very charming—especially that of *Nant-y-Mor*, after crossing which we ascend slightly over copsy ground, and then, turning abruptly to the right, descend again to *Cwm Bychan* and *Pont Aberglaslyn*.

This scene is fully described in the Beddgelert and Portmadoc route (*p.* 161). The approach to the bridge from this side winds between a rocky wood-crowned knoll and the side of the stream. The suddenness of the transition from the open country to a ravine so narrow as to barely afford room for the road and the river, is very effective. We cross the bridge, turn to the right (for the best view go a few yards to the left), and in less than a mile emerge from the pass on to the level meadow-land, in the midst of which is "Gelert's grave," and at the far end of it the village and church of Beddgelert. The *Goat Hotel* is 200 yards short of the village, the *Llewelyn Arms* and the *Saracen's Head* in it. Beyond Pont Aberglaslyn a corner may be cut off by an obvious foot-path commencing where the road quits the side of the stream.

For **Beddgelert**, see p. 58.

Ffestiniog Village to Maentwrog, 3 m; Harlech, 13 m; Barmouth, 23 m. by road.

Since the construction of the railways this road has been comparatively little traversed, and those who have already explored
the immediate neighbourhood of Maentwrog will gain more than
they lose by adopting the railway route (*see above*).

For the route as far as *Maentwrog, see p.* 174.

On approaching the village you bend to the left instead of
crossing the bridge to Tan-y-Bwlch. At the turn a milestone tells
you how far it is to everywhere.

Maentwrog (Hotel: *The Grapes. Post arr.* 8.30 *a.m., dep.* 4.20
p.m.) lies close under a low almost sheer rock that partly blocks the
valley and forms a perfect screen to the village from the east. When
the tourist has viewed Rhaiadr-du and the Raven **Fall** (*pp.* 172
173), there is nothing special to do except to take a peep into the
churchyard and, perhaps, mount to the top of the rock, which he
may attain by turning out of the Trawsfynydd road about 100
yards up it. In the *Churchyard* are three fine yews, and at the
south-west angle of the church is the *Stone* (Maen) *of Twrog*, an
unadorned monument 4 feet high, which throws no light on its
own history. Pronounce "Men," or, rather, "Man-toorog."

A mile beyond Maentwrog we cross the lovely *Rhaiadr-du*
("Black Fall") *glen* at its mouth, whence the old road to Harlech
starts up through the wood *, and then for some miles the road
passes close between the hills and the river, here widening into
its estuary, which is flanked by rocks and picturesque. The rest
of the way to Harlech is over a flat, the road skirting the hills a
little way from the railway. At *Talsarnau* there is a fair little inn
a little distance from the station.

The road from Harlech to Barmouth keeps more or less near
the railway (*p.* 169), rather above it, and calls for no separate
description.

Ffestiniog Village to Bala (*by road*), 19 m., or to **Penmachno,**
9½ m; and Bettws-y-Coed (*by road*), 14 m.

What little tourist traffic there ever was along these roads has been almost
entirely diverted, first by the railway from Bettws-y-Coed, and then by that
from Bala to Ffestiniog. They both pass over high ground for a great part of
the distance, and afford good distant views, but the foreground is for the most
part bare and featureless. Exception must be made in favour of the last few
miles into Bettws-y-Coed, which are described in the Corwen and Bettws route

---

* This road (about 10 m. in length) reaches in a mile the shores of *Llyn Tec-
wyn-uchaf* (the "higher Tecwyn Lake"), a considerable sheet of water in the
midst of low hills. *Moel Tecwyn* is a little to the right of its near end, and
commands a good view, including Snowdon, almost due north, and the Lleyn
promontory. *Llandecwyn Church* and *Llyn Tecwyn-isaf* ("lower") are then
passed, and a small glen is entered, at the end of which, after crossing the stream
we gain high ground and command a fine all-round prospect. Finally, we
wind down to *Harlech* by the lane that leads from that village to Glen Artro
and Cwm Bychan.

(*p. 126*), and, in a smaller degree, of the last part of the Bala route, where the road threads a pretty valley alongside of the stream and the railway. There is a small road-side house, where the two roads part, 3¼ *m*. from Ffestiniog ; also one or two inns at Penmachno on the Bettws road, and one at Rhyd-y-fen (10 *m. from Ffestiniog*) on that to Bala. Rhyd-y-fen lies directly between the two Arenigs, and is the best starting point for them (*see* Part II.).

Ffestiniog Village to Bala (*by rail*); *Ffestiniog Village to Maentwrog-road*, 2 *m*; *Trawsfynydd*, 5 *m*; *Arenig*, 13½ *m*; *Frongoch*, 19 *m*; *Bala* (*town*), 21½ *m*; (*Junction*), 22½ *m*.

This line, starting at a height of 700 ft. above sea-level, is carried over high ground for the greater part of its course, reaching its summit-level near Llyn Tryweryn (1,196 *ft.*), whence it drops rapidly by the side of the Tryweryn stream, which it follows all the rest of the way to Bala. The first part commands a succession of fine prospects, the middle portion passes between barren and lofty mountains, and for the last six or seven miles the line threads a pleasant valley. For the first half of the distance it forms an irregular semicircle, going several miles south of the road.

Quitting Ffestiniog we have a fine view down the valley, and in about a mile cross the Cynfael glen, a short distance above the waterfalls. Then, as we approach Maentwrog-road, 2 m. above Maentwrog village, Moel Hebog comes into view to the left of Moelwyn. Northwards, to the right of Moelwyn, between it and the bulky Manods, the peak of Moel Siabod appears in the distance, and as we proceed towards Trawsfynydd, a long line of mountains comes into view on the right front. This is the Rhinog range, and consists of a line of notched heights with wild rocky slopes, and little variation in height. Half way between Maentwrog-road and Trawsfynydd we see on the left hand Tomen-y-mur, a double-headed little hump crowning a small green eminence. This was, we are told, a meeting-place of Roman roads, whereof the chief was Sarn Helen (the " causeway of Helen," variously stated to have been the wife of Maximus, of Constantine, and not a woman at all). It ran from North to South Wales, and crops up in all manner of places, distracting alike to the tourist and the guide-book writer. Here, too, says an old authority, in a somewhat vague way, " the English kings used to encamp when they came against Wales." We give the statement for what it is worth.

Trawsfynydd (inns : *Cross Foxes*, &c.) lies about a mile to the west of its station, and a little north of the largest and dreariest plateau in Wales. The village, which is itself placed in pleasant scenery, consists of one long street running north and south.

Trawsfynydd to Dolgelley, 13 *m*.

This road for the first 5 miles is the essence of dreariness ; the rest of it delightful. After crossing the Prysor stream, at the south end of the village.

Guide VIII.

N

it rises slightly and pursues an almost perfectly straight course over a bare moorland, at the end of which it enters the deep and beantifully wooded **Ganllwydd Glen.** The moorland rises on the west to the Rhinog line of summits, of which the chief are the two Diphwys—one opposite Trawsfynydd —the most northerly height of the range; the other at the extreme south overlooking the Mawddach estuary. Between these are Rhinog-fawr, and Rhinog-fach, two massive humps of broken rock separated by a semi-circular dip called Bwlch-Drws-Ardudwy; then, south of the latter, Llethr, a flat-topped hill of equal elevation to the others. Cader Idris is in front, and far away in the rear Moelwyn and Moel Siabod rise over the head of the valley. On entering the Ganllwydd Glen the stream is crossed by *Pont Dolgefeiliau,* 1½ miles beyond which the valley in which are Pistyll Cain and Rhaiadr Mawddach converges on the left. This is, perhaps, the most beautiful part of the route. Steep hills, wooled to their summits, rise on every side, and the stream falls rapidly over a rock-strewn bed. In another ¼ mile it is joined by the Water of *Cwm Camlan,* half-a-mile up which and easily reached by a cart-road succeeded by a path on the north side of the stream, is *Rhaiadr-du,* a waterfall of considerable volume in itself, and most picturesque in its surroundings. Beyond the bridge over the Camlan stream the finely timbered grounds of *Dol-y-Melynon* are on the right, and beyond these we reach the **Tyn-y-Groes Inn,** as delightfully situated a hostelry as can be imagined. Beyond it the *Precipice Walk* is seen high upon the hill-side across the river—now the Mawddach—and in three miles we enter the Barmouth and Dolgelley road 2 m. west of Dolgelley. After crossing the bridge the remnant of *Cymmer Abbey* is on the left.

The last half of this route is more fully described as an excursion from Dolgelley in " Part II."

*** The intense sameness of the first part of this route may be partly avoided, and the falls of Pistyll Cain and Rhaiadr Mawddach visited on the way by turning to the left as soon as you enter the straight reach of road beyond the Prysor Bridge at Trawsfynydd. A winding track leads over the hill and down into the Cain glen. This will add, perhaps, an hour to the time of the walk.

For *Pistyll Cain* and *Rhaiadr Mawddach see* " Part II."

From Trawsfynydd the line turns east, and continues ascending high up above the green but bare *Prysor valley.* Rhinog fawr and Rhinog-fach, separated by the depression of Bwlch-drws-Ardudwy, are well seen across the treeless Trawsfynydd plateau, and Cader Idris appears in the far south. The highest point is reached at *Llyn Tryweryn,* situated in a scene of desolation such as the dreariest recesses of Dartmoor can hardly match. From it a rapid descent is made into the Tryweryn valley. *Arenig-fawr* now rises commandingly on the right, and the heavy looking *Arenig-fach* on the left. Beyond *Arenig Station,* which is at the foot of the former, we pass *Mynydd Nodol* on the right, and proceeding through more fertile ground and between lower hills, soon reach **Bala Town** (*Part II.*) station. The *Junction Station* is a mile further.

The Palmerston Slate Quarry.—(*From a correspondent describing a visit in 1883.*)—" While at Blaenau Ffestiniog we made our way to the Palmerston Slate Quarry, which we were told was the largest and most productive in

Wales. The landlady of the Baltic Hotel found us a highly respectable guide, who conducted us up the great heaps of shale, and past the "finishing" sheds to a narrow-gauge line, along which the huge blocks of slate are brought from the pit's mouth on trucks. On one of these we were bidden to take our seats, the guide sitting just behind us and holding us on carefully, whilst two lads pushed us along through a tunnel about 50 yards long, dark and rather moist. On reaching our destination, where we came to more sheds filled with machinery, we alighted and walked down some steps into the first chamber of the black smoky mine; there are nine beneath it, right into the bowels of the earth. The miners, who number between seven and eight hundred, were then enjoying the open air during their dinner hour, and were sitting or lying about near the pit's mouth. Considering the fearful atmosphere so many of them have to work in from six in the morning till 5.30 in the evening, they, most of them, looked very robust and healthy; they were all very civil and well behaved to us as we passed in and out amongst them, and there seemed a great deal of kindly feeling and good fellowship between themselves. The miners earn from 23s to 25s. a week, and the slate finishers 45s. This mine made £83,000 clear profits last year (1882), but this was unusually good. It yields an average profit of £50,000 or £60,000. The shaft we went down was pitch dark, and the air was most disagreeable to breathe. A miner lad went before us with a lantern; our guide held me by the arm and my sister followed us closely, carrying a bit of lighted candle, set in a lump of clay, in her hand. We came upon bridges across shafts letting air down to the chambers beneath, where we saw, dimly burning, ever so far down, the lights of the poor miners. The quality of the slate in this quarry is very good, and the mine has already been worked 80 years. Our guide showed us the water-works which pump the water out of the mine, and the slate just as it is after it has been blasted, huge blocks worth about £4 each, which are conveyed to the pit's mouth on trucks, part of the way drawn by horses and then by machinery with wire ropes up the steep incline to where the narrow-gauge line takes it on to the finishing sheds where it is split, cut in squares, and then sent off to the railroad, to be forwarded to all parts of the world. We took a look at the great engine which sets all the different machinery in motion in the finishing shed, where nothing is done by hand now-a-days except the actual splitting of the blocks of slate, which is an easy task when once the two wedges are driven in. The guide has a fixed charge of 5s. for taking people over the mine, and we were glad to give it to him—he was so civil and so careful over us."

Mountain Section.

————◆————

Introductory. We shall here give a description of those separate mountains which are most convenient and most remunerative to ascend, and of such ranges as, from their position between places of popular resort, offer temptations to those who like to spend whole days on the high ground. There are numbers of other heights easy of access, and affording delightful views to visitors who happen to be sojourning near their feet, but not of sufficient general interest to call for special description. The region described in this volume comprises the whole Snowdonian range, the heights that rise between Nant Gwynant, Nant-y-Gwryd, and the Ffestiniog and Lledr valleys, and the Clwydian hills. Of these Snowdon itself affords the greatest facilities, either for a rapid up-and-down journey, or for a full day's ramble. Moelwyn and Cynicht, taken together, will occupy as much of a day as you like to give to them; the Glyders may either be accomplished in a few hours from Pen-y-gwryd, or made the climax of a good day's excursion between Capel Curig, Llanberis and Bethesda. Moel Siabod, Moel Hebog, and the Rivals are worthy objects of a separate excursion, and Moel Fammau will proportionately repay the smaller amount of labour involved in surmounting it.

The eastern part of Snowdonia, between the Conway and Llugwy valleys and Nant Ffrancon, is better adapted for full-day excursions. The mountains that compose it are hardly of sufficient interest in themselves to repay the labour which their great height and comparative remoteness from the surrounding tourist resorts entail for their ascents separately. Delightful ridge-rambles, however, may be made by starting from one of the watering places between Bangor and Conway, or from one of the stations in the Conway valley, and crossing their highest summits —Carnedds Llewelyn, and Dafydd—to Bethesda. The shortest excursion over them to be recommended is the tour of the Carnedds, from and to Bethesda.

₊ As many tourists gain their first mountaineering experience in Wales, we may be excused for tendering a word of advice which will appear quite superfluous to those who have already "found their mountain legs." Briefly, then, always have a good margin of daylight before you; take a compass and a flask of spirits (the latter, if needed, is all the more effective should you happen to be an habitual abstainer); be sure to be stoutly and comfortably shod, and, if you lose your way in a fog, do not be in a frantic hurry to get down.

The following is a list of the mountains specially described in these pages. A fuller one is given in our introductory pages :—

	ft.	page.		ft.	page.
Snowdon - - - -	3571	203	Elydr-fach - - - -	2500*	189
Carnedd Llewelyn -	3482	181	Moel Wnion - - - -	1905	{ 76 / 101
" Dafydd - -	3430	181	Yr Eifl (the Rivals) - -	1887	144
Glyder-fawr - - -	3275	191			
" fach - - -	3250*	191	Moel Fammau- - - -	1823	{ 37 / 14
Y Garn - - - -	3107	194			
Y Foel Fras - - -	3091	185	Penmaenmawr- - - -	1553	{ 62 / 71
Elidyr Fawr - - -	3033	189	Llanfairfechan Hill - -	1200*	70
Y Tryfan. - - - -	3009*	210	Y Foel Llys - - - -	1181	65
Moel Siabod - - -	2865	197	Gallt-y-foel - - - - -	900*	122
Penllithrig - - - -	2623	116	Conway Mountain - -	800*	57
Moel Hebog - - -	2578	195	Great Orme's Head - -	750*	464
Moelwyn - - - -	2529	200	Moel-y-Gest - - - -	750*	165
Cynicht - - - - -	2400*	202	Holyhead Mountain - -	719	97

* *Approximate.*

CARNEDD LLEWELYN AND CARNEDD DAFYDD.

Carnedd Dafydd, 3,430 ft.; Llewelyn 3,482 ft.

These twin heights, if we may so call them, rank next to Snowdon in elevation. Seen in combination from the lower part of the Ogwen valley, between Bangor and Bethesda, or from other viewpoints in the same direction, they present a very effective appearance, though their peaks are only slightly tapering and the dip between them is very shallow. From other points of the compass, they are merely the highest parts of a long and lofty range. A description of the various ways of ascending them is almost tantamount to one of the entire hill-district of Eastern Snowdonia.

At present there is only the ruin of a cairn on Carnedd Llewelyn, but on Carnedd Dafydd one has recently been raised to a height of 14 or 15 feet, higher, if we mistake not, than any in Great Britain, except that on Ben Lawers in Perthshire. This cairn overlooks Bethesda, but is not seen from the Capel Curig side.

In individual interest these two mountains are inferior to most of those described in this section, but as the culminating points of a good day's walk over the hills, they can hardly fail to satisfy the pedestrian.

The nearest and most convenient starting-place for both is Bethesda, whence you may either simply make the tour of the two or, after reaching Carnedd Llewelyn, descend to Capel Curig.

Aber or Llanfairfechan, or to Tal-y-Cafn on the Bettws-y-Coed branch railway, half-way between Conway and Llanrwst. We shall endeavour to accommodate our description to the requirements of tourists making any of these places their starting point.

Ascents.

(1.) *From Bethesda, taking Carnedd Llewelyn first.*
(2.) ,,   ,,   ,,   ,, *Dafydd first.*
(3) ,, *Capel Curig to Carnedd Llewelyn.*
(4) ,,   ,,   ,,   *Dafydd.*
(5) ,, *Aber (or Llanfairfechan) to both.*
(6) ,, *Llandudno (or Llanrwst) by Tal-y-Cafn to both.*

(1) **From Bethesda to Carnedd Llewelyn**, 3-4 hrs. This is the best way to make the tour of the Carnedds, because the best views are generally in front. The first and only difficulty in it is to steer one's way successfully through the by-ways and footpaths of Bethesda itself. Follow the main (Capel Curig) road for 300 yards or so beyond the "Douglas Arms." Then, close to the fifth milestone from Bangor, take the lane on the left, and at cross-roads, 250 yards further, turn to the right round some one-storied cottages, beyond which you enter a cart-track through a gate. This track becomes almost at once a foot-path by which, bending to the left, you pass more cottages, and enter a lane close to a bridge over the *Caseg stream*, which is your guide for the next 3 miles, till you are fairly at the foot of the mountain. Do not cross the bridge, but of three tracks that confront you when you enter the lane, take the middle one which passes through an iron swing-gate and ascends to another lane (avoid left fork) by some neat cottages. Cross this lane and continue upwards along a rough twisting lane, till you are clear of another group of cottages, and come to a gate across the lane. Hence there is a good retrospect over Anglesey to Holyhead Mountain. The shortest, and perhaps, the best route from this point is to cross the wall by a stone step-stile, and to follow a faint green track, which at first runs parallel with the stream a little way from it, and then alongside it. The alternative, and rather drier route, is to continue up the lane, which turns to the right at the highest wall and then keeps a few hundred yards above the footpath. Both routes bring you, after an hour's walk, to a cluster of sheep-pens. During this part of the walk the precipitous height of Yr Elen, which hides the summit of Carnedd Llewelyn from Bethesda, is a fine object on the right front, and the Carnedd itself rises nobly from the hollow on the left of it.

From the sheep-pens you mark a green zig-zag, working up the left-hand slope of a smaller shoulder, *Clogwyn-yr-helwyn*. It is quite worth while to climb this, and walk along the ridge for

the sake of the view down into the wild corrie formed by the projection of Yr Elen, but our nearest onward route is rather to the
left, till we breast the main ridge near an abandoned hut,
sheltered by a rude group of rocks. This makes the slope as
gentle as possible, and, once on the ridge, we have only to plod
along it to the right till we gain the cairn at the top of Carnedd
Llewelyn. The last part of the ascent is stony, and in places
steep; upright stones mark it intermittently. On the left the
hills slope down irregularly to the Conway valley. *For the view
see p.* 186 *and the route on to Carnedd Dafydd, and back to Bethesda
p.* 187.

(2.) **From Bethesda to Carnedd Llewelyn by Carnedd**
Dafydd, 3-4 *hrs.* There are several ways of starting up Carnedd
Dafydd from Bethesda. One is to follow the above-described
route till you reach the Caseg stream (p. 182); then *cross* the
bridge and turn to the left a few yards beyond it to a farm called
Tyddyn-du, whence a path goes straight on with a stream below
on the left, and the rest of the way to the huge cairn on the top
is plain enough.

A *second route* is to follow the Capel Curig road for half-a-mile
beyond the "Douglas Arms," and then take the left turn opposite
the road that crosses the Ogwen to the slate-quarries; then, right
again in a few yards, and so on to the ridge, from which the cairn
is plainly visible. The *simplest way*, however is to go up
Nant Ffrancon by the high road to the hamlet of *Tyn-y-*
Maes, 1¾ miles beyond the "Douglas Arms," and thence to climb
to the ridge by a steep pitch on the left, through fields on the
south side of the stream that has a larch plantation on its north
side; (by continuing along the high road to *Ty-gwyn*, a mile further,
and there bending very sharply back, you may gain the same point
on the ridge by a cart-track).

From this ridge the cairn on Carnedd Dafydd is conspicuous.
The cart-tract doubles round through a wall, and by bending to
the right, and following this wall all the way up you will reach
the summit of **Braich-du**, the southern shoulder of Carnedd
Dafydd. Before going further, it is worth while to walk to the
right for a few hundred yards till you can see down the crags to
the top of Nant Ffrancon. Llyn Ogwen and Llyn Idwal, en-
vironed by the Tryfan, the Glyders and Y Garn, compose one of
the most grandly wild pictures in Wales.

The way from Braich-du to Carnedd Dafydd is unmistakable
and there is scarcely any depression between the two. In the
hollow on the right is the little tarn of *Ffynnon-y-Lloer.* *For the
view from Carnedd Dafydd, see p.* 186; *descent to Capel Curig,
p.* 188.

Hence to Carnedd Llewelyn it is nearly an hour's walk and
some of the first part is beset with boulders. If you avoid them
by making a circuit to the right, you lose the best part of the view,
which is down the crags of "Dafydd" into the deep hollow between

it and "Llewelyn": about half-way the route turns to the left and crosses a narrow saddle. *Ffynnon Llugwy*, a large tarn, is in the hollow on the right; beyond it the bare upper valley of the Llugwy and, to the left of it, the steep ridge of Penhelig, with Penllithrig beyond. From the end of the "saddle" an easy ascent of a few hundred feet leads to the top of Carnedd Llewelyn. *For the view and routes down, see 186 and following pages.*

(3 and 4.) **From Capel Curig to Carnedd Llewelyn**, 2½–3 *hrs.*; **Carnedd Dafydd** 2½–3 *hrs.* These ascents up the dull sides of both mountains are quite devoid of special interest and will be as easily made by observing the dotted lines on our map as by following any verbal description. The route is for 3 miles or more along the Bangor road. If you are going the round of the two, do not leave the road until it has crossed the Llugwy and passed the 36th milestone from Holyhead. Then take the farm-road that leads to *Glan Llugwy Farm*, but before reaching the house turn to the left and climb *Craig Llugwy*. Hence it is a long trudge north-westwards to the cairn on Carnedd Dafydd, which, notwithstanding its size, is not visible till you are close upon it. The way thence to Llewelyn is described above. If bound for Carnedd Llewelyn only, pass the farm and then climb northwards till you have crossed a wall and got a view of Ffynnon Llugwy on the right. Thence, skirting a ridge on its eastern side, you will attain the saddle between the two Carnedds at its south end, and join the route already described (*p.* 183) from Bethesda. *For descents from Carnedd Llewelyn, see pages* 187, 188.

(5.) **From Aber or Llanfairfechan to Carnedd Llewelyn**, 4–4½ *hrs.* These are long but interesting ascents, and those who contemplate crossing the entire range will do best to commence from this side, or from Tal-y-Cafn (*p.* 183). (*From Llanfair-fechan, see p.* 183).

(a) *From Aber.* Take the road up the glen as far as *Pont-newydd* (*p.* 75); cross the bridge and follow the Bwlch-y-deufaen route (*p.* 72) till you come on to open ground and see the green track to Llyn-yr-Afon as therein stated.

A *shorter Route*, affording a close view of the Aber Fall but missing Llyn-yr-Afon, is up the glen to the smaller fall, nearly a mile west of the chief one, and thence up the hill to a green track which doubles round the northern end of *Y Drosgl* and ascends to the rocky height of *Bera-bach*, half-way between the ridge and the stream of Afon-bach. The all-round view from the ridge of Y Drosgl and Bera-bach is very fine. Northwards it extends over the sea from the Great Orme in the east, over Holyhead Mountain to the triple-peaked Rivals in the west; the deeply hollowed sides of Carnedd Llewelyn and Carnedd Dafydd are close at hand to the south and just right of the latter, the peak of Snowdon peers over its mighty shoulder, Crib-y-ddysgyl. Eastwards the loftier heights of Y Foel Fras and Llwyomor shut out further view.

From Bera-bach we continue along the ridge and, crossing Yr Arryg, join the Llyn-yr-Afon route, described below, nearly 2 miles short of Carnedd Llewelyn.

The Llyn-yr-Afon track soon bends to the left and you come into a solitary upland valley enlivened by the sparkling stream which descends from Llyn-yr-Afon. When the path becomes faint and intermittent keep to the left of the stream till, bending to the right and climbing a stony slope, you come suddenly to the shore of Llyn-yr-Afon. This is a remote tarn, 1,600 feet above sea-level, and strangely over-rated by some writers, who have gone as far as to compare it with Llyn Idwal. It is surrounded by grassy slopes, broken in the south-west by crag. Its seclusion is perfect but it has scarcely an element of grandeur.

From the lake a smart climb southwards up a broken hollow lands us on the ridge that connects Drum on the left with Y Foel Fras on the right.

At this point the **Route from Llanfairfechan** strikes in. Briefly described, the first part of this route is identical with that to Carreg-fawr (*p.* 70). Thence it continues south and, crossing the Bwlch-y-ddeufaen route from Aber (*see map*), continues upward by a fairly marked track to the ridge of *Yr Orsedd* and *Y Drosgl* (not to be confused with the Y Drosgl passed in the ascent from Aber by the Falls). From this ridge you look down upon Llyn-yr-Afon on the right, and, continuing high up above that lake, join the Aber track as above described.

Along the ridge we have now reached (2,300 *ft.*) is an iron fence running south-west to the flat summit of **Y Foel Fras** (3,091 *ft.*). During the ascent—a gradual grass slope—we look eastwards over a featureless expanse of moorland into the Conway valley, beyond which the Clwydian range bounds the prospect.

From Y Foel Fras Carnedd Llewelyn is in sight, its steep side dropping eastward and its northern buttress, Yr Elen, projecting boldly to the right. Beyond this buttress Carnedd Dafydd with its lofty cairn is conspicuous, and to the right of Yr Elen, Elidyrfawr rises to a perfect cone between Nant Ffrancon and the Llanberis valley—one of the finest outlines in the country. Northwards you may see, weather permitting, the Isle of Man and Cumberland. Yr Orsedd hides all Llanfairfechan except a row of houses alongside the shore, to the right of which are Penmaenmawr and the Great Orme. The sky-line of Llwydmor just cuts the far side of the Menai straits.

Between Y Foel Fras and Carnedd Llewelyn the dip is very slight and the going very good. In about a mile we join the route past the Aber Falls already described, and, half-a-mile further, we come to the abandoned hut at which the Bethesda route converges. For the rest of the way, see p. 183.

(6.) **From Llandudno or Llanrwst** (4–5 *hrs. walking from Tal-y-Cafn.*) The rail should be taken to Tal-y-Cafn station. Thence there is a ferry (1*d.*) over the Conway river, on the far side of which is a public-house. From the ferry Y Foel Fras, which is about 2 *m.* due north of Carnedd Llewelyn, appears S.W. by W., and Clogwyn Eira with crag about it nearly S.W. Our route lies

hard by the eastern foot of the latter, and passes a cottage seen
high up in this direction, called Rowlan. Take the road straight
on from the ferry, and when this, in about ¾ m. runs into that from
Conway to Bettws-y-Coed, turn to the left. At *Tal-y-Bont*, 1¾ m.
further, is a small inn just beyond which, after crossing the
bridge, we turn to the right and zig-zag up the hill, having a
pleasant little glen and burn on our right, and obtaining a good
view of the vale of Conway both up and down. When the road
turns sharply to the left, the prospect up the glen we are ascending becomes wilder, and Y Foel Fras (3,091 ft.) is prominent at
its head. A few steps further, the lower part of the Conway
valley comes finely into view, a soft and pretty scene well diversified with timber. Thence onward for a while, we need only
remark that the road—a fair one of its kind—cannot be mistaken
and is not to be quitted. As it reaches the top of the ridge that
divides the glen we have ascended from the valley of the Afon
Porth-lwyd, the square summit of Penllithrig comes suddenly into
view on the left-front. Due west we now see the abrupt western
side of the cwm in which Llyn-Dulyn lies, and to the left of this
the top of Carnedd Llewelyn appears over the bold crags of Clogwyn Eira. **Llyn Eigiau** is hidden away under the latter and
does not come into sight until we reach a bridge over the Porth-
lwyd stream that issues from its farther end. It is about a mile
long but except for the fine and precipitous rocks on its far side
is lacking in interest. We now have a disused quarry tramway on
our left and the deserted slate-works are just ahead. The road,
hitherto fairly good, now rapidly deteriorates but the combe up
which it still runs, bending to the right, for another mile or so to
further slate works is a grand amphitheatre of cliffs. Penhelig is
above the last quarry and Carnedd Llewelyn presents its sternest
front beyond the *col* to its right. It is obvious that all the cliffs
are unscaleable and so from the mine-buildings (1,600 ft.) we
begin to breast the rough grass hill on the right. There is now no
further guidance needed. Perhaps the best way is to keep the
stream on the left hand for about ½ hour, and then to make for
the slopes that on the left front gradually rise to the ridge. All
the going, what with long grass and patches of bog, is fatiguing,
and the last pull is somewhat steep, but there is no other source
of difficulty and no danger. When the ridge is gained bear to the
left and you will reach the summit by the route already described
from Bethesda (*p.* 183).

View from the summits. The views from *Carnedd Llewelyn*
and *Carnedd Dafydd* are so similar in general character and particular features that to describe them separately would be useless
repetition. The chief difference is that from Llewelyn, Bethesda
is not visible. By traversing the rocky plateau, however, south-
westwards for a few minutes we get a view of the village—a very
small matter,—and—a far greater one—look down into the deep
and wild corrie from which Yr Elen rises. A muddy little tarn
at the bottom somewhat detracts from the impressiveness of this
scene.

The most unique object in the view—especially from Llewelyn
—is the Tryfan, which rises to a height of 2,000 feet above the
Ogwen Valley, in front of Glyder-fach, in the form of an almost
perfect pyramid. To the right of it, over the rocky Glyders, the
peaks of Snowdon are seen, and this is the only direction in
which the view is shut in by superior heights. North of Snowdon,
Elidyr-fawr presents the conical outline on which we have already
commented, and from Carnedd Dafydd the length of the Lleyn
promontory and, possibly, Bardsey island may be seen, the peaks
of the Rivals appearing over the gap to the left of Elidyr-fawr.
Then comes a wide expanse of lowland and sea extending over the
Menai Straits and Anglesey, westward to the two Ormes, and
onward to the north end of the long Clwydian range. South-eastwards, parts of the Llugwy valley appear above and below Capel
Curig, and beyond it is the level line of the Berwyns, with the two
peaks of Arenig-fawr on their right and nearer at hand. The
Arans and Cader Idris continue the sky-line south and south-westwards. Moel Siabod is over the eastern extension of Glyder-fach.
Ffynnon Llugwy (seen from Llewelyn), the source of the Llugwy,
lies just below in the hollow to the south and to the left of it—the
narrow ridge of Penhelig connects Carnedd Llewelyn with Penllithrig. This ridge is a possible descent, but tourists must adopt
it on their own responsibility. We have never tried it. Ireland,
the Isle of Man and Cumberland are, of course, within the possibilities of the prospect.

Descents. After the full description we have given of the
ascents these require little description. We start from "Llewelyn."

(1.) To Bethesda by Carnedd Dafydd. Start along the
side of a fragmentary wall which descends to the narrow saddle
that connects the two Carnedds. From the end of the saddle climb
to the right. The rocks may be avoided by keeping well to the
left of the ridge. From Carnedd Dafydd the most attractive route
is to proceed still in a south westerly direction over the ridge
called *Braich-du*, and then, before turning northwards, to have a
look down to the head of Nant Ffrancon (*p.* 183). From the
view-point bend sharply back to the right and keep a wall on the
left as you descend the ridge. After a sharp drop, succeeded by
a comparative flat, you come to an iron-gate in a rail-fence. The
cart-track that goes through this gate doubles back and enters the
main road at *Ty-gwyn Farm*, but by dropping straight into Nant
Ffrancon from about the point at which it bends back you will
enter the valley at the hamlet of *Tyn-y-maes*, and reach Bethesda
in another 2 miles.
Instead of descending to Tyn-y-maes you may continue along
the ridge all the way to Bethesda.

(2.) To Bethesda (direct). The ridge that runs due west
from the cairn on Carnedd Llewelyn must be avoided, as it ends
in the precipitous cliffs of Yr Elen. Take the north-eastern

ridge for about 1¼ miles, and then descend the humpy ridge of *Clogwyn-yr-helwyn*. (In case of mist coming on, go on beyond this ridge until a shepherd's **hut adjoining a** jumble of rocks is just below the **main** ridge on **the left. Thence** make down the slope. There is no **crag,** and the stream in the bottom is the best guide to Bethesda.) From Clogwyn yr-helwyn a **fine view** of the crags of Yr Elen, and of the wild corrie it guards, **is** obtained. It is advisable to make down the northern flank of the end of this ridge to the stream. A fine echo can be awoke as we descend. A curious circular group of stone sheep-pens is seen below close to the stream, and thence an intermittent path descends the right bank, and about a mile from Bethesda enters a rough road. When the houses above Bethesda are reached, keep as much down-hill as you can by road or foot-path, and you will enter the high road, 300 yards south of the Douglas Hotel. *For precise directions, see reverse route, p.* 182.

(3.) **To Capel Curig.** Descend the ridge that commences at the south end of the saddle between the two Carnedds, and from its foot make for the farm of *Glan Llugwy*, whence a cart-track enters the main road in less than a mile, 3½ miles short of Capel Curig.

(4.) **To Aber or Llanfairfechan.** Go north-eastwards as far as the hut mentioned in the direct Bethesda descent (*No.* 2). Then either bend round to the north-west along the ridge, passing the top of Yr Arryg and Bera-bach (*p.* 184), and descend from the latter to the Aber Glen by the smaller fall (*p.* 76); or continue north-eastwards over Y Foel Fras, whence an iron fence shows the way to the hollow between that mountain and Drum. From the hollow (*a*) for *Aber* descend to Llyn-yr Afon on the left, and keeping the stream that issues from that lake on the left, continue down the valley to the Bwlch-y-ddeufaen route (*p.* 60). (*b*) For *Llanfairfechan* continue along the ridge looking down to Llyn-yr-Afon on the left. You will soon come to a track that descends a little to the right of the ridge, and, crossing the Bwlch-y-ddeu'aen track descends by the side of Carreg-fawr to Llanfairfechan (*p.* 72).

(5.) **To Tal y Cafn (for Llandudno or Llanrwst.)** Follow the last-named route north-eastwards till, after passing some humps of rock on the right, half-a-mile from the summit, you can comfortably descend into the valley on the right. At the foot of the descent into this valley are some disused quarry-huts, and hence there is a cart-track, improving as it goes on, all the way to the Llanrwst and Conway road which is entered close to the *Tal-y-Bont Inn*, 2½ miles short of **Tal-y-Cafn Station.** (*See reverse route, p.* 185).

ELIDYR-FAWR, 3,033 ft., and ELIDYR-FACH, about 2,550 ft.

From Llanberis, 2¼-2¾ *hrs. From Bethesda*, 3-3½ *hrs.*

Seen from the high ground on the east or west Elidyr-fawr is a natural pyramid, and presents one of the finest outlines in Wales. Intervening heights, however, hide it from the low ground in these directions, and the full broadside which it displays to the north is far less attractive. On the Llanberis side slate-quarries abound up to a height of nearly 2,000 feet, but, admitting this drawback, the ascent is well worth making. From Bethesda the walk is rather tedious.

(1.) **From Llanberis.** Take the road between the two lakes as in the route to Bethesda (*p.* 138), and ascend to the left. For the first eight minutes in every hour the road hereabouts is kept clear because of the blasting above. Then passing the *Quarrymen's Hospital* on the left the road turns sharp to the right, and very soon becomes a footpath to the left again where a noticeboard forbids direct progress. Avoid the next sharp bend to the right, and a second one, which descends somewhat to the left. Then, at the next fork, take the left branch. This goes over the level top of a slate-heap for several hundred yards, and you now look straight up to the cairn on Elidyr-fach. Beyond the slate-heap enter a lane; take the right hand turn, and keep on ascending. A main road is soon crossed some way to the right of a chapel. Continuing the ascent you reach another road which goes up to the highest quarry. Follow this towards the quarry till it becomes a path, then climb to the left, and, making your way between the slate-heaps, you will gain, by a sharp ascent, the cairn that is all but on the top of **Elidyr-fach.** All the way up there is a wide view northwards over Carnarvon and Anglesey, and the peaks of the Rivals are a feature westwards. That of Snowdon is also visible. Close below is the dull upland called a "Turbary," that is "peat-common," between Llanberis and Bethesda, with a small sheet of water in the midst of it.

From Elidyr-fach the "fawr" comes into view, rising to a fine peak in front. The ascent is slantwise, up a steep scree of gravel changing to boulders as you approach the ridge, which is a long and very rough one.

From the cairn which marks the summit of **Elidyr-fawr,** besides the objects already named, we see the range that extends from above Penrhyn slate-quarries to the top of Nant Ffrancon; Moel Perfydd, round and grassy; then a deep break and Moel-goch, succeeded by the much loftier Y Garn, beyond which the Glyders and the Tryfan appear. This side of the range is a vast sheepwalk, sloping steeply. Across the Ogwen valley are Carnedds Dafydd and Llewelyn, the former crowned by a huge cairn; and more to the right we have a peep into the valley that leads to

Capel Curig. Penmaenmawr is seen in the north west, over the gap between Moel Wnion and Y Drosgl. The Straits, the Bridges, Penrhyn Castle, and the Holyhead Mountain are all included in the prospect.

(2.) **From Bethesda.** The ridge-route from the slate-quarries is a tiresome heathery one, and it is best to take the road up Nant Ffrancon for nearly two miles till the bridge a little short of the hamlet of *Tyn-y-maes* is reached. Cross this and, after pursuing the road on the other side for about ¼ m., turn up by the side of the stream on the right and make for the ridge between Bronllwyd and Carnedd-y-filiast. This part of the route requires care, as a little further south the mountain descends to Nant Ffrancon in enormous slabs of smooth slate, and in the other direction (northwards) the ascent is very steep and strewn with huge boulders.

The top of Carnedd-y-filiast is crossed by a high wall. From about here the view into Nant Ffrancon is very fine, and on the other side the sharp ridge of Elidyr-fawr stretches away at right angles. Close beneath it is a large tarn, called *Marchlyn-mawr*, and the way onward is by the narrow ridge which, after you have descended some distance, leads round this tarn up to the top of the Elidyr. The drop to the tarn is almost sheer, and it is best in places to keep a little to the left of the top of the ridge.

Descents. (1) **to Llanberis.** This may be made (*a*) over Elidyr fach, as in the ascent, and thence between the highest quarries, first to the upper and then to the lower (main) road or (*b*) by the bwlch that overlooks Marchlyn-mawr, and then along the green hill side called *Esgair-ceunant* to *Old Llanberis*, which is seen at the bottom of the valley.

(2) **To Bethesda.** Descend the ridge to the **bwlch** overlooking Marchlyn-mawr, keeping in places a little to the right of the edge. Thence bend to the left up to Moel Perfydd and Carnedd-y-filiast, both of which present green slopes westward, and smooth precipices of slate to Nant Ffrancon in the east. After crossing a huge wall and descending some distance, it is best to pick your way down to Nant Ffrancon, as the rest of the ridge over Bronllwyd to the Penrhyn slate-quarries is beset with stones and heather. Once in the valley, you may cross the Ogwen to the high-road by a bridge almost opposite the hamlet of *Tyn-y-maes*, and nearly 2 miles south of *Bethesda*.

GLYDER-FAWR, 3,275 ft., and GLYDER-FACH, about 3,250 ft.

These are the culminating heights of the rugged chain which separates the Llanberis valley and Nant-y-gwryd from Nant Ffrancon and the upper Llugwy valley. They are well worth ascending, not only for themselves, but also for the magnificent view of Snowdon they afford across the head of the pass of Llanberis.

There is probably no rougher mountain in the kingdom than the Glyder-fach. The last few hundred feet of the ascent, whichever way it may be made, is over a chaotic assemblage of rocks and boulders that might, to all appearance, have dropped down from the sky on this particular spot.

The easiest ascent of the Glyders is from Pen-y-gwryd, and the hardest from the top of Nant Ffrancon. From Llanberis and Capel Curig the way is fairly easy, but much longer. As to the Pen-y-gwryd route a word of caution! At first sight the simplest ascent seems to be by the hollow that leads to the slight gap between the two heights; but, writing after some experience, we have no hesitation in pronouncing this one of the most distressing climbs we have ever made. The going consists of stones and ruts concealed by heather to such an extent that almost every step is a matter of careful consideration.

The height of Glyder-fach, reckoning to the "top of rocks," is on the authority of the Ordnance Survey Office given above as within 25 ft. of Glyder-fawr. Without this dictum many observers might be inclined to think the suffixes should be reversed.

⁎ Those who wish to prolong the walk over the Glyders may, without difficulty, continue from Llyn-y-Cwm and the top of the Devil's Kitchen over Y Garn and Moel-goch, and, at the foot of the latter, join the route from Llanberis over Elidyr-fawr to Bethesda, described on page 189; or, of course, they may start from Bethesda and go over the entire length of the range, or as much of it as they please, to Capel Curig. *See* "*Descent 3.*"

Ascents. (1.) **Pen-y-gwryd** (or **Corphwysfa**) to **Glyder-fawr**, 1½—2 *hrs.* Go for a good 200 yards along the Llanberis road from Pen-y-gwryd; then pass through an opening near a shed and go north-westwards with the little height of Y *Foel-perfedd* between you and the road on your left and the stream issuing from *Llyn-y-cwm-Ffynnon* some distance on the right. Cross this stream as it issues from the north-east end of the lake, and make straight ahead for the ridge which leads up to the Glyder-fawr. Hereabouts the ground is thickly strewn with moraine débris. The climb to the ridge is steep but easy, and when once you are on it you have only to bear away slightly to the right till you reach the top of the mountain.

From Cor; hwysfa you may get on to the ridge at once and follow it all the way to the summit.

The **View from the** top is extensive and varied. Northwards we look down into Llyn Idwal with Nant Ffrancon and Bethesda beyond it. In this direction Penrhyn Castle is seen and, further away, Beaumaris, the east corner of Anglesey. and Puffin Island. To the right of this the superior heights of Carnedd Dafydd and Carnedd Llewelyn stop the way, but eastwards the prospect extends to the sea-board near Rhyl. Then come the sharp-pointed Tryfan and the precipices of Glyder-fach close at hand, to the right of which is the depression of the Llugwy valley extending to the high ground between Bettws-y-Coed and Corwen, beyond which Moel Fammau tops the Clwydian range. Over Moel Siabod we see the long Berwyn chain and, to the right of the latter. the Arenigs and (farther away) the twin peaks of Aran. Cader Idris is almost due south and the Rhinogs nearer at hand a little to the right of it with Cynicht and Moelwyn still closer. Then, more sea stretching away beyond Aberystwith and, between Cynicht and Snowdon, Harlech Castle and the Portmadoc viaduct. Then the peaks, combes and cliffs of Snowdon, by far the finest feature in the whole view—and, to the right of them, the Llanberis Lakes, Carnarvon Castle, the Menai Straits and the plain of Anglesey rising to its only eminence in the Holyhead promontory.

Between this and the Nant Ffrancon valley the range upon which we are standing is continued over the summits of Y Garn and Y Foel-goch till it sinks to the plain in the direction of Bangor.

From Glyder-fawr to Glyder-fach the direction is due east along the ridge of the precipice called Y Waen-oer, "the cold mountain flat," as expressive a name as could be given. The distance is 1¼ miles, but this is no index to the time. The first part of the journey is over a kind of natural pavement—a strange contrast to the last. On the left hand, about half-way, a sharp edge of the mountain shoots out northwards, between the hollows in which lie Llyn Idwal and Llyn Bochlwyd respectively. This is the shortest way down to Nant Ffrancon (*see below.*) A little beyond this spot the stones of the Glyder-fach begin, and there is nothing else to be looked at, or thought of, except the best way through them. If ever Cyclops took it into his head to upset one of his own walls, the result would probably have been the Glyder-fach. Arrived at the summit, and looking eastwards, we have a much more extensive view than from the Glyder-fawr. In other directions the prospect is pretty much the same, except that Snowdon is not such an absorbing feature in it.

(2.) **Pen-y-gwryd to the Glyder-fach direct**, 1½-2 *hrs.* By adopting this route you may save nearly an hour's walking, but

the one we have already described is considerably the pleasanter
of the two, besides having the advantage of including both summits and the glorious walk between them.

For this direct route, leave the road opposite a mile-stone,
about 250 yards on the Capel Curig side of the inn, and make for
the bend in a wall which goes some way up the mountain. Then
bear to the right, and on attaining the highest ground visible
from the inn, turn a little to the left again. A terribly rough
walk up the stones will take you to the summit. (*See also p.* 211).

(3.) **From Pen-y-Benglog at the top of Nant Ffrancon**,
1½-2 *hrs. to Glyder-fawr*. The ascent of the Glyders from this
side requires care, in consequence of the precipitous character of
their northern slopes. The more usual route is by Llyn Idwal
and the "Devil's Kitchen" (*Twll-du*, "the black hole"), but a
shorter and very interesting one is by the sharp ridge which separates the Llyn Idwal and Llyn Bochlwyd hollows. This is as
follows:—Start from Pen-y-Benglog by a path which strikes up
the hill southwards from the west side of the cottage, in a line
with the road up Nant Ffrancon. This goes above and some
distance to the right of the stream issuing from Llyn Bochlwyd.
Y Tryfan rises on the left, and Glyder-fach in front. When
Llyn Bochlwyd comes into sight, turn to the right and make for
the lateral edge on the same side. This reaches the main Glyder
ridge about half way between the "fawr" and the "fach." The
first part is intermittently steep, but fairly easy going. In the
last part, just before achieving the ridge, there is some rough
clambering amongst the crags, free from danger, but calling for
discretion in picking the way. The best plan, we think, is to keep
a little to the right of the edge, as the drop on the left to Cwm
Bochlwyd is sheer. Once on the ridge, it is twenty minutes'
walk west to Glyder-fawr, and half-an-hour east to Glyder-fach.
This is a route which should on no account be taken in any but
clear weather.

(4.) **From Capel Curig direct to Glyder-fach**, 2-2½ *hrs.*
For this ascent you may either follow the ridge all the way,
striking up it directly from the hotel, or (shorter and better) you
may take the Pen-y-gwryd route for about 1½ miles, passing the two
lakes, and then turn up the fell by the farm-house of *Dyffryn
Mymbyr;* whence, after crossing a wall, you will come to a long
smooth ascent over grass to the part of the ridge which overlooks
Nant-y-gogo. Hence the Tryfan comes into prominent view. A
stretch of level swampy ground, containing a few tarns, is crossed,
beyond which, passing another northward spur you look down
into the desolate *Cwm Tryfan.* Glyder-fach is now directly in
front, and you must pick your way up through the stones as you
best can.

(5.) **From Benglog (head of Nant Ffrancon) to Glyder-
fawr by Twll-du (the Devil's Kitchen)**, 2½-3 *hrs.*
This route, as far as the top of Twll-du and Llyn-y-Cwm, is

fully described on page 103.   Thence it is a sharp climb of from
1,000 to 1,200 feet to the plateau of Glyder-fawr, the direction
being south-east.

(6.) **From Llanberis to Glyder-fawr**, 3½ to 4 *hrs.*   Tourists
who have not already walked up or down the Pass of Llanberis
will probably make Corphwysfa, at the head of it, their starting
point for the trackless part of the ascent.   The route thither
from Llanberis is described on page 139, and the ascent itself on
page 191.   Otherwise the following is a very pleasant route :—
Take the 'pass" road as far as *Old Llanberis* (2 *m.*), and there
turn to the left, about 200 yards beyond the inn, by a slate-fenced
road that leads to a group of cottages, and then, becoming a
mere path, winds up past one or two more.   From the last cottage ascend the steep green slope with a wall on the left for
several hundred feet, and when the wall turns bend to the right,
near the side of a tributary rill.   There is a vestige of a green
track just beyond the wall, but this soon ceases, and all you have
to do is to continue eastwards till you cross the ridge of Y Garn,
about half-a-mile south-west of its summit.   The peaks to the
left and behind are Moel-goch and Elidyr-fawr, and a fine view of
Snowdon is obtained on the right.

Beyond the ridge of Y Garn it is a slight descent to *Llyn-y-Cwm*
and the head of the *Devil's Kitchen*, and the rest of the way is, as
stated above, up a steep rocky slope of from 1,000 to 1,200 *ft.*

The **View** and the route onward to Glyder-fach are described
on *p.* 192.

Descents.   (1) To Pen-y-gwryd.   From either peak avoid
the heathery hollow that descends due south from the slight depression between them.   It is full of hidden stones and ruts.

(1.)   From *Glyder-fawr*, go almost south along the highest
ground for a while, until you can comfortably descend to the left
to the north end of *Llyn-y-Cwm-ffynnon*—a rough but not difficult
walk.   From the lake keep the stream issuing from it considerably on the left, and you will enter the main road a little on
the Llanberis side of the *Pen-y-gwryd inn.*   For *Corphwysfa*, keep
along the ridge without descending to the lake.

From *Glyder-fach*, take a south-easterly direction, rather left of
Siabod, for a while and then, bearing to the right, you will
presently come to the bend in the wall mentioned in the ascent
(*p.* 193).

(2.) **To Capel Curig.**   Keep along the ridge till you have
passed the two hollows of *Cwm Tryfan* and *Nant-y-gogo.*   Then
leave it and descend a smooth grassy slope to *Dyffryn Mymbyr*, a
farm just above the high-road and a little west of the Capel Curig
lakes.

(3.) **To Benglog (head of Nant Ffrancon.)**   There are two
ways of getting down in this direction, but neither should be
attempted in anything but clear weather, as the whole range is

extremely precipitous on this side. The one is down to *Llyn
Bochlwyd* by the narrow rocky ridge that strikes northwards between
the "fawr" and the top of the hollow in which that lake lies—
the other by the *Devil's Kitchen*. For the latter the slope
that goes down to Llyn-y-Cwm must be descended. Then, after
tracing the stream that issues thence to the top of the "Kitchen,"
you must go along the ridge to the right till you come to a steep
stony slope by the side of a rill. Where this rill plunges down a
ledge of a rock, keep a little to the left, and you will soon reach
the narrow outlet of the kitchen. The rest of the way will be
fully understood from the description given on p. 103.

From the **Glyder-fach** to **Benglog**, a descent may be made
through the gap between the "fach" itself and Y Tryfan; but
this gap must, we believe, be approached by a somewhat circu-
itous route to the right. The writer has not descended this way.

Lastly, for **Llanberis** either the Corphwysfa route by the top
of the Pass may be taken, or, starting in a westerly direction, you
may cross the ridge of Y Garn about half-a-mile south of its
summit, and thence descend in the same direction to a wall from
which you look down into *Old Llanberis*, at the bottom of a steep
grass slope. Do not be in too great a hurry to commence this last
part of the descent. From Old to New Llanberis the distance is
2 miles.

MOEL HEBOG, 2,578 ft.

From Beddgelert, 1½–2 *hrs.; from* Criccieth, *3–4 hrs.*; *Tremadoc*,
2½–3½ *hrs.*

Moel Hebog is the presiding mountain of Beddgelert, though
its actual summit is not to be seen from the village. It is bold
and abrupt in character, but not peaked. The ascent from Criccieth is long and somewhat tedious, and Tremadoc is an equally
good starting-point, the mountain part of the route being pretty
much the same from both places. From Beddgelert you may
ascend by one way and descend by another. The view from the
top is a very good one.

(1.) **From Beddgelert** (a). Take a track that begins on the north
side of the Goat Hotel. Looking up the stream-course that comes
down from the hollow on the south side of the summit you will
see a gap in the wall. It is best to make for this gap as the wall
is otherwise an awkward one to surmount. On the way to it you
pass a little farm called *Cwm Cloch-uchaf*, and thence you may
follow either bank of the streamlet. Beyond the gap bend to the
right up the rough and steep ground and make for the ridge above
some way east of the highest part of it visible. The last part of
the ascent is very steep and requires care in picking your way.
Having attained the ridge a few minutes rough walking places
you on the cairn, which is close to the angle of a wall.

(b.) Follow the Carnarvon road for a short distance and then cross the Colwyn stream by a bridge, beyond which is a small farm, *Cwm Cloch-isaf*. From about here you bend to the right and, avoiding the shoulder that comes down almost directly towards Beddgelert, make for the one beyond and to the north of it. Some new larch-plantings occupy the lower skirts of the mountain in this direction. It is best to pass above and to the left of these, and then to attack the shoulder, bending to the left when you have attained its ridge. This is accounted the easiest way up as its higher part is not so steep as the one we have described from the "Goat."

(2.) **From Criccieth or Tremadoc.** From *Criccieth*, the road described on page 148 as leading to the first Cromlech must be followed as far as the *Ynys-ddu Farm* turn. Hence, keeping straight on, you come to an octagonal *Lodge*. Go to the left of this, and a little further on, turning to the right a few yards short of a gate in front, you pass through a farm between a villa and an old chapel. The peak of Snowdon is now just visible beyond the tower of Brynkir, and our road descends to two other roads, both leading from Tremadoc to *Dolbenmaen*. The latter village is seen on the left. Cross the first road, and on reaching the second, turn to the right and go towards Tremadoc for about half-a-mile, to a small inn at a point where the road from Llanfihangel comes up from a bridge on the left. Continuing towards Tremadoc from the inn, you come in ¼ mile to some cottages on the left (*this point is nearly 3 miles from Tremadoc.*) Here cross the stream by some large stepping-stones, and make for a farm among some trees on the other side. Pass to the left of this farm. Moel Hebog has been conspicuous in front nearly the whole way, and now you have only to choose your course up its long green shoulder to the summit. At first you pass one or two more farms, and then cross a tramway, beyond which it is best perhaps to work round to the left of a green hillock called *Moel Isallt*. Some tiresome walls have to be got over and, as you proceed, you may see below you on the right a large tarn called *Tal-y-llyn* lying in the hollow between Hebog and Moel-ddu.

View from the top. The great charm of this is the bird's-eye view of Beddgelert obtained by walking a few yards north-eastward. Beyond the village is the valley leading up to Pen-y-gwryd with Llyn-y-Ddinas and Llyn Gwynant reposing in its depths, and Siabod rising beyond it. Snowdon blocks the way north-eastwards, Y Wyddfa and Yr Aran being its most prominent peaks, while over the gap between the former and Moel Eilio, Elidyr-fawr, between the Llanberis Lakes and Nant Ffrancon, is seen. Northwards the view over Llyn-y-Gader up the valley along which the high-road to Carnarvon goes is of a duller character. Part of Anglesey appears in the distance. Then turning westwards you command a great part of the Lleyn promontory with St. Tudwal's Isles to the south of it, and the Rivals almost due

MOEL HEBOG. 197

west. Southwards the view of Cardigan Bay is most extensive, and the mountains stretching southwards from Beddgelert include Cynicht, Moelwyn, the Rhinogs and Cader Idris. Pont Aberglaslyn is hidden.

Descents. *To Beddgelert.* These require care in starting. You descend a little way north-east along the stony ridge, and then (*a*) pick your way down rough and steep débris to the gap in the wall pointed out in the description of the ascent from the Goat, or (*b*) you turn to the left and work round along the shoulder that descends towards the larch plantings. By the former route the high road is entered at the "Goat;" by the latter a bridge is crossed a little north of the village.

To Criccieth or *Tremadoc.* Go down the long green slope in a direction a little south of south-west. After crossing several walls and a tramway, you will traverse a rough pasture, comparatively flat, and enter the Tremadoc and Dolbenmaen road. Hence to Criccieth, the map and the description of the route up (*p.* 196) will give sufficient guidance.

MOEL SIABOD (pron. "Shabod") 2,865 ft.

From Bettws-y-Coed, 2½-3 hrs.; Capel Curig, 1½-2 hrs.; Dolwyddelen, 1¾-2¼ hrs.; Pen-y-gwryd, 1¾-2¼ hrs.

Rising apart from all other mountains, with the valleys of the Llugwy and the Lledr, Nant-y-gwryd and Nant Gwynant as distinctive boundaries, Moel Siabod possesses an individuality that is denied to many neighbouring mountains of equal or greater height. Looked at from the Lledr or the lower part of the Llugwy valley, it has a particularly graceful and striking outline, and from more than one view-point in these directions it bears a distinct resemblance to that most shapely of Scotch mountains, Schiehallion. From other points of view, it is little more than a steep green slope with a long level top.

Of the starting-points which we have enumerated above, there can be little doubt that Dolwyddelen is the most favourable one from an artistic point of view. In making the ascent this way, we have the southern scarp of the mountain in front, whereas, however pleasant the long green slopes of the northern and western sides to Capel Curig and Pen-y-gwryd respectively, may be to *descend*, they are very tedious to *ascend*. The direct route from Bettws-y-Coed involves a walk or drive of 4 miles along the high-road before the foot of the mountain is reached. We, therefore, advise tourists to take the train to Dolwyddelen, and thence to cross to any one of the three other places mentioned.

Ascents. (1.) **From Bettws-y-Coed** (*direct*). The first 4 miles, as far as Pont-gyfing, are described on *p.* 129. Thence

(a) you may cross the bridge and take the second turn to the right. The track, thus entered, goes in the direction of the summit and to the right of a tramway which serves a couple of slate-quarries. Some distance short of the last quarry it is best to bend to the right out of the track and climb the ridge to the peak which was visible from the last part of the road to Pont-gyfing. It is a sharp climb up the ridge and a long but very interesting half mile of rock and boulder from the top of it to the actual summit, before reaching which you cross the top of two deep gullies. The roughness may be avoided, at the expense of the interest, by keeping under the rocks along the top of the green slope that drops towards Capel Curig on the right of the ridge. The top is distinguished by a large cairn, or rather, half-cairn.

(b.) *An easier route.* Instead of crossing Pont-gyfing continue along the high-road for nearly half-a-mile to the *Tan-y-bwlch Hotel*, and there cross the river by a rustic foot-bridge, turning to the right beyond it through an oak-coppice. After crossing a wall turn up to the left and climb till you reach open ground broken with boulders and heather. The stony ridge of the mountain now appears in front, and a long slope, in ascending which you cross a wall and join the Capel Curig route, leads to it.

(2.) **From Capel Curig.** Cross the stream issuing from the lakes by the bridge on the south side of the hotel. Hence the path ascends to a cottage, beyond which you cross and follow up a streamlet that comes down through rough, broken ground. Passing between slate refuse on the left and the hollow of the stream on the right, you go through a gateway in a wall and reach the long grass slope that rises almost to the summit. The actual top is not visible but by making for the western extremity of the rocky ridge that forms the sky-line you cannot miss it. During the ascent there is a fine view of Snowdon and the Glyders.

(3.) **From Dolwyddelen.** Take the main road up the Lledr valley for half-a-mile, and then the by-road that goes up to the Castle on the right. Nearly opposite the Castle a rough cart-track diverges to the right. By this you cross a stream and continue over boggy and almost level ground to a farm-shed. Snowdon and its offshoot Lliwedd are now in view. At the shed the bog ceases awhile, but again occurs before you commence the actual ascent. During all this time Siabod presents its steepest side on the right hand, but you must be careful not to make for it until you can be sure of escaping its escarpment. Then, leaving the hollow, climb the green broken slope and reach the ridge by a rough terrace that ascends almost to the top. The only risk is that of getting too much to the right. During the ascent you look back, across the dip over which the road to Ffestiniog goes, to the Rhinog range in the direction of Barmouth. Moelwyn and Cynicht appear on the left.

(4.) From Pen-y-gwryd. Follow the Dolwyddelen route (p. 140) till you look down on the two lakes called *Llyniau-duwaunedd.* Hence, instead of descending, turn to the left, and you will reach the top of the mountain by a long and tedious grassy shoulder.

View from the Top. This is exceptionally good. Eastwards is a rich stretch of the Llugwy valley, extending to the Swallow Falls, and terminated by a strip of the Conway valley close to Bettws-y-Coed, which village, however, is unseen. A chain of lakes to the left of the Llugwy is a feature, and to the right of it, separated by moorland, is the Lledr valley, with the road that climbs to the plateau between Bettws-y-Coed and Corwen. The Clwydian and Berwyn ranges bound the view in this direction. The two peaks of Arenig-fawr are prominent in the south-east, and, a little to the left of them, in a direct line with the level top of Arenig-fach, is Llyn Conway, the source of the Conway river. To the right of these and farther away are the Arans and Cader Idris, the latter due south. Then comes a rocky range with Moelwyn and Cynicht at its northern extremity and close at hand. A peep into the Beddgelert valley is obtained, Llyn-y-Ddinas commencing it and Moel Hebog forming a fine background. Snowdon, the Glyders—with Y Tryfan showing 3 peaks to the right of them—and Carnedds Dafydd and Llewelyn monopolise the prospect to the west and north-west. Northwards part of the Llandudno promontory may be seen.

The ridge of Moel Siabod extends eastwards for half-a-mile. It is of the roughest character imaginable, and, as you proceed along it, two rocky gullies that drop to *Llyn-y-foel,* are specially noteworthy. Explore it by all means.

Descents. (1.) To Bettws-y-Coed direct. Follow the ridge eastwards, or keep in a line with it on its left side along the top of a grassy slope. At its end a steep descent will take you to a broad path that passes to the left of a tramway and some slate quarries, and reaches the main road at *Pont-gyfyng,* 4 miles short of Bettws (*see p.* 129).

(2.) **To Capel Curig.** You will catch sight of the hotel by walking a few yards north-east of the summit. There is no difficulty in reaching it.

(3.) **To Dolwyddelen.** Go south-west, descending from the ridge when you see a favourable opportunity. The route passes close to Dolwyddelen Castle, ¾m. west of the village.

(4.) **To Pen-y-gwryd.** A long gradual descent almost due west leads over a round grassy shoulder to *Bwlch-Rhiw-'r-ychain,* which overlooks the two lakelets, *Llyniau Duwaunedd.* Hence the route is described on page 128.

MOELWYN, 2,529 ft.; CYNICHT, about 2,370 ft.

These mountains rise abruptly at the head of Traeth-mawr, and about midway between Ffestiniog village and Beddgelert. From the former they are the highest ascents within easy walking distance, and from the latter they offer a pleasant climb free from the inevitable draw-backs of Snowdon when " in season." Cynicht from the neighourhood of Portmadoc appears as a sharp and steep peak and has, not inappropriately, been styled the Welsh Matterhorn. The summits of the two mountains are, as the crow flies, about 1½ miles apart, and those who do not object to a steep down and up course can proceed pretty direct from one to the other—a stiff hour's work. If, however, the intervening dip of Cwm Croesor be passed at its head, the additional mile or so in distance will involve no extra time, and save a good deal of fatigue. The walk from Ffestiniog village to Beddgelert or *vice versâ* over both summits is about 13 to 14 miles, and the time required not less than 6 to 7 hours. The Ffestiniog narrow-gauge railway may be utilised by taking the train either to or from Tan-y-Grisiau or Tan-y-Bwlch; the former station is about 620 feet above sea-level, and the latter about 400 feet.

It is difficult to advise the tourist who can only afford time for one ascent which mountain to give the preference to. Moelwyn is a few feet the higher and commands the Vale of Ffestiniog, but it is much cut about by slate-quarries. Cynicht on the other hand is nearly intact, affords the better view of the fine southern escarpment of Snowdon, and if it be approached, as it should be, along its southern ridge, has towards the top just sufficient abruptness to add interest to the climb.

Ascent of Moelwyn, 2,529 ft.

(*a.*) *From Tan-y-Grisiau.* (*b.*) *From Tan-y-Bwlch.* (*c.*) *From Beddgelert.*

(*a.*) **From Tan-y-Grisiau,** *about 1½ hrs.* This is an easy climb that, without much extra effort, can be accomplished in an hour, and the route is almost wholly in sight from the station, whence before starting it will make matters quite simple if we just note a point or two. Looking down the line, *i.e.* towards Portmadoc, high up on the left of the mountain-side is seen an inclined-plane with the usual erection across its top. To the right of this, and somewhat below, we make out a water-wheel and the white streak of a small cascade. Our way lies just to the right of this cascade. Thus prepared, we start down the line, having first asked leave to do so, and made sure that no train is due. The line is so narrow, that to be overtaken by a slate train —they run down swiftly, and often without stopping at the station —is dangerous. About 250 yards below the station, where the

second tram-line on the right joins company, we get over a gate
on that side and turn at once to the left, following a wall, past a
new cottage. Thence a rough path, which is more troublesome
to trace than to take one's own course, may be followed. The
ascent is over rock-broken grassy ground, and the burn from Llyn
Trwstyllon keeps us more or less close company. When the cascade mentioned above is close by on our left, a wall has to be
scaled, and the water-wheel and disused quarry-works are then
seen. In a minute or two the desolate **Llyn Trwstyllon** is
reached, and the tramway is observed winding round it on the
left, and so up the mountain-side beyond.

Before reaching the Llyn, a green slope on the right offers a tempting way up,
but this must not be taken.

From the shore of the lake the rounded summit of Moelwyn is
on our right-front and the best way up is to attack the easy ridge
from the foot of the lake and then to turn to the left along it.
The cairn on the top of the mountain is not seen from below.
The **view** is a very wide one owing to the comparatively isolated
situation of the mountain, but it does not rival in beauty that
commanded from the hills behind Harlech. Immediately below,
on the north side of the mountain, is Cwm Croesor, with Cynicht
steeply cragged and screed across it, and beyond this Snowdon is
well seen, the fine peak of Yr Aran rising above Cwm-y-Llan.
The coast as far as Bardsey is like a map below us, and on a clear
day a peep of the sea is obtained between Moel Siabod and the
monument-crowned Moel Fammau. On the south-west we command the upper part of the vale of Ffestiniog, and in the distance
beyond Ffestiniog village are the two Arenigs. The wall-like
face of Cader Idris is due south.

(b.) **From Tan-y-Bwlch station** cross the wall by the wooden
steps, close to the down platform. The old mountain-road from
Maentwrog—at best but a mule-track the greater part of the way
—is then entered on, and has to be followed for about 2½ miles.
Moel Hebog is soon prominent in front, Moelwyn-bach is on our
right, and on the left we get a wide view over Traeth-mawr to the
sea about Portmadoc. Then, about two miles from the station,
we cross the mouth of the great combe that runs up between
Moelwyn-bach and Braich-y-Parc (the western ridge of Moelwyn)
and get a full view of Moelwyn. Still following our mountain-
road, after the next steep, we turn to the right along the road that
ascends the southern flank of Cwm Croesor to the Moelwyn slate-
quarry. **Cwm Croesor** is a fine glen, but has lost much of its
original wildness. A considerable collection of quarrymen's
houses occupies its mouth, and a tramway runs up it. Cynicht
rises almost precipitously on its north side, and is on its southern
flank scarred by a quarry. After reaching the Moelwyn quarry
our course bends sharply round to the right and a steep, but not
difficult climb, brings us to the cairn on the top of the mountain.
For the view see above under (a).

From **Moelwyn** to **Cynicht**. The most direct way is to descend to the head of Cwm Croesor and climb the steep screes that rise from the combe just east of the summit of Cynicht. There is no danger, though it is a stiff ascent to the ridge, which is gained a few hundred yards east of the top of the mountain. A longer, but easier route, is to descend Moelwyn by its northern flank—Moel-y-Rhudd—to *Bwlch-cwm-orthin*, the pass at the top of the combe running up from Tan-y-Grisiau. Thence climbing gradually to the lakelet-sprinkled and somewhat boggy watershed that divides Cwm Croesor from the Lledr valley and is about 1¼ miles due north of the pass, we gain the northern ridge of Cynicht and have below us, close at hand, the uninteresting Llyn-yr-Adar.   Turning left, along the ridge, we pass just above Llyn-y-Biswail and reach the summit of Cynicht in a few hundred yards more.

(*c*.) **From Beddgelert**. This is identical with the ascent of Cynicht (*p*. 202) as far as Cwm Croesor, and from the far side of that glen the route is the same as that from Tan-y-Bwlch, described above under (*b*).

Ascent of Cynicht, about 2,370 ft.

(*a*.) *From Beddgelert*; (*b*.) *from Tan-y-Bwlch*; (*c*.) *from Tan-y-Grisiau*.

(*a*.) **From Beddgelert**. By far the most interesting ascent is by the south-west ridge of the mountain. Follow the Portmadoc road through Aberglaslyn, cross the bridge, and, shortly afterwards, just beyond a burn, take the old mountain-road (on the left) to Tan-y-Bwlch and Maentwrog. About 1½ miles from Pont Aberglaslyn we cross *Nant-y-mor*.

The track on the eastern side of the combe—*Nant-y-mor*—runs up to the foot of *Cwm-Celli-Iago*, ascending which to *Bwlch-y-batel* the summit of Cynicht may be reached by its western ridge.

Then our track crosses the southern spur of *Yr Arddu*, and drops to the small *Afon-dulif*. The next ascent places us on the end of the ridge just short of *Cwm Croesor*, and by it, quitting the road, we ascend. This ridge commands a fine view of that combe, and of Moelwyn, and on our left Snowdon rises to a noble peak. After following the top of the ridge for some way it is easier going to keep along its northern slope past a deserted cottage or two. The ascent now soon becomes stiffer, but offers no real difficulty though it may appear to the tourist unused to such exploits to be dangerously steep. After passing the cottages just mentioned we have first to climb a shoulder, and in so doing we lose sight for a while of the final peak. The way up this shoulder is diagonally along its western side, on which the parsley fern grows abundantly. Do not be tempted to descend and to make for the

western ridge of the mountain, but keep up till the top end of a
wall is reached, after crossing which mount again (a matter of a
few yards) to the ridge. **Here we** get a fine view into the depths
of Cwm Croesor, to which the ridge falls precipitously. From
the point we have **now attained we** have known more than one
timid climber turn back, but **with** the smallest **amount of** nerve
and care the **rest of** the ascent is quite **free from** danger. As
we **stand with our** back to the rocks that **here crest** the ridge a
few rocks are seen on our right front. Up these we make our
way, and then attain a **stone-strewed turf slope.** The summit is
only a few minutes further.

(*b.*) **From Tan-y-Bwlch.** Cross the **wall at the back** of the
down platform of the railway **station** by the stair-ladder. The
rough road beyond is the old mountain-road **to** Beddgelert. The
route is the same as that for Moelwyn (*p.* 201). Instead, however, of turning to the right when Cwm Croesor is **reached** we
cross that valley and climb the ridge beyond, quitting the road
just beyond a chapel. Thence the ascent is the same as that
given above under (*a*).

(*c.*) From **Tan-y-Grisiau.** This route ascends the quarry-
spoilt *Cwm Orthin* and passes *Llyn Orthin.* Beyond the lake the
main combe turns westwards, and in about 2¼ miles from the station
we reach the Bwlch. Thence we can either descend to the head
of Cwm Croesor and mount the steep screes east of the summit or
make the circuit by *Llyn-yr-Adar* described p. 202 in going from
Moelwyn to Cynicht.

N.B.—The walk from the top of Cynicht by the Lledr valley to Roman
Bridge, which some may be tempted to take in order to strike the rail to
Bettws-y-Coed, is not to be recommended. There is no difficulty in finding the
way, as, it is due north-east for about two miles, and then down the valley,
dropping to which, Dolwyddelen Castle is seen, 4 or 5 miles away at the foot of
Moel Siabod. The objection to the route is the hopelessly swampy nature of
the valley until we strike the railway just north of the great Blaenau tunnel.

SNOWDON, 3,571 ft.

Snowdon is not only the highest mountain in the southern
part of Great Britain, but also the finest. The group of peaks
and ridges which constitute it has no rival, and the only single
peaks which can enter into competition with its highest one are,
perhaps, Schiehallion in Perthshire ; Bowfell, Great Gable and the
Langdale Pikes in the Lake District; and Elydir-fawr, Cynicht
(viewed from between Portmadoc and Beddgelert) and the Tryfan
in Wales. In Scotland, the mountains of Skye and Arran and
the Teallach heights in Ross-shire present bolder rock scenery,
but the only mountain-mass which can compare with the Welsh
Monarch in combined grace and boldness of outline is that of Ben
Cruachan.

Snowdon has five distinct peaks:—*Y Wyddfa*, the central and highest one; *Yr Aran* and *Lliwedd*, to the south of Y Wyddfa; *Crib-y-ddysgyl* and *Crib-goch* to the north-east of it. The best view-point for the whole group is Capel Curig; for the main peak, the neighbourhood of Portmadoc. There is also a very fine and famous view of Y Wyddfa from the western end of the Nantlle valley, the flanking hills of which serve as a frame to the picture. From the north, Crib-y-ddysgyl interposes its huge shoulder and either hides Y Wyddfa altogether or only admits of the last hundred feet or so of it being seen.

The view *from* the summit is a most extensive one of both land and sea, but its finest features are the grand ridges and subsidiary peaks of Snowdon itself, and most visitors will be of opinion that the comparative absence of rich valley scenery in the mid-distance places the prospect in other respects at some disadvantage with those which are obtained from Cader Idris in Wales, and from the general run of the mountains in the Lake District.

There are four recognised ascents of Snowdon:—From Llanberis, Capel Curig (Pen-y-gwryd or Corphwysfa), Beddgelert (or Rhyd-ddu Station) and Snowdon Ranger. All these are free from danger. The Llanberis ascent is the easiest and least interesting; that from Capel Curig the steepest and finest. The Beddgelert route (joined by the Rhyd-ddu track soon after the high-road is quitted) traces for the last half-mile the top of a sharp ridge called Bwlch-y-maen. The Snowdon Ranger route calls for no comment. There are other practicable routes—but, with the exception of those given on page 211A, and the alternative descent to Beddgelert over Yr Aran, which is perfectly safe, they are hardly of a character to be described in a general guide-book.*

Ascents. (1.) **From Llanberis,** 5m. *Pony 5s., Guide 5s.*; 2-3 *hrs.* There is a pony-track, just passable by carts for the greater part of the distance, all the way to the top. From the village or station you either go south by the main road as far as the Victoria Hotel, and then turn up a lane to the right, or you may take the alternate lane and foot-path from near the Dolbadarn Hotel past the new church and, after crossing the stream that comes from the Fall, join the road from the Victoria. Then the road enters a wood and ascends steeply with the Fall a little way off and unseen on the right. At the top of the steep ascent the track passes through a gate on to open ground, and a

---

* In the great majority of cases, such ascents or descents are successfully accomplished, but, in comparison with the number of times they are essayed, the instances of disaster are, even with experienced climbers, far too numerous. Some winters ago, the writer, halting at Wasdale Head, in Cumberland, noticed in the Visitors Book the record of a successful ascent of the Pillar Rock (the most dangerous bit of crag work in the Lake District) by an Alpine climber. Underneath was a cutting from a Welsh newspaper, describing the death of the same gentleman on Crib-goch in the following year. The fatality occurred on Clogwyn-person (Cwm-glas), and but for this addition to it the record would have encouraged the idea, so often put forward by fairly practised climbers, that such cliffs and rocks do not present any serious danger.

little further turns abruptly to the left. (The direct route onward leads to an upland chapel.) From this point there is no mistaking the way. The topmost peak, Y Wyddfa, peers over the broad shoulder of Crib-y-ddysgyl ("thizgil") in front; on the right is a shallow valley, with the track to Snowdon Ranger and the dull outline of Moel Eilio beyond it; in the rear the prospect—a featureless one—extends over Anglesey. For the next two miles there is little change in the view. Over a dip on the right Moel Hebog, overlooking Beddgelert, appears; the dark cliffs of Clogwyn-du'r-Arddu, above which goes the path from Snowdon Ranger to the summit, are in front, and on the left higher ground shuts out the Llanberis valley.

About two-thirds of the way up in distance, and half in height, we come to the *Refreshment Huts* (*see p.* 211A), beyond which the track bends to the left and ascends steeply to a point whence there is a striking view into Cwm-glas-bach and the Llanberis valley.

From this point the ordinary track again passes out of sight of the Llanberis valley, and commands no view in that direction until, within half-a-mile of the summit, it reaches the top of the Glaslyn hollow (*Cwm Dyli*), up which comes the zig-zag path from Pen-y-gwryd. At the expense of an extra 20 minutes, however, and a rather stiff climb up some stony ground, you may cling to the ridge and gain a splendid view down the larger *Cwm-glas*—one of the finest hollows in Wales, similar in character to that in which Llyn Idwal lies, and to the Llyn-y-cau corrie of Cader Idris. At the top of this ascent you are on **Crib-y-ddysgyl**; thence a razor-like edge strikes away to the left to *Crib-goch*, which is immediately over the Pass of Llanberis. Then, bending to the right round the Glaslyn hollow (Cwm Dyli), you descend about 100 feet and rejoin the beaten track close to the convergence of the Snowdon Ranger and Capel Curig routes. Hereabouts, close to some ruined huts, is a spring. The view westwards now includes Llyn Cwellyn, the road from Carnarvon to Beddgelert, and the Nantlle Lakes—the last-named being seen through the narrow opening of the Nantlle valley. Y Wyddfa rises directly in front, and a sharp climb of ¼ hour places you on the summit. *For the view see p.* 207.

(2.) **From Beddgelert.** 6½ *m* ;* or **Rhyd-ddu,** 3½ *m.* The opening of the little narrow-gauge railway (*p.* 141) to Rhyd-ddu has brought the latter of these two into existence as a popular route. The meeting-place is about ¾ *m.* from the Carnarvon and Beddgelert road. From *Beddgelert* you follow this road (*p.* 159) for a long 2½ miles, and then, a few yards short of Pitt's Head, take a track to the right up to *Ffridd-uchaf farm*, beyond which the path ascends a green slope, with a hollow on the right. From *Rhyd-ddu*, you commence the ascent at a crossing a little north of the station, and follow a quarry-track till it joins the Beddgelert path, in about ⅜ mile. Thence continuing the ascent over

* *Guide from Beddgelert, 7s. 6d., Pony 10s.*

some broken ground, the **path** goes through a wall close to a sheep-fold, and soon passes a cairn, which marks the spot where a tourist lost his life from exhaustion in 1859. The view northwards now extends over **Llyn** Cwellyn, Carnarvon and Anglesey to Holyhead Mountain. Continuing upwards, we pass through walls again on to a shoulder of the mountain, called *Llechog*, precipitous on the left hand and looking over a hollow, in which are several small lakes, to Y Wyddfa itself. Westwards, the Nantlle lakes have come into view, between the bold heights of Mynyddmawr and Y Garn. Then, bending **left** along the side of a steep slope, the **path** reaches the narrow **ridge** of **Bwlch-y-maen**, which leads directly to the summit. From this edge the drop on both sides is almost precipitous, **and** occasionally the path, being for a few yards unprotected, is rather awkward in **a** high **cross-wind**, reminding one of the Patterdale ascent of Helvellyn. Otherwise this is by far the most interesting part of the ascent. The hollow on the right is *Cwm-y-Llan*, opening on to the Beddgelert and Capel Curig road between **Llyn** Gwynant and Llyn-y-Ddinas. Beyond it is the abrupt edge of Lliwedd. Moel Siabod and the Capel Curig lakes are now in sight, and a great part of the prospect which we shall describe from the top. Bwlch-y-maen widens out at its upper end to the centre-piece of the whole, *Y Wyddfa. For the view see p. 207.*

(3.) **From** Pen-y-gwryd **Hotel**, 5 *m.* (**Capel Curig**, 9 *m.* **Corphwysfa** Hotel, 4 *m.*), 2-3 *hrs. Pony*, 5*s. Guide*, 5*s.* Pen-y-gwryd is about 950 feet above sea-level, and Corphwysfa (the " Resting-place ") about 1,200 ft. From Capel Curig, the Llanberis road (*p.* 131) is followed past Pen-y-gwryd to *Corphwysfa*, which is exactly at the top of the Pass of Llanberis. [For " upper track " see p. 211ʌ.] Here, a few yards short of the **inn**, the path, at first a cart-track, passable for two miles by carriages, strikes off on the left, and continues on a very slight ascent round the smaller height of *Pen-y-lan* to *Llyn Llydaw*. On the left it commands the upper part of Nant Gwynant and, as it bends to the right, the summit of Snowdon appears towering with noble effect in front.

Llyn Llydaw is a large sheet of water, 1,500 feet above the sea, and surrounded, except on the east, by the precipitous arms of Snowdon. On approaching it, the pedestrian may cut off **a** sharp angle in the road. A stone *causeway* crosses the lake a short distance from its eastern end, and beyond this the road is continued along its **northern** shore almost to its far end.

From Llyn Llydaw there is a sharp ascent of 500 feet to the smaller tarn of *Glaslyn* in Cwm Dyli, at the outlet of which are the old mine-works, a great disfigurement to the scene. Here the cart-track ceases, and the rest of the route is a very rough and steep zig-zag one up the rocky hollow between Y Wyddfa, which all the way presents a magnificent appearance in front, and the sharp ridge connecting Crib-y-ddysgyl with Crib-goch—a grand walk, but requiring no description, as the path, though occasionally breaking into two, cannot well be missed. In the lower part of the hollow there are abundant evidences of glacial action.

On the sharp ridge at the top of the combe we join the Llanberis track ½ mile short of the summit of Y Wyddfa.

From Snowdon Ranger 1½ to 2 hrs; 4 m. Pony 7s. 6d. Guide 7s. 6d.

This ascent is for the first quarter of an hour identical with the route from Snowdon Ranger to Llanberis (p. 141). When the path reaches a gate in a wall and becomes smaller as it bears up the hill to the left, quit it and go through the gate on to the sodden hill-side beyond. Snowdon is right ahead, and in clear weather no mistake can well be made. By keeping well up the hill-side the worst of the wet ground can be avoided. On the right hand a large isolated block of rock, *Maen-bras*, is seen on the bottom of the slope and presently, after crossing a gully or two, an inter-mittent path may be followed. *Llyn Ffynnon-y-gwas* is seen below on the right, and we gradually ascend the green slope until we reach the top of the ridge, Clogwyn Du'r Arddu, whose northern face is a wall of precipitous crags at the foot of which are the little tarn *Llyn Du'r Arddu* and the workings of an abandoned copper mine. Below, on the right, is the solitary Cwm Clogwyn with its three wee tarns, and the peak of Snowdon at its head. After a zig-zag ascent by a defined path, the Llanberis path is joined about 80 yards short of the junction of that route with the one from Pen-y-gwryd.

At the summit is the so-called **Snowdon Hotel**—a rude collection of huts not "raised in nice proportion," but providing, besides beds, simple fare at a charge which, considering the diffi-culties of transport, cannot be fairly called excessive. "Bass" and "Guinness" are one shilling a pint bottle, and other things in proportion.

The **View from the Top of Snowdon** is mainly dependent on atmospheric conditions for its extent. The foreground is occupied by the rocky arms of the mountain itself ramifying in all directions ;— *Crib-y-ddysgyl* and *Crib-goch* north east, *Lliwedd* south-east, *Yr Aran* south, *Llechog* south-west and *Clogwyn-du'r-Arddu* north-west. In the way of water we have Glaslyn, Llyn Llydaw, and the Capel Curig lakes east ; Llyn Cwellyn, Llyn-y-Gader, with two smaller and partly artificial sheets of water between them, and the Nantlle Lakes between the rocky heights of Mynydd-mawr and Y Garn, west ; the lower part of Llyn Padarn, north ; and a girdle of sea from beyond Rhyl to the farthest extremity of Cardigan Bay. The southern part of the Menai Straits, a portion of the Tubular Bridge, and almost the whole of Anglesey—in appearance as flat as a pancake, except for the Holyhead mountain—are included in the prospect.

The only bit of really green valley visible is a strip of Nant Gwynant between Llyn Gwynant and Llyn-y-Ddinas, though the whole of Nant-y-Gwryd, between Pen-y-gwryd and Capel Curig, and a part of the valley near Llyn Cwellyn, form part of the panorama.

Mountains are naturally the most abundant, if not the most attractive objects in the prospect from this monarch of them all, and premising that mountains (like men), to be appreciated, should be looked up to and not down upon, we must admit the comparative excellence of the view in this respect. The finest effect within the writer's memory was obtained on the occasion of a winter ascent many years ago, when nothing but mountain tops was visible. The lowlands were shrouded in fog, but the sky above was beautifully blue, and each separate peak floated in mid-air like the "baseless fabric of a vision." Beginning in the north, a little to the right of Llyn Padarn, we have the sharp peak of Elidyr-fawr succeeded by Carnedd Dafydd and Carnedd Llewelyn, the loftiest summits in the whole environment. Penmaenmawr is just visible to the left of the two latter, and to the right of them the Glyders appear close at hand over the edge connecting Crib-y-ddysgyl with Crib-goch. Eastwards the billowy Clwydian range bounds the prospect, and Moel Siabod shows its least effective side to the right of the Capel Curig Lakes. Far away to the right of Siabod is the featureless line of the Berwyn Hills, and you may possibly detect Llyn Conway in front of them. Arenig-fawr, near Bala, is just over Lliwedd, and to the right of the latter the Arans, between Bala and Dinas Mawddwy, cut the sky-line. Moelwyn and Cynicht are nearer at hand between these and Cader Idris, which is the farthest height visible southwards, except a bit of Plynlimon. Then comes Cardigan Bay, stretching far away to the Precelly Hills in Pembrokeshire, and having St. David's Head beyond Moel Hebog, as its southern, and the long Lleyn promontory as its northern limit. Harlech Castle stands close to the water a little left of Yr Aran. Westwards, along the Lleyn promontory, the sharp peaks of the Rivals, on the left of Nantlle Lakes, afford the most striking mountain outline.

In clear weather the prospect is bounded by the Wicklow Mountains rising from the sea between the Nantlle valley and Anglesey, the Isle of Man almost due north over Llyn Padarn, and Scafell and Black Combe rather more to the east and just above the top of Penmaenmawr.

Descents. (1.) **To Llanberis,** 5 m. There is no chance of mistaking this well-defined track, except that in foggy weather it is just possible to get on the Snowdon Ranger path, which diverges to the left nearly half-a-mile from the summit, and 80 yards beyond the point at which the Pen-y-gwryd path commences its plunge into the depths of Cwm Dyli. Pedestrians who have not already seen Cwm-glas are strongly advised to turn out of the track to the right a few yards beyond these divergences, and ascend about 100 feet to the top of **Crib-y-ddysgyl** (see p. 205), whence, after inspecting the narrow ridge leading to Crib-goch, they may keep along the edge that commands Cwm-glas, and rejoin the ordinary track at the point where it commences the steep pitch down to the *Refreshment Huts* (3 *m. from Llanberis*). This is the only point on the ordinary track that commands a view down into the Llanberis valley. It is at the head of Cwm-glas-bach (the "little" Cwm-glas). From the lower hut the route is dull, unless you climb to the edge of the cliffs on the right, and there is nothing calling for more description than we have given in the ascent (*p.* 204) until we enter the main road opposite the Victoria Hotel, and a little south of the station and village of *Llanberis* (*p.* 137).

(2.) **To Beddgelert** (6½ *m.*), **or Rhyd-ddu Station**, 3½ m The track down the sharp ridge of Bwlch-y-Maen (*p.* 206) is unmistakable. In ¾ of a mile it swerves to the right, along the steep slope of Llechog.

The alternative route to Beddgelert over **Yr Aran** should be commenced about here. To accomplish it you have only to go up and down along the ridge and, after surmounting *Yr Aran*, either to continue down the shoulder called *Y Graig-wen* to the Carnarvon and Beddgelert road, or to return a little way to *Bwlch-cwm-y-llan*, and thence drop into the valley of the same name to the mines which are connected by a cart-road with Nant Gwynant.

Beyond the precipitous cliffs of Llechog the regular track bends to the left again, and about a mile further, after passing some sheep-folds, crosses the quarry-track which descends to the railway a few yards from *Rhyd-ddu Station*. For *Beddgelert* you keep straight on, with a hollow on the left and, after passing *Ffridd-uchaf Farm*, enter the main road a few yards south of *Pitt's Head* (**p.** 158), and nearly 3 miles short of *Beddgelert*.

(3.) **To Corphwysfa**, 4 *m*; Pen-y-gwryd, 5 *m*; and **Capel Curig**, 9 *m* [for the "upper track" see *p.* 211A]. A great part of this route is in sight from the top. It quits the Llanberis track in about ⅓ mile, and zigzags abruptly down into the depths of *Cwm Dyli*, which is flanked by Y Wyddfa and Lliwedd on the right and the Crib-goch spur on the left. At the tarn, called *Glaslyn*, some hideous old mining works are reached, and from them a cart-track descends 500 feet to Llyn Llydaw, which is crossed by a causeway near its eastern end. From the other side you may save a bit by taking a path in front instead of bending back by the cart-track, which is, however, rejoined almost at once, and comes out on to the main road at the top of the Pass of Llanberis, opposite the *Corphwysfa*, 1 mile short of the *Pen-y-gwryd*, and 5 miles short of *Capel Curig Hotel*. For the route from *Corphwysfa* to *Llanberis, see* **p.** 132; to *Capel Curig*, **p.** 140; and to *Beddgelert*, p. 132.

(4.) **To Snowdon Ranger**. The inn may be seen from the top. It lies in a little belt of trees nearly half-way down the east side of Llyn Cwellyn. The track for it leaves the Llanberis one in a short half-mile, 80 yards beyond the abrupt commencement of the Pen-y-gwryd descent. Then, after descending the smooth side of *Crib-y-ddysgyl*, it continues a little south of the top of the steep cliff called *Clogwyn-du'r-Arddu*, at the foot of which is the small lake of the same name. From the end of this cliff a steep descent takes us above the north side of *Llyn Ffynnon-y-Gwas*. The rest of the way is easy going over grass, the last bit being a sharp descent to the inn. When in doubt, keep on eastward in the direction of Mynydd-mawr, which rises from the far side of Llyn Cwellyn.

Y TRYFAN ("The Three-headed Peak"), 3,009 feet.

From Pen-y-Benglog (top of Nant Ffrancon) 1-1½ hrs.

The **Tryfan** is perhaps the most remarkable mountain in Wales. It is a pyramid of rock rising 2,000 feet above the upper Llugwy valley. As seen from various points of the compass, it shows one, two, three or even four peaks, or rather humps. The only ascents are from Pen-y-Benglog—the cottage at the head of Nant Ffrancon—or from Pen-y-gwryd by the dip between Glyder-fach and Y Tryfan itself. The writer's recollection is of an ascent made several winters ago under very peculiar circumstances. The lower ground, almost as far as the top of Nant Ffrancon, was shrouded by mist and drizzling rain, but above this height there was a sky of the purest blue and a frosty atmosphere. All the mountains of Wales floated on a sea of mist.

From Pen-y-Benglog ascend by the rough track that leads to Llyn Bochlwyd and the Glyders (*p.* 193). Then, leaving Llyn Bochlwyd on the right, and bearing a little more in that direction, you scramble up to the summit. Minute guidance is not needed, because you cannot go far to the left without coming to sheer crags, and on the right a wall, ascending the mountain from the gap between it and Glyder-fach, forms the limit of deviation in that direction. This wall is the object to be aimed at by those who make the ascent from Pen-y-gwryd.

Most of the ascent is over scree and boulders, and the top is a perfect wilderness of rocky débris, the two crowning rocks being several yards in perpendicular height, very narrow-topped, and a yard or two apart. Mr. Bingley, who wrote his experiences at the beginning of the century, tells us of a "friend who leapt "from one to the other and then back again." Commenting on the performance, the writer quaintly adds: "A body thus pro-"jected, without great management in its counteraction, would "have sent him a step farther than he intended to have gone, that "is, down the precipice." *Verb. sap.*

The *View from the Top*, though somewhat circumscribed by loftier heights, is very striking. The head of Nant Ffrancon, immediately below, is its chief feature. Llyn Ogwen looks as if you might almost throw a stone into it, and beyond it, in the hollows formed by the shoulders of Carnedd Dafydd and Carnedd

Llewelyn respectively, are the solitary lakelets of Ffynnon-y-Lloer and Ffynnon Llugwy (*Ffynnon* signifies "a fountain," and these lakes are the sources of the Ogwen and the Llugwy.) Westwards, beyond Llyn Bochlwyd, Llyn Idwal lies in the arms of Glyder-fawr and Y Garn. Snowdon is hidden by the former, but to the right of Y Garn the finely-cut ridge of Elidyr-fawr is seen. More to the right a part of Nant Ffrancon appears, and beyond it a portion of Anglesey, to the east of the Tubular Bridge. Westwards the prospect is extensive, reaching over the lower hills between the Llugwy valley and Llanrwst to the Clwydian range and, further south, to the Berwyns. In this direction the deep hollow of Cwm Tryfan is close below, and over the ridge beyond we catch Moel Siabod, itself over-topped by Arenig-fawr in the far distance.

The *Descent of Y Tryfan* is necessarily the same as the ascent.

From **Pen-y-gwryd** to **Llyn Ogwen**. This walk may be accomplished in from 2 to 2½ hours by following the direction for ascending Glyder-fach, on page 193, to the corner of the wall and a small cairn visible further up the hill a little to the right. Hence a succession of such cairns gives a good line to the top of the ridge.

From this point descend to the screes coming down from Glyder-fach, and make for the lowest part of the wall on the *col* between Glyder-fach and Tryfan. There is a track, but in many parts it is ill defined. From the wall proceed about west, to the outlet of Llyn Bochlwyd, over rough rocks at first, and rather boggy ground lower down. Cross the stream flowing out of the lake and follow it down until the steep ground is passed. Then make for the lower end of Llyn Ogwen by the track mentioned on page 193, line 17.

ADDITIONAL SNOWDON EXCURSIONS.

Snowdon from Llanberis, p. 204. **Cwm Brwynog** is worth
visiting, if only for the enormous heap of moraine matter bounding
the N. and W. edges of the two little pools under Clogwyn d'ur
Arddu. The shortest approach is to turn to the right just short
of the *Refreshment Huts, p.* 205, and to make straight for the
cliff in front. Another way is from Llanberis to keep close to the
stream in the bottom of the valley, and follow it up to the
moraine heap. A short scramble up the larger blocks of rock will
land the visitor on a level with or somewhat above the little pools.

Cwm Brwynog may be quitted at the eastern or western extremity.

(*a*) *Eastern.* Turn your back on the cliff, and go obliquely to
the right for the Llanberis path.

(*b*) *Western.* There is a small gully, a little distance short of
Bwlch Cwm Brwynog, up which it is not difficult to scramble,
although the stones are many and loose. It is easier, however, to
make for the bwlch. On reaching the top of it turn to the left
and pass over the top of Clogwyn d'ur Arddu, along the Snowdon
Ranger track, *p.* 207.

Snowdon from Pen-y-gwryd, p. 206. Instead of the usual route
there given there is another known as the **Capel Curig upper
track**. This starts some 250 paces along the ordinary track and
zigzags up the hillside, eventually striking up between two little
grassy peaks, which lie about S.-W. from Pen-y-pass (Corphwysfa)
Inn. Thence the route crosses to the Llydaw side of the ridge,
but keeps high above the water's edge. The path is now fairly
well marked, but where it is indistinct for a short distance, the
traveller should remember that it winds along the base of Crib-goch,
and, as a rule, rises throughout its length. It joins the usual
Pen-y-gwryd zigzag above Glaslyn.

This track affords a lovely view of the Pass of Llanberis, and
after heavy rains is practicable when the *Causeway* (*p.* 206) over
Llydaw is submerged.

N.B. Anyone descending from Snowdon by this route (especially in winter) is strongly advised to get well down towards the
main track before **darkness sets in,** particularly when there is
mist about.

Ascent of Snowdon by Cwm-glas. This route will be appreciated by those who find the ordinary routes too hackneyed. It
is perfectly safe and has been taken by ladies. There is no path,
and one or two walls have to be crossed, but there is no difficulty worth
mention from beginning to end. If Pen-y-gwryd be the starting point,
follow the Llanberis road for about ½ *m.* beyond (*i.e.*, W. of) Pont-y-
gromlech, then cross over **two** rustic bridges on the left [on the

right, of course, if coming up from Llanberis] and make for the great rounded grass-grown mound in the centre of the foreground. Pass on either side of this mound, and just beyond it you will see, on the left (*i.e.*, the E. side of the valley), a black wet cliff. Turn to the left when past this and keep the first stream beyond it on your left hand, until nearly on a level with the crags, which lie a few yards to your right. Bend slightly round these and in a few minutes the Lower Lake in Cwm-glas is reached. From its outlet proceed S.-W., close to the cliff which runs down between the two lakes. Having reached the Upper Lake stand so as to face, in the direction of its length, up the cwm. Close to the cliff on your left is a dark looking gully. Now take a half turn to the right and breast the steep and wet grass for the ridge, some distance on the other side of which is the Llanberis path. It will save time if on reaching the top of the ridge you bear rather to the left and so approach the Llanberis path obliquely instead of making straight for it.

Another ascent by Cwm-glas. From the Lower Lake in Cwm-glas (*above*) there is an easy passage, nearly due south, over *Bwlch-goch*, to the "Capel Curig upper track" (*p.* 211A). When you reach the top of the bwlch bend slightly to the right.

On reaching Bwlch-goch from Cwm-glas, a turn to the left and a rough scramble will land the tourist on the first pinnacles of **Crib-goch**, and from this point a fair notion of the ridge is obtained. Thus far there is no difficulty or danger, but the traverse of the ridge is not to be recommended indiscriminately.

INDEX.

N.B.—Where more than one page is referred to, that on which a locality is particularly described is given first.

Telegraph Offices are indicated by an asterisk; *Railway Stations* by a dagger. The names enclosed in square brackets are required to complete the Postal address.

†**Aber** [Bangor], 74, 21.
,, Falls, 75.
Aberdaron [Pwllheli], 152.
*†**Abergele** [Denbighshire], 40, 19.
Aberglaslyn (Pont), 161, 164.
Abersoch [Pwllheli], 152.
†Afonwen Junction, 146.
Aire Point, 19.
Allt-wen, 58, 66.
Alyn, River and Glen, 14.
*†Amlwch [Anglesey], 95.
Anglesey, 83.
,, Column, 85.
Aran, Yr, 209, &c.
Arenig Station, 178.

*†**Bala** [Merioneth], 177, &c.
*†**Bangor**, 79, 21, &c.
Bardsey Isle, 154.
*†Barmouth, 169.
Baron Hill, 92, 89.
Basingwerke Abbey, 17.
***Beaumaris** [Anglesey], 90, 88, &c.
Beddau-gwyr-Ardudwy, 171.
Beddgelert [Carnarvon], 158, 128, 132, 142, &c.
Bedd Taliesin, 112.
Beeston Castle, 1.
Benarth Hill, 59.
Bera-bach, 184.
Benglog (Pen-y-), 103, 193, 210.

*†**Bethesda** [Bangor], 100, 78, 99, 131, &c.
Bettws Garmon, 141, 160.
*†**Bettws-y-Coed** [Carnarvonshire], 118, 104, 113, &c.
*†**Blaenau Ffestiniog** [Merioneth], 167, 128, 161, 168, &c.
Bodelwyddan church, 28, 19.
†Bodfari [Rhyl], 38.
Bodlondeb, 53.
†Bodorgan, 95.
Bodrhyddan, 26.
Boduan Hall, 156.
Bod-yscallen, 52.
Borth (Portmadoc), 163.
Braich-du, 183, 187.
,, -y-Parc, 201.
†Bridge End, 13.
Britannia Bridge, 85, &c.
Bronllwyd, 190, &c.
Bryn Euryn, 53, 48.
,, Maelgwyn, 53, 48.
Bryniog Isaf and Uchaf, 116.
Brynkir, 146.
Bryntyrch, 130.
Bryn-y-neuadd, 69.
Bulkeley Monument, 93.
Bull Bay, 95.
Bwlch-chediad, 128.
,, -cwm-orthin, 202, 203.
,, -pen-barras, 14, 39.

Bwlch - rhiw-'r - ychain, 128, 140.
  „   -y-ddeufaen, 59, 70, 75.
  „   -y-maen, 206, 174.
  „   -y-maes-cwm, 138.
  „   -y-rhiw, 152, 154.
Bwrdd Arthur, 93.

Caegwilym-ddu, 75.
Caer Estyn, 12.
Caergwrle Castle, 13.
Caerhun, 106, 126.
*†Caerwys [Holywell], 38.
  Capel Curig [Bettws-y-Coed], 130, &c.
  „   Garmon, 122, 119.
Careg-lefain, 156.
  „   -y-defaid, 151.
  „   -y-llam, 156.
  „   -y-rimbill, 151, 149.
Carn Boduan, 156.
  „   Fadryn, 155.
*†**Carnarvon**, 133, 87, &c.
  Carnedds Dafydd and Llewelyn;
      From Aber, 184.
      „   Bethesda, 182, 183.
      „   Capel Curig, 184.
      „   Llandudno or Llanrwst, 185.
      „   Llanfairfechan, 184.
Carnedd-y-Filiast, 190.
Carreg-fawr, 70, 69.
  „   -y-gwalch, 125.
Caseg, Afon, 182.
Castell Bodafon, 51.
  „   Caer Seiont, 57.
  „   Lleiniog, 92.
  „   Odo, 155.
Cefn Caves, 31.
  „   -yr-Ogof, 41.
Cernioge, 126.
Cerrig-y-Druidion [Corwen], 126.
*†**Chester**, 3, &c.
†Chwilog, 145.
Cilcain, 38.
Clogwyn-du'r-Arddu, 205, 207.
  „   -y-gureg, 146.

Clogwyn-yr-helwyn, 182.
Clunllom, 112, 113, 114.
Clwyd, Vale of. 19.
Clynnog [Carnarvon], 143, 142.
  „   -fawr, 144.
*†**Colwyn** [Colwyn Bay], 42.
*†   „   Bay, 42, 20, 53.
  „   Glen, 142.
*†Connah's Quay, 13.
*†**Conway**, 55, 20, &c.
  „   Falls, 120.
  „   Mountain, 57.
  „   River, 115, 119.
Corphwysfa, 142, 132, 206.
Crafnant, Valley and Lake, 114.
Craig-cwm-bychan, 138, 141, 157.
Craig-Eigiau, 186.
  „   Llwyd Farm, 64.
  „   y-Dinas, 143.
  „   y-Fodwch, 67.
  „   y-Gleision, 116.
  „   y-Llan, 162, 159.
  „   y-wen, 115, 116.
Creuddyn, 48.
Crib-goch, 205. 208, 84, 130, 132, 159, 211B.
Cribiau, 128.
Crib-y-ddysgyl, 205, 130, 139.
*†**Criccieth** [Carnarvonshire] 147, &c.
Cromlechs ;   Bwlch-y-ddeufaen, 73, 79 ; Capel Garmon, 123 ; Clynnog, 144 ; Criccieth,148; Pass of Llanberis, 132, 139 ; Plas-Newydd, 87.
Cwm Brwynog, 211A.
  „   Camlan, 178.
  „   Celli-Iago, 202.
  „   Clogwen, 141.
  „   Croesor, 201, **161**, **174.**
  „   Cwlyd, **116.**
  „   Dyli, 132.
  „   Glas, 139, **132**, 205, 208.
  „   Nantlle, **142.**
  „   Orthin, 202, 203, 161.
  „   Tryfan, 104, 193, 211.
  „   -y-glo, **136.**

Cwm-y-llan, 160.
„ -yr-Afon-goch, 76.
Cynfael Falls, 170.
Cynicht. 200, &c.

†Deganwy [Conway],105,125, 53,
*†Denbigh, 33.
Devil's Kitchen, 103, &c.
Dick of Aberdaron, 153, 30.
†Dinas [Carnarvon], 140, 143, 145.
Dinas [Llanfairfechan], 71.
Dinorwic Quarries. 139.
Dolbadarn Castle, 137.
Dolbenmaen, 142, 148.
Dolgarrog Falls, 106, 125, 107.
*†Dolwyddelen, 127, 140, 168, &c.
Drysgol-fawr, 102.
*†Duffws (Blaenau Ffestiniog), 161, 167, 168.
Dwyfawr Stream, 148.
Dwygyfylchi, 58, 65, &c.
Dwyryd Stream, 166, 174.
Dyserth [Rhyl], 27.

Eaton Hall, 10.
Edeyrn, 155.
Eglwys-Fair, 153.
„ Rhos, 54, 51.
„ Wen, 46.
Elidyr-fawr and-fach, 189, &c.
Elwy Glen, 31.
Esgair-felyn, 132.

Fairy Glen (Penmaenmawr), 66. 58, 65.
Fairy Glen (Bettws-y-Coed), 120.
Falcon Rock, 107.
*†Ffestiniog, Blaenau, 167, 128, &c.
*†Ffestiniog, Village, 169, &c.
Ffestiniog, Railway, 165, 167.
Ffestiniog, Valley, 162, 166, 171.
Ffos Noddyn, 120.

Ffos Rhufeiniaid, 101.
Ffridd, 128. 140.
„ Denomddydd, 65, 62.
„ du, 75.
Ffynnon Fair, 153, 32.
„ Llugwy, 184, 211.
„ -y-Lloer, 104, 211.
„ Wen, 27.
*†Flint, 17.
Foel-goch, 102, 130.
„ -lwyd, 70, 72.
„ -Llys, 58, 57, 65, 64.
†Foryd, 24.
Four Crosses, 145, 143.

†Gaerwen Junction, 95.
Gallt-y-foel, 122.
„ -y-wenalt, 132.
Ganllwyd Glen, 178.
Garth [Bangor], 87, 80, 88.
Gelert's Grave, 159, 164, 175.
Gimlet Rock, 151.
Glan Conway, 106, 126.
„ Llugwy Farm, 184.
Glaslyn, 206, 132, 159, 163.
Gloddaeth, 51, 48.
Glyder-fach and -fawr.
From Bethesda (Pen-y-Benglog), 193.
„ Capel Curig, 193.
„ Llanberis, 194.
„ Pen-y-gwryd, 191, 192.
Glynllyfon Park, 143.
Glyn-y-garth, 87, 88.
Gogarth Abbey, 47.
Gorddyn-mawr, 41.
Gored-goch, 85, 89.
Great Orme's Head, 46, 47.
GreenGorge(Penmaenmawr), 65, 67.
Gray Mare's Tail, 111.
†Groeslon, 142, 143.
Gwaenysgor, 27.
Gwrfai Stream, 141, 143, 157.
Gwrych Castle, 40, 19.
Gwydir (Llanrwst), 110, 113, 125.
Gwydir Chapel, 113.
Gwynant Valley, 128, &c.

Gwrtheyrn, Nant, 156.
Gyffin, 59.
Gyffiniau Stream, 174.
Gyrn, 77, 101.

Happy Valley (Llandudno), 46.
*†Harlech, 169.
*Hawarden, 11.
Hell's Mouth, 152.
Henar Farm, 71.
Heriri Mons, 172.
Holland Arms, 94.
*†Holyhead, 96, &c.
*†Holywell, 17.
†Hope, 13.
Hornby Cave, 47.
Hugh Lloyd's Pulpit, 170.

Lavan Sands, 21, 112.
Little Orme's Head. 49, 48.
Llanaelhaiarn, 142, 143, 145.
    „ beblig, 135, 157.
    „ bedr (Conway), 39, 15, 105.
    „ bedrog, 151, 154.
*†Llanberis, 137, 132, &c.
    „ Pass, 139, 132.
Llanddona, 93.
† „ ddulas, 41.
   „ degai, 82, 99.
   „ degfan, 89.
   „ disilio, 86.
   „ drillo-yn-Rhos, 43, 52.
*†Llandudno, 44, &c.
Llandwrog, 143.
    „ fair, P. G. (Anglesey), 84, 94.
    „ faes Priory, 92, 82.
*†Llanfairfechan, 69, 21, &c.
Llanfihangel, 93, 149.
    „ -y-Pennant, 142, 149.
*†Llangefni, 85.
   „ gelynin, 59.
   „ gybi. 142, 143, 145.
   „ rhaiadr, 35.
   „ rhwchwyn, 111, 113.
*†Llanrwst, 109, 104, 107, 124, &c.

Llanwnda, 143, 145.
Llechog, 206, 207.
Lledr Valley, 121, 123, 127, 168, 203.
Llefn, 101.
Lleyn Promontory, 150.
Llithfaen, 145.
Lliwedd, 130, 132, 160.
Llugwy Valley, 124, 104, 107, 119, 129.
Llwyd-mor, 185, 21.
Llyn Bochlwyd, 193, 210.
   „ Conway, 120.
   „ Coron, 95.
   „ Crafnant, 114, 111.
   „ Cwellyn, 157, 141, 146
   „ Cwlyd, 116.
   „ du'r Arddu, 207.
   „ Dulyn, 106.
   „ Eigiau, 186.
   „ Elsi, 123.
   „ Faelog, 95.
   „ Ffynnon y-Gwas, 207.
   „ Geironydd, 112.
   „ Gwynant, 132, 128.
   „ Idwal, 103, &c.
   „ Llydaw, 206.
   „ Melynllyn, 106.
   „ Ogwen, 104, 131.
   „ Padarn, 136, 137.
   „ Peris, 132, 137.
   „ Tecwyn, 176.
   „ Trwstyllon, 201.
   „ Tryweryn, 178, 177.
   „ -y-cwm-ffynnon, 191.
   „ -y-Ddinas, 128, 132, 159, 160.
   „ -y-Dywarchen, 146, 141.
   „ -y-Foel, 199.
   „ -y-Gader, 142.
   „ -y-Parc, 116, 124.
   „ -yr-Adar, 202, 203.
   „ -yr-Afon, 185.
Llyniau Duwaunedd, 128, 110.
Llysfaen Hill, 41.
Loggerheads Inn, 14.

Machno Falls, 121.
Maen-bras, 207.

*Maentwrog [Tan-y-Bwlch, Merioneth], 176, &c.
†Maentwrog-road, 172.
Maes Cwm, 138, 141.
  „ -y-Gaer, 75, 21.
Malldraeth Marsh, 95.
  „ Sands, 95.
Manod-mawr and -fach, 162, 168.
Marchlyn-mawr, 196.
Marl House, 52.
Meini Hirion(Penmaenmawr) 67.
Meliden, 27.
Melynllyn, 106.
*†Menai Bridge, 86, 89.
  „ Suspension Bridge, 86.
  „ Straits, 86, 85.
  „ Tubular Bridge, 85.
Miners' Bridge, 121, 117, 119, 124.
†Minffordd Junction, 166.
Min-y-don (Red Wharf Bay), 94.
Moel-ddu, 163.
  „ Eilio, 157.
  „ Faban, 101, 77.
  „ Fammau, 37, 14.
  „ Hebog, from Beddgelert 195; from Criccieth and Tremadoc, 196.
  „ Hiraddug, 27.
  „ Penllechog, 144.
  „ Pen-y-Bryn, 121.
  „ Perfydd, 21, 102.
Moel Siabod, 104, 113, 128.
  From Bettws-y-Coed, 197.
  „ Capel Curig, 198.
  „ Dolwyddelen, 198.
  „ Pen-y-gwryd, 199.
Moel Wnion, 76, 101.
  „ -y-Ci, 101.
  „ -y-Gaer, 38, 39.
  „ -y-Gest, 163.
Moelfre, 64, 93.
Moelwyn.
  From Beddgelert, 202.
  „ Tan-y-Bwlch, 201.
  „ „ -y-Grisiau, 200.
*†Mold, 93, 13.

Mona, 94.
Morfa Nevin, 156.
  „ Rhianedd, 54.
*†Mostyn (Holywell), 54, 18.
Mynydd Anelwog, 153.
  „ Daulyn, 114.
  „ Nodol, 178.
  „ Pentre, 48, 49.

Nanhoron, 151, 155.
†Nannerch, 38.
Nant (Aber), 76.
  „ Bodlas, 151.
  „ Ffrancon, 102, 129, &c.
  „ Gwrtheyrn, 145.
  „ Gwynant, 132.
  „ Mill, 157. 141.
  „ -y Gwryd, 140.
  „ -y-mor, 159, 202.
†Nantlle [Carnarvonshire]146, 142.
Nelson Statue, 88, 94.
*Nevin [Pwllheli], 155, 142, 145.
Newborough, 95.
Newmarket Cop, 27.
North Stack, 97.

Ogwen Bank, 102.
  „ Falls, 102.
  „ Lake, 104, 131.
  „ River, 99, 138.
Old Llanberis, 139, 132, 137, 194.
Old Meredith, 146.

Pabo Hill, 48, 51.
Palmerston Slate Quarry,178.
Pandy Mill, 121.
Pant Bridge, 120.
  „ Rhydderch, 86.
Parwyd, 154.
Parys Mountain, 77.
Peckforton, 1.
Pen-caer-Helen, 73.
  „ helig, 187.
  „ llithrig, 113, 186.
  „ 'r Allt, 124.
Pengwern, 27.
Penmachno, 120.

Penmaenan, 63.
Penmaenbach, 57, 21.
*†Penmaenmawr, 61, 21, &c.
„ Mountain.
From Llanfairfechan, 71.
„ Penmaenmawr vill., 62.
Penmon Priory, 92.
Penrhyn Castle, 99, &c.
† „ Deudraeth, [Merioneth], 166.
„ Slate-quarries, 100, 131.
*†Pensarn [Denbighshire], 40, 19, &c.
Pentraeth, 94.
Pentre-Voelas, 126, 120.
Pen-trwyn, 46.
„ -y-Benglog, 131, 193.
„ -y-Bryn, 123.
„ -y-Cafn, 64.
„ -y-Dinas, 47.
„ -y-Ga'ler, 59.
„ -y-Gaer, 106, 72.
*† „ -y-Groes, 142, 143, 145.
Pen-y-Gwryd [Llanberis], 131, 103, 128, 140, 160, 206.
Pen-y-gyffiniau, 162.
Pistyll, 145, 156.
„ Cain, 178.
Pitt's Head, 158, 141, 160.
Plas (Tan-y-Bwlch), 162, 166, 169, 174.
Plas-mawr (Conway), 56.
„ Newydd (Anglesey), 87, 84, 22, 85.
Pont Aberglaslyn, 161, 164.
Pont Dolgefeiliau, 178.
„ Newydd, 75, 73, **143.**
† „ Rug, 136.
„ -y-Cim, 143.
„ -y-Coetmor, 99.
„ -y-Gromlech, 132.
„ -y-Gyfyng. 104, 130.
„ -y-Pair, 119, 117, 121, 124.
„ -y-Pant, 127, 168.
„ -y-Rhyd-goch, 145.
„ -yr-allt-goch, 32.
„ -yr-Onen, 31.

*†Port Dinorwic, 133, 22, 88.
„ Nevin, 156.
„ Penrhyn, 79, 100.
*†Portmadoc, 163, 128, 134.
Porth Ceiriad, 152.
„ Dinlleyn, 156, 155.
„ Llwyd Falls, 106, 125.
„ Nigel, 152.
†Prestatyn [Rhyl], 19.
Priestholm, 93.
Prysor Valley, 178.
Puffin Island, 93, 92.
*†Pwllheli, 149, 142, 145, 154.

†Queen's Ferry, 11, 17.

Raven Fall, 172, 173.
Red Wharf Bay, 93, 94.
Rhaiadr-cwm, 171.
„ -du, 172, 173.
„ Mawddach, 178.
„ -mawr, 107.
„ -y-Wennol, 122,
Rhewl, 35.
Rhianfa, 87, 88.
Rhiw Hill, 152.
Rhiwiau-uchaf Farm, 70.
Rhiwlas, 75.
Rhos Hirwawn, 155.
Rivals, The, *from* Llanaelhaiarn, 144; *from* Nevin, 156.
*†Rhuddlan [Rhyl], 25.
†Rhyd-ddu [Carnarvon], 140, 141, 146, 160.
Rhyd-y-fen, 177.
†Rhydymwyn, 38.
*†Rhyl, 23, &c., 19.
Roe-wen, 59, 73.
Roman Bridge, 128, 127.
*†Ruthin, 36.

Sarn Helen, 177, 128, 172.
Sarn [Pwllheli], 155, 151, 154.
Segontium, 134.
Seiont, River, 135, 133, 143, 145.
Siamber-wen, 27.
Skerries Lighthouse, 98.

Slate Quarry, description of,
178, 100.
Snowdon, 203.
From Beddgelert, 205.
 ,, Capel Curig,206,211A.
 ,, Cwm-glas, 211A, 211D.
 ,, Llanberis, 204.
 ,, Pen-y-gwryd, 206.
 ,, Rhyd-ddu, 205.
 ,, Snowdon Ranger,207.
†Snowdon Ranger [Carnar-
von], 138, 141.
South Stack, 98.
St. Ann's Chapel, 138.
*†**St. Asaph**, 29.
St. Hilary's Church, 33.
St. Tudno's Church, 46.
Suspension Bridge [Conway],
54, 53.
Suspension Bridge [Menai],
86.
Swallow Falls, 122, 121, 104.
Sychnant Pass, 57, 66.

Talargoch Mine, 27.
Taliesin, 112.
Talsarnau, 176.
Tal-y-Bont, 73, 106.
 ,, -y-Cafn, 58, 70, 72, 73,
126.
 ,, -y-fan, 21, 72, 59, 70.
*†**Tan-y-Bwlch** [Merioneth],
161, 162, 166, 174.
Tan-y-Bwlch [Bettws-y-
Coed], 112.
 ,, -y-Grisiau, 169, 161, 167.
Tocia [Aberdaron], 151, 154,
155.
Tomen-y-mur, 171, 172, 177.
Tower Hill, 93.
Trallwyn, 145.
Traeth-mawr, 162, 169.
†Trawsfynydd [Tan-y-Bwlch,
Merioneth], 177.
Treborth, 83, 84, 85, 86.
*†Trefnant, 32, 31.
*†**Trefriw** [Llanrwst], 110,
114, 113, 107, 125, 108.
  Spa, 106.

Tremadoc [Portmadoc],
164, 163.
Tremeirchion, 32
Tre'r-castell, 92
Tre'r Ceiri, 144, 142.
Trwyn-y-fawch, 50.
 ,, -y-wylfa, 65.
Tryfan, Y, 210, 85, 163.
 ,, Junction, 141.
Tubular Bridge (Conway),
54, 53.
Tubular Bridge(Menai),85.
Tudweiliog, 155.
Twll-du, 103.
Twt Hill, 134.
Ty-Hyll, 104, 113, 114.
Tyn-y-Coed, 123, 130.
 ,, -y-Groes Inn, 178.
 ,, -y-ffrith, 64.
 ,, -y-llwyfan, 71.

Upper Bangor, 80.
Vaenol Park, 22, 84.
†Valley, 94, 95.

Waenfawr, 141, 157, 160.
Waterloo Bridge, 119, 107.
Whitchurch, 34.

Y Drosgl, 184, 185.
,, Foel-perfydd, 132.
,, Foel-fras, 186, 48, 20, 57,
101.
,, Garn, 194, 102, 146, 133,
142.
,, Mwd, 75.
,, Y Ro, 59.
,, Wyddfa, 130, 132.
Ynys-ddu Farm, 148.
 ,, Enlli, 154.
 ,, Gwylan, 153.
 ,, Seiriol, 92.
Yr-allt-wen, 164.
 ,, -Aran, 209, 122, 128, 160.
 ,, -Arryg, 184.
 ,, -Eifl (see Rivals).
 ,, -Elen, 186, 99, 183.
 ,, -Ogof Cave, 41, 20.
 ,, -Orsedd, 60.

TOURIST TICKETS.

(Issued from May 1st to October 31st. Available for Two Calendar Months.)

** These Tables are corrected annually. There is very little alteration in the fares from year to year.

From LONDON, LIVERPOOL, MANCHESTER, AND BIRMINGHAM.

Complete List.

To	LONDON 1 Cl.	2 Cl.	3 Cl.	LIVERPOOL 1 Cl.	2 Cl.	3 Cl.	MANCHESTER 1 Cl.	2 Cl.	3 Cl.	BIRMINGHAM 1 Cl.	2 Cl.	3 Cl.
	s. d.	s. d.	s. d.	s. d.	s. d.	s. d.	s. d.	s. d.	s. d.	s. d.	s. d.	s. d.
Aberdovey	67 6	49 6	32 6	26 0	18 6	11 6	31 0	21 9	14 0	36 3	25 9	16 0
Aberystwith	70 0	53 0	34 0	31 0	22 0	14 0	36 0	25 9	16 0	40 0	28 0	17 0
Bala (or Llanuwchllyn)	61 6	45 3	31 0	19 11	14 5	9 0	25 0	18 6	12 0	31 6	22 9	14 6
Barmouth	67 6	49 3	32 6	26 0	18 6	11 6	31 0	21 9	14 0	36 3	25 3	16 0
Borth	68 0	50 11	33 3	29 0	21 0	13 3	34 0	24 0	15 3	37 3	26 3	16 6
Corwen	57 6	42 3	31 0	14 11	11 11	7 2	20 0	15 9	10 0	27 3	20 3	12 0
Dolgelley	67 6	49 3	32 6	26 0	18 6	11 6	31 0	21 9	14 0	36 3	25 9	16 0
Harlech	70 9	51 6	34 0	29 3	20 9	14 6	34 3	24 3	15 6	39 6	28 6	17 6
Llangollen	54 0	40 0	31 0	12 5	9 5	6 0	18 0	13 0	8 6	23 9	17 9	10 6
Towyn	67 6	49 3	32 6	26 0	18 6	11 6	31 0	21 9	14 0	36 3	25 9	16 0
(a) N. Wales Circular	84 0	62 0	—	41 0	29 0	—	46 0	33 0	—	50 0	40 0	—
(b) " "	71 0	54 0	—	30 0	22 0	—	35 0	26 0	—	45 0	33 0	—
(c) N. & S. Wales "	106 0	76 0	—	76 0	54 0	—	79 0	56 0	—	79 0	56 0	—
(d) N. S. & Mid W. Circular	118 0	83 0	—	87 0	61 0	—	91 0	63 0	—	91 0	63 0	—
(e) N. & Mid Wales "	87 0	64 0	—	51 0	37 0	—	56 0	41 0	—	58 0	42 0	—
(f) Snowdon Tour	84 0	62 0	—	41 0	29 0	—	46 0	33 0	—	50 0	40 0	—
(g) S. & Mid W. Circular	95 0	70 0	—	65 0	46 0	—	69 0	49 0	—	68 0	48 0	—
(h) Mid Wales "	71 0	52 0	—	27 6	19 6	—	34 6	24 6	—	38 6	28 6	—
(i) S. & Mid Wales "	96 0	71 0	—	66 0	47 0	—	70 0	50 0	—	69 0	49 0	—
(j) " "	109 0	79 0	—	79 0	55 0	—	83 0	58 0	—	82 0	57 0	—

a, b, c, d, e, f, g, h, i, j. For these Routes see p. 4 of this sheet.

From	1 Cl.		2 Cl.		3 Cl.		1 Cl.		2 Cl.		3 Cl.		1 Cl.		2 Cl.		3 Cl.	
	s.	d.	s.	d.	s.	d.	s.	d.	s.	d.	s.	d.	s.	d.	s.	d.	s.	d.
Bath	54	0	38	6	23	6	54	0	38	6	23	6	50	9	36	3	23	6
Bedford	55	0	40	9	26	6	58	0	42	9	28	0	58	0	42	9	28	0
Birkenhead	26	0	18	6	11	6	26	0	18	6	11	6	31	0	22	0	14	0
Blackburn	36	0	26	0	16	6	36	0	26	0	16	6	40	0	28	6	18	6
Bolton	31	0	22	6	14	6	31	0	22	6	14	6	36	9	26	3	17	0
Bradford	40	0	30	0	19	0	40	0	30	0	19	0	43	0	32	6	21	0
Brighton	85	0	61	3	39	0	85	0	61	3	39	0	85	9	61	0	40	6
Bristol	54	0	38	6	23	6	54	0	38	6	23	6	50	9	36	3	23	6
Burton-on-Trent	37	9	26	8	16	6	40	9	28	9	18	6	40	0	28	9	18	6
Cambridge	63	9	46	9	30	6	66	9	48	9	32	0	66	9	48	9	32	6
Cardiff	43	6	30	4	19	0	43	6	30	4	19	0	43	6	30	4	19	6
Carlisle	62	6	44	6	28	6	62	6	44	6	28	6	68	6	49	7	31	0
Cheltenham	44	0	33	3	22	6	44	0	33	3	22	6	44	0	33	6	21	6
Chester	21	9	15	0	10	0	21	9	15	0	10	0	28	6	18	6	11	6
Colchester	78	3	58	4	37	10	81	3	60	9	39	6	81	3	60	9	39	6
Coventry	42	0	30	0	19	3	45	0	32	0	20	6	45	0	32	0	20	6
Darlington	56	2	43	6	28	3	56	2	43	6	28	3	59	8	47	3	30	9
Derby	39	0	27	11	17	0	41	0	29	6	18	6	41	0	29	3	18	6

Newport (Mon.)												
Northampton	47	9 34	0 22		6 28	9 18	6	39	0 19	0 25	0 36	
Norwich								74	10 57	1 35	4 59	
Nottingham	50	6 37	3 23 6	43 0	3 20	3 20 6	42	9 31	9 19	11 20	
Oxford	56	6 41	3 26 0	48 0	3 36	3 23 6	56	6 40	6 25	9 26	
Peterboro'	98	2 72	6 43 0	89 11	69	5 40 0	54	0 41	6 25	0 43	
Plymouth							100	3 72	6 43	3 70	
Portsmouth Harb.							87	0 62	9 40	9 62	
Preston	29	3 21	0 13 6	21	6 16	0 10 6	31	3 24	9 16	6 28	
Reading†	58	6 43	3 27 6	50	9 38	0 24 6	63	6 46	6 29	3 48	
Sheffield	38	3 27	8 18 6	30	6 22	2 14 6	45	4 33	3 20	4 35	
Shrewsbury	18	3 12	9 7 6	10	0 7	5 4 6	22	6 15	9 9	0 17	
Stoke-upon-Trent	27	0 20	6 11 9	22	6 18	0 9 9	30	3 21	9 12	0 25	
Sunderland	57	10 46	8 31 9	53	4 41	8 28 3	64	10 50	8 33	4 54	
Swansea	45	6 32	0 19 0	43	9 32	0 19 0	33	6 22	9 13	0 20	
Wakefield	33	0 25	0 17 6	27	9 20	9 13 6	40	0 30	0 18	6 33	
Warrington	21	0 15	0 9 6	13	6 10	0 6 0	27	0 19	3 12	0 22	
Wigan	24	6 17	9 12 0	16	9 12	0 9 6	30	0 21	6 14	6 24	
Wolverhampton	27	3 19	9 12 6	19	3 14	0 9 0	32	0 23	0 14	0 25	
Worcester†	36	3 25	9 15 0	28	3 20	6 12 0	43	9 31	3 18	0 31	
York	39	8 31	0 21 6	35	6 26	10 18 0	46	8 35	6 21	6 24	

*Borth.—Tourist Tickets are issued to **Borth** at (generally speaking) a slightly lower rate than to Aberystwith; also to **Corwen** and **Harlech.**

† To Towyn and Aberdovey (from Reading), 65s, 47s., 29s. 6d.; (from Worcester), 42s., 20s. 6d., 17s.

4

Circular Tours.

————◆————

The following are the Circular Routes referred to on p. 1, and by which tickets are granted from most places on pp. 2 and 3.

(a) By **G. W.** or **L. & N. W.**, *via* Chester, Ruabon, Llangollen, Bala, Dolgelley, Barmouth, Portmadoc, Carnarvon, Bangor, Chester; or *vice versâ*.

(b) By **G .W.**, *via* Ruabon, Llangollen, Bala, Blaenau Ffestiniog, Bettws-y-Coed, Llandudno Junc., Rhyl, and Chester; or *vice versâ*.

(c) By **L. & N. W.**, *via* Shrewsbury, Llandrindod, Builth Road, Carmarthen (Tenby), Strata Florida, Aberystwith, Barmouth (Dolgelley), Portmadoc, Carnarvon (by Afonwen, or by Bedgelert and Llanberis), Bangor, Chester; or *vice versâ*.

(d) By **L. & N. W.**, same as (c) with addition of Builth Road to Brecon and back, and Builth Road to Llanidloes and back.

(e) By **G. W.**, *via* Ruabon, Llangollen, Bala, Blaenau Ffestiniog, Bettws-y-Coed, Llandudno Junc., Bangor, Carnarvon, Portmadoc, Barmouth, Machynlleth, Welshpool, Oswestry (or Shrewsbury); or *vice versâ*.

(f) By **L. & N. W.**, *via* Shrewsbury, Welshpool, Machynlleth, Barmouth (Dolgelley), Portmadoc, Carnarvon (by Afonwen or Beddgelert and Llanberis), Bangor, Chester; or *vice versâ*.

(g) By **G. W.**, *via* Ruabon, Llangollen, Bala, Dolgelley, Barmouth, Aberystwith, Carmarthen (Tenby), Newport; or *vice versâ*.

h) By **G. W.**, *via* Ruabon, Llangollen, Bala, Dolgelley, Barmouth, Machynlleth, Welshpool and Oswestry (or Shrewsbury); or *vice versâ*.

(i) By **L. & N. W.**, *via* Shrewsbury, Welshpool, Machynlleth, Aberystwith, Carmarthen (Tenby), Llandrindod, Shrewsbury; or *vice versâ*.

(j) By **L. & N. W.**, same as (i), with addition of Builth Road to Brecon and back, and Builth Road to Llanidloes and back.

For (g) (i), and (j) see also "Thorough Guide to South Wales."

London : J. S. LEVIN, Steam Printing Works, 75, Leadenhall St., E.C.

NORTH WALES

(PART II.)

LLANGOLLEN, BALA, DOLGELLEY, BARMOUTH,
OSWESTRY, SHREWSBURY, WELSHPOOL, LLANIDLOES,
MACHYNLLETH, AND ABERYSTWITH SECTIONS.

BY

M. J. B. BADDELEY, B.A.,

AUTHOR OF "THE ENGLISH LAKES," "HIGHLANDS OF SCOTLAND,"
"NORTHERN HIGHLANDS," "PEAK OF DERBYSHIRE," AND
"SOUTH DEVON AND SOUTH CORNWALL,"

AND

C. S. WARD, M.A.,

AUTHOR OF "NORTH DEVON AND NORTH CORNWALL," "SOUTH DEVON AND
SOUTH CORNWALL," AND "EASTERN COUNTIES."

MAPS AND PLANS

By BARTHOLOMEW.

SECOND EDITION, REVISED.

" From Tudno's cell to Mynach's deep-toned glen."

LONDON:
DULAU & CO., 37, SOHO SQUARE, W.
1887.

CONTENTS.

	Page
Map **Index**	vii
Introduction	viii
The Scenery.	viii
Geology	ix
Accommodation	xi
Fishing	xii
Glossary	xii
Height of Mountains	xiv
Skeleton Tours	xv
G. W. R. ROUTE TO BARMOUTH AND FFESTINIOG	1
LLANGOLLEN SECTION: **Llangollen**	8
Plas Newydd	9
Castell Dinas Bran	10
Barber's Hill	11
Valle Crucis Abbey, &c.	12
Moel-y-Gamelin	14
Eglwyseg Rocks	16
Y Fron-fawr	17
Glyn Ceiriog	17
„ to Llanrhaiadr and Pistyll Rhaiadr	17
„ to Llanfyllin	18
Wynnstay	18
Chirk Castle	20
„ to Llangollen	23
Corwen	23
„ to Rhyl	24
„ to Bettws-y-Coed	25
„ to Bala by road	27
BALA SECTION: **Bala**	28
Tour of the Lake	29
Llanuwchllyn	30
Bala to Dinas Mawddwy by road	31
„ to Pistyll Rhaiadr and Llanrhaiadr	32
„ to Liverpool Reservoir ("Lake Fyrnwy")	33
The Reservoir to Llanrhaiadr	34
DOLGELLEY SECTION: **Dolgelley**	36
Torrent Walk	37
„ to Precipice Walk	37
Nannau and Precipice Walk	38
Rhaiadr-du, Pistyll Cain, Rhaiadr Mawddach	40
Pandy and Aran Glen	42

Page

Abergwynant Valley 42
Dolgelley to Ffestiniog by road 43
  ,, to Bala, road or rail 43
  ,, to Tal-y-Llyn and Towyn, &c. . . . 43
  ,, to Dinas Mawddwy and Machynlleth 44
  ,, to Barmouth by road 46
Ferns 47

BARMOUTH SECTION : **Barmouth** 48

Barmouth Bridge 50
Panorama Walk 52
Cors-y-Gedol, &c.. 52
    to Barmouth over the hills . . . 54
Pant Einion, Llwyngwril, &c. 55
Barmouth to Dolgelley by rail 55
  ,, ,, by road 56
  ,, to Harlech and Portmadoc . . . 57
Dyffryn Station to Cwm Bychan, &c. . . . 57
Mynffordd Junction to Duffws (Toy Line) . . 59
Barmouth to Cwm Bychan by Pensarn Station . . 60
Ascent of Rhinog-fawr 61
Harlech 65
  ,, to Cwm Bychan 66
  ,, to Talsarnau by the hills . . 67
Barmouth to Aberystwith, &c. 68
Towyn 69
Excursions from Towyn 71
Aberdovey 72

CAMBRIAN RAILWAY TO BARMOUTH AND ABERYSTWITH . 73

Oswestry 74
Llanfyllin to Llanrhaiadr, &c., by road . . . 76
Llanrhaiadr to Bala, &c., by road . . . 77
  ,, to Liverpool Reservoir, &c. . . 78
Shrewsbury 81
Breidden Hills 84
Welshpool 85
Llanidloes 88
  ,, to Plynlimon 89
  ,, to Aberystwith by road . . . 89

MACHYNLLETH SECTION : **Machynlleth** . . . 92

Machynlleth to Dinas Mawddwy 93
Dinas to Dolgelley 94
  to Llanuwchllyn (road) and Bala . . 94
Machynlleth to Tal-y-Llyn and Dolgelley . . 95
  ,, to Towyn 96
  ,, to Llyfnant Glen, &c. . . 97
  ,, to Barmouth (rail) . . . 99

Page

ABERYSTWITH SECTION : **Aberystwith** 100
   Pen Dinas 102
   Constitution Hill 103
   Allt-wen 103
   Twll Twrw 104
   Nant Eos 104
   Strata Florida Abbey 105
   Aberystwith to Borth 106
   Borth 106
      Borth to Bᵒ ld Talicsin 107
   Aberystwith to Machynlleth 108
    ,,   to Devil's Bridge 109
   Devil's Bridge 113
   Devil's Bridge to Hafod, &c. 115
      Pont Rhyd-y-Groes to Devil's Bridge 116
   Aberystwith to Plynlimon and Llanidloes . . . 117

MOUNTAIN SECTION : Heights and Introductory . . . 118
   Aran Mawddwy and Aran Benllyn 118
   Arenig-fawr and Arenig-fach 123
   Cader Idris 125
   Diphwys and Licthr 136
   Rhobell-fawr 139

MAP INDEX.

Opp. P

Index Map (inside cover).
Wrexham, Oswestry, Barmouth, Harlech 2
Llangollen and neighbourhood 8
Barmouth, Dolgelley, Cader Idris, &c. 48
Towyn, Aberdovey, Borth, Machynlleth 70
Shrewsbury, Dinas Mawddwy, Llanidloes 82
The coast from Barmouth to Aberystwith, &c. . . . 92
Plan of Aberystwith 100
Aberystwith, Borth, Devil's Bridge, Hafod . . . 110

Introduction.

The District described in this volume comprises the southern half of North Wales, and such an extent of Cardiganshire as falls within range of easy excursions from Aberystwith. It may be briefly defined as the country served by the Great Western and Cambrian Railways.

Starting from Ruabon, we follow the G.W.R. by Llangollen, Bala and Dolgelley to Barmouth, diverging on our way—*northward*, to places of popular resort fully described in *Part I.*, and *southward*, as far as the main Cambrian line.

Next, setting out from Oswestry and Shrewsbury, we travel by the Cambrian Railway through to Aberystwith, Barmouth, Dolgelley and Harlech, turning aside as opportunity offers—*northward*, till we again join the Great Western, and *southward* so as to include the South Wales borderland lying between Llanidloes, Plynlimon and Aberystwith.

The coast is described from a little north of Harlech to a little south of Aberystwith, and includes, besides Harlech and Pensarn, the favourite watering-places of Barmouth, Towyn, Aberdovey, Borth, and Aberystwith.

The Scenery.—We need not repeat the general remarks made in *Part I.* on the distinctive characteristics of North Wales scenery. Here it may suffice to say that those who fairly explore the area treated of in these pages will find within it all the several kinds of scenery that have won for the Principality its deservedly high place among holiday playgrounds. They will indeed come across fewer examples of rugged and impressive grandeur than are to be seen in the neighbourhood of Snowdon, as, for instance, in the passes of Llanberis and Nant Ffrancon, but they may wander literally for weeks amid ever fresh scenes of an exquisite and varied beauty of a distinctly richer type than any to be found in Carnarvonshire. Not that there is any lack of sterner pictures. The valleys of the Dee, the Wnion and the Dovey have certainly comparatively little of rugged mountain to enhance the verdure of their straths and the silvan luxuriance of the hill-slopes that flank them, but in the sheer escarpment and corries of Cader Idris the incomparable Mawddach estuary, with its broken margin of wooded glen and heathery hill, has a background well nigh as stern as any in the Snowdon region. Llyn-y-Cau, too, in the heart of the Cader Idris range, is the perfection of a mountain tarn, surpassed neither by Llyn Idwal nor in Cwm Glas, while for naked wildness few scenes equal the sombre chasms and pitiless crags in the inmost recesses of the Rhinogs.

To the South of the Cader Idris range the richness rapidly diminishes, but there is still much soft and beautiful valley scenery about the Dovey and its tributaries, especially in the neighbourhood of Machynlleth. Beyond this the country degenerates as it rises again to the wide and bare upland that attains its highest level in Plynlimon. Yet further south comes a break in the dreary hill-country of North Cardiganshire, where at the Devil's Bridge the impetuous Mynach stream plunges nearly at a bound into the almost unequalled ravine of the Rheidol.

The south-eastern portion of North Wales is chiefly occupied by the Berwyns, which, cut up by deep and green valleys, ramify in all directions. These hills present little or no beauty of outline, and are mostly covered with heather, very wearisome to the ordinary pedestrian — grouse-moors, in fact, and best left to the enjoyment of the sportsman. Were it not for Pistyll Rhaiadr, the highest waterfall of any size and in some respects the most beautiful in Wales, and the interest attaching to to the conversion of the desolate valley of the upper Fyrnwy into a vast reservoir for the water supply of Liverpool, they would call for scant notice in a work of this kind. We do not, of course, mean that they possess no beauty, but only to suggest that for the general run of travellers their attractions are few.

Geology. The stratified rocks of our present area all belong to the Palæozoic (*i. e.*, ancient life) period, and include nearly all the distinctive formations of that period. The missing formations are the Devonian and the Laurentian, unless the former is represented by the red and grey sandstones resting on quartz conglomerate, to be found about three miles north of Llangollen, and the latter by certain pre-Cambrian rocks in the neighbourhood of Dolgelley.

Could we obtain a continuous section of the country from a trifle east of Wrexham to St. George's Channel, between Barmouth and Harlech, we should see the several formations succeeding one another, from the newest to the most ancient, as we passed from east to west. North Wales has, however, been subjected to two distinct epochs of volcanic disturbance since the deposition of its oldest strata, and these have so dislocated the sedimentary rocks over large areas that, although the general structure is simple enough, its details present problems of the most complex nature.

(1) The district bounded on the west by the coast between Barmouth and Harlech, and extending eastward across the Dolgelley and Trawsfynydd road to *Craig-y- Penmaen* is the **Cambrian** area of the Geological Ordnance map. This is traversed from North to South by the wild mountain range of which the Rhinogs are about the centre. "The rocks are mostly greenish-grey grits, with some bands of slate, traversed by many dykes of igneous rock ; except worm-tracks and worm-borings, no fossils are known from this district," but a considerable variety has been found in the same rocks near St. David's. Harlech Castle stands on a fine cliff of this formation, and the neighbourhood of Cwm Bychan, as well as the verdureless passes through the mountains, afford unusual facilities for its examination.

(2) At Aberrhamffroch, close to Barmouth, may be seen the junction of the "Cambrian" with the Menevian beds (so named from Menevia, a Roman station near St. David's, where they were first examined), and the Lingula flags, both of which are now held to form part of the Cambrian system. The *Lingula flags* may be traced along the Mawddach estuary to Dolgelley and thence northward by Rhobell-fawr to Maentwrog. *Rhobell-fawr* is a huge mass of intrusive "greenstone," but the "flags" consist of "black and grey micaceous slates and sandstones."

(3) Passing to the **Silurian** system we have its lowest formation, the *Arenig beds* "of grit and black slates" well developed, near Tai-hirion, southwest of Arenig-fach, about a mile from Rhyd-y-Fen Inn on the road towards Ffestiniog.

(4) Cader Idris, the Arans and the Arenigs are mainly composed of black shales and slates (*Llandeilo flags*) interbedded with various kinds of igneous rock and volcanic ashes, referable to the earlier of the two eruptive epochs mentioned in our prefatory remarks. The summit of *Cader Idris* is "greenstone," and columnar porphyry is well developed in the rocks of the Saddle to the westward and in Mynydd-mawr to the eastward. The cliffs of *Llyn-y-Cau* afford a good example of these Llandeilo slates traversed by igneous dykes.

(5) Of the *Bala beds*—"black and blue slates and sandy beds" with a great series of ash-beds and lavas above them—probably the most interesting features to the amateur are the two bands of limestone, the Bala (or Rhiwlas) and the Hirnant. The fossils of the beds below the Bala limestone are to be found on the Dinas Mawddwy road, about 3½ miles from Llanuwchllyn, between the farms *Pai-yn-y-nant* and *Tyn-y-fron*, the latter on the old road in the bottom of the valley. For the Bala limestone *Moel-y-Garnedd* and *Pen-y-Rhiw*, respectively 2 miles west and ¾-mile north-west of Bala town, are good points. The Hirnant limestone fossils can be found about 3½ miles from Bala, up the Hirnant valley, at the foot of *Craig Moel-y-Ddinas*, the steep which the road climbs immediately after passing the house of Aber Hirnant.

The igneous rocks and ashes of the Bala beds belong to the second volcanic epoch above mentioned. The centre of activity was in the Snowdon district, and the igneous rocks of that neighbourhood are consequently later by a long interval than those of the Llandeilo age.

(6) In the neighbourhood of Llangollen a great variety of formations is found within a comparatively small area. The town itself stands upon the *Wenlock Shales* (Upper Silurian), but the three great divisions of the **Carboniferous System** are within easy reach to the eastward. Of these the mountain limestone forms the fine escarpment of Eglwyseg Rocks. The Berwyns belong to the Bala beds already described, but at Pistyll Rhaiadr the waterfall is flanked by cliffs of the underlying Llandeilo beds.

(7) The desolate upland culminating in Plynlimon is formed of undulations of the *Bala beds* and the *Lower Llandovery rocks* next in order above them. About Aberystwith the contortions of these strata are well seen in the cliffs, but beyond this they present little of interest to the amateur, particularly as fossils are but rarely to be found in them.

(8) The Breidden Hills consist of a mass of igneous rock intruded through the *Llandeilo flags*, and are, therefore, to be ranked in age with Cader Idris, &c., *see* (4).

*** In the foregoing paragraphs free use has been made of *Geology of the Counties of England and Wales* (Kelly), and *Records of the Rocks* (Murray).

Accommodation.

In the body of the book will be found particulars as to hotel and inn accommodation, and here it need only be mentioned that the economically minded tourist can almost everywhere get good treatment for 10s. to 12s. per diem, and in several cases may arrange to pay an inclusive sum from 2½ to 3 guineas per week. As a whole our present district is perhaps somewhat less expensive than that further north, and exclusive of liquors the following items are about the average :

Breakfast	1s. 6d.	to	3s.
Luncheon	1s. 6d.	„	2s.
Dinner	2s. 6d.	„	5s.
Bed	2s.	„	3s. 6d.
Attendance	1s. 6d.	„	1s. 6d.

9s. 0d. „ 15s. 0d.

Lodgings vary much in price, and are, as one would expect, most expensive where they are in the greatest demand, *i.e.*, at the best known watering-places. During the height of the season Barmouth is somewhat more expensive than Aberystwith. At the minor places (Towyn, Aberdovey, Borth) on the coast, fair quarters may be obtained at 15s. a room, and even less. The several inland resorts—Dolgelley, Bala, Llangollen, Machynlleth, &c.— are, as a rule, cheaper than the watering-places, while those who like to be "quite in the country" and are content with cottage lodgings or a village inn, have an abundant choice. The Welsh housewife, though not perhaps quite a paragon of neatness in her domestic arrangements, is, generally speaking, a liberal and sedulous caterer for the requirements of her visitors and takes a personal pride in their comfort, which one often misses in more sophisticated places.

Fishing. The angler who is a stranger to North Wales will find in the *The Angler's Guide* (price 1s.), issued by Mr. W. Pritchard, Talbot Road, Hirdir, Wrexham, a list of the chief waters arranged under the names of the principal places. The pamphlet is rather out of date, but is at present the only publication on the subject. Owing to the facilities afforded by the railway companies, it matters little where the fisherman locates himself, and most of the waters are either open free or on a moderate payment. The fish range from salmon, sewin, sea-trout and trout to the "coarse" fish that swarm in Bala Lake. It should be mentioned, however, that the curious fish, the *Gwiniad*, so called from the whiteness of its scales, is peculiar to this lake.

Glossary.

. For General Remarks on Welsh place-names and pronunciation the reader is referred to *Part I.*

Aber, a confluence, river-mouth.
Afon, a river.
Allt (from *Gallt*), a cliff.
Aran (or *Arran*), a high place, an alp.
Bach | masc. *Fach* | fem.
Buchan | *Fechan* | little.
Bala, an outlet.
Bedd, a grave.
Ber, a hill-top.
Bettws, Bead house, *i.e.* house of prayer, chapel; corruption *of English.*
Blaen, pl. *Blaenau*, a summit.
Bod, a dwelling, abode.
Borth, see *Porth.*
Braich, an arm.
Bron (*fron*), pap or breast.
Bryn (*fryn*), a hill.
Bwlch, a mountain pass.
Bwrdd, a table.
Cader (*gader*), a seat, a chair.
Cae, a meadow.

Caer (*Gaer*), a fort.
Cain, fair.
Careg, a rock or stone.
Carn, *Carnedd*, a cairn, heap of stones.
Cau, a hollow.
Cefn, a ridge.
Celli (*Gelli*), a bower, grove.
Cil, a recess.
Clogwyn, a precipice.
Clunllom, a haunch.
Clynog, bosky, bushy.
Coch, fem. *Goch*, red.
Coed, a wood.
Cor (*gor*), a choir, church.
Cors, a bog.
Craig, pl. *Creigiau*, a craig.
Crib, pl. *Cribiau*, a crest.
Croes (*Groes*), a cross.
Cwm, a valley.
Cymmer, a confluence.
Dau, fem. *Dwy*, two.
Din, *Dinas*, a hill-fort.
Dôl, a dale.
Drosgl, a hump (*lit.* awkward).

Drws, a door.
Du (ddu), black.
Dwfr (dwr), water.
Dyffryn, a valley.
Eglwys (Lat. *Ecclesia*), a church.
Esgair, a shank, a leg.
Fach, fechan, see Bach.
Fawr, see Mawr.
Ffordd, a (high) way.
Foryd (from *Moryd*) an estuary.
Ffridd, a forest.
Ffynnon, a well, a spring.
Gelli, see Celli.
Glan, a bank, a shore.
Glas (las), blue or green.
Glyn, a glen.
Gogof (Ogof), a cavern.
Gwalch a hawk, or heron.
Gwern, a swamp, an alder-grove.
Gwy (wy,) water.
Gwyn (wyn), fem. *gwen (wen)*, white.
Hafod, a summer dwelling.
Hên, old.
Hir, long.
Isel, low; *is*, lower; *isaf*, lowest.
Llam, a stride, step.
Llan, a churchyard, church.
Llech, a rock, a flag-stone.
Lleyn, a peninsula.
Llwyd, brown.
Llyn, pl. *Llyniau*, a lake.
Llwyn, a grove.
Llys, a court, a hall.
Maen (Faen), pl. *Meini*, a stone.
Maes (Faes), a field.
Mawr (Fawr), great.
Melin (Felin), a mill.
Moel (Foel), a bare hill.
Morfa, a marsh, lit. a place by the sea.

Mynach, a monk.
Mynydd (Fynydd), a mountain, a moorland.
Nant, a brook, hence a vale.
Neuadd, a hall.
Newydd, new.
Pant, a hollow.
Pen, a headland.
Pentref (Pentre), a village.
Perfedd, a centre.
Pistyll, a spout.
Plâs, a palace.
Pont (Bont), a bridge.
Porth (Borth), a port, a harbour.
Prysor, brushwood.
Pwll, a pool.
Rhaiadr, a waterfall.
Rhiw, a slope, a brow.
Rhos, moorland.
Rhudd, red.
Rhyd, a ford.
Sarn, a causeway.
Sych, dry.
Tal, a headland, a point.
Talar, a headland in a point.
Tan, under.
Tomen, a mound.
Towyn (Tywyn), a strand.
Traeth, a beach.
Traws, cross (adj. and noun).
Tref (Tre), a house.
Tri, three.
Trwyn, a point.
Twll, a pit.
Ty, a house.
Tyddyn, a farm.
Uchel, high; *uch (uwch)*, higher; *uchaf*, highest.
Wen see Gwyn.
Y (Yr before a vowel), the; *Yn* in, at, into.
Ychain (pl. of *Ych*), oxen.
Ynys, an island.
Yspytty, a hospital, an inn.
Ystrad, a vale.

HEIGHT, &c., OF CHIEF MOUNTAINS.

Name.	County.	Feet.	Meaning.
Snowdon	Carnarvon	3571	Hill of Snow.
Carnedd Llewelyn	,,	3482	Llewelyn's Cairn.
„ Dafydd	,,	3430	David's Cairn.
Y Glyder-fawr	,,	3275	————
„ fach	,,	3262	————
Y Garn	,,	3107	Heap of Stones.
Y Foel-fras	,,	3091	Humpy Mount.
Elidyr-fawr	,,	3033	————
Y Tryfan	,,	3009	Three-headed (hill)
Aran Mawddwy	Merioneth	2970	High place.
Yr Arryg	Carnarvon	2874	————
Cader Idris	Merioneth	2929	Chair of Idris.
Aran Benllyn	,,	2902	High place at head of
Moel Siabod	Carnarvon	2865	———— [lake
Pen Helig	,,	2850	————
Arenig-fawr	Merioneth	2800	Great Arenig.
Y Foel-goch	Carnarvon	2726	Red Mount.
Moel Perfydd	,,	2750*	Central Mount.
Carnedd-y-Filiast	,,	2694	Greyhound Cairn.
Moel-sych	Merion.&Montg.	2718	Dry Mount (sych).
Pen Llithrig-y-Wrach	Carnarvon	2623	Slippery Hag's Head.
Llwyd-mawr	,,	2600*	Big brown (hill).
Drum	,,	2579	Ridge.
Moel Hebog	,,	2578	Falcon Mount.
Cader Fronwen	Merion.&Montg.	2573	White-breasted Seat.
Moelwyn	Carnarvon	2529	White Mount.
Y Drosgl	,,	2478	Hump.
Diphwys	Merioneth	2467	————
Plynlimon	Cardigan	2469	Five Beacons.
Rhobell-fawr	Merioneth	2409	————
Llethr	,,	2475	Smooth.
Rhinog-fawr	,,	2362	————
Cynicht	Carnarvon	2362	————
Y Garnedd-goch	,,	2315	Red Cairn.
Moel Eilio	,,	2382	————
Mynydd-mawr	,,	2293	Great Mount.
Manod-mawr	Merioneth	2171	Great Mass.
Moel Wnion	Carnarvon	1905	————
„ -y-gamelin	Denbigh	1897	Mount of the winding stream.
Yr-Eifl (Rivals)	Carnarvon	1887	The Forks.
Moel Famman	Denbigh, Flint	1823	————
Penmaenmawr	Carnarvon	1553	Big stone headland.
Moel Offrwm	Merioneth	1328	Mount of Sacrifice.
Breidden Hills	Montgomery	1250*	————
Carn Madryn	Carnarvon	900*	Fox Cairn.
Conway Mountain	,,	800*	————
Great Orme's Head	,,	750*	————
Holyhead Mount.	Anglesey	719	————

* *Approximate*

SUGGESTION FOR TOURS.

. North Wales affords scope for the gratification of so many different tastes in touring that a list of tours adapted to each taste would occupy many pages. Lovers of sea and land in combination will include Llandudno, Penmaenmawr, Llanfairfechan, Beaumaris, Barmouth and Aberystwith in their tour; mountaineers will be at pains not to omit Snowdon or Cader Idris, and will appreciate the other ascents described in our "Mountain Section"; archæologists will lay stress on the castles of Rhuddlan, Conway, Beaumaris, Carnarvon, and Harlech, not forgetting Valle Crucis Abbey. The ancient town on the Rivals, and a number of cromlechs, will also attract them; while everybody will wish to see as much of the districts of Snowdon, Ffestiniog, Barmouth and Dolgelley as time permits. The following outline tours only profess to secure the tourist who wishes to make the most of his time against going wrong. He might go right in a hundred different ways. We must also draw attention to the circular tours of the railway companies, the routes of which are noted in our yellow sheet.

A FORTNIGHT FOR NON-PEDESTRIANS.

DAY.

        1.   **Chester.**
  2 and 3.—**Llandudno.**
  4 and 5.—**Bettws-y-Coed.**
  6 and 7.—**Menai Bridge.**
        8.—**Llanberis.**
        9.—**Beddgelert.**
       10.—**Ffestiniog.**
 11 and 12.—**Barmouth.**
 13 and 14.—**Dolgelley.**
 15 and 16.—**Llangollen.**
                or,
 13 — 16.—**Aberystwith** and **Machynlleth.**

A WEEK'S TOUR FROM RUABON. (For fair walkers.)

Sleeping Quarters in Italics.

Day.

1. Rail to Llangollen, visit Castell Dinas Bran, walk over Geraint (Barber's) Hill to Chain Bridge Inn (Berwyn Station); back by Llantysilio and Valle Crucis Abbey to *Llangollen* (or *Chain Bridge*).

2. Rail to Llanuwchllyn, ascend Aran Benllyn and Aran Mawddwy, descend to Drws-y-Nant (rail to Dolgelley), or to Dinas Mawddwy and walk to *Dolgelley.*

3. The Torrent walk, thence to Nannau, the Precipice walk and Pistyll Cain and Rhaiadr Mawddach, returning by road by Tyn-y-Groes Inn and Llanelltyd to *Dolgelley.*

4. Ascend Cader Idris by the Aran brook and descend to *Barmouth* (a ridge-walk the greater part of the way—ascent by Foxes' Path shorter, but misses Mynydd Moel; pony-track involves going twice over the higher part of the mountain.)

5. Train to Harlech, walk to Cwm Bychan and thence by Roman steps and Pass of Ardudwy to Dyffryn Station; rail to *Barmouth, Towyn, or Aberdovey.**

6. Train to Glandovey Station (*not* Junction), walk up Llyfnant Valley to Pistyll-y-Llyn and thence to Machynlleth; train home by Welshpool.

* A finer route, but not allowing the return home to be begun till the evening of the sixth day (*mail leaves Aberystwith abt. 6 p.m.*; *Llanidloes abt. 7.30 p.m.*) is the following :—

5. Continue by rail to *Aberystwith.*

6. Walk or drive (by direct road) to the Devil's Bridge; return to Abery t-with by Pont Erwyd, or Hafod, or walk on to Llanidloes.

A PEDESTRIAN FORTNIGHT.

Sleeping Quarters in Italics.

Day.

1. Chester to Mold by train; walk over Moel Fammau to *Ruthin*, 12 m.

2. Denbigh by train; walk to Cefn Caves, &c., and St Asaph; train to *Llandudno Junction* or *Conway.*

3. Llandudno by train; walk round Great Orme; rail to Llanfair (Anglesey); walk to Bangor; train to *Bethesda.*

4. Walk up Nant Ffrancon to Llyn Idwal and, by the Devil's Kitchen, over Glyder-fawr to Capel Curig and *Bettws-y-Coed.*

5. Walk by Fairy Glen, Conway Falls, the Cromlech and Capel Garmon back to Bettws-y-Coed; train to *Dolwyddelen.*

6. Over Moel Siabod to Pen-y-gwryd and *Llanberis.*

7. Over Snowdon to *Beddgelert.*

8. Walk to Portmadoc or Tan-y-Bwlch; rail to Duffws; walk to *Ffestiniog Village.* Or walk all the way by Tan-y-Bwlch, or over Moelwyn.

9. Walk by Cynfael Falls, Rhaiadr and Raven Fall to Talsarnau Station; rail to *Harlech*, or by old road from Maentwrog to *Harlech.*

10. Walk by Cwm Bychan, Roman Steps, Bwlch Drws-Ardudwy to Dyffryn Station; train to *Barmouth.*

11. Over Cader Idris to *Dolgelley.*

12. Walk to Tal-y-llyn and Corris, train to *Machynlleth.* Or train to Berwyn; walk to *Llangollen.*

The Great Western Route to Barmouth.

Chester to Wrexham, 12¼ m; Ruabon, 17 m. (Shrewsbury to Ruabon, 25¼ m.)

Ruabon to Llangollen, 6 m; Corwen, 16½ m; Bala Junction, 27 m; Dolgelley, 44½ m; Barmouth Junction, 52 m; Barmouth, 54 m.

— Bala Junction to Bala Town, ¾ m; Ffestiniog Village, 22 m; Blaenau Ffestiniog, 25½ m.

Time from Ruabon to Barmouth, 2¾—3 hrs.

General Remarks. For mingled beauty and richness of valley scenery this line is hardly surpassed in the kingdom. Between Bala and Dolgelley, too, the sterner features of nature present themselves in the bold outlines of the Arans, Arenig and Cader Idris. All these mountains are comprehensively seen during the journey, but none of them are prominent enough to interfere with the pervading impression of soft luxuriance which is created by the general character of the country immediately bordering upon the line. In the tourist regions of Scotland the valleys threaded by the railways are of secondary interest to the mountains which flank them; in the Peak of Derbyshire it is the narrowness of the ravines, and the sheer walls of limestone cliff towering above them, that hold the eye of the traveller; in Devonshire the wide out-look over uplands teeming with cultivation and furrowed by deep silvan stream-courses claim his admiration, but in Wales, and in no part of it more than on the route we are about to describe, the centre of attraction is the valley itself, with its happy combinations of water, wood, and meadowland, presenting themselves to the eye in a succession of pictures as varied as they are delightful.

As far as Dolgelley the line belongs to the Great Western Company, which runs its comfortable and well-appointed trains through to Barmouth. From Dolgelley to Barmouth the Cambrian are the owners, and from 7 in the morning till 10 at night, there is a constant service of trains during the season.

The Route. The first 9 miles of this route as far as Gresford, may be dismissed in a line. As we quit the route for Holyhead, and turn southward, the wooded ridge of Hawarden is the nearest high ground on our right, and to the left of it, and much further off is Moel Fammau, with its Jubilee monument. About *Gresford* the valley of the Aleyn river is prettily wooded, but we soon quit it, and stop at *Wrexham Station.*

Wrexham (Principal Hotel : *Wynnstay Arms*) is a busy and rapidly growing town on the edge of the North Wales coal-field.   It is in no wise a tourist's resort but offers one inducement to him to break his journey or to pay its visit from Llangollen, namely, its fine **church** (a good half-mile from the station), the tower of which, a richly decorated Perpendicular work of six stages and 135 feet high, is worthy of Somersetshire, and is accounted one of the "Seven wonders of Wales."   Its peal of bells, ten in number, is also of rare quality.   The church was completely restored by Ferrey in 1867 and is not, except for its tower, of any particular architectural interest.   That it originally terminated eastward at the present chancel-arch is proved by the fragments of window-tracery still remaining.   Of *monuments*, &c., there are several worth examination.   In the north-west porch is the effigy of a Knight in armour "Keneverike ap Horel" of uncertain date, and a fragment of a fresco of the Crucifixion, and a portion of another fresco, the Day of Judgment, has been brought to light over the chancel-arch.   Roubillac's famous monument to Miss Mary Myddelton of Croesnewydd (d. 1747, daughter of Sir Richard Myddelton, of Chirk Castle) is in the north aisle.   One quaint epitaph (there are several more) may be quoted:

" Here lies interr'd beneath these stones,
The beard, the flesh, and eke the bones
Of Wrexham clerk, old Daniel Jones, 1668."

It was for the first missionary service in Wrexham church, on Whitsunday 1809, that Reginald Heber, son-in-law of the then vicar, Dean Shipley, composed his missionary hymn " From Greenland's icy mountains."

Between Wrexham and Ruabon there is nothing calling for notice.   The latter station is the junction for Llangollen on the Great Western Railway branch to Dolgelley, and passengers have to change trains.   *For Wynnstay, see p.* 18.

Ruabon Station (*Refreshment Room*) is on the high ground, and from it to Llangollen, a little short of which the level of the Dee valley is reached, there is an almost continuous descent. At first the line passes through the mining and quarrying district of *Acrefair* (*pron.* " Akryvire ").   During the descent there is a good view on the left hand across the valley, the railway viaduct of the main Shrewsbury and Chester line and the aqueduct of the Ellesmere canal being conspicuous.   The latter, called *Pont-y-cysylltau*, was constructed by Telford between the years 1795 and 1805 at a cost of nearly £50,000.   It is 120 ft. above the river and has 19 arches of a total length of about 350 yards.

Two miles short of Llangollen we reach the side of the Dee. On the right are the limestone bluffs called Eglwyseg Rocks and then *Dinas Bran*, crowned by its rude castle, rises like a pyramid ; while on the left is the prettily wooded little hill called *Pen-y-Coed*.   **Llangollen** is approached by a narrow dell occupied by the river, the railway, the canal and two roads.   *For a a description of the town, see p.* 8.   It looks its best from the

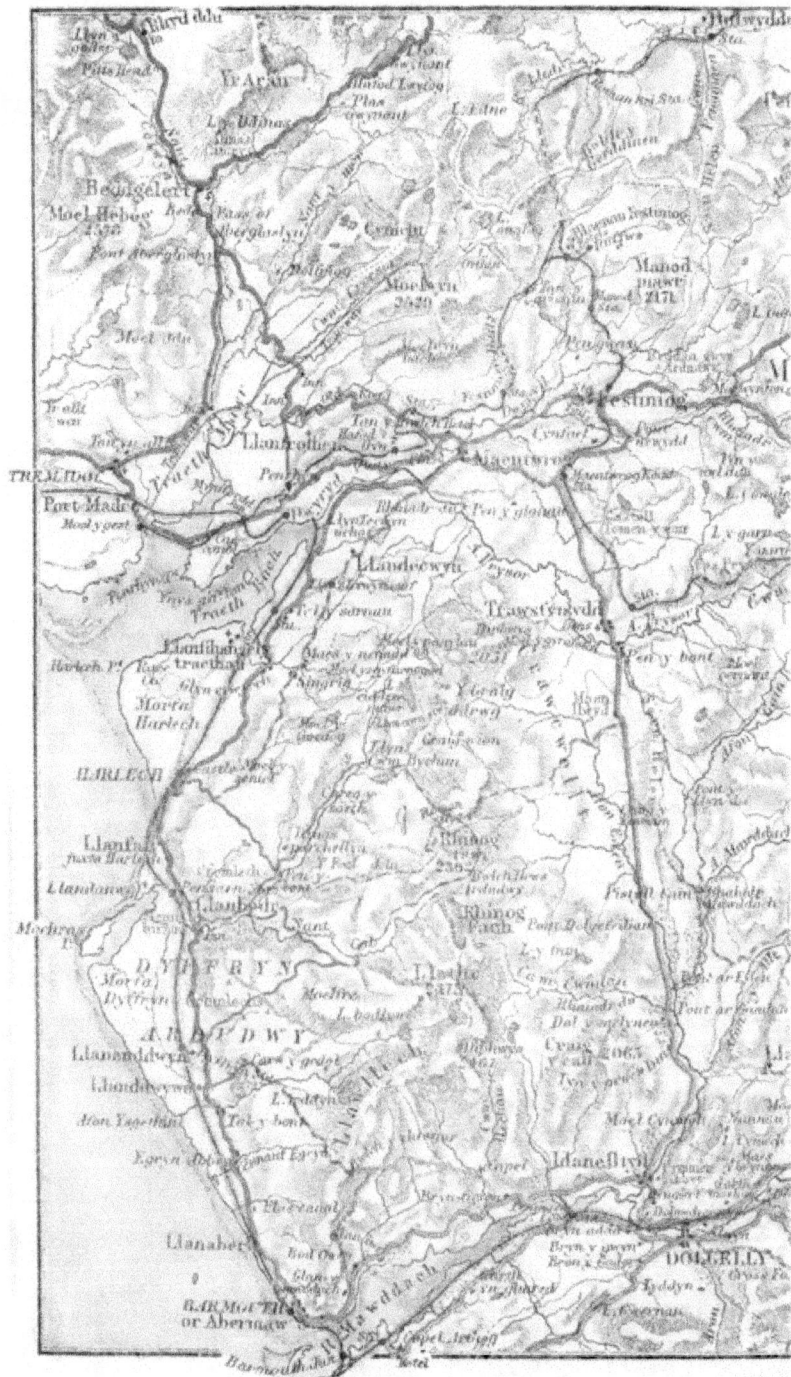

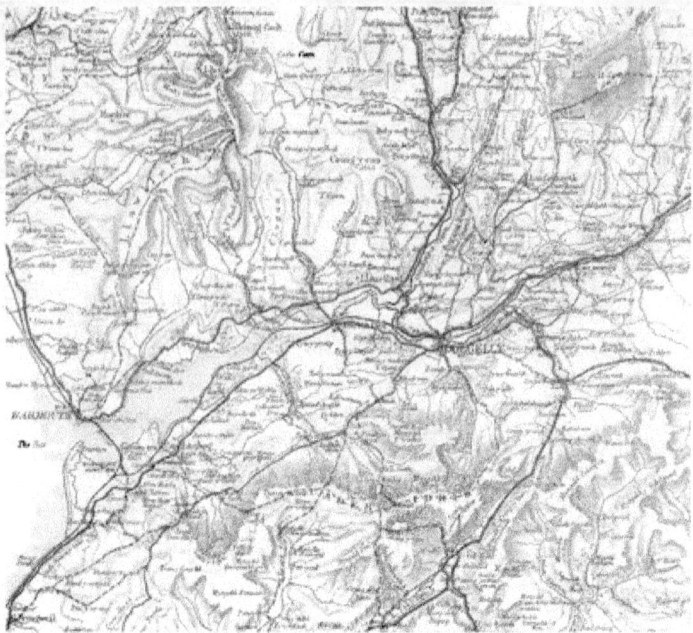

station, with which it is connected by the *old bridge*, an irregular structure with arches of graduated height. This bridge is one of the traditional "Wonders of Wales," and was built in 1345. On both sides of it the stream pursues a broken and picturesque course.

One of the most charming parts of the Dee valley is that between Llangollen and the next station, *Berwyn*, 2 miles distant. Dinas Bran opposes its western slope to the line, and across the river rises *Barber's Hill*. About half-way, as the line turns sharply to the left and crosses a viaduct, a view is presented up the *Valle Crucis* glen on the right. A glimpse, and nothing more, of the Abbey may be obtained. The right-hand side of the carriage is now the one to look out from. Close below is the river, fretting and foaming, if there has been a fair rainfall, over a bed of broken rock; beyond it the rustic little canal, as clear as the river, and affording passage for one boat only. On popular holidays there is often quite a boat procession. At **Berwyn** **station** is a small hotel, charmingly situated and called the "Chain Bridge" after the bridge which connects it with the station, while behind it we catch sight of *Braich-y-Gwynt*. the summer residence of Sir Theodore and Lady Martin, the former well-known as a man of letters, and the latter, perhaps, still better remembered as Miss Helen Faucit.

Beyond Berwyn station the main valley strikes away to the right. *Llantysilio Church* and *Hall* in park-like woodland and backed by the boldly outlined Moel-y-Gamelin heights constitute a charming picture, seen for too brief a moment—perhaps the sweetest bit of scenery during the whole journey. Another minute and we are whisked into and through a tunnel, emerging from which we come upon an entirely fresh reach of the river. Where we have travelled half-a-mile it has wound three miles round the green tongue of *Rhisgog*. Looking up it as soon as the tunnel is quitted, we see its direct course now broken by the wooded knoll of *Ty-newydd*. The Holyhead road goes to the south of this, but the railway accompanies the stream round its northern slope to *Glyndyfrdwy (*pron.* "Glyndov'rdwy") station (*inn*). Hence to Corwen, road, rail and river keep company along a comparatively direct course: on the left the Berwyn range rises at once from the valley; on the right a lower range runs parallel to it from Moel-y-Gamelin. One mile and a half beyond Glyndyfrdwy, a fir-clad eminence on the right, between and close to both rail and road, is called "*Owen Glyndwr's Mound.*" It is apparently a burial mound and is said to have been used as a look-out by the Welsh patriot. The whole valley hereabouts was his hereditary possession. Half-a-mile further we come to *Carrog station*, and then, on the north side of the river, the village of *Llansaintffraid*, to which, if we add its distinguishing cognomen.

---

* This is a good starting point for Moel Morfydd and Moel-y-Gamelin, see reverse route *p.* 15.

Glyndyfrdwy, we get a very pretty little name which means "Saint Bride's Church in the valley of the Dee."

At **Corwen** (*Refreshment Room*) there is a wide break in the line of hills on the right of the river, which forms an arc round an expanse of flat meadow-land. Here the Vale of Clwyd extension line (L. & N. W. R.), from Rhyl and Denbigh and Ruthin, runs into the Great Western. On the other side, a cliff, just enough out of the perpendicular to admit of its being covered with trees to the summit, rises to a height of several hundred feet. The cairn on the highest point commemorates the marriage of the Prince of Wales. *For the town and excursions from it see* *p.* 23.

Half-a-mile after leaving Corwen we go under the Holyhead road, which is carried across the Dee by a six-arch bridge close to the line on the right. Next, on the left, the poor little church of *Llangar*—more like a long cottage than a church—is passed, and then *Cynwyd station*, close to which is another Dee bridge.

Cynwyd is the starting point for a pleasant glen walk up the *Afon Tryston* which, about ⅜ m. from the station, forms a pretty cascade.

The valley of the Dee, hereabouts and for the next few miles, widens into a green strath, and the bounding hills, fringed with woodland, present no marked features. All trains, up and down, stop at **Llandrillo station**, which is a starting point for Pistyll Rhaiadr, in some respects the finest waterfall in North Wales. The route to it through Llandrillo village and over the Berwyns is given under Bala excursions p. 32.

Crossing the Dee, in a mile or so **Crogen**, a seat of the Earl of Dudley, is on the left, where, after a sweep southward, the river again approaches the line before we recross it and run to *Llandderfel station*, another starting point for a walk over the Berwyns to Pistyll Rhaiadr.

Llandderfel village, half-a-mile from the station, across the river, takes its name from St. Derfel, a 6th century worthy whose image was in great repute as an object of pilgrimage down to the Reformation period, when it was carried off and burnt at Smithfield. The *Church*, which has been restored, has had its ancient rood-loft reinstated. In the porch are the so-called *Derfel's Horse* and *Derfel's Staff*, the former being really the decapitated body of a wooden stag.

The valley now becomes narrower and well clothed with fir and larch. The large house on the left is *Palé* (H. Robertson, Esq.) and opposite to it *Fronheulog*, charmingly placed on the hill-side. Then we catch sight of a pretty reach of the Dee, and after a short tunnel come in view of Bala, with the foot of the lake beyond and the peak of Arenig-fawr peering over an intervening ridge. The church on the far side of the valley, just short of Bala Junction, is *Llanfor*, and close to the junction the Dee is joined by its tributary the Tryweryn.

At Bala Junction those bound for Bala itself and the Ffestiniog line change trains.

For **Bala town** and the road-routes thence, see p. 28.

Bala Junction to Ffestiniog, by rail.

Bala Junction to Bala Town, ¾ m; Frongoch, 2¼ m; Arenig, 8½ m; Trawsfynydd, 17¼ m; Maentwrog-road, 20½ m; Ffestiniog Village, 22 m; Blaenau Ffestiniog, 25½ m.

This branch of the G. W. R. was made principally to get at the Ffestiniog slates. It passes for the first few miles along a pretty pastoral valley; for the next ten or so it traverses a wild upland, relieved only from utter dreariness by the finely-shaped Arenig-fawr, and for the rest of the way affords beautiful views across and down the vale of Ffestiniog.

As we quit the **Town Station** the Calvinistic Methodist College, well-placed on the hill-side to the left, attracts our attention. Then we enter the Tryweryn valley at once, and Arenig comes into view. Passing Frongoch Station, we get more than one pretty peep as we cross the river itself, or catch glimpses of its tributary glens. Mynydd Nodol shows a dark heathery side on the left, and soon the cliffs of Arenig-fawr over Llyn Arenig (not seen) appear on the same side. On the other side is a fine view of the deep gorge of Afon Gelyn, and then we come to **Arenig Station** (Inn ¾ m. away, under Arenig-fach; for ascent of Arenig see "Mountain Section"). Hereabouts the dreary part of the route begins, the line reaching its summit-level (1196 ft.) near Llyn Tryweryn. Beyond this we look down on the le t into the green but bare Cwm Prysor. The rocky Rhinogs are seen in front and, as we proceed, Cader Idris comes into view in the south, over the barren plateau of Trawsfynydd. At Trawsfynydd Station the line turns north and soon we see the two little green humps of Tomen-y-mur (Part I.) on the right, while in front the peaks on the far side of the Vale of Ffestiniog appear,—Moelwyn the chief of them. Beyond **Maentwrog-road** Station (2 m. from Maentwrog, Part I) the Vale of Ffestiniog opens on the left, and beyond it we may note Moel Hebog and the little Moel-y-Gest—the latter marking the position of Portmadoc. The view is very charming as we cross the Cynfael stream a little above the falls. Then comes **Ffestiniog Village** beyond which the line winds along the hill-side for 3½ miles more to **Blaenau Ffestiniog**. Duffws Station, the starting point of the Ffestiniog "Toy" line is 200 yards away from the G.W. terminus; the L. and N.W., and the "Toy" Blaenau Ffestiniog nearly half-a-mile. All these places are fully described in "North Wales, Part I."

A little beyond the junction, as we pass the site of the old Bala station, now disused, we have on the right, close at hand, Castell Gronw, a small mound or tomen, similar to the one in Bala town, and like it attributed to the Romans. Then **Bala Lake** comes into view on the same side, and for 3½ miles we follow its eastern shore, keeping close to the water all the way. Near its foot, on the opposite side, is the yew-girt little church, Llan-y-cil, with Arenig rising boldly against the sky in a steep escarpment. Then, a couple of miles onward, we pass on the left the little church of Llangower, while across the lake the valley of the Afon Llafar affords a pretty peep towards the Arenigs. Close to the opening of this valley, and just to the west of it, is Glan-y-llyn, one of the residences of Sir Watkin Wynn, whose private station we run through without stopping. Looking out on the left, the ridge of the Arans foreshortened rises in a cone at the head of the lake, which gives the name Benllyn, "head of the lake," to the peak in sight. **Llanuwchllyn Station**, with the good little *Goat Inn* close by, is a convenient starting-point for several pleasant mountain excursions—the Arans and Arenigs, and for the wild walk over the hills by Bwlch-y-Groes to Dinas Mawddwy. *For the former of these see our " Mountain Section "; for the latter,* p. 31.

In the course of the journey from Llangollen the line has gradually ascended from about 50 ft. to 550 ft. above sea-level, but we have yet to reach the *col*, 760 ft., by which road and rail cross from the valley of the Dee to that of the Wnion. This we do by ascending the bare valley of the *Dwfrdwy*, and as the engine feels the tug up-hill the traveller has an interval of rest from sightseeing. When the *col* is passed, a rapid run brings us to **Drws-y-Nant Station**, the nearest railway approach to the summit of the Arans, which are well seen on the left, just past the station. The line now winds down the lovely wooded glen of the *Wnion*, and a look out should be kept on the left hand for a magnificent full length view of the Cader Idris range. Mynydd Moel appears from this point to be the apex, but the peak to the right of it is the actual summit. A mile beyond **Bont Newydd**, where tickets are called for, the glen of the Dolgelley Torrent Walk is seen above the demesne and house of Dolserau, and then the top of Cader Idris is soon lost to sight, and we arrive at **Dolgelley** (*p.* 36).

We now enter on the Cambrian Railway, and across the sparkling stream of the Wnion, here grown to a considerable river, get a good view of Dolgelley, with its delightfully-wooded and broken surroundings. Mynydd Moel forms a noble background, and for a moment the top of Cader Idris is again seen, with the Saddle (Cyfrwy) to the right of it, and still more to the right, blocking a narrow glen, the steep profile of Tyrau-mawr. We now turn our attention for the rest of the journey to the right-hand side, where, as the Wnion valley runs into that of the Mawddach, a charming mountain outline of many folds, and clad below with abundance of varied woodland, is seen across the richly green but marshy meadows that border the main river.

At **Penmaenpool Station** (*small hotel, the " George," close by*), if the tide be in, we reach the margin of a sea-loch, and henceforward, all the way to Barmouth, the scenery vies both in colouring and beauty of form with any, not only in Wales but in the kingdom. Of course the foreground is dependent for its charm on the tide, but even at low water the far side of the estuary suffers little disadvantage. Glen after glen opens out, each leading by a silvan defile up into rich purple valleys, themselves overtopped by the Llawllech range, of which Diphwys (2,467 feet) is the dominant height. Our advice to all travellers by this route is to put away the book and enjoy the prospect.* Just short of *Artoy Station* the line quits the water-side, and crosses a marsh, not as other marshes are, but broken by knobs of rock, and then winds round to *Barmouth Junction*, whence, by the long bridge that for the last part of the journey has been seen stretching across the estuary to **Barmouth**, we reach our destination. The view from the bridge, unrivalled certainly in Wales, is described in detail on p. 50

* We should mention that there is a bridge over the river at Penmaenpool, by which a road reaches Barmouth in 7 miles (*see p. 47.*)

Llangollen.

Hotels : *Hand, Royal*, overlooking the Dee, and opposite the station ; *Eagle, Grapes, Cambrian*, a little further away from the station.

Post : Del. abt. 7 a.m. and 4.30 p.m. ; *Sunday* 7 a.m. ; desp. abt. 10 a.m. and 8.30 p.m. Office open : *Week days*, 7 a.m. to 8 p.m. ; *Sundays*, 7 to 10 a.m.

Population : abt. 3,000. **Boats** ply on canal to Berwyn.

Distances : (*rail*), Ruabon (for Wynnstay), 6 m. ; Berwyn, 1¾ m. ; Glyndyfrdwy, 5½ m. ; Corwen, 10½ m. ; Bala, 22 m. ; Dolgelley, 38½ m. ; Barmouth, 48 m. (*Road or footpath*, reckoning from the Bridge), Valle Crucis Abbey, 2 m. ; Chain Bridge (Berwin) 2 m. ; Chirk Castle (nearest way), 4 m. ; Glyn Ceiriog, 3 m.

The neighbourhood of Llangollen may be briefly described as decidedly the most beautiful in the hill as contrasted with the mountain district of Wales. Some tourists, on arriving at the little town, may be disappointed to find that they are still, say, five and twenty miles short of real mountain scenery, but if they once realise this fact and still feel dissatisfied, they must be hard indeed to please. To be sure, the Berwyn range, which reaches a height of 2700 feet, commences close to Llangollen and the outline of Moel-y-Gamelin, only a few miles away to the north-west, is bold as well as graceful, but the Berwyns are moors rather than mountains, and Moel-y.Gamelin is less than 2000 feet high. The valley of the Dee, however, of which Llangollen may be said to be the capital, is perhaps, of its kind unsurpassed in the kingdom, and its loveliest scenes are in this immediate neighbourhood. The *town* itself has been greatly improved of late years. Opinions differ, but we fancy that no one will disagree with us when we assert that, except from the accident of situation and when seen from a distance, as in the case of Dolgelley, Welsh towns have but little of the picturesque in themselves, and therefore every step in the direction of comfort and cleanliness may be welcomed with approval untinged by regret.

As to the hotels, the *Hand* and the *Royal* are the chief ones, and the former has a long established reputation, while the latter (previously known as the King's Head) is intimately associated with the " Ladies of Llangollen," who expected their visitors to patronise it.

Llangollen Bridge, which connects the station with the town, is one of the so-called " Wonders of Wales." It is of four

SECTION MAP No. 7

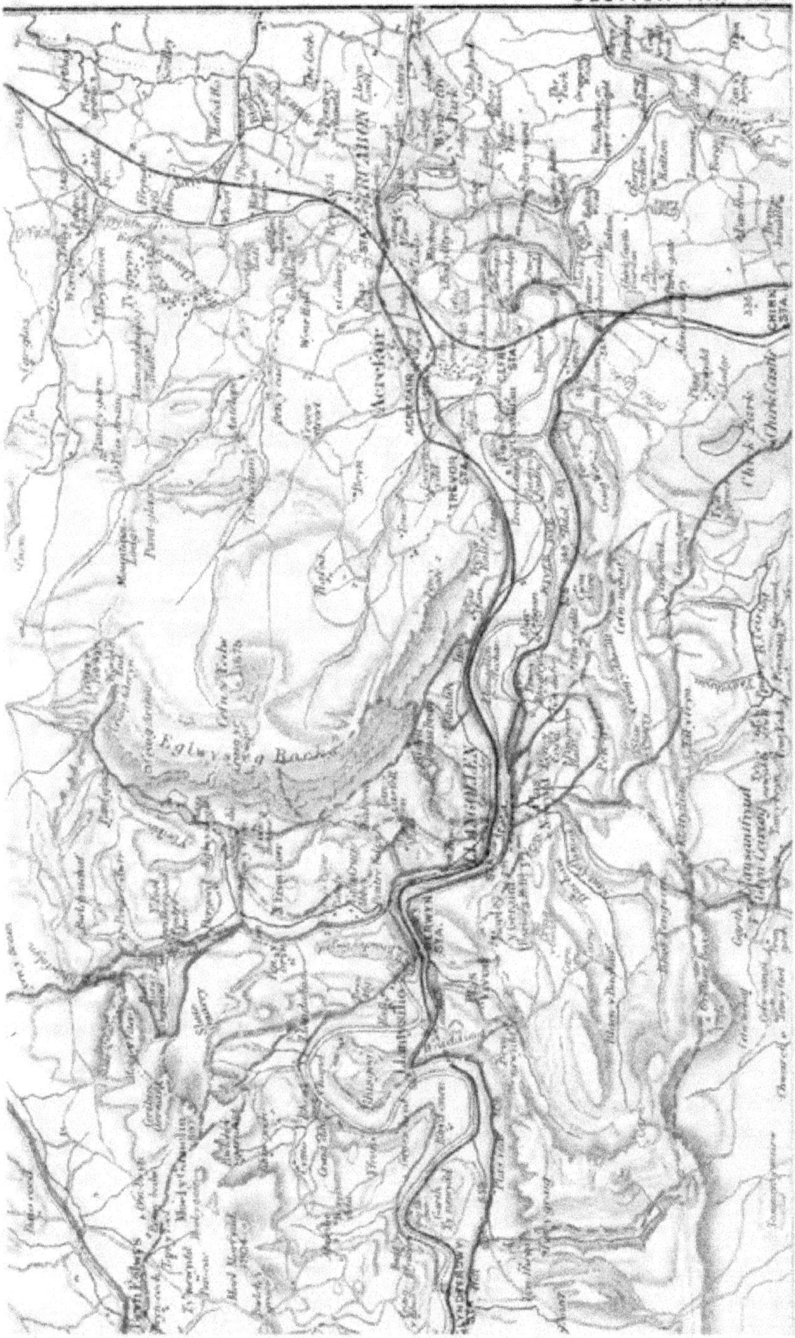

pointed **arches**, the end ones being wider than the central pair, and was originally built in 1345-46, by John Trevor, afterwards Bishop of St. Asaph. The Dee hereabouts is delightful, and flows down over a series of up-turned edges of rock that, except when long draught has unduly shrunk the stream, break its waters into a turmoil of rapids. The **Church**, dedicated to St. Collen, whence the town gets its name, has no striking features. In the church-yard is a three-sided monument to the Ladies of Llangollen and their old servant Mary Carryl, and the graves of the post-boys whose fortunes they made are also pointed out.

Llangollen beer is widely and favourably known, and flannel was, rather than is, a staple product.

Walks in the Neighbourhood.

For beautiful and varied walks of from an hour's to a day's duration few places in the country can surpass Llangollen. The only difficulty in describing them arises from the ease with which they may be in part interchanged one with another, or extended at will. We shall endeavour to arrange them so as to avoid as far as possible going over the same ground twice.

(1) **Plas Newydd** = New Place (General Yorke, C.B.) is about half-a-mile from the station and bridge. The most direct way to it is to turn to the left at the top of Castle Street and then at the *Grapes Hotel* to take the narrow street on the right hand. Presently a railed off path on the left leads to the house, or the drive can be entered by proceeding a few yards further. Visitors enter at the principal entrance (*admission 6d.*), and after examining the interior of the house can explore its surroundings. The interest of the place is twofold, first in connection with the Ladies of Llangollen, whose story, a romance without a hero, is briefly told below; and secondly on account of the large and varied collection of curiosities of all sorts and qualities, with which the house has been crammed by the present owner.

The **Ladies of Llangollen.** In 1776 two unmarried Irish ladies, Lady Eleanor Butler, then about 38 years old, and the Honourable Sarah Ponsonby, 17 years her junior, the latter attended by a trusty maid, Mary Carryl, discontented with their home-life, left Ireland, and, concealing their destination from their respective families, took up their abode at Denbigh. Two years later they moved to a four-room cottage called Pen-y-Maes, at Llangollen. This cottage they enlarged and renamed it Plas Newydd. Gradually under their tasteful care the humble dwelling became a charming cottage ornée, and in it they received visits from many of the celebrities of the day. Every one is familiar with the costume of the Ladies—beaver chimney-pot hats, and blue coat-bodied riding-habits—and to it and their short-cut powdered hair is probably due the general notion of their eccentricity. Two such personages were, of course, a great power in the village, but their 50 years' sway, if despotic, was beneficent. Visitors were expected to mark their coming by a contribution of old oak or by the gift of some curiosity, and when not otherwise employed, the Ladies' joiner scoured the district on their behalf to buy up relics for the adornment of the cottage. Mary Carryl died in 1809 and left her savings, including the freehold of Plas Newydd, which she had purchased out of them, to the Ladies, and it was after that date that the exterior carvings of the house were added. Lady Eleanor died in 1829, aged 90, and Miss Ponsonby in 1831, aged 76, and in 1832 the contents of their dwelling were dispersed under the hammer of the grandiloquent George Robins. Since then the house has frequently changed hands. It was for a time again the residence of two spinster ladies—Miss Lolly and Miss Andrew, both since dead ; the latter was buried at Llantysilio (*page* 14) where there is a window to her memory—but is now in the possession of General Yorke, C.B., who has altered the old part of the house and added a wing.

It would exceed our space to describe Plas Newydd and its contents in detail, and be, too, a work of supererogation, since for 6d. a pamphlet and appendix, written by the General and giving a full catalogue, can be obtained in the town or at the house. Suffice to say that, outside and in, the house is a mass of carved oak. Of objects belonging to the Ladies there are only a few, and none of intrinsic merit. A window recess in the "Oak room" is lined with the oak of their old pew in Llangollen church.

From the grounds the return can be made by the Chester and Holyhead road, but the walk may be extended with advantage so as to include the circuit of **Pen-y-Coed**, the isolated wood-crowned hill which rises south-east of the town. There is a footpath round its northern slope. but none over its summit. *Route :*— Half-a-mile beyond Plas Newydd, as we continue along the road by which we left Llangollen, we pass a few hundred yards to the right of *Pengwern Hall*, now only a farm-house. The original mansion was built as early as the 10th century, by Tudor Trevor, ancestor of the Mostyn family, who afterwards occupied it. Hence the road winds round *Pen-y-Coed* (the "head of the wood"). passing on the right hand, a little after it has turned again in the direction of Llangollen, the handsome modern mansion of *Tyn-dwfr*, an effective example of timber-built architecture. A short distance beyond this a pathway diverges to the left into the wood and past a cottage. Either this may be taken, or the road itself followed into the town. The length of the round is about three miles.

2. **Castell Dinas Bran** ("Crow Castle "), 910 *feet*, 1 *hour up and down*. This singular ruin, perched on a still more singular hill, is certainly one of the most striking features of the vale of Llangollen. and its tremendous popularity with "trippers," who love above all things a slope which they can pant and puff up and alternately run and tumble down, must not tempt us to disparage it. Even to more sober-minded visitors the information that sure-footed donkeys stand for hire at the foot may not be in all cases unwelcome.

From the town you cross the bridge, the railway and the canal in quick succession, and then enter a footpath, which ascends through two fields, crosses another road and is resumed in another

field whence it enters a third road. Go up this and past another
crossing till you gain the open hill-side through a gate-way.
The rest of the climb is short but steep. to be zig-zagged at
pleasure. The ruins themselves are of the rudest and most
featureless character, but the view from them, though limited in
extent by the superior height of the surrounding hills, is very
delightful. Its greatest extent is eastward, in which direction the
eye ranges over the widening portion of the vale, past the viaduct
of the Shrewsbury and Chester railway to the level plain of north
Shropshire. North-eastwards the limestone scarp of the Eglwyseg
Rocks rises above a deep and narrow depression, which extends
northwards till it reaches its limit at the suggestively-named
" World's End." Then, turning westwards, we look up the beautiful Dee valley to the shapely ridge of Moel-y-Gamelin. Below,
due south, we have Llangollen itself, and to the right of it, Barber's
Hill, in front of the dark heathery Berwyns, on which the shooting-
box tower is a conspicuous object. Guide-books of well earned
repute speak of Snowdon as visible in clear weather. If so, it
must be looked for to the left of Moel-y-Gamelin in a direction a
little north of west. The hill on which Dinas Bran stands has
the peculiarity of being steep on all sides, especially the northern.
The name has been derived from the little river Bran, which
flows beneath and signifies a crow. It is a common one in Scotland also. Historically the extreme rudeness of the architecture—
if architecture it can be called—points to a very early foundation.
In the thirteenth century the castle was occupied by Gryffydd ap-
Madoc ("Griffith, the son of Madoc"), who " basely sided with
Henry the Third and betrayed his country." A century later it
was the residence of a fair maid, by name Myfanwy Fechan
(Vaughan), a connection of the Mostyn family. To her, Howell-
ap-Eyricon Llugliw, an illustrious bard, played the part of Claude
Melnotte, but Wales was not a republic at the time, and it all
ended in an ode. Shortly afterwards the castle became a ruin.

3. **Barber's Hill** (*about* 1000 *ft.*) &c., 20 *minutes' walk from
the town.* This is a delightful excursion, especially if it be
extended to the valley beyond, which opens on to the main Dee
valley, close to Berwyn station. Here refreshment may be
obtained at the *Chain Bridge Hotel*, and the return to Llangollen
may be agreeably varied by taking Valle Crucis Abbey on the way.
The entire round will be one of from 6 to 7 miles.

Barber's Hill is so called from a story, as false as it is repulsive, of
a homicidal barber. the morbid interest in which is probably the cause
of the disuse of its true and pretty name, *Moel-y-Geraint*, " the
hill of the kindred." It rises due west of the town, and the way
up is by a lane which ascends steeply from near the *Grapes Hotel*,
and to the south of the main road. In ascending, avoid a stile
approached by steps, on the left hand, and turning sharply to the
left a little further on, close to a seat, climb by the side of an iron
fence. This is the direct cut and very steep. To ease it you must
proceed further along the road before taking to the open ground.

The *View* from the top, on which is a small cairn, is strikingly beautiful, but eastwards the best part of it is seen during the ascent, as the foreground of valley, river and town in that direction is hidden before you reach the actual summit. Beyond them are the widening valley, the canal and railway viaducts, the towers and grounds of Wynnstay, and the plains of Shropshire as far as the atmosphere admits of their being seen. North-east are Castell Dinas Bran and the long line of the Eglwyseg rocks; northwards, Valle Crucis Abbey, beautifully placed at the opening of its woody little vale; north-west the three summits of Moel-y-Gamelin, and the grassy knoll of Rhisgog, almost encircled by a horse-shoe bend of the Dee. In the west, the mansion of Vivod with another grassy knoll behind it, occupies a pleasant looking little valley, to which we must descend, if our route is for Berwyn. To reach that hamlet still follow the railing, and, entering a lane, turn sharp to the right and then still more sharply to the left. From a farm a little way along this last lane you may either make direct for Berwyn, by a lane that skirts the hill-side and overlooks the valley, or you may keep on up the valley by a road which gradually approaches, and in about a mile crosses its stream. For some way below the crossing, the water flows through a prettily wooded little glen, which may itself be crossed by an obvious foot-path. From the bridge by which the road crosses, you turn sharp to the right and pursue a winding road which passes at its highest point a group of farm-buildings and then descends above the mansion of Vivod to Berwyn. From the green hill to the left of this road a.ter winding round the little glen in which Vivod stands, an almost incomparable valley-view in both directions is to be had. The spot is over the Berwyn tunnel, and we must add, is private.

From Berwyn we may either take the train back to Llangollen (2 *miles*) or walk on the far side of the river by the canal-side. By diverging up the Ruthin-road about half-a-mile beyond Chain Bridge, we may visit *Valle Crucis Abbey*, the détour only adding a mile to the distance. This, however, is the subject of our next description.

4. Valle Crucis Abbey, Chain-Bridge, &c. This is entirely a valley excursion, though it may be extended so as to include hill-climbing at pleasure. We advise those who really want a breakfast-to-dinner walk, to take a morning train to Berwyn, thence visit Llantysilio Church and ascend Moel-y-Gamelin, drop down to the Ruthin road, and return to Llangollen by Valle Crucis and the canal-side. *For the ascent of Moel-y-Gamelin see page* 14. All the best scenery in this direction from Llangollen is visible from this route, and we may add that north of Moel-y-Gamelin the country degenerates into the uninteresting upland which supplies the head waters of the Vale of Clwyd. For " easy-goers" let us recommend the train to Berwyn, thence a stroll to Llantysilio, and up the pleasant little green hill behind the hotel at Chain

Bridge, whence the return may be made by Valle Crucis and the canal-side. The walking distance in this case will be about 5 miles.

Valle Crucis Abbey (*admission* 6d.) is nearly 2 miles by road from Llangollen. The pleasantest way for pedestrians is to cross the bridge and railway at the station, and thence to proceed by the towing-path of the canal, till, in about a mile. it turns abruptly to the left for Chain Bridge. This canal, be it noted, is not as other canals. It is a narrow, clear, avenue shaded stretch of water, issuing from the Dee a little above Chain Bridge. At the turn, enter the Ruthin high-road, and in a short half-mile you will have the Abbey one field away on the right hand.

Those who take the train to Berwyn (2 m.) must, on arriving there, cross the Chain Bridge to the hotel just beneath the station, and thence return by canal-path and road to the Ruthin road, which is entered a third of a mile short of the Abbey.

This ruin, though it has no pretensions to rank with the most famous of the monastic remains of Great Britain, such as those of Tintern, Fountains and Furness, is the finest object of its kind in North Wales, and occupies a situation inferior to none ; in fact, the venerable trees which overshadow its entrance, and the verdant growth which clothes part of its walls are its not least picturesque attributes. It was founded about 1200 by Madoc-ap-Gryffydd Maelor, whose homestall was, as before stated, Castell Dinas Bran, and who was a hearty supporter of Llewelyn in the cause of Welsh independence. The style is early English, and the finest parts of the remains are the west-end with dog-tooth ornamentation, three lofty Decorated windows over the doorway, and a beautiful round window in the gable. The *chancel* has also a trio of lancet windows and in the south-side of the *south transept* are the remains of a piscina and wide canopy. The monastic buildings, which extend at right angles from the south side of the abbey-church, long occupied as a farm-house, have been purged and the chapter-house is now cleared to the floor level. A round headed doorway and an elaborate window are the chief exterior features of this part of the buildings.

A little east of the Abbey and in the grounds is a still pool of water in which the reflection of the east-end is decidedly effective, and from this point the singular form of the buttresses which bifurcate and envelop the lancet lights is well seen.

Re-entering the road and proceeding as far as the second milestone from Llangollen, we have in a field on the right hand, **Eliseg's Pillar**, accounted one of the most remarkable memorial stones in the country. Eliseg was a lord of Powys and is said to have taken part in the battle of Bangor Iscoed A.D. 607. The old inscription is effaced and a modern one records the restoration of what remained of the original pillar (overthrown by the Puritans, as a popish symbol) by Mr. Lloyd of Trevor Hall, in 1779. It stands on a mound in a little grove of a half-a-dozen oak trees.

Those who are making the expedition this way may cross the little green hill west of the Valle Crucis to *Llantysilio Church*, which is otherwise reached direct from Chain Bridge in a few minutes. The small *hotel* at Chain Bridge is built on the narrow strip of land between the river and canal, the latter a narrow pellucid stream flowing beneath a face of rock and supplied by the river a little way higher up.

If we ascend the last-named hill behind the Inn—and it is as pleasant a way of spending an hour as can be imagined—we pass to the right of *Braich-y-Gwynt* (*p.* 3).

To reach **Llantysilio** itself, we follow the course of the canal westwards from the Inn, and after passing a wide circular weir at which its waters issue from the river, reach the *Church*. Architecturally there is nothing remarkable about this fabric but its position in a grove of ancient yews, with a wych-elm or two, and in the richest part of the lovely Dee valley, makes it the bourn of a delightful walk. The east window commemorates Miss Andrew, and was given by Miss Lolley. These " Ladies of Llangollen " occupied Plas Newydd and repeated the experiment of the more famous pair. *Llantysilio Hall* is hard by.

From Chain Bridge a return may be made by the route we have already described the reverse way, over Barber's Hill (*p.* 11). Those who care to see perhaps the most perfect *Valley* view in the Kingdom should—under privilege—climb the green hill which rises above the tunnel a little west of Berwyn station. A gateway from nearly the highest point of the Corwen road, a mile west of the station, shows the way up to it. From it the view westward extends to Corwen, and eastward to the centre of Shropshire.

5. **Moel-y-Gamelin** (*pron.* Gamélin; 1897 ft.), **Moel-y-Gaer** (camp), and **Moel Morfydd** (1804 ft.). Maps *p.* 2 and 8.

Berwyn Sta. to top of Gamelin, 3½ *m.*, 1¼ *hr.*; thence either (i) back by Ruthin road past Valle Crucis (*p.* 13) to Llangollen; or (ii) by Gaer and Morfydd and down to Glyndyfrdwy Sta. (Inn) whence rail 5½ *m.* to Llangollen. The total walk in each case about 8 *m.* or 3 *hrs.*

N.B. Public-house at *Pentre-dwfr*, 3¾ *m.* from Llangollen on the *old* Ruthin road, and another at *Pen-y-bryn*, a mile nearer that town.

Moel-y-Gamelin is the chief of the two peaks seen N.W. from Llangollen. *Moel Morfydd* (better view point) is a full half-hour to the W.S.W. of Gamelin. The minor height nearly midway between them is Moel-y-Gaer. Either walk indicated above is worth taking and the return (ii) to Glyndyfrdwy Station is most enjoyable. There are, of course, opportunities for longer walks by taking the mountain road from Gamelin to (abt. 2¼ *m.*) *Bryn Eglwys* and thence by the high-road (6½ *m.*) to *Corwen*; or a by-road from *Bryn Eglwys* to *Llansaintffraid* and *Carrog Sta.*, 5½ *m.* The round from Gamelin by *World's End* and the *Eglwyseg Rocks* to *Llangollen* is a long one and at first both devious and rather dull.

The route (i) may, of course, be taken the reverse way, in which case it is best to follow the Ruthin road for a little over 4 miles, and then ascend by the Oernant slate-quarries. This road forks nearly 3 miles from Llangollen, the right-hand branch, or old road, continuing along the valley for some way, and then rising to the watershed by a tremendous hill, while the left hand one ascends gradually round the Oernant combe. The latter is the one to be followed.

Route from Berwyn Station. Cross the Chain Bridge and turn left between the inn and the canal. The latter has its beginning at the wide circular weir erected in order to keep it supplied with water from the main stream. A short d.stance further the road is joined close to *Llantysilio Church* (*p.* 14). The scenery about here is, perhaps, the richest and loveliest in the whole valley of the Dee. The river has just made a horse-shoe bend round the the green hill of *Rhisgog*, and beyond the head of the bend the Moel-y-Gamelin range affords a fine background. West of the church is *Llantysilio Hall* in a beautifully green park.

Three-quarters of a mile beyond the church our road forks. The left-hand branch is the nearest way to the summit of the mountain—in fact, it passes over the *col* between Moel-y-Gamelin and Moel Morfydd to the village of Bryn Eglwys in Nant Morwynion—but the right-hand affords the finer route. Proceeding by it we soon enter a footpath which ascends above a little wooded ravine on the left, and leads to an extensive slate-quarry. This quarry is worth a few minutes' exploration. From it the top of Moel-y-Gamelin is easily reached, either by making straight for it or by taking a path to the left which leads round the slope of the hill to the *col* on the west of it. Those who are disposed to somewhat shorten their walk to Glyndyfrdwy Station will not lose much if instead of ascending to the top of Moel-y-Gamelin they proceed from the *col* just mentioned to Moel-y-Gaer and Moel Morfydd. The view from the last named hill is distinctly better than from Moel-y-Gamelin, *see next page.*

The **View** from Moel-y-Gamelin is rather disappointing. By far the best part of it is that down to the beautiful Llantysilio bend of the Dee, and over Llangollen, but this has been well seen during the last part of the ascent. In the distance, immediately over Llantysilio, the peaked Breidden Hills of Montgomeryshire may be detected, and some distance to the left of them, in clear weather, the whale-back of the Wrekin in Shropshire; north-eastwards Cyrn-y-Brain, a dull and flat topped continuation of the Gamelin range, bounds the view, and northwards the garden-like vale of Clwyd stretches far away to the sea. Ruthin and Denbigh may be made out, and to the east of it Moel Fammau, always recognisable by its huge monument, overtops all its fellows in the billowy Clwydian range. The foreground, however, in this direction is bare and too elevated to give any impression of depth. Snowdonia displays its varied outline a little north of west, the peak of Snowdon itself rising just left of the nearer summit of

Moel Siabod. Then, further south and closer at hand, are
Arenig and the Arans, to the left of which the dusky Berwyns
form the horizon, till we come again to the Breiddens.

In descending to the Ruthin road you may either make for its
nearest point at the O*rnant Slate-quarry, almost due east, or
strike north-eastward and cross the neighbouring height of Moel-y-
Faen, on the far slope of which and just above the road is another
extensive range of slate-quarries. The latter is the route if you
want to keep on high ground, and go the entire circuit by the
" World's End."

(ii) By the camp on Moel-y-Gaer to Moel Morfydd is a stiff ½ hr.
of thick heather, etc., but the view from the latter is better than
from Gamelin, being wider to the S. and more directly down the
valley towards Llangollen. Descend the steep S. side of Morfydd
and you will strike a delightful grass road which presently joins
the road on the N. side of the Dee. About a mile up-stream cross
the bridge to Glyndyfrdwy Sta. and Inn (good).

6. **Eglwyseg Rocks**. These rocks, which were described many
years ago by Pennant ("Tour in Wales") as the only disfigurement of the Llangollen scenery, consist of a fine limestone escarpment about 1,200 ft. above sea-level and 4 miles long from end to
end. Their nearest point is about two miles from the town, from
which, however, Castle Dinas Bran all but hides them. Once on
the top you may enjoy a breezy walk over short grass as far as
you like. Perhaps the pleasantest way is to attack them at
their east end, which may be reached either by following the
Ruabon road for about 1½ miles, or by crossing the canal beyond the
station and taking the lane to the right, which works round to the
east side of Dinas Bran. The view of the main valley and its
little tributary subordinate ones is very pleasing, and the only
parts of the rocks themselves which we think will justify the
word "disfigurement" are those on which quarrying operations
have produced a raw appearance in the face of the cliff. The
most conspicuous mountains visible are Arenig and the Arans,
which rise beyond the Berwyns and the Moel-y-Gamelin peaks.

Eastwards, from the edge of this long cliff, stretches a table-
land, as dull and featureless as limestone uplands usually are.
Its highest point, Cefn-y-fedw (1,765 ft.), will hardly tempt us to
quit the edge, from which it is more than half a-mile distant.
Better to continue northwards till cliff and valley merge into one
at the fine recess, between Craig-y-Forwyn, N., and Craig Aderyn,
S., known as the **World's End**. You will easily find your way
down into this and from it a fair road descends to Llangollen
(abt. 5 m.) giving the choice, abt. 2 m. down the valley, of continuing on below the Eglwyseg Rocks viâ Dinbren to the town; or
turning W. and following the left bank of the stream-valley to the
Ruthin road just N. of Pen-y-bryn (Inn). In the latter case
(World's End to Llangollen, 6 m.) do not make the mistake of
taking the lane which follows the right bank of the stream when
it turns off W. It is pleasant enough but involves a sharp climb
out of it to Bergoed (Farm) and a great détour N. to Pentre-dwfr
(Inn) before we can conveniently get across the valley.

7. **Y Fron-fawr** (3 *m.*). This is the delightful little green hill north of the town, between the valleys which are threaded by the Ruthin road and that to "World's End." To reach it cross the river, the railway and the canal, and beyond the canal take the road to the left instead of proceeding by the footpath to Dinas Bran. In ⅓ mile the road bears to the right and then left again round *Dinbren Hall*, on passing which you go to the right for a few yards, then left, and so up the green slope to the summit of the hill. On the way up, there is a very pleasing view of the Abbey and glen of Valle Crucis, and from the top the view, though confined by higher hills. is charming all round. You may descend towards the far end of the ridge and return to Llangollen by the Ruthin road and the Abbey.

8. **Glyn Ceiriog** (3 *m.*), **and the Berwyns.** Fine air and good views are the inducements for this walk. Little of special interest is passed close at hand. The return may be made from Glyndyfrdwy (pron. "Glyndov'rdwy") station, 5 miles west of Llangollen. There is an *inn* a little way from the station.

Quit Llangollen by the road which goes to the right of the Grapes Hotel and passes Plas Newydd (*p.* 9), ¼ mile beyond which, and after crossing a brook. turn sharp to the right and ascend by a road that is carried up the hill on the left hand of the dell containing the brook. There is a fine retrospect as soon as you get high enough to overlook Pen-y-Coed, Eglwyseg Rocks and Wynnstay Park being prominent. The range of hills which we are now ascending is thickly planted with fir trees. At cross-roads at the top keep straight on.

Glyn Ceiriog (Principal Inn : *New Inn Hotel*), usually shortened into Glyn, but whose full name is Llansantfraid Glyn Ceiriog, is reached by a steep descent. It is a busy little village, connected with Chirk by a tramway made for the carriage of slates, but also conveying passergers. The distance is 5½ miles, but the terminus of the tramway is at Pontfaen, a long half-mile from Chirk station. There are about three trains each way in the summer months, occupying three-quarters of an hour on the journey. (*See* "*Bradshaw.*")

Glyn Ceiriog to Llanarmon, 5 *m* ; **Llanraiadr-yn-Mochnant.** 12 *m* ; **and Pistyll Rhaiadr,** 16 *m.*

The road onward descends to the Ceiriog river, in which there is good fishing. and continues side by side with it to **Llanarmon** (Inn), 8 *m.* from Llangollen. Here it leaves the Ceiriog glen and ascends, having on the right hand a shoulder of *Mynydd Tarw* (2,236 *ft.*), one of the chief Berwyns. From the top of the hill, which forms the watershed between the tributaries of the Dee and the Severn, two roads lead to Llanrhaiadr-yn-Mochnant. The one bending to the left round Mynydd-mawr is the nearest. The other reaches that village by the valley of the Twrch. **Llanraiadr-yn-Mochnant** (Hotel : *Wynnstay Arms*) is chiefly visited on account of its proximity to Pistyll Rhaiadr, one of the most striking waterfalls in Wales. Unfortunately, the situation of the fall is wide of ordinary through-routes. About 4 miles from Llanrhaiadr down the

Tanat valley is Llangedwyn, where there is a good inn much frequented by any ers

Llanrhaiadr to Llanfyllin, 6 m. Leave the village at its east end, and in a short mile take the road on the right, and at cross-roads, a few hundred yards further, keep straight on and cross the *River Tanat*, a good sized trout stream. Thenceforward the road, a main one, is unmistakable. As the higher ground is reached the view backward of Llanrhaiadr and the Tanat valley is of much beauty of the softer kind. The peak that presently becomes prominent to the nort.-west is *Gyrn Moelfre*, 1,719 feet.

For **Llanfyllin** *see Index.*

To Glyndyfrdwy station. Instead of going off at the finger-post to Glyn Ceiriog, keep on till the top of the ridge is reached, and then turn to the right and keep westward along the high ground. In a mile you will pass the *Grouse Box* (1715 ft.) so conspicuous from the heights on the other side of Llangollen. From it there is a wide view, but a still better one from the loftier height that rises on the north side of the road a long mile further on. The peaks of Snowdon are seen W.N.W., and to the right of them the Glyders and the tamer ridge of which Carnedd Dafydd and Llewelyn are the highest points. Moel Siabod rises a little nearer, between Snowdon and the Glyders.

Half-a-mile beyond this height we may turn to the right and, **after a descent** of about two miles, enter the Llangollen and **Corwen** road, a mile short of Glyndyfrdwy Station. The *Berwyn Hotel* is a good little inn.

9. **Wynnstay** (Sir Watkin Williams-Wynn, Bart., M.P.) adjoins the town of Ruabon, 6 miles distant by rail from Llangollen. The *House* is not shown, but, except on special occasions either there or in the Park, no respectable applicant is denied admission to the latter at the Ruabon Lodge, which is close to the town.

Should the Ruabon Lodge happen to be closed there is a public way across the park from the Broth Lodge, which is about half-a-mile from the former up the hill past Ruabon Vicarage. This leads to Nant-y-bellan Tower, but misses the Bath grounds.

The following round of 4 to 5 miles embraces all that is best worth seeing, and supposes the tourist to enter at the *Ruabon Lodge* and to quit the grounds at the Waterloo Lodge, close to Cefn Station on the main line, 1¾ miles south of Ruabon by road or rail. Chirk Station and village (Hotel : *Hand*) are 4 miles south by rail and 3¼ miles by road, and the return thence to Llangollen *viâ* Chirk castle is under 5½ miles. If Chirk Castle (*page* 20) is included in the round, then a public day should be chosen for the excursion.

To prevent disappointment we may begin by saying that Wynnstay Park proper is not in itself of any very remarkable beauty, and the House, which is well seen in the course of the walk, was rebuilt some years ago after a fire. It is the situation of the Park at the entrance of the Vale of Llangollen that is its chief charm, and the Dee valley from Nant-y-bellan to Cefn is certainly delightful. Entering at the Ruabon Lodge, we are at the end of the *Great Avenue*, about a mile long, which leads to the House. Instead of pursuing it we turn sharply to the right through an iron-gate and enter the *Bath grounds*. Keep to the left along the upper path. On the right are delightful peeps of an ornamental piece of water seen through trees of noble growth. In about 5 minutes turn down to the right to the Bath. Here is a house for the attendant, a portico, and the bath itself about 40 feet by 20 feet. The whole is rather dilapidated, moss and weeds and a scarcity of water telling of disuse. Leaving the Bath, take a path south-west up a gentle ascent to an arbour. Here we command a view of the lake, and continuing on, with the lake on the right, from the highest part of the walk a small cascade appears on its far side. Abundance of seats enable us to take matters as easily as we like. Still pursuing the path, a slight deviation to the left brings us to the *Pillar*, a Doric column, 101 feet high, erected to the memory of the 5th baronet (d. 1840) by his mother. Leaving the Bath grounds by a gate close to the Pillar, a few minutes brings us in full sight of **Wynnstay** itself, and westward is a fine view up the Vale, while abundance of deer, red and fallow, lend grace and life to the Park. We now follow the drive southwards and quit the Park proper, passing on the right a small lodge. Then by the first turn to the right, and past another lodge the public road is struck. Following this road and facing westward we see close at hand a large stuccoed mansion, *Pen-y-nant*, which we pass on our left. Then, a few yards beyond a cottage, we take a drive or broad path through a field into a wood and so in a few yards reach the **Nant-y-bellan** Tower, erected to the memory of the officers of the "Ancient Britons" regiment, commanded by the Sir Watkin of that day, who fell in the Irish troubles of '98. It is not, however, this memorial that is the attraction here, but the "Marten's Dingle," for that is the interpretation of Nant-y-bellan. At the foot of the steep and wooded declivity sparkles the Dee, its opposite bank also richly clad, but of less elevation. Westward is a lovely view, the chief points in which are the Viaduct, Castell Dinas Bran, the sharply defined extremity of Cyrn-y-Brain and the Berwyns beyond Llangollen. The tower to the right of the viaduct is the *Waterloo Tower*, which is the next point to be made for. The best way to it is to retrace our route as far as the mansion Pen-y-nant. Opposite this go through a gate and follow the path across the field and through a wood to a broad drive. This drive leads to the Waterloo Lodge and affords delightful views of the Dee, seen through the trees on the left hand. From the Waterloo Lodge a path on the right leads to the *Waterloo Tower*, which, though out of sight, is only about 200 yards off. This monument, built by the late baronet to commemorate the battle, is in no wise remarkable, and its foot commands no view both on account of the comparative lowness of its site and its environment of trees. From the summit there is a fine one, greatly marred, however, by the immediate neighbourhood of collieries. **Cefn Station** is close by, but if the walk is to be extended to Chirk, then from the Lodge gate we turn to the left and cross a fine iron bridge. The high-road to Chirk is unmistakable.

A corner may be cut off by turning up a road on the left, about ½ m. from the iron bridge, near some yellow cottages. About 100 yards along it take the second of two stiles, not the first on the right, but the one in front.

On the left as we follow the road the prospect is dull, but on the right is the beautiful demesne of Chirk Castle. The first large building we come to in **Chirk** village is the *Hand Hotel* (comfortable) and a turn to the right, just short of it, is the way to the station, 5 minutes' walk distant.

If **Chirk Castle** is to be visited on the return to Langollen, then any doubt as to the days on which it is shown can be solved by applying at the Chirk Castle Office, at Chirk, where under certain circumstances a special order can be obtained on non-public days. The Castle is described and the several routes to it from Llangollen are given below. From Chirk village its distance is about 1¼ m. and from the station 1½ m.

The traveller with half-an-hour to spare should, from the south end of the village, turn to the right in order to see the *viaduct* and *aqueduct* that cross the beautiful valley of the Ceiriog.

To reach the castle from the *Hand Hotel* we pass the station and beyond the railway take a stile on the right, and then, when a lane is reached, turn right and then left through a gate into the Park.

10. **Chirk Castle** (*Admission on M., W., and F., 2s. 6d. for a party of five or less, and 6d. for each additional person; Schools 5s. per 100 persons; the money is given to the local charities. Special orders for which double fees are charged can be obtained for non-public days by applying to the Agent, Chirk Castle Office, Chirk*), the noble seat of Mr. Middleton Biddulph, is approachable from Llangollen by several routes:

(i) By rail to Chirk Station, 10 m.; and thence walk 1½ m. (*above*).

(ii) By rail to Trevor Station, 3½ m.; and thence walk across the valley by Pont-Cysylltau (aqueduct), and then by London and Holyhead road to Chirk village, 8 m. from Trevor Station, and 1½ m. from the Castle.

(iii) By London and Holyhead road all the way, 9 m.

(iv) By mountain-road *vid* Pennant, 6 m.

(v) By bridle-road over east end of Glyn Hill (Cefn-uchaf), 4 m.

Of these routes (iv) and (v) are the only ones here demanding description, but in regard to (ii) it should be mentioned that the view from the aqueduct up the Vale is beautiful. The walk to the castle from Chirk village and station is given sufficiently above, and Wynnstay and Chirk from Ruabon station, whence walk to Llangollen, on *page* 18. Pedestrians equal to a walk of 10 miles are recommended to take route (iv) on the outward, and route (v) on the homeward journey. The steepness of the ascent will cause plenty of pauses to admire the backward view during the former, and then an easy descent will enable the full beauty of the Vale to be enjoyed in returning. Those who only walk from Chirk to Llangollen should take route (v) which is given in that direction *page* 23. Here we describe both (iv) and (v) *to* Chirk.

(iv) **To Chirk Castle viâ Pennant**, 6 *m.*

Take the road on the right of the *Grapes Hotel*, and about ¼ mile past *Plas Newydd* in full view of Pengwern Hall (farm) take the second road on the right. As the higher ground is reached, a fine backward view is obtained in which Crow Castle is the dominant feature. Presently, when the road bends to the left, a finger post " to Glyn " is passed, and then in a few hundred yards the top of the ridge is gained at a junction of roads. Here turn left, and then almost immediately to the right. The road soon becomes a broad green lane, and branch-roads on either hand are to be eschewed. Soon after passing between some fir-plantations it swerves a little to the left and drops quickly to *Pennant*, a farmstead whose only importance is to define the route. Just past the farm-buildings turn up to the right and over a brow to a second farm, and then by a short and final climb to a third. Here, where route (v) converges, Chirk Castle and the lake in front of it are in full view and form a fine foreground to a far-stretching prospect. Descend the hill and enter the park by a gate close to a cottage and follow the road which leads, with the lake on our left, to the Home Farm close under the castle. Keep on along the road as it winds. *Offa's Dyke*, a not very noticeable green swelling, is crossed and a high gate is passed through, and then we bend round to the left, past a range of offices, and through another gate. Here, instead of following the drive round to the front, we ascend some steps on the right to a door up a short passage. *For a description of the castle, see page* 22.

(v). **To Chirk Castle direct**, *pedestrian route*, 4 *m.*

Leave the town by the road on the left of the *Grapes Hotel*, and at a fork beyond the Llangollen turnpike take the right-hand branch, and at the next fork the right-hand branch again. The road skirts the prettily-wooded hill, *Pen-y-Coed*, and passes to the right of the handsome and modern timber-built mansion, *Tynwr*. A little further cross roads are reached, and the road from the town past Plas Newydd and Pengwern Hall comes in on the right. We keep straight on, and ascend steeply, and at a junction of tracks some way up bend to the left. Henceforward no mistake is possible. Two fine beeches are passed, and the track—a cart-road little used—near the top of the winding ascent joins a road by

which we keep straight on over the brow. The views of the Vale
and away eastward are wide and beautiful all the way up. A long
descent past a cottage brings us to a junction of roads at a farm,
and Chirk Castle is in full view below on the left. The way to it
is obvious, but see end of (iv).

Chirk Castle is rectangular in plan, with a massive round
tower at each angle. The north front, in which is the principal
entrance gateway, is well seen as we approach from Llangollen
by the routes described above. At a distance the many chimneys
detract somewhat from the dignity of its appearance, but close at
hand its massive bulk gives an impression of great strength. The
present castle is the successor of a much older work, and dates
from the time of Edward I. After having belonged to many noble
owners, it was bought in 1595 by Sir Thomas Middleton, the Lord
Mayor, who having himself later on joined the Roundheads, had
to besiege his own castle when it was occupied for a time by the
Cavaliers. A little while afterwards, Sir Thomas, having returned
to his allegiance, was himself besieged, and the castle was taken,
and suffered great damage. After the Restoration, Sir Thomas
came by his own again, and repaired the works at great cost. It
is still in the possession of his family, in the female line.

Entering by the door up the steps on the right of the approach
to the main entrance, we find ourselves in a *quadrangle* about 160
by 100 feet, of which the south side is unrestored, but in excellent
preservation, the windows throughout being Elizabethan. On
entering the castle the *billiard-room* first calls for notice. Around
the walls is a grim collection of matchlocks, old armour, and
sundry antlers. Notice at one end of the room an inlaid picture
of the castle in 1735, " done by the porter, Roberts," who was
porter at Ruthin Castle, then in the possession of the Middletons.
Another object of interest is the illuminated grant of a baronetcy
to Sir Thomas, 1661.

A fine staircase, restored like the rest of the principal rooms
by Pugin, leads to the *State apartments*, and here the explana-
tions given by the intelligent cicerone relieve us of the task of
description. The chief items of interest are the portraits which
adorn the walls, and amongst these, in addition to family portraits,
are the easily recognised faces of Charles I., Charles II., William
III. and Queen Mary, and the Duke of Monmouth. The bedroom
in which Charles I. slept is shown, and also the bed, removed long
since to another room. To obtain an idea of the massiveness
of the structure one has only to step into a room opening from the
royal bed-chamber. This apartment has, in recent years, been
made in the thickness of the walls. Two female portraits by Lely
are subjects of great beauty, but the gem of the objects shown
is an ebony *cabinet* with tortoiseshell exterior panels. Inside it
is embellished with exquisite silver plaque work and a series of
sacred pictures, painted on copper and attributed to Rubens. It
is insured for £5,000, probably far below its marketable value.

The tradition is that Charles II offered a peerage to Sir Thomas Middleton, which was declined by him, and that thereupon the King gave him the cabinet as a mark of his regard. A fine view from the ramparts is a fitting conclusion to our visit.

Chirk Castle to Llangollen, *direct* 4 *m.*

The last half of this walk commands a fine view of the Vale. Leave the Castle by the Farm road (*i.e.* bear round to the right after passing through the drive gates) and on quitting the Park ascend the hill. At the junction of roads at the top turn to the right and still ascend. A cottage is passed, and keeping straight on over the brow, a gate which seems to block the way is seen ahead. Here the road turns to the left, but we pass through the gate and follow a cart or bridle-road which, passing two fine beeches half way down, leads without possibility of mistake to cross-roads at the east end of Pen-y-Coed. Here the left-hand road will take us by Pengwern Hall and Plas Newydd to the town, while the one straight onward winds past the handsome timber-built mansion of Tyndwr. round the prettily wooded height of Pen-y-Coed, and enters Llangollen through the turnpike on the Holyhead road.

Corwen.

————◆————

Hotel: *Owen Glyndwr*, 5 min. walk E. of the station. **Post** *arr. abt.* 7 *a.m.*; 3.45 *p.m.*; *dep.* 9.30 *a.m.*, 5 and 8 *p.m.* *Pop. abt.* 2,500.

For route from Llangollen, see p. 3.

Corwen is in itself a dull-looking, old-fashioned town, but a not unimportant railway junction. The hotel is a good one of the old sort. The place as a whole, when compared with the generality of popular resorts in North Wales, possesses no special attraction except for the sportsman. The Dee and its tributary, the Alwen, which joins it about 1½ miles west of the town, afford good sport and may be fished on moderate terms.

The **Church** lies back from the main street near the hotel. It is a plain building with a long nave. There is nothing remarkable inside, unless it be a monument of *Iorwerth Sulien*, one of its early vicars. Outside, however, are two noteworthy objects : the shaft of a cross accredited to the 8th century near the S.W. corner, 8 feet high and inscribed with the figure of a dagger ; and, on the lintel of the south door, the mark of Glyndwr's dagger thrown, says tradition, from the heights above to mark the temporary displeasure of the great national hero at whose birth "the frame and "huge foundations of the earth shaked like a coward." A row of

almshouses on the edge of the church-yard shows the comfortable
provision made by a Mr. Eyton for the widows of six Merionethshire
ministers. Corwen was the head-quarters of Owen Glyndwr, and
to him it owes its place in history. It was here that he gathered
his forces before the battle of Shrewsbury, and standing on the top
of the rock behind the town, beheld "nearly 40 square miles of
his own land." We cannot do better than visit his view-point. It
is the spot marked by the obelisk-like cairn we have already
seen from the railway. To reach it we pass the hotel, and in
about 100 yards turn up a lane to the right. This takes us at
once through a gate from which we may attack the hill by a steep
footpath at once, or by continuing straight on for a while and then
bending sharp to the left, modify the steepness of the ascent. The
summit is a green little area or terrace, railed round and having
as its centre-piece a cairn, 20 feet high, erected as a memorial
of the marriage of the Prince of Wales. The view is a very
pleasing one and the best to be had in the immediate neighbourhood of Corwen. Below, the town and the church are conspicuous:
beyond them the river sweeps round a flat expanse of meadow-
land. Looking across the railway bridge we see the many-peaked
Clwydian range with Moel Fammau, indicated by the Jubilee
monument, for its crowning height. The view down the Dee
valley extends to the green hill which is over the Llantysilio
tunnel, 7 miles away, the gap between which and Moel-y-Gamelin
is partly occupied by Castell Dinas Bran. In the other direction
the main river bends from the south and the valley seen is that of
its tributary, the Alwen, descending from the high ground between
Corwen and Bettws-y-Coed. The crowning summit some way
south of this valley is Arenig. Northwards the prospect has no
special feature, and southwards the Berwyn moors shut out all
view.

Sojourners at Corwen may tramp to their hearts' content over
the heathery Berwyn hills, some of their chief summits, Moel
Ferna (2,070 ft.), Cader Fronwen (2,573 ft.), and Moel Sych (2,716 ft.)
to wit, being all within range of a day's walk. They command
fine distant views of the chief mountains of North Wales, but in
themselves are hardly of sufficient interest to call for special description in a general guide-book. Their carpeting of heather
makes them very tiresome going for the ordinary mountaineer,
who may gracefully and without personal sacrifice acquiesce in the
claims of the sportsman to their sole proprietorship.

**Corwen to Ruthin, 12 m; Denbigh, 18½ m; St. Asaph, 24 m;
and Rhyl, 30 m. By rail (L. & N.W.).**

Route fully described between Rhyl and Ruthin in "North Wales, Part I."

Between Corwen and Ruthin there is little calling for special remark. The
line affords a prospect of undulating country westwards as far as Arenig, and,
after crossing the Dee, enters a shallow valley in which is Gwyddelwern Station.
Between this and the next station, Derwen, is the watershed of the Dee and
Clwyd respectively, which here forms the boundary-line between the counties

of Merioneth and Denbigh. The church stands a little west of the line, and though small, contains a handsome 15th century screen and rood-loft. In the graveyard is a much weathered 13th century cross.

The next station is *Nantclwyd*, near to which, on the right-hand side, in a well-wooded park, stands *Nantclwyd Hall*. The narrow glen of *Nantclwyd* is then entered, and after passing under the *Eyarth Rocks* (limestone), through which there is a pretty peep westwards, we reach *Eyarth* Station. Hereabouts the Vale of Clwyd, flat and fertile, opens out on the right, and the long Clwydian range, with the monument-crowned Moel Fammau as its highest peak, is seen stretching away to the north.

Ruthin, Denbigh, and St. Asaph are described in the Rhyl section of Part I, and as we pass along the Vale of Clwyd between those towns there is nothing to detain the tourist. As seen from the line the valley is chiefly interesting to the agriculturist.

Corwen to Cerrig-y-Druidion, 10 m; Pentre Voelas, 15½ m; and Bettwys-y-Coed, 22 m.

This portion of the famous Holyhead road has been almost entirely extinguished as a tourist route by the railways. The greater part of it is over a monotonous upland, without any height or boldness of outline in the surrounding hills to compensate for the lack of the softer features of scenery.

The Holyhead road, described with such gushes of admiration by some writers, is very trying to the pedestrian. On many parts of it you may travel mile after mile without finding a blade of grass on either side to relieve the monotony of the "hard high road," and the stone walls which flank it are, in their rigid regularity, only surpassed by the poplar rows of France and the Low Countries. The greater part of it, however, passes through very fine scenery, and even in that part which we are now describing we must admit some redeeming features. There are good homely inns at Cerrig-y-Druidion and Pentre-Voelas; between Corwen and the former place a charming river-bit is passed, and the last 3 miles to Bettws-y-Coed command as beautiful views as one could wish to see. The road is also, after the gradual ascent to Cerrig-y-Druidion has been mastered, a good one for bicyclists.

The Route. Quitting the town at the station, our road is identical for half-a-mile with that to Dolgelley. Then it turns sharply to the right and crosses the railway and the river *Dee*. The *Alwen*, a tributary stream, is also crossed a little more than a mile further, and kept close on the right hand for another two miles. This river comes down from the hilly and little-visited country between Ruthin and Cerrig-y-Druidion, and as far as the point at which we abandon it for its little feeder, the *Geirw*, it forms the boundary between the counties of Denbigh and Merioneth. The Geirw is crossed immediately beyond the point at which the valley of the larger stream strikes away to the north. Just beyond the crossing we pass the *Goat Inn*; and 1½ miles further we reach the best bit of scenery between Corwen and Pentre Voelas. This is where a road comes in on the left hand across **Pont-y-Glyn**. The bridge consists of one arch thrown over a rocky part of the river, at a height of 50 or 60 feet. Above and below, the stream is broken by cataracts, of which the chief one is beneath the bridge, and the precipitous banks on either side are richly clothed with fine timber. The comparatively uninteresting character of the country for several miles around makes this beautiful little scene a particularly grateful one to the traveller. After quitting it he will meet with little to arrest the eye until, in

4 miles, he approaches *Cerrig-y-Druidion*. The last mile of the road is perfectly straight, and to the right of it, ¾ m. away, is the British Camp, *Pen-y-Gaer*, the moat of which may still be traced. Hither, says tradition, Caractacus fled for refuge after his defeat by the Romans in the Western counties, and here he was betrayed by Cartismaudna. The extent of the camp is 6 or 7 acres.

Cerrig-y-Druidion—or, the "stones of the Druids," if we are to accept the vulgar interpretation—lies slightly to the right of the high-road, which swerves to the left a little short of it. To pass through it adds a few yards to the distance, and nothing to the interest of the journey. There are two very fair inns, the *Lion* in the village, and the *Saracen's Head* on the high-road.

From the village the road is again painfully straight—two miles without a bend, and no scenery. Here we cross the watershed of the Dee and the Conway, and in another mile arrive at a spot which has possibly roused our curiosity for some miles past—*Cernioge*, to wit. In the good old days when 10 miles an hour was rapid travelling and the "Wild Irishman" not even a dream of the future, this was a change-house on the great Holyhead track and the milestones, in both directions, still remind us of the fact. Now it has subsided into a farm with a few sycamores to break the force of the winds to which it is exposed on all sides. A similar example on this same route of the effect of rail on road is that of the "Mona Inn" in Anglesey, which still figures on about twenty milestones between Bangor and Holyhead, though the roof has fallen in years ago. This last snare is a serious one to the unfortunate tourist who puts his faith in milestones and is foolish enough to waste precious time in tramping Anglesey, since there is no entertainment for man or beast within 7 or 8 miles in either direction. On our present route, however, ample atonement is made by the pleasant and comfortable old hostelry at **Pentre Voelas**, 2 miles beyond the treacherous Cernioge. Here, too, the scenery begins. From the crest of the road beyond the inn two peaks of Snowdon come into view a little left of the nearer and lower Moel Siabod; then we cross and recross the Conway as it descends from the wild hill-solitude of Llyn Conway, and changes its nakedness for a fringe of woodland flowers and foliage. From the second crossing, *Paddock Bridge*, 2 miles beyond Pentre Voelas, there is a very pretty peep up a little affluent on the left, and in another mile the mountain prospect opens up finely in front. Hereabouts, too, we are not far from Glan Conway, a residence of Lord Penbryn, which occupies a wooded height on the north of the road. As the mountains come into view we have Carnedd Dafydd and Llewelyn directly in front of us, then the sharp summit of the Tryfan, between which and the unmistakable peaks of Snowdon the Glyders appear. Nearest and most prominent of all, however, is Moel Siabod, whose graceful peak shows to great advantage at the far end of the Lledr valley. Its position as seen from here, is between Snowdon and the Glyders.

Two miles short of Bettws, 4½ beyond Pentre Voelas, a road strikes away to to the left for Penmachno and Ffestiniog. A few yards further the Conway **Falls** are seen at the bottom of a deep ravine on the same side. (They are reached by a footpath which leaves the road 175 yds. beyond the Penmachno turn, *see Part I., p.* 120.) The view up the Lledr valley from this part of the road is very fine. All this scenery, however, is described under the head of Bettws-y-Coed (*Part I*). Those who wish to visit the *Fairy Glen* on the way may take a broad green path which strikes to the left out of the main road at the same place as the turn for the Conway Falls, and runs parallel with it on a lower level. The wicket-gate by which the glen is reached is about ¾ m. down this track and beyond a cottage.

Our main road now descends rapidly and, crossing the Waterloo Bridge and the railway, enters **Bettws-y-Coed** close to the station.

Corwen to Bala (a) by the *old* road 12 *m*; (b) by the *new* road 13 *m*. *For route by rail see p.* 4.

The above roads, except for half-a-mile at starting and a mile at the end, are distinct throughout. The *new* road which ascends the valley of the Dee through the "Vale of Edeyrnion" is to be preferred alike by the pedestrian, the cyclist, and those who drive; the scenery along it is more varied, and the road-gradients more easy than by the *old* road.

(a) The *old* road, 12 *m*. About ½ mile west of Corwen station turn to left and cross the railway and the Dee by the Holyhead road. In half-a-mile the road to Ruthin goes off on the right, and a short distance along it on the left is **Rug Chapel**, "which contains some curious carving and painting of the period to which its foundation belongs, 1637." Our way lies past the grounds of Rug, once belonging to Owen Glyndwr and later a seat of the Vaughan family. Then the Alwen is crossed at *Pont-melin-rug*, and ¾ mile west of it we reach the *Druid Inn* and turn to the left up the Nant Ffrauan valley, which is of only commonplace character. About 3 miles up it, and about half-a-mile beyond the point where the stream is crossed for the third time, on a hill on the north side, is the vitrified fort of *Caer Cruyni*, and a tower which was erected in 1841 on the occasion of Sir Watkin Wynn's majority. About 7 miles from Corwen near the summit of the route a small public-house is passed. The descent towards Bala is pleasantly wooded and affords peeps of the lake and of the mountains around its head, chief of which are the Arans and Arenig-fawr. As we enter the valley of the Dee the "new" road, described below comes in on the left and, passing *Llanfor*, we enter Bala over the *Treweryn* stream close to the station.

(b) The *new* road 13 *m*. This passes through the villages of Cynwyd and Llandrillo, where there are inns, and crosses the Dee close to Llandderfel Station where there is also an inn. The scenery, without being remarkable, is pretty, especially about and beyond the last named point. The railway, which is never far removed from the road, enables the pedestrian to abbreviate his walk at will at any of the intermediate stations of Cynwyd, Llandrillo or Llandderfel.

Take the road going west from Corwen Station, and where the Holyhead road goes off on the right keep straight on. In a trifle over a mile the poor little church of *Llangar* is on the right, and at 2 miles from starting the village of **Cynwyd** (Inn, *Prince of Wales*) is reached. [Here, by proceeding about half-a-mile up the Trystion stream, a pretty bit of glen and a waterfall can be seen. The waterfall is ¾ m. from Cynwyd Station.] At **Llandrillo**, 5 *m*., there is a good inn, the *Dudley Arms*, but nothing else of much interest to the tourist. Turning to the right a little beyond the inn, the road in a rather long mile approaches the Dee, and then ascends, winding round a spur that projects towards the river and having the charming seat *Crogen* below on the right. When the top of the ascent is reached the view ahead of the well clad and here shut-in Vale of Edeyrnion is delightful. At **Llandderfel Station** (*Inn*) we cross the railway and the Dee. The new mansion, a short distance up stream on the south bank, is *Palé* (H. Robertson, Esq.), and opposite to it is another seat, I' *Fron-heulog*, backed by a richly-wooded hill. Llandderfel village (*page* 4) is a quarter of a mile on the right after crossing the river. We however turn to the left, and then for the next 3 miles keep close company with the Dee, as it comes down through a narrow well-wooded glen from the meads below Bala, which is entered a short mile beyond Llanfor.

BALA SECTION.

𝔅𝔞𝔩𝔞.

Hotels : *White Lion, Plasgoch, Bull's Head ;* all in High Street, within 4 minutes walk of the Station, which is at the bottom of the street.

Post : *Arr. abt. 7 a.m., 6 p.m. ; dep. 9 a.m., 7.30 p.m. Open (weekdays) 7 a.m. to 9 p.m. ; (Sundays) 8 to 16 a.m.*

Population : *abt.* 1,500.

Distances : *(By rail)* Arenig Station, 8 *m.* Bettws-y-Coed, 38 *m.* Corwen, 12 *m.* Dolgelley, 17½ *m.* Ffestiniog, 21½ *m.* Llangollen, 22½ *m.* Llanuwchllyn, 5¼ *m.* *(By road)* Dinas Mawddwy, 18 *m.* Llanfyllin, 21 *m.* Llanrhaidr-yn-Mochnant 17 *m.* Fyrnwy Valley (Liverpool Reservoir), 13 *m.* Pistyll Rhaiadr 7½ *m.* on foot from Llandrillo Station.

Bala is a small market town, pleasantly situated on the meads a quarter of a mile from the lower end of Bala Lake. The river Treweryn, coming down from the dreary watershed that is crossed by the Ffestiniog branch railway, flows past the station on its way to join the Dee close to Bala Junction. The town, both in size and population only a big village, has no " lions," but the main street, about a quarter of a mile long, has a certain picturesqueness, due to a sprinkling of trees on either side of it. As we leave the station the prominent building away on the right is the *Calvanistic Methodist College* for the training of ministers, and close by, on our left, is the *Grammar School.* Just beyond this is **Tomen-y-Bala**, a small artificial mound, planted with evergreens and said to be of Roman origin, like the similar one to the south of the town, on the near side of the *old* and now disused station. The one we are passing is a capital view-point for the lake and the valley of the Dee. On the same side, just beyond this, is an *old church* in a ruinous condition, but noticeable for the complete mantle of ivy that enwraps its tower. With the mention of the handsome modern *Church*, by Ferrey, and a word of praise for the *White Lion*, our say about the town itself is completed.

As a tourist rendezvous, Bala has suffered by the opening in 1882 of the branch line to Ffestiniog, because many who used to break their journey before proceeding by coach now hurry through to Bettws-y-Coed, &c. without getting even a hasty glance at the lake.

Bala Lake (Llyn Tegid) is the only sheet of water of any considerable size in the Principality. Its extreme length is 3½ miles, and the breadth, which varies but little from end to end, a trifle over half a-mile. The scenery on its banks is softly beautiful, and in no wise grand, but the lofty ridge of the Arans, seen end-on as a cone beyond the head of the lake, and the steep escarpment of Arenig-fawr to the north-west of it, though both too far removed to be said to dominate it effectively, prevent the reproach of tameness. Indeed, from nowhere else do these mountains appear to such advantage as from the water, a fact not always easy for the visitor to verify owing to the scarcity of boats—a due supply of which would, we fancy, do much to reinstate Bala in public favour, in spite of the fishing being chiefly for " coarse " fish. The circuit of the lake is worth making, either by road, 11 miles, or by rail to *Llanuwchllyn Station*, and back by road, 6 miles along the western shore. The views from the eastern bank, rail or road, are identical, and are briefly noted (*p.* 5).

Llanfor Church is only a mile beyond Bala Station, and thereabouts as well as up the Treweryn valley pleasant strolls are near at hand.

Excursions from Bala.

Except the tour of the Lake there are not many excursions that belong pre-eminently to Bala as headquarters, though its situation close to a railway junction brings a large district within reach of a day's outing by train. Of road-routes that by the Vale of Edeyrnion to Corwen and Llangollen is described the reverse way *p.* 27, and the mountain road viâ Llanuwchllyn and Bwlch-y-Groes to Dinas Mawddwy *page* 31. The only other routes that here call for description are to Pistyll Rhaiadr (*p.* 77), the highest waterfall of any volume in Wales, and to the Liverpool reservoir (*p.* 79) in process of construction in the upper valley of the Fyrnwy Verniew). In either case the tourist is recommended to look out the above references before starting on expeditions which, if too high hopes are entertained beforehand, may possibly prove disappointing. We may, however, add that Pistyll Rhaiadr is well worth seeing even at the cost of having to trudge over the highest point of the Berwyns, and that the interest of the reservoir is thus far only an engineering one as the water is not yet in. When it is, then Bala Lake will lose its pride of place, at any rate in regard to size if not in picturesqueness.

Tour of the Lake. *Bala to Llanuwchllyn by S.E. shore, road,* 5 *m.* (*rail* 5½ *m.*); *Llanuwchllyn to Bala by N.W. shore, road,* 6 *m.*

From the centre of the town the road strikes south-east, and in a third of a mile reaches the foot of the lake, of which a full-length view is afforded, with Aran Benllyn (" Head of the lake ")

rising from its upper end, and Cader Idris in the far distance;
eastward, Arenig presides over the scene. Then the Dee and the
railway are crossed, the former at its outlet from the lake, and the
latter ¼ mile further. Hence road and rail, running side by side,
hug the shore till its end is reached, 1½ miles short of Llanuwchllyn. The few objects of special interest on the way are named
in the description of the railway route (p. 5). Nearly a mile
beyond the end of the lake the Dinas Mawddwy road (v. 31)
diverges to the left, while our route descends to and crosses the
Twrch stream at the foot of a little glen (see below), whence,
turning to the right, we go under the railway, and if bound for the
station or inn, bend back on our previous course by another turn
to the right, recrossing the Twrch.

Llanuwchllyn (Inn : *Goat*, close to station) is a pleasant little village,
about a mile from the head of Bala Lake. For the general tourist the inn is a
good starting-point both for the ascent of the Arans (*see* " *Mountain Section* ")
and for the walk or drive over Bwlch-y-Groes (abt. 1950 feet) to Dinas Mawddwy.
The trout-fisher has also close at hand three streams: the *Lliw*, coming down
from Arenig, and passing about ¼ m. north of the village ; the *Dyfrdwy*, flowing through the village and having its source on the watershed over which the
railway climbs on its way to Drws-y-Nant ; and the *Twrch*, which rises amid
the wild moorland under the east flank of Aran Mawddwy, and is crossed by the
railway just west of the station. The lover of hill-tops may, without difficulty,
make the ascent of the Arans from the upper valleys of either of the last
named streams.

The pedestrian who finds himself at Llanuwchllyn Station with half-an-hour
to spare is advised to get a peep of the picturesque **Twrch glen** and of the
fine eastern crags of Aran Benllyn. To do this turn left at the end of the
station road, cross the bridge over the Twrch, and just beyond go through a
wicket-gate on the right and mount the foot-path to its junction with the
Dinas Mawddwy road. In returning, descend to the stream, cross it (an easy
matter, except in a spate), and return to the bridge by the left bank.

Of short walks in the neigbourhood the best, perhaps, is up the **Lliw
Valley** by road on the left bank. About 2½ miles from the station cross the
stream by a foot-bridge to the foot of *Carn Dochan*, of gold mining repute.
The ascent to the " Castle " on the summit is only a few minutes' climb, which
is rewarded by a lovely view. Distance, out and home, 6½ miles.

For **Caer Gai** see below.

From the station, entering—or regaining—the main road, we
turn to the right through Pandy hamlet, and then cross the
Dyfrdwy (Dee) to Llanuwchllyn village, a quarter of a mile
beyond which the *Afon Lliw* is crossed at *Pont Lliw*. Thence
we turn our back on the mountains, and the only further
direction that need be given is to avoid branch roads and
keep to the main one. After a picturesquely ivied house is
passed on the left, there is on the same side the reputed
Roman outpost of *Caer Gai*, now a tree-clad knoll, with a
house upon it and the faintest possible trace of a ditch on the
lower slopes close to the road. On the right the high ground

about Bwlch y-Groes soon comes into view, followed immediately
by the head of the lake, with a flag-staff on the far side marking
the private railway station used by the lord paramount of these
parts, Sir Watkin Wynn, when resident at *Glan-y-Llyn*. The
House is below on the right, where the road makes a short
ascent. On emerging from the trees we command a delightful
full-length view of the lake, and of Llangower combe across ft.
In the descent to the *Llafar* stream the cliffs of Arenig-fawr rise
boldly on the left, and to the right rear is the cone of the Arans.
From the bridge the flat top of Arenig-fach shows a trifle to the
right of his big brother. Onward the road keeps well above the
lake, which for awhile is only now and again to be seen through
the foliage. When the view opens, the eastern bank, dotted with
plantations, is very like the north side of the upper part of Loch
Tay, only with the part of Ben Lawers left out. About half-a-
mile from the foot of the lake, and $\frac{3}{4}$ m. short of Bala, at a turn
of the road, we reach **Llan-y-Cil**, the comely and restored little
parish church of Bala. Here, in the pretty yew-shaded grave-
yard, is the tomb of the saintly Thomas Charles, the John Wesley
of Welsh methodism. In the church the epitaph to the poet,
Rev. Evan Lloyd, is by Wilkes.

"Mr. Charles, setting himself whilst curate of Llanymawddwy, about the year
1783, to put down some bad practices that prevailed in that parish, began to
renew the old custom of catechising, but being looked upon as an innovator, was
complained of by his parishioners to their non resident rector and by him dismissed the curacy. Being suspected of Methodism, he was unable to obtain any
other curacy, and finding himself at length precluded from all hopes of preferment,
and almost all opportunity of usefulness in the Church, he joined the Methodists,
though in heart he still clung to the Church."—*Thomas*. Not his least title to
remembrance is the fact that he suggested the formation of the British and
Foreign Bible Society. He died in 1814.

Just as we leave the side of the lake, Cader Fronwen (2,573 ft.),
some 10 miles distant, peers over the intervening hills due east,
and looking back the summit of Aran Mawddwy (2,972 feet) rises
sharply behind Aran Benllyn.

Bala to Dinas Mawddwy over Bwlch-y-Groes, 18 *m.*; *road all the way.*

The pedestrian is advised to make use of the railway as far as
Llanuwchllyn (5$\frac{1}{2}$ *m. Route described p.* 5), whence, starting
from the inn or station we turn to the left when we reach the
main road, and proceed to the bridge over the Twrch, after
crossing which an angle of road may be cut off by taking a foot-
path up the fields on the right hand. In about 2 miles *Cwm Croes*
comes in on the right, and we get a fair view of the eastern
escarpment of Aran Benllyn, and then the steady 3-mile ascent
to the col begins. This part of the route is rather monotonous,
but when the summit-level, about 1,950 feet, is crossed, 5 *m.* from

Llanuwchllyn, the interest of the walk begins. For 1½ m. we descend rapidly a fine wild combe, down whose abrupt sides foam many rill-cascades—a pretty feature after rain. At the foot of the descent we find ourselves in a charming hill-environed amphi-theatre brightened by more cascades. We are now in the *Dyfi* (*Dovey*) *valley*, which is well wooded, but so completely shut in by abrupt hills of moderate elevation as to afford no extent of view except a peep of Aran Mawddwy from the turn of the road at the foot of the pass. In 9 *m.* we reach *Llanymawddwy*, a poor village with a roadside inn, and some 4 miles from it arrive at **Dinas Mawddwy**.

Bala to Pistyll Rhaiadr, *pedestrian route from Llandrillo Station, abt.* 7½ *m*; Llanrhaidr-yn-Mochnant (*good hotel*) 11½ *m.*

This route is breezy and crosses the Berwyns at their highest point. Owing to the heather which covers the upper parts of the range it is rather fatiguing, and it is only a good walker who will reach the waterfall in 3 hours from Llandrillo village.

From **Llandrillo Station**, 7 miles from Bala, it is ten minutes' walk to the village, for which we turn to the left at the junction of the station-road with the main one. The *Dudley Arms* is a good inn a few yards to the left when the village is entered. If a call there is not required, then we bear to the right past the church, cross the *Ccnding* stream, and turn to the right again up the valley. In about a mile we bear round to the left, and the rough road enters *Cwm Dywyll*, and when this subdivides, ascends the *Clochnant cwm* that comes down from under Cader Fronwen. Then the best way is to cross the *Clochnant* and follow the track over the spur on the south side of it to *Cwm Dywyll* again. At an abandoned slate-quarry the track comes to an end, and a stiffish climb through the heather in a direction south-east to the spur on the south side of the *cwm* lands us in about half an hour on the top of the ridge, along which we bear to the right to **Cader Berwyn**. The ridge is comparatively narrow and the view a wide one, but not of very great interest, as all the higher mountains are too distant. The Aran range is seen full length due west, and to the right of it is Arenig-fawr with the flat topped Arenig fach still more to the right. Southwards range upon range of apparently parallel ridges of undulating outline bespeak a district unattractive to the mountaineer. The summit close by, south-west, is Moel-sych, 2,716 feet, but there is no inducement to pro-long the heathery walk, and it is best to make down the steep intervening combe to the foot of *Llyn Llync-caws*, a lonely tarn whence a stream issues. On the left of the stream a path des-cends the green combe, and on reaching the main valley we get as best we may across the brook and find the waterfall only a short distance up the stream it joins. Close to the fall is a cottage where light refreshment may be obtained. For **Pistyll Rhaiadr** and **Llanrhaiadr**, *see pp.* 77, 76. The route to the latter is a fair road down the left side of the valley and quite unmistakable.

Bala to **Liverpool Reservoir,** "Lake Fyrnwy;" 10 *m. to
Rhiwargor,* its nearest point; 13 *m. to Llanwddyn,* about midway
down; 15 *m. to the embankment* at its foot.

There is no inn short of Llanwddyn, where are two or three public-houses.
The nearest sleeping accommodation to Llanwddyn is at Llanrhaiadr-yn-
Mochnant, good hotel, 12 *m.* by high-road (10 *m.* for pedestrians), or Llanfyllin,
12½ *m.*

As an excursion out and home from Bala, the distance, a good
30 miles if the great embankment at the foot be visited, is
almost prohibitive except for those who ride or drive. Pedestrians bound for the district served by the main Cambrian line,
can include a visit to Pistyll Rhaiadr by sleeping at Llanrhaiadr-
yn-Mochnant and thence making for Llanfyllin station, 6 *m.*

It is not every day, however, that we have the opportunity of
seeing the process of manufacturing a lake 12 miles in circuit,
and so even a long and not very interesting walk may be condoned;
and if we are to make acquaintance at all with the at present
humble village of Llanwddyn, we must not wait for the hotels
that will doubtless soon spring up after the filling of the lake, for
then it will be too late, as the village, or rather its present site,
will be deep below the waters.

Routes. (a) *From Bala by the Hirnant valley and over Bwlch
Rhiw Hirnant, a fair mountain road;*

(b) *From Llanuwchllyn station over Bwlch-y-Groes and then by
mountain-road too rough to drive over.*

The distances given at the head of this excursion refer to route
(*a*); that from Llanuwchllyn is about a mile shorter. The two
routes unite about 1½ *m.* short of Llanwddyn, and there is not
much to choose between them in respect of scenery. The
strongest epithets that either of them deserves are pretty and
solitary.

Route (a). After passing the foot of Bala lake and crossing
the railway, at a fork in the road we take the right-hand branch.
This leads over the hill to *Rhos-y-gwaliau,* where church and
parsonage are prettily placed above the stream, which we cross
and then ascend the wooded and narrow valley. Two miles from
the village the house and grounds of *Aber Hirnant* are passed on
our left. The road, as we continue up it, for a while becomes
rough, but affords a good view of the glen, in which a small pool
has been formed by a dam across the stream that has now shrunk
by subdivision to the dimensions of a burn. Then the valley loses
its wooded character and we drop to some cottages called *Moel-
y-ddinas,* just short of which we cross a burn by a foot-bridge. On
bearing round to the left a fine combe, locally called the *Horse-
shoe,* is at first sight the end of the glen, but on nearer approach
the road is found to bend round to the left and soon again to the
right into a desolate and bare combe, up which, first on the right

hand and then on the left, it ascends to the *bwlch*. This part of the walk is unredeemed dulness, and the descent on the other side is for two miles or more of a like quality. After crossing the Fyrnwy, on approaching *Rhiwargor Farm*, things improve, and when the new lake is an accomplished fact, this farm, which just escapes being inundated, will be delightfully situated. At present the fine bit of crag that overhangs the stream, some distance below the farm, is the only feature of any moment.

About a mile up the burn that joins the Fyrnwy at Rhiwargor, is a considerable waterfall, but it is not worth the tramp to obtain a near view of it. The road down the main valley leads to **Llanwddyn**, where the *Powis Castle* is the best of the poor inns. A grocer's shop hard by will, however, supply a biscuit, &c.

The road continues down the valley, and in about 1¼ m. from the village another road comes in from a side valley on the left. Up this valley, about 1¼ m., are the *quarries* whence the stone for the dam is obtained, and those who take the pedestrian route from the Reservoir to Llanrhaiadr, described in the small print next following, will pass them presently. For the foot of the Reservoir keep on down the main valley another ¾ m. *For details of the Reservoir see page* 79.

The best road for driving from the **Reservoir** to **Llanrhaiadr** or to **Llanfyllin** is identical for the first nine miles, reckoning from Llanwddyn. It turns to the left up a tributary valley about a mile below the dam and, keeping a general direction north-west, gradually climbs and crosses the watershed (between the Fyrnwy and Tanat basins; about 2½ m. beyond the summit the road for Llanfyllin goes off up-hill on the right, and in about 2¼ m. joins the direct one between that place and Llanrhaiadr). For Llanrhaiadr we keep straight on and cross the Tanat and then the Rhaiadr stream. A turn left a few hundred yards beyond the latter, and then after a like distance left again, brings us to **Llanrhaiadr** village. The hotel is close to the church.

Pedestrian route from the Reservoir to Llanrhaiadr. 10 m. from Llanwddyn ; 9½ m. from embankment ; 7½ m. from the Quarries.

From the foot of the Reservoir a lift may be obtained in the guard's van of one of the frequent return stone-trains that bring down material from the quarries. Mount the steep green hill above, (*i.e.*, north-east of) the quarries. A line of telephone wire gives the direction when near the top of the hill, the actual top of which, only a trifle higher than the course of the wire, is worth reaching for the sake of the good general view of the bed of the future lake. The Aran range with its fine escarpment, is well seen nearly due west, and to the left of it Cader Idris presents an end-on profile above an intervening ridge. Between south and south-west a long easy left-hand slope leading up to a slight point enables us to identify Plynlimon. After following the wire over the brow bear to the right down and across a bit of wet ground to a road which, when struck, follow to the left. Beyond some farm-buildings it soon drops to **Hirnant**, a tiny hamlet with church and parsonage, chapel and public-house all on the same small scale. Here we turn to the right, and keep to the road that descends the valley, with the stream below on our right, to

Pen-y-Bont (small inn, *Railway*), a hamlet on the main road between Bala and Llanfyllin, and distant from the latter town 6 *m*. Passing through the hamlet our road turns off on the left, crosses the Afon Tanat, and takes a straight course regardless of gradients. Happily, the steepest and longest hill is that by which, with a pretty view in front, we descend into **Llanrhaiadr**, where the comfortable *Wynnstay Arms Hotel* is close to the church, a few yards beyond the bridge over the Rhaiadr stream.

Route (b). From Llanuwchllyn station to Bwlch-y-Groes is described on p. 31. A short distance beyond the top take a rough road on the left and keep to it. At the first cottage reached a bottle of ginger beer can be had. Down a solitary glen, with a bright stream making frequent cascades, we drop to *Eunant* (which will be overflowed by the lake), and then cross the stream below the house. Route (*a*) is joined in about a mile across the main valley.

For ascents of the **Arans** *and* **Arenigs** *from Bala see " Mountain Section."*

Dolgelley.

Hotels : *Golden Lion, Ship, Angel,* all within ¼ m. of station.

Post : Chief deliveries *abt.* 8.20 *a.m.,* 6.40 *p.m.* ; *Sundays,* 9 *a.m.* ; despatches, 8 *a.m.,* 7 *p.m.* ; *Sundays,* 4 *and* 6 *p.m.* Open: *Weekdays,* 7.30 *a.m. to* 8 *p.m.*; *Sundays,* 8 *to* 10 *a.m.*

Population : *abt.* 2,500.

Distances : Arthog *(rail or road),* 7 *m.* ; Bala *(rail),* 18½ *m.* ; Barmouth *(rail),* 9½ *m.,* *(road),* 10 *m.* ; Dinas Mawddwy *(road),* 10¾ *m.* ; Drws-y-Nant *(rail),* 6¾ *m.* ; Ffestiniog *(rail),* 39 *m.,* *(road),* 18½ *m.* ; Harlech *(rail),* 20 *m.* *(road),* 20 *m.* ; Llanuwchllyn *(rail),* 13 *m.* ; Machynlleth *(rail),* 31¼ *m.,* *(road to Corris* 11 *m., thence rail)* 16 *m.* ; Penmaenpool *(rail or road),* 2 *m.* ; Pistyll Cain *(road),* 8 *m.* ; Rhaiadr-du *(road),* 6 *m.* ; Tal-y-Llyn *(road),* 10 *m.* ; Towyn *(rail),* 18 *m.,* *(old road)* 16¼ *m.* ; *(coast-road)* 20 *m.*

Breaks make the round of the Torrent and Precipice Walks during the season.

Greatly improved though **Dolgelley** has been as a town during the last few years, it is still entirely to its surroundings that it owes its popularity as a tourist resort, and in this respect it is almost unrivalled, speaking of Wales only. The valley in which it is placed may not be quite so romantic as that of the Dee at Llangollen, the rock and wood not so striking as at Bettws-y-Coed, and the mountain amphitheatre may be inferior to that of Beddgelert, but the distinctive features of the scenery round the three places we have named are nowhere more happily combined than about Dolgelley. The valley of the Wnion, the rocks of Mynydd-y-Gader and the towering heights of Mynydd Moel (the eastern peak of Cader Idris) and Rhobell-fawr afford a picture as varied in its general as it is beautiful in its particular character, and in whatever direction the visitor, be he tourist or artist, directs his steps from the town, he will hardly travel a dull yard.

The name Dolgelley is said to mean the "vale" or "meadow of hazels," but there is now no special appropriateness about it. Politically, the town is the capital of Merionethshire, and there are only five smaller capitals in Great Britain,—Cromarty, Inveraray, Dornoch, Dingwall, and Beaumaris. It is irregularly built and old-fashioned, the open square in the centre being the only thoroughfare which could be fairly called a main street. The river Wnion skirts it on the north and is joined close to the station by the Aran brook, which comes down from a tarn of the same name under Cader Idris.

The only **public buildings** are the *Church* (containing the recumbent effigy of "Maurice, filius Yngr Vychan") and the *County Hall* (some portraits of local magnates, including one of Sir Robert W. Vaughan, *d.* 1843, by Sir Martin Shee). The old *Parliament House*, in which Owen Glyndwr is said to have assembled his Parliament, was pulled down in 1882, and in 1887 the old jail, no longer needed, made way for a row of lodging-houses.

The season at Dolgelley is, of course, at its height during August, but, unlike its popular neighbour Barmouth, it attracts a good many visitors—anglers and others—from Easter onwards. Most of the people who let lodgings do so as a supplementary, rather than as a sole, means of subsistence, and so the charges for rooms are on the whole distinctly lower than in resorts where the year's income has to be gathered during the six weeks' rush. On the score of healthiness the place can safely be recommended —it draws its water supply from Llyn Cynwch, a small lake which we shall see on our way to the Precipice walk.

Excursions from Dolgelley.

The following excursions include only those in the immediate neighbourhood or such as are most conveniently commenced from Dolgelley. For longer expeditions, in which the railway is made use of, the reader is referred to the index. The ascents of Cader Idris, the Arans, and Arenig are given in the "Mountain Section."

Besides the walks we give, there are many little rambles near at hand which the traveller, who makes Dolgelley his head-quarters, will need no guide to discover.

(1) The **Torrent Walk**, *abt.* 2 *m.* to the foot of the "walk," which is itself about a mile in length. The round out and home is about 5½ miles, and carriages can drive to both ends of the "walk." Leave the town by the Machynlleth road, which at once crosses the Aran stream. A long mile onward turn down a road on the left, and, on the near side of a bridge over the "Torrent" stream, enter the "walk" by a private gate. Thence we steadily ascend the glen by a footpath that keeps the stream on the left hand all the way. The combination of water, rock and woodland is perfect. Just before reaching the second swing-gate across the path, a short turn to the left affords a particularly sweet view. Soon the stream for a short distance becomes less tumultuous and flows through a charming glade, and then a fine high fall, exqui-sitely broken and draped, can be contemplated at leisure from the seat conveniently placed by the side of the path, which is now high up above a deep gorge. As we near the top of the "walk," we get fine views down-stream. The house of *Caerynwch* is at the head of the glen, which we leave by crossing a footbridge into the road. Then, turning to the right, we drop quickly to the main valley and re-enter Dolgelley at the point we left it.

The Torrent Walk to the Precipice Walk, *abt.* 4 *m.* This is a delightful but rather intricate stroll—much to be recom-

mended as the most varied route by which the two "walks" may
be accomplished in one easy day—the entire distance from and to
Dolgelley not exceeding 12 miles. The "half-way house" (no inn)
is Bont Newydd station, to reach which you go east from the top
of the Torrent Walk, just after crossing the foot-bridge over the
stream, and in rather less than a mile turn down to the left at the
Pen-y-Groes Post Office. There are several houses on the way,
and it is best to make sure by enquiry. Crossing the river and the
rail at *Bont Newydd*, turn to the left and ascend to a bridge over
a tributary stream. Cross this, and, turning again to the left,
follow a winding road round the south side of Moel Offrwm till
you reach Nannau Park. Here there is a great intricacy of routes,
and you may pass either to the south or the north of the mansion.
Llyn Cynwch, on the opposite (western) side of which runs the
tame part of the Precipice Walk, is a little west of the mansion,
and the rest of the way will be understood from the following
description of the direct route to it from Dolgelley.

(2) **To Nannau (2¼ m.), the Precipice Walk (3 m.), and
back to Dolgelley,** 6—7 *m. in all.*

A multitude of by-roads, never going in the right direction for
many yards together, and the interposition of a low green
eminence between Dolgelley and the places above named, make
the routes hereabouts rather difficult to find. Find or lose, however, the whole country-side will well repay a full day's exploration,
while those to whom time is an object will do best to observe the
following directions :—
Cross the railway at the station and follow the right-hand
(Bala) road for ¼ *m.*.* Then turn up to the left by a road that
runs for nearly half-a-mile above and almost parallel to the one
you have quitted. During the ascent there is a fine back-view of
Cader and its bold continuation Tyrau-mawr. Then, turning to
the left again, we make a slight ascent into an upland valley. The
Arans form an imposing mass on the right, and in another short
half-mile our road joins a cross one. Here turning to the right,
we reach in a few minutes the ivied gateway of *Nannau Park.* It
has an open arcade on each side. The public road goes through
a gate just beyond and runs almost side by side with the one
through the park till a milestone (2 *m. from Dolgelley*) is reached.
From this point you may either (*a*) turn to the left and, crossing
the drive, go through an archway bearing the inscription "This
arch was finished the day good King George III. died," to a farm
called *Maes-y-Brynar,* where carriages may be put up, and whence,
turning to the right, you reach in a few hundred yards the foot of
Llyn Cynwch; or (*b*) you may keep along the road past and round
the mansion of Nannau, to the head of Llyn Cynwch.

* There is an alternative foot-track commencing about a furlong on this road
and ascending past a house and through a wood. The course of this is best
learnt from the map.

Nannau House (*abt.* 780 *ft. above the sea*), so called from the family which originally inhabited it, but now the residence of the Vaughans, stands in the midst of a park which has the silvan luxuriance of an English demesne in combination with hill-surroundings remarkable for beauty and variety even in Wales. In the old house, of which no trace remains, lived Howel Selé, cousin and bitter enemy of Owen Glyndwr, and in the park, according to a legend repeated with some variation in poetry and prose, an encounter took place between the two cousins, which ended in the remains of the less famous one being shut up in an oak tree, celebrated both by Sir Walter Scott and Lord Lytton as the " blasted " tree. A sun-dial placed in the kitchen-garden marks the position of this tree, and a brass plate thereon bears a representation of it.

Moel Offrwm (1328 ft; if correctly spelt, means the " hill of sacrifice ") rises steeply from the east side of the park, and well repays the half-hour's exertion of ascending it. On the summit are the remains of a considerable *hill-fort* of rough stones, which, by the way, has not been improved by the addition of some trumpery little cannons. The all-round view from the top is charming, though difficult to get from any one position in consequence of a high wall. Nannau Park spreads itself out delightfully on one side, and on the other is the remote little village of Llanfachreth, with a graceful spire. There is a peep into the woody Mawddach glen about Tyn-y-Groes, and the mountain girdle includes Cader Idris, the Arans, Rhobell-fawr, and Craig-y-Cau, while the vista of the Mawddach estuary extends to Barmouth Bridge. **Llyn Cynwch** lies immediately behind and to the west of Nannau House, and may be reached by either of the routes described *p.* 38. It is a long, narrow sheet of water, with low hills diversified with larch and a sprinkling of oak on each side. It has no pretension to be anything more than pretty, but Cader Idris makes a fine background to its southern end. A part of the **Precipice Walk** skirts its east side, and we may go in either direction along it ; our present one is northerly, that is through the plantation, and so round Moel Cynwch—a low hill, of which the walk makes the circuit. As we keep bending to the left, the precipice, or, rather, very steep slope, begins below us. The track is somewhat narrow, but quite safe. From about its commencement a steep descent may be made to a wood, and thence a track may be followed over two streams to a bridge that crosses the Mawddach a few yards beyond Tyn-y-Groes Inn. Over and above the abundant wood the scenery is greatly improved by heather.

We have now doubled the north end of Moel Cynwch, and are going southward. Several hundred feet below is the narrow Ganllwyd glen, down which the Mawddach comes—one branch from the bare plateau of Trawsfynydd, another from the woody defiles in which are Rhaiadr Mawddach and Pistyll Cain. Southward, the cliffs of Cader rise pre-eminent. Then, rounding the south end of Moel Cynwch, we come to a step-stile, from which the track turns east.

[Those who keep along the track from this point soon come to another step-
stile at the south end of Llyn Cynwch close to the end of the route above
described from Maes-y-Brynar Farm.]

After crossing this stile, turn down-hill at once in the direction
of the top of "Cader." So doing, you skirt the right side of one
wood, and then, after passing through a gateway at which a cart-
track commences, the left side of another. There is a full view to
the right up the Mawddach estuary, and close below are Llanelltyd Bridge and Cymmer Abbey. Then you sight a road to which
the track winds round to the left. Cross this road and follow a
broadish green track that drops to a barn. Here a wicket on the
left opens on to a good path which crosses a field and, continuing
to the left of a cottage with two tall chimneys, bends round a
beech wood and enters a lane that descends directly to Dolgelley
station.

(3) **Tyn-y-Groes** (*Inn*), 5 *m*; and the waterfalls **Rhaiadr-
du**, 6¼ *m*; **Pistyll Cain** and **Rhaiadr Mawddach**, 8 *m*.

The main road from Dolgelley to Trawsfynydd (13 *m*.) misses
Pistyll Cain and Rhaiadr Mawddach, but pedestrians pursuing
that route can include them both at the cost of an extra mile and
a half. The only inn between Dolgelley and Trawsfynydd is at
Tyn-y-Groes. Carriages can approach within about half-a-mile of
these falls, and those who are driving to Trawsfynydd may, if an
additional 4 miles for the horses and a walk of 3 miles be not
objected to, visit them and avoid twice traversing the same ground
by ordering the carriage to return to Pont ar Eden and, thence
proceeding 3 miles along the main road towards Trawsfynydd, to
wait at the point where the hill-road from Pistyll Cain joins it.

As an excursion from Dolgelley carriage-folk have no choice but
to go and return the same way, but pedestrians may with advantage return by the eastern side of the Mawddach glen. A glance
at the map will show that either the Precipice Walk, or Nannau
and Moel Offrwm, may thus, with little addition to the distance
be included.

This is, perhaps, the finest glen excursion within easy reach of
Dolgelley, and not only is the scenery for the greater part of the
distance of a high order of beauty, but Pistyll Cain is a waterfall
second to none in the Principality for gracefulness.

The Route. After crossing the bridge over the railway close to
Dolgelley station turn to the left and keep to the Barmouth road,
which presently winds round into the open valley of the Mawddach, here a tranquil stream bordered by rich meadow-land set
in a charming environment of wooded hills.

Just short of *Llanelltyd Bridge*, a farm-road on the right leads, in
about 500 yards, to *Cymmer Abbey* *, so named from its position
near the confluence of the Wnion and the Mawddach.

* A more direct approach is by the steep lane that starts from above Dolgelley
Station and passes behind Hengwrt.

Cymmer Abbey was a Cistercian foundation dating from about 1200, but does not appear to have ever risen to any great degree of importance. Of the ruins the only noteworthy portion is the church, but this contains very few features of interest. The north side is barricaded for its whole length (about 100 feet) by a row of cow-houses. The east end contains a recess with 3 lancet windows, and on the south side are remains of an arcade. A fine sycamore grows in the north-west corner, and, outside, an avenue of limes and a row of wind-bent walnut trees increase the seclusion of the spot. In the farm-buildings west of the church there is a large room called the *Abbot's Hall*.

After crossing the bridge at Llanelltyd, where there is nothing to detain us, our road turns to the right out of the Barmouth road and ascends the Mawddach valley, soon reaching the river-side. Across the stream rises the steep hill, along the face of which, high up, the Precipice Walk (p. 38) is carried. In about two miles the road trends to the left, and the valley becomes a glen, having on its far side the bulky form of Penrhos, which, with its mantle of bracken and heather, is perfect of its kind. Then, passing through a wood, we come to the charmingly situated *Tyn-y-Groes Inn*, a favourite angling resort.

Hence, crossing the river by a bridge a little beyond the inn we may bend back and return to Dolgelley by the *Precipice Walk*, or by *Nannau*, or by both (*see p. 39*).

Beyond Tyn-y-Groes we pass on the left the finely-timbered grounds of *Dolmelynllyn*, backed by the stern scarp of *Craig-y-Cau*, and a little further we cross the *Camlan stream*. **Rhaiadr-du** is half a mile up this, and may be reached by a rough cart-track that commences on the north side of the bridge. It is a water-slide rather than a fall, and the height is between 50 and 60 feet. The détour is well worth making.

Returning to the road we shortly turn to the right, cross the bridge over the *Eden*, pass through a gate and enter the charmingly-wooded glen of the upper Mawddach, which is heard rather than seen as it rushes down its rock-bound gorge through the trees a few yards on our right. It is worth while, should the river be in flood, to make our way now and again to its bank, as there are many fine bits of rock and cascade. For the rest of the way the road keeps close to the stream, and no mistake can be made. A house is passed, and, a little beyond it, the buildings pertaining to a deserted mine.

Beyond this mine the road becomes a cart-track through the wood, and when it forks we take the right-hand branch, which soon descends to the *Afon Cain* and crosses it by a bridge about half-way between the Fall and the confluence of its waters with the Mawddach.

Pistyll Cain is only a few yards from the bridge by the narrow path up-stream. The fall is coy and we come suddenly upon it. Owing to the narrow gorge bending abruptly at the point where the water dashes over a rugged crag 150 feet high, we get a half-face view of the cataract, which is broken in its descent by projecting rocks into a singularly graceful form. The surroundings, too—a cool deep rocky dell draped and overhung and happily quite unspoiled—are perfect. Returning to the cart-road we see a few yards down-stream the confluence of the Cain and Mawddach, close to which the appurtenances of a "gold-mine," including a slim waterwheel are a sad disfigurement. A trifling distance up the main stream is **Rhaiadr Mawddach**. There is nothing particularly beautiful about this fall, but in times of flood it gives the impression of power, and at all times the glen, in spite of the mining gear, is a good example of a wooded ravine.

A little above the fall the Mawddach is crossed by a bridge. If, instead of crossing this, you ascend by the cart-track to the left you may reach Traws-fynydd in about 6 miles, crossing the Afon Cain by *Pont-y-Llyn-du* about 2½ m. on the way.

We may return towards Dolgelley by the eastern bank of the Mawddach. About ¾ mile below the junction with the Cain the track ascends through the wood and winds round the hill-side into a tributary valley, where is an old copper-mine below which is a bridge across the Mawddach. Keeping up this valley we might cross the minor watershed and descend the glen of the *Afon-yr-allt* to near its junction with the Mawddach, and then either keep down the main valley, near the river, and so by Cymmer Abbey to Llanelltyd Bridge, or strike up the hill-side to the Precipice Walk, or, as a third course, turn eastward towards *Llanfachreth*, whose little spire soon comes into view up the valley. Either *viâ* Llanfachreth or by a road across the wooded valley we make for Nannau (*p.* 39). There is a little *Inn* at Llanfachreth.

From Pistyll Cain to the Trawsfynydd road, 3 m. Returning a short distance down the right bank of the stream, we ascend through the wood and strike a lane that ascends along the side of the valley. Then, after passing a lonely cottage and one or two poor outbuildings we emerge on to the open hill-side, and the track, now a fair mountain-road, bends to the left and ascends to and crosses the top of the ridge and runs into another similar road, said to be the Roman road from Trawsfynydd to Dolgelley. Following it northward for about a quarter of a mile, at a fork we take the left-hand branch, which gradually descends to the main-road, joining it 4 miles beyond Tyn-y-Groes Inn, and about the same distance short of Trawsfynydd, to which place it is a dreary walk along a straight road that runs parallel to the rugged but unpicturesque Rhinog range.

(4.) **Pandy and the Aran glen.**—A delightful stroll described in our "Mountain Section" as the first part of a route up Cader Idris.

(5.) **Abergwynant Valley,** 4 *m. from Dolgelley by road*; 1½ *m. beyond Penmaenpool Station and Inn.*

This charming little glen, a feature in the view from Cader Idris, is crossed at its lower end by the Towyn (coast) road, whence a lane leads up its east side, first rising steeply; then, at a school-house, descending to and twice crossing the stream. A return may be made to Dolgelley by the old road, up to which, however, the paths beyond the second crossing are intricate (*see map*). The whole round is about 10 miles.

Dolgelley to Maentwrog and Ffestiniog.

Dolgelley to Tyn-y-Groes Inn, 5 m ; Trawsfynydd (Inns), 13 m ; Maentwrog-road Station, 16 m ; Maentwrog, 18 m ; (or Ffestiniog Village, 19 m.).

The first part of this route is fully dealt with in Excursion 3 (*page* 40). A little beyond *Pont Dolgefeiliau*, $2\frac{1}{2}$ miles past Tyn-y-Groes, the road enters a desolate plateau bounded on the west by the rocky Rhinog range, and continues in a straight line all the way to *Trawsfynydd*. Here (10 min. walk to the right of the village), or at *Maentwrog-road*, the rail may be taken to Ffestiniog, and the route either to that village or to Maentwrog affords fine views across the Ffestiniog valley. It is described on page 5, but for a detailed description of the district see "North Wales, Part I.," in the Ffestiniog Section.

Dolgelley to Bala by road or rail.

Dolgelley to Bont Newydd, 3 m ; Drws-y-Nant (inn, 1 m. beyond station), $6\frac{3}{4}$ m ; Llanuwchllyn (inn at station), 13 m ; Bala Junction, 18 m ; Bala Town, 19 m. (18 m. by road).

This route is fully described the reverse way on page 5. Road and rail are close together as far as Llanuwchllyn, whence the rail skirts the south-east, and the direct road the north-west shore of Bala Lake.

Between one and two miles from Dolgelley the lie of the Torrent Walk may be detected amongst the trees on the right hand across the grounds of Dolserau. For several miles the route gradually ascends the lovely valley of the Wnion, whose stream the rail crosses a little beyond *Bont Newydd*. The long grassy slope of the Arans then appears on the right, and on the left that of Rhobell-fawr. Cader Idris is a grand object in the back view. Gradually the country becomes more wild and bare, and 2 miles beyond *Drws-y-Nant* the highest point on the line (*abt.* 760 *ft.*) is passed. Hereabouts the valley widens, the peak of Arenig comes into view on the left, and the road quits the side of the line for *Llanuwchllyn village*, half-a-mile north of that *station*. The Arans, ascending by a succession of rocky knobs, now present their finer side, the whole length of *Bala Lake* is skirted, and at *Bala Junction* we change trains for *Bala Town*, to which the road (*p.* 30) from Llanuwchllyn goes direct. For Bala see *p.* 29.

Dolgelley to Tal-y-Llyn and Towyn ; Dinas Mawddwy or Machynlleth.

Dolgelley to Cross Foxes Inn, $3\frac{1}{4}$ m ; Tal-y-Llyn Hotel, $9\frac{1}{2}$ m ; Abergynolwyn Station, 13 m ; and Towyn, 20 m.
—Cross Foxes to Dinas Mawddwy, 7 m. Cross Foxes to Corris Station, $7\frac{1}{4}$ m ; Machynlleth, $12\frac{1}{2}$ m.

All these routes are identical as far as the small Cross Foxes Inn, for which point a hill-road, shorter by half-a-mile, starts on the right hand about $\frac{1}{4}$ mile out of Dolgelley. The Dinas Mawddyw-

road diverges to the left at "Cross Foxes," and the Machynlleth road strikes off on the same side a little short of Tal-y-Llyn
Lake. Tal-y-Llyn village stands at the south end of the lake, and
three miles short of Abergynolwyn Station, whence there is a railway of the " toy " gauge to Towyn, for which place the last train
has hitherto left about half past four.

The only tourist resort of any importance on these routes is the
Tal-y-Llyn Hotel, ¼ mile short of the south end of the lake of that
name. There is, however, another very fair little inn at the outlet of the lake, *Pen-y-Bont*, and one of equal merit a little way
above the station at Abercorris, or Corris, as it is now called.

The Rôute. Winding out of the town by the road that goes to
the left from the south end of the square, we cross the Aran
stream, and begin an ascent which continues with little intermission for nearly six miles. At first the beautiful Wnion valley
is on the left and a gentle green eminence on the right. In 1¼
miles the route to the foot of the Torrent Walk diverges on the
left, and 2½ miles from the town, after passing the grounds of
Caerynwch, another road in the same direction crosses the stream
a little above the head of the same walk. The **Cross Foxes**
(650 *ft. above sea-level*) is a mile further.

Cross Foxes to Dinas Mawddwy, 7 m. *Described the reverse way,*
(p. 94). The first 2½ miles of this route is only remarkable for the fine retrospect which it commands of Cader Idris and the mountains north and north-
west of Dolgelley. Then, crossing the pass called *Bwlch-oerddrws* ("Cold Door
Pass," *abt.* 1,200 *ft.*) a descent is made into the deep valley, flanked by green hills,
which joins the main Dovey glen at *Dinas Mawddwy* (*Index*). The last part of
the route is bold and beautiful.

From Cross Foxes to the highest part of the route, 860 feet
above the sea, a desolate tract of country is crossed, having as its
western flank the long and rocky eastern shoulder of Cader Idris.
At the top of the Pass the small lake of *Llyn Trigraienyn* is to the
left of the road, under the steep cliffs of Craig-y-Llam (the " rock
of the step "). Tal-y-Llyn comes into view in front, and the
descent to it down a narrow glen, with the cliffs of Cader on the
right, is very fine, though the top of the mountain is not in sight.

The road to **Corris** and **Machynlleth** (pub. convey. to Corris St. from
Tal-y-Llyn in summer) forks to the left about a mile short of the lake, of which,
during a steep ascent, a comprehensive view is afforded on the right-hand. Still
finer is the retrospect into the Llyn-y-Cau hollow of Cader Idris with Cader
itself and Craig-y-Cau beyond it. About the top of the Pass (660 *ft.*) the slate-
quarries of Abercorris begin and they continue with little intermission on both
sides of the road to the *Station* and *Inn* of *Corris*. Thence the route by rail or
road to *Machynlleth* is through a narrow, well-wooded and in every respect
charming valley. *For description, see* " *Machynlleth*."

Nearly half-a-mile beyond the Machynlleth branch of the road
the Tal-y-Llyn carriage-road turns square to the left. (The road
that goes straight on through a gate, and is marked as the more
important one on the Ordnance Survey, skirts the western side of

the lake, and in the last ¾ m. to Tal-y-Llyn village is barely even a cart-track). On the right is the Llyn-y-Cau hollow of Cader Idris, with picturesque waterfalls close at hand.

Tal-y-Llyn (pron. almost "Tathlinn," 1¼ m. long by ¼ m. wide), rather disappoints the expectations formed on its first appearance from the top of the pass. It is a fine sheet of water, and the hills on both sides are steep and lofty; but there is no variety or mystery about it—no sudden disclosure of unexpected beauties. It is chiefly noteworthy for the abundance of its trout, and the two inns (see p. 44) on its shore are frequented by anglers. The carriage-road skirts its south-eastern side, and at times is almost under water. *Convey. to Corris (for Machynlleth) in summer.*

For the ascent of Cader Idris from Tal-y-Llyn, see "Mountain Section."

A low green mound blocks the valley a little beyond the outlet of the lake, and then the road very gradually descends a fairly wooded and almost straight valley to **Abergynolwyn** (*public house*). Here the main valley strikes away to the right, but it is only a few yards' ascent into another which forms a direct continuation of the one we have been descending. *Abergynolwyn Station* is 10 minutes' walk beyond the village, and from it Towyn is reached by a gradual descent in 7 miles. The line affords peeps of one or two pretty waterfalls on the left. Its passenger terminus is nearly a mile from the Cambrian station of the same name. For Towyn, see page 69.

Dolgelley to Towyn. *other routes.* There are two other carriage-roads from Dolgelley to Towyn besides the one by Tal-y-Llyn. The pony-track over the ridge of Cader Idris should also be remembered.

(a) **By the Coast.** *Penmaenpool* 2½ m; *Arthog,* 7 m; *Llwyngwril,* 12 m; *Llanegryn,* 16 m; *Towyn,* 20 m.

Except for the distance between Penmaenpool and Arthog and the last six miles this road follows the line of railway. It is not much used by tourists as a through route, but parts of it form a very pleasing variety in connection with excursions from Dolgelley or Barmouth.

Following the right-hand road from the S.W. end of the town, we soon reach *Penmaenpool,* where there is a good little tourist hotel. Hence the bridge may be crossed and Barmouth reached by the road along the north side of the estuary (*p.* 46) in 7 miles.

From Penmaenpool the road passes between luxuriantly wooded hills, and in a short 1½ miles crosses the *Gwynant* stream, which comes down a charming little glen from the lakes under Cader Idris. *See* (5) *on p.* 42.

Continuing our way still through fine woodland scenery, we reach Arthog (*hotel, see p.* 54), and again come in sight of the estuary, which is seen across a richly tinted marsh. From Arthog

station we may take train to Barmouth, or, turning out of the road
about a mile further, we may walk across (there is no regular
road) by the station at the Junction, beyond which, side by side
with the line, is the path leading on to the bridge (*toll*, *2d.*, **see**
p. 50).

The rest of the road is described under Barmouth excursions
(*p.* 55). It has an advantage over the railway in breasting the
Friog promontory at a greater height above the sea. Beyond
Llwyngwril (*station and road-side inn*), the road turns inland and
the walk is tedious.

(b) **By the old mountain road**, 16¼ m. This is a fine bracing
walk in its highest part (about 1,700 feet above the sea), but when
the alternative route by pony-track over the ridge of Cader Idris
(either diverging to the top or merely crossing the *col*) may be
comfortably accomplished, few tourists will choose the road.

At the fork of the roads at the S.W. end of Dolgelley take the
left-hand branch. In 3 miles the route to "Cader" (*see* "*Mountain
Section*") by the Foxes' Path quits the road opposite a temperance inn, and a little further the pony-track above-named goes off
in the same direction. The craggy front of the mountain is well
seen, and presently Tyrau-mawr rises steeply on our right, but
there is no extent of view until in 6 miles we begin the stiff
ascent to the ridge, which is crossed a little west of its prominent
shoulder *Craig Cwm-llwyd*. Then the view opens up across the
Mawddach estuary to the Llawllech range ; Barmouth is seen and,
from the highest part of the road, the Carnarvonshire promontory
from Bardsey Island to the double-peaked Rivals and the saddle-
shaped hills between them and Snowdon. Beyond this the road
descends a long green valley called *Cwm-llwyd*, and before reaching *Llanegryn* (*inn p.* 72) commands a view across the Dysynni
valley of the mountains from Cader Idris to the sea between Towyn
and Aberdovey. The rest of the way across the *Dysynni* flats is
literally as dull as ditch-water.

(c) **By pony-track over the Cader ridge**, abt. 18 m. The
ascent of Cader Idris from Dolgelley, and the descent to Towyn
described in the " Mountain Section " give full particulars of this
route, and we need only here repeat our advice to the tourist to
cross from Llanfihangel-y-Pennant (about half-way between Dolgelley and Towyn) to Abergynolwyn Station (*abt.* 2½ m.) rather
than to walk all the way, because the last four or five miles of the
route are quite uninteresting.

Dolgelley to Barmouth by road. *Dolgelley to Bont-ddu*
(*hotel*), 5 m ; *Barmouth*, 10 m. *Route fully described the rev.rse
way*, p. 56.

As far as Llanelltyd (2 m.) this route coincides with that to
Pistyll Cain, &c. (*p.* 40). For the rest of the distance it winds along

the north side of the Mawddach estuary passing close or near to
the water-side for about 2 miles; then going somewhat inland
past the picturesque and charmingly situated "*Half Way House.*"
There is a splendid view of Cader Idris, and the steep but regular
slope of the Foxes' Path is very noticeable. Everyone should
walk a few yards up the *glen* at Bont-ddu (*p.* 56). As we proceed
the water-side is again reached 2 miles short of Barmouth, which,
however, is hidden by a projecting rock until we enter the town
itself.

Ferns. The neighbourhood of Dolgelley is a good hunting-
ground for some of the rarer species, or, to speak more exactly,
for some of the kinds that are found only or chiefly in subalpine
habitats. Amongst these may be mentioned the Beech Fern
(*Polypodium Phegopteris*), the Green Spleenwort (*Asplenium
Viride*), the two Filmy Ferns (Tunbridge and Wilson's), and the
Brittle Bladder Fern (*Cystopteris Fragilis*). We refrain, for obvious reasons, from naming the precise localities in which these
kinds may respectively be found, but we may state generally, that
the slopes and rocks of Cader, between the old Towyn road and
the summit, and the neighbourhood of Nannau, are regions of
more than ordinary interest for the collector. It may be added
without fear, however, that the Parsley Fern (*Allosorus Crispus*),
the commonest, and at the same time the uncommonest of ferns—
the easiest to grow and the hardest to rear—almost carpets the
ground about Llyn-y-Gader and at the foot of the Foxes' Path.
Somewhere in the neighbourhood one dealer professes to find the
Forked Spleenwort (*A. septentrionale*), but where is a close secret
to all besides himself. That he occasionally has a specimen for
sale is certain, and that the skirts of Cader Idris have been
searched a hundred times by the keenest eyes without success, is
also certain, but then the broken lower slopes of the range are so
extensive and so suited to it, that it is quite possible some nook
may harbour the rarity.

The Holly Fern (*P. lonchitis*) is not, we believe, to be found in
this neighbourhood. What is sold as such by the dealers is the
not uncommon pinnate form of the Prickly Shield Fern (*P. aculea-
tum*). A plant, abundant on the mountain, and locally known as
the False Maidenhair, is not a fern at all.

BARMOUTH SECTION.

Barmouth.

—✦—

Hotels : *Corsygedol*, 200 yards south of Station ; *Marine* (recently enlarged), close to the sands ; *Lion, Barmouth*, south of station ; *Talydon* (private, opposite the station.

Post Office : ¼ *m.* south of station. Chief del. abt. 8.30 *a.m.*, 7.15 *p.m.*; Sundays, 11.30 *a.m.* Despatches, abt. 7.20 *a.m.*, 2.30 and 6.35 *p.m.*; Sundays, 4.35 *p.m.* Open, Weekdays, 7 *a.m.* to 8 *p.m.*; Sundays 10.15 to 11.30 *a.m.*

Pop : abt. 2000.

Distances : Aberdovey (*rail*), 16 *m* ; Aberystwith (*rail*), 38 *m* ; Bala (*rail*), 28 *m* ; Beddgelert (*rail to Portmadoc*, 19 *m* ; *thence coach*), 27 *m* ; Blaenau Ffestiniog (*rail*), 28 *m* ; Cwm Bychan (*rail to Llanbedr*, 8 *m* ; *thence road*), 14 *m* ; Dolgelley (*rail*), 9½ *m.* (*road over Penmaenpool Bridge*) 9 *m*, (*by Llanelltyd*), 10 *m* ; Ffestiniog Village (*rail or road to Harlech*, 10½ *m* ; *thence road*), 23 *m*, (*rail all the way*), 32 *m* ; Harlech (*rail or road*), 10½ *m* ; Machynlleth (*rail*), 25½ *m* ; Tal-y-Llyn (*by Dolgelley*), 20 *m*, (*by Towyn*), 23 *m* ; Tan-y-Bwlch (*rail*, 22½ *m* ; *thence road*), 23¼ *m* ; Towyn (*rail*), 12 *m*.

Barmouth, or *Abermaw*, the "mouth of the Mawddach," is situated just where the long billowy Llawllech range of hills sinks abruptly to the water in the angle formed by the open sea and the Mawddach estuary. In front is a wide expanse of firm sand entirely covered at high tide. There is nothing very remarkable in the appearance of the town itself, which consists of one long and irregular street running parallel with the shore, a varied group of smaller dwellings perched high and low behind it, wherever a break in the cliff affords room for foundations, and a sea-frontage of good modern lodging-houses on the edge of the sands.

If the visitor has come from inland or by the coast-route from the south he will hardly require to be told what we are about to add ; but if from the north, he must walk half-a-mile southward from the station before he discovers that Barmouth is, in respect of its neighbourhood, the most beautiful watering-place in the country. This pre-eminence it owes entirely to the proximity of the Mawddach estuary, which may be briefly described as the one spot in England or Wales where scenery of the very highest class begins immediately from the sea-shore. The surroundings of Lynton and Lynmouth, incomparable in their way, lack the breadth and the dignity which those of Barmouth acquire from the wide-spreading, almost landlocked Mawddach estuary and the noble screen of mountains behind it, just far enough away to admit of an interval of richness and cultivation, yet near enough to display their height and ruggedness to full advantage. Other

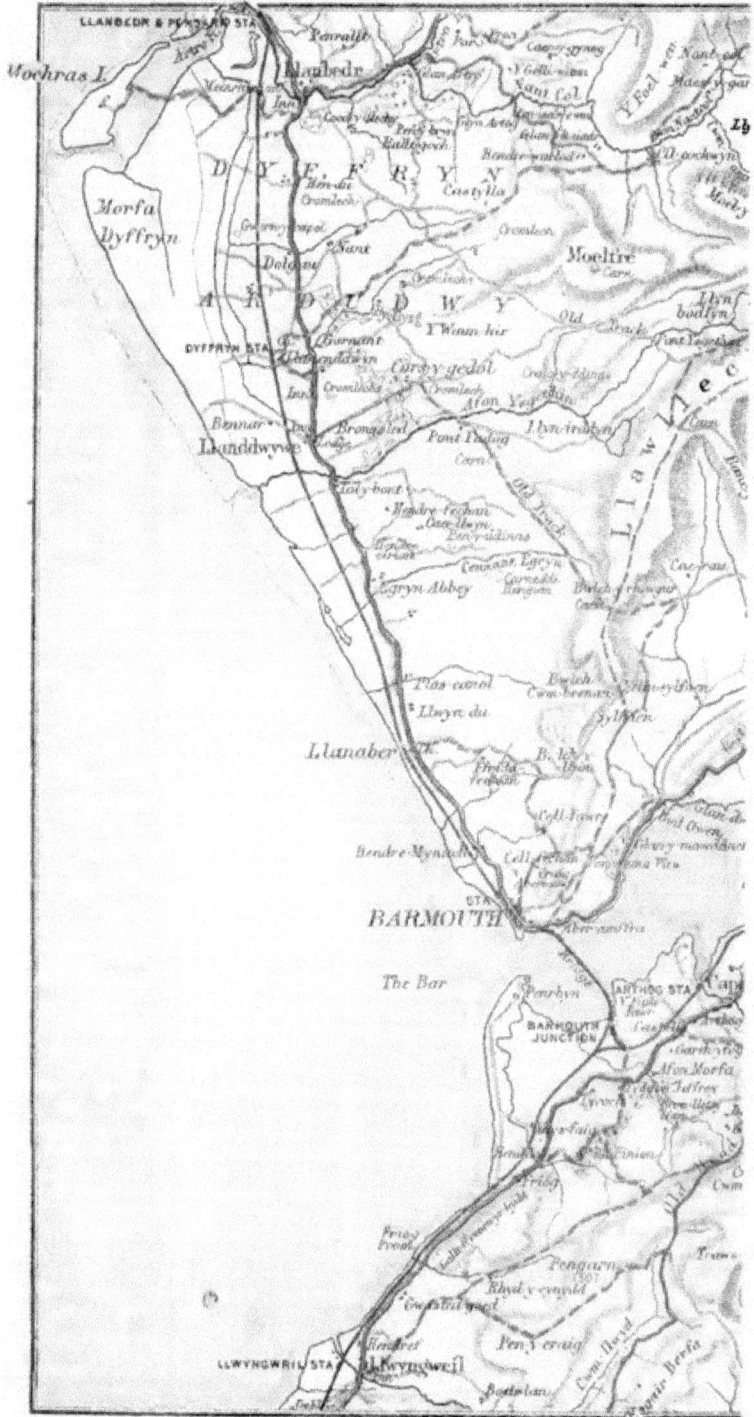

LLANBEDR & PENSARN STA.

Penrallt

Moehras I.

Llanbedr

Glan Aber

Caer-y-synog

Y Gelli-wion

Nant Col

Y Foel-wen

Nant col

Maes-y-gar

Meirionddu Inn

Gloddvaethu

Glan Fenai

Glan-y-nant

Coed-y-ddaehy

Pen-y-bryn

Fron Arda

Bron-y-wion

Cochwyn

Rallwgoch

Bendre-waelder

Mody

D Y F F R Y N

Morfa Dyffryn

Hen-dee Cromlech

Castylla

Cromlech

Gwern-y-mynydd

Sarn

Moeltre

Carn

A R D U D W Y

DYFFRYN STA.

Dolgau

Bryn-inche

Ffinant

Old   Track

Llyn bodlyn

Ynt laethan

Inn   Fen-du

Cwrnant

Y Wann hir

Old   Track

Bron-y-waun

Cors-y-gedol

L l a w

Inn   Cromlech

Cromlech

Afon Ysg   Inn

Orddy-dange

Bennar   Drys

Brongoled

Pont Fadog

Llyn irddyn

Cwm

Llanddwywe

Corn

Old Track

Tony-bont

Hendre-fechan

Gors-llwyn

Pen-rhiwlas

Caerau

Hafoty   vrisus

Cefnau   Egryn

Egryn Abbey

Carneddu   Hengwm

Bwlch-y-rhiwgyr

Plas canol

Bwlch-   Cwm-brenan

Rhiw-gyllan

Llwyn du

Dyffwn

Llanaber   Pc

Frefa   traiam

B. Ichen   Uchn

Hendre-Mynach

Cell-fawr

Coll Owen

Rhiw Gian

Tilwny mawddwn

Cell arddu

Croes   y   mwalch

Llwyn-gwra View

BARMOUTH   STA.

The Bar

Aberamffra

Penrhyn

ARTHOG STA.

Cae

Y   Figla   Fawr

BARMOUTH JUNCTION

Garth-angh

Afon Morfa

Bryn-gafroy   Jeffrey

Gwern

Pen-y-faig

Finian

Priel

Friog   Fruog

Pengarn

Glanaber farm

Rhyd-y-cerydd

Cwrt

Gwastad-goed

Pen-y-craig

Cwn-Hesd

Cwm Berfa

LLWYNGWRIL STA.

Llwyngwril

Bottalan

Inn

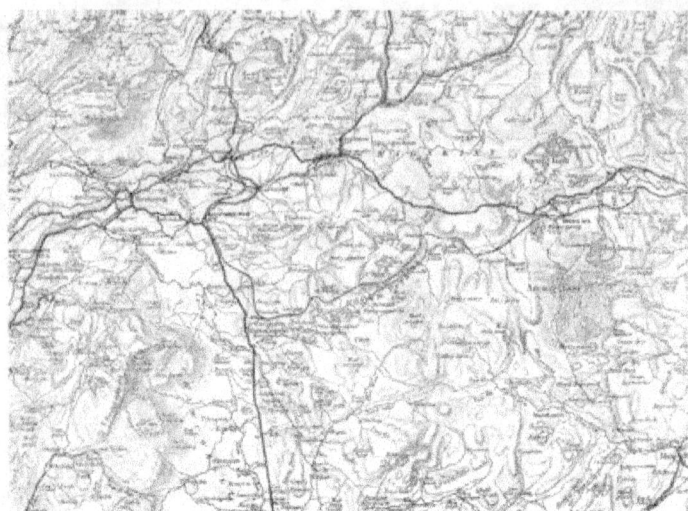

watering-places, which include scenery in the list of their attractions—such as Llandudno, Tenby, Torquay, Ilfracombe, Falmouth, Scarborough, and Whitby—may claim superiority to Barmouth in their actual situation, but not one of them combines so delightfully the attractions peculiar to the seaside with the less artificial ones of inland scenery. The man who suffers from *ennui* at Barmouth need never trouble himself again about Nature during the rest of his life. If you doubt this, look at the merry groups of visitors who crowd the platform on a fine summer's morning—some for Arthog and " Cader ;" others for Pensarn and Cwm Bychan; a detachment for Dolgelley with its Torrent and Precipice Walks; another for Ffestiniog by the " Toy " line; artists, to get into their foregrounds the rich colouring afforded by the Arthog marshes ; anglers to whip the streams of Towyn, Machynlleth, Tyn-y-Groes and Glen Artro—in short, frequent trains and cheap fares in all directions have made Barmouth a centre from which a large portion of the best scenery of North Wales is accessible in a day's outing. Those who can only appreciate the beautiful in solitude may leave the train at way-side stations and lose themselves in a dozen nooks and corners, where the only accompaniment to their day-dreams will be the bleating of the sheep, the soughing of the wind and the music of the waterfall.

As a town Barmouth has its peculiarities. Thirty years ago, when a drive from Carnarvon, or across the breadth of Wales, was necessary to reach it, these peculiarities were summed up in the one word " queer." In the hands of the modern architect this queerness—and, we may add, a great deal of picturesqueness—has nearly vanished, but traces of it may still be detected in a scattered remnant of tiny low-roomed cottages, which here and there crouch between the lofty three and four storied shops and lodging-houses that have, generally speaking, superseded them. The " queerness " arising from its site, however, must ever remain. One personal experience will tell more than a page of description.—" I was once," said a friend, " taking a walk on the " cliff behind the town just as it was getting dark, and lost my " way in returning. At last I came to a steep flight of steps " which offered an obvious escape from my awkward position on " the edge of a precipice. At the bottom of the steps progress " was blocked by a door. I knocked, and presently a servant " appeared. When I had duly explained and apologised she led " the way through the house, down three flights of stairs, and " showed me out of the front door into the main thoroughfare."

Sand is the staple commodity of Barmouth ; sand here, there, and everywhere to an extent which, when the wind is blowing strong from the sea, sorely tries the temper of some visitors, and for a long time to come is apt to qualify their otherwise delightful reminiscences of the place. Of late a fairly successful attempt has been made to reduce the sand nuisance on the esplanade, but many tourists who have walked the whole distance from the town to the top of " Cader " will agree with us that the hardest part of

the excursion is the sandy 500 yards between the railway bridge
and the Junction. There is a floor of firm sand extending, perhaps, half-a-mile at low water, in front of the town as well as
a similar stretch south of the river-mouth, but for all that the
supply of loose sand seems never to fail.

The **Hotel accommodation** of Barmouth is good, though not
very extensive. The *Cors-y-Gedol* is a large well appointed house,
the *Marine* offers a wide sea-view and adjoins the esplanade, which
is now much improved (*p.* 49). The *Tal-y-Don*, a nice little private
hotel, the *Lion* and the *Barmouth* are in the main street in the
order named.

Lodgings are in great request during August and September,
when prices are high, but earlier in the year good quarters can be
obtained at a moderate cost. *Porkington Terrace* (½ *m. south of
station*) commands the best view. There is also a little accommodation of a humbler sort at the " Junction," on the south side
of the Bridge.

For the **botanist**, the neighbourhood of Barmouth is full of interest. A
list of Wild Flowers (3*d.*, *published by J. Kynoch*), found in bloom during the first
half of August, 1884, contains 500 names.

Barmouth Bridge. (*Toll* 2*d.* ; *weekly ticket*, 6*d.*) It must
be admitted that the railway from Barmouth to Dolgelley, which
crosses this bridge, has done a minimum amount of damage to
the scenery through which it passes. Except for the steam-wreath
from a passing train, its course can scarcely be detected in any
general view, while by the erection of the bridge itself visitors
have obtained one of the finest promenades in Europe.

The bridge is a plain wooden structure, with an iron drawbridge
over the stream-course at its northern end. It is 800 yards long,
and is crossed by a single line of rails and a footway about 8 feet
wide, both of which belong to the Cambrian Company. A short
footpath starting from the Dolgelley road, half-a-mile south of the
station, leads on to it, and the path beyond is continued nearly
another half-mile to Barmouth Junction Station.

As we pass through the entrance-gate the view up the estuary
opens at once. In front we have a prominent shoulder of the
Cader range, which sinks to the sea westwards at the Friog promontory, and is skirted by the Machynlleth railway. Immediately
below this range, hardly visible in the woods, are one or two
pretty waterfalls. Behind us, on the left, the little harbour of
Aberamffra is a pleasing feature. Eyes front again, and we follow the Cader range eastward to Tyrau (*Tirry*) -mawr, its most
prominent peak as seen from here and just over Tyn-y-Coed, a
conspicuous mansion which marks the position of Arthog. The
hotel there nestles amongst the trees to the right of this house.
Then, beyond the Arthog hills, comes the topmost peak of Cader,
and Mynydd Moel rises from the hollow between Mynydd-y-Gader
and the Arthog hills. Very singular is the outline of the lower hills
further east, especially that of the " Giant," from whose face,

supine, protrudes a nose which might have won a marshal's
baton from Napoleon. Beneath this are the sweetly wooded pro-
montories which, breaking the regularity of the shore-line on
both sides, give to the prospect its peculiar richness and diversity.
Beyond them, as we continue our walk, we may mark, filling up
the vista, the comparatively low height of Moel Cynwch, round
which runs the Precipice Walk. Moel Offrwm is behind it, a little
to the right, and the mass of Rhobell-fawr on the left. The
gently sloping Aran heights, which are well seen in the far east
from the Barmouth end of the bridge, have disappeared behind
the "Giant" ridge, and the only part of them now seen is
a peak which fills up a slight gap between Rhobell-fawr and
Moel Offrwm.

We are about half-way over the bridge, and the hills on the
north side of the estuary have come into full view. On the one
next to the Precipice Walk, the tramway leading up to the gold
mines may be recognised by its straightness. Then, nearer to us,
are two lower hills remarkable for their lovely colouring of purple
rock and heath. Lastly, we have in the background the long
Llawllech range, culminating in the round top of Diphwys.
Looking seawards, the heights of the Lleyn promontory of Carnarvonshire display their usual graceful outline.

No one, we fancy, can look on this scene under favourable
conditions of tide and weather without owning that he has spread
before him as noble a combination of water, wood and mountain,
as is to be found in Great Britain.

Excursions from Barmouth.

Pleasant strolls over the rough gorsy upland, which forms the
beginning of the Llawllech range, and is only a few hundred feet
above Barmouth, may be enjoyed by starting up the narrow
tortuous lane from the north side of the Cors-y-gedol Hotel. The
hill that blocks the way in front as you ascend is called *Craig
Abermaw* ("Barmouth Hill ").

(*a*) If you keep to the left of this, you will reach in less than
half a mile the farm of *Cell-fechin*, whence you may bend to the
right, and, crossing a slight depression, proceed by *Gwastadannes*
farm into the lane by which the Panorama Walk is most quickly
reached. On entering this lane you may either go straight back
to Barmouth, or, turning to the left after going a very short distance in that direction, proceed to the " Walk." (*See p. 52.*)

(*b*) Keeping to the right of Craig Abermaw, after a short ascent
from the Cors-y-Gedol, we enter the last mentioned lane some
way short of the turn for the Panorama Walk.

(*c*) From Cell-fechan farm a winding lane goes to *Cell-fawr*
farm (¼ *m. further*), and then works round the breast of the hill to
Llanaber church (3 *m.* from Barmouth this way), whence it is less
than two miles back by the main road.

(1) **The Panorama Walk.** The prospect from this favourite view-point may be described as a bird's-eye edition of that from the bridge. The Walk is on the breast of a steep slope down to the water's edge, and about 200 feet above it. Consequently the immediate shores of the spreading estuary are seen in much greater detail, and the view is, as a whole, more comprehensive ; whether more beautiful is a matter of taste.

From the far end of Porkington Terrace, which is half-a-mile south of the station on the Dolgelley road, turn up the steep lane to the left, and where the lane forks at the top of the rise take the right-hand branch, which passes through a gate. Half-a-mile further turn sharp to the right, and, bending back a little, you pass between two hillocks and reach the lodge and gate opening on to the walk. A penny is charged for admission, and the view discloses itself at once. From the Friog promontory, which shoots down into the sea southwards beyond the bridge, the mountain girdle extends eastward as far as the end of the Cader range, the most prominent heights being Craig-cwm-llwyd (rather east of south), Tyrau-mawr, the Saddle, Cader itself, and Mynydd Moel ; then it bends northwards to the slightly tapering twin Aran peaks—the farthest heights visible ; then returning westwards it includes Rhobell-fawr, Craig-y-Cau, the green and round summit of Diphwys, from which the Llawllech range sinks in a waving line to its abrupt end over Barmouth, and only a little in the rear of our standpoint.

From the gate at which we entered the " Walk," we may continue along the lane down to the Dolgelley road, entering it about two miles from Barmouth. This is a delightful stroll all the way round, the total distance being about 4 miles.

(2) **Llanaber Church**, 1¾ *m.* ; **Llanddwywe Church**, 3½ *m.* (from Dyffryn station, 1 *m.*) ; **Cors-y-gedol**, 4 *m.* by road.

Small inns : One close to Llanddwywe Church ; *King's Head* ¼ m. N. of it on the main road, ⅔ m. S.E. of Dyffryn Station.

Two churches, sundry cromlechs, and the fact that the once important but now extinct family of the Vaughans of Cors-y-gedol had their seat at the mansion so named, are the inducements to this excursion, which, commanding, as it does throughout, a wide view over the whole sweep of Cardigan Bay, is a favourite drive. On pedestrians in search of scenery, and with only limited time at command, its claims are less, but they, by combining it with the inland ramble back to Barmouth, indicated in the small type, page 54, may find their account in the fine prospect from the Llawllech range, even if they do not include Diphwys (2,467 feet), as they easily may, in the day's round.

Leaving Barmouth by the Harlech road, in about 1¾ *m.*, we reach **Llanaber**, the parish church of Barmouth (*key at cottage close by*). It is Early English in style, and externally very plain. Inside it is both beautiful and interesting, and the work of restoration has been well done. A remarkable feature is the east window of a single lancet. Here, too, is preserved an inscribed stone variously read as " Cal*xtus*," or " *Cœlextus monedo regi*," of which the date and intention are unknown. It is said to have been found long ago on the shingle, near Barmouth, and removed to *Ceilwart-isaf* farm, where it long served as a footbridge.

About 1¼ *m.* beyond Llanaber the *Eqryn Abbey* of the map indicates the site of a religious house that has wholly disappeared, after which, passing through the hamlet of *Tal-y-bont,* we reach at 3½ *m.* from Barmouth the entrance lodge of Cors-y-gedol, opposite to which is **Llanddwywe Church**. (*Key at the Parish Clerk's, Coed-coch, ½ m. distant, and a little off the way to Dyffryn Station.*) The church is, architecturally, of minor importance ; the porch is dated 1593, while 1668 indicates a still later addition to the fabric. The Cors-y.gedol chapel, begun by Gryffydd Vaughan in 1615, contains, amongst others, his monument designed by Inigo Jones.

Nearly opposite the *King's Head Inn* are two **Cromlechs.** To reach them go 80 yards towards Harlech and over a stile on the right. Then double back. One of the cromlechs is fairly perfect, and they are close together.

The approach to **Cors-y-gedol** is by a straight drive nearly a mile in length and at first steep. As we ascend, the view expands and embraces the whole of Cardigan Bay from Bardsey to Strumble Head. Then follows an avenue, begun in 1734, and we are soon in front of the mansion (interior not shown.) There is here not much to detain us. The *gateway,* attributed to Inigo Jones, and a coat of arms on the house, are nearly all that witness to the long tenure of the Vaughans.

The **Vaughans of Cors-y-gedol** traced their descent from Gerald de Windsor, keeper of Pembroke Castle, in the time of Henry I., through Osborn, a son of Maurice Fitz Gerald, the first Geraldine lord of Decies and Desmond. Osborn, in the latter half of the 13th century, came over from Ireland and served under Llewelyn, who gave him the heiress of Cors-y-gedol to wife. The slight remains of a camp at *Berllys* (abt. a mile N.W.) are attributed to him. One of his descendants, about 1400, married a daughter of Tudor Vaughan, brother of Owen Glyndwr, and a son (Gryffydd) of hers was the first who took the surname of Vaughan. This Gryffydd was one of the defenders of Harlech Castle in 1468. A later Gryffydd in 1592-3 rebuilt Cors-y-gedol, and the far from smooth course of his love-story may be read in the Archæol. Camb., Jan., 1875, from which we take these details. Richard Vaughan (d. 1636) was M.P. for the county, and of him it is related that he "was so very fat and unwieldy that the folding doors of the House of Commons were opened to let him in." It was this gentleman's father who began the Cors-y-gedol Chapel and whose tomb has been already mentioned. He himself had the gate-house erected in 1630. A successor, who died in 1734, remodelled the mansion, and began planting the avenue, and with his son, William Vaughan, the house became extinct at the close of the 18th century, when the property passed to the Mostyn family, but has since more than once changed hands.

Near Cors-y-gedol is a cromlech known as **Arthur's Quoit** (*Coetan Arthwr*). To reach it, turn to the right opposite the gate

leading to the House, and then bear to the left round the outbuildings into a road, along which proceed to the left and soon turn
again to the right up a cart-road. At the top of this go through
a gate on the right into a grass-field. The quoit is about 300 yards
direct from the gate, and on it is the impression of Arthur's
fingers, left there when he hurled the block from the summit of
Moelfre !

Cors-y-gedol to Barmouth over the hills, abt. 1¼ hrs. direct, or
4½ hrs. including the ascent of Diphwys.

Proceed as above directed to Arthur's Quoit and keep on along the cart-track
to the bridge over the *Afon Ysgethin*, and at a fork about 200 yards on the far
side, if bound direct back to Barmouth, take the right-hand branch. The hill
a mile away on the left is *Craig-y-ddinas*, on which are the remains of a hill-fort.
The cart-track gradually climbs to the top of Llawllech ridge at *Bwlch-y-
rhiwgur*, whence it drops obliquely to another, along which we turn to the
right and, avoiding upward tracks, enter Barmouth at its south end.

If the ascent of Diphwys, or a visit to the lakelets that feed the Ysgethin, is
desired, then at the above-mentioned fork take the left-hand branch. In about
half-an-hour *Llyn-irddyn* is just above, on our right, and by continuing up the
valley, another half-hour will bring us to *Llyn-bodllyn* a somewhat larger lake.
From this a stiffish pull of yet another half hour lands us on the summit of
Diphwys, or we may proceed to the head of the valley to the tiny tarn *Llyn-
dulyn* and thence mount to the ridge connecting Llethr with Diphwys. For
Diphwys and the return to Barmouth *see Mountain Section*.

(3) **Arthog** (Hotel, *Arthog Hall*, abt. ¾ m. from the station) is a
small village some 2½ miles S.E. of Barmouth by rail or on foot.
In itself it has nothing to show the tourist, but it is situated at
the foot of well wooded, broken ground, with lovely rambles close
at hand, and the fair-sized hotel, finely placed on the hill-side,
is a favourite one. From it the view of the Mawddach estuary, and
of Barmouth and the hills behind it, is delightful. There is no
road from Barmouth, and pedestrians cross the bridge and usually
follow the rails to Arthog Station. In so doing there is passed a
view point of the estuary equal to, if not better than, the bridge,
namely, the top of the rocky knoll, Y *Figle-fawr*, on the left
of Barmouth Junction Station. The farmer, whose house is on
the far side of the knoll, demands a small fee.

Arthog lakes—*Llyn Creigenen* and a smaller one hard by—
are about a mile east of the hotel, to which the fishing belongs,
and are reached by the same route as that by which we begin
the climb towards Cader Idris, namely, by a lane a little to the
right of the hotel. This lane joins the direct one from the village,
after ascending which for some distance we bear to the left, and
soon cross a small stream hard by *Llys Bradwen*, once the palace
of a Welsh chieftain, of which, however, as well as of a stone circle,
nothing noteworthy is left. The lakes are just beyond the ridge
in front of us as we cross the brook, and over their rugged and
broken surroundings we may scramble *ad libitum*.

Within the grounds of the hotel are two cascades (*tickets*, 6d. *each, at the hote*) hardly worth the fee, perhaps, after a drought, but at other times of considerable beauty. On the tickets full direction how to find them are given. For the ramble towards Henddol and Llwyngwril, *see below*, and for the ascent of Cader Idris *see Mountain Section*.

(4) **Pant Einion. Llwyngwril**, &c. The road between Barmouth Junction and Llwyngwril is part of the Dolgelley and Towyn road, already described (*p.* 46) as being carried in this part along the breast of the promontory, higher up than the railway, and thereby affording a better view.

The best way to make this excursion is to take train to Barmouth *Junction* and then, entering a farm-road beyond the loop-line, to cross the main road and ascend a winding lane by which you may either (a) go through the prettily-wooded *Pant Einion*, which contains a waterfall, and rejoin the main road at the house of *Henddol*, 3 miles short of Llwyngwril; or (b) bearing more to the left in about ¾ mile, and again left the same distance further on, reach the old Towyn road (*p.* 46) near its highest point and just under *Craig-cwm-llwyd*—a bluff of the Cader range, and worth the slight extra trouble of ascending. Hence, the return is best made by Henddol, as Llwyngwril has nothing attractive in itself. The road between it and Henddol, however, commands a fine panorama of the Carnarvonshire hills from Bardsey to Snowdon, and, in the other direction, of the sweep of Cardigan Bay to Strumble Head. At **Llwyngwril** there is a small village inn (*Garthangharad Arms*), and ¼ mile short of the village, a few yards west of the road, is an old *Friends' Burial Ground*, with a new plate, inscribed 1646, on the entrance gate. There are a few small lodging-houses about Llwyngwril; the neighbourhood, much cut up by stone walls, is dull, but healthy, and the high ground commands wide views. You can return to Barmouth by train.

Barmouth to Dolgelley by rail.

Barmouth to Barmouth Junction, 2 *m*; Arthog, 3 *m*; Penmaenpoool, 7½ *m*; Dolgelley, 9½ *m*.

Route described the reverse way, p. 6.

The details of this route have entered into so many of our descriptions, and so soon become familiar to the sojourner at Barmouth, that we shall here give only a bare outline of it.

Diverging from the coast-line at *Barmouth Junction*, we turn sharp to the left and cross the Arthog marsh-land to *Arthog* station. Half-a-mile further the side of the estuary is reached, and its windings are followed all the way to Penmaenpool; across it, and beyond the varied border of meadow, wood and purple hill that fringes the northern shore, rises the Llawllech range to the green, round bluff of Diphwys, Craig-y-Cau and Rhobell-**fawr** continuing the mountain outline eastward. On our own

side, the wooded knolls only just admit space for the line. In
this and other respects Scotch tourists may be reminded of the
Skye line as it skirts the southern shore of Loch Carron.

At *Penmaenpool* (*Inn*; *Bridge over the river*) the navigable part
of the Mawddach ceases, and the remaining distance to Dolgelley
is over a green, cattle-feeding strath, across which, on the left,
there is a good view up the narrow Ganllwyd valley.

For **Dolgelley** *see p.* 36.

Barmouth to Bont-ddu (*Hotel*), 5 *m*; and Dolgelley, 10 *m*. (*by road*),

*A mile saved by crossing Penmaenpool Bridge (6¾ m. from
Barmouth*).

This is justly accounted one of the most beautiful drives in the
kingdom. When the tide is up it is certainly the finest in Wales,
though of late years the greater part cf the traffic has been
diverted to the equally fine railway-route along the south side of
the estuary.

Quitting Barmouth at its south end, the road drops to the
pleasant Aberamffra harbour, and the view up the estuary opens out
at once, attaining its climax in the first two miles. Looking across
the water, we have Arthog on its woody slope, and behind it the
whole range of Cader Idris, extending from the Friog promontory
over Craig Cwm-llwyd and Tyrau-mawr to its crowning heights of
Pen-y-Gader and Mynydd Moel, to the left of which, in the far
distance, the Arans are seen. The minor ridge, in which the
Giant's Nose is the most striking object, forms a kind of terrace
between Cader and the strath at the head of the estuary. Then,
after crossing the outlet of a narrow valley on the left, up which
we obtain a passing view of Diphwys, the road retires from the
water, and for almost all the rest of the way to Bont-ddu (pron.
"Bont-the") is separated from it by meadows and low-wooded
eminences. Occasional glimpses of the estuary and of Cader are
obtained, but there is nothing of remarkable interest until
Bont-ddu is reached, and beyond it the picturesque little hotel
which is known as the *Half-way House*.

Bont-ddu (the "black bridge"). Entering a field through a
gate on the west side of the hotel you reach the Bont-ddu glen.
It is a delightfully wooded dingle, and down it, at a considerable
depth, the stream rushes between perpendicular rocks. A very
little distance up it there is a fine waterfall. All this is well seen
from a gravel walk, which, beyond the waterfall, winds up to a
summer-house.

From the hotel a diversion may be made up the valley to the
Llawllech range, and the summit of Diphwys reached in about
1½ hours.

Beyond Bont-ddu the road draws nearer to the estuary again,
and in a little over a mile reaches a picturesque spot where it
narrows to the width of a river and is crossed by a bridge leading

to Penmaenpool station. A wide stretch of pasture now intervenes
on the right, and on the left the narrow and beautiful *Cwm-mynach*
strikes northwards. Cader Idris is still a fine object to the south,
the inclined plane of the Foxes' Path being very clearly defined a
little to the left of the summit. Then we pass through the village of
L'an-lltyd (*no inn*), and cross the wider opening of the Ganllwyd
valley, down which come the main Mawddach stream and the road
from Ffestiniog and Maentwrog. The abrupt hill to the east
of this valley is Moel Cynwch, and round it goes the celebrated
Precipice Walk.

  Descending to the bridge the road now crosses the Mawddach,
passing just beyond it the entrance to Cymmer Abbey (*p.* 41),
which is seen on the left. Then, by a wide sweep round the hilly
ground on the left, it enters Dolgelley by the railway station and
across the river.

Barmouth to Harlech and Portmadoc by rail.

Barmouth to Llanbedr (*for* Cwm Bychan), 7½ *m* ; Harlech, 10 *m* ; Minffordd
Junction (*for* Ffestiniog railway), 17 *m* ; Portmadoc, 18½ *m*.

4-5 trains a day. Time, abt. 1 *hr.*

This part of the Cambrian railway follows the coast-line nearly
the whole distance, and after the first few miles presents a succession of charming views.

  Quitting Barmouth Station we have a wide view across the head
of Cardigan Bay to the long Lleyn promontory of Carnarvonshire, which discloses a graceful outline of hills on a descending
scale from the two peaks of Yr eifl (the "Rivals"), to the remote
cliffs of Bardsey Island. On the right is the but-end of the
Llawllech range, but the general appearance of the country on
this side is somewhat dull and bare, and the hill-slopes between
Barmouth and Harlech are mostly intersected by stone walls.

  Two miles on our way Llanaber Church (*p.* 52) is conspicuous
on the right. Then the shore, low and swampy, recedes. The
woods of Cors-y-gedol, and the green round top of Moelfre, come
into view before we reach **Dyffryn Station** (4½ *m*). This is the
nearest point at which to leave the train for Bwlch Drws Ardudwy
(the "Pass of the door of Ardudwy"), but we have preferred to give
a full description of the route the reverse way (*p.* 61).

Dyffryn Station to Bwlch Drws Ardudwy, 7¼ *m* ; Roman
Steps, 9½ *m* ; Cwm Bychan, 11½ *m* ; Llanbedr Station, 18 *m*. (Cwm
Bychan to Harlech, 5 *m*.)

  The *Inn* at Dyffryn is on the Barmouth road, 10 minutes' walk from the
Station and just that much out of our direct way. There is no other inn or
refreshment-house till you reach Llanbedr, nearly a mile short of Llanbedr
Station.

  For the direct route take the first turn to the left after leaving the station
and pass round the *Church*. This (parochially *Llanenddwyn*) occupies the site
of one which we are told existed in the sixth century. It was restored in 1883

The pulpit is made of cherry-wood. In the grave-yard, S. of the church, is the tomb of the regicide, Colonel Jones, brother-in-law to Cromwell. A few hundred yards beyond the church turn right again and you will presently cross the Barmouth and Harlech road, whereon is the chief part of the village. A sharp ascent begins at once. The road, a fair one at first, with a stream a little way on the right, soon reaches open ground and skirts at a considerable height the northward slope of Moelfre, affording an extensive view over the wooded glen of the Artro below, and of the mountains beyond from the Lleyn heights to Rhinog-fawr, including Snowdon and the nearer peaks of Moelwyn and Cynicht. Rhinog-fawr shows a dark rocky front, straight ahead. Our route is to the south of it. After a long hour's walk the road drops to the *Nant-col* valley and crosses it at right angles, turning to the right again beyond the crossing and, ¾ mile further, passing between the last two farms in the valley. After this it is a rough pony-track, at first faintly marked, but afterwards clear enough. In front is the pass (**Bwlch Drws Ardudwy**), a semi-circular depression separating Rhinog-fawr from Rhinog-fach. On our way up to it we pass the mouth of two little valleys on the right, whose streamlets flow down from Llethr. The whole scene is one of rocky desolation, most striking before the top of the pass is reached, because from that point the wide and featureless moor of Trawsfynydd dwarfs all the bolder parts of it. [The path we are on crosses this moor, and by it you may reach Trawsfynydd village (*inns*) in less than two hours, but there is nothing to recommend the walk.] For the Roman Steps, turn to the left out of the path as soon as you can do so without much climbing, and then go round the base of Rhinog-fawr. You will soon drop into another depression, watered by a little stream. Crossing this and climbing a steep pitch beyond you will strike into the **Roman Steps** path a few hundred yards east of its highest point. Turn north-west, *i.e.* to the left along this path, leaving a rock-strewn hollow below. The path descends, in many places by steps, through a narrow defile more than half-a-mile long. The rough slope of a hill succeeds, and you drop down, with a rapidly deepening valley on the right, to an outbuilding of a farm-house which is ¼ mile east of the lake of **Cwm Bychan**. *For a description of this lake, see p.* 61. Beyond it the route, now becoming a carriage-road, keeps along the right-hand of the stream all the way to the inn at Llanbedr, from which it is a short mile along the high-road to *Pensarn Station*. Between Cwm Bychan and Pensarn the valley is of a silvan character. By taking a turn to the right about half-way, just short of the bridge at *Pen-y-bont*, you may reach *Harlech* by a tortuous hill-road in about 3 miles from the point of divergence.

Beyond Dyffryn we have Moelfre close at hand on the right, and further off, as we proceed, the dark brow of Rhinog-fawr, separated from Rhinog-fach by the semi-circular depression of Bwlch Drws Ardudwy; on the left the shore-line trends still further away, the intervening space being occupied by *Morfa Dyffryn* ("the marsh of the water-plain.") At the northern end of these sands is *Mochras*, an island at high tide, and at low much visited for shells.

The scenery on the right greatly improves as we pass the outlet of the Artro glen with its foreground of fir-trees. Beyond it is Llanbedr, where the morning trains usually drop a number of tourists to fish in the Artro, to pick up shells on Mochras, or to make the Cwm Bychan excursion, for which see p. 60. Antiquarians, too, may by turning up the lane to the right, a few yards north of the station, then left and right again as opportunity offers, find, about a mile from the station, as noteworthy a *cromlech* as any of the numerous ones marked on the Ordnance survey in this neighbourhood. It is close to a barn, and now—" to what base uses do we come!"—has had its interstices filled up, and been turned into a pigstye!

From Pensarn the line enters a shallow cutting and emerges close to the sea again a little north of the ruin of *Llandanwg Church*, which is seen close to the sea. Two miles further **Harlech** is reached. Here the road, going considerably above the railway, has a corresponding advantage. For a description of the town and castle see *p.* 65. The station is just below the frowning rock on which the castle stands. Leaving it, we pass over *Morfa Harlech*, a flat expanse of tillage and pasture land, 2 miles wide. The name Y *las-Ynys* (the "green island"), by which a little mound on the right of the line, a mile beyond Harlech, is known, carries us back to the time when all this flat was over-flowed by the tide. Beyond this, in the left front, is Snowdonia—a very fine view,—the peak of Snowdon itself showing a beautiful pyramidal outline, with Cynicht and Moelwyn to the right of it. The next station is *Talsarnau*, whence, looking across the estuary, we see Portmadoc and, behind it, a hill-outline resembling that of the Giant's Nose as seen from Barmouth Bridge. Further away and more to the right, Moel Hebog is the conspicuous mountain. Then we sweep suddenly to the left round the opening of the Ffestiniog valley. The bare rocky scene presented at this point is more Scotch than Welsh in character, resembling a remote sea-loch on the Sutherland coast.

Penrhyn Deudraeth, the next station, is a large untidy village occupied principally by quarrymen. Beyond it the line, now running westward, skirts for a short distance the north side of the bay, and then turns inland to **Minffordd Junction**. Here the Ffestiniog line is carried over the Cambrian, and passengers for Ffestiniog change carriages and walk a few yards to the upper station.

This celebrated "Toy" railway is fully described in *Part I.*, *p.* 166, but for the benefit of day-visitors from Barmouth we here repeat so much of the description as explains the scenery on the route.

Mynffordd Junction to **Penrhyn**, 1¼ m; **Tan-y-Bwlch**, 5¼ m; **Tan-y-Grisiau**, 9½ m; **Blaenau Ffestiniog**, 10¾ m; **Duffws**, 11 m.

As the train quits Mynffordd, Cynicht and Moelwyn are prominent on the left. Then comes *Penrhyn* (called *Penrhyn Deudraeth* on the Cambrian line). It lies below us on the right, and is the abode of quarrymen. A stretch of dullish moorland succeeds. Then, as we ascend, lovely peeps are obtained through intervals in the oak-copse, which skirts the line for a long distance, into the lower part, or strath of the Ffestiniog valley, watered by the winding stream of the Dwyryd, which is seen flowing through a low rocky defile into the sea.

We pass immediately above and behind the finely placed mansion of *Plas*;
Maentwrog appears at the foot of a rocky knoll far below, and the steeple of
Ffestiniog church crowning a green hill at the far end of the valley. Another
minute, and we are going almost back again—right away from the depths into
which the line seemed about to plunge. This, the sharpest curve upon it, works
round the Tan-y-Bwlch glen, on the far side of which is **Tan-y-Bwlch** station.
If our train happens to be crossing another there, the latter will very likely be
seen running in the same direction, and parallel with us. Tan-y-Bwlch station
is 400 feet above the sea, a long mile above Tan-y-Bwlch Hotel, and 1¼ miles
from Maentwrog. Just beyond it a little fall is noticeable on the left, and a
lake on the right. Then we pass through a short tunnel and, on emerging from
it, get a pretty view of Ffestiniog village. The next bend affords a more extensive one down the green strath seawards, and then comes a tunnel ⅜ *m.* long.
Issuing from it, the valley has vanished, and we are traversing barren hollows
at the foot of Moelwyn. On the left, the mountain-side is strewn with rocky
débris. **Tan-y-Grisiau** station, 630 feet above the sea and the best starting
point for the summit of Moelwyn, is soon reached, and beyond it comes a green
upland over which Ffestiniog Church re-appears, but our journey is almost
over. Cyclopean walls of slate pierced by black caves, break-neck inclines, and
tramways that look as if they were off in search of the moon, indicate our
arrival at the new **Ffestiniog** :—The old one is 4 miles further, on the
Great Western line to Bala. If bound thither, we must go on to the "Toy"
terminus, **Duffws**. The platform at Blaenau Ffestiniog is adjacent to the L.
and N.W. station, for Bettws-y-Coed, &c.

Beyond Mynffordd the line crosses, side by side with the road,
the long embankment by which the wide alluvial flat of Traeth-
mawr is protected from the sea. As we cross, there is a rich and
grand mountain view on the right, comprising Moel Hebog, the
peak of Snowdon, Cynicht and Moelwyn. Snowdon from this
point looks its very best. *For Portmadoc, see Part I., p.* 163.

Barmouth to Cwm Bychan, &c., by Pensarn (Llanbedr).

For Barmouth to Pensarn by Rail, 7½ *m., see p.* 57.

Llanbedr (Inn: *Victoria*, ¾ *m.* S. of Station. *Post arr. abt.* 8.15
a.m.; dep. 2.35 *and* 4.30 *p.m.; vehicles meet principal trains during
the season*), a favourite resort with anglers, is pleasantly situated
on the Afon Artro, one of the best fishing waters in Wales.
Lodgings are fairly plentiful, and are increasing in number as the
place, in addition to its attractions for the fisherman, is the most
convenient starting point for exploring the wild summits and
recesses of the Ardudwy. The neighbourhood also abounds in
cromlechs and other ancient remains, a notable specimen of which
—two Longstones and another with an Ogham inscription—may
be seen between the river and the road from the station just short
of the village. Mochras, the peninsula that forms the seaward
bulwark of the Artro estuary, is a short two miles from the village,
and is famous for rare and beautiful shells. It should be visited
at low tide.

Llanbedr to Llyn Cwm Bychan 5½ *m* ; top of **Bwlch-y-Tyddiad (Roman Steps)**, 8 *m* ; top of **Bwlch Drws Ardudwy**, 10 *m* ; and back to **Llanbedr**, 18 *m* ; or to **Dyffryn Station**, 19 *m*.

Carriages can proceed nearly to Llyn Cwm Bychan and also towards Bwlch Drws Ardudwy as far as the farm Maes-y-Garnedd. There is no inn on the round.

This route includes the finest and most interesting scenery in the neighbourhood. Nothing is gained by walking to Cwm Bychan, and the pedestrian will do well to husband his powers by driving so far. In the course of our description we indicate in the proper place the divergences that may be made. If the ascent of Rhinog-fawr is to be included in the round an early start should be made, as the rugged character of all but its western flank and the remoteness of its position make it one of the least desirable spots in which to be overtaken by darkness.

We leave Llanbedr by the road that goes off up-stream close to the bridge and inn. The way for some miles is pleasantly shady, the stream keeps us company as far as Cwm Bychan, out of whose Llyn it issues, and we get many delightful river-glen peeps. About 1 *m*. from the start we reach the junction of the *Artro* and *Nant-col*, just above which the former is spanned by a well ivied bridge.

N.B.—The Nant-col comes from the tarns under Rhinog-fach and Llethr, on the south side of Bwlch-Drws-Ardudwy ; the Artro from Cwm Bychan. The Ordnance Map wrongly names the former "Afon Artro."

We do not cross the bridge, but keep straight on, having the stream still on our right. At *Pen-y-bont*, 1¾ *m*., is another bridge, and the road which crosses it gives the easiest and most direct approach to Rhinog-fawr.

Ascent of Rhinog-fawr from Pen-y-bont, *abt. 4 m. or 2 hrs.* Cross the bridge and, avoiding branch-tracks going off on either hand to farms, keep to the mountain-road that winds up on to the ridge of *Mynydd Llanbedr*. Soon, after a sharp turn to the left, the track divides, and we take to the left branch. (That to the right gradually winds down under *Y Foel-ddu* to Cwm Nant-col, up which lies the direct route from Llanbedr to Bwlch Drws Ardudwy.) A mile or so along the ridge we turn to the right, and leave on our left the rounded summit of Y Foel-ddu. The track ceases soon after this, but the route, though quite obvious in the main, cannot well be described. The only point is to get on to the open as directly as may be, *see p. 62.*

Our road now passes under an avenue of beech trees, and the scenery becomes wilder. Across the stream the craggy flank of the mountains contrasts finely with the foliage along their base. *Craig-y-Saeth* is the principal height in this direction, and it is around its western offshoot that our course now lies. Bending to the right for **Llyn Cwm Bychan**, we catch sight of a mountain burn coming down on the left in pretty cascades. The Llyn, as we approach it, seems to be enclosed on three sides by a girdle of

well nigh impassable rocky crags. and Saeth rises in a precipitous
cone from its southern verge. Further back appear the summit
and cairn of Rhinog-fawr. At the end, beyond a fringe of reed,
backed by a tiny meadow or two, with a little oak-scrub on the
lower slopes, Craig-wion rears itself ledge upon ledge. The Llyn
is not more than ⅓ m. in length, and about 250 yards wide. It
contains trout, but they seldom sport well. At the east end is a
small farm-house and a few outbuildings, which, instead of de-
tracting from the stern picture, lead one's thoughts to the terrible
loneliness of such a domicile when wintry storms are howling and
echoing from the crags. The last is no fancy touch, for Craig-y-
Saeth gives back one of the best of echoes.

Our route onward passes along the north side of the lake, and
when, a few hundred yards beyond it, a shed is reached, we turn
to the right through a gate and, avoiding a cart-track going off
on the left, ascend the green slope ahead. A ruined cottage is
passed, and then by a wall and through a bit of coppice we reach
the open hill-side, and strike the path that we are to follow
through Bwlch-y-Tyddiad. The crags of Craig-wion are on our
left, and looking back there is the bold cone of Moel-y-panylau,
2,051 feet.

If, when the combe divides, instead of following the path we strike up over
the ridge on our right, *Gloywlyn* or *Glowlyn*, a bright little lake lying between
Craig-y-Saeth and Rhinog-fawr, can be reached in about 20 minutes. The
ground, however, is exceedingly rough, cut up by gullies and covered with
stones, heath and whortleberry. There is a fine view of the Snowdonian mountains northward, Moel Hebog and the Glyders being the most prominent, and
the sea is in sight to the westward. By mounting the ledge-broken slope at the
south end of the lake, and then bearing to the left, the summit of Rhinog-fawr
is within a steady ¾ hr. climb from Glowlyn.

Rhinog-fawr (2,362 ft.; two cairns) is one of the finest view-points, being
the centre of an amphitheatre of heights. We look N. and S. to the peaks of
Snowdon and the cliff-line of Cader Idris respectively. Left of Snowdon, Moel
Hebog and the whole range stretching thence to Bardsey island are in sight, the
two-peaked Rivals a bold outline. Pwllheli, Criccieth (recognised by its castle),
and Portmadoc line the coast. W. is a sea-view to a far-off horizon ; S., Bwlch
Drws Ardudwy, close below, and beyond it the line of Rhinog-fach, Llethr,
and Diphwys. Then, more eastwards, the slightly tapering Arans and (north
of east) the bolder Arenig-fawr, with the table-topped Arenig-fach to the left
of it—all these across the wide and dreary plain of Trawsfynydd. Lastly,
turning northwards, we may see Blaenau Ffestiniog, and Ffestiniog spire, but
the Vale of Ffestiniog is hidden. Manod-mawr (heavy-topped) is to the right
of, and Moel Siabod behind Blaenau. Left of Siabod the sharp peak of Tryfan
and the Glyders, and nearer at hand, due north, Moelwyn. The return from
Rhinog-fawr to Llanbedr can be made by descending the W. slope and striking
the track that runs from the S. side of Y Foel-ddu to Pen-y-bont. The point
is not to descend too much into the Naut-col valley. To Dyffryn Sta. *see pp,* 63, 64.

After passing through a wall that crosses the entrance to the
pass, we come upon the so-called **Roman Steps**. Whether
British or Roman, they are an interesting and well preserved

memorial of much intelligent engineering toil, and for a great part of the distance appear to be as sound as on the day they were made. The pass narrows as we ascend, and the sides rise sheer to some height on either hand. Apparently, considerable cutting of the rock had to be done to form what even now is a fairly easy way through a defile which is by nature of the roughest description. When the top of the pass is reached, a wide but, in any but bright weather, dreary prospect, suddenly bursts on the view, extending over the wide plateau of Trawsfynydd towards Cader Idris.

A bit of paved way goes to the right at the top of the pass. Its object is not obvious, as it stops short in a few yards and can never have led anywhere Possibly it was paced by the sentry who kept watch against the enemy's approach in time of war. It is useless attempting to round the cliff by it as a deep and impassable depression is on the far side.

The descent from the *col* is by a steep rough path leading to Trawsfynydd village. Quit this path about half-way down and, dropping direct into the valley, cross it above the boggy ground that occupies its lower part. Then, striking due south over the slopes below Rhinog fawr, we find on the far side another path that, followed to the right hand, leads through the celebrated **Gate of Ardudwy**. This path is also in part a rude staircase, but is far less perfect and far more fatiguing to descend than its neighbour is to climb. The pass is wild and sombre rather than beautiful. The twin masses of the Rhinogs rise bare and stern on either hand, and when, after descending about ½ m., we look up a huge cliff recess on the right, the scene is fairly entitled to the epithet savage.

About ½ m. from the top of the pass a narrow combe on the left comes down from *Llyn Howel*, the principal source of the Nant-col. Rhinog-fach rises finely from the margin of the lake. By ascending the slope at the head of the combe the top of Llethr may be reached and the walk be continued over Diphwys to Penmaenpool or Barmouth. *For these routes, see " Mountain Section."*

A bit of boggy ground has to be crossed at the exit from the pass, and leaving *Nant-col farm* above us on the right, we soon arrive at another farm called *Maes-y-Garnedd*, whose meadows, watered by the Nant-col, are pleasant to look upon after the barren desolation of the defiles we have threaded. This farmhouse was the birth place of Col. Jones, the regicide, executed 1660. Our route now becomes a road, rough indeed, but practicable for driving, and some travellers order the conveyance that sets them down at Cwm Bychan to meet them again hereabouts. A mile or so from Maes-y-Garnedd we cross the stream to another farm, beyond which the road to Llanbedr drops to and recrosses the *Nant-col* and rejoins the outward route at the junction of this stream with the Artro, a mile short of Llanbedr. The road to

Dyffryn **Station** continues nearly due **west** over a spur of Moelfre. From the top of this spur the road to Dyffryn station steadily drops in a general direction south-west. A lane for Llanbedr goes off on the right about a mile down the hill. The map sufficiently indicates the routes. In the village of *Llanenddwyn*, through which we pass ½ mile short of Dyffryn station, there is a village inn on the Barmouth road, about half-a-mile south of our direct route, where it crosses that road.

The ascent of Moelfre is worth making either from Dyffryn Station or Llanbedr. The antiquarian will find two cromlechs on its lower western slopes, and on Craig-y-ddinas, about a mile due south from it, overlooking the Ysgethin valley, are the remains of a hill-fort.

Harlech.

Hotel: *Castle*, good ; and smaller inns.

Post: *Arr. abt.* 8 *a.m.* ; *dep.* 6.50 *a.m.* ; 4.30 *p.m.*

Though technically a corporate town, Harlech is in fact only a small and rather mean-looking village of a few hundred inhabitants, and with limited lodgings' accommodation. As the name implies (*ar llech* = " on the rock "), the site is a commanding one, and every season many hundreds of tourists pay it a flying visit on account of its castle and the fine sea and mountain view thence obtainable. Materfamilias, laying her plans for the summer outing, should, however, be told that it is no place for the bairns to enjoy the seashore—here a fertile and cultivated, but ugly marshland. Even for pedestrians, and still more for anglers, it is a less convenient base of operations than its neighbour Llanbedr (*p.* 60), which is the point whence public conveyances start for Cwm Bychan and the wild scenery of the Rhinogs. Indeed, the good hotel and the view it commands are the sole recommendation of Harlech as a resting-place, for even its celebrated castle has little of interest within it to detain the traveller. One view-point there is, however, within a walk or drive of a mile and a half, which all should endeavour to reach, Moel-y-Senicl, since the prospect from it, over Traeth-mawr to the mountains of Snowdonia, is of rare beauty. This and the route to Cwm Bychan and the Rhinogs will be found on pages 66-68.

Harlech Station is close below the fine crag on which the castle stands, and of the latter we get a good view as we wind round its base up to the village. **Harlech Castle** (*admission*, 4*d.*), both in position and appearance, is the ideal castle of childhood—high-perched, four-square, round-towered, and impressively massive. Its *history* may be told in a few words. Like so many other Welsh strongholds it owes its origin to Edward I., and dates from 1280 to 1310. In 1404 it was seized by Glyndwr, but re-taken by the royal forces four years later. In 1460 it afforded temporary shelter to Queen Margaret after Henry VI.'s overthrow at Northampton, and only yielded to the victorious "White Rose" after a protracted siege in 1468. This siege, says Mr. Pughe, gave rise to the martial strain known as the " March of the Men of Harlech." From that time it was allowed to become dilapidated, but was put into a state of defence and held for the King at the opening of the Civil War. In 1647, however, it was taken by General Mytton, and since then has played no part except in tourist story.

Crossing the deep and broad ditch which defended the east side'
we enter the middle ward between two bartisan towers. This
ward, which is of varying width, runs round the entire building
and is a pleasant grass-walk. On its northern side was a postern,
now closed. The main entrance to the inner ward is beween two
huge round towers, and the passage was defended at its outward
end by two, at its inner extremity by a third portcullis. Just short
of the latter we have entrances right and left to what must have
been the almost dark quarters of the guardians of the gate. Here
the staircases are broken and the floors gone, but the principal
chamber, which occupied the first floor and extended over the left
hand room and the passage, has well preserved and typical
Edwardian fire-places. Entering the central quadrangle, an area
gloomy beyond most of its kind, the main stairs enable us to
ascend and judge of the proportions of the chamber just mentioned.
The *great hall* was on the opposite side of the court, and was
apparently a lean-to structure but poorly lighted. Adjoining it
on the north, next to a corner space now partitioned off, was the
chapel. The ascent to the top of the walls is made by a stair in the
south-east angle of the court, near the foot of which are a few inscribed stones and some querns (hand-mill stones), collected by the
late Mr. Wynne, of Peniarth. The battlements form a well protected promenade, and from them two of the towers, inaccessible
from below, can be examined. The view of the sea, the coast and
the mountains is as comprehensive as it is beautiful. Across the
bay, 7 miles off, rises the sister stronghold of Criccieth, and to the
left of it are the graceful Rivals. the commencement of a glorious
range of heights, culminating in the peak of Snowdon due north
of us and ending near at hand in Moelwyn and the Manods. If
the tide be up and the day be bright, the islet-broken waters of
Traeth-bach and the deep empurpled combes in the mid-distance
make the picture perfect.

Before quitting the battlements the outermost line of defence
should be noticed. It still shows the position of its gates : the
upper gate below the south-west tower and the water-gate lower
down beyond the north-west angle.

For **Mo-l-y-Senicl**. the view-point already mentioned as 1½ m.
from the town, we turn up-hill from the Castle past the Post
Office When, after a walled-in bit of road, an iron gate across
the road is reached, a good view backwards is obtained of the
mountains running down the Lleyn peninsula. Pass through the
gate. From the top of the rise Y Foel ddu is the green height
prominent ahead, and to the left of it Rhinog-fawr. When cross-
roads are reached we turn to the left, and ascend past some
cottages.

Harlech to Cwm Bychan, 5 *m.,* **and Rhinog-fawr,** 3 *hrs.*

The road straight on from the above cross-roads leads, in 2 *m.,* into the Artro
valley route for Cwm Bychan, which it joins a few hundred yards beyond Pen-
y-bont at a point 2 *m.* from Llanbedr village, and 3 *m.* from the lake.

SECTION MAP No. 10

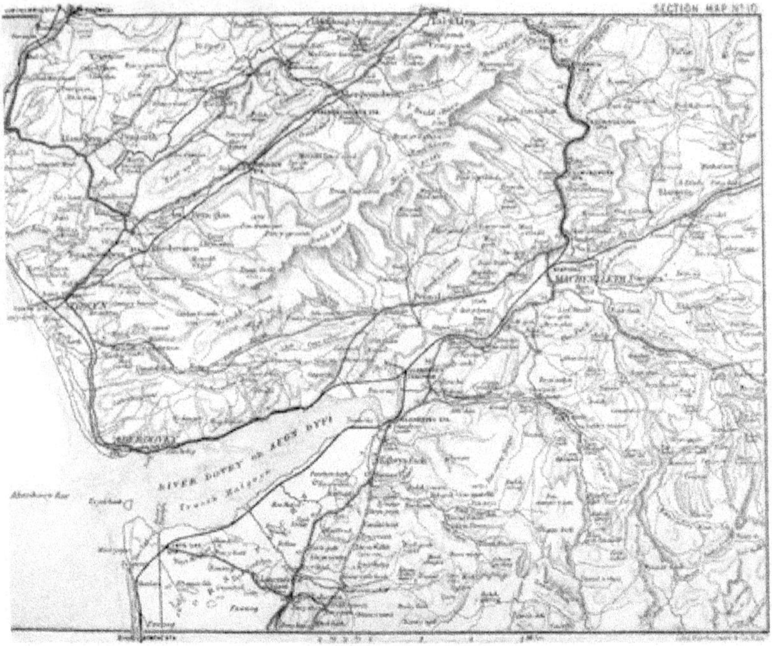

By crossing the Artro at Pen-y-bont, and following a mountain cart-road that
bears to the left up the green ridge of Mynydd Llanbedr to the foot of the final
steeps of Y Foel-ddu, which must be passed on our left, we may reach the summit of Rhinog fawr (p. 62) by an easy walk of 7 m. from Harlech. There is
no wilder and more solitary spot in North Wales. Immediately below us, on
the south side of the summit, is the savage pass Bwlch Drws Ardudwy, while on
the opposite side, round an intervening bluff, is the entrance to Bwlch-Tyddiad,
through which, by the "Roman steps," is the path from Trawsfynydd to Cwm
Bychan. The fair-sized lake at the foot of the broken north-west slopes is
Gloyllyn with Craig-y-Saeth immediately beyond and over it. It is an easy
descent to Gloyllyn, and thence a rough scramble bearing to the eastward over
rock and heather into the valley at the head of the Cwm Bychan lake. The
descent direct from Rhinog-fawr into the gorges immediately guarding it may
be fit for goats, but not for reasonable beings who value their necks.

Soon on the right we get a fine view of Craig-y Saeth and of the
cliffs in the upper part of the Artro valley. The step notched
ridge more to the left is Craig Wion, at the head of Cwm Bychan,
and the line of wild and scarcely graceful crags is continued
northward to Moel-y-Panylau. On the other side of our road
a gap in the hills shows us Moel Hebog, bulky and almost flat-
topped. The object of our walk is the summit of the little rocky
knoll on our left front, and to attain this we turn through a gate
beyond a rill soon after passing an upright stone. The easiest
way is to make for the upper of two gateways seen in a wall on
the ridge. The view of Traeth-bach, with its islet, and of Traeth-
mawr and its mountain girdle (Moelwyn nearest and Cynicht, the
knobby ridge beyond), above all of the broken ground immediately
about Traeth-mawr, is not unlike and scarcely inferior to the
beauties of the Mawddach estuary, whilst the coast-view, far more
extensive than any to be had thereabouts, stretches from Bardsey
(seen over the promontory west of St. Tudwal's Islands) past
Pwllheli, Criccieth, and Portmadoc to Strumble Head. The return
to Harlech cannot be varied with any advantage. *Cwm Bychan*
is about 3 miles east of Moel-y-Senicl.

Harlech to Talsarnau, by the hills, 5 m., 2 hrs.

This is an extension of the walk to the summit of Moel-y-Senicl
described above. From the top of the hill rejoin the road, now
only a cart-track, and follow it northward about half-a-mile to
where it divides. The left-hand branch, affording a pleasant view
of the Traeths and the mountains beyond, leads down into the
main road, and so to *Talsarnau station* in three miles from the
fork, about two miles from which, at Singrig hamlet, we have to
turn sharply to the left, and when the road is reached follow it to
the right.

Alternative route. If from the fork of the cart-road mentioned above
we take the right-hand branch, and where this, almost at once, again divides,
the right-hand branch once more, *Talsarnau Station* may still be reached by a
rough walk of 10 miles, all told, from Harlech, that will delight those who like
to get into an unfrequented district—such as this—dotted with solitary tarns,
and broken up by ridges that flank the western side of Moel-y-Panylau.

The green hill immediately in front at the bifurcation of the tracks is Moel-y-gaedog, and the Ordnance Map shows a camp upon it. It can, of course, be easily climbed and our route rejoined by following the top eastward, but there is no special object in the ascent, as the view does not differ much from that already obtained from Moel-y-Senicl and the camp is scarcely traceable. It involves, moreover. the getting over two or three awkward walls. Keeping, therefore, the track, we soon come in sight of the poor little tarn *Llyn-y-fedw* on our left, and then, after passing through an iron gate, about half-a-mile onward, the track comes to an end. From this point the map and compass will be our best guides. The boggy valley immediately below is not to be crossed direct, but bearing a little to the left up a rock-strewn depression, with a little burn in it, we make for the top of the minor ridge on its east side, and then have before us the dreary lake *Llyn-ciddeu-maur* with its tiny namesake *-bach,* a mere pool, a quarter of a mile to the north of it. From the latter a cart-track begins and runs into another (the second left-hand one we did *not* take when starting from the bifurcation near Moel-y-gaedog; it goes through the hills by a gap N. of Moel-y-Panylau to Trawsfynydd) by a short détour to the eastward. Our better route, however, is to cross the ridge, north-west, to *Llyn Caerwych*, another insignificant tarn. Beyond this, after climbing a little hump, we gain the water-parting between the Artro tributaries and the brooks flowing to the Traeth-bach. Making our way down the valley a track is soon struck by which, passing a farm or two by a winding lane running close to *Llyn Tecwyn-isaf,* we gain the old road from Harlech to Maentwrog, when turning to the left and shortly after to the right, by a lane down through *Talsarnau* village, we reach the *Station*.

Barmouth to Machynlleth or Aberystwith by rail.

Barmouth to Barmouth Junction, $1\frac{3}{4}$ *m*; Llwyngwryl, $5\frac{1}{2}$ *m*; Towyn, 12 *m*; Aberdovey, 16 *m*; Glandovey Junction, 22 *m*; Borth $30\frac{1}{2}$ *m*; Aberystwith $38\frac{1}{2}$ *m*.
— Glandovey Junction to Machynlleth, $3\frac{1}{2}$ *m*.
Passengers for Aberystwith usually change carriages at Glandovey Junction. Route described the reverse way in the "Cambrian Route to Barmouth and Aberystwith" (p. 73).

After crossing **Barmouth Bridge**, with its magnificent view up the Mawddach estuary, the line reaches **Barmouth Junction**, where passengers from the Dolgelley branch are taken up. Then, passing between wooded hills on the left and a wide marsh on the right, it reaches the *Friog* promontory and is carried along the face of the rock for about two miles at a considerable height above the sea. The view extends from Bardsey Isle to Snowdon, the most marked intervening height being the double-peaked Rivals. After going a little inland at **Llwyngwril** (*p.* 55), we run close to the sea again till a descent is made to the bridge over the *Dysynni* and the *Towyn marsh* ("Morfa Towyn"). The peak of Cader Idris and the precipitous little "Bird Rock" now come into view, the former at the head of the **Dysynni Valley**, the latter to the right of its entrance.

For **Towyn** (*refr. room*) *see p.* 69. The town is on the left-hand as we pass, and shows nothing noteworthy except its massive church-tower. Then, on the same side, we have a view up the long, straight depression which leads to Tal-y-Llyn, and Cader Idris is again seen for a few moments. The next opening (1¼ m. beyond Towyn) is the Happy Valley, traversed by the old road to Machynlleth. Sand-heaps and marsh are now on the right till the line reaches the shore again and sweeps round to **Aberdovey Station**, ¼ m. short of the town, for a description of which see page 72. The large building near the station was built for an hotel.

Tunnels and cuttings only admit of stray peeps into the town as we pass behind it, but on emerging from them a fine view opens across the Dovey estuary and the Borth marsh to the graceful hills beyond. Borth village is seen at the foot of a little headland, and there will probably be a wreath of steam to indicate the course of the railway from Aberystwith, as the train that connects with ours at Glandovey Junction comes rushing along the south side of the water. Our route hugs the north side throughout, and, as the estuary narrows, the wooded little glens that pierce the barer hills on the far side are pleasant to behold. On one little knoll we may note Glandovey Castle, and then, crossing the Dovey itself, we reach **Glandovey Junction** (temp. refr. room).

For the rest of the route to **Aberystwith**, see p. 91.

For *Machynlleth* the line crosses a marsh, and then enters the narrower portion of the Dovey valley, keeping near the river between green and graceful hills of moderate elevation.

For **Machynlleth**, see p. 92.

Towyn.

Hotels: *Corbet Arms*, short ½ m. from station ; *Cambrian*, ½ m. from station.

Post Office, near the church : Del. abt. 8.15 a.m. and 6.15 p.m. ; desp. abt. 5.20 p.m. Open : *Week days*, 8 a.m. to 8 p.m. ; *Sundays*, 8 to 10 a.m.

Distances : Aberdovey (*rail or road*), 4½ m. ; Aberystwith (*rail*), 27 m. ; Barmouth (*rail*), 12 m. ; Borth (*rail*), 18½ m. ; Dolgelley (*rail*), 17½ m. ; (*coast road*), 20m. ; (*hill-road*), 16½m.; (*by Tal-y-Llyn rail and road*), 20m.; Machynlleth (*rail*), 18½ m. ; (*old road*), 12 m. ; Tal-y-Llyn, 10 m.

Towyn is a well-built little town greatly improved of late years, and possessed of a well-earned reputation for healthiness. As a sea-side resort its weakness is that from the town the sea is hardly, if at all, visible, while the number of lodging-houses overlooking the water is very limited. It occupies the southern end of the Dysynni flat (*Morfa Towyn*)—an alluvial tract measuring nearly 1½ m. from north to south and extending some miles inland.

The flatness of this tract adds considerably to the effect of the screen of surrounding mountains, amongst which Cader Idris, rising from the head of the valley 12 miles away, and the small but precipitous Bird Rock (" Craig Aderyn ") about half that distance, are the most conspicuous heights. The railway on a low embankment passes between the town and the sea.

The beach at Towyn is of firm, hard sand and very extensive, offering excellent bathing facilities. There is, however, no shelter for boats as at Aberdovey. The *Corbet Arms* is a good hotel, and lodgings are comparatively cheap.

The **Church**, founded by and dedicated to St. Cadfan, is one of the most interesting and ancient in North Wales. It is cruciform in plan, with a central tower, and was carefully restored, and in part rebuilt, in 1882. Of old work are the Early Norman nave, aisles, clerestory, and North transept. The South transept and the chancel (except the north wall, which is the original Early English), together with the tower, are new, but re-produce old work destroyed by the fall of the old tower in 1692.

Among the *Monuments*, notice : 1. the effigy of a knight in armour (14th cent.), Griffith Adda, of Dolgoch and Ynys-y-Maengwyn (*see p.* 71), according to the inscription placed above it by the late Mr. Wynne, of Peniarth ; 2. the effigy of a priest (14th cent.), remarkable, says Mr. Bloxam, as an almost unique example : " the *amice*, instead of being folded about the neck, is worn on the head as a hood " ; 3. the famous, so-called. **St. Cadfan's Stone.** This venerable relic, formerly outside the church, is now on the floor at the west end of the north aisle. It was once thought to have been part of the tomb of St. Cadfan, the co-founder and first abbot of the monastery on Bardsey, in the 6th century ; but against this is the tradition that the Saint was buried on the island. The Rev. J. Williams, in *Archæologia Cambrensis*, 1850, translated what he supposed to be a double memorial, as follows :

1. The body of Cyngen is on the side where the marks will be.
2. Beneath a similar mound is extended Cadvan. Sad that it should enclose the praise of the earth. May he rest without blemish.

More recent examinations have, however, all but demolished this interesting rendering, and antiquaries no longer profess to find the name of Cadfan, which is held to be a misreading of Adgan, whoever he may have been. " The body of Cyngen " (a name borne by more than one 6th century saint) is almost the only part of this inscription now considered to be beyond reasonable doubt.

" *St. Cadfan's Well*," in the pleasure-grounds close by, is another memorial of the virtues of Towyn's benefactor.

Llwyngwril

Goiewen

Castell
y gaer

Bodilan

Yr Ogof

Rhollei
Lôn

Y Fignoer

Allt-lwyd

Pen-y-gorlun
1266

Craig Epryn
Llewelyn

Pen-y-gorlun

Pen-y-bryn

Cerrig

Llanlloyd

Pant ywyn
Rhiw felen

Cwm

Glan-y-wern

Pont-y-gareth

Craig
yr Aderyn
(Bird Rock)

Gwlch
y maen

Llangelynin

Llanegryn

Pennarth

Pen-y-cood
Aber
tryweryn

Bwlch

Bryn-llwyd

Castell Maer
Camp

Dysynni

Morfa
trwydol
Tyfnydd

Pen-y-Cemaes

Foel-wyllt

Dolgoch
STA.

Bryn-glas

Bron-dyvy

Tal-y-bont

Pont Dysynni

Bryn
Craig

River

Afon Fathew

STA.

1679

Pen trum

Pant

Rhyd-y
owenfeld

Pen-y-wern

Cil-y-owys

Ynys-maengwyn

Kenfal

STA.

Rhydyronen

Mynydd
y Gaer

Trum Gell
1713

Tre'r
ddôl

STA.

Morfa Towyn
(Towyn Marsh)

Pall Well

Bryn-llin

Hendy

Penbryn
y llog

Pant cynfal

Bathi

TOWYN STA.

TOWYN

Bron-gwyn

Craig y barcut

Corlan fraith
1334

Mynydd
bychan

Glan-y-don

Ffriddil

Cefin

Haföd

Y tyn-y-cornel

Maes-porth
Gaethle Bodfa
Moel
Gaethle Llanerch-lorn

Maeslorth Pant-lwonen

Maes-y-bryn-glaws

Tyn-y-berth

Cefin rhos isaf

Cefn-rhos-uchaf

Bwlch

Efraid

Sychnant

Brynhowel

ABERDOVEY

STA.

Pen-helig

RIVER DOVEY OR A

Aberdovey Bar

Tryni-bach

Traeth Malgwyn

B

Moel-ynys

Gorse
Pen-sarn

YNYS-LAS
STA.

Glan-Dyfi
Pen-y-bont

Ynys

Ynys Morlo

Fawnog

Llwe
Gynfelin

Aber Lenny

Frynnon-las

Gwynfryn

Gelly

Fawnog

Excursions from Towyn.

These are mostly given under the heads of Barmouth, Dolgelley and Machynlleth, and being nearly all road or rail expeditions will be readily understood from the descriptions given the reverse way, except the rail to Abergynolwyn and the ascent and descent of Cader Idris, which will be found in full detail in the "*Mountain Section.*"

1. **To Llanegryn**, 4½ *m* ; **Bird Rock**, 7½ *m* ; **Llanfihangel-y-Pennant**, 10 *m*, by road.

Llanfihangel to Abergynolwyn (village 2¼ *m* ; Tal-y-Llyn, 5½ **m.**) Station, 3 *m.* whence by rail or road it is 7 *m.* to Towyn.

— to Tal-y-Llyn direct by Bwlch Cedris, 3 *m.*

Towyn to the Bird Rock (Craig Aderyn), 6 *m.* by nearest way, *see* "*Mountain Section*" under "*Cader Idris from Towyn.*"

We start by the Dolgelley road, and on the right, about a mile from the town, is the ancient stone *Croes-jaen*. On the other side, half-a-mile further, are the mansion and grounds of *Ynys-Maengwyn* (John Corbet, Esq.), long a seat of the Corbett family. The house, part of which only is old, after having been fortified by the Royalists in 1645, was almost immediately burnt by them, lest it should fall into the hands of the Roundheads. About a mile onward the road bends to the left, and crosses two streams to *Bryn Crug*, or *Pont Fathew* (public-houses), where the direct route for the Bird Rock and Llanfihangel turns to right. We take the left turn for *Pont Dysynni*. Some 500 yards below this bridge and on the right bank of the river is a small mound *Tomen Ddreiniog*, while Tal-y-bont, on our left as we begin to ascend, is on the site of a mansion associated with Llewelyn and Edward I. **Llanegryn** is about a mile from the bridge, a few hundred yards on the right from the point where the old and new roads to Dolgelley diverge right and left respectively. The **Church**, well restored by the late Mr. W. W. E. Wynne, of Peniarth, "the Mæcenas of Welsh literature," has a good roof, an interesting Norman font, and a superb roodscreen. For Llanfihangel we continue another ¾ *m.* along the old Dolgelley road, down past the entrance to *Peniarth* (since 1859 the home of the Hengwrt MSS.) to Bryn-gwyn, and there turn to the right, and about ½ *m.* onward to the left. The road now skirts the north of the Dysynni valley, gradually nears the river, and crosses it at *Pont-y-Garth* opposite **Craig Aderyn** ("Bird Rock"), which we keep on our right as we go up the main valley to *Pont Ystumaner*, the bridge over the stream issuing from Tal-y-Llyn. A direct course of a mile then brings us to **Llanfihangel-y-Pennant** (*Peniarth Arms*), a sequestered village at the foot of Cader Idris. On the hill, left of the road as we approach it, are the remains of *Castell-y-Bere*, once one of the largest castles in Wales. It was visited by Edward I., but little is known of its subsequent history.

Llanfihangel to Abergynolwyn Station, 3 m. by road (*Pedestrians* should enquire for a footpath which saves ½ m.), involves a return almost to Pont Ystumaner, just short of which turn to the left up the valley. At Abergynolwyn village, half-a-mile from the station, there is a public house.

Llanfihangel to Tal-y-Llyn (direct pedestrian route), 3 m. This is over *Bwlch Cedris*, abt. 1½ m. E. of the village. A word of enquiry before starting will make matters clear. From the top of the pass we command the Tal-y-Llyn valley and drop quickly to the main road from Towyn.

(2.) To **Barmouth** (12 m.), by rail p. 99.

(3.) To **Dolgelley** by coast-road, p. 45; by hill-road, p. 46; over Cader Idris, *see "Mountain Section."*

(4.) To **Abergynolwyn** (rail), 7 m., p. 132; **Tal-y-Llyn** (road), 10 m.; **Dolgelley** (road), 20 m., p. 143. N.B.—The station for the narrow-gauge line to Abergynolwyn is at the east end of the town, ¾ m. from the Cambrian Station.

(5.) To **Machynlleth** by the Happy Valley (12 m.), p. 96.

(6.) To **Aberdovey**, 4 m.; **Machynlleth**, 13½ m.; **Borth**, 18½ m.; and **Aberystwith**, 27 m. (by rail), p. 68.

Aberdovey (Hotels: *Dovey, Raven, Britannia. Post, arr. abt. 8 a.m., 6.30 p.m.; dep. abt. 7 a.m., 5.40 p.m. Office open, Weekdays, 7 a.m. to 8 p.m.; Sunday, 8 to 10 a.m.*), is a pleasant little port and watering-place, undisturbed by fashion, peaceful, but at the same time accessible. It can boast of a wide extent of firm sand and very fair bathing. Of walks peculiar to itself there are only those on to the low hill-range that rises between the sea and the "Happy Valley" route from Machynlleth to Towyn, including Llyn Barfog, 4 m., and Pennal (*Inn*), 6 m., p. 96. The railway, however, brings many excursions which we have described in connection with other places within the range of a day's outing; the Llyfnant valley (p. 97) and Tal-y-Llyn may be visited and even Cader Idris ascended, while the glories of Barmouth and Dolgelley only involve from 1½ to 2½ hours' railway travelling there and back. Special cheap fares are an additional inducement. The climate of Aberdovey is exceptionally mild and equable.

The town itself follows the curvature of the shore, and is only intermittently visible from the railway, which passes through cuttings and tunnels behind it. The station is half-a-mile to the west of it, just beyond a large building which was erected as an hotel, and was afterwards for some years a Jesuit college.

The Cambrian Route to Barmouth and Aberystwith.

Whitchurch to Oswestry, 18 *m* ; Welshpool, 34 *m*. (Shrewsbury to Welshpool, 19¼ *m*.), Newtown 47¼ *m* ; Moat Lane Junction, 52¼ *m*. (Llanidloes, 60 *m*.) ; Cemmaes Road, 70 *m*. (Dinas Mawddwy, 77 *m*.) ; Machynlleth, 75½ *m*. (Corris, 80¾ *m*.) ; Glandovey Junction, 79 *m* ; Borth, 87¼ *m* ; Aberystwith, 95½ *m*.
— Glandovey Junction to Aberdovey, 6 *m* ; Towyn, 9¾ *m* ; Barmouth Junction, 20 *m*. (Dolgelley, 27¾ *m*.) ; Barmouth, 21¾ *m*.

Through carriages between London and Aberystwith, *vid* Shrewsbury, throughout the year ; also, during the season, between London and Barmouth ; Manchester, Liverpool, and Aberystwith ; Hereford and Aberystwith (*by Mid Wales route*).

Refreshment rooms at Whitchurch, Oswestry, Shrewsbury, Welshpool, Moat Lane Jnc., Llanidloes, Machynlleth, Glandovey Jnc. (Temp.), Towyn (up platform), Barmouth Jnc., Dolgelley, Borth, and Aberystwith (Temp.).

The approach to Central and North Wales by the Cambrian railway does not plunge into the heart of the scenery at once, but it is interesting throughout, and on a gradually increasing scale of beauty which secures the tourist's attention during the whole journey. The watershed between the Severn and the streams that flow west into Cardigan Bay is crossed at a height of 692 feet between Moat Lane Junction and Cemmaes Road, and for the rest of the way, especially to Barmouth, the prospects are brimful of beauty.

From Glandovey Junction the Barmouth and Dolgelley line hugs the coast nearly all the way. Magnificent views of the peerless Mawddach estuary are obtained, and that of the Dovey is skirted throughout by the Barmouth line on the north and the Aberystwith one on the south.

There is an abundant service of trains from both Oswestry and Shrewsbury. The two routes unite at Buttington Junction, 3 *m*. short of Welshpool, but the trains from both starting-points run through to Welshpool, whence the main part goes on to Aberyst-with, but through carriages are run from Shrewsbury to Barmouth. The Cambrian line itself starts from Whitchurch on the Crewe and Shrewsbury branch of the L. & N. W., and there is direct communication by it from Manchester and Liverpool. Passengers from G. W. R. stations north of Shrewsbury change trains at Gobowen, and proceed thence *viá* Oswestry.

The Route.—Between Whitchurch and Oswestry the line passes through an ordinary rural district, and presents no special objects of interest, except perhaps the large mere on the left, just short of Ellesmere Station, and the old mansion of Hardwick on the same side a few miles beyond it. *For continuation of route,* *see p. 75.*

Oswestry.

Hotels: *Wynnstay Arms, Queen's, Matthew's Temperance,* abt. 5 min. from stations.

Post: *Arr. abt.* 7 *a.m.,* 2 *and* 5 *p.m.* ; *dep.* 5 *and* 10 *a.m.,* 8.15 *p.m.*

Population : 7851.

Distances: (*By road*) Llanrhaiadr-yn-Mochnant, 12 *m.* direct, 13 *m. vid* Llangedwyn ; Pistyll Rhaiadr, 16 *m* ; Old Oswestry (Caer Ogyafan) 1 *m.*

During the summer a **Coach** leaves Llanrhaiadr for Oswestry (Wed. and Sat. only) at 9 *a m.*, and returns from Oswestry at 5 *p.m. Fares*: Single, 2s. ; return, 3s.

Oswestry, variously interpreted as " Oswald's tree " (Oswald of Northumbria was killed here in battle against Penda of Mercia in 642. and his body, tradition says, was afterwards crucified on a tree), or " Oswald's town " (in which case the name is a hybrid, and the last syllable *tre*) is a flourishing market-town in Shropshire, 3 miles from the Welsh border, but in the diocese of St. Asaph. Situated in a pleasant but in no wise remarkable neighbourhood in regard to scenery, its chief importance to the tourist bound for North Wales is its comparatively easy access to that out of the way but fine waterfall, Pistyll Rhaiadr. In the town itself the Church, 10 minutes' walk from the station, is the only object of sufficient interest to induce the passing traveller to break his journey, and this will not detain him long Those who arrive by the G.W.R. *vid* Gobowen, and are bound westward by the Cambrian Railway, have to change stations, because the lines, though they approach within a stone's throw of each other, do not actually join. By scme of the trains there is an interval of ½ to ¾ of an hour, and even the shorter time is enough to permit a sight of the chief feature of the **Church**, its fine *tower*, which is very picturesque, and has almost the character of a venerable rock on account of the abundant growth of yew bushes from its crevices. This tower, during the Civil War in great part pulled down, was rebuilt some years after the Restoration. The body of the building was restored by the late Mr. Street, and the interior is somewhat striking in appearance, owing to the nave-aisles being of the same width as the transept-arms are long, and divided from them by an arcade. From the floor of the church rises the massive tower, and its walls have been covered with memorials, but none of them of any general interest. The only tomb of any

moment is in the wall of the north aisle. This is to Hugh Yale
(d. 1616) and his wife, who were buried "within the chancel of
this church, commonly called St. Mary's before its demolition in
the late wars." In the south chancel-aisle is some good modern
glass. About half-a-mile west of the church, and close to the Grammar School, is **St. Oswald's Well**, of little interest, and about
a mile to the north is *Caer Ogyafon*, or *Old Oswestry*, a fine and
well preserved earthwork with a triple line of defences.

Route continued. *Oswestry to Welshpool*, 16 m. There is
nothing to detain the tourist on this part of the Cambrian Railway, unless he choose to climb the Breidden Hills from Buttington
Station. They are, however, more conveniently ascended from
Middletown Station on the Shrewsbury and Welshpool line (*see*
p. 85).

Quitting Oswestry, the bold scarp of a limestone hill, marred
by works, is noticeable on the right hand. Then we proceed
through a pleasant pastoral country to **Llanymynech** (6 m; Inn,
Lion), where the Llanfyllin branch diverges to the right, and on
the left a grass-grown line, no longer used, is a portion of the
" Potteries and North Wales " railway. We do not remember to
have been favoured with a prospectus of this line, but we should
fancy that even the lively imagination of a promoter must have
been sorely taxed to furnish the public with inducements for
taking shares in it. One day it may possibly become a connecting
link in an Irish route through the Berwyns, but at present it is a
very " poor relation " of the surrounding lines.

For the route hence to Llanfyllin, Pistyll Rhaiadr, and Lake
Fyrnwy (Liverpool Reservoir), see p. 76.

A few yards beyond this station the line crosses the Fyrnwy,
an important feeder of the Severn, which it joins a few miles
further east at the foot of the **Breidden Hills**. These hills are
conspicuous features in the landscape from many parts of North
Wales They rise from the level strath of the Severn to a height of
1,250 feet in three peaks, and are in parts wooded almost to the
summit. The most northerly of them, *Breidden Hill* proper, is
crowned by a lofty obelisk in honour of the celebrated Admiral
Rodney, who died in 1792. The other hills are called *Cefn-y-*
Castell and *Moel-y-Golfa* respectively, and, as we proceed, the
latter presents the appearance of an almost perfect cone with its
southern slope wooded from head to foot. It is due east of our
course as we cross the Severn a mile short of **Buttington**
Junction (13 m. from *Oswestry*). *For the Breiddens, see p. 84.*

Here the Shrewsbury line comes in, and 3 miles further we are
at Welshpool. *For description of the town, &c., see p. 85; for*
continuation of route, p. 87.

Llanymynech to Llanfyllin (*rail*), 9 *m* ; "Lake Fyrnwy," &c.

The scenery along this branch is pleasant, but in no wise re-markable. Soon after starting, the Tanat river is crossed, and the Fyrnwy is then followed for a mile, after which the line ascends the valley of its tributary, the Afon-cain. Just short of Llanfyllin, near *Bryngwyn* station, the Breidden Hills are well seen towards the left rear. Llanfyllyn is pronounced " Thlanvuthlin."

Llanfyllin (Inn, *Wynnstay Arms*) is a small, uninteresting town, famous for its beer and for the sweet bells of its ugly red-brick church. Pedestrians bound for Llanrhaiadr-yn-Mochnant, 6 *m.*, and Pistyll Rhaiadr, 10 *m.*, pass both the church and the " hotel." The latter is the last house of entertainment short of Llanrhaiadr.

Llanfyllin to Llanrhaiadr-yn-Mochnant, 6 *m.*

This is a pretty walk, with a good inn at its terminus. The road leaves Llanfyllin at the west end, and then has on the right the unremarkable house but picturesque demesne of *Bodfach*. When the road forks, take the right-hand branch. [The left-hand one goes to Cann Office and Dinas Mawddwy.] About a mile from the fork there is a *tomen* above the road on the right amongst the trees, and then, as the road ascends, we soon get a charming view of the Cain valley on our left. Thenceforward, the scenery is soft and pretty all the way to Llanrhaiadr. When at a fork, about a mile beyond the tomen, a road goes off up-hill on the left, take the lower or right-hand road. This is the only point where any doubt as to the route can occur. About 3½ miles from Llanfyllin the scenery is at its best, and if the day be bright the view of the Tanat Vale, with Llanrhaiadr on the left-front and the hill Gyrn Moelfre (1,707 feet), a fairly pronounced summit on the right-front, is very beautiful. Beyond the bridge over the Tanat river we come to cross-roads, and can either continue straight on, and then in a few hundred yards turn to the left, or, turning left at the cross-roads, we can take a field-path on the right, from the near side of *Pont Aber Khaiadr*. In each case the distance to the village is about a mile.

Llanrhaiadr-yn-Mochnant (Hotel : *Wynnstay Arms*) is a poor little place, and the hotel (good), which is close to the church, owes its prosperity chiefly to summer visitors to Pistyll Rhaiadr, 4 miles distant. The church was restored in 1879, when an ancient cross, still to be seen, was discovered. *In summer there is a public conveyance on Wednesdays and Saturdays to and from Oswestry. Single fare, 2s. ; return, 3s.*

Llanrhaiadr to Pistyll Rhaiadr, 4 *m.*

Take the road on the right that ascends from the main street, just short of the bridge over the Rhaiadr. The way cannot be missed, as it keeps the stream below on the left throughout. In about a mile and a half we first get sight of the waterfall, some two miles off, as the bird flies. It suffers somewhat by being so long in sight before it is reached, and the valley by which we approach it is rather commonplace. Happily, just before the full beauty of the fall is revealed, it disappears for a while and then, when it again comes into view, its upper part is well framed by the walls of the road. The road presently deteriorates, and at a gate becomes a cart-track. Here take the lower track, which leads to a small farm-house (where light refreshment can be obtained) close to the fall. Pass the house and ascend by the side of the stream to a foot-bridge. Cross this and mount the hill-side, bearing to the right. In this way the best view-point is reached. **Pistyll Rhaiadr,** by adding its successive leaps, is credited with a height of 230 feet, but it is a fall whose merits ought not to be judged either by height or volume. In fact, it is remarkable on neither of these accounts, and never is its sterling beauty seen to greater advantage than when the stream is comparatively small. Then the dark cliff with its crest of firs is graced by a lace-like ribbon that descends with scarcely perceptible motion. The main portion of the fall is nearly perpendicular and may be 120 feet. It is received into a cup which is hidden from view by what may be termed a portion of its rim. Through a hole beneath this rim the water issues in a true Pistyll, that is a " spout," and then makes successive descents of insignificant altitude to the bottom of the valley. It is this "rim" under which the steam reissues, that is the much maligned " bridge," so often said to mar the beauty of the waterfall. It does, indeed, interrupt what from a distance would otherwise appear as one continuous cataract, but from the view-point to which we have mounted, he must indeed be difficult to please who is not satisfied.

The cliff on either side of the fall is abrupt and picturesquely wooded. By passing above the farm-house a steep ascent, first eastward and then bending back again, enables us to reach the top of the fall. If we ascend the burn that comes down the green valley east of the farm-house, we soon reach the little tarn, *Llyn Llync-y-Caws,* whence it issues. The hills above it are *Moel-y-Sych* (2716 feet), and *Cader Berwyn,* and from them **Llandrillo** can be reached in about seven miles ; *see* p. 32 (*reverse route*).

Llanrhaiadr-yn-Mochnant, *viâ* **Llangynnog,** 7 *m.*, **and Milltirgerig Pass** to **Bala,** 19 *m.*, **or Llandrillo Village,** 20 *m.* (**Station,** 20½ *m.*)

The only recommendation of this route across the Berwyns is that it is the most direct, and by a fair road, for a mountainous one, all the way. The distances given above are for driving. On foot Bala may be reached in 18 miles, and Llandrillo in 14 miles ; the curtailment being due in each case to the use of a more hilly road at starting, and in the case of Llandrillo to a rough by-road to end with.

The *best carriage-road* ascends the Tanat valley the whole way, *viâ* Pen-y-Bont, 4¼ *m.*, to Llangynnog. *The more direct road*

leaves Llanrhaiadr at the top of the village, and at once
mounts a stiff hill and joins the carriage road at Pen-y-Bont
(Inn : *Railway*), 3 *m*. The scenery of the *Tanat* valley is pleasant,
and near **Llangynnog** (*Inn*), the archæologist may examine
the remains of a British village, situated on a small plateau
west of the summit of Craig Rhiwarth, the steep hill above the
village.

From Llangynnog the road ascends the east side of the combe
of the *Afon Eiarth*, which it follows almost to its source, and then
crosses the dreary moorland that extends on both sides of *Milltirgerig Pass*. About 1¼ *m*. beyond the summit-level a solitary
cottage is passed on the left, and then in about another mile a
rough road (too prominently marked on Ordnance diverges on the
right to **Llandrillo**, which village (*p*. 27) is four miles from the
turn, and the Station half-a mile further. If we are bound for
Bala we keep to the fair road by which we have crossed the pass,
and are still about three miles distant from the main road. When
that is reached, turn left for **Bala**, or right for **Landrillo**,
distant respectively 3¾ and 4¼ miles.

Llanrhaiadr-yn-Mochnant to "Lake Fyrnwy" (Liverpool Reservoir) and **Llanwddyn** (pron. " Thlanoothin ") *by
road* 12 *m*. Pedestrian route, *via* **Hirnant to the foot of the
"Lake,"** and thence to Llanwddyn, 11½ *m*.

    Llanwddyn to Bala (*mountain-road*), 13 *m*.

    ... **To Dinas Mawddwy** (*mountain-road too rough to drive over*), 14 *m*.

Neither of these routes offers anything very remarkable in the
way of scenery, and the interest of " Lake Fyrnwy " is, and for
some years to come will continue to be, chiefly an engineering one.
The manufacture of a lake some 12 miles in circuit is, however,
so vast an undertaking that a good many will be tempted to
inspect the process. The road-route (described the reverse way
page 34) goes pretty direct to the embankment at the foot of the
" Lake," and travellers bound for Dinas Mawddwy *via* Bwlch-y-
Groes and Llan-y-Mawddwy may abridge their walk to 11½ miles
by driving as far as Eunant, abt. 2½ *m*. above Llanwddyn.

Pedestrian route. From the hotel proceed up the village,
and beyond the bridge follow the road up the hill. In 3 miles we
reach **Pen-y-Bont**, and beyond the *Railway Inn* take the left-
hand road. A tributary of the Tanat keeps us company on the
left as far as **Hirnant** (*small public-house*) 5½ *m*., where we
turn to the left and, crossing the stream, gradually ascend the
other side of the valley. Beyond some out-buildings the lane
reaches the open country, and on the right the posts of a telephone wire indicate our route over the hill. After a bit of somewhat wet ground, a gate in a wall is reached and a cart-track
struck which crosses the hills and leaves no doubt as to the
route. When, however, the track forsakes the wire, follow the

LAKE VYRNWY.

Postal Address : Vyrnwy Hot l, Llanwddyn, Oswestry.

Nearest Railway Station and Telegraph Office : Llanfyllin, 10 miles.

The completion of this undertaking **has rendered** some portions of pages 33-35 and 78-80 obsolete. The annexed map shows the limits of the lake, the **roads** around **it**, and those leading to Bala, Bwlch-y-Groes (for Llanuwchllyn and Dinas Mawddwy), Llanrhaiadr-yn-Mochnant, and Llanfyllin. At the time of writing (Feb , 1889) the water is being collected and the Vyrnwy Hotel is being built. The winter thus far has been dry in Wales, otherwise the lake might have been full by Easter. It is not now expected that it will be so before August.

The reader is requested to **note the** following modifications **of** routes :

P. 33. Llanwddyn village **has been** destroyed. In approaching from Bala the road on the east side of the lake **is** the shorter to the Vyrnwy Hotel.

P. 35. From Llanuwchllyn, the west **arm** of the lake is **reached just above** where Eunant was, and **the** road down the **west side** and along the dam **at** the south-end **leads** to the hotel.

P. 34, small print, and p. 78, "Pedestrian **route.**" The map indicates **the** route between Hirnant and the hotel. Coming from Hirnant you cross the stream, as stated in the text, and follow the lane till it reaches the open. At the **point** where the fences cease you turn along a path **to** the right. **After** crossing a bit of wet ground you pass through **a gate, and bear** up the hill, presently bending to the **left** to the hotel.

It is satisfactory to be able to say that Lake Vyrnwy (*pron.* Vernew) promises **to be a real addition** to the scenery and to look "quite at home." **The masonry of the works is** massive and free from meretricious ornament. **The Vyrnwy Tower (100 ft. above** the level of the water and 60 ft. below it) is a short distance from the east shore, with which it is connected by arches. Its design is at once **dignified and** picturesque. The lower part of the Tower admits the water to the aqueduct from near the surface of the lake, whatever its level may be. The upper part of the Tower contains hydraulic machinery **for** working the valves and drawing up and washing the great strainers, through which the water is passed. **Mr. Hawksley** retired in 1885, and Mr. Deacon, his coadjutor, **is** now sole engineer.

In the bed of the lake the rock showed abundant traces of glacier carving and, at the close of the glacial period, it is almost certain that the high ledge of rock, on which the Great Dam has been built, marked the foot of a lake. The mountain-streams would bring down great quantities of detritus, shattered by the frosts of the still severe winter climate of a later (yet prehistoric) date, and thus the deep bed was filled up. The Vyrnwy, before the works began, here wound along an alluvial flat fringed with beds of peat and scanty groves of alder.

The area of the lake, when full, will be 1121 acres, and the greatest depth 84 feet. The Dam is expected to be practically completed in 1889. It rises more than 100 feet above the ground, and the foundations lie some 60 feet below. Along the top is a carriage road, 1200 feet long and 20 feet wide, supported on 33 arches and intersected by towers used in connection with the regulation of the outflow.

The *village* of Llanwddyn is not to be rebuilt on a fresh site, because the lake has appropriated the valley lands of its people. The new church, vicarage, hotel, and the houses of the waterworks' officials, all near the south end of the lake, will probably be known as Llanwddyn. The hotel (150 feet above the water-level) commands a fine view up the lake as far as its bifurcation, 4 miles off, on either side of the precipitous spur of Moel Eunant. To the west rise the Aran mountains. With the growth of the plantations—landscape gardening on a gigantic scale—and the Vyrnwy Tower in mid-distance the scene bids fair to be genuinely beautiful; the lake is to be stocked with fish.

As stated in the text the total length of the aqueduct between the lake and Liverpool is 67 miles. The *Aqua Marcia* and the *Anio Novus*, the two longest of the aqueducts of ancient Rome, measured 57 and 54 miles respectively; the *Aqua Claudia*, $42\frac{1}{2}$ miles. Of those in this country Glasgow gets its supply from Loch Katrine, $34\frac{1}{2}$ miles distant, and the Manchester and Thirlmere aqueduct is estimated to be $95\frac{3}{4}$ miles long.

SECTION MAP Nº 1

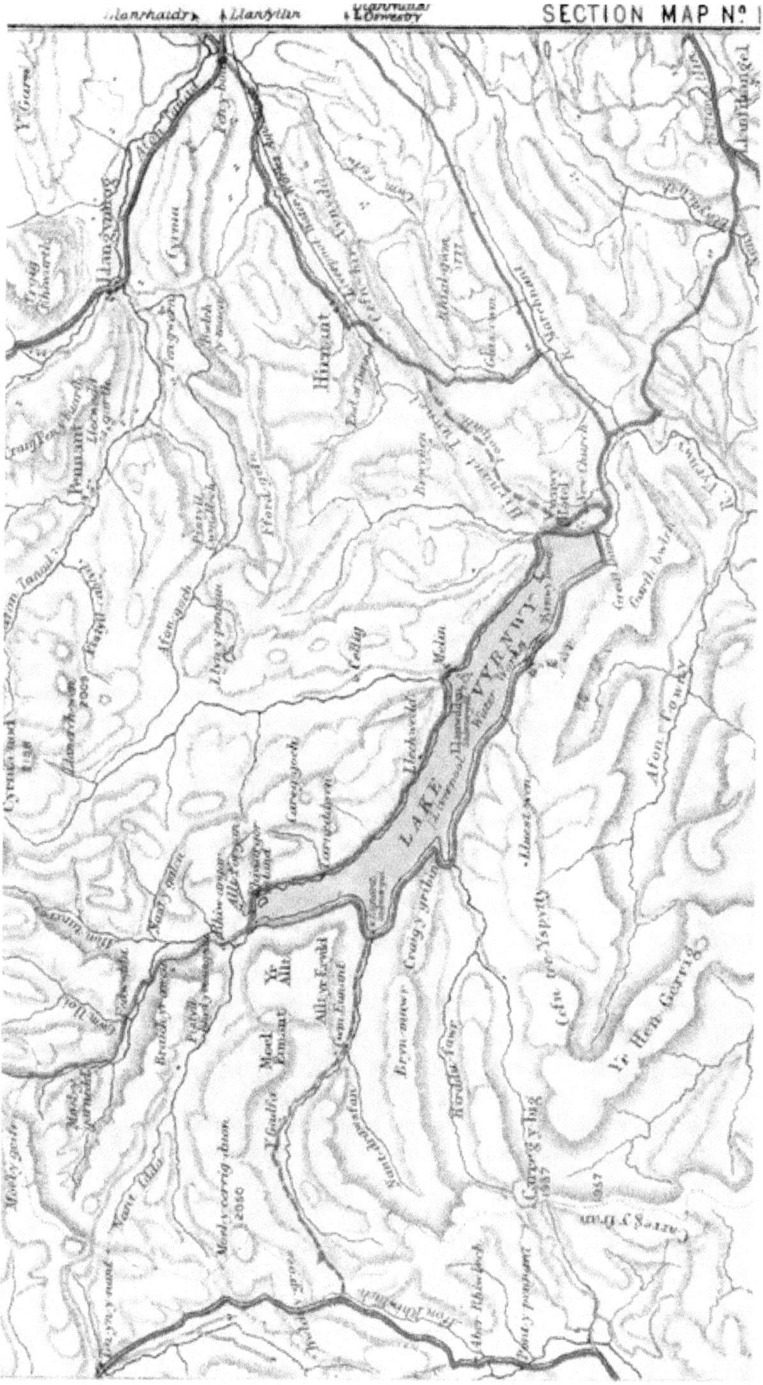

latter or, better, make for the top of the hill that it crosses. Thence, nearly the whole of the bed of the future lake is over-looked, and the village of Llanwddyn is seen a trifle north of west, with the finely scarped flank of the Arans above and beyond it. W.S.W. Cader Idris appears end-on above an intervening ridge, while in a S.S.W. direction is Plynlimon (a long left-hand slope leading up to a slight peak).

In descending from the hill, leave the wire and make in the direction of Llanwddyn. Soon the top of the quarry is reached whence the stone for the great embankment at the foot of the "Lake" is obtained. Making our way down the quarry (where, it will be noticed, every block is carefully washed before being despatched) the tramway is reached by which the stone is carried to the embankment, and a lift can be had in the guard's van of one of the frequent trains.

"**Lake Vyrnwy**," by which name the great reservoir for the supply of Liverpool is to be known, will, when completed, be slightly the largest sheet of water in Wales, viz., 1,115 acres, as against the 1,100 acres of Bala Lake, and bids fair to be a genuine improvement. We have no love for gigantic schemes of water-supply, whereby such scenes as Loch Katrine or Thirlmere are tampered with, but in the present instance the engineers (Mr. T. Hawksley and Mr. G. F. Deacon) have to deal with a featureless boggy valley, at an average height of 780 feet above sea-level, which with considerable probability is said once upon a time to have been occupied by a lake. This valley contracts, 2½ miles below Llanwddyn, to a width of about 300 yards, and it is here-abouts that the **Embankment**, the largest of its kind in the kingdom and a colossal work (a trifle over 400 yards in length, 100 feet wide at its base, and intended to rise 84 feet above the bottom of the valley) has been in process of erection since 1881. The head of the "Lake" will extend nearly as far as Rhiwargor Farm house on the Bala road and just beyond Eunant on the Dinas Mawddwy route. The site of the little village of Llanwddyn will be deep beneath its waters, whose circuit will be about 12 miles, with a maximum length of 4¾ miles. At present new roads on both sides of the "Lake" are nearly completed, and another is intended to be carried on arches along the top of the embankment. The storage capacity of the reservoir (i.e., the maximum amount of water above the level of the outflow aque-duct) is estimated at 12,000 millions of gallons, and the area of the Vyrnwy watershed (exclusive of those of the Cowny and the Marchnant, which may be impounded and brought into connection with it by tunnels should the need arise), is set down as 17,583 acres. The Liverpool Corporation, at whose instance the work is being effected, are compelled by their Act of Parliament so to regulate the supply of water to the river below, that riparian owners shall not suffer, and. to enable this to be done, tunnel-sluices will be carried through the embankment.

The conveyance of the water to Liverpool, distant, as the bird

flies, 46 miles, is to be partly by tunnels and partly by pipes, and
the former are being made of the full size of 7 feet diameter, but
pipes equal only to about ½ of that capacity are all that are at
present being laid down. The tunnel from the reservoir to the
Hirnant valley will be 2¼ miles long, and the aqueduct, when completed, will measure 67 miles.

If on the completion of the works judicious planting on the
flanking hills be, as is promised, carried out, then not even the
soul of Mr. Ruskin will be vexed by this giant " improvement."

From the embankment it is about 2½ miles up the valley by the
east-side road to **Llanwddyn**, a little village with a restored
Church, and two or three poor public-houses, of which the *Powis
Castle* is perhaps the best.

The road from **Llanwddyn to Bala**, or Dinas Mawddwy, keeps
straight on up the valley, and, when this is made to bifurcate by
the fine crags of Allt-yr-Erydd, for Bala we continue up the right-
hand combe past *Rhiwargor Farm*, whence the road over the
Berwyns is unmistakable, and is sufficiently described *page* 33.

For **Dinas Mawddwy** we leave the main road just before
the valley forks (*see above*) and, turning down into the bottom
of it, cross the Fyrnwy, here a somewhat sluggish trout
stream. In a little over half-a-mile, the house and farm of
Eunant (doomed to be submerged) are reached, and we ascend the
combe by a rough road that for a while is fairly picturesque, owing
to the merry brook that hurries down alongside in frequent little
cascades. Before the road becomes rougher than ever, and all
trees are left behind, a cottage offers " ginger beer," and this is
the last chance of refreshment short of Llan-y-Mawddwy. It is a
monotonous climb to the summit of the route, which enters the
road from Bala to Dinas Mawddwy a trifle south of Bwlch-y-Groes,
whence the route onward is given *page* 31.

Shrewsbury.

Hotels: *Raven, Lion, George.*

Post: Chief del. abt. 7 a.m., 1.30 and 6 p.m.; desp. 10 a.m., 12 noon, and 9.30 p.m.

Population: About 27,000.

No traveller with time at command, and on pleasure bent, should pass through Shrewsbury without paying it a visit. The town is so compact that a few hours will suffice for a cursory inspection of the chief objects of interest, but many days may be profitably spent in and about it, and the merits of the Raven Hotel, as a resting place, are too well known to need a word of commendation. The following brief description is all that can find place in a Guide to North Wales. and for fuller particulars we must refer our readers to the shilling Handbook (with plan), by the late Mr. H. Pidgeon.

Walk through the Town, 2 to 3 *hrs.*; *a round of about* 3½ *miles.* Shrewsbury is built on a peninsula of rising ground, within a loop of the Severn. On the isthmus, which is less than a quarter of a mile in width, is the Railway Station, built in the Tudor style. Immediately above it stands the red sandstone **Castle**, the shell of which is in part as old as the reign of Edward I. We turn to the left from the station, and the entrance to the Castle is by gates close to a chapel, on the left-hand side of the street. Strangers are allowed to visit the grounds as far as the tower, built by Telford, on a mound overlooking the river. The interior of the Castle, which is a private residence, is not shown. Returning to the street, on the opposite side we have the old buildings (now a free *Museum and Public Reading Room*) of **Shrewsbury School**, founded by Edward VI. in 1551. Here Sir Philip Sidney was educated, though not in the existing structure, which dates from 1595–1627. The prosperity of the school, under a succession of able scholars—Butler, Kennedy, and Mr. Moss, the present headmaster—has necessitated new buildings on a fresh site at Kingsland, a suburb south-west of the town, across the Severn.

Beyond the School, on the same side of Castle Street, is Plimmer's, the confectioner, where Pailin's "**Shrewsbury Cakes**," immortalised by Ingoldsby, in "Bloudie Jacke," may still be had, and beyond this is the *Raven Hotel.* At the Post-Office, we turn to the left to **St. Mary's Church**. The lofty tower and spire 222 feet, is the chief feature of the exterior,

which, as a whole, is interesting rather than beautiful, owing
to the fact that its component parts, ranging in style from
Norman to Late Perpendicular, lack unity. Inside, however,
the general effect is delightful. The *nave*, of four bays, has
round arches springing from clustered columns, and is Transitional between Norman and Early English. The *transept* is
Early English, and the south arm has a good blind arcade below
its graceful triplet of slightly splayed lancets. The north arm of
the transept is occupied by the organ, and the Blakeway window
behind it is the only one in the church that is harsh in colouring
and unsatisfactory. The *Jesse Window*, at the east end, is 14th
century glass, and was removed from Old St. Chad's in 1788, after
that church had been wrecked by the fall of the tower. The
"St. Bernard" triplet, on the north side of the chancel, and part
of the middle window in the south aisle of the nave, came
originally from the Abbey of Altenburg, and are early 16th
century glass.

On the south side of the chancel is *Trinity Chapel*, mainly 15th
century, but with earlier and later portions. It contains a mutilated tomb supposed to be that of Thomas Percy, Earl of Worcester, beheaded in 1403, whose headless skeleton was discovered
beneath it when the tomb was opened years ago; and Bishop
Butler's monument, by E. H. Bailey, R.A. Dr. Butler, before his
appointment to the See of Lichfield, was Head Master of Shrewsbury School.

On leaving St. Mary's we see at its south-east corner the *Salop
Infirmary*, and then in a few steps reach *St. Alkmund's* with a
good tower and spire, and a fine timber-built house hard by on the
north side. A trifle south of St. Alkmund's is the uninteresting
St Julian's church, past which we descend to the old fashioned
and steep street, *Wyle Cop*, and so down to **English Bridge** and
across the Severn. The river is here divided into several channels
by green ridges, but is scarcely picturesque. Keeping straight on
and under the railway, we arrive at *Holy Cross*, in front of the
Abbey Church, whose red sandstone tower, rising from the west
end of the nave, which has lean-to Norman aisles, completes a
really venerable west-front. The great *west window* is Early Perpendicular, and of seven lights, with an enriched ogee label rising
to a finial. The base of the tower is part of the Norman church
of Roger, Earl of Shrewsbury's foundation. The figures under the
canopies on either side of the window represent St. Peter and St.
Paul, and that above is supposed to be Edward III, but is past re-
cognition. The present building consists of the nave and aisles
only of what once was a cruciform church, and the exterior, with
the exception of the west front, calls for no special notice. We
enter by the south porch. The *nave* consists of three Norman and
two Early English bays, and is divided from the tower by a fine
arch in the latter style, and the interior, as a whole, is, considering its shorn dimensions, exceedingly beautiful. There are a good
many *monuments* worth examining, as other churches have from

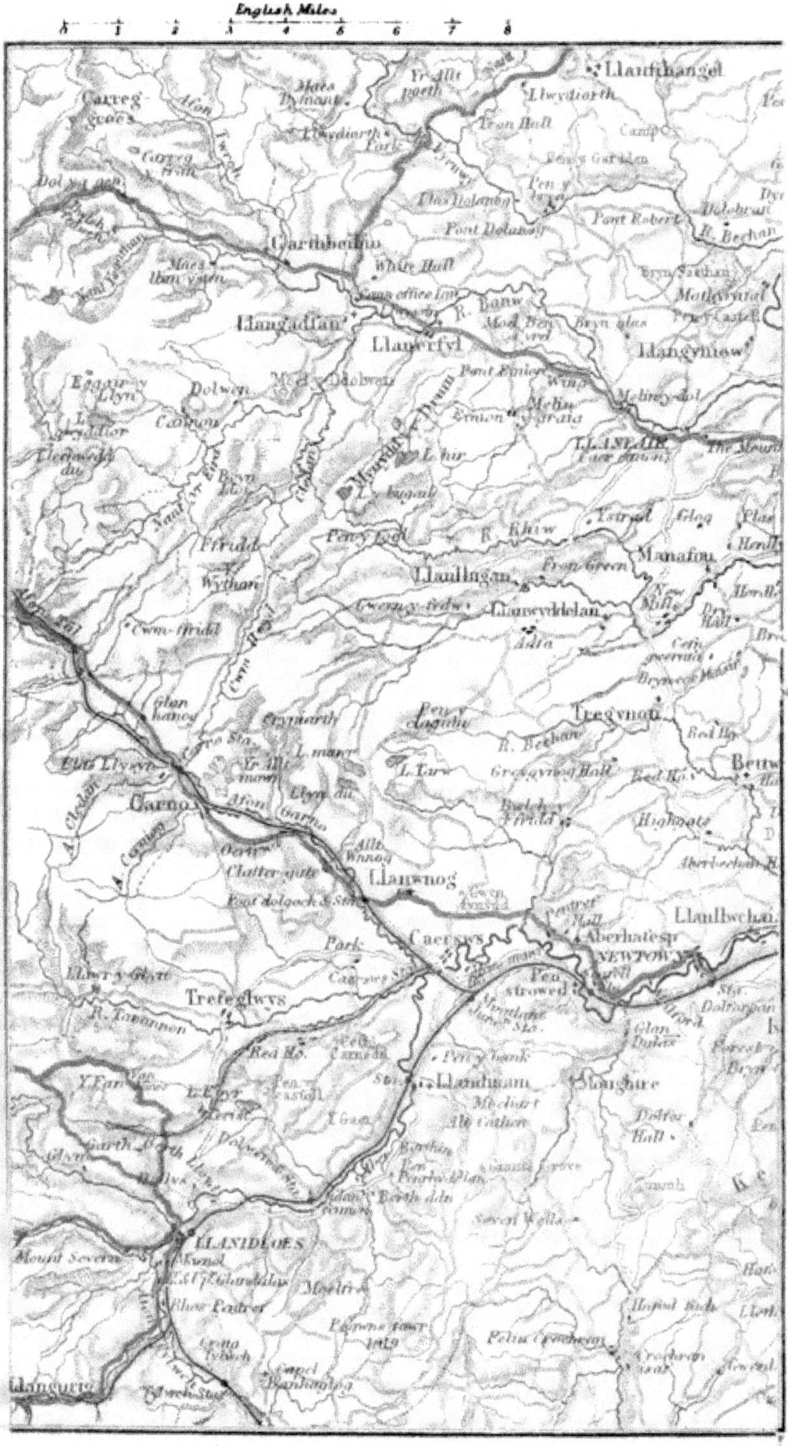

English Miles
0
1
2
3
4
5
6
7
8
Llanfihangel
Llwydiarth
Carreg-y-gros
Dol-y-gan
Garthbeibio
Llangadfan
Llanerfyl
R. Banw
Pont Robert
R. Bechan
Llangyniew
Llanfair
Dolwen
Ffridd
Wythan
Cwm-ffridd
Glan hanog
Carno
Afon Carno
Llanwnog
Caersws
Park
Trefeglwys
R. Trannon
Llanllugan
Llanwyddelan
Adfa
Manafon
New Mills
Tregynon
Gregynog Hall
R. Bechan
Highgate
Llanllwchaiarn
Aberhafesp
Newtown
Penstrowed
Moat Lane Junct Sta.
Llandinam
Penybank
Dolfor Hall
Llanidloes
Mount Severn
Rhos Padrec
Maeltrw
Felin Cresheinant
Red Ho.
Pen y castell
Y Fan
Llangurig
Dolwen
Glyn

time to time contributed memorials. Behind the organ is a mailed effigy, supposed to be Earl Roger, *d.* 1094, the founder of the abbey. Within the screened-off west end of the north aisle are three tombs with effigies, viz.: (From Old St. Chad's), Richard Onslow, *d.* 1571, in his robes as Speaker of the House of Commons, and his wife; (from St. Alkmund's), Alderman Jones, *d.* 1612, and his wife; and (from Wellington, Salop) William Charlton, *d.* 1522, and his wife. In the vestry is a fine collection of the well known Oxford almanacks.

Of the monastic buildings the only remnant of much interest is the Early English **stone pulpit** of the refectory. This is across the road, south of the church, in a stone-mason's yard.

By continuing eastward by Abbey Foregate we could visit *Lord Hill's Monument*, a Doric column surmounted by a colossal statue. The view from the gallery is worth the small fee charged, but the tourist with only 2 or 3 hours at his disposal will hardly have time to extend his walk so far from the town. Turning to the right at the column, we reach in a short distance *St.Giles' Church*, which is in part of early 12th century date and originally belonged to the Lepers' Hospital.

Returning to the town by the way we left it, instead of proceeding up Wyle Cop, where it bends to the right up the hill, we take the by-street, Beeches Lane, straight on and follow the course of the **town walls**, which command a view of the river, past the square tower, *Murivance*, the only one remaining of the twenty that once defended the town. In a short distance a road on the left leads down to the river past the handsome new buildings of the *Ear and Eye Hospital* to *Kingsland Bridge*, but we keep straight on till we reach **New St. Chad's** Church, a huge heathenish structure, erected in 1792, manifestly for an auditorium rather than for worship. From the terrace there is a full view of the delightful lime-avenues of the **Quarry**, a public promenade, on the bank of the Severn, of which Shrewsbury is justly proud. If we make our way down to the main avenue we can follow the river on to **Welsh Bridge**, and thence return to the centre of the town up *Mardol*, another of the many curiously named streets, after which, crossing the High street, we may take a hasty look at *Market Square* with its fine old **Market House** and the statue of Lord Clive, by Marochetti. Returning to High Street a straight course to the right will take us direct to the station in less than 10 minutes.

Shrewsbury to **Welshpool**, *rail*, 19¾ *m.*

From the departure platform at Shrewsbury we get a fair view of Lord Hill's column, rising above the trees, south-west, and from the bridge over the Severn the castle is seen high up on the right rear. Then look out on the left for the Abbey Church and the stone Pulpit, which are close to the line. Shrewsbury itself, with the lofty spires of St. Mary's and St. Alkmund's, shows to

advantage on the other side, and then for a few miles there is
nothing of much moment unless Lyth Hill and the Stipperstone
range on the left be so accounted.

Approaching *Middletown*, 15 *m*, just short of which the railway
enters Montgomeryshire, the Breidden Hills come into view close at
hand on the right. Their most striking appearance is from the
west side as the train slackens for Buttington Junction, 17¼ *m*.

Breidden Hills.

This finely shaped group of mountains in miniature consists of three ridges.
The railway skirts two of these in succession: first (*i.e.*, eastward) *Middletown
Hill*, green and furze-patched with the trace of an old camp, *Cefn-y-Castell*, on
its bare summit, and next *Moel-y-Golfa*, whose steep southern flank is beauti
fully clad with firs and other trees. Behind (*i.e.* north) and parallel to these
is *Breidden Hill*, surmounted by the *Rodney obelisk*, which is a conspicuous
feature when the group is viewed from the westward.

Middletown Station (*small inn*) is the nearest point from which to
ascend any one of the three hills, but those who would appreciate one of the
most charming hill-outlines in all Wales should approach the group end-on from
the south-west. **Buttington Junction**, the station next west of Middletown, is about 1½ miles from the foot of Moel-y-Golfa, and from it, or better
still from Welshpool, the pedestrian is recommended to start. The road from
Welshpool to Middletown is between 6 and 7 miles, and passes close to Buttington Junction. Quite apart from any satisfaction to be derived from the ascent
of these hills, the road from Welshpool to Buttington Junction affords so
delightful a view of them nearly all the way, that a brief indication of it is here
given.

Welshpool to Buttington Junc. (3 *m. road*, 2½ *m. rail*) and the
Breidden Hills.

Take the Oswestry road, which leaves the town east of the Parish Church
In about 1½ miles, at *Buttington Cross*, turn to the right and cross the Severn to
Buttington Church and the Shrewsbury road. This road soon bears to the
left and passes close to Buttington Station. About a mile beyond that station
is a roadside inn, the *Plough and Harrow*, a quarter of a mile past which we
come to a junction of by-roads. Here we take the one on the left hand. This
ascends at once and winds round a little knoll, and so reaches the west flank of
Moel-y-Golfa, which, as compared with the side towards the railway, is
sparsely wooded. No minute directions are really needed for the ascent either
of Moel-y-Golfa (*abt.* 1,300 *ft.*) or Breidden Hill (*abt.* 1,200 *ft.*). The former can
be attacked at several points, obvious enough when we are on the ground. The
easiest way to **Breidden Hill** is to keep to the road up the depression on
the north side of Moel-y-Golfa and then to take a cart-track, left, to a cottage
where a stile and field-path lead to another stile and cottage. After this it is
only a matter of taste how far the pedestrian may choose to lessen the gradients of the climb to the Rodney Obelisk by a devious ascent. The *view* includes
the spires of Shrewsbury eastward; Gyrn Moelfre (1707 *feet*) north-west, with
the range of the Berwyns behind and to the left of it. At our feet and stretching far away is the rich green vale of the Severn and the Fyrnwy.

Ascent from Middletown Station (*small inn*). Follow the railway a few hundred yards towards Shrewsbury and then take a field-path on the left to the main road, where left again and then up on the right past a bit of a quarry to the dip between Cefn-y-Castell (right) and Moel-y-Golfa (left).

For the top of *Golfa* bear round to the left, and then the way through the fields is obvious. For *Breidden Hill* turn to the right by a cart-track to a cottage, whence by stile and foot-path to another stile and cottage (*see p.* 84).

If from Breidden Hill we wish to strike the railway abt. 4 miles distant, either at Pool Quay or Arddleen Stations, then Criggion, the terminus of the defunct potteries line, is the point to make for down the north end of the ridge. At Criggion ask the way to Rhyd Ergyn (*ferry*), and when across the Severn enquire again, if bound for Pool Quay. If Arddleen be the destination, then by turning to the right about a quarter of a mile up the river from the ferry it is almost a straight road to that station.

From Buttington Junction, and still better from a little beyond it, the Breiddens appear to great advantage, looking out on the right-rear. The Rodney Obelisk is conspicuous on the left hand summit. Then the Severn is crossed, and with a good view on the right of the modern Norman church, *Christchurch*, we run into *Welshpool station*. Here through-carriages are attached to the Oswestry portion of the train.

Welshpool.

----◆----

Hotel : *Royal Oak*, ¼ m. from station.
Post : *Del. abt.* 7 *a.m.*, 3.30 *p.m.* ; *Desp. abt.* 10.50 *a.m.*, 7.45 *p.m.*
Population : *abt.* 5,000.

Welshpool is the largest and most prosperous-looking town in Montgomeryshire, being a chief centre of the flannel trade, and of considerable agricultural importance. Beyond its pleasant situation, however, in the wider part of the upper Severn valley, it is only interesting to the tourist as possessing a good local museum, and being the point at which to leave the train for Powys Castle. The town takes its name from a small pool, or rather pond (*Llyn-ddu*, the "black-pool,") now within the policies of Powys Castle.

The **Powys-land Museum** (*open* 10 *to* 4 ; *admission* 3*d.*, *Sat.* 1 *to* 4, free) is just east of the old *Church* (restored by Street) and about 8 minutes from the station. It contains a fine collection of local fossils and a large one of shells. There are a good many stone implements as well as a fair number of Roman and other antiquities. The antiquarian library (open to the public under certain regulations) consists of about 1,000 volumes, and there is also a news-room. The *School of Art* is well supplied with casts, but thus far has no original works. The Powys-land Club dates from 1867, since which year the "Montgomeryshire Collections" have been regularly issued ; the Museum was started in 1874.

Powys Castle (Earl of Powis. *Park always open; Castle shown in the absence of the family.*) This mansion, striking both in itself and in its situation, is on the hill-side a long mile south-west of the town, from which it is reached by turning to the left out of the main street some way beyond the hotel and post-office, just where the street begins to curve to the left. The park is entered at once, and the drive soon passes *Llyn-ddu.* Some of the timber is very fine. Enquiries should be made in the town as to whether admission may be obtained to the Castle, but in any case it is worth while to walk through the park. By turning up the right-hand drive a little before reaching the house, and ascending to an eminence, a fine view westward may be obtained, including in clear weather, Cader Idris and the Arans.

The **Castle** is entered through a gateway between two towers on the side remote from the town. On the left of the court-yard is the ivy-grown *Ball Room.* On entering, the visitor is shown into the *Dining-Room,* which contains tapestry representing Antony parting from Cleopatra. The ceiling has for its subject the **Four Seasons.** Thence we pass into the *Drawing-Room* and *Bed-Rooms,* one of which was occupied by Charles II., and is still kept furnished as it was at the time of his visit. Amongst the many interesting objects of art which are shown, we may mention a statue from Herculaneum, 2,000 years old ; a Byzantine cup that belonged to Mary of Modena ; tapestry representing Nebuchadnezzar and the Fiery Furnace ; an inlaid table presented by a Pope; Florentine marbles; bed-carving of the early part of the 17th century; Chinese and Japanese cabinets; some Indian curiosities presented by Lord Clive, and a looking-glass carved by Grinling Gibbons. From one window there is a picturesque look-out over the N.E. gate, which was formerly the entrance to the Castle, and is entirely hand-work ; while from the *Saloon,* the prospect down the Severn valley to the Breidden Hills is one of great beauty, chiefly owing to its silvan luxuriance. A noteworthy feature of the building is the thickness of the walls. The grounds were laid out by Capability Brown (d. 1783).

Guilsfield Church, three miles north, should be visited by all who make any stay at Welshpool. The *south porch,* with its parvise, is the most noteworthy external feature. Inside, the 15th-century *chancel-roof* is a fine work, beautifully restored by Street.

Welshpool to Llanfair, 7½ *m ;* **Cann Office,** 14 *m ;* **Mallwyd,** 24½ *m ;* and **Dinas Mawddwy,** 26 *m.* 'Bus to Llanfair.

This route is more traversed by sportsmen than tourists, the scenery, though pleasantly diversified for the first part of the way, being nowhere of a sufficiently high order to induce searchers after the picturesque to incur the delay attendant on adopting it. The comfortable inn at *Cann Office* is a favourite resort of anglers, and beyond it the road rises to a dreary pass, *Bwlch-y-Fedwen,* over a southern arm of the Berwyns.

Welshpool to Aberystwith (rail), 61½ *m.* *Route continued from pp. 75 and 85.*

Newtown, 14 *m*; *Moat Lane Junction,* 18½ *m*; *Machynlleth,* 41½ *m*; *Borth,* 53½ *m*; *Aberystwith,* 61½ *m.* *For other distances, Refreshment Rooms, &c., see p. 73.*

Immediately on leaving Welshpool we get peeps on the right of Powys Castle (*page* 86), rising above the rich woods of its park, while on the left the spire of Leighton Church and the tower of Leighton Hall are conspicuous. Then, having recrossed the Severn, the line follows it closely for a mile or more, but again quits it before reaching *Forden Station* (*small inn*), beyond which the valley of the Camlan, a tributary of the Severn, is crossed. At the head of this valley *i.e.,* on the left, and just across the Shropshire border, the pointed Corndon Hill (1,685 feet) appears, while due south we get a peep of the church-tower and a bit of the castle of Montgomery. **Montgomery** Station is nearly two miles from the town, which from it is out of sight.

Montgomery is a sleepy place of about 1,100 inhabitants, but has a good inn, the *Green Dragon.* The only attractions for the tourist are the remnant of the Edwardian *Castle* and the beautiful view from *Ffridd Faldwyn,* an old encampment on the hill between the station and the town, and overlooking the latter. Lymore Park is about 1 m. S.E.

The valley of the Severn now contracts, and the rail and highroad keep close company between sweetly wooded slopes along it southward to **Abermule Station** (*small inn*), where a branch, 3¾ miles long, goes off on the left to *Kerry* (Inn: *New*), whose station is 1¼ *m.* E. of the village, which is 3 *m.* S.E. of Newton on the same road.

Kerry church, re-opened in October, 1883, after restoration from the designs of the late Mr. Street, is interesting, both architecturally and from the fact of its being the subject of the celebrated dispute between Adam, Bishop of St. Asaph and Giraldus Cambrensis, the historian, who was Archdeacon of Brecon. The occasion was the dedication of the Norman church (of which the tower and an arcade remain) in 1196, and the subject of dispute was whether the church belonged to St. Asaph's or St. David's diocese. Both parties came prepared to support their cause by force, and the Bishop was defeated and driven off.

Another short run of four miles brings us to **Newtown** (Hotel: *Boar's Head*), where a considerable manufactory of flannel is carried on by Mr. Pryce Jones, whose mills are close to the line, as is the ugly new church. In this church is preserved the fine *screen* that was formerly in the old church in the centre of the town, but it has been turned into a reredos.

Beyond Newtown the valley again widens, and at its widest part we come to **Moat Lane Junction.** (*Refreshment Room.*)

Main route continued on p. 90.

Moat Lane Junction to Llanidloes, 7¾ m.

Llanidloes is the starting point for those who wish to cross the wilds of Central

mines were a source of wealth to their proprietors; at the present time they are only intermittently worked owing to the fall in the price of lead.

The *Distances* from Llanidloes westwards are as follows :—

To **Machynlleth** by road, pretty at both ends but bleak and uninteresting in the middle, 20 m. Roadside inn at *Stay-a-little* (8 m.), whence it is about 7 m. to Llanbrynmair village, 9 m. to the Station.

To **Aberystwith** by Dyffryn Castell Inn, and Pont Erwyd, 30 m. by Dyffryn Castell and the Devil's Bridge, 32 m.

To the top of **Plynlimon**, abt. 13 m.

Llanidloes.

❦

Chief Hotel : *Trewythen Arms*, 300 yds. from Station.

Post Office (*opposite hotel*): *Chief del. abt. 7 a.m.; desp. 7.10 p.m. Open on Sundays, 8 to 10 a.m.* **Pop.**, *abt.* 3,500.

Llanidloes has the advantage of a fairly picturesque situation, but as a town it is rather below than above mediocrity. Internally there is little or nothing to detain the tourist. From the old *Market-House*, which forms a centre-piece, streets diverge to the four points of the compass : East to the station ; South for Rhayader and Aberystwith (by Llangurig) ; West for the Upper Severn valley and Plynlimon ; North for Newtown and Machynlleth. Following the northward one for a few yards you will find the **Church** a little to the left. It has a short ivy-grown tower, surmounted by a wooden turret. Inside, the roof of carved oak is said to have been brought from the Abbey of Cwm Hir in Radnorshire. From the churchyard, close to which the Clywedog joins the Severn, there is a pretty view up the valley of the former stream.

The *Trewythen Arms*, between the Station and the Market House, is a fair hotel of the Commercial order, with first class charges.

Llanidloes was the scene of serious Chartist riots in 1839.

The celebrated **Van Mines** are 2½ miles on the Machynlleth road. To reach them cross the main bridge at the end of the street leading northward, and a mile further take the right-hand turn. It is not many years since these mines were a " golconda " of lead to their proprietors ; at the present time they are, we believe, only intermittently worked.

The *Distances* from Llanidloes westwards are as follows :—

To **Machynlleth** by road, pretty at both ends but bleak and uninteresting in the middle, 20 m. Roadside inn at *Stay-a-little* (8 m.), whence, it is about 7 m. to Llanbrynmair village, 9 m. to the Station.

To **Aberystwith** by Dyffryn Castell Inn, and Pont Erwyd. 30 m. by Dyffryn Castell and the Devil's Bridge, 32 m.

To the top of **Plynlimon**, abt. 13 m.

An alternative route to Aberystwith is to take the train (Mid-Wales) to Rhayader, and thence to walk up the Wye valley, joining the direct route from Llanidloes at Llangurig, 5 m. from Llanidloes and 10 m. from Rhayader.

The most remunerative route as a whole is that from Rhayader by Devil's Bridge, 37 miles in all, but advantageously broken by staying a night at the *Hafod Arms*, a good hotel at Devil's bridge.

Compared with the average of mountains, Plynlimon is not worth climbing. The place it occupies in geography books is probably due to the number of rivers of which it is the "nursing mother," certainly not to its own height or beauty. The tourist will avoid risk of disappointment by bearing in mind that the entire mountain-range south of the Dovey valley as far as the Beacons of Brecon and Carmarthen, is of inferior attractiveness, being mostly vast sheep-walks. Many of the valleys, however, are very beautiful.

Llanidloes to Plynlimon *direct.* Go straight through the town from the station or hotel, cross the Severn by the upper bridge, and turn to the left. For the next seven miles or so the road to be followed is that which keeps nearest the river and on its northern side. It is unmistakable except when, about 3 miles from Llanidloes, and within sight of a chapel by the river-side (*see below*), it turns at right angles to the right, and becomes for a while very narrow. The valley is contracted and flanked by low, prettily wooded hills. The road is a good one at first, then fair, and ultimately degenerates into a cart-track ending at the farmstead of *Rhyd-dib-enuch*, where the hollow of the main stream bends sharply to the right. From this farm, crossing the water and keeping a westerly direction, you will reach the top in about 5 miles. A little short of the first top (2,430 ft.) the lonely combe in which the infant Wye utters its first lisp is passed on the left. The highest top (2,469 ft.) is nearly 2 miles further on, S.W.W. of the lower one. The *view* is an extensive one of land and sea, but the dull monotony of the foreground in all directions, and the absence of interesting objects near enough to be seen in detail, make it an unsatisfactory reward for the toil of the ascent. It is best, perhaps, towards the south-west, in which direction a good deal of the coast of Cardigan and Pembroke is seen.

The best descent is to Dyffryn Castell Inn, 3½ miles south along the ridge. Hence it is 16 miles by Devil's Bridge and 14 by Pont Erwyd into Aberystwith, *see below and pp.* 111 *and* 112.

₊ From the point mentioned above, at which you turn short to the right, 3 miles from Llanidloes, you may go straight on and, crossing the Severn by the chapel, ascend on the right of a very pretty dell, past some farms, to the ridge which separates the Severn from the Wye valley. Here the route, previously a cart-road, becomes indistinct for a few yards, but recovers itself in descending to a tributary of the Wye, *Afon Biduo*, which is crossed by a foot-bridge. Between this and the main Wye valley there is another ridge up which goes a cart-road bending slightly to the right from the foot-bridge and leaving an upland farm on the left. On the top there is, for a while, little or no track, but, bending to the left again from the highest wall, you will drop steeply into the high-road, near a chapel a little short of the eighth milestone from Llanidloes.

Llanidloes to Aberystwith by road. *Direct,* 30 m. ; *by the Devil's Bridge,* 32 m. (*5 m. more from Rhayader.*)

The railway, marked on the Ordnance map from Llanidloes to Llangurig, does not exist. It was intended to form part of the "Manchester and Milford," and

was constructed up to the point of laying the permanent way as far as Llangurig, where, for want of funds or other cause, the enterprise at this end of the
line collapsed ; from the other (Carmarthen) end it was made as far as Strata
Florida, and thence diverted to Aberystwith.

The roads from Llanidloes and Rhayader unite at **Llangurig** (2 *inns*), 5 *m.*
from Llanidloes, 10 *m.* from Rhayader.   The latter route is up the Wye valley
and, during its first part especially, goes through fine, bold scenery.   From
Llangurig upwards the valley is fairly cultivated as far as the *Glonseern Inn*, a
good roadside house, 9½ miles from Llanidloes.   Half-a-mile further the road
crosses the Wye, which comes down a lonesome combe from Plynlimon on the
right, and thence the road follows the north side of a tributary stream to **Steddfa
Gurig**, the highest point on the route (1,358 *ft.*), and the nearest point on any
road to the summit of Plynlimon (2½ *m. off*) ; so near, indeed, that a former proprietor of the now closed inn wrote on his sign-board: " The notorious hill of
Plinlimmon is on the premises, and will be shown to any gentleman travellers
who wishes to see it."   Steddfa Gurig now consists of an inhabited house or two,
and two parallel rows of deserted miners' cottages.   The word Steddfa means
seats and   may allude to the peculiar formation of the bed of the river, which
here descends over a succession of rock-terraces.

From Steddfa Gurig the road winds down the north side of a bare valley containing a multitude of abandoned lead-mines, which have been foisted on the
public as *El Dorados* in disguise.   In 2½ miles we reach the welcome inn of
Dyffryn Castell (*guide to Plynlimon*, 3½ *m. distant ; 3d. a head for parties;
minimum charge, abt. 3s.*)   The two roads to Aberystwith by Pont Erwyd and
the Devil's Bridge respectively, diverge a little beyond this.   They are described
in the *Aberystwith Section* (*pp.* 111, 112).

A mile beyond Moat Lane Junction we cross the Severn for the
last time, a few yards short of *Caersws Station*, whence the mineral
line to the Van Mines (*p.* 88) diverges to the left.   Continuing
along the tributary stream called Afon Carno, which threads a
charming valley, we come to *Pontdolgoch* Station.   On the right
is the round, wood covered height of Allt Wnnog, and four miles
further we reach *Carno* Station (*inn*), whence the ascent to the
summit-level of the line (692 feet) is slow and tame, but the
Talerddig cutting, which has been hewn out of the rock at the top
of the pass, is impressive, and, as we emerge from it, the strata
on the left exhibit a fine example of an anticlinal axis that has the
appearance of an arch of masonry.

From this point the scenery becomes distinctly Welsh, and for
three miles we descend the narrow and lovely glen of the *Afon Tâl*.
The pace almost prevents our noticing the details of this charming
valley, the depths of which are on the left of the line.   About two
miles down it there is on the right hand a graveyard where, we
are told, the persecuted Puritans assembled in the days of Charles I.
Looking out on the other side, we may descry the peak of Cader
Idris over the smooth-topped hills in front.   At *Llanbrynmair*
Station (Inn : the *Wynnstay Arms*, an angler's resort), where the
surroundings are pleasant green meadows and hills, we enter the
Twymyn valley, and that stream, as we near Cemmaes Road,

affords another charming bit of river-glen. At **Cemmaes Road** (Inn : the *Dovey Hotel*, close to the station) we enter the Dovey (Dyfi) valley. *For Cemmaes Road to Dinas Mawddwy, &c., see p. 93.*

We have now reached the green vale of the Dyfi (Dovey), and that fine fishing river is close to the line all the way to **Machynlleth.** (*Refreshment Room.*) *For description of town and routes from it, see p. 92.*

As we quit Machynlleth, the sky-line of its towers and spires is very graceful, and a run of four miles down the Dovey valley, which soon becomes a flat and somewhat marshy strath between picturesque combe-riven hills dotted with farmsteads and little plantations, brings us to **Glandovey Junction** (*Ref. Room. Temp.*). where the line bifurcates, right to Barmouth and the north ; left to Borth and Aberystwith. Here we have due east the mouth of the Llyfnant valley (p. 97), but the next station, Glandovey, less than a mile off on the Aberystwith branch, is the one most convenient for those who would explore it.

For the route hence to **Barmouth** *and* **Dolgelley,** *see p. 98.*

From Glandovey Junction the Aberystwith line proceeds by the side of the Dovey to *Glandovey Station*, which is just below the prettily placed little castle whence it derives its name. Then for five miles the Dovey estuary is skirted and, as we proceed, the view across it to Aberdovey and over Pennal in the right-rear, becomes, when the tide is up, very beautiful, though none of the mountains in sight are known to fame. On our left is the dreary salt-marsh, Cors Fochno, and Ynys-las (*Station*), at its north-west angle was, until the railway was made, the usual crossing place by ferry to Aberdovey. The original hamlet has been in great part destroyed by an encroachment of the tide. Next, turning southward, the open sea is close by on the right, and **Borth** (p. 106) is reached, whence the only view from the railway is towards the hills on the left hand. From Borth we turn away from the coast and ascend a prettily wooded valley past *Llanfihangel.* The little village and church are on the right hand, close by the station. The next station is *Bow Street*, whence we can almost see the sea down a hollow on the right, while on the left the Plynlimon heights soon become visible. The scenery, however, is rather suggestive of Devonian orchards than Welsh mountains. A little further we come to the Rheidol, winding down a wide alluvial strath on the left, and then, bending suddenly to the west, the line passes close by Llanbadarn, with its fine Early English church well seen on the right, and the Wellington Monument on Pen Dinas conspicuous across the valley nearly opposite to it. Though arriving from the north, we enter Aberystwith from the south-east. The shore is a quarter of a mile from the station. Hotel omnibuses await the trains.

For **Aberystwith,** *see p. 100.*

MACHYNLLETH SECTION.

Machynlleth.

(Pron. Mach-unth-leth.)

Hotels: *Lion*, abt. ½ m. from Station; (smaller) *Eagles, Glyndwr*, near Station.

Post Office in Maengwyn Street, near Clock Tower. *Chief del., 7.30 a.m., 5.30 p.m. (Sundays, 9.45 a.m.); Desp., 6.20 p.m. (Sunday, 5.50 p.m.) Open on Sunday, 9.45—10.45 a.m.*

Pop.: abt. 2,500.

From Machynlleth, rail to Corris and conveyance in connection, to Tal-y-Llyn, and *vice versâ*, two or three times a day in summer; see bills at Station, etc.

No place in Wales has had so little justice done to it in guidebooks as Machynlleth. As a town it has no superior of its size in the principality, and its surroundings are delightful. In addition, it is a most convenient head-quarters for the angler, and the tourist may, within six miles on each side, avail himself of five different railway routes. These are—the main line to Welshpool, along which we have just travelled; its continuation to Aberystwith; the coast branch from Glandovey Junction to Barmouth, Dolgelley and Portmadoc; the Dinas Mawddwy branch from Cemmaes road, and the "toy" line which threads a charming little valley to Aber Corris, whence it is only about four miles to Tal-y-Llyn and the foot of Cader Idris.

The two main streets of Machynlleth are wide, and have been in parts planted with trees; the houses are exceptionally well built, and several buildings of considerable architectural merit have lately been erected. A special feature is the graceful sky-line presented by the group of spires and towers, from the railway.

Walking into the town from the station, we pass, on the right hand, the *Old Church* (restored) which is mainly Perpendicular and somewhat squat but has an ivy-clad tower, and a picturesque churchyard. Then, where Maengwyn street strikes off to the left a handsome *Clock-tower* stands in the middle of the road. It was erected in 1873, in commemoration of the coming of age of the present Marquis of Londonderry.

A little way down Maelgwyn Street we pass a new *church*, Early English in style, and a considerable distance further on the same

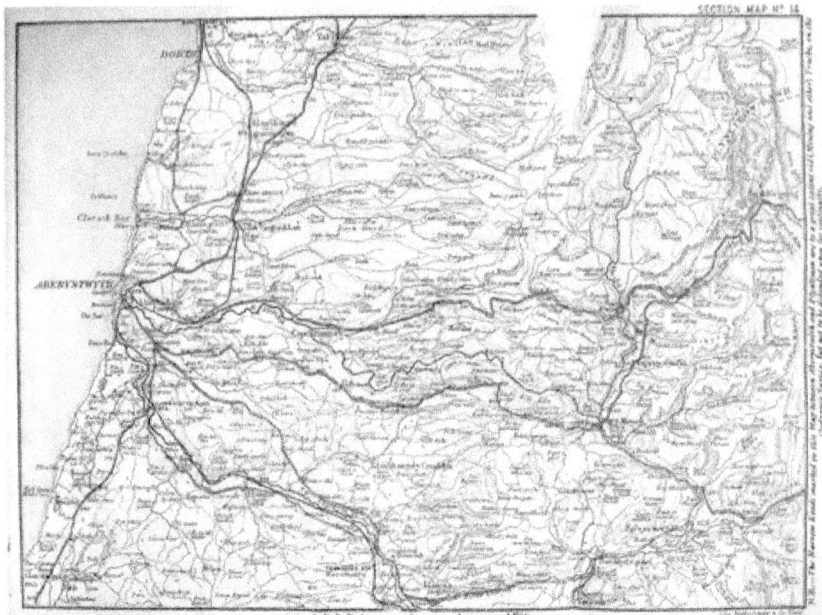

side, a picturesque old cottage with dormer windows, and the
mysterious inscription—

1628 | OWEN

P V Q H I O V X O Y

In Machynlleth, Owen Glyndwr was crowned King of Wales at
a Parliament held in 1402.

At the south end of the town, is *Plas Machynlleth*, the seat of
the Marquis of Londonderry.

Routes from Machynlleth.

(1) Machynlleth to Dinas Mawddwy, &c., by rail. *Machynlleth to Cemmaes Road, 5¼ m. ; Dinas Mawddwy, 12 m.*

This route follows the valley of the Dovey throughout. To
Cemmaes Road it is a part of the main Cambrian line, and
beyond that an independent branch line made chiefly for the
conveyance of slate from the quarries at Dinas Mawddwy. The
scenery, without any attributes of grandeur, is increasingly
beautiful throughout. From the terminus, Dinas Mawddwy,
there are good mountain-roads to Dolgelley and Bala, and mountaineers may enjoy a capital walk over the Arans (*upwards of 3,000
feet*) to Llanuwchllyn or Drws-y-Nant station on the Bala and
Dolgelley line.

The *railway* from Cemmaes Road soon crosses the Dovey and continues more or less close to its western bank all the way. Low green
hills are on the right, and steeper, well wooded ones on the left,
the most effective bit of scenery being the opening of the Angell
glen at the station of *Aber Angell* and, two miles further, the view
across a romantic bridge to Mallwyd. By the road route, you pass
through *Cemmaes* (Inn: the *Penrhos Arms*) in 1½ miles, and
through **Mallwyd**, 4¼ miles further. Here is a fair-sized hotel,
the *Peniarth Arms*, chiefly frequented by fishermen. The *church*,
both in itself and its situation, is interesting. It has a wooden
slate-covered tower, a porch bearing date 1641, and something
"very like a whale" over the doorway. In the churchyard are
some fine yews—one with a circumference of 7 or 8 yards, and no
less than six trunks. A road, of no special interest to the tourist,
goes from here across the hills to Welshpool *see p. 86.*

Dinas Mawddwy (Hotel: the *Buckley Arms*, close to the
station. *Post arr. 7.30–8 a.m., dep. abt. 5.55 p.m.*) is an old and
rather dilapidated-looking village in a very picturesque situation at
the junction of the Afon Geryst with the Dovey. It is deep-set
amongst hills which almost rise to the dignity of mountains. A
slate-quarry is the source of what little commercial account
it possesses, and the chief patrons of its large hotel are sportsmen.
Passing tourists should certainly take a stroll to Mallwyd (*see
above*).

Dinas Mawddwy to Cross Foxes Inn, 7 m ; **Dolgelley,** 10¼ m.
A fairly interesting route, dull in the middle, but beautiful in the last part.
Half-a-mile may be saved by taking the hill-road from Cross Foxes, but it is
far better to add half-a-mile and turn aside down the Torrent Walk between
Cross Foxes and Dolgelley.

From the Station or Hotel go northward for half-a-mile through the village,
and turn to the left at the end of it, opposite the entrance to *Plas.*   Hence,
the first 4 miles are on an ascent, somewhat severe in the latter part, to the pass
called *Bwlch-oerddrws,* about 1200 ft. above the sea.   Steep green mountains flank
the road on both sides, and cultivation ceases in about 3 miles.   At the top of
the pass Cader Idris comes into view in front, and to the right of it we see the
Diphwys range.   Hence, to *Cross Foxes*—a fair roadside inn—there is a descent
of 600 feet.   At Cross Foxes the Tal-y-Llyn road is entered.   The old and
nearer road onward ascends again, but by the newer one we reach the upper
end of the *Torrent Walk* in about a mile.   *For a description of the rest of the
way, see p.* 44.

Dinas Mawddwy to Llanuwchllyn, (road), 13 m. ; *and*
Bala (rail, 5 m.), 18 m.

Route described the reverse way, p. 31.

On this road is one of the highest passes (about 1,950 feet) in
Wales, Bwlch-y-Groes (the " Pass of the Cross "), about which a
great deal of exaggerated language has been used.   " The face of
the country here," says one writer, " puts on a terrific appearance
as if warning the traveller to proceed no further. . . . The
mountains rise one above another in tremendous grandeur," and
so on.   The only thing remarkable in the pass itself, except
its height, is the dull and bare character of its surroundings.
The walk up to it, however, from Dinas is well worth taking ; the
valley on the Bala side is deep and impressive, and there is
a fairly good view of the Aran ridge during the descent.
   The Route.—Half-a-mile from the station and hotel. just where
the Dolgelley road (*see above*) turns to the left, the Bala one turns
to the right, passing the modern mansion and grounds of *Plas.* A
little further it crosses the *Geryst* stream, which comes down the
valley traversed by the Dolgelley road.   Then, more than a mile
on our way, we cross the *Cowarch* water close to its confluence with
the Dyfi (Dovey).   Near the bridge it forms some pretty cascades.
Our route onward, fenced on both sides, is through a narrow and
fertile valley, well timbered in its lower parts.   Lofty hills, green
to the summit, and only here and there diversified by rock. flank
it so closely as to render it a scene of almost perfect seclusion.
   Four miles from Dinas is the small and poor-looking village of
Llan-y-Mawddwy, with a road-side inn, and a church dedicated to
St. Tydecho ab Amwn Ddu, a cousin of St. Cadfan.   A mile or so
onward the valley widens, and becomes an amphitheatre enclosed
by a singularly picturesque environment of hills, from which,
after wet weather, several burns fall in pretty Staubbach-like
cascades.   Then we quit the Dyfi, which comes down a narrow
ravine from the Arans on the left,—admitting the only glimpse of

Aran Mawddwy obtainable all the way to the top of the pass,—
whence our road swerves to the right under the craggy height of
Yr Eryr (the "Eagle's height "), and commences the long and
steep ascent to Bwlch-y-Groes, which owes its name, we are
told, to a stone cross that formerly marked its summit. As we
climb, the hills on the other side of the valley assume greater
boldness. [A little short of the top, a cart-road strikes away on
the right, and enters almost at once a tributary valley of the
Severn. This road goes to Llanwddyn and the Fyrnwy reservoir
(p 79). It may be noted that although the gathering ground of
England's longest river does not occupy a square foot of Merionethshire, it comes up so close in several places, that a chance breath
of wind may change the destination of a drop of water from
the Bristol Channel to the Irish Sea.] At the top of the pass,
the boundary line between Merioneth and Montgomery touches
the road, whence it strikes west and follows the ridge of the
Berwyns for many miles.

Hereabouts Aran Benllyn comes into view over the rough
boggy ground on the left, and, as we begin the descent towards
Bala, the deep hollow of Cwm Cynllwud lies at our feet in front.
In the distance, looking down the valley, we see the peaked and
lofty Arenig. The road, new in comparison with the old track,
which kept to the bottom of the valley till it was almost close
beneath the pass, is well engineered along the sides of the hills
which shut it in on the east, and the descent, though long,
is nowhere excessively steep. The most impressive part is about
a mile beyond the bwlch, from which point it gradually becomes
prettily sprinkled with wood. Indeed the flourishing condition of
the deciduous trees that are here found at an elevation of from
1,000 to 1,100 feet is remarkable. Tai-yn-y-Nant Farm, two
miles from the top of the pass, is just 1,000 feet above the sea.
Nearly two miles further, Cwm Groes, descending from Aran
Benllyn, comes in at a sharp angle on the left. Nothing else calls
for remark, unless it be the rough and knotty outline of the ridge
of the last named mountain, as it descends in a straight line from
its summit to Llanuwchllyn. About half-a-mile before reaching
that village, we may cut off an acute angle of the road by taking
a foot-path on the left, which drops abruptly to the bridge over the
Twrch, as the stream which threads Cwm Cynllwyd is called. A
few yards further we pass under the railway and, taking a turn to
the right, reach the inn and station of **Llanuwchllyn**, 5½
miles from Bala, to which town there are roads on both sides of
Bala lake.

Machynlleth to (Aber)corris (rail or road) 5 m., and **Tal-
y-Llyn** (road; convey. in summer), 9 m., or **Dolgelley**, 16 m.

The terminus of the little Corris line, made for the conveyance
of slates from Abercorris, is a few yards beyond the Cambrian
Station, and is reached by going under the line to the west of that

station. The carriages are constructed with special regard to
tourists, and the route is an exceedingly pretty one. For the
whole distance to Corris both rail and road follow closely the
windings of the river, which flows through a narrow valley flanked
by steep and abundantly wooded hills. More than one charming
glen strikes away on the left to the mountain-ridge which separates this valley from that of Tal-y-Llyn, and, looking back soon
after starting, we have a view of the Plynlimon moorland. At
the **Corris** terminus the line is considerably below the road, and
on the latter there is a very fair inn, commanding a view of the
upper part of the valley, which has, to an almost unique degree
the typical configuration of the valleys hereabouts—the segment
of a circle. For *Tal-y-Llyn see p. 45.*

From Abercorris the road ascends to the left by the side of a
small tributary, and for the next mile or two Nature is entirely
sacrificed to slate-quarries. The highest point reached is 660
feet (300 feet above Abercorris), and Tal-y-Llyn is about 350 feet
below it. Cader Idris, with the Llyn-y-Cau hollow in front of it,
is a noble object as the road rapidly descends. The *Tal-y-Llyn*
and *Tal-y-bont* inns are at the far (south) end of the lake, but for
Dolgelley we keep straight on and, after dropping to the **strath**,
climb 500 feet by a good road to the pass which lies between that
town and Tal-y-Llyn. The easternmost cliffs of Cader are on the
left, and on the right, near the highest point, we pass the lakelet
of *Llyn Trigraienyn,* also under steep cliffs. The descent to *Cross
Foxes Inn,* 3½ m. short of Dolgelley, is desolate, but there is a view
in front over the Wnion valley to Rhobell-fawr. *For the route
from Cross Foxes, see p. 44.* By taking the main road we may
include the Torrent Walk in the expedition.

Machynlleth to Pennal, 4 m., and **Towyn,** 12 m., *by old
road through the Happy Valley.*

This is a pleasant walk, to be recommended as a variation on
the railway route to such tourists as are going from Machynlleth
to Towyn and back, or *vice versâ.* Those who are only travelling
one way between those places will hardly find it worth the extra
time spent upon it.

Leaving Machynlleth by the railway station, you cross *Pont-ar-
Dyfi* and turn sharply to the left. The retrospect over Machynlleth during the ascent of the hill between it and Pennal is particularly pleasing. At *Pennal* there are one or two small inns, and
three-quarters of a mile further the main road to Aberdovey is
quitted and a sharp ascent commenced, with a prettily wooded
glen on the right, to the highest point in the route (350 *feet*).
From hereabouts there is a good view, but nothing more of special
interest occurs until, about 9 miles from Machynlleth, you cut
off a corner of the road by crossing a field on the right, and enter
the narrowest part of the valley, which, however, soon opens out
again, and enters the main Aberdovey road a good mile south of

Towyn village, and 1½ miles from the station. *For* **Towyn**, *see* p. 69.

(5) **Llyfnant Glen** and **Pistyll-y-Llyn**. *By rail to Glandovey,* 4½ *m. Thence walk back to Machynlleth, about* 9 *m.*

Glandovey is also the starting point of the walk for those making the excursion from Aberdovey, Borth, or Aberystwith.

This is a charming little excursion, which should be made by every one who stays any time in Machynlleth or Aberdovey. The point at which Pistyll-y-Llyn comes into full view—and there is little to be gained by going any further—is about 4½ miles from Machynlleth by direct hill-road, but by adopting that route we only see the lovely Llyfnant glen from its upper end. It is far better to take train to Glandovey *Station* (not *Junction*, whence there is no path).

From the station return along the Machynlleth road for nearly half-a-mile. At this distance a sign-post directs you up a narrow lane to the right into the "Llyfnant Valley." When this forks, take the branch to the right.

The left branch leads to a bridge across the stream, whence a cart-track keeps near the water as far as an old mine-bank about a mile up it. The walk that far might be mistaken for a bit of North Devon except for the colouring of the stream-bed which is less rich. By mounting a path just beyond the mine-bank to the top of the wood a fine view is obtained of the glen with a peep of the Dovey estuary and Aberdovey. The huge *Craig Cyfarthfa* that here rises abruptly from the glen can only be surmounted by trespassing, while the view it commands is marred by the desolate moorland at the head of the valley. The walk up-stream comes to an end at the mine-bank, but in ordinary conditions the water can be crossed, dryshod, to the road on the south side, next described.

As we proceed, the strath suddenly narrows, and the valley becomes a deep glen, its sides feathered with wood to their summits. The road (just practicable for carriages) ascends, and a little short of its highest point, a wooded hill projects boldly on the left side. It is worth while to turn aside to the rocky knob which forms its crest. Then we drop to the valley again, where for a little space it affords room on one side for a few green fields, but only again to become very narrow as through a bower of oak and birch we approach **Glas Pwll**. This sequestered and beautifully placed little residence is on the north side, and almost immediately beyond it, after crossing a foot-bridge over a tributary brook, there is a choice of routes : (*a*) To the Rhaiadr gorge and falls, half-a-mile up the main stream ; (*b*) to Machynlleth, either direct (about 3 miles by a fair hill-road), or inclusive of the view-point for Pistyll-y-llyn, about 6 miles. These routes can with advantage be combined at the cost of a slight climb from Cwm Rhaiadr, and without any increase of mileage. If the tourist is pressed for time, and the weather has been dry (in which case Pistyll-y-Llyn shrinks to the dimensions of a thread-water), he is recommended to give the preference to route (a).

(a.) Bear a little to the right by some cottages, and pass through a gate on the left to a meadow track. At a flimsy foot-bridge cross the stream, and follow it up to the gorge. The falls are not seen till we reach another foot-bridge, which was made to furnish a view-point. Some dilapidated steps enable us to ascend the gorge, and from the path above it the main fall, a water-slide of about 50 feet, is best seen. Hence, we can scramble up to the road along the north side of the valley, and turning to the right along it, proceed to the view-point for Pistyll-y-Llyn, described under (b), or turning to the left, strike the road to Machynlleth (*see below*).

(b.) Cross the second foot-bridge (over the main stream), and for Machynlleth direct keep to the hill-road, but to see Pistyll-y-Llyn turn sharply to the right after ascending about 150 yards. From this point, a good road, which first drops to the stream again, and then ascends steeply, brings us in about 1½ miles to the little farm of *Gallt-y-Bladur*, near which we get the best view of the fall.

The position and surroundings of **Pistyll-y-Llyn**, somewhat resemble those of the Aber Falls, but the fall itself, being over a shelving rock, is not so impressive. Below the point at which we are standing, the glen has widened into a green valley, which is brought to a sudden end by an amphitheatre of green hills, and the water falls from the level of the moorland above into its depth. There is no accessory attraction of foliage, and few visitors will think it worth while to proceed to the fall itself, unless they are minded to climb to the moorland, which they may do by working back a little at first, and visit *Llyn Pen Rhaiadr*, 7 miles from Machynlleth, or are bound for Plynlimon. All the upland, however, about here—Plynlimon included—is very featureless. The house conspicuous between our view-point and Pistyll-y-Llyn, is *Cwm Rhaiadr*.

For Machynlleth we retrace our steps towards Glas Pwll and there, instead of turning down to the two foot-bridges, continue along a very fair road, which in about 1½ miles, after affording a very pretty peep into the Dovey valley on the left and crossing a small stream that flows down to it, ascends steeply past a few cottages only to drop with equal abruptness into the Aberystwith road, close to Machynlleth. An obvious foot-path, beginning at a cottage, cuts off a sharp corner in the lower part of the descent. The view in descending is delightful, and many will loiter on the smooth-cropped green hill to the left of the road.

This walk is specially fine in late autumn.

For the road from **Machynlleth** *to* **Aberystwith**, *see p.* 108.

Glandovey Junction to Aberdovey, 6 m; **Towyn**, 9¾ m; **Barmouth Junction**, 20 m; (**Dolgelley**, 27¾ m.) **Barmouth**, 21¾ m.

This branch, the most beautiful of the Cambrian system, is carried along the coast or across river-estuaries the whole way, and from the elevated position which it maintains for several miles, it affords very extensive views over the sea.

Starting from the **Junction**, the line crosses the Dovey just where that river widens into its estuary. On the right is a belt of pasture and silvan lowland in the direction of Pennal and the Happy Valley—as the old route from Machynlleth to Towyn is called; on the left Glandovey Castle peers above the woods on the hillside, beyond the entrance to the Llyfnant valley.

The hills now close in on the right, and the line winds along the shore passing through several short tunnels. On the far (south) side of the estuary is the wide Borth marsh, properly called Cors Fochno, with the Aberystwith line traceable along its shore as far as Ynys-las and Borth itself, at its south-western extremity. In bright weather, with the tide up, the estuary of the Dovey yields to none in Wales, except the incomparable Mawddach. At its north-east extremity we come to **Aberdovey**. The line passes behind the town, which is only seen in the intervals between cuttings or tunnels, and the *station* is some distance beyond it.

For a description of Aberdovey, *see p.* 72. Between it and Towyn low hills rise on the right of the line, and on the left is a widening salt-marsh. In 2½ miles, however, the hill-line is broken by the entrance to the Happy Valley, and a little short of **Towyn** there is a view up the straight valley that leads to Tal-y-Llyn, with the peak of Cader Idris prominent to the north of it. For *Towyn, see page* 69. Beyond it the line continues northwards in a straight line across the *Dysynni* flat for 1½ miles. Cader Idris again comes into view, and underneath it the boldly scarped Bird Rock (*Craig Aderyn*) rises almost sheer from the valley. Then, crossing the Dysynni river, we ascend to the cliff and, looking over the sea, have the whole line of the Carnarvonshire promontory revealed to us from Bardsey Island to the Rivals—a hill-outline of great beauty. Barmouth and its bridge, with the Llawllech range rising in front of Moelfre, also come into view before the next station, *Llwyngwril*, is reached, and the same view with variations which include the peak of Snowdon, continues till the descent to the flat sea-board and *Barmouth Junction* commences. About here the seaward end of the Cader range sinks very steeply into the sea at the Friog promontory, and the railway skirts it at a considerable height. Extensive works have been executed to minimise the chances of landslip.

Barmouth Station is 1¾ miles beyond the Junction, and from the bridge between the two, about half-a-mile long, the view is superb, Cader Idris holding the pride of place. *For a description, see p.* 50; *for* **Barmouth**, *p.* 48; to **Dolgelley**, *p.* 55.

ABERYSTWITH SECTION.

Aberystwith.

———◆———

Hotels: *Queen's, Belle Vue*, on the Parade, ½ *m.* from the Station; *Lion, (Cogerddan Arms), Talbot*, in the town, ¼ *m.* from the Station.

Post Office (Terrace Road): *Chief deliveries abt.* 8.15 *a.m.*, and 6.30 *p.m.* (*Sundays*, 11.10 *a.m.*). *Box closes abt.* 7.30 *a.m.*, 5 *p.m. Open on Sundays*, 8—10 *a.m.*, 12¾—1½ *noon.*

Population: about 6,700.

Distances: Aberdovey (*rail*), 22¼ *m.*; Barmouth (*rail*), 38½ *m.*; Borth (*rail*), 8½ *m.*; Devil's Bridge (*road*), 1 ½ *m.*; Hafod (*road*), 16 *m.*; Machynlleth (*rail*), 20½ *m.*; (*road*), 18 *m.*; Strata Florida (*rail and road*), 16½ *m.*

Aberystwith is not only the oldest watering-place of any importance in the Principality, but also the commercial capital of Mid Wales. At a time when the little Church of St. Tudno, on the bleak wind-swept slope of the Great Orme, with a surrounding population of 318 souls, was all that represented the modern Llandudno, and Rhyl consisted of a few fishermen's huts far from any thoroughfare, coaches were traversing the long and now deserted leagues of highway from Hereford to the busy port at the mouth of the Ystwith, which was the largest town in the county of Cardigan, and had a bi-weekly market, a shipping register of nearly 10,000 tons, a " handsome Town-hall, and a play-house."

Though the accident of situation has prevented the town from maintaining this supremacy, Aberystwith is still in high and deserved favour as a watering-place, and if it does not advance at the tearing pace of several of its more quickly accessible competitors, it maintains a steady advance both in outward appearance and inward prosperity. Though by no means free from the regular peripatetic nuisances of watering-places, it enjoys comparative immunity from the irregular ones, being one of the hardest places in the kingdom for the restless and resistless day-tripper to patronize. The monotony, again, which attaches to watering-places pure and simple is here modified by the mixed character of the town. The sea-frontage, a natural crescent lately extended northwards by the addition of a handsome line of lodging-houses, affords as good a promenade as can be wished for, but you can vary the routine of promenading and bathing and

ABERYSTWITH.

pebble-hunting (Aberystwith is famous for its pebbles) by a stroll through the town, and on market-days you may see "Taffy" in all his glory. The interior is a very fair specimen of a Welsh town, though you may not feel inclined to turn your steps towards the harbour a second time.

The drawback to Aberystwith, when compared with its rivals further north, is undoubtedly its scenery. The bay itself, round which the town clusters, is of a graceful outline, and the hills that rise at each end are nearly 500 feet high, but the colouring is dull and unattractive. The valleys of the Rheidol and the Ystwith, whose streams have been artificially united just as they enter the sea to the south of the town, would make the fortune of a Lancashire or Lincolnshire watering-place, but in competition with the estuaries of the Mawddach, the Dovey and the Conway, they rank only as Plynlimon — that wonderful mountain so much read of and so little seen— ranks with Snowdon and Cader Idris. There is, however, one piece of scenery, almost matchless of its kind, which Aberystwith may fairly claim as exclusively its own—the scenery of the Rheidol and the Mynach at the Devil's Bridge; the routes to this are given on page 109.

The **beach** at Aberystwith is mostly of pebbles, with a certain quantity of dark sand, and at low tide a considerable exposure of dark, weedy rock. The bathing, however, is good, and in the genuine open sea. There is a good **pier** (*admission*, 2*d.*), though the sharp slope of the shore has saved the expense of building a long one. South of it the beach is all rock, and at its edge is the **University College of Wales** (*open to Visitors, July 1 to Sept. 14, 10—1, 2—5; rest of year, M., W., F., 3—5. Admission, 6d. Handbook to Museum, 3d.*), a large modern building of considerable architectural pretensions, and originally intended for an hotel.

Still more south, and forming the southern horn of the bay are the **Castle grounds.** The street running from the Parade, along the east side of the College is the shortest way to them. The *Castle* consists of four more or less ruined towers and a few fragments of walls. It has, itself, no beauty, but the walks afford a pleasant stroll, and in clear weather the peak of Snowdon may be seen from them, a little to the left of Constitution Hill. The long Carnarvonshire promontory extending to Bardsey Island is a graceful feature from whatever view-point it may be seen, and in the other direction the southern sweep of Cardigan Bay may be traced to its farthest extremity, the Precely Hills in Pembroke-shire being included in the prospect.

The *history* of the Castle is ordinary enough. It was originally built by Gilbert Strongbow, early in the 12th Century; destroyed by Owen Gwynedd; built again by Edward I.; it declared for Charles I., and was finally dismantled by Cromwell.

Aberystwith has only been known by its present name since the days of Elizabeth, and, as late as 1861, it was a part of the parish of **Llanbadarn-fawr.** The old church of this parish should be visited. It lies a little north of the railway in the

midst of orchard-like surroundings, suggestive of Devonshire
rather than Wales, and is about a mile along the right hand
branch from the fork of the road at the end of North-
gate-street (*see Plan*). The church is cruciform, with an unusually massive central tower, and is almost entirely Early
English, but has suffered much in interest at the hands of
restorers. The parish takes its name from St. Padarn, a companion of St. Cadfan, who, "at the head of a large company of
saints from Armorica," came into Wales about the year 516. St.
Padarn founded the original church here, which became episcopal
under him as its first bishop. After an absence of 21 years
he returned to his native country, and his name is found among
the subscribers of the Council of Paris, 557. The last mention of
the see of Llanbadarn is in 720, when, according to the Welsh
Chronicles, the diocese was ravaged by the Saxons, and soon after
was merged in that of Menevia (St. David's). The only monument of more than local interest, is a flat slab in the chancel which
marks the grave of Lewis Morris, the Welsh antiquarian and poet,
who died in 1765. In the grave-yard, near the S.W. entrance, are
two old crosses.

Walks, &c., about Aberystwith.

¸ Before describing these, we would avoid the risk of causing disappointment by stating that for some reason or other the best view-points within
strolling distance of Aberystwith are not as accessible to visitors as such points
have been made by local enterprise at most watering-places of equal pretensions. Northwards, there is a good path along the breast of Constitution Hill,
but southwards, from which side the views are better, no walk has been laid out
up Pen Dinas, while the direct route up Allt-wen, which would be a delightful
stroll, has been cut off altogether at the foot of the cliff.

(1.) **Pen Dinas.**—This is the tower-crowned hill, a mile south
of the town, and about 400 feet above sea level. To reach it, cross
the bridge at the end of Bridge-street (*see Plan*), and after going
under the Manchester and Milford railway, turn along a lane to
the right at once, and in less than 200 yards commence the ascent
between two turf fences. (A longer but less steep way, is to keep
to the lane for a few hundred yards until, after you have passed an
occupation bridge over the railway on the right, a track strikes up
to a cottage on the left ; a third way is to continue along the main
road for 200 yards, and then to take a farm-road, just past a white
cottage.) Towards the top there is no clearly defined path. The
column—a very ugly memorial of the Duke of Wellington—soon
comes into sight, and on the near side of it are the remains of an
ancient camp.

The view from the tower includes the lower part of the Rheidol
and Ystwith valleys, the long southern sweep of Cardigan Bay,
and northwards, as great an extent of the mountains of North
Wales as the atmosphere will permit. Very little of Aberystwith

itself is seen. Rather north of east, Plynlimon may be just recognized as the highest part of a long featureless range.

The westward slope of Pen Dinas is very steep, but you may continue your wa k eastward to the hamlet of Piccadilly, or southward to the road that crosses from the Rheidol to the Ystwith valley.

(2.) **Constitution Hill** (*Pen Glais*), is about 450 feet high, and forms the northern flank of the hollow in which the town lies. An obvious track commences at the extreme end of the esplanade, and ascends at once above the cliff to a height of 300 feet. There is a fine retrospect of the town and Cardigan Bay during the ascent ; and the Carnarvonshire heights, from Snowdon to Bardsey come into view in front. Just as we lose sight of the town, the peak of Cader Idris appears rather more to the right. In about a mile the path descends to the shore again at a narrow strath called *Clarach Kay*. Looking up this to the right, we may see in the distance all the summit that Plynlimon can boast of. Then we may return to Aberystwith up the valley by Bow Street, station 2 *m*. distant, or over the hill (the routes are unmistakable), or we may continue up the cliff, and descend in another mile to the narrower little opening at *Wallog* (a country villa). Hence it is three-quarters of a mile to the hill-road between Aberystwith and Borth, and for the sake of the front views across Borth Marsh and the Dovey estuary, it is well worth while to continue the walk to *Borth* station (*p.* 106), returning to Aberystwith by train. By this route it is about seven miles from Aberystwith to Borth.

(3.) **Allt-wen** (the White Cliff," a by-no-means appropriate name), 2-2½ *m. south of the town*.

This is a capital view-point, but it is difficult to describe a route to it, as the direct one (*see below*) is closed by the proprietor at the foot of the hill itself. Except at high tide, it is possible to scramble up the débris of the cliff from the beach just below the top, but visitors should make themselves sure on these points before starting for the ramble.

In any case cross Rheidol Bridge at the end of Bridge Street and turn to the right a little further on for the stone pier, whence cross the Ystwith by a wooden bridge. Then go along the sea-wall, which extends across about half-a-mile of the level strath of the Ystwith to the foot of the cliff. The house among the trees on the breast of the hill is *Tan-y-Bwlch*. Then you may either (if allowed) ascend the cliff at once, or walk under it for some distance t ll a steep slope offers access to the top. (The round-about route turns left from the sea-wall at Pen-y-Ro, about two-thirds of the way along it.) The *view* is best from a stile about half-a-mile short of the highest point. Looking north we have the town and castle backed by Constitution Hill, beyond whose cliff the northern shore of the Dovey estuary projects. The white building just over the foot of the same cliff is near the station at Aberdovey, and further left, at the end of the next promontory in that direction, stands **Towyn**, exactly underneath the peak of Snowdon. A lower peak, **more** to the left, is Moel Hebog, below which, still further left, the Friog promontory, with Llwyngwril in front of it, hides all the coast between itself and the far side of Cardigan Bay. Along this—the Lleyn promontory—all the heights from Moel Hebog to Bardsey Island appear like separate islands, the curvature of the earth hiding the low ground that intervenes between each. Most prominent in the graceful outline is that of the double-headed Rivals.

Turning eastward from Snowdon, we detect the peak of Cader Idris some way left of the monument on Pen Dinas and, nearly over the same landmark, the eastward scarp of **Aran Mawddwy**. Then comes the long range of Cardiganshire uplands culminating in the humps of Plynlimon. The Ystwith valley is a rich and pleasant foreground to the east, and southward we have the full sweep of Cardigan Bay, with Precelly Top appearing over it about half way, to Strumble Head, which projects to the south of Fishguard.

Quitting our view-point, we may continue along, or rather to the right of the ridge for some distance, and then, turning to the left, make our way to the Aberayron **road**, about a quarter of a mile beyond Llanrhystyd-road Station (3 *m. from Aberystwith*) or, dropping to a high valley a little east of the ridge, go on southward till we join the same road a little short of the 5th milestone from Aberystwith. The roads and cart-tracks about here can only be learnt from the map, but those who wish to include another ' lion ' of Aberystwith, the Monk's Cave, should note the following description :—

(4.) **Twll Twrw** (the " Monk's Cave," or " Thunder Hole,") is a remarkable cavity in the cliff, about five miles south of Aberystwith. It is most comfortably visited by boat in calm weather (*charge, about* 10s.), but to reach it on foot you may either proceed over or under (a very rough walk) Allt wen, as in the foregoing description, or follow the Aberayron road (*mail-cart about* 8 *a.m.*) for 5½ miles, and then **turn** to the right by a winding track that leads to the shore near the cave, which is from 15 to 20 yards long, and a fair height.

(5.) **Nant Eos** (W. B. Powell, Esq.). This fine seat, the name of which means the Nightingale's Brook or Vale, is about 4 miles south-east of Aberystwith. The public are not at present allowed to visit these grounds except by special leave of the proprietor. Supposing that obtained, quit the town by the bridge, and at Piccadilly toll-bar take either the middle or the left-hand road. Nant Eos lies between them, and in the former case we turn to the left about a mile onward, and in the latter case to the right in about ¾ mile, or if we prefer the high-road, at about 3½ *m*. from Aberystwith. The best plan is to go by the first named and to return by the last, which commands the Rheidol vale.

(6.) **Strata Florida Abbey**, rail 14 *m.*, thence 2¾ *m.* by road.

People who avail themselves of the " Manchester and Milford " railway to reach this remote spot, may well say with Shakespeare " What's in a name ? " To explain briefly, we may state that the original intention of this line was to form the shortest possible route between Manchester and Milford Haven, by connecting the Cambrian at Llanidloes with the Great Western at Pencader near Carmarthen. From Llanidloes to Llangurig, a distance of six or seven miles, the line was actually made, but from Llangurig to Strata Florida mountains and lack of money together proved an insuperable obstacle, so the last resource was a diversion of the line from the latter place to Aberystwith—the only possible terminus within thirty miles.

A further difficulty—of nomenclature—arose with regard to this particular spot. Pontrhydfendigaed (" the bridge of the blessed ford ") is the name of the village, but no English porter could be found to pronounce it, and no Welsh one to render it intelligible, so a compromise was effected and Strata Florida—the Monkish name for the abbey, properly called Mynachlog-fawr — was adopted.

There is neither scenery nor ruin to draw visitors to Strata Florida, but those who like to see " Wild Wales," as it is, apart from all tourist influences, will not regret devoting half a day to an expedition to this most primitive part of it.

The railway journey to Strata Florida Station is fairly interesting. First the line passes between Dinas and the sea ; then it pursues for some time the Ystwith valley, affording a good view of Crosswood Park (Earl of Lisburne) and, where the main valley turns away to the left towards the recesses of Hafod, it climbs to a height of about 500 feet, looking down into a pretty tributary stream which flows through a deep wooded combe. This combe comes to an abrupt end at the fall of *Pwll Caradoc,* so called from the story of a prince of that name having, in mortification at losing a battle, thrown himself over the precipice into the pool below.

Beyond this the line goes through a tunnel, whence it emerges on to the wide upland strath (600 *ft. above sea-level*) of the Upper Teifi. The air up here is always pleasant, and under its influence one may thoroughly enjoy a grateful respite from the excitement of sight-seeing.

Strata Florida Station is in the parish of Yspytty Ystrad Meurig, and 1¼ miles north of Pontrhydfendigaed, whence a conveyance (*fare,* 6*d.*) meets every train. The *Black* and (very) *Red Lion* in the latter village are the only inns in the neighbourhood, and they are very small. The conveyance belongs to the Black Lion. **Strata Florida Abbey** (*Mynachlog-fawr*), called also *Ystrad-flur,* " the Strath of bloom," is 1¼ miles further on (2¾ *m. from the station*), and is reached by turning to the left by the smithy at the south end of the village. Nothing remains of this once great monastery—the largest in Wales, and the chief store-house of her learning—but a *Late Norman arch* (its members curiously tied together by crosiers), and the fragment of a wall. The rest of the area which it presumably occupied, now contains a poor-looking church and a graveyard. The Teifi (one of the best trout-streams in Wales) comes out of the shallow peaceful valley, wherein are its "pools" among the low hills westward, and flows close by through green pastures with a fair sprinkling of trees on the higher ground. The only incongruous object in the scene is a lead-mine.

The original abbey is said to have been a Cistercian House founded by one of the Princes of Wales, and to have been destroyed by Henry IV. out of spite towards Owen Glyndwr. Its successor did not survive the dissolution in the reign of Henry VIII. Another account is that the site of the original abbey was 2 miles away at a place called *Yr Hen Fonachlog* (the "old monastery"), and that the scanty ruin of to-day is the remnant of one that only existed for about 40 years.

Aberystwith to Borth, by rail, 8¼ m.

We have already (*p.* 103) described a pedestrian route, mostly along the coast, to Borth. The railway route is described the reverse way on page 91. Taken this way we need only note Llanbadarn Church (l.), the view up the strath of the Rheidol (r.), the valley extending left from *Bow Street* (4 m.) to the sea and, opposite to it on the right, the prospect over the glades of Cogerddan to Plynlimon. Beyond Bow Street, the line, continuing along a shallow valley, passes *Llanfihangel* station and church, and then descends to Borth Marsh, a little way up which stands the village.

Borth (large *Hotel* close to the station ; *Post arr.* 7.30 *a.m.* (*Sunday.* 10 *a.m.*) ; *dep.* 6 *p.m.* (*every day*). *Office open, Weekdays,* 8 *a.m.* to 8 *p.m.* ; *Sunday*, 8 to 10 *a.m.*) owes its popularity to its healthiness and the fine stretch of firm sand which extends in front of it. The village, described a century ago as a " miserable fishing cottage," begins at the foot of the low cliffs which extend all the way from Aberystwith. It consists of one straight street more than half-a-mile in length and running alongside the shore, and a short one of lodging-houses between the hotel and the station. Except at the north end, near the hotel, there is little or no sea-frontage, as the main street has houses on both sides. Inland, Borth Marsh, *Cors Fochno*, stretches for three miles, and the view is bounded by the hills beyond the Dovey estuary, with Aran Mawddwy in the far distance, north-east, and those which rise southward therefrom towards Plynlimon.

The recommendations of Borth are firm sands, good bathing, lodgings cheaper than the average, easy communication by rail with other places, and a quietude unknown to more popular and populous resorts. It was the temporary sojourn of Uppingham school at Borth that brought it chiefly into notice a few years ago.

The stumps of trees discoverable in the sands about here at low tide, give colour to the tradition that this part of Cardigan Bay was once a fair and fertile champaign protected by an embankment, and it would doubtless have continued so to this hour had not a drunken watchman opened the sluices and permanently deluged the whole in a single night.

Borth to Bedd Taliesin (pron. *Tilly-essin*), 5-6 m. This interesting spot, the reputed grave of the first and foremost of the Welsh bards (*but see p.* 108), may be reached by several routes from Borth. One is to take the train to Llanfihangel, whence the road joins the main Aberys'with and Machynlleth road in about 1¾ miles, the total walking distance being 5 miles (*see p.* 108.) Another, to take the train to Ynys-las, whence a road reaches Tre-Taliesin (*see below*) in 3 miles, while two others are along the slopes that skirt the south side of Borth Marsh. For the first two miles or so these last two are identical; after that you bear slightly to the left for Taliesin village, and to the right for Tal-y-Bont. The course we recommend is to go by Llanfihangel and to return by Taliesin. Those who prefer walking all the way should take the foot-path that crosses the line just south of the Borth platform. This leads to a new church, on approaching which it bends to the left and crosses the straightened course of the Afon Lery by a white foot-bridge. Thence, bearing right, it quits the marsh and joins a cart-road leading to a farm called *Pont-y-dwn*. Beyond the farm pass through a gate on the left and continue along a cart-track which passes several other little farms. The tracks are very devious, but the one thing to be avoided is descending to the marsh, which is almost, if not quite impassable. (*a*) For Tal-y-Bont turn to the right about 1½ miles beyond Pant-y-dwn ; for Taliesin village keep the road nearest to the side of the marsh. The Tal-y-Bont route joins the Aberystwith and Machynlleth road opposite the narrower road which ascends to Bedd Taliesin and ¾ mile north of the *Black Lion Inn*. *For the rest of this route see p.* 108.

(*b*) The Taliesin route joins the Machynlleth road a few yards south of the *Royal Oak Inn*, a neat little roadside house, in Taliesin village (*p.* 108). Behind the inn a track ascends in the direction of a lead-mine, whose débris is seen high up among the trees. Ascend by this track, turning to the right by an iron fence, and on entering the wood bend to the left and keep ascending till you reach the mine. Here level ground is gained, and passing to the left of a large wheel you enter a cart-track which soon bends to the right and then, close to another wheel, turns up left again towards a farm (*Pen-y-Sarn*) and a small chapel. Leaving these on the right bear left again, and where the track forks take the right branch. **Bedd Taliesin** lies a few yards to the right of the track. It may be recognised by a flat slab resting on three or four smaller stones, close to which is the reputed grave—a narrow trough, nearly 6 feet long (*see p.* 108).

To descend to Tal-y-Bont take the road which goes parallel with the chapel and farm some distance below them. This descends a narrow valley, crosses its stream in ¾ mile and enters the considerable village of Tal-y-Bont at its north end, ½ m. north of the *Black Lion Inn*, (*see p.* 118). For Llanfihangel station (3 m. *further*) you turn to the right in another mile.

Aberystwith to Machynlleth (*pedestrian or carriage route*).

The distance by road from Aberystwith to Machynlleth is 18 miles. Pedestrians, however, will save five miles and lose nothing by taking the train to Llanfihangel, and on arriving at Tal-y-Bont diverging to Bedd Taliesin (*pron.* Tally-essin) whence they may either descend direct into the high-road near Taliesin village, or continue by bye-roads, and not rejoin it for 3 miles further. This makes a very interesting walk, the distances being as follows :—

Aberystwith to Llanfihangel (rail) 6 m. *Llanfihangel to Tal-y-Bont (road),* 3 m; *Bedd Taliesin,* 5 m; *Taliesin Village,* 6½ m; *Tre'r-ddol,* 7 m; *Derwen-las,* 13 m; *Machynlleth,* 15½ m.

Hotel at Tal-y-Bont; roadside inns at Llanfihangel, Taliesin Tre'r-ddol and Derwen-las.

From Llanfihangel it is 1½ miles into the main road, which a long mile further crosses the Lery river, a fishing stream of some repute, coming down from the region of Plynlimon. The *hotel* is a few yards beyond the bridge. **Tal-y-Bont** is a large village with several lead-mines in its vicinity. The road to Bedd Taliesin diverges to the right at the north end of it, and is on the rise all the way. In three-quarters of a mile it crosses the stream. and a mile further, passing a little below and to the left of a small farm (*Pen-y-Sarn*) and chapel, turns up to the right for a few yards; then left again, forking almost at once. Taking the right-hand branch, you are close on **Bedd Taliesin** (the " Grave of Taliesin "). A rough mound with a flat slab resting on three or four small stones marks the spot, and close to it is a narrow trough, nearly six feet long and flanked by two stones. This is the veritable grave, but it is to be noted that there is another Bedd Taliesin, on the shore of Llyn Geirionydd, between Trefriw and Capel Curig (*see* " North Wales, Part I.," *p.* 112).

Taliesin was the father of Welsh bards, and flourished in the 6th century. The story of the circumstances immediately succeeding his birth is, *mutato nomine,* almost identical with that of Moses. If you sleep on his grave, you rise either a madman—no great mental change !—or a poet.

The views from the high ground about here are very fine, especially across the Dovey estuary. Moel-y-Gaer, a fortified hill, 1½ miles due west of the " Bedd," is a good point for comprehending them.

In descending to Taliesin village, retrace your steps for a short distance, and then turn to the right by a cart-track just below a large wheel. This track soon bears to the left, and passing another wheel, becomes a foot-path, which at once crosses the débris of a lead-mine, and, bearing again to the left, descends abruptly through a wood to the village, entering the main Machynlleth road close to the *Royal Oak Inn.*

From Bedd Taliesin you may go northwards, and crossing a stream, continue along a small valley for about 3 miles, till you join the main road a little short of the church of Eglwys-fach, and 6 miles short of Machynlleth (*see map*).

From Taliesin village, the road passes for some miles between wooded knolls, leaving Borth Marsh on the left. In about 3½ miles at a place called *Furnace*, a waterfall, part y artificial, is noticeable on the right, and a mile further we pass under the woods of Glandovey Castle, and reach *Glandovey statiom*. Then comes the entrance to the narrow Llyfnant valley (*p.* 97) on the right. After crossing Pont Llyfnant, at the far end of this, pedestrians should ascend by the old road (the right hand branch of two rough ones that start together). After climbing for about 200 feet, a charming prospect up the green Dovey valley reveals itself, and the new road is joined close to the little *Black Lion Inn* at Derwen-las, and 2½ miles short of Machynlleth, which soon after displays its picturesque skyline at a sudden bend of the road.

Aberystwith to the Devil's Bridge.

(*a*) *By direct road*, 11¼ *m.*   (*b*) *By north road, vià Pont Erwyd*, 15 *m.*   (*c*) *Rail to Trawscoed*, 9 *m* ; *thence road, vià Hafod*, 12 *m*. 21 *m. in all.*

Mail-cart (*Fares* : single, 3s., return, 4s.) carrying a limited number of passengers leaves P. O., Aberystwith, the year round, at 8 *a.m.*, and starts back from Devil's Bridge at 3 *p.m.* It takes the Pont Erwyd route on both journeys ; *time* abt. 3 hrs. each way.

Excursion breaks (*return fare*, 4s.) leave Aberystwith daily during the season, going by the direct road and returning by Pont Erwyd.

At the luncheon-rooms annexed to the *Hafod Arms Hotel*, Devil's Bridge, a substantial cold luncheon is provided at 2s. each, including attendance ; children half-price.

For those who stay the night at the hotel : bed, breakfast, and attendance, 5s.

For visiting the waterfalls (including charge for guide) 1s. each ; children half-price.

The object of this excursion is very inadequately indicated by the name—the Devil's Bridge—by which it is universally known. The old arch over the Mynach has, indeed. certain more or less vague legendary and historical associations and, in connection with the deep and narrow gorge which it spans, forms a striking picture, but it is not on these accounts that the spot to which it lends its name has acquired its reputation. *That* rests on the ideal glen of the Rheidol and the fine falls of the Mynach. Not only is there no scenery within 20 miles of Aberystwith that can for a moment bear comparison with this, but, of its kind, there is no finer glen in Great Britain than this portion of the Rheidol valley. In the winding character of its course and the abruptness of its flanking hills, it will recall to the Devonshire tourist the ravine of the Teign about Fingle Bridge, whilst in depth and richness of woodland it has much of the charm of the East Lyn glen, seen from the road or hills overlooking Watersmeet. These

Devon scenes, especially the latter, have the advantage of their
Cambrian rival in the character of their upper slopes, which in
the case of the Lyn are diversified by bold bits of crag protruding
through the foliage, but on the other hand the considerable
cascade on the Rheidol itself, and the fine chain of falls down
which its tributary, the Mynach, plunges to join it, are features
in which neither of the southern streams we have named can
seriously be said to compete.

Choice of routes. Of the three approaches to the Devil's Bridge
mentioned in the small print at the head of this " Excursion," by
far the best is the *direct one*, which for the greater part of the
distance traverses the high ridge bounding the valley of the
Rheidol on the south. The views it commands are both wide and,
in favourable weather, of considerable beauty, though nowhere
attaining to the first rank. The Pont Erwyd route, for 12 out of
the 15 miles, is distinctly uninteresting: first we have 6 miles on low
ground, with commonplace surroundings, and then 6 more over a
watershed once, no doubt, of a certain unsophisticated and lonely
wildness, but now irretrievably marred by that bane of this part
of Wales, the moribund lead-mines ; the last 3 miles leave the
mine scars behind and gradually increase in interest as sundry
peeps are gained into the narrow and deep ravine of the Rheidol.

The route by Trawscoed station and Hafod is intermediate in
quality between the above two. The short railway journey of 9
miles, as well as the two roads of about the same length, all con-
verge just short of Trawscoed station, where the scenery, after being
distinctly poor, becomes pretty, owing to the woods of the Earl of
Lisburne's domain. The Ystwith itself has been ruined by the
detritus and dusky outpourings of the Crogwinion and Lisburne
lead-mines higher up its valley, and so the 6 miles from the
station to Pont Rhyd-y-Groes (where the Hafod property is
entered), though in parts distinctly pleasing, lack the attractions
of a virgin mountain-stream. The Hafod domain once entered
on, the journey becomes thoroughly beautiful, and so continues for
the 3 miles through the park, after which an unsullied, if not a
very interesting 2¾ miles brings us to the Devil's Bridge.

The majority of tourists avail themselves of the excursion-
breaks from Aberystwith, and so traverse the direct route on the
outward, and the Pont Erwyd route on the return journey but
they miss Hafod, which is too distant to be visited in the interval
between the two. Those who fail to find special charm in the
miscellaneous company and "high spirits" incidental to public
conveyance at low fares, should arrange to tarry for at least one
night at the *Hafod Arms Hotel* (well managed, reasonable in its
charges, and magnificently situated close to the Bridge). Supposing
two days to be allotted to the excursion, then a good arrangement
of the traveller's time would be to take the mail-cart *viâ* Pont
Erwyd as far as Yspytty Cynfyn church. This is a trifle over
1½ miles from the Hotel and close to the Parson's Bridge,

where the Rheidol glen is exceedingly fine. Exploring thereabouts a while, he will have time to walk by the road, which
affords good peeps of the glen, to the hotel and get an early
luncheon before the arrival of the caravans. After luncheon,
leaving the beauties of the Rheidol till later in the day, when the
excursionist will have departed, he should walk to Hafod. seeing
Eglwys Newydd church and the Piran Fall on the way, and continue down the Ystwith as far as Pont Rhyd-y-Groes, where the
Bear Inn offers the chance of passing refreshment. Thence
either by the way he came (the Hafod grounds will bear twice
seeing), or over the hills by Llantrisant, a breezy but rather dull
4 miles, he will get back to his inn and have the evening to enjoy
its romantic surroundings. Next day an early morning ramble
down the glen followed by a leisurely walk into Aberystwith by
the direct road will finish up an exceedingly pleasant round.

Those who can only allot one day to the excursion, and who
also want to see Hafod, should drive by the direct road from
Aberystwith and then walk down the Ystwith valley to Trawscoed
(Crosswood) station, whence a late evening train can be taken
back to Aberystwith.

(i.) **The Direct Route.**—This leaves the town by Bridge Street,
and after crossing the Rheidol near the harbour, passes under the
M. & M. R., profanely called the "wheelbarrow line." Then
a gradual ascent past the monument-crowned Pen Dinas (on the
right) brings us in 1½ miles to *Piccadilly* toll-gate, where we
take the left hand of three roads in front. Another ¾ mile
of climbing suddenly opens up a fine and wide view of the
Rheidol valley, which, though on closer acquaintance found to be
hereabouts utterly lacking in really beautiful details, has, under
favourable conditions of atmosphere and as viewed from the high
ground above it, a softness of aspect which is very pleasing.
The only objects here calling for mention are the fine old church
of Llanbadarnfawr immediately across the vale, and the little Pen
Parciau bridge that nestles close under the ridge by which we have
climbed to our present position. Onward for a while nothing of
moment appears. About the fourth milestone, we pass through
a poor little hamlet, *Capel Sion*, and presently get on the right a
peep down a green little glen, a tributary of the Ystwith valley.
Soon after passing the fifth milestone, looking back, a well-defined
peak rises nearly due north above an intermediate ridge; this
is Cader Idris, some 20 miles off, seen over the top of the hills
about the lower Dovey. At 7 miles from starting, we pass the
Henffordd Arms, a poor road-side public-house, the only place of
entertainment on the route. Just beyond it, the ridge we are
pursuing suddenly narrows, and from Bwlch Heble, as the little
l is named, we look down on the one side into the Rheidol
valley, and on the other into a thickly wooded tributary glen of
the Ystwith. Now for two miles the Rheidol vale is really
beautiful, and the road commands it fully. Aberystwith, which

presented its least picturesque side when the valley was first caught sight of, is now no longer in view, but its position is indicated by the too chimney-like monument on Pen Dinas. Approaching the summit-level of the route, 989 feet above the sea and 9 miles on our way, the two peaks of Plynlimon (really a mile or more apart, but here foreshortened) appear to the north-east, a very flattering presentation of a really bog-sodden and un-interesting mountain. The road then begins a gentle descent, and we get peeps now and again of the Rheidol, rapidly narrow-ing from a valley to a tortuous glen. Beyond it the hills present a knob-like outline, very characteristic of much of the South Wales scenery, on the confines of which we are now trespassing. As we near our destination, the larch-woods on the road to Hafod are in front on the right, and across a tributary stream on the left is the cone-like knoll of Castell-fan-Grach. The Devil's Bridge scenery, is coy, and the last mile or so of our journey is almost ugly, when suddenly, as we stop at the *Hafod Arms Hotel*, the full glory of what we have come to see bursts upon us.

(ii.) **The Pont Erwyd Route.**—This leaves the town by the Llanbadarn road, and passes through that village close to the fine church, which even as we pass it is seen to have been sadly tinkered by restorers. The first 6 miles are very tame, then nature gets a little pleasanter, but man becomes more vile. The main Rheidol valley was left behind at Capel Bangor, 5 miles from starting, and the stream in the valley whose south side we are gradually climbing is called the Afon Melynddwr. At *Goginan*, a mining hamlet, with a *shop* (so marked in Ordnance Map) and a small inn, the *Miner's Arms*, the mail-cart makes a more or less prolonged halt, and more than ample time is afforded to take in the lead-spoilt features of the valley below. Once more on our way the scenery somewhat improves, and a wildish valley opens on the left, but lead is still fatal to all beauty. The summit-level is reached at Bwlch Nant-'r-Arian, about 850 ft., and thence the road descends a bare green valley, wholly abandoned to lead mines, to **Pont Erwyd**, about ½ *m.* short of which is the *Gogerddan Arms*, a fair inn in a wild but not unpicturesque situation, thanks to the Rheidol, which here winds with many loops at the bottom of an abrupt little ravine. After crossing the river by the single arch which gives its name to the hamlet, the Devil's Bridge road strikes off at once on the right, and in about half-a-mile fords a tributary burn. Gradually the Rheidol ravine becomes more and more the dominant attraction, a really fine little chink—it is scarcely more here—in the desolate upland. A mile and a half from Pont Erwyd and the same distance from the Devil's Bridge, is **Yspytty Cynfyn** *Church*, where those who adopt the sug-gested two-days route, indicated above, should leave the mail-cart, sending on their *impedimenta* to the hotel with orders for luncheon to be ready in an hour's time. The church just named has no features of interest, but the antiquarian should look, perhaps, at certain ancient stones set in the graveyard wall. The **Parson's**

Bridge is only a few hundred yards by foot-path from the church—a romantic spot in a savage little gorge through which the Rheidol, when in flood, tears its way with great impetuosity. [Those who make a more or less prolonged stay at the Devil's Bridge—and no one could do better than give it a week—will do well to cross the stream here and follow it downwards—no road, but sundry paths—at least as far as the first bridge beyond the inflow of the Mynach. Owing to the character of the defile, there is no track on either bank along the water-side at its narrowest part, and from the Hotel the only means of crossing the river is by this Parson's Bridge, or by the one below called Pont-pren-Plwcca. The two are about 2½ miles apart, reckoning by the course of the water, but a fair hour's walk by the only available track.]

After passing Yspytty Cynfyn the scene is still on the whole bare, but approaching the end of the drive, first one thread-water and then another is caught sight of, as the steeps of the main valley, clad with oak-scrub, come into view. Just before crossing the (New) Devil's Bridge, the beauty of the spot unfolds itself, and thirty yards beyond, at the hotel, is fully revealed.

(iii.) **The Trawscoed and Hafod route.**—This, as far as Pont Rhyd-y-Groes, requires no further description than that given in our introductory remarks. The Hafod grounds, which are there entered, will be found fully described on p. 116, as well as the road thence to the Devil's Bridge.

Those who desire to drive from Trawscoed must bespeak a conveyance from the Hafod Arms Hotel, as there is no posting-house nearer at hand.

The Devil's Bridge.

Hotel: *Hafod Arms*, close to the Bridge and Falls, and overlooking the Rheidol Glen.

Post *arr. abt.* 11 *a.m., dep.* 3 *p.m.* *Post Town* : *Aberystwith.*

Distances : *Aberystwith (direct)* 11½ m. ; (*viâ Pont Erwyd, 3 m.*) 15 m. *Hafod,* 4½ m. *Trawscoed Station,* 12 m. *Llanidloes Station,* 20½ m.

Of the scenery of the Rheidol glen enough has already been said on pp. 109, 110. For that of the Ystwith valley, about Hafod, see page 116. In this place it only remains for us to add, that the general character of the higher ground bordering these streams is deficient in beauty, and that all interest is confined to the glens, which are as delightful as the country through which they wind is bare and commonplace.

Now let us take the general round usually followed by day-visitors. First comes the 1s. fee, for no sight of the old bridge is possible, nor of the gorge of the Mynach, except from the grounds of the hotel, and these are only accessible on payment.

We must confess that on our first visit this none too modest charge was only grudgingly produced, for we abominate the lock-and-key cavern and petrifying well style of thing.   It is, however, only just to the landlord of the hotel to give his explanation of the matter, viz., that his rent is calculated on the assumption that he gets these shillings, and that but for this fee many of the hundreds who flock from Aberystwith would not spend a farthing in a spot which, as a tarrying-place, is not improved by their patronage.   This defence is sound, and when we add that no better shilling's worth is to be had in the Principality, we have, we hope, said enough to discount annoyance.

We cross the bridge close to the hotel, enter a gate immediately beyond it on the right hand, and descend the steps to the water's edge.   The overhanging trees, and the cool, deep shadows of the winding pool, in which for a moment the waters linger, are very beautiful, but the turmoil below, where the very heart of the rocks has been eaten out by eternal grinding, is weird and impressive. Above is the storm-weathered arch of the *Monks' Bridge*, over which Archbishop Baldwin may have passed 800 years ago, when he went to visit the monks of Strata Florida.   The *new bridge* that now carries the road is just above the old one, which has thus lost nothing of its charm by a juxtaposition that renders it inaccessible.

Returning to the road, in a hundred yards or so we pass through a door-way on the left.   Hence a path descends through a scanty copse to a rocky spur projecting into the main valley towards the junction of the two streams.   From this spur the *Fall of the Rheidol* is well seen, together with the pathless gorge out of which it leaps.   Just above it, on the farther bank, comes down a silvery streak, one of the several graceful thread-waters that diversify the richly clad steeps of the ravine.   Following the footpath along and down the ridge, the *Upper falls of the Mynach* (or *Rhyddnant*) come full into view; but the main fall, which is the lowermost of the chain, is nearly hidden by the foliage.   Looking right down the Rheidol glen, another silver thread is observed descending from the hill-side that closes the valley in.

Descending yet further we gain the top of a steep flight of 100 steps, and some way down them pause at a point that commands the *chief fall* with a less perfect view of the three above it.   It is a lovely sight when the stream is small and of crystal purity, but in times of flood what is lost in delicacy is gained in grandeur, for then, instead of fall above fall, we have one huge cataract plunging with the voice of thunder into the sheer gulf beneath our feet.   At the bottom of the rocky staircase the stream is crossed by a frail iron bridge, about which a word of caution to the exhilarated excursionist may not be out of place, and it is this.   The bridge is very slight, though quite strong enough for any amount of legitimate foot-traffic, but it is not strong enough to stand the swaying process to which foolish "trippers," pleased to fancy themselves in a swing at a fair, endeavour sometimes to subject it. To prevent what, if a rod thus unduly strained were to break, might prove a fatal catastrophe, we ask all reasonable people to support the authority of the guide.

From this foot-bridge irregular steps lead up alongside the falls. At the foot of one of them are the remains of a cave, now a shallow affair, but connected in local story with certain children blood-thirsty beyond their years. Near the top, by going out on a spur overhanging the stream, we can get a peep, but no more, except when the trees have shed their leaves, of the old bridge, which by-the-way is called by the natives, not the Devil's, but the Monk's bridge.

The **Parson's Bridge** (p. 112) across the Rheidol gorge, near Yspytty Cynfyn, 1½ miles up the valley, should on no account be omitted, and, time permitting, the ramble thence down the far side of the glen already mentioned should be taken. From the hotel grounds it is quite possible to scramble somehow down to the main stream, but there is no path, and no advantage to be gained, if there were. It is the view of the Mynach ravine and falls that is a great feature from the opposite bank.

The Devil's Bridge to Hafod, 4½ m., and Pont Rhyd-y-Groes, 6 m.

Instead of crossing the Devil's Bridge, we take the road that strikes uphill on the hotel side of it, and ascend the green and peaceful valley of the Rhyddnant, and when that rends more to the left, a prattling tributary burn keeps us company. Gradually this tributary valley takes a more barren aspect, but towards the top we enter the larch-woods that are, in this direction, the outliers of the groves of Hafod. At the summit of the pass, nearly 2 miles from the hotel, a rough-stone pointed arch spans the road. It commemorates the Jubilee of the reign of George III. and the loyalty of Colonel Johnes, the creator of Hafod. After passing a spruce-fir plantation on the left, about 1½ miles beyond the arch, take a road (not shown on Ordnance) through a gate on the right hand, just short of a small burn.* Under the shade of a beech-grove, and accompanied by the brook, we descend past Eglwys Newydd parsonage, and are then fairly within the inner circle of the Hafod estate. Here the plantations lose their artificial character, and the valley becomes exceedingly pretty. When a lodge is reached, ask for the key of the church, which is only a few yards up the upper of the two roads. **Eglwys Newydd** architecturally is mean and ugly, but the shaggy old yews in its little grave-yard, and its sequestered situation are delightful. The interior of the building is as poor as the outside, but the monument to Miss Johnes (d. 1811), by Chantrey, is a faultless work. It represents the daughter on a couch, with

* The road we quit crosses another stream 230 yds. further onward, and then bearing to the right soon reaches the Ystwith valley, near the head of which it strikes south-west across the hills to the Wye valley at Rhayader.

the mother weeping at the foot, and the father behind supporting her head. The east window of Dutch glass is good in colour and of curious design.

The **Piran Fall** is in the glen just below the church, and is approached by a tunnel through the rock; it is of no striking height or volume, but worth the trifling *détour* necessary to visit it. From it we follow the drive (*i.e.*, the lower road from the lodge), and soon have below on the left the "Flower Garden" of the Ordnance Map, a charming group of rhododendron and other greenery around a cedar. Then to the right of the road on the bluff above it is the vase-surmounted *Bedford Obelisk*, another of Colonel Johnes' memorials, after passing which, in a few yards, we come suddenly upon the *mansion*. This is a curious mixture, one-half being arabesque, with a dome that might form part of an Indian shrine, the other half Italian and plain, with a lofty clock-tower or campanile. The former part was by Nash, the latter by Salvin. The view from the house, down the Ystwith valley, is charming, but the river itself has been marred by the mine detritus. Onward, the road is well wooded and follows the stream to **Pont Rhyd-y-Groes** (*Bear Inn*).

Hafod, as already intimated, was the creation of Col. Johnes, who purchased the estate, then a desolate and almost treeless glen and waste, in 1783. He planted, literally, millions of trees, and built a mansion, wherein he collected priceless treasures of art and literature, and established a printing press. The whole was destroyed by fire in 1807. Then Nash built the grotesque mansion part of which we have already described, and this the colonel once more filled with costly rarities, but on his death, in 1816, the estate got into Chancery and so remained till 1841, when it was bought by the Duke of Newcastle for £62,000, who, 4 years afterwards, sold it to Mr. Hoghton for half as much again. This gentleman made great improvement and built the Italian portion of the mansion, but in 1857 it once more changed owners and became the property of Mr. Chambers, who, holding it only 14 years, parted with it to the Company that built or, rather, enlarged the hotel at the Devil's Bridge. At present the estate, in whole or in part, belongs to Mr. Waddingham, who occupies the mansion.

Pont Rhyd-y-Groes by Llantrisant to the Devil's Bridge, abt. 4 m. over the hills.

This is only given as an alternative route, and is of little interest in itself, though it serves to confirm the impression that all the beauty of this part of Cardiganshire is confined to the valleys. Take the road down the valley on the right bank of the Ystwith, and avoid rough roads on either hand. The church prominent on the sky-line ahead is Ysputty Ystwith, and if we were bound for Strata Florida we should pass close to it. The gorge of the Ystwith, as we turn to the right up-hill away from it is rather pretty. We ascend by the side of a lead-murky brook; and the hills are at first fairly wooded, chiefly with larch. When a bare plateau is reached keep straight on for a while, and then turn to the right to and through some lead-works, and so to the little church of **Llantrisant**, long in ruins but now restored This lonely edifice would, but for the mines, have been left to decay, but it is now probably more useful than ever, and is served by the Parson of Llanfihangel-y-Creiddyn, a village neaily 5 miles away to the westward. From Llautrisant the Devil's Bridge is about 2 miles distant, and presently the ravine of the Rheidol with the group of houses that constitutes the hamlet comes in sight, and an obvious foot-path on the right cuts off an angle of the road. The country beyond the Rheidol presents a curious outline of knob-like hills.

Aberystwith to Plynlimon and Llanidloes.

See the description of routes the reverse way on page 89.

The nearest inn to the summit of Plynlimon is *Dyffryn Castell,* a few yards beyond the junction of the Devil's Bridge and Pont. Erwyd routes to Llanidloes. 4 miles from Devil's Bridge and 2 miles from Pont Erwyd. Hence it is $3\frac{1}{2}$ miles to the top, and a guide can be had for about 3s., or 3d. each for a large party. The inn offers fair country accommodation and, if only from the convenience of its situation, merits the patronage of climbers of Plynlimon, on whom it is to a great extent dependent, and who might in rough weather fare very ill without it, the surrounding country being exceptionally desolate.

From the inn you may either attack the slope of the mountain at once and reach the summit by the ridge, or continue $2\frac{1}{2}$ miles on the road to its highest point at Steddfa Gurig (1,358 ft.). The mountain is not so boggy on this as on the east side. *For further description and the view, see p.* 89.

Mountain Section.

———◆———

In the part of Wales described in this particular volume, the mountains which tempt the tourist to the exertion of climbing them are interesting but not very numerous. Cader Idris, the Arans, Arenig-fawr, the Rhinog and Diphwys range, the Berwyns, and Plynlimon almost exhaust the list, and but for the fictitious interest which Plynlimon has obtained from the fact of its giving birth to so many rivers, we might certainly omit it altogether, for a more featureless and less interesting mountain of its height it would be difficult to find. If we wanted to exemplify the fact that, as regards scenery, the form of a mountain is a much more important consideration than its height, we should contrast the Langdale Pikes in Westmorland with Plynlimon—the former, the most effective feature of perhaps the handsomest scene in the country, the latter, a mere sheep-walk; yet both within a few feet of the same height. The Berwyn summits, too, are rather the highest points of elevated moors than mountains, and such of these as come in the tourist's way we have already described under the head of those resorts which are nearest to them. On the contrary, there is hardly a finer mountain-walk in the kingdom than that which embraces the whole, or part of the Cader Idris range, while the Arans, Arenig-fawr, and the various heights extending from Diphwys to Rhinog-fawr, are one and all very enjoyable, besides being within easy reach of good accommodation.

	ft.	page.		ft.	page.
Aran Mawddwy - - -	2972	118	Diphwys - - - -	2467	136
Cader Idris - - - -	2929	125	Rhobell-fawr - - -	2409	139
Aran Benllyn - - - -	2902	118	Llethr - - - - -	2475	136
Arenig-fawr - - - -	2800	123	Rhinog-fawr - - -	2390	61, 62, 67
Moel-sych - - - - -	2718	32	Moel Ferna - - -	2070	24
Cader Fronwen - - -	2573	24	Moel-y-Gamelin - -	1897	14
Plynlimon - - - - -	2469	89, 117	Moel Offrwm - - -	1328	39

———◆———

ARAN MAWDDWY, 2,972 ft.; and ARAN BENLLYN, 2,902 ft.

These twin summits crown the highest mountain ridge in Wales outside Snowdonia, Aran Mawddwy being, according to the Ordnance Survey, 40 feet higher than Cader Idris, and 60 feet higher than the Brecon Beacons in South Wales. They are both fine heights, especially as seen from the direction of Bala, but suffer from the disadvantage of presenting their front, or scarped elevation, to a high and barren moorland which dwarfs their stature, and whose intersecting valleys are too deep and narrow to admit of anything more than their own immediate environments being seen from them. To compare great things with small, the Arans are not unlike a picture with its face turned to the wall. In this respect they are as disadvantageously placed as Cader Idris is the reverse.

There are three places which may conveniently be made the starting or finishing point of a walk over the Arans—Llanuwchllyn or Drws-y-Nant on the Bala and Dolgelley Railway, and Dinas Mawddwy at the end of the branch line from Cemmaes Road on the Cambrian. Those who do not contemplate extending their tour into the Dinas Mawddwy and Machynlleth district will do best to ascend from Llanuwchllyn and descend to Drws-y-Nant, or *rice versâ*, but the descent to Dinas Mawddwy is a very interesting one, and the first bit of it, as described below, should be made in any case.

There is a good-sized hotel — the *Buckley Arms*—at Dinas Mawddwy, a comfortable inn at Llanuwchllyn Station, and a fair road-side house one mile on the Bala side of Drws-y-Nant. Also a small way-side house at Llanymawddwy, 4 m. from Dina-Mawddwy on the road to Bala. All the trains stop at Llanuwchllyn, and nearly all at Drws-y-Nant.

Ascents.

(1) **From Llanuwchllyn.** From the station or inn, which is close at hand, cross the Twrch river by the bridge, and on reaching the main road turn to the left and pass under the railway. A few yards further you come to the river again, which is crossed by a bridge at the lower end of a very pretty little dell. Hence there is a choice of routes.

(a) *The shortest and roughest.* Do not cross the bridge, but enter a cart-track through a gate on the near side of it. This soon brings you to the foot of the long line of ascending knots, more or less rugged, which you cannot fail to have noticed from the station. Taking these knots in succession, with a slight inclination to the right where the straight course is uncomfortably precipitous, or, if you prefer bog to rock, keeping them on the left all the way up, you will reach the top of *Aran Benllyn* (not visible till you are close upon it) in from 1½ to 2 hours. During the ascent there is a full-length view of Bala Lake, and the valley extending from it to Dolgelley opens out as we approach the top. The double-crested mountain across the valley northwards is Arenig, and to the left of it the principal peaks of Snowdonia from Moel Siabod, with the Carnedds farther back, to Snowdon itself, form an imposing array, which is continued by

the Rhinogs and the Llawllech range to Barmouth. The front of
Cader also appears in the south-west.

(b) *Longer and easier.*   2-2½ hrs. to *Aran Benllyn.*   Cross the
bridge and avoid the sharp angle made by the road by entering a
footpath which starts on the other side of it and re-enters the
road after a sharp ascent.   Hence you follow the Dinas Mawddwy
road (*p.* 31), having the Twrch stream and Cwm Cynllwyd on the
right hand, and the mountain rising like a giant step-ladder
beyond them.   The ridge may be gained at several points, but the
simplest plan is to continue along the main road for nearly two
miles, and then to cross the Twrch and strike up *Cwm Croes* (the
" hollow of the cross ") by a rough farm-track, keeping the stream
on the left hand.   This valley is flanked by a long and steep line
of cliff.   One mile and a half up it you come to the farm of *Nant-
y-barcud,* whence the onward route is obvious.   It passes to the
south of Llyn-lliwbran and gains the ridge half-a-mile short of
the top of **Aran Benllyn,** which is reached by climbing the last
step of the " ladder."

The view. The most pleasing feature of this is the full
length of Bala lake, with Bala town at its extremity, and the
billowy Clwydian range, emphasized by the monument-crowned
Moel Fammau, in the far distance.   Eastwards, the dark moorland of the Berwyns spreads for miles, and to the right of it the
sharp peaks of the Breidden hills between Welshpool and Shrewsbury may be seen, possibly the Wrekin also—a vague undulation
in the sky-line to the left of the Breiddens.   Northwards, the
double-crested Arenig disputes with the height we occupy lord-
ship over the Bala district, and to the left of it, thrice as far
away, Snowdonia extends from the dull outline of the Carnedds
to the crowning peak of Snowdon itself.   Between them are the
Glyders, with the lower summit of Moel Siabod immediately in
front of them.   To the left of Snowdon come Moelwyn, Moel
Hebog (farther off) and, much nearer, the rugged range in which
Rhinog-fawr, Rhinog-fach. Llethr and Diphwys seem all of a
height.   Just across the valley and in a line with Rhinog-fawr is
Rhobell-fawr.   From Diphwys the Llawllech range drops gradually to Barmouth Bridge (Barmouth itself is not seen), and then
the cliffs of Cader rise in a long line above and some way south
of the Mawddach estuary.

Continuation of walk. From Aran Benllyn to the higher
peak of Aran Mawddwy the distance is 1½ miles, and the walk will
occupy from a half to three quarters of an hour.   The way is over
a rocky débris, plentifully interspersed with grass.   On the left
the crags sink abruptly in broken and splintered masses, but about
half way a green tongue descends at a fairly easy slope to the side
of *Llyn Dyfi,*—the source of the Dyfi, or " Dovey " as it is called
lower down.   A little beyond this tongue we attack the last pitch,
and after a short effort reach the cairn on the top of **Aran
Mawddwy.** Hence the landscape opens up southwards, but it

has few special features. Plynlimon may be known by its trio of smooth green humps, and the Carmarthen Van and the Brecon Beacons may possibly be recognised far away to the left of it. Cardigan Bay is seen beyond the level marsh of Borth, south of the Dovey estuary.

Looking eastwards we have immediately below us the com-mencement of a valley which is typical of this part of Wales, deep and concave,—scooped out, it would seem, by a gentler agency than that which has shaped the rugged combes of Snowdonia and North Wales generally. At its end there is a glimpse of the Bala and Dinas road at the foot of Bwlch-y-Groes, and on its south side a long and almost level spur of the mountain projects several hundred feet below our stand-point. By whichever route we are returning, we should certainly go far enough along this spur to gain a view down *Hen Gwm*, for the reason implied in our descrip-tion of the descent to Dinas Mawddwy given on p. 122.

(2.) **From Drws-y-Nant**, 1¼–1½ *hrs*. This is at once the easiest, shortest and least interesting ascent. As from Llanuwchllyn, the height to be climbed is something less than 2,500 feet, owing to our starting-point being itself close on 500 ft. in elevation. From the down-side of the station we cross the bridge over the Wnion, and then, after a short rise, enter the fields and, passing to the left of a small homestead, strike a cart-track which, running a short distance above and to the left of the wooded little glen of *Afon-hirnog*, soon becomes a rough stony path. Follow this path for a mile or more till it passes through a wall on to the unenclosed hill-side. Here we can either bend round to the right and so on to the western spur, or at once attack the ascent in front, passing, a little way up, between two stone posts. No further direction is needed as it is now only a question of steadily mounting to the ridge, which is reached after a somewhat boggy tramp just south of the summit of Mawddwy. Before climbing the last steep pitch of the mountain, however, the tourist who contemplates descend-ing to Llanuwchllyn is advised to cross the green plateau south of it and called *Drws-bach*, till from the narrow spur called *Dyrysgol* (*see descent to Dinas Mawddwy*) he obtains the view down Hen Gwm on the right.

(3) **From Dinas Mawddwy**, 2½–3 *hrs*. This is a very in-teresting ascent, especially if the walk be continued over Aran Benllyn to Llanuwchllyn Station. Quitting the station and hotel, we reach, in half-a-mile, the village of *Dinas Mawddwy*, at the head of which, opposite the entrance to *Plas* (Sir Edmund Buckley), take the right-hand (Bala) road, and, after following it for another half-mile, during which the *Geryst* stream is crossed, turn up a lane on the left, which for a short distance runs just above the road you have quitted, and then strikes more to the left up the *Cowarch* glen. This little valley is about 2 miles long, flanked by steep green hills, except

where the break of Cwm Terwyn occurs on the right hand, and
headed by the fine cliffs of Craig Cowarch. The bottom is cultivated, and sprinkled with a number of farmsteads. At one of
them, *Bryn-glas*, 1½ miles up the valley, a small rill, coming from
Craig Cowarch, joins the main stream. Cross the rill at *Bryn-
glas*, and the main stream at *Pont-faen* (foot-bridge), half-a-mile
further and towards the end of an alluvial flat. Hence you turn
to the right, up the bowl-shaped recess of *Hen Gwm*, of which
more anon. The track, made for peat-carriage, goes some way to
the right of the stream, and presently commences a long, straight,
and regular climb along the steep side of the hill which forms the
south-east flank of the combe. When it ceases, you are on the
comparatively level spur called **Dyrysgol**, and almost at once the
stony summit of Aran Mawddwy appears in front. As you proceed to the left, round the head of Hen Gwm, Dyrysgol becomes so
narrow that in one place there is a little rift across it, caused by
the edge giving way. The slopes, however, are not dangerously
steep on either side, and you can enjoy the sweetly pretty view
down Hen Gwm, with its green meadows and glimmering skein-
like streamlet, to your heart's content before essaying the last tug
up the mountain. Further direction is unnecessary.

For the **view** see p. 120.

Aran Benllyn is 1½ miles beyond Aran Mawddwy. The route
is a rough one, but there is only a dip of about 200 feet.

Descents.

(1) **To Llanuwchllyn.** Keep over Benllyn and down the
knotty humps all the way (now and then it is smoother going a
little to the left) till you come to a cart-track that enters the road
between the Twrch stream and the railway bridge, and within
¼ m. of Llanuwchllyn Station and Inn, for both of which turn to
the right after going under the railway.

⁂ The directions given for the ascent by Cwm Croes (*p.* 120)
will suffice for those who prefer descending by that route.

(2) **To Drws-y-Nant** go due west from Mawddwy in the
direction of the round top of Diphwys. After trudging over a
boggy flat you will descend to a cart-track, by which, keeping to
the right of the wooded little Harnog glen, you will soon reach the
station. For the inn, keep more to the right throughout. The
next stream in that direction goes towards it.

(3) **To Dinas Mawddwy.** Drop southwards to the *col* which
connects the green plateau of *Dyrysgol*, extending due east, with
the main ridge. This *col* is so narrow that in one place it has
actually given way, and there is a little rift across it. The slope
on both sides is very steep but grassy. From Dyrysgol *Hen
Gwm* comes into view far below, on the right—a fresher and

sweeter little scene we could not wish to behold. It is a deep boat-shaped hollow encircled by steep green hills with here and there a crest of crag, and threaded by a bright streamlet which scarcely goes a dozen consecutive yards in the same direction. There is a sprinkling of wood, and a few cottages at its lower end, where the valley bends abruptly to the left, give it a pleasant homeliness. Looking down we see a plainly marked path slanting regularly down its eastern flank. This is the route to follow—unless we wish to go by *Llanymawddwy*, in which case it is, perhaps, best to pick our way down the steep green slope which descends to the Dyfi stream, and to skirt the latter till in about 2 miles we come out into the Bala and Dinas road at *Pont-y-Pennant*, about a mile north of the village, and 5 miles from Dinas.

For Dinas *direct* we cross the stream at the foot of *Hen Gwm*, close to the farmstead of *Pont-faen*, and then, crossing a flat patch of ground, proceed along a narrow, hilly lane to the right of the stream, passing several farms. In a couple of miles this lane joins the Bala and Dinas road half-a-mile short of the *village* of Dinas, and one mile short of the *hotel* and *station*.

ARENIG-FAWR, 2,800 ft.; ARENIG-FACH, 2,264 ft.

Until the opening of the G.W.R. branch from Bala to Ffestiniog, in 1882, these mountains were comparatively inaccessible. Now they lend their name to the little " Arenig " station, situated in the valley between them, and distant from Bala 8 m.; from Ffestiniog, 13½ m. Arenig-fawr is a finely peaked mountain, and its central position gives a specially comprehensive character to the view from it. The smaller height (Arenig-fach), on the contrary, is flat-topped and uninteresting. About half-a mile from the Arenig station, and marked by a little grove of sycamore, is the *Rhyd-y-Fen Inn*, on the main road. It can be reached direct across the fields by a path that is carried over the Tryweryn stream by a bridge made in 1883 to save the détour by the old bridge some distance higher up. The scenery hereabouts is dreary enough, as neither mountain, when viewed from the valley, presents any beauty of outline, but during the latter part of the summer the hedges of *spiræa salicifolia* in bloom are a pleasant feature. The ascent of **Arenig-fach** is a favourite one with picnic-folk, and can be made at once from the inn in ¾ hr. Owing to the elevation of the valley, the actual climb is not more than 1,200 feet. No description or guidance is necessary. Under the N.E. slope lies *Llyn Arenig-fach*, a tarn in some repute with anglers.

The ascent of **Arenig-fawr** may with advantage be made the beginning of a delightful walk of 9 miles (abt. 5 hrs.) to Llanuwchllyn (*page* 30), whence the road along the west side of the lake can be followed to Bala (*page* 28), or the train taken. The route can of course be reversed, but the direction in which we first take it has the double recommendation of starting from high ground (about 1,100 ft. above the sea), and presenting the principal view in front. We will describe the walk both ways.

(1.) **From Arenig Station** *to the top*, 2 *m.*, 1-1½ *hrs.* ; **to Llan- uwchllyn Station**, 9 *m.*, 5 *hrs.* The ascent begins by a rough path on the near side of *Milltergerrig Farm*, about ¼ mile west of the station along the old road to Ffestiniog. When the path ends there is a choice of routes : (*a*) if it be desired to get a view of *Llyn Arenig*, a large, deep tarn lying between the north-east spurs of the mountain, we must bear up the green slope to the left and, when the ridge is reached, go well over it, as the Llyn is close under the crags. Thence we turn back along the ridge south-west to the cairn on the summit. (*b*) *To the summit direct.* From the end of the path bear up the steep green slope on the right towards the rock-strewn ridge. When the rocks are reached the rest of the ascent is comparatively easy, and very pleasant going. The cairn soon comes in sight. (N.B.—The top of the mountain cannot be seen from the inn, but only its east-and-west ridge.) The **view** from the summit is a very wide one, owing to the absence of competing heights near at hand. Far away to the north, beyond Arenig-fach, is the Conway valley below Bettws-y-Coed, with Llyn Conway, the principal source of the river of that name, in the mid-distance, and the Orme promontory as the limit. North-east we see the Clwydian range, attaining its summit in the tower-crowned Moel Fammau. South-east, beyond a dull area of moorland, extends the full length of Bala Lake, with Bala and Llanuwchllyn at each end, and the Berwyn range beyond. Nearly due south the twin peaks of Aran appear, and to their right, over Rhobell-fawr, which hides Dolgelley, is the long cliff-line of Cader Idris. Turning south-west we have in succession,—to the right of Rhobell-fawr—Diphwys, Llethr, Rhinog-fach and Rhinog-fawr, the last two divided by the Ardudwy dip. Then, across a dreary foreground, the railway may be traced past Llyn Try-weryn, and over a viaduct towards Cwm Prysor and Trawsfynydd. Further away, the sea is in sight about Portmadoc, with Moelwyn hard by on the right. Next comes the unmistakeable peak of Snowdon, separated from the Glyders by the Pass of Llanberis. Moel Siabod is nearer at hand, and over it the double peak of the Tryfan is a feature in the scene. Carnedds Dafydd and Llewelyn, almost level-topped, complete the panorama.

Descent to Llanuwchllyn. From the summit a sharp drop, followed by a rise to a secondary peak, places us on the southern ridge of the mountain, down whose hillocky crest we steadily make our way for a mile or more, having on our right, across the deep valley of the *Afon-yr-Wynt*, the boldly scarped mountain called Moel-llyfn-Nant. Then, leaving the cairn on *Moel-y-nenyn* three parts of a mile on our left, we drop to a lower part of the mountain and, entering a rough track, in less than a mile further descend still more abruptly to a very boggy bit of ground, on the far side of which is a rough road forking in a few yards. The left branch takes us round to the east side of the hill past a small plantation to *Trawscoed Farm*. Hence a farm-road going due south descends in a mile or so to the foot of the hills close to the pleasantly timbered bank of *Afon Lliw*, a charming streamlet, on the far side of which rises a picturesque bluff marked by some remains of *Castell Carndochan*, as well as more recent works in connection with gold mining. Of the "Castell" we have no authentic information. No further direction is needed except to say that a field-path on the right, just short of a chapel and graveyard, cuts off an angle of the road and comes out on to the Bala road at *Pont Lliw*, whence it is ¼ mile to the *Village* of **Llanuwchllyn** and one mile to the *Station* and the comfortable *Goat Inn* hard by it.

(2.) **From Llanuwchllyn Station**, 7 *m.* 4 *hrs.* **Descent to Arenig Station**, 2 *m.*, 1 *hr.*

Pass through the village of Llanuwchllyn and, ¼ mile further, take the field-path on the far side of *Pont Lliw*. This leads on to a by-road close to a chapel. Turn to the left and keep along the road, north of the *Afon Lliw* stream, for nearly 1½ miles. Then, at a very picturesque spot, under *Castell Carndochan (see above)* the road quits the stream and ascends past some small farms to *Trawscoed*, the last habitation on the route. Here turn to the left. A rough road continues for nearly a mile and then reaches a boggy hollow, from which you make an abrupt ascent on to the ridge, coming to another rough track at the top. This, too, ceases in less than a mile near the foot of another rise, which takes you on to the southern spur of the mountain. This attained, you have only to keep on pretty straight over some comparatively level hillocky ground, and then attack the green stone-sprinkled slope which rises first to a smaller, and then, after a slight descent, to the main summit.

Descent to Arenig Station. Continue northwards round the combe on the left and, after following the ridge a little, descend in the direction of the lumpy summit of Arenig-fach. You will enter a road at the farm of *Militergerrig*, about ½ *m.* west of the *Station*. The *Rhyd-y-Fen Inn* is among the sycamores on the far side of the marsh, a good half-mile away.

CADER IDRIS, 2,949 ft.

Next to Snowdon, the most popular mountain in Wales with tourists is Cader Idris (the "Chair of Idris." Idris was a giant of the heroic age in Wales), and in this instance there can be no doubt that tourists have fixed their affections in the right place.

There are few more finely scarped mountains in the British Isles, and the views from the entire length of its ridge—a distance of some 6 miles—are certainly more beautiful than those from any other noteworthy height in Wales. This superiority is entirely due to the position which the mountain occupies with reference to the Mawddach estuary and the valley extending thence towards Bala lake. To these it presents its northern flank, a long wall of almost sheer precipice, broken here and there, as at the Foxes' Path, by a short interval of scree. Southwards, also, the mountain presents a splendid semi-circular crater in the direction of Tal-y-Llyn. South-westwards it descends by a gradual slope to the Dysynni valley and Towyn, and westwards the ridge drops somewhat more abruptly to the sea at the Friog promontory.

The ascent is usually made from Dolgelley or Barmouth, but Towyn and the Tal-y-Llyn Hotel are also good starting points. A very enjoyable day may be spent in ascending from Barmouth and following the ridge almost the entire way to Dolgelley, or by reversing the route. The following descriptions include all these routes.

Ascents.

(1) **From Barmouth**, 8½ m., 4 hrs.* Take the train to *Arthog* (2½ m.), or cross the railway-bridge (*toll* 2d.) and walk along the line as far as a lane which crosses it ¼ m. short of *Arthog station*. Then, in either case. make for the road which runs parallel to the line a few hundred yards south of it, and commence the ascent by a lane starting from the east end of a long row of cottages (*Arthog village*). This lane rises steeply between trees, on leaving which, after passing through a gate, you continue up-hill for a while and then, turning to the left, take a footpath on the same side, which leads to the bank of a stream. Do not cross this stream, but continue along the path to a farm-house (*Pant-y-llan*) in a slight hollow threaded by a tributary rill. Then, still keeping the stream on the left. you cross a couple of fields by an ill-defined track into the old Dolgelley and Towyn road, beyond and parallel to which runs the ridge of Cader. Its most prominent height from hereabouts is *Tyrau-mawr* ("Tirrymowr"), a craggy acclivity a little to the left of the line we have hitherto followed. The ridge must be gained a short distance to the right of this, and the best route to it is to follow the road eastwards as far as a gate which opens on to some boggy ground (almost opposite the farm *Hafod-y-fach*), crossing which you escape an awkward wall by bending to the right and passing between some iron railings and a new planting on to the open hill-side. All perplexity is now over; you have only to make for the top of the ridge and follow

* If time or other cause prevent the whole ascent being made, the first part of it, as far as Tyrau-mawr (2000 ft., 1 hr. from Arthog), will be found as fine an excursion as can be taken in the neighbourhood. The Arthog guide usually meets the 10 a.m. train.

it, with slight variation, all the way to the top of the mountain, which comes into view as soon as the ridge is gained. The direct line is along the southern slope of *Tyrau-mawr*, a little below the plateau which forms the summit of that peak, but it is quite worth while to diverge to the edge of this plateau for the sake of the glorious view it commands—finer perhaps than that from Cader itself. It embraces the Mawddach estuary, with the Llaw-llech range culminating in the round summit of Diphwys (Diffoos), beyond it : to the left, across a wide expanse of sea, the graceful outline of the Carnarvon promontory extends to Bardsey Island. The peak of Snowdon rises a little to the left of Diphwys. Close at hand, below, are the two Arthog lakes. Rhobell-fawr and Arenig are the chief heights in the north-east. Cader itself blocks the way eastwards, and to the south the ground slopes gradually to the Dysynni valley. The sheer-looking scarp, south-east, drops to Tal-y-Llyn, but the lake itself is hidden.

The height of Tyrau-mawr is about 2,000 feet, and beyond it, pursuing the ridge, we drop to about 1,700, joining at the lowest part the pony-track from Dolgelley, which comes up between two stone posts. This track also connects Dolgelley and Towyn, the route to the latter town being down the hollow on the right, in the direction of a conspicuous little crag called the Bird Rock.

From a little beyond this point the final part of the ascent commences, and the ground becomes thickly strewed with stones. It is best to follow the right-hand track as being rather smoother than the more direct one, and passing in about half-a-mile a spring of water. Then at the foot of the peak itself we come to the tethering place for the ponies, and a few minutes' struggle up a winding path lands us on the top cairn. Oddly enough, the Ordnance map does not place the height on the highest point, but upon the "Saddle," which projects a little to the west, and is from 100 to 200 feet lower. The recorded height of the next peak eastwards, Mynydd Moel, 2,835, will hardly in the eyes of an observer, favour the assumption that any point in the range exceeds 3,000 feet. N.B.—Avoid the Augean hut at the summit.

View from the Top. This is of the highest order, and the formation of the mountain affords the best possible opportunity for enjoying it. Northwards, in which direction we have the finest scenery in Wales, there is an almost perpendicular fall of several hundred feet from the cairn. At the foot of this mural precipice lies the dark and still Llyn-y-Gader, beyond which the rugged hill-side sinks gradually to the upland valley threaded by the mountain-road from Dolgelley to Towyn. Between this valley and the Mawddach estuary rises a minor ridge of broken outline and intersected by the exquisitely wooded little glen of Abergwynant. From the far side of the Mawddach several valleys, competing with each other in silvan luxuriance, strike northwards to the long Llawllech range and the bare moorland of Trawsfynydd.

Chief amongst these is the Ganllwydd valley, along which goes the road from Dolgelley to Ffestiniog, and to the right of which, high up on the hill side, is the Precipice Walk. Some way to the left of this valley the Llawllech range attains its summit in the round top of Diphwys, beyond which it continues northwards to Llethr, Rhinog-fach and Rhinog-fawr. The deep and narrow "V" in this range lies between Llethr and Rhinog-fach. The view in this direction is bounded by the whole Carnarvonshire range from Bardsey Island to Carnedd Llewelyn. The peak of Snowdon, rising above the Rhinog-fach depression, cannot be mistaken; to the right of it, separated by the dip which marks the Pass of Llanberis, the Glyders appear, and beyond them Carnedd David and Llewelyn. Moel Siabod is nearer and a little to the right. Left of Snowdon the chief heights are Moel Hebog and the Rivals.

North-eastwards a singularly rich prospect presents itself. Dolgelley is hidden, but the valley of the Wnion, extending from it almost to Bala Lake, is shown in its full length. To the left of the Bala depression the two peaks of Arenig-fawr, and to the right of it Aran Benllyn and Aran Mawddwy, separated by a very slight depression, command the scene. In the far distance, beyond the lake, Moel Fammau, crowned by the Jubilee monument, marks the centre of the Clwydian range. Then, south of the last named, the dark heather-clad Berwyn range, without any peak to emphasize it, extends for many a mile. Due east the sharp peaks of the Breidden Hills, only a dozen miles short of Shrewsbury, break the evenness of the sky-line. Then there is nothing of note unless it be the green little vale of Abercorris close at hand, till, looking due south we see the two or three green humps of Plynlimon. Far away to the right of these, the Carmarthen Van, forming the western buttress of the Black Mountains of South Wales, may be detected in clear weather. A considerable part of the coast between Aberystwith and St. David's Head is also visible.

Tal-y-Llyn is hidden by a shoulder of Cader itself, but south-westwards there is a very pretty glimpse down the level strath of the green Dysynni valley to the sea close to Towyn. The Bird Rock is a feature of this valley.

The tourist who is descending to Barmouth or Dolgelley should not leave the top without picking his way southwards among the boulders for a short distance till he looks down upon Llyn-y-Cau, as impressive a mountain tarn as is to be found in Britain and overlooked by the most abrupt crag of the mountain, Craig-y-Cau.

•*• Standing on the top of Cader one clear day the thought occurred to the writer, "With how many, or rather how few bounds can the eye travel from Scotland to the English Channel?" The answer (open to question) was "7." From Scafell Pike it can see Criffell in Dumfriesshire and Snowdon ; from Snowdon, Cader Idris; from Cader, the Carmarthen Van; from the Carmarthen Van, Dunkery Beacon on Exmoor ; from Dunkery, Brown Willy in Cornwall from Brown Willy, the English Channel.

(2) **Ascents from Dolgelley.** There are three ways of climbing Cader Idris from Dolgelley : (a) By the ordinary pony-track, 6 m. —a pleasant and easy ascent; (b) by the Foxes' Path, 4½ m.— disagreeably but not dangerously steep in the last part; (c) by the ridge of the mountain, 6 m.—a delightful walk for those who appreciate high ground and fresh air, especially if it be continued over Tyrau-mawr to Barmouth.

If time be a consideration, pedestrians will do best to ascend by the pony track and return by the Foxes' Path. Variety is thus obtained at the sacrifice of a very few minutes.

(a) By the **Pony-track**, 6 m. 2½-3 hrs. *Pony*, 7s. 6d., *Guide*, 6s. The first three miles of this route are along the old Towyn hill-road, which goes south-west from the church and ascends at once into a minor valley, separated from the main Wnion valley by a low range of hills. The bold bluff of the Cader range visible as we quit the town is Mynydd Moel, 1 mile east of the summit. In 2 miles a small lake—*Llyn Gwernan*—is reached. At the far end of it is an *Inn*—now *Temperance*—opposite to which the track for the Foxes' Path starts. Our present route continues along the road a good half-mile, and then, just short of the second of two little bridges, turns up a lane to the left. After passing Llyn Gwernan the summit of Cader itself has come into view, with the Saddle standing boldly out to the right of it, succeeded by a green depression, which rises again to Tyrau-mawr. The lowest part of this depression is the point at which we gain the ridge, the exact spot being marked by two stone posts. In making for it, the path, after crossing the stream out of the lane by which we left the road, ascends through a little wood, and continues in a direction a good deal to the right of the summit ridge ; but no further guidance is needed, except to follow the path up to the two posts—you may cut off an angle by diverging a little short of them—and then to turn sharp to the left along the ridge. During this part of the ascent the Llawllech range has come into view behind us, and the end of the Carnarvonshire promontory across a wide stretch of sea westward. At the posts the Barmouth route is joined, and the rest of the way, as well as the view from the top, is described on page 127. The bridle-path beyond the posts descends to *Llanfihangel-y-Pennant* (4 m.), in the valley, and is continued thence by a road to Towyn (about 13 m.). Total distance from Dolgelley to Towyn, 17-18 m., a dull six of which may be saved by crossing from Llanfihangel-y-Pennant to Abergynolwyn Station p. 72).

(b) By the **Foxes' Path**, 4½ m., 2¼-2¾ hrs. This, though the most interesting, and except for the Foxes' Path itself the easiest route, is rather to be recommended in coming down than going up. It is also the shortest, and entails the crossing of only a bit or two of wet ground. The Foxes' Path rises 900 feet at a continuous angle of about 35°.

Follow the old Towyn road to the far end of *Llyn Gwernan*

($2\frac{1}{4}$ m.), and then, opposite the Temperance House, take the foot-path on the left through a bit of copse-wood. This path is quite unmistakable until we come in view of the Cader range, after which the broad incline on the left of the summit shows us the Foxes' Path, and the direction we are to take. A tumble-down bridge, at the head of a very pretty little glen on the right, is to be avoided. Short of it the path goes a little to the left and reaches the open fell. As we ascend, a fine view opens westward over the broken ground that intervenes between the Mawddach estuary and the mountain-wall of Cader itself, which rises before us with imposing sternness. To the right of the principal peak is the Saddle. A little stream is soon crossed by stepping-stones, and then, over a small bit of bog, we reach the foot of **Llyn-y Gafr**, a shallow, reedy lakelet, full of trout, beyond which there is no path. Crossing the stream issuing from it we breast the rock-strewn ridge that rises between us and the foot of the final climb, and at the top of this ridge, passing between two hillocks, we reach the east side of **Llyn-y-Gadr**, the small lake that occupies the stern and echo-yielding combe between the Saddle and the highest part of the mountain. It is rather a rough bit of walking along the lake-side, but the fern-collector will find the tedium of it relieved by the presence of the parsley fern, which grows here more abundantly than anywhere else in the neighbourhood. Down the steep scree, known as the Foxes' Path, there is for a considerable distance a small water-course, and after the first few feet of the ascent have been mastered this stream-bed offers, per-haps, the easiest route. When it becomes somewhat difficult there is nothing for it but to scramble up the loose stones and *detritus* that extend to the grassy top of the ridge. There is absolutely no danger, but where the party is at all numerous care must be taken to avoid falling stones. Turf at the upper part of the climb makes the finish easy. From the top of the ridge the summit-cairn is about 300 yards on the right hand.

(c) By the **Ridge from East to West**, $3\frac{1}{2}$-$4\frac{1}{2}$ *hrs.*, 7 *m.* For a couple of miles or so this route is along a lane which strikes south out of the Dinas Mawddwy road just as it issues from the town, and on the far side of the bridge over the Aran brook. The first few yards are unpleasantly suggestive of the proximity of tan yards. In half-a mile we bend to the left, opposite *Pandy Mill*, and a little way further double back again, very sharply, through a gate to the right, keeping the main stream close below on the right all the way. The little glen through which it flows is made musical and picturesque by a succession of waterfalls almost hidden by dense and varied foliage. About $\frac{3}{4}$ m. beyond Pandy the lane quits the stream and, becoming very narrow, passes a farmstead or two, beyond which we reach the open hill side. Mynydd Moel, the eastern buttress of the highest ridge of Cader, and about a mile from the summit, towers a little to the right of our course during this part of the walk. Our route lies over it, but it is best to gain the ridge as soon as possible in order to

avoid the boggy hollow through which the Aran stream flows.
The ridge once gained, by a steep clamber up a rocky slope, we
have only to follow it all the way round this hollow. On the left
hand it sinks precipitously to the valley containing the Tal-y-Llyn
road. Presently Llyn Aran is seen far below on the right, and then,
bending to the right, we climb to the cairn on **Mynydd Moel**
(2,835 ft.), from the top of which a magnificent view presents
itself. Westwards the rocky scarp of the mountain, dropping
rugged and abrupt for nearly 1,000 feet, is seen as far as Cader
itself and the Saddle; beyond it the opening of the Mawddach
estuary and Barmouth Bridge; then over the wide expanse of
Cardigan Bay, the long and graceful sky-line of the Carnarvon
promontory extends, with Bardsey like a little cock-boat at its
extremity. Northward is Snowdonia, the peak of Snowdon rising
a little to the right of the deep and narrow rift which separates
Llethr from Rhinog-fach. In this direction Dolgelley itself,
nestling in its luxuriantly wooded valley at our very feet, gives a
variety and animation to the scene which is lost in the view from
the highest peak of the mountain. Beyond the town the little
Cynwch Lake, with the park of Nannau to the right of it, is a
landscape in itself. Further away, and slightly to the left of
these, the eye ranges over the bare plateau of Trawsfynydd to Moel
Siabod and the Glyders, to the right of which the conical Tryfan
rises in front of the bulky masses of Carnedd Dafydd and Carnedd
Llewelyn. Then, turning to the north-east, we look up the woods
and meadows of the Wnion valley to Bala Lake, north of which
Arenig-fawr, and south of it the Arans, are the chief heights.
Eastwards, a dull outline of wavy hill-tops is broken by the
Breidden Hills, on the borders of Shropshire. Southwards, the
upper part of Tal y-Llyn and the pleasant little vale of Abercorris,
fast losing its pleasantness in slate-quarries, lie deep-set in the
hills, and between the former and Cader itself the sheer precipice
of Craig-y-Cau overhangs the hollow in which lies the tarn of the
same name. The three humps of Plinlimmon are visible beyond
Tal-y Llyn, and to the right of them the Carmarthen Van may
sometimes be descried on the horizon.

From Mynydd Moel to the crowning cairn of " Cader," the
distance is about a mile, easy going. A few hundred yards short
of the cairn the top of the Foxes' Path is passed.

(3) **Ascents from Tal-y-Llyn**. The most interesting route to
a fair climber is that by Llyn-y-Cau, but it should be remembered
that the ascent thence to the summit is exceedingly steep,
more so, indeed, than the Foxes' Path. Those who select the
much easier route, which we shall describe first, will miss very
little that is seen from the more ambitious one. Both introduce
the tourist to Craig-y-Cau and Llyn-y-Cau.

(a) **Easy route**, 4 m. 2—2½ hrs. From the hotel pass round
the south-west corner of the lake, and ¼ mile beyond its outlet
enter a wood by a path which leads steeply up to a farm called

Rhiwrogof. Hence continuing up you will gain the ridge which extends from Craig-ddu to Mynydd Pencoed. Below and to the right of this ridge is *Cwm-ammarch*, after doubling the head of which you will gain the summit of *Pencoed*, and look down from the top of Craig-y-Cau into the dark waters of Llyn-y-Cau, perhaps the finest tarn in Wales, just as Craig y-Cau, descending for about 700 or 800 feet almost sheer into its waters, is one of the grandest crags. Between the latter and the top of Cader there is a dip of about 100 feet. The walk along the edge of the cliff is very fine. At its lowest part the Llyn-y-Cau route comes up by a narrow gully. Beyond this it is best to turn away to the left hand from the cliff so as to avoid as much as possible the stony wilderness which entirely occupies the direct route to the top. By so doing you will join the Dolgelley bridle track at the foot of the last steep pitch, and a few minutes' walk short of the cairn.

(*b*) By **Llyn-y-Cau**, 5 *m.* 3 *hrs.* Follow the Dolgelley road for nearly 2 miles—1 *m.* beyond the head of the lake. Then, ¼ *m.* beyond an abrupt turn to the right, take a lane on the left which leads in a few hundred yards to the farm-house of *Minffordd.* Above this the Llyn-y-Cau combe has been visible for some time. There is a path on both sides the stream, which in descending from the upper part of the valley makes more than one very picturesque fall—worth turning aside for after rain. Of the two paths take the one which winds steeply up on the right of the stream, and on reaching the moraine-heaps in the upper and more level part of the combe, cross the water and make for the south-east corner of the basin in which Llyn-y-Cau evidently lies, though the lake itself is not to be seen until you are close to it. The scene, as you approach it, is most impressive. Cader itself flings down a precipitous and rocky slope on the right, while on the other side Craig-y-Cau responds with a sheer 700 or 800 feet of cliff, rising black almost from the water's edge. Between the two the cliff-line slightly drops, but the abruptness is maintained all the way, and it is hard at first to detect any practicable way of overcoming it. Round the south of the tarn, however, there is a narrow path, and at the west end, just beyond the precipice of Craig-y-Cau, comes a gully up which you may scramble bearing a little bit to the right in its higher part. This lands you in the dip between Craig-y-Cau on the left and Pen y-Gader (the "head of Cader") on the right. From this point follow the direction given in the last described route (the "easy" one).

(4) **From Towyn** (*Pendre Station*). *Rail to Abergynolwyn,* 7 *m.*, 40 *min. Thence walk to Llanfihangel-y-Pennant,* 2½ *m*; *Top of Ridge,* 6½ *m*; *Top of "Cader,"* 8 *m. Walking time,* 3½-4 *hrs.*
Public-house at Abergynolwyn; Village Inn at Llanfihangel-y-Pennant.

There is an alternative route by road all the way to Llanfihangel, but this simply handicaps the tourist with half-a-dozen profitless miles over the flat before the interest of the walk begins. The route goes north-east out of the town, and after crossing *Pont Fathew* (2 m., *one or two small public-houses*) turns to the right, and then, in a few yards, left again where a mass of exposed rock serves as a pavement. On the left spreads the wide strath of the Dysynni, and in 6 miles we pass close under the **Bird Rock** (*Craig Aderyn*). This is a bold, terraced scarp only a few hundred feet above the sea, but striking not only from its form, which contrasts finely with the flat expanse below, but also as occupying the position of an outpost to the mountain-land in the rear. Two miles further the road from Abergynolwyn Station is joined.

The line from Towyn to Abergynolwyn gradually ascends nearly all the way, the terminus at Abergynolwyn being only a short distance beyond a minor watershed. It was made chiefly for the conveyance of slates, and is of a narrow ("Toy") gauge—a little wider than the Ffestiniog. There are about three passenger trains a day, and to tourists visiting Cader Idris, or the Tal-y-Llyn district, from Towyn and neighbourhood, they afford great convenience by saving them some seven miles' tiresome walking or hiring.

Except for here and there a pretty streamlet tumbling down from the hills on the right—as at *Dolgoch* (4½ m.)—and the summit of Cader, seen on the left front, there is nothing noteworthy either during the railway journey, or at **Abergynolwyn** itself, which is simply a straggling collection of quarrymen's houses. The *station* is half-a-mile short of the *village* and *inn*.

Though the valley between Towyn and Tal y-Llyn, as seen from either end, appears from its straightness and continuity the outlet for the waters of Tal-y-Llyn, it is only so in the upper part, as the stream that issues from that lake turns sharp to the right at Abergynolwyn, and flows between low hills into the Dysynni. Our road onward from Abergynolwyn follows its course till in 1½ miles it joins the Towyn and Llanfihangel road—but tourists should, at Abergynolwyn, ask the way by foot-path to Llanfihangel, as half-a-mile may thus be cut off.

From the comfortable little inn (*Peniarth Arms*) at **Llanfihangel** to the top of Cader, the route is interesting, though there is no immunity from the tedium inseparable from climbing a mountain on its dull side. In half a-mile we cross the stream. The school-bell hung in a sycamore tree suggests primitiveness. Then our route, becoming a cart-track, bends to the right after passing a farm, and for the rest of the way to the ridge keeps to the left of the stream, and within a few hundred yards of it for about two miles, when it makes a sweep to the left to get over a tributary rill (*but see map*). The top of the mountain has been in view for some time, and the climber may use his own discretion about "making tracks" for it. The only advantage of the round-about route by the *col* is that which is afforded by a fairly marked path.

* * From the *col* the track is continued down to the Dolgelley road (*p. 135*).

Descents.

(1) **To Barmouth**, 8½ *m.*, 3–3½ *hrs.* This is almost or quite
a ridge-walk for the first 2½ miles. The easiest route, after
dropping steeply to the little level plot where the ponies are
tethered, proceeds a few hundred yards to the left of the ridge,
passing a little way further a spring, but it is worth while to keep
along the ridge to the top of the **Saddle** (*Cyfrwy*), which hangs
most effectively over Llyn-y-Gader. In any case the green depression in the ridge between the top of the mountain and Tyrau-
mawr has to be crossed. From this depression two stone gate-
posts mark the divergence of the Dolgelley route, and from them
it is possible to drop direct to the old Dolgelley and Towyn road
in the direction of Barmouth, visible in front; but the descent is
steep, and beset with stone walls. The better plan is to keep along
the ridge over the top, or a little to the left of Tyrau-mawr, after
passing which there is no difficulty in striking the above road a
little beyond a small farm, conspicuous on its far side. By making
a small angle before entering the road, and passing through a gate
close to a small planting and some iron railings, you may avoid
walls. A few yards after entering the road you will cross a small
stream. Pass through a gate on the right beyond this stream,
and cross a couple of fields by an indistinct cart-track to a farm,
Pant-y-Llan, in the hollow formed by a tributary streamlet. Hence
a footpath alongside the main brook takes you into a lane, which
descends between trees to the high-road at Arthog village. For the
station turn sharp to the right on entering this road, and left again
in a few yards; for Barmouth Junction or town continue past the
row of houses, and make for the railway by an old lane beyond
them. There is no regular road from Arthog to Barmouth, but the
railway takes the place of one for pedestrians, and there is a
recognised footpath (*toll*, 2*d.*) across the bridge.

(2) **To Dolgelley.** (*a*) *By the Foxes' Path*, 4½ *m.*, 1½—2 *hrs.*
This is the popular route *down* Cader. The **Foxes' Path.**
which is an inclined plane of loose scree, lying at an angle
of about 35 degrees, is very steep but quite safe. It begins a
short distance E. of the summit on the left of a direction-
cairn. In its highest part, the scree is interspersed with grass,
down which it is best to zigzag. At the foot of it lies *Llyn-y-Gader*,
after leaving which on the left hand, the path goes between two
small hillocks, and then bends to the right to the foot of another
tarn, *Llyn-y-Gafr*. Beyond this it crosses another stream, which
it keeps on the left all the way to the old Towyn and
Dolgelley road. Where it forks, take the right branch. This
first winds up over a hillock, and then drops to the road opposite
a *Temperance Inn*, at the west end of *Llyn Gwernan*, passing on
the way a prettily wooded little ravine. From the inn to Dolgelley
the distance is 2¼ *m.*

(b) *By the Pony-track*, 6 m., 2-2½ hrs. This route is the same as the Barmouth one as far as the two gate-posts. Hence an abrupt descent brings you into the old Towyn and Dolgelley road (*see p.* 134), nearly 3 miles short of Dolgelley.

(c) *By the Ridge eastwards*, 7 m. 3-3½ hrs. This introduces those who have reached the top by any other route to several fresh view-points. First there is **Mynydd Moel**, one mile on the way and conspicuous from the summit. *For a description see p.* 131. Then dropping steeply, you pass round the head of a wild combe down which the little river Aran flows from *Llyn* Aran. A little further, after crossing some rough ground, you look down upon the upland valley containing the Dolgelley and Tal-y-Llyn road. The main ridge now drops towards the *Cross Foxes Inn*, but after following it for a mile past the head of the Aran combe it is best to descend to some farmsteads which are seen a little to the right of the Aran stream and in the direction of Dolgelley. From them a lane, at first very narrow and tortuous, leads to the town, passing during the last mile or more through a wood just above and to the right of the stream. Several charming little waterfalls seen through the foliage enhance the beauty of this part of the walk, but the entrance to the town is, to say the least of it, unsavoury.

(3) **To Tal-y-Llyn.** (*a*) *By Llyn-y-Cau*, 5 m. 2-2½ hrs. This is the most interesting route, but the first part of it, down to Llyn-y-Cau, is excessively steep and requires great caution. The point to make for is the lowest part of the depression between the top of the mountain and Craig-y-Cau, and to reach this—the direct route is terribly rough—it is best to follow the Barmouth track (*p.* 134) as far as the level little plot where the ponies from Dolgelley stop, a few hundred yards below the summit, and then to turn to the left, working round the stones till you reach the top of the cliff at its lowest point. Beyond this point the sheer precipices of Craig-y-Cau render descent impossible, but from it, looking down into Llyn-y-Cau there is a practicable route commencing with a little natural grass track which goes a trifle to the left of the gully, and is continued by equally steep scree, from the bottom of which a narrow path doubles round the south side of the tarn. Beyond the tarn the ground is humpy and consists of moraine matter for a while. If you cross the stream in about half-a-mile, you will light on a track which winds steeply down at some little distance above it to the farm-house a few hundred yards short of the Dolgelley and Tal-y-Llyn road. A quarter of a mile after entering this, turn to the left by the road which passes along the south side of the lake to the Tal-y Llyn hotel.

(b) *By the easy route*, 4 m., 1½-2 hrs. Proceed as in the Llyn-y-Cau route to the top of the gully. Instead of descending this, rise again along the edge of the cliff to the top of *Mynydd Pencoed* (*Craig-y-Cau*, as this end is called). Hence strike obliquely, rather west of south, across the smooth grassy ridge of Pencoed, until, in about half-a-mile, you have reached the head of *Cwm-ammarch*. Double round this and descend by the ridge which keeps the combe on the left, bearing to the right where it becomes steep, so as to reach the farm-house called on the map *Rhiwrogof*. Hence a cart-road drops aslant through the wood and enters the Abergynolwyn road nearly a mile beyond the Tal-y-Llyn hotel. A steep footpath, dropping to the road that hugs the shore of the lake, saves nearly a mile.

(4) **To Towyn**. The Dysynni valley, along which this route lies, is seen from the top of the mountain to the sea-board, and the way is easy to find. You may either follow the Barmouth track (*p.* 134) as far as the two stone posts at the top of the col, and then stick to the bridle-path to Llanfihangel-y-Pennant, or you may shorten the distance by taking a somewhat steeper course direct into the Dysynni valley. In either case, half-a-dozen uninteresting miles of walking may be saved by taking the train from Abergynolwyn station (abt. 2½ *m.* from Llanfihangel, *see Route up from Towyn*). Hitherto the last train to Towyn has left about 4.30.

DIPHWYS (2,467 ft.), **LLETHR** (abt. 2,400 ft.), and the Llawllech Range, from Dolgelley or Barmouth.

The central point of this expedition, wherever it be begun and ended, is Diphwys, which, next to the unrivalled Cader, is the best and most convenient mountain-climb from Barmouth, and though hardly so handy from Dolgelley, may easily be ascended by such as make that town their head-quarters. The abundant service of trains between Barmouth and Dolgelley, nearly all stopping if required at Penmaenpool, enables sojourners in either town to make the excursion, one way or the other, with almost equal convenience. The plan we recommend is to take train to Penmaenpool, thence climbing Diphwys by the Cwm-mynach valley, and descending to Barmouth by the Llawllech ridge. This plan, besides giving the hardest part of the work to the early part of the day, has also the advantage of presenting the successive views more suddenly and effectively than the reverse route. Beyond Diphwys the route may be varied in one or two ways which we shall briefly describe, but the only addition to it to be recommended is the détour to the neighbouring height of Llethr. There is a good inn at Penmaenpool station, but no other on or near to the route.

(1) Starting from **Penmaenpool**, 2¼ *m. from Dolgelley*; 7 *m. from Barmouth*.

Penmaenpool to Diphwys, 5½ m. 2½-3 hrs.; Barmouth, 12 m. 5-6 hrs.

Détour to Llethr, 3 m. there and back.

Leaving Penmaenpool station by the bridge over the Mawddach (*toll*, 1d.) we cross in half-a-mile the Dolgelley and Barmouth road, and at once enter a rough cart-road which ascends the *Cwm-mynach* glen. On the left hand the sound of the stream tumbling down its rocky bed through a deep embowered ravine invites us to a few minutes' trespass on the intervening meadow-land. A little further, and we come to an ideal waters-meet—two little torrents leaping over boulders in noisy rivalry. Then side by side with the left-hand one we proceed past one to a second square-arched bridge, after crossing which a green upland valley, containing one or two farmsteads, is entered. Half-an hour's more walking brings us to the source of our pleasant little stream in *L'yn Cwm-mynach*, a sheet of water so full of reeds, and otherwise disappointing, that it is a relief to quit the track and traverse the few hundred yards of ground which lie between us and the steep slope of Diphwys, rough and boggy though they be. And now, before getting too much under the mountain, let us pick our route. Those crags to the right must be avoided, and the steepish but regular line of ascent to the left of them preferred. Above the upper extremity of this a still steeper green slope will place us on the ridge of the range considerably below, and to the right of the summit. Once on this ridge, we can wander whither we list. Along it there runs a wall, by following which northward the rival height of **Llethr** may be reached after a very slight depression. The going is rough, but the détour is worth making, though the views obtained on the way are not of a character to linger over. The bare, unlovely plateau of Trawsfynydd extends mile upon mile below, and except Arenig beyond it and the Cader ridge southward, there is little to admire in the mountain shapes. Peeps of the sea westwards are a pleasant relief. Llethr means a declivity, but on breasting it we find an area so level and smooth that a day or two's labour would turn it into a bowling green or a tennis lawn. Smoothness, however, is not a general failing of Welsh mountains, and if we follow this particular one to its northern end (a few paces onward) we shall come suddenly to a dip so steep and rugged that even the wall has to stop short. This is the deep hollow so conspicuous from the ridge of Cader, but not, as some climbers of the latter mountain would have it, the famous "pass of the men of Ardudwy." That lies behind and beyond the next height, **Rhinog-fach** (the "little" Rhinog, very little inferior in stature, by the way, to its big brother, Rhinog-fawr). If we would reach it we must bend to the left and pick our way down the slope to *Llyn Howell*, a gloomy little lake, with a sheer wall of rock on its eastern side, whence we may either drop down the valley and strike the Ardudwy Pass, about half-a-mile west of its *col*, or, crossing the wall, which begins again near the lake, zig-zag up Rhinog-fach, and come down near the *col* by bending to the right from the top of the mountain. The routes from the pass are described on pages 58 and 63: one is to Dyffryn Station, between Barmouth and Harlech; another is to Cwm Bychan and Harlech or Pensarn, by the Roman Steps, and a third over the "dreary, dreary moorland" of Trawsfynydd to the village of the same name.

We have enumerated three routes beyond Llethr for complete-
ness' sake, but as the fag end of the excursion we are now
describing they are things to " do "rather than to enjoy. The interesting parts of them, such as Cwm Bychan, are too good to come
so late in the day. Tourists who prefer enjoyment to exploit will
stop short either where the wall crosses their path on Diphwys,
or where it ends on Llethr. In returning from the latter it is
better to take a more direct line for the summit of the former than
that indicated by the wall. On the way you will be struck by the
regular semi-circular course of the strata on this side of **Diphwys**.
The top of that mountain is marked by a ruinous cairn protruding
from the wall. When we reach it the richness of the Mawddach
scenery breaks upon us, all the more striking from its contrast
with the barrenness we have left behind. The grand line of the
Cader cliffs is in full view, and the twin Arans rise to the left of
them and to the right of Rhobell fawr. Westward, there is a
wide expanse of sea, bounded by the long Carnarvonshire range
and Bardsey.

And now for the **descent**. Two walls, if we recollect aright,
have to be crossed, and a third—the one which tracks the course
of the Llawllech range all the way—has to be hugged for a long
distance. The going is easy and the descent very gradual for at
least three miles, during which the sea-view continues. Then,
just short of a sudden rise in the range, we come to a gateway in
the wall, from which an easily-followed path slants down the
mountain-side to the farm-house and buildings of *Sylfaen*, which
lie a mile below, almost in a line with Arthog on the far side of
the estuary. From Sylfaen a very fair cart-road carries on the
descent to Barmouth, passing to the right of the Panorama walk
about a mile before it drops into the Dolgelley road at the east end
of the town.

This part of the walk is treated with greater detail in the following description of the route taken the reverse way.

(2) *Reverse Route.* **Barmouth to Diphwys** (*direct*), 6½ m
2½—3½ *hrs.*; **Penmaenpool Station**, 12 *m*; (— *Barmouth, by
rail*, 19 *m*.); **Dolgelley**, *by rail*, 14½ *m*.

The Llawllech range of hills, which extends all the way to
Diphwys, may be climbed by any of the steep lanes leading upwards from Barmouth, or by following the Dolgelley road for
2 miles and then turning upwards. Considerably the simplest
way, however,—and those who contemplate going the entire round
will not want to waste time at the commencement—is to leave the
town by the lane which leads up from the end of Porkington
Terrace — half-a-mile from the station Dolgelley way—to the
Panorama Walk. Where this forks at the top of the steep pitch
by which it begins, avoid the left-hand branch, and passing
through a gate beyond which there is a charming little peep on
the right, continue up the little valley and out into the more open
country as straight as the lane will take you to the *Sylfaen Farm*,

2¾ miles from Barmouth, and the largest of a succession of little farmsteads passed on the way. Charming views across the estuary enliven this part of the walk, and the round summit of Diphwys rises some miles ahead. From Sylfaen we may continue for about 1½ miles below the Llawllech range before beginning the steeper part of the ascent, but the best way is to leave the farm-buildings a few yards on the right and to make at once for the top of the ridge by a broken track which rises slantwise to a gateway visible on the sky-line. During the ascent—an easy and pleasant one—the view eastwards increases in beauty and extent, the Aran peaks being prominent beyond Dolgelley. On breasting the ridge at the gateway, a view opens to the north and north-west. In the former direction the green top of Moelfre rises beyond the Ysgethin valley, and the peak of Snowdon is seen in the distance ; in the latter the eye ranges over the sea to Criccieth and Pwllheli on the far-reaching Carnarvon promontory, the double peak of the Yr Eifl (the Rivals) rising between the two. To the left of Moelfre the woods and mansion of Cors-y-Gedol may be noticed.

From this point to the top of **Diphwys** the distance is nearly 3½ miles. A wall extends along the ridge the whole way, and a little short of the summit one or two cross ones are encountered. The bracing air and the beauty of the view on both sides, especially the southern, are fair compensation for what would otherwise be a monotonous walk. Two tarns relieve the bareness of the valley on the left—*Llyn Irddyn* and *Llyn Bodtlyn*. The summit of the mountain and the possible détours from it to Llethr, Rhinog-fach, &c., are described in the reverse route (*p.* 137). If you are in a hurry to get back to Barmouth, you may gain variety without sacrificing much time by starting due south from the top and striking the Dolgelley and Barmouth road near its half-way house, the Hotel at Bont-ddu (*page* 56; *total distance abt. 9 m.*), or by descending the Ysgethin valley on the north side of the range to Cors-y-Gedol and Dyffryn Station. (*Inn* ¾ *m. short of station. Distance,* 6–7 *m.*)

For *Penmaenpool* and *Dolgelley* proceed down the ridge to the first little hollow in it, nearly half-a-mile distant. Then turn to the right down a steep grass-slope, bending left again in a few minutes and entering a rough cart-track, close to *Llyn Cwm-mynach*, a reedy little lake at the head of the valley of the same name. This track, which is fully described on page 137, will take you in 3½ miles on to the Barmouth and Dolgelley road, just opposite to the cross-road to *Penmaenpool Bridge* and *Station* (*good inn*), half-a-mile further.

RHOBELL-FAWR, 2,409 feet.

Dolgelley to Nannau and thence direct 7 m., 3 hrs. ; or through Llanfachreth (small inn) 7½ m.

This mountain, conspicuous in all views from the higher ground about Dolgelley is of minor interest to the climber. The way to

it lies past *Nannau* (*page* 38). When after leaving that mansion
on our left a junction of many roads is reached, there is a choice
of routes, (*a*) by the road bearing to the right, or (*b*) by the road
straight on.

(*a*) *Direct*, by the road to the right. This forks in about half-a-
mile, and we take the left branch and keep to it up past *Cors-y-
garnedd* Farm to *Bwlch-gorwaered*, 3 miles from Nannau. Here a
track, which soon comes to an end, goes off on the right towards
the summit and involves a mile and a half of collar work in a
direction a trifle to the north of east.

(*b*) *By Llanfachreth.* At the junction of roads at Nannau keep
straight on and descend to the village. At the church, whose
spire is a pretty feature as we approach it, turn to the right.
Route (*a*) is joined about three quarters of a mile from Llanfachreth.

The view from the summit of Rhobell-fawr includes all the
chief mountains between Snowdon and Cader Idris, as well as a
peep of Bala Lake.

In **returning** a descent can be made, in $3\frac{1}{2}$ miles southwards,
by a track that runs north and south about a mile east of the
summit, to the Bala and Dolgelley road, which is struck at a point
about half-way between Drws-y-Nant and Bont Newydd stations.

INDEX.

N.B.—Where more than one page is referred to, that on which a locality is particularly described is given first.

Telegraph Offices are indicated by an asterisk; *Railway Stations* by a dagger. The names enclosed in square brackets are required to complete the Postal address.

Aberamffra, 50.

†Aberangell, 93.

*†Abercorris (see Corris).

*†**Aberdovey** [Merioneth], 72.

   To Aberystwith, 60, 91.

   „ Barmouth, 99.

   „ Machynlleth, 60.

   „ Towyn, 99,

Abergwynant, 42.

†Abergynolwyn, 133, 45, 72.

Aber Hirnant, 33.

†Abermule [Montgomery], 87.

*†**Aberystwith**, 100.

   To Aberdovey, Towyn, Barmouth, &c. 91, 99.

   „ Borth, 106.

   „ Devil's Bridge, 109.

   „ Hafod, 116.

   „ Llanidloes, 117.

   „ Machynlleth, 108.

   „ Plynlimon, 117.

   „ Strata Florida, 105.

†Acrefair, 2.

Afon Bidno, 89.

   „ Cain, 41.

   „ Carno, 90.

   „ Eiarth, 78.

   „ Gelyn, 5.

   „ Harnog, 121.

   „ Lery, 107.

   „ Llafar, 5.

   „ Lliw, 125, 30.

   „ Melynddwr, 112.

   „ Tal, 90.

   „ Tanat, 35.

Afon Trystion, 4, 27.

   „ -y-Wynt, 124.

   „ -yr-Allt, 42.

   „ Ysgethin, 54.

Aleyn, River, 2.

Allt-wen, 103.

   „ Wnnog, 90.

   „ -yr-Erydd, 80.

Alwen, River, 25, 27.

Arans (Benllyn and **Mawddwy),**

   From Dinas Mawddwy, 121.

   „ Drws-y-Nant, 121,

   „ Llanuwchllyn, 119.

†Arddleen, 85.

Ardudwy, Gate of, 63, 58.

Arenig (-fawr and **-fach),**

   From Arenig Station, 124.

   „ Llanuwchllyn, 125.

†Arenig Station, 5.

†Arthog [Dolgelley], 54, 7, 55, 126.

Arthur's Quoit, 53.

Artro, Glen and River, 61, 58. 66.

*†**Bala** [Merioneth], 28, 5.

   To Arans, 119.

   „ Arenigs, 124, 125.

   „ Corwen, 4, 27.

   „ Dinas Mawddwy, 31.

   „ Dolgelley, 5.

   „ Ffestiniog, 5,

   „ Liverpool Reservoir, 33.

   „ Pistyll Rhayadr, 32.

†Bala Junction, 5, 43.
   „   Lake, 29, 5.
Barber's Hill, 11, 3.
*†**Barmouth** [Merioneth], 48.
   To Aberdovey, 68.
      „ Aberystwith, 68.
      „ Cader Idris, 126.
      „ Cwm Bychan, 60, 57.
      „ Dolgelley, 55, 56.
      „ Ffestiniog, 57.
      „ Harlech, 57.
      „ Machynlleth, 68.
      „ Portmadoc, 57.
      „ Towyn, 68.

Barmouth Bridge, 50.
*†   „   Junction, 50, 7, 55, 68, 99.
Bath Grounds, 19.
Bedd Taliesin, 108, 107.
Bedford Obelisk, 116.
†Berwyn [Llangollen], 3, 12.
Bird Rock, 133, 68, 71.
*†Blaenau Ffestiniog, 5, 60.
Bodfach, 76.
Bont-ddu [Dolgelley], 56, 47, 139.
Bont newydd, 38, 6.
*†**Borth** [Cardiganshire], 106, 91.
   To Aberdovey, Towyn, **and** Barmouth, 91, 99.
      „ Aberystwith, 91, 106.

†Bow Street, 91, 106.
Braich-y-Gwynt, 3, 14.
Bran, River, 11.
Breidden Hills, 84, 75.
Bryn Crug, 71.
   „   Eglwys, 15.
   „   -glas, 122.
   „   -gwyn, 71.
†Buttington Junction, 84, 75.
Bwlch Cedris, 72
   „   Drws Ardudwy, 63, 58, 67.

Bwlch Heble, 111.
   „   Nant r-Arian, 112.
   „   Oerddrws, 44, 94.
   „   -y Fedwen, 86.
   „   -y-Groes, 94, 31, 35, 80.
   „   -y-Tyddiad, 67, 62.

Cader Berwyn, 32, 77.
   „   Fronwen, 24.
Cader Idris : 125.
   From Barmouth, 126.
      „ Dolgelley, 129, 130.
      „ Tal-y-Llyn, 131, 132.
      „ Towyn, 132.
Caer Crwyni, 27.
   „   Gai, 30.
†Caersws Station, 90.
Caerynwch, 37.
Cain valley, 76.
Camlan valley, 41, 87.
Cann Office [Welshpool], 86, 76.
Capel Bangor, 112.
   „   Sion, 111.
Carn Dochan, 30.
†Carno [Montgomery], 90.
†Carrog, 3.
Castell Dinas Bran, 10.
   „   Fan Grach, 112.
   „   Gronw, 5.
   „   -y-Bere, 71.
Cefn Carnedd, 88.
†   „   Station, 18, 20.
   „   -y-Castell, 75, 85.
   „   -y-Fedw, 16.
Ceiriog, River, 17.
Cell-fawr, -fechan, 51.
†Cemmaes, 93.
†Cemmaes Road [Montgomery-shire], 91, 93
Cendiog stream, 32.
Cernioge, 26.
Cerrig-y-Druidion [Corwen], 26, 25.
Chain   Bridge   [†Berwyn Llangollen], 3, 14, 11, 13.
*†Chirk [Ruabon], 20, 18.
   „   Castle, 22.
Clochnant Cwm, 32.
Clywedog, River, 88.
Coed coch, 53.
Constitution Hill, 103.
Conway Falls, 25.
*†Corris [Montgomeryshire], 96, 44.
Corsfochno, 91.
Cors-y-Gedol, 53.

*†**Corwen**, 23.
   To B.la, 3, 27.
    ,, Bettws-y-Coed, 25.
    ,, Llangollen, 4.
    ,, Ruthin, 24,
Cowarch Glen, 94, 121.
Craig Abermaw, 51.
   ,, Aderyn, 133, 71.
   ,, Cwm Llwyd, 46, 55.
   ,, Cyfarthfa, 97.
   ,, Rhiwarth, 78.
   ,, Wion, 62.
   ,, -y-Cau, 128, 131, 41.
   ,, -y-Ddinas, 54.
   ,, -y-Forwen, 16.
   ,, -y-Llam, 44.
   ,, -y-Saeth, 62, 67.
Criggion, 85.
Croes-faen, 71.
Crogen, 27, 4.
Cross Foxes Inn, 44, 94.
Crosswood Park, 105.
Crow Castle, 10.
Cwm Ammarch, 132.
Cwm Bychan, 61, 58, 63.
Cwm Cynllwyd, 95.
   ,, Croes, 31, 95.
   ,, Dywyll, 32.
   ,, -llwyd, 46.
   ,, Mynach, 137, 57.
   ,, Proesor, 5.
   ,, Rhayadr, 97, 98.
   ,, Terwyn, 122.
Cyfrwy, 134, 6.
Cymmer Abbey, 41.
Cynfael stream, 5.
Cynwyd, 27, 4.
Cyrn-y-Brain, 19, 16.

Dee valley and river, 19, 24.
†Derwen, 24.
Derwen-las, 109.
Devil's Bridge [Aberystwith], 113.
   From Aberystwith, 109.
    ,, Llanidloes, 89.
*†**Dinas Mawddwy,** 93, 121, 30.
Dinbren Hall, 17.

Diphwys,
   From Barmouth *or* Dolgelley, 136.
*†**Dolgelley,** 36.
   To Bala, 43.
    ,, Barmouth, 6, 46.
    ,, Cader Idris, 129, 130.
    ,, Dinas Mawddwy, 43.
    ,, Ffestiniog, 43.
    ,, Machynlleth, 43.
    ,, Tal y-Llyn, 43.
    ,, Towyn, 43, 45.
Dolmelynllyn, 41.
Dolserau, 43, 6.
Dovey Estuary, 99, 91.
Druid Inn, 27.
Drws-bach, 121.
   ,, -y Nant, 119, 6, 121.
*†**Duffws** (Blaenau Ffestiniog), 5, 60.
Dwyryd Stream, 59.
Dyffryn Castell Inn, 117, 89, 90.
†Dyffryn Station, 57, 64.
Dyfi Valley, 32, 91.
Dyfrdwy Valley, 30, 6.
Dyrysgol, 122, 121.
Dysynni Valley, 46, 68, 99, 133.

Eden, River, 41.
Edeyrnion, Vale of, 27.
Eglwyseg Rocks, 16, 2, 14.
Eglwys Newydd, 115.
Egryn Abbey, 53.
Eliseg's Pillar, 13.
Eunant, 35, 80.
†Eyarth Station, 25.

Fairy Glen, 26.
*†Ffestiniog, 5, 60.
†Forden (Welshpool), 87.
Foxes' Path, 134, 129.
Friog Promontory, 52, 46, 68, 99.
†Frongoch, 5.
Fronheulog, 4.
Furnace, 109.
Fyrnwy, " Lake," 79, 29, 33.

Gallt y Bladur, 98.
Ganllwyd Glen, 39, 57.
"Gate" of Ardudwy, 63, 58, 67.
Geirw Stream, 25.
Geryst Stream, 94.
"Giant's Nose," 50.
Glan Conway, 26.
†Glandovey, 97, 109.
†   ,,   Junction, 73, 91, 69, 99.
Glansevern Inn, 90.
Glan-y-Llyn, 5, 31.
Glas Pwll, 97.
Gloyllyn, 62, 67.
Glyn Ceiriog, 17.
†Glyndyfrdwy, 17, 3.
Goat Inn, 25.
Gogerddan Arms, 112.
Goginan, 112.
Grouse Box (Llangollen), 18.
Guilsfield Church, 86.
Gwastadannes, 51.
†Gwyddelwern (Corwen), 24.
Gwynant Stream, 45.
Gyrn Moelfre, 76.

Hafod, 116, 110.
Hafod Arms (Devil's Bridge), 110.
"Half-way House," 47, 56, (see Bont-ddu.)
Happy Valley, 96, 72.
*†Harlech [Merioneth], 65, 58, 59.
Harnog Glen, 122.
Henddol, 55.
Henffordd Arms, 111.
Hen Gwm, 122, 121.
Hirnant, 34, 78, 80.

†Kerry [Montgomeryshire], 87.

Ladies of Llangollen, 9.
"Lake of Fyrnwy," 79, 29.
Leighton Hall, 87.
"Liverpool Reservoir," 79, 29.
Llafar stream, 31.

Llanaber Church, 52, 51.
Llanarmon [Llangollen], 17.
Llanbadarn-fawr, 101, 91.
Llanbedr [Merioneth], 60, (see also †Pensarn).
*†Llanbrynmair [Montgomeryshire], 90, 88.
Llandanwg, 59.
†Llandderfel [Corwen], 27, 4.
†Llandinam, 88.
Llanddwywe Church, 53.
*†Llandrillo [Corwen], 32, 4, 27, 77, 78.
Llanegryn, 71, 46.
Llanelltyd, 40, 42.
Llanenddwyn, 57, 64.
Llanfachreth, 140, 42.
†Llanfihangel [Aberystwith], 107, 91.
Llanfihangel-y-Pennant, (Towyn), 71, 133, 46.
Llanfor, 27, 4, 29.
*†Llanfyllin, 76, 18, 33
Llangar Church, 4, 27.
Llangedwyn [Llanfyllin], 18.
*†Llangollen, 8.
    To Bala, 3.
    „ Corwen, 3.
    „ Llaurhaiadr, 17.
Llangower, 5.
Llangwrig, 90, 89.
Llangynnog, 78, 77.
*†Llanidloes [Montgomeryshire], 88, 117.
Llanrhaiadr-yn Mochnant [Oswestry], 76, 17, 34.
*†Llanrhystyd, 104.
Llansaintffraid, 3.
Llantrisant, 116.
Llantysilio, 14, 12, 3.
*†Llanuwchllyn [Merioneth], 30, 6, 95, 119.
Llanwddyn, 80, 34, 33.
Llan-y-Cil, 31, 5.
    „ -y-Mawddwy, 94, 32, 80, 123.
Llawllech Range, 6.
Llethr, 136, 58, 63.
Lliw, River, 30, 125.
†Llwyngwril, 55, 46, 99.

Llyfnant Valley, 97.
Llyn Aran, 131.
,, Arenig, 124.
,, ,, -fach, 123.
,, Barfog, 72.
,. Bodllyn, 54, 139.
,. Ciddew, 68.
,. Conway, 26.
,. Caerwych, 68.
,. Creigenen, 54.
,. Cwm Bychan, 61, 58, 63.
,, Cynwch, 39, 38.
,, Dulyn, 54.
,. Dyfi, 120.
,. Gwernan, 129.
,. Howell, 137.
.. Irddyn, 54, 139.
,, Llyne Caws, 32, 77.
,. Pen Rhaiadr, 98.
,, Tecwyn, 68.
,, Trigraienyn, 44, 96.
,. Tryweryn, 5.
,. -y-Cau, 128, 132, 135.
,. -y-Fedw, 68.
.. -y-Gader, 130, 134, 47.
,, -y-Gafr, 130, 134.
Llys Bradwen, 54.

*†Machynlleth [Mont-
gomeryshire], 92.
To Aberdovey, 91, 99.
,, Aberystwith, 91, 108.
,, Corris and Dolgelley, 95.
,, Dinas Mawdwy, 93.
,, Llyfnant Glen, 97.
,, Tal-y-Llyn, 95.
,, Towyn, 91, 99, 96.
Maentwrog (*†Tan-y-Bwlch,
Merioneth), 43, 5.
Maes-y-Brynar, 38.
,, -y-Garnedd, 63, 61.
Mallwydd [*†Dinas
Mawddwy], 93, 86.
Mawddach Estuary, 48, 6,
50, &c.
†Middletown, 84.
Milltirgerrig, Pass. 78.
,, Farm, 124.
Minffordd Farm, 132.
†Moat Lane Junction, 87, 88.

Mochras, 60, 58.
Moel Cynwch, 39.
,, Ferna, 24.
,, Morfydd, 15.
,, Offrwm, 39.
,, Sych, 24, 32. 77.
,, -y-Ddinas, 33.
,, -y-Faen, 16.
,, -y-Gaer, 15.
,, -y-Gamelin, 14, 3.
,, -y-Geraint, 11.
,, -y-Golfa, 84, 85, 75.
,, -y-Se nicl, 66.
Monk's Bridge, 114.
,, Cave, 104.
*†Montgomery, 87.
Morfa Dyffryn, 58.
,, Harlech, 59.
,, Towyn, 68.
Mynach Falls, 114.
†Mynffordd Junction, 59.
Mynydd Moel, 131, 135, 6.
,, Nodol, 5.
,, Pencoed, 132, 135.
,, Tarw, 17.

Nannau, 39, 38, 41.
†Nant Clwyd, 25.
Nant-Col, 61, 58, 63.
,, Eos, 104.
,, Farm, 63.
,, Ffrauan Valley, 27.
,, Morwynion, 15.
Nant-y-Barcwd, 120,
,, -y-Bellan Tower, 19, 18.
*†Newtown, 87.

Oernant Slate Quarries, 15.
Offa's Dyke, 21.
*†Oswestry, 74.
To Pistyll Rhaiadr, 76.
Owen Glyndwr's Mount, 3.

Paddock Bridge, 26.
Palé, 27, 4.
Panorama Walk, 52.
Pant Einion, 55.
Pant-y-dwn, 107.
,, -y-Llan, 126, 134.

Parson's Bridge, 112, 115.
Pencoed, 132.
Pen Dinas, 102, 91.
Pengwern Hall, 10.
Peniarth, 71.
†Penmaenpool [Dolgelley], 45,
	6, 136, 139.
Pennal [Machynlleth], 96. 72.
Pennant, 21.
Pen Parciau Bridge, 111.
Penrhos, 41.
*†Penrhyn Deudraeth, 59.

rentredwfr, 14.
Pentre Voelas [Bettws-y-
	Coed], 26.
Pen-y-Bont (Glen Artro), 58,
	61.
	„	„	(Tanat Valley),
		78, 35.
„ -y-Bryn, 14.
„ -y-Coed, 10, 2, 21.
„ -y-Groes, 38.
„ -y-Nant, 19.
„ -y-Sarn, 107, 108.
Piccadilly, 111.
Piran Fall, 116, 111.
Pistyll Cain, 41, 40.
	„	Rhaiadr, 77, 32, 4, 17.
	„	-y-Llyn, 98, 97.
Plas, 121, 94.
	„	Newydd, 9.
Plynlimon;
	From Aberystwith. 117.
	„ Llanidloes, 89.

Pont Aber Rhaiadr, 76.
	„	ar Dyfi, 96.
	„	ar Eden, 40.
	„	Dolgefeiliau 43.
	„	Dysynni, 71.
	„	Erwyd, 112, 110.
	„	Fathew, 71, 133.
	„	Llyfnant, 109.
	„	Melin-rug, 27.
	„	-pren-Plwcca, 113.
	„	Rhyd-y-Groes 116.
	„	-y-Cysylltau, 2.
	„	-7-Garth, 71.
	„	-y-Glyn, 25.
	„	-y-Llyn-du, 42.

Pont Ystumaner, 71.
†Pontdolgoch, 90.
†Pontfaen, 17.
Pontrhydfendigaed, 105.
†Pool Quay, 85.
Powis Castle, 86.
Precipice Walk, 39, 38.
Pwll Caradoc, 105.

Rhaiadr-du, 41.
	„	Mawddach, 42.
*†Rhayader, 89.
Rheidol Glen, 109, 112, &c.
Rhinog-fawr, 61, 62, 67,
	137.
	„	-fach, 137, 63.
Rhisgog, 3, 15.
Rhiwargor Farm, 34, 80.
Rhiwrogof, 132. 136.
Rhobell-fawr, 139.
Rhos-y-gwaliau, 33.
Rhid-dib-enwch, 89.
Rhyddnant Valley, 115.
Rhyd Ergyn, 85.
	„	-y-Fen, 123.
Rodney Obelisk, 84, 85.
Roman Steps, 62, 58, 67.
*†Ruabon, 2, 18.
Rug Chapel, 27.
*†Ruthin 24.

Saddle [Cader Idris], 134.
Severn, River, 89.
*†Shrewsbury, 81.
Singrig, 67.
Stay-a-little Inn, 88.
Steddfa Gurig, 90, 117.
†Strata Florida, 105.
Sylfaen, 138.

Tai-yn-y-Nant Farm. 95.
Talerddig Cutting, 90.
Taliesin, 108.
†Talsarnau, 59, 67.
Tal-y-Bont [Cardigan], 108.
Tal-y-Bont (Tal-y Llyn), 96.
Tal-y-Llyn [Corris, Mont-
	gomery], 45, 72, 96, 131.
Tanat Valley, 78, 18, 76.

*†Tan-y-Bwlch [Merioneth],60.
† „ -y-Grisiau, 60.
Thunder Hole, 104.
Tomen Ddreiniog, 71.
„ -y-Bala, 28.
„ -y-Mur, 5.
Torrent Walk, 37, 94, 44.
*†**Towyn** [Merioneth], 69,45.
To Aberdovey, 69.
„ Aberystwith, 69, 91.
„ Barmouth, 99.
„ Cader Idris, 132.
„ Dolgelley, 72, 43.
„ Machynlleth, 69.
†Trawscoed, 110.
*†Trawsfynydd, 58, 39, 63, 43.
Trystion Stream, 27.
Tryweryn, River, 28.
Twll Twrw, 104.
Twrch Stream, 30, 95.
Twymyn Valley, 90.
Tyndwr, 21, 10.
Ty-newydd, 3.
Tyn-y-Coed, 50.
Tyn-y-Groes Inn [Dolgelley],
41, 39, 40.
Tyrau-Mawr, 126, 127, 134.

Vale of Clwyd, 25, 12.
„ „ Edeyrnion, 27.
„ „ Llangollen, 19, 21.
Valle Crucis Abbey, 13, 11.
Van Mines, 88.
Vivod, 12.
*†**Welshpool**, 85. 75.
*†Whitchurch, 73.
Wnion Valley, 43, 44, 6.
World's end, 14, 16.
*†**Wrexham**, 2.
Wye, River, 89.
Wynnstay Park, 18.

Y Figle-fawr, 54.
Y Foel-ddu, 61.
Y Fron-fawr, 17.
Y Fron-heulog, 27.
Y las Ynys, 59.
Ynys-las, 91.
Ynys Maengwyn, 71.
Yr Eryr, 95.
Ysgethin Valley, 64.
Yspytty Cynfyn, 112, 110.
„ Ystwith, 116.
Ystwith Valley, 110, 101, 104.

London: J. S. LEVIN, Steam Printing Works, 75, Leadenhall Street, E.C.

www.ingramcontent.com/pod-product-compliance
Lightning Source LLC
Chambersburg PA
CBHW031828270326
41932CB00008B/591